How to Prepare for the

CBEST™

California Basic Educational Skills Test

Fourth Edition

Model Tests by
Decision Development Corporation
Concord, California

Coordinating Editors
Fred Obrecht, M.A.
Allan Mundsack, M.A.
John Orozco, M.A.
Louise Barbato, Ph.D.

BARRON'S

Portions of this book from:
*Barron's How to Prepare for the Graduate
Record Examination* by Brownstein, Weiner,
and Green
*Barron's How to Prepare for the California High
School Proficiency Examination* by Green and
Siemon
*Barron's How to Prepare for the Scholastic
Aptitude Test* by Brownstein, Weiner, and Green
*Barron's How to Prepare for the Law School
Admission Test* by Bobrow and associates
*Barron's How to Prepare for the California State
University Writing Proficiency Exams,* ed. by
Obrecht, Mundsack, and Green

All inquiries should be addressed to:
Barron's Educational Series, Inc.
250 Wireless Boulevard
Hauppauge, New York 11788

Library of Congress Catalog Card No. 96-35268

International Standard Book No. 0-8120-9731-9

Library of Congress Cataloging-in-Publication Data
How to prepare for the CBEST. California Basic Educational
Skills Test / coordinating editors, Fred Obrecht . . . [et al.]. —
4th ed.
    p. cm.
  At head of title: Barron's.
  "Model tests by Decision Development Corporation, Concord,
California."
  ISBN 0-8120-9731-9
  1. California Basic Educational Skills Test—Study guides.
I. Obrecht, Fred. II. Decision Development Corporation. III.
Barron's Educational Series, Inc.
LB3060.33.C34B37 1997
370'.7'76—dc20
                        96-35268
                        CIP

PRINTED IN THE UNITED STATES OF AMERICA
9876543

Contents

Introduction

So you want to be a teacher. Who can blame you? After all, who could resist the high salary, the social status, and, of course, the catered lunches? With all the media attention given to our educational system, you should have a good idea as to what it is you are getting into. All kidding aside, teaching is a noble profession. Society needs good teachers who will help our next generation rise to the responsibilities of adulthood.

Whether you've just started your college education or have completed your degree, all you have to do now is survive educational theory, student teaching, and the CBEST™, the California Basic Educational Skills Test. Passing the CBEST™ will give you credibility in your chosen profession. With preparation, it should be no more than a confirmation of the skills you have already acquired from your undergraduate studies.

A passing score on the CBEST™ is 51.25 percent in each section. If you fail one section of the exam, you do not need to retake the sections you passed previously. In other words, you can pass one section at a time if you wish, but it will cost you forty dollars each time you take the exam.

The most important thing you can do before taking this exam is to give yourself an honest self-assessment. So, take the diagnostic test in this book. Once you know your weaknesses, you can then prepare for the exam. Work on one section an hour each day until you feel comfortable. If you know of other candidates who are planning to take the CBEST™, work in a small study group. Whatever your strategy, if you prepare ahead of time, passing the CBEST™ should be easy.

Chapter 1

What You Should Know About the CBEST™

The CBEST™ has changed since August 1995. The use of time is more flexible now.

1. You are no longer restricted to the old system in which you were allotted 65 minutes for the reading section, 70 minutes for the mathematics, and 60 minutes for the writing.

2. You can use your four hours any way you wish. For example, you are allowed to spend a half hour more on the writing portion than on the reading.

3. If you wish, you might use the entire allocated time for only one portion of the exam.

GENERAL GUIDELINES

1. The exam is given six times a year.

2. Contact your local college, school district, or county board of education for specific dates and locations.

3. There is no limit on the number of times the exam can be taken.

4. The test covers reading, writing, and mathematics.

5. A passing score is 51.25 percent per section.

6. Your score will be sent to you and nobody else. The National Evaluation Systems (NES) will forward your scores to specific California colleges and universities if you request them to do so on your registration form.

7. If you retake the exam, you do not have to repeat those sections you have passed. It will cost you forty dollars each time.

8. You can cancel your CBEST™ score by notifying the supervisor at the test center before you leave.

9. You are not penalized for guessing on the exam. A blank answer is as costly as a wrong answer.

10. You can write on the exam booklet. Note taking, outlining, and calculating on the booklet are good test-taking methods.

11. The CBEST™ is only one step in becoming a teacher.

    a. Even with an emergency credential, you will still need at least a B.A. degree.

    b. You will need to complete educational courses and student teaching.

    c. For further information regarding teacher certification, contact the Commission on Teacher Credentialing, P.O. Box 944270, Sacramento, CA 94244-2700, (916) 445-7254. Their offices are open from 8:00 A.M. to 4:30 P.M. Monday through Friday.

12. The CBEST™ is required in the state of Oregon. You can reach the Oregon Teachers Standards and Practices Commission at (503) 378-6586.

13. The CBEST™ is administered by NES, P.O. Box 340880, Sacramento, CA 95834-0880.

    a. Send a money order of forty dollars payable to NES.

    b. For further information, call (916) 928-4001.

    c. Representatives will answer questions from 9:00 A.M. to 3:00 P.M. Monday through Friday.

    d. During phone-in registrations, representatives will answer your questions from 9:00 A.M. to 5:00 P.M.

    e. If you require special arrangements to take the test, NES may be able to help (916) 928-6150.

STRATEGIES FOR TAKING THE EXAM

1. Concentrate only on taking the CBEST™ for several days prior to the test. If you have prepared for the exam, you need only review your skills prior to the test date.

2. Exclude any social activities or stressful events on your calendar near exam day that might cause you to be preoccupied. Avert your attention from problems that might cloud your reasoning.

3. Pacing yourself is important. You only have so much time to complete your tasks. If you have taken timed exams in preparation, you should have a sense of how long it takes you to read questions and write the answers.

4. Listen carefully to the instructions given. Make certain that you are answering the right questions. In other words, make sure that if you are reading question number 7, that you fill in the answer space for number 7. If you skip a question, skip the corresponding answer space.

5. Carefully read the questions. Following directions is half the battle.

HELPFUL HINTS

The One-Check, Two-Check System

Many people score lower than they should on the CBEST™ simply because they do not get to many of the easier problems. They puzzle over difficult questions and use up the time that could be spent answering easy ones. In fact, the difficult questions are worth exactly the same as the easy ones, so it makes sense not to do the hard problems until you have answered all the easy ones.

To maximize your correct answers by focusing on the easier problems, use the following system:

- Work through the whole section, answering only the easy questions (those that you are able to answer in 30–40 seconds). If you run across a problem that is too difficult or time-consuming, mark it on your answer sheet with one check (✓). If you run across a problem that you can't even *begin* to solve, put two checks next to it (✓✓). (You may wish to take a guess now.)

- After you have answered all the easy questions in any one section, go back and try your one-check problems, solving as many of them as you can during your remaining time.

- If you finish your one-check problems and still have time remaining, go back and try the two-check problems. In many cases you will find yourself able to solve some of these problems, which looked so impossible at first.

- Finally, a few minutes before time is called, *erase the check marks from your answer sheet* and make a guess for each unsolved question. There is no penalty for guessing on the CBEST™.

You should use this system as you work through the practice tests in this book; such practice will allow you to make "one-check, two-check" judgments quickly when you actually take the CBEST™. As our extensive research has shown, use of this system results in less wasted time on the CBEST™.

The Elimination Strategy

Faced with four or five answer choices, you will work more efficiently and effectively if you *eliminate unreasonable or irrelevant answers immediately.* In most cases, two or three choices in every set will stand out as obviously incorrect. Many test takers don't perceive this because they painstakingly analyze every choice, even the obviously ridiculous ones.

The wise test taker, aware that most answer choices can be easily eliminated, does so without complicating the process by considering unreasonable possibilities. To summarize the elimination strategy:

- Look for unreasonable or incorrect answer choices first. Expect to find at least two or three of these with every problem.

- When a choice seems wrong, cross it out in your test booklet *immediately,* so that you will not be tempted to reconsider it.

Eliminating choices in this fashion will lead you to correct answers more quickly, and will increase your overall confidence.

Marking in the Test Booklet

Many test takers don't take full advantage of opportunities to mark key words and draw diagrams in the test booklet. Remember that, in the reading comprehension section, *marking key words and phrases will significantly increase your comprehension and lead you to a correct answer.* Marking also helps to keep you focused and alert.

Further, more specific hints about marking are given in the introductory chapters that follow. The important general point to stress here is that active, successful test taking entails marking and drawing, and that passive, weak test takers make little use of this technique.

The "Multiple-Multiple-Choice" Item

You are sure to encounter a number of test problems that contain two sets of multiple choices. Here is an example:

> According to the theory of aerodynamics, the bumblebee should be unable to fly. But it flies anyway.
>
> Which of the following can be logically inferred from the above statement?
>
> I. The bumblebee's behavior contradicts scientific theory.
> II. The bumblebee is not really able to fly.
> III. Some theories don't hold true in all cases.
>
> (A) I only
> (B) II only
> (C) I and II
> (D) I, II, and III
> (E) I and III

When faced with a problem of this structure, begin by considering the Roman numeral choices. Label each as "TRUE" or "FALSE" (or "yes/no" or "correct/incorrect"), and eliminate final answer choices accordingly.

With the above problem, you should proceed as follows:

Statement I: TRUE—Eliminate (B) because it does not contain I.
Statement II: FALSE—Eliminate (C) and (D) because they do contain II.
Statement III: TRUE—Eliminate (A), and choose (E).

HOW TO USE THIS BOOK EFFECTIVELY

Take the Diagnostic Test

In the following chapter you will find a CBEST™ diagnostic test. Your results on this test will indicate the sorts of problems which you need to practice. Some of them you may already recognize as troublesome to you. You will become aware of others as you work through the test. This book thoroughly reviews the basic educational skills covered by the CBEST™. Your results on this test will pinpoint which parts of the book demand the most attention from you.

Study the Appropriate Chapters

You will discover that Chapter 3 includes worthwhile advice on how to go about answering the sorts of reading questions you will find on the CBEST™ (literal, logical, and critical comprehension questions). Chapter 4 is devoted to a comprehensive review of the mathematical skills you need to do well on the CBEST™. Chapter 5 provides guidelines and extensive practice for writing the essays on the test. Chapter 6 contains a handy outline of the elements of grammar, and Chapter 7 includes more grammar practice for ESL students. The remainder of the book provides you with practice answering simulated CBEST™ questions. Three model tests comparable to the actual CBEST™ in format, number of questions, level of difficulty, and time allowed are provided.

Take the Model Tests

Each model test includes 50 reading comprehension questions, 50 quantitative questions, and 2 essay topics. You will probably find that the actual CBEST™ follows this pattern.

Use the model tests in this book as a means of confirming your strengths and diagnosing your weaknesses. Correct answers and thorough explanations follow each model test: use them as you continue your analysis of your skills.

Follow this pattern. First, take the diagnostic test and pinpoint your weak areas. Concentrate on these weak areas during your general review (Chapters 3–7). Then take each model test in turn, being sure to analyze your results and review newly revealed weak spots before you go on to the next model test. If you follow this study plan assiduously, you will be able to face the CBEST™ with confidence.

Chapter 2

A Diagnostic Test

This chapter contains a short version of a typical CBEST™. Take the test and then check your answers in the Answer Key. Give yourself one point for each correct answer. Then use the Analysis of Errors table to help you determine the areas in which you scored low and are weak so that you may concentrate your studies on this material.

This test, like the CBEST™, is divided into three sections: Reading, Mathematics, and Writing. Allow yourself 100 minutes for the entire test.

READING

Time: 20 minutes

Directions: Each passage in this test is followed by a question or questions about its content. Select the best answer to each question from among the five choices given. Answer all questions on the basis of what is stated or implied in the passage.

Questions 1–2

The new tax law supplies some important incentives for saving. Whether you are an inveterate saver or one who has never been able to keep over $1,000 in the bank at one time, it is advisable to investigate some of these incentives for saving. One category of incentives includes tax-exempt "All-Savers" certificates; a second category consists of tax-deferred retirement accounts, the provisions for which are very generous.

1. Saving incentives are, according to the author,

   (A) only appropriate for a certain class of savers.
   (B) available only to someone with more than $1,000 in the bank.
   (C) categorized according to financial advantage.
   (D) all tax-exempt.
   (E) important to know about.

2. The word "inveterate" as used in this selection, means

   (A) infrequent.
   (B) habitual.
   (C) haphazard.
   (D) prominent.
   (E) impoverished.

Questions 3–5

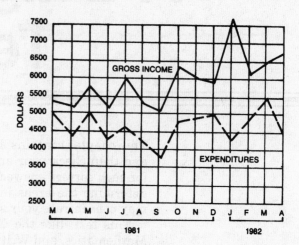

The graph represents the gross income and expenditures for a small business for each month of one year. Refer to the graph to answer the questions.

3. The graph shows that the greatest net profits for this business were in

   (A) March 1981.
   (B) April 1981.
   (C) January 1982.
   (D) August 1982.
   (E) January 1981.

4. From this graph, one may conclude that

   (A) there is a direct relation between income and expenditures.
   (B) this business has been successful for each month shown.
   (C) profits must be increased if the business is to survive.
   (D) the summer months are usually best for this business.
   (E) 1981 was a better year than thus far in 1982.

5. If the owner of this business used the year shown as an indication of its health, he could conclude that

   (A) the "ups" are outweighed by the "downs."
   (B) he is spending too much on new goods.
   (C) the losses it is showing for some months must be eliminated.
   (D) it is showing a healthy trend.
   (E) there is little hope of the business surviving.

Questions 6–8

Fear is by no means the only obstacle to learning the language of computers. The language used by humans is replete with vagueness. Not a sentence uttered can be considered to be free from some degree of ambiguity. Computers, on the other hand, require a precision of expression or exactness that is extremely rare in ordinary language. The use of language in normal discourse assumes some shared experiences, and we take for granted that a listener has some common sense. The computer, unfortunately, has not shared our experiences, and it has absolutely no common sense.

6. The writer makes his point by use of

   (A) exaggeration.
   (B) examples.
   (C) generalization.
   (D) sarcasm.
   (E) comparison.

7. According to the author, a computer has

   (A) many flaws.
   (B) no intelligence.
   (C) few uses.
   (D) a memory bank.
   (E) a common language.

8. The writer implies that one barrier to using a computer is

   (A) the complexity of the equipment.
   (B) the lack of educational materials.
   (C) the ambiguity of the instructions.
   (D) the uniqueness of computer language.
   (E) a general lack of familiarity with its operations.

Questions 9–10

Young children have mastered language through a complex process of trial and error. In fact, they have had to be wrong many times in order to learn the right responses. More importantly, they are not usually penalized for being wrong when learning to use oral language. This atmosphere, which was pervasive in their homes, should be carried over to the classroom. Teachers should do the following: emphasize questions that have more than one correct answer; reinforce attempts to find an answer by crediting any part that is right; solicit reasons for responses that are incorrect; allow students to see that their teacher can be wrong or that teachers don't always know the answer. Let them prove the teacher wrong or find the information needed to resolve an issue.

9. The author compares learning in the classroom to

   (A) a very complex process of questioning.
   (B) learning to speak.
   (C) the attempt to solve problems.
   (D) taking a risk in life.
   (E) trying to respond to questions without answers.

10. It is possible to conclude that the author would agree that

   (A) classroom teachers do not ask enough questions.
   (B) children should not be taught at home.
   (C) the teacher must serve as a model for students by having the content well in hand.
   (D) the opportunity to make mistakes is essential to learning.
   (E) the way children learn oral language cannot be adopted in the classroom.

Questions 11–13

Latin, with its fossilized beauties, unfolds a wealth of meaning that lazy, linear English, worn smooth of almost all grammatical inflections, tends to gloss over.

11. One can conclude from the passage that

   (A) Latin is a more difficult language than English.
   (B) English is distorted by lazy writers.
   (C) English has changed more than Latin.
   (D) Latin has more inflections than English.
   (E) more and deeper meaning is conveyed by English.

12. Latin's "fossilized beauties" are

   (A) former beauty queens.
   (B) archaic grammatical elements.
   (C) old coins.
   (D) words that are obsolete.
   (E) ancient ruins.

13. The author's main point is that

   (A) English has lost many grammatical features that add to the depth of meaning in Latin.
   (B) Latin is no longer a spoken language anywhere in the world.
   (C) many people who speak English make grammatical errors.
   (D) English is linear, and Latin is indirect.
   (E) if Latin were spoken today, fewer communication problems would arise.

Questions 14–15

In contrast with the country's centers of population, the Pacific slope of its isthmus to the west of the interoceanic route presents a linguistic picture with relatively few complicating factors. The population, although sparse, has been stable, and non-Hispanic influences on its speech have not been significant until recent times, when communication with the larger cities of the country has affected the dialogue.

14. The author's main point is that

   (A) the geography of this part of the country isolated the inhabitants.
   (B) the language of city-dwellers is subject to a wider range of influences.
   (C) the language of populations which are not stable reflects a variety of influences from other languages.
   (D) the language of this section of the country has not been affected by many external factors.
   (E) population shifts produce drastic changes in language and produce dialects.

15. This paragraph was probably taken from

   (A) a selection describing linguistic factors which inhibit communication.
   (B) an essay on the influences of geography on linguistic development.
   (C) a paper describing the dialects of a specific Spanish-speaking country.
   (D) a report on the difficulty of carrying out improvement projects in countries where language barriers exist.
   (E) an encyclopedia article detailing the geography and linguistic history of a country.

MATHEMATICS

Time: 20 minutes

Directions: Select the best answer to each of the following questions. Any figures provided are there as reference; they are approximations and are not drawn to scale except when stated.

You may refer to the following information during this section of the test.

= is equal to
≠ is unequal to
< is less than
> is greater than
≤ is less than or equal to
≥ is greater than or equal to

√ square root of
° degrees
‖ is parallel to
⊥ is perpendicular to
π pi, approximately 3.14

Circle: Radius = r; Circumference = $2\pi r$; Area = πr^2; a circle contains 360°

Triangle: In triangle ABC, $\angle BDA$ is a right angle,

Area of $\triangle ABC = \dfrac{AC \times BD}{2}$;

Perimeter of $\triangle ABC = AB + BC + CA$
Sum of the measures of the three angles is 180°.

Rectangle: Area = $L \times W$;
Perimeter = $2 \times (L + W)$

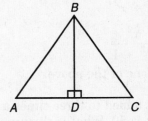

1. What is the value of $\dfrac{6a^2b^3}{18}$ when $a = 3$ and $b = 2$?

   (A) 12
   (B) $\frac{17}{3}$
   (C) 1
   (D) 24
   (E) 36

2. A block of wood is 5 inches × 10 inches × 15 inches. What is the *surface area* of the block? (Refer to the diagram.)

   (A) 750 square inches
   (B) 750 cubic inches
   (C) 550 square inches
   (D) 75 square inches
   (E) Not enough information given

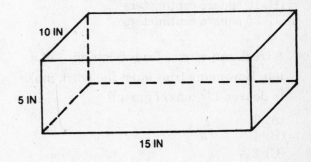

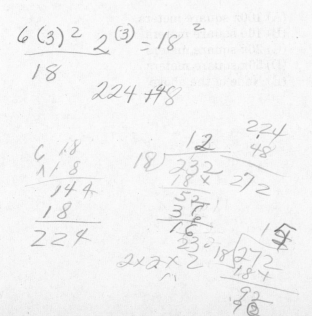

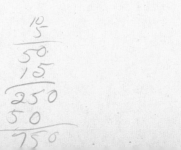

3. A recipe for 6 servings of potato soup calls for 3 cups of milk. How many cups of milk should be used to make 15 servings of soup?

(A) $7\frac{1}{2}$ cups

(B) 9 cups

(C) 13 cups

(D) 14 cups

(E) 30 cups

4. Which of the following expressions is equal to $\dfrac{x}{x + 1/x}$?

(A) $\dfrac{x}{x + 1}$

(B) $1 + x^2$

(C) $\dfrac{1}{1 + x^2}$

(D) $\dfrac{x^2}{x^2 + 1}$

(E) None of the above

5. If 5 is added to three times a number, the result is 80. What is the number?

(A) 30

(B) 25

(C) 13

(D) 28

(E) None of the above

$3x + 5 = 80$
$-5 \quad -5$
$\dfrac{3x}{3} \qquad \overline{15}$

6. The perimeter of a square is 20 centimeters. What is the area of the square?

(A) 40 square centimeters

(B) 20 square centimeters

(C) 16 square centimeters

(D) 10 square centimeters

(E) 25 square centimeters

7. A truck can carry a load weighing $\frac{3}{4}$ of a ton. How many trips must the truck make to deliver $1\frac{15}{16}$ tons of gravel?

(A) 3

(B) 4

(C) $2\frac{7}{12}$

(D) $1\frac{3}{16}$

(E) $3\frac{7}{8}$

8. Sharon worked a total of 40 hours one week at two jobs. One job paid her $4.50 per hour and the other $5.00 per hour. She made $189.00. How many hours did Sharon work at the job with the lower hourly wage?

(A) 22 hours

(B) 20 hours

(C) 18 hours

(D) 15 hours

(E) Cannot be determined

9. Put the following numbers in order from smallest to largest:

$$.6, \frac{57}{100}, .625, \frac{4}{7}$$

(A) $\frac{57}{100}, .6, .625, \frac{4}{7}$

(B) $.625, .6, \frac{57}{100}, \frac{4}{7}$

(C) $\frac{57}{100}, .6, \frac{4}{7}, .625$

(D) $\frac{57}{100}, \frac{4}{7}, .6, .625$

(E) $\frac{4}{7}, \frac{57}{100}, .6, .625$

10. Ron has 58 cents in his pocket in dimes, nickels, and pennies. If he has a total of 11 coins and the same number of dimes as pennies, how many nickels does he have?

(A) 1

(B) 3

(C) Either 1 or 3

(D) 5

(E) 10

11. How many square meters of pasture does a goat have for grazing if he is tied to a stake by a 10-meter rope?

(A) 100π square meters

(B) 100 square meters

(C) 20π square meters

(D) 50π square meters

(E) None of the above

12. In a bicycle shop the number of 10-speed bicycles is 25 more than twice the number of 3-speed bicycles. Which number sentence is a correct expression of this information? (Note: Let x represent the number of 10-speed bicycles and y represent the number of 3-speed bicycles.)

(A) $2x = y + 25$
(B) $x + 25 = y$
(C) $x - 25 = y$
(D) $x = 2y + 25$
(E) $x = 2(y + 25)$

13. Robinson, Simpson, and Thornton are stamp collectors. Robinson's collection is worth $25,000, which is twice the value of Simpson's collection. Thornton's collection is worth three times the difference in the values of Robinson's and Simpson's collections. How much is Thornton's stamp collection worth? Answer: $75,000

Which statement best describes why the answer given for this problem is *not* reasonable?

(A) Simpson's collection is worth $50,000.
(B) $75,000 is 3 times the value of Robinson's collection, not 3 times the difference of Robinson's and Simpson's collections.
(C) $75,000 is not twice the value of Robinson's collection.
(D) Thornton's collection is worth $112,500.
(E) Because there is not enough information to answer the question.

14. Mr. Hernandez has taught 7th grade for 9 years. His salary over these 9 years has averaged $23,400.

With only the information given, which of the following questions can be answered?

 I. What was Mr. Hernandez's salary during his 1st year?
 II. What was Mr. Hernandez's salary during his 5th year?
III. How much money has Mr. Hernandez earned during the past 9 years?

(A) I only
(B) II only
(C) III only
(D) I and II only
(E) I, II and III

Note: Refer to graph below to answer item 15.

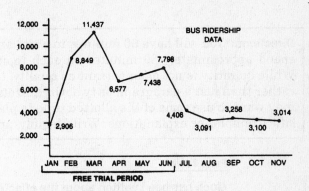

15. The graph shows the change in bus ridership in a small city during an eleven-month period. The greatest percent decline in ridership in a one-month period was from

(A) June to July
(B) March to April
(C) January to February
(D) July to August
(E) None of the above

WRITING

Directions: You will have 60 minutes to write an essay on each of the following two topics. Try to spend approximately 30 minutes on each topic, as they are of equal value in the evaluation. While quantity is not as important as quality, the topics selected will probably require an essay rather than just a paragraph or two. Organization is an integral part of effective writing, so you may want to use some of the allotted time to plan your work. Support your ideas with clear, specific examples or explanations. Write legibly, and do not skip lines.

FIRST TOPIC

Much has been written about the effects of television on the present generation. Discuss the positive and negative effect you believe television has had on children.

SECOND TOPIC

In a democracy, one of the greatest challenges is for people to work together to reach a decision. Describe an experience you have had, whether working on a committee, attending a town meeting, or planning a reunion, in which people were or were not able to work together to achieve their goal.

ANSWER KEY

Reading

1. E	4. B	7. B	10. D	13. A
2. B	5. D	8. D	11. D	14. D
3. C	6. E	9. B	12. B	15. C

Mathematics

1. D	4. D	7. A	10. D	13. B
2. C	5. B	8. A	11. A	14. C
3. A	6. E	9. D	12. D	15. A

ANALYSIS OF ERRORS

You now have completed your diagnostic test and checked your answers against the answer key, giving yourself one point for each correct answer. If you scored 12 or less on either the reading or the mathematics sections, you need to spend some time studying the review chapters in this book. In this diagnostic test, 11 correct answers to 15 questions approximates a *marginal* passing score; however, you want to enter the testing room knowing you can do better than just a borderline pass.

Go over the test answer explanations and correct any of your answers that are wrong.

If you scored better than 12 on both the reading and mathematics sections of the test, see how you do on one of the lengthier model tests.

If you scored 12 or below on either multiple-choice section, use the following chart to help you in your review. Find the question numbers that you got wrong and study the subject matter covered in those questions. Then do the sample exercises at the end of the appropriate review chapter.

SECTION	QUESTION NUMBERS	SUBJECT AREA
READING	1, 13, 14	Finding the Main Idea
	7, 9	Finding Specific Details
	8, 10, 11, 15	Finding Implications
	2, 12	Determining the Meaning of Strange Words
	6	Determining Special Techniques
	3, 4, 5	Interpreting Tables and Graphs
MATHEMATICS Arithmetic	9	Whole Numbers
	7, 9	Fractions
	9	Decimals
	15	Percentage
	14	Averages, Medians, Ranges and Modes
Algebra	1, 4, 8, 12	Algebraic Expressions
	5, 12, 13	Verbal Problems
	3	Ratio and Proportion
Geometry	11	Circles
	2, 6, 11	Area, Perimeter, and Volume
	10	Trial and Error (see Answer Explanations)

ANSWER EXPLANATIONS

Reading

1. **E** The author suggests that saving incentives are worth investigating, regardless of one's financial status.

2. **B** In making the contrast between types of savers, the writer refers to the other type as those who are inconsistent about saving.

3. **C** The letters at the bottom represent the months from March 1981 to April 1982. Net profits are gross income (solid line) less expenditures (dashed line). The difference between income and expenditures was greatest for the month of January 1982.

4. **B** The graph shows that profits were greater than expenditures each month of the period shown.

5. **D** Since the business profits are good each month and generally increasing, it appears to be in good health.

6. **E** The writer compares computer language to the language of normal discourse or the language used by humans.

7. **B** The writer states that the computer has no common sense and implies that it cannot reason about vagueness or make assumptions and is, therefore, not intelligent.

8. **D** As the writer explains, computer language requires exactness and precision, unlike human language; as such, it is unique.

9. **B** The author describes the process of mastering language in the home; then, in lines 5 and 6, he relates this directly to effective teaching techniques.

10. **D** It is the author's main point that risk-taking behaviors are important in learning.

11. **D** Since the writer states that English is "worn smooth" of inflections, it can be concluded that Latin has more.

12. **B** Although the figurative expression, "fossilized beauties," may be unclear in isolation, the later reference to "grammatical inflections" makes B the best answer.

13. **A** If the reader understands that Latin's "fossilized beauties" are grammatical elements that have been lost in English, then it will be clear that the writer means that they add to the depth of meaning in Latin. The author does not go so far as to imply, as in answer (E), that Latin would be a viable substitute as a spoken language.

14. **D** The author describes a geographical area where the language of the inhabitants has not been affected to any great extent by external factors.

15. **C** The passage is specific enough and includes references to other sections of the country so that one can conclude that it is presenting a linguistic picture of a Spanish-speaking country.

Mathematics

1. **D** $\dfrac{6a^2b^3}{18} = \dfrac{6 \cdot 3^2 \cdot 2^3}{18} = \dfrac{6 \cdot 9 \cdot 8}{18}$

$\phantom{\dfrac{6a^2b^3}{18}} = \dfrac{432}{18} = 24$

2. **C** *Surface area* refers to the combined areas of the 6 surfaces on the block of wood.
2 surfaces have area = $10 \times 15 = 150$ square inches
2 surfaces have area = $5 \times 15 = 75$ square inches
2 surfaces have area = $5 \times 10 = 50$ square inches
$(2 \times 150) + (2 \times 75) + (2 \times 50) = 550$ square inches

3. **A** $\dfrac{6 \text{ servings}}{3 \text{ cups milk}} = \dfrac{15 \text{ servings}}{x \text{ cups milk}}$

$6x = 45$

$x = 7\tfrac{1}{2}$ cups of milk

4. **D** $\dfrac{x}{x + 1/x} = \dfrac{x}{(x^2 + 1)/x}$

$\dfrac{x \cdot x}{x^2 + 1} = \dfrac{x^2}{x^2 + 1}$

5. **B** Let N represent the number.
$3 \cdot N + 5 = 80$
$3 \cdot N = 75$
$N = 25$

6. **E**   Perimeter = $4s$, so $20 = 4s$ and $s = 5$. Area = s^2, so Area = $5^2 = 25$ square centimeters.

7. **A**   To find how many $\frac{3}{4}$ ton loads are in $1\frac{15}{16}$ tons, you divide $1\frac{15}{16}$ by $\frac{3}{4}$.

$$1\tfrac{15}{16} \div \tfrac{3}{4} = \tfrac{31}{16} \div \tfrac{3}{4} = \tfrac{31}{16} \times \tfrac{4}{3}$$
$$= \tfrac{31}{4} \times \tfrac{1}{3} = \tfrac{31}{12}$$

$\frac{31}{12} = 2\frac{7}{12}$ loads. Consequently, it will require 3 trips to deliver the gravel.

8. **A**   Let A = number of hours worked at $4.50 per hour and B = number of hours worked at $5.00 per hour.
$$A + B = 40$$
and $4.50 \times A + 5.00 \times B = 189.00$
$$B = 40 - A$$
so $4.50A + 5.00(40 - A) = 189.00$
This equation simplifies to:
$4.50A + 200.00 - 5.00A = 189.
$4.50A - 5A = 189. - 200.
Thus $- .50A = -11.00$
so $A = 22$ hours

9. **D**   The correct order is $\frac{57}{100}$, $\frac{4}{7}$, .6, .625

(Note: $\frac{57}{100} = .570$, $\frac{4}{7}$ is approximately .571 and .6 = .600)

10. **D**   Let x be the number of pennies and dimes, and n be the number of nickels. Solve the following system of equations:
$x + n + x = 11$
(The total number of coins is 11.)
$10x + 5n + x = 58$
(The value of the coins is 58 cents.)
Simplify both equations first.
$2x + n = 11$ (*)
$11x + 5n = 58$
Multiply both sides of the first equation by –5.
$-10x - 5n = -55$
$11x + 5n = 58$
Add the left sides and the right sides of the two equations.
$x = 3$ (Ron has 3 dimes and pennies.)
Substitute $x = 3$ into a previous equation (*) above.
$$2(3) + n = 11$$
$$6 + n = 11$$
$$n = 5$$
Ron has 5 nickels.

11. **A**   The 10-meter rope allows the goat to graze over the area of a circle of radius 10 meters. The formula for the area of a circle is πr^2, where r is the radius. So, $\pi(10)^2 = 100\pi$ square meters is the area.

12. **D**   Twice the number of 3-speed bicycles is $2y$. 25 more than $2y$ is $2y + 25$. So, x, the number of 10-speed bicycles, is $2y + 25$. $x = 2y + 25$.

13. **B** $75,000 = 3 \times 25,000$, not $3(25,000 - 12,500)$, which is the correct expression to use.

14. **C**   There is no way to determine Mr Hernandez's salary for any particular year. However, since the average is the sum of each year's salary divided by the total number of years (i.e., $23,400 = $ sum $\div 9$), the sum or total salary earned is found by multiplying $9 \times 23,400$.

15. **A**   The percent decline in ridership from June to July was 43.5%
($7798 - 4406 = 3392$ and $\frac{3392}{7798} \times 100\%$ $= 43.5\%$).

Writing

The following essay and essay outline have been written to demonstrate a well-written answer and the planning of a well-written answer. Use these only as guidelines to evaluating your own writing and organization. Many different organization patterns and plans could work equally well for the topics given.

FIRST TOPIC

Much has been written about the effects of television on the present generation. Discuss the positive and negative effects you believe television has had on children.

Essay

Newspapers and magazine articles, as well as professional journals, frequently report on studies which examine the effects of television on children. If we review these studies' findings, we begin to believe that we can prove whatever we wish: that television has contributed to the deterioration of students' spelling ability or that it has stimulated interest in reading or other classroom activities. Television is a medium which permits us to sit at dinner with a president and to experience visually many situations and places. At the same time, it makes only limited demands on our thinking ability. Television supplies even the laughter for situation comedies so shallow in plot that the purpose of the laugh track can only be to convince us that the program content is, in fact, humorous. A general review, then, of studies and commentaries on television's effects would demonstrate that both positive and negative effects exist.

It is, in fact, difficult to distinguish between the positive and negative effects of television viewing since any effect we identify as positive we can rather easily reinterpret as negative, or at least possessing negative side-effects. As an example, we might say that television helps to broaden experience, exposing children to situations and events to which they might not otherwise have access. By means of television, they experience the excitement of the Olympic games, as well as the horrors of the latest military confrontation in the world. They see parts of the world whose names and locations they have not yet learned in school. From television, they learn words, concepts, behaviors, and facts they wouldn't otherwise know. There is a drastic difference between what a child growing up in the 1940's knew and what the child of the 1990's knows. Certainly there is value in all of this. A child with a broader background of knowledge learns more and learns it faster. But how much of this knowledge is information we would rather children did not have? How much violence, injustice, and adult sexual behavior do children "experience" before they are ready to do so? The most common criticism of television viewing is that it does not allow children to remain children in knowledge.

Some advocates of television point out the higher-quality dramatic productions as stimuli to reading. The popular "Party of Five" series is often cited in this regard. Television producers have made some effort with certain quality productions to encourage children to "read all about it" by suggesting readings related to the topic of the program. On the other hand, some detractors suggest that these efforts are minimal, that television viewing merely absorbs time better spent in reading. They also suggest that reading which has been stimulated by a pre-digested television program is more shallow than independent reading and less open to individual thinking and interpretation.

The effects of television viewing—positive and negative—seem to revolve around one crucial problem. It is true that television allows us to see excellent productions of Shakespeare and to be present at a presidential inauguration, but television bombards us with such an array of experiences that we get little opportunity for any creative contemplation. Children move from one experience to another, often ones that they do not fully understand, without ever responding creatively or reacting to any of these experiences. It is a process of passive "viewing," not active "seeing," in which children participate. No ferment of ideas takes place. No implications are considered. No questions are posed. Children are exposed to an excess of experiences which are improperly digested.

It seems quite certain that television will remain part of our lives and that comments on television viewing and its effects will remain as well. For every positive effect that is cited, a negative value will be assigned by those who interpret it differently. Parents and teachers alike will share the responsibility of controlling the quantity of children's viewing and of helping children to assimilate what they view.

Second Topic

In a democracy, one of the greatest challenges is for people to work together to reach a decision. Describe an experience you have had, whether working on a committee, attending a town meeting, or planning a reunion, in which people were or were not able to work together to achieve their goal.

Essay Outline
A. Introduction
 1. Give background for the theme of the paper.
 2. Present thesis or main point of the paper.

B. Description of experience
 1. Context
 2. People involved
 3. Group goals and strategies

C. Explanation of problems or absence of problems
 1. Describe, in general, how your experience progressed.
 2. Give examples to support the description.

D. Summary and conclusions
 1. Restate your theme in brief terms.
 2. State conclusions you could draw from this experience, implications for viability of the democratic procedure, or recommendations.

Chapter 3

Reading Skills Review

The reading questions on the CBEST™ test your ability to

1. Find the main idea of a selection.

2. Find specific details mentioned in the passage.

3. Draw inferences or logical conclusions from a text.

4. Determine the meaning of unfamiliar words from their context.

5. Determine special techniques the author uses to achieve effects (methods of organizing a passage).

You may have to apply ideas or information in a passage to situations that are not included in the passage or make generalizations on the basis of information in the passage.

You have up to four hours to complete this section. Organize your time in any manner that is convenient to you. To simulate test conditions, give yourself 60 minutes when doing the practice exams. You do not need any outside knowledge to answer these questions; you can choose the best answer simply by analyzing whatever is stated or implied in the particular passage. The passages will vary in length from 200 words to just a sentence or two.

When you prepare for the test, read through the following review. Then work your way through the sample passages, taking time to study the answer explanations for approaches that might be new to you. In general, before tackling a particular passage, you may want to skim the questions to get a general sense of what is wanted. Then read the passage keeping those questions in mind. *Answer every question:* remember, the CBEST™ has no penalty for guessing.

REVIEW

Do not take this section for granted. When interviewing teachers who passed the CBEST™ on their second attempt, I was surprised to learn that it was not the math or the writing portion that confounded them; it was the reading section that troubled them the most. What happened? They either failed to take this section seriously, perhaps stemming from overconfidence, or they took it too seriously and psyched themselves out.

The first thing you must do to prepare for the exam is to sharpen and manage your sense of time. If you are like most of us mortals, your sense of time seems different under stress. You often have more time than you think. Learn to pace yourself without panicking, working quickly and efficiently. A good way to evaluate your sense of time is to time yourself as you take the practice exams.

The second thing you must do to prepare is evaluate your reading score on the diagnostic exam. On the sections you scored lower, identify your weaknesses. Did you misunderstand the directions? Sometimes the only problem you may have is a misunderstanding of what was asked of you. Were you confused by the meanings of words? Did you lose track of the line of reasoning in the essays?

If the problems are based on reading comprehension, there are several solutions. One step is to follow the long-term planning offered in this chapter. The other is to cover the short-term by looking at the test-taking tips.

Long-Term Planning for the CBEST™

When we read for pleasure, we are not tested or held accountable for understanding the text. Most readers tend to skim. In fact, today's newspapers, magazines, and popular novels are usually written with monosyllabic words, and rarely venture beyond simple and compound sentence structures. The average newspaper in the U.S. is written at a sixth grade level. So, if you have not read a demanding text in some time, you may not be ready for the CBEST™.

Reading is based upon understanding inferences, identifying main ideas, making accurate interpretations, and having a reasonable vocabulary. Each of these skills can be developed. There are practical strategies for understanding questions and answering those questions effectively.

There are numerous ways you can prepare for the reading and writing portions of this test. Reading good essays, poetry, short stories, novels, histories, and biographies can help you with your reading as well as your writing. There are two commonly used techniques many English teachers employ that can help any candidate improve reading and writing abilities. One is a unique vocabulary journal, and the other is a dialectic notebook.

The vocabulary journal is a tool for acquiring new words. The type of vocabulary journal I recommend notes the new word by underlining. It then cites the page and paragraph the word comes from, defines the word with the use of a good dictionary, and quotes the sentence, clause, or phrase the new word was found in. On the next line, the journal writer paraphrases the sentence with a familiar word. Note the following example:

VOCABULARY JOURNAL

The Call of the Wild by Jack London and the *Webster's II: New Riverside Dictionary.*
1. dominion (*C.W.* pps. 173 par. 6). Definition: n. 1. Supreme authority or control: sovereignty. 2. A territory or sphere of control or influence: realm.
  Direct quote—
  a. "...he watched them pass under the dominion of the man in the red sweater."
  Student paraphrased response—
  b. He watched them pass under the control of the man in red.

The journal entries identify new words. The journal also gives you a dictionary definition of the words you are acquiring. More importantly, it shows how the word is used in context. And last, it allows you to associate new words with those you commonly use. Remember, no vocabulary journal will work well unless the words in it are used in writing and speaking.

The vocabulary journal might be too long and time consuming for some candidates. A more commonly used technique is to merely list the newly acquired words and define them. Some students do well memorizing long columns of new words, but there is at best a short-term benefit from such a process.

The dialectic journal requires no more than paper, a ruler, and a straight line drawn down the center of the page. At the top of the left-hand side write *Note Taking*. At the top of the right-hand side write *Note Making*. Whenever you read an interesting passage, note it in the *Note Taking* side. Use direct quotations, ellipses, and brackets to identify key words and phrases. On the *Note Making* side, follow a process of *why* and *because* questioning and answering. For example, ask yourself why the passage was important. Answer it with an implied because. Continue this line of questioning until you are satisfied with your answers. After reading an entire book, you will have many pages of clear notes. On one side will be direct quotations, and on the other side will be your ideas. This process creates a lively dialogue between the reader and the text. From this dialogue, the reader will discover issues of importance for the purpose of further discussion. This technique can also help you improve your reading skills by helping you find the main idea as well as interpret and explore meanings through inferences.

The journal should look like this:

A Dialectic Journal on
The Call of the Wild by Jack London

p# / ¶#	Note Taking	Note Making
173 6	"He [Buck] was beaten… he was not broken…. he stood no chance against a man with a club."	Buck understood his limitations. This is important because it shows his intelligence. This intelligence sets him apart from others, making him special.

The above journal helps you identify important passages. It also helps you to interpret what the passages mean.

Both vocabulary and dialectic journals take time. They require practice, but they improve reading and writing abilities. The vocabulary journal not only gives you a list of new words, it shows how the words are used in context and how to relate the words to common terms you might use often. The dialectic journal helps you read accurately for meaning.

Another way of developing a strong vocabulary is to understand root words, suffixes, and prefixes. But a memorized vocabulary in itself has a short shelf life. Applied skills are often retained much longer.

Whether using a list or the above journals, begin using them long before you take the exam.

Short-Term Planning for the CBEST™

Finding the Main Idea

Questions testing ability to find the main idea often take the following forms:

1. The title that best expresses the ideas of the passage is ...

2. The main idea of this selection may be best expressed as ...

3. Which of the following best states the theme of the passage?

4. This passage illustrates ...

5. The author's purpose in writing this passage is ...

Since a paragraph is defined as a group of sentences revolving about a central theme, any title that is appropriate must include the thought that each of the sentences of the paragraph is developing. It should not be too broad or too narrow in its scope: it should be specific and yet comprehensive enough to include all the essential ideas presented by the sentences.

Note: **A good title for a passage of two or more paragraphs should include the thoughts of *all* the paragraphs.**

Often, authors provide the reader with a sentence that expresses the main idea succinctly. Such *topic sentences* may appear anywhere in the paragraph, although we are accustomed to looking for them in the opening or closing sentences. However, in the kind of reading that you are expected to be able to handle, topic sentences are often implied rather than stated.

One Way to Identify the Main Idea

If you cannot identify a topic sentence, you can find the main idea in other ways. One way is to write a mental headline, as if to summarize the passage for the readers of a newspaper. A quick way to do this is:

1. Decide the person, place, or thing which is the subject of the reading passage. The subject can be something abstract, such as an idea. It can be a process, or something in motion, for which no single-word synonym exists. This *person, place, thing, idea,* or *process* then becomes the subject of the headline sentence.

2. Decide the most important thing that is being said about the subject. Either the subject must be *doing* something, or something is *being done* to it. This action becomes the verb of the mental headline.

ILLUSTRATION I

The much-maligned profit motive may not be the only or even the most basic incitement for the development of trade in human societies. Very likely the enjoyment of variety accounts sufficiently for those early, unrecorded exchanges—one family's beans for another's squash, for instance, or a blue feather for a red one. In addition, the differences between human beings naturally caused one person to manufacture a better reed flute, another to be a superior discoverer of good scraping stones, a third to know, by an unself-conscious acuteness of observation that could almost be called instinct, where the choice berries and fruits were to be found. Trade encouraged each to become still more proficient in his or her specialty. So commerce has encouraged the development of skills and, over the long run, an ever-increasing quality of goods. Yet it may be questioned whether the human being is implicitly greedy, as might be supposed by a superficial study of economics. Many human needs have been filled by the exchange of goods we now call business.

A good title for this passage would be:

(A) *The Maligned Profit Motive.*
(B) *Trade—Society's Basic Need.*
(C) *Why Trade?*
(D) *Reasons for Trade.*
(E) *Shallow Economic Theories.*

All of the above choices have something to do with the passage. A question which asks for a title, however, is asking you to select the *main* idea from several subsidiary ones. First, find the person, place, thing, idea, or process which is repeated throughout the passage. Are there any words in the second sentence which repeat something in the first sentence? *Exchanges* repeats the idea of *trade.* Go on to the third sentence. The idea of trade is not repeated in words. However, the three skills mentioned imply three products for trade. *Trade* occurs in the fourth sentence, *commerce* in the fifth, and *exchange of goods* and *business* in the last. The subject, then, must be something about trade, and the idea will include the most primitive forms of trade as well as modern business.

Now, look for the verb of the headline. What is trade *doing,* or what is *being done* to it? Look again for a repetition of ideas. The first sentence tells us that the causes of early trade were *more than* the profit motive, which must, then, be one cause. The second sentence gives us another cause of trade—the enjoyment of variety. Still another cause—superior products—is implied, though not stated, by the third and fourth sentences. The next sentence gives us some results of trade. Then, another possible cause—man's implicit greed—is doubted in the sixth sentence. The final sentence is a summation and a correction of a misconception—trade fills several needs.

The subject of our mental headline is *trade* and the predicate of the headline sentence is *has several causes* or *fills a variety of needs.* A number of headlines can be built on these ideas: TRADE IS PRODUCT OF HUMAN NEEDS, or SEVERAL HUMAN CHARACTERISTICS CAUSE TRADE, etc. Note that the last sentence of the passage is now clearly seen to be a topic sentence.

Which of the proposed titles fits the headline best? Choice A can be rejected for it is only one cause of trade. Choice B is not stated in the passage. Trade may be a basic need of society, but this passage does not say so. Choice E may be rejected for it is not part of the main idea as stated in the mental headline. We must choose between Choice C and Choice D. Choice C can imply a decision to be made in the future or an argument against trade. Choice D is directed more toward the past, which accords better with the passage. The answer is Choice D.

Another Way to Identify the Main Idea

Another way to find the main idea is mentally to order the ideas presented, deciding which are equal, which subordinate. We could also say that we weigh them, separating the heavy from the light. Using this approach with the same passage, we find: In the first two sentences, *profit motive* is equal to or possibly less than *enjoyment of variety. Superior products* (implied by the third sentence) are equal to the first two ideas because of the words *in addition.* Sentence 6 denies the importance of *greed,* despite appearances. It cannot be superior to the others. The final sentence refuses to place any of these motives first, so they must all be balanced in the statement of the main idea: *People have several motives for trade.* We

Answer Sheet— A Diagnostic Test

Reading

6/15

1. Ⓐ Ⓑ Ⓒ Ⓓ Ⓔ
2. Ⓐ Ⓑ Ⓒ Ⓓ Ⓔ
3. Ⓐ Ⓑ Ⓒ Ⓓ Ⓔ
✗4. Ⓐ Ⓑ Ⓒ Ⓓ Ⓔ
5. Ⓐ Ⓑ Ⓒ Ⓓ Ⓔ

6. Ⓐ Ⓑ Ⓒ Ⓓ Ⓔ
✗7. Ⓐ Ⓑ Ⓒ Ⓓ Ⓔ
8. Ⓐ Ⓑ Ⓒ Ⓓ Ⓔ
9. Ⓐ Ⓑ Ⓒ Ⓓ Ⓔ
10. Ⓐ Ⓑ Ⓒ Ⓓ Ⓔ

11. Ⓐ Ⓑ Ⓒ Ⓓ Ⓔ
✗12. Ⓐ Ⓑ Ⓒ Ⓓ Ⓔ
13. Ⓐ Ⓑ Ⓒ Ⓓ Ⓔ
✗14. Ⓐ Ⓑ Ⓒ Ⓓ Ⓔ
✗15. Ⓐ Ⓑ Ⓒ Ⓓ Ⓔ

Mathematics

7/15 ✗

1. Ⓐ Ⓑ Ⓒ Ⓓ Ⓔ
✗2. Ⓐ Ⓑ Ⓒ Ⓓ Ⓔ
3. Ⓐ Ⓑ Ⓒ Ⓓ Ⓔ
✗4. Ⓐ Ⓑ Ⓒ Ⓓ Ⓔ
5. Ⓐ Ⓑ Ⓒ Ⓓ Ⓔ

✗6. Ⓐ Ⓑ Ⓒ Ⓓ Ⓔ
7. Ⓐ Ⓑ Ⓒ Ⓓ Ⓔ
✗8. Ⓐ Ⓑ Ⓒ Ⓓ Ⓔ
✗9. Ⓐ Ⓑ Ⓒ Ⓓ Ⓔ
10. Ⓐ Ⓑ Ⓒ Ⓓ Ⓔ

11. Ⓐ Ⓑ Ⓒ Ⓓ Ⓔ
✗12. Ⓐ Ⓑ Ⓒ Ⓓ Ⓔ
13. Ⓐ Ⓑ Ⓒ Ⓓ Ⓔ
✗14. Ⓐ Ⓑ Ⓒ Ⓓ Ⓔ
✗15. Ⓐ Ⓑ Ⓒ Ⓓ Ⓔ

$R = 2 \times 25{,}000$

$S =$

$\dfrac{25}{31\overline{)7}}$ $41\overline{)\begin{smallmatrix}1.75\\7.00\end{smallmatrix}}$ $.75$ $\dfrac{43}{75}$

$D\dfrac{3}{45} = \dfrac{30}{25}$

$\dfrac{6}{15}$ $\begin{smallmatrix}30\\28\\20\end{smallmatrix}$ $75.1\overline{)193}$ $\dfrac{150}{43}$ $.93$

$9\ 3 = 34$

75.00
144
60
48

$50¢$ $\dfrac{3}{4} \div \dfrac{3R}{16} =$ $6\overline{)1.00}$ $\dfrac{1.0 \times 10}{2}$ $\dfrac{100}{2}$

$\dfrac{3}{4} \times \dfrac{16\ 4}{32} = \dfrac{12}{31}$ $\dfrac{.15}{.16}$ 3.1 $\dfrac{100}{2}$ 50

$\dfrac{4.50}{40}$ $\dfrac{5.00}{40}$

$X = 10 sp$ $\dfrac{2000}{1800}$ $200\ 0$

$X = 3 sp$ $25{,}000$ $3\overline{)\dfrac{1}{32}}\ \dfrac{2}{3}$ 150.00

$X + 25$

then look for the title that most nearly reflects this balance of ideas, or ordering of importance.

Note: **Some common words to indicate *equality* of elements:**

again	another	first	moreover
also	as well as	furthermore	similar
and	besides	likewise	

EXAMPLES

Laxity of application is, *again,* one reason for ...
The salubrious climate was *also* ...
Promptness *and* neatness are requisites ...
Another earth-renewing crop is ...
A visit by the chief engineer *as well as* a government inspection sent shivers of apprehension ...
Besides the delay in ratification, the committee ...

Note: **Some common words to point out elements of *greater value*:**
above all   importance
deciding   significantly

EXAMPLES

The quick application of justice is, *above all,* the determining ...
The *deciding* factor was to be found not in ...
A technique of *importance* in the Impressionist movement ...
Significantly, the bearer of this news ...

An important note: **If you are like most people, you often lose your place while you are reading. This happens because about every 90 seconds the mind goes blank. For some people, a blank mind can last a lifetime, but for most of us it only lasts seconds. I have known of diligent students who have returned to the beginning of a reading passage fully determined to concentrate, only to lose their focus at the same spot they did previously. By making brief notes onto the side of your readings, you help yourself mark where you have left off when your mind wearies or wanders. Instead of returning to the beginning of the passage, look at your notes and return to the location just before your mind drifted. For example, observe the following breakdown:**

Jerry & Joyce disagree on how to spend district $ Unlike Jerry, Joyce remained uncommitted to any compact that would appropriate the school district's resources it required for indispensable services. Jerry, the visionary, saw the need for arts and music. Joyce wondered if the money could be better allocated on remediation, or even saved for future programs. Neither could come to a quick concordance on what the district's priorities should be.

The best title for the above passage is

(A) *The Need to Raise Taxes for Schools.*
(B) *Difficult Personalities.*
(C) *Hard Choices.*
(D) *Foolish Decisions.*
(E) *Indispensable School Services.*

Using the note taking techniques should help you come to a quick conclusion. The question asks for an answer that will sum up what the passage is about. One answer encompasses the main issue of the passage. The best answer is C because, as the notes to the side state, the two personalities cannot come to an agreement. Not coming to an agreement is the same as recognizing the hard choices Jerry and Joyce have to make. Nowhere does the passage suggest the need to raise taxes, therefore, A is incorrect. Little is revealed about personalities other than that Jerry prefers art and music, and Joyce prefers helping remedial students. Therefore B is ruled out. The passage does not suggest that either decision will be foolish, so D is eliminated. The passage has not come to a conclusion as to what indispensable school services are, so E is incorrect. That leaves us with C.

Finding Specific Detail

In the development of ideas, a writer will make statements in support of his or her point of view or the message he or she is trying to convey. The questions most frequently found in reading tests merely require you to identify one of these statements, often expressed in different words. This kind of question may take one of these forms:

1. The author states that ...

2. The writer mentions all of the items listed below EXCEPT ...

3. Which of the following statements is correct, according to the reading passage?

Note: **The answer to questions of specific detail must be in the passage. You must be able to find a word or sentence or group of sentences which justifies the choice. You must not call on information from other sources. You must not let yourself be hurried into making unfounded assumptions.**

EXAMPLE

In Illustration I on page 27, the author states that

    (A) the profit motive is the cause of trade.
    (B) differences between human beings cause envy.
    (C) men sometimes work by instinct.
    (D) people have generally become more skillful.
    (E) studying economics leads to wrong ideas.

Choice A: Reject. The first sentence states that the profit motive is not the only cause of trade. This expression in the question—"is the cause"—does not allow for other causes. Choice B: Reject. Differences between human beings may cause envy, but the passage does not say so. Choice C: The passage says that one may work by a process that could almost be called instinct—but it is not. Reject. Choice E: Only one kind of study—superficial—will lead to wrong ideas. "Eating leaves leads to death by poisoning?" Only a certain kind of leaf. Choice D: The author states that "commerce has encouraged the development of skills." Skills do not develop alone, but in people, so people must be more skillful. The word *generally* allows for interruptions by war, natural disasters, etc.

Finding Implications and Drawing Inferences

This is a more difficult kind of question since you must draw forth an answer not stated in the text—a process which is open to many errors. You may not be able to find words or sentences which clearly support your choice, as is possible in questions which ask for identification of detail. Nevertheless, by grasping the author's ideas, you should be able to reject inferences which can *not* be made.

Note: **How to draw inferences:**

1. *Reason*—If X is true, Y must also be true.

2. *Perceive Feelings*—If the author feels this way on one subject, he probably feels a certain way about another subject.

3. *Sense a Larger Structure*—This passage is part of an argument for a proposal, or part of a description, or part of a longer story.

A question which calls on the reader to make inferences could be stated in any of these ways:

1. The author probably feels that...

2. The passage is intended to...

3. It may be inferred from this passage that...

4. An inference which may not be made from this passage is...

5. The paragraph preceding this passage probably states that...

EXAMPLE

In Illustration I on page 27, the author seems to be

(A) defending business against accusations of greed.
(B) preparing for an indictment of business.
(C) skeptical of recorded history.
(D) proficient in his specialty.
(E) ashamed of his ignorance of economics.

The author says that the profit motive has been *maligned*. He *questions* whether humans are greedy, which implies that someone has said that they are. This passage—a collection of various motives for business—may then be aimed at a defense against the accusation that there is only one motive for business—greed. However, we must be sure to consider all the choices. Choice A is possible. Choice B must then be wrong. There is no basis in the reading for Choices C and D. Since he says that others have a superficial knowledge of economics, he must feel that he is in a position to judge. Therefore, Choice E is rejected. Choice A is the only possibility.

Determining the Meaning of Strange Words

When a question in the reading part of an examination asks for the meaning of a word, it can usually be deduced from the context. The purpose of this kind of question is to determine how well the student can extract meaning from the text, not how extensive his general vocabulary is.

Note: Sometimes the unknown word is common but used in one of its special or technical meanings.

EXAMPLE

He *threw* the pot in an hour. The wheel turned busily and the shape grew quickly under his forming fingers. (*Throw* here means to shape on a potter's wheel.)

Note: At other times, the unknown word may bear a deceptive semblance to a known word.

EXAMPLE

He fell *insensible* to the ground. (He was unconscious. He did not fall foolish or without common sense to the ground.)

Note: Sometimes a word may be completely new. Punctuation and surrounding words can form clues.

EXAMPLE

Japanese do not talk comfortably or freely about the *burakumin,* the social outcasts. (Burakumin = social outcasts.)

Note: Do not assume that you know the meaning if you know *one* meaning of a word. The student must find the meaning of that word as *used* in that passage. He must look within the reading for clues. Often the thought is repeated in the same sentence or near it.

ILLUSTRATION II

He laughed and shrugged. "I have no choice," he said. "I must bow to the *ineluctable.*"

The word *ineluctable* is closest to

    (A) impermissible.
    (B) unavoidable.
    (C) unknown.
    (D) terror.
    (E) evil.

If a person has *no choice,* he probably wants to avoid something, but it is *unavoidable.* This does not necessarily mean that he does not permit it, or does not know it. *Terror* and *evil* are not implied. The ineluctable could be an unwanted dessert thrust on a guest by an implacable hostess.

Note: Sometimes the opposite of the meaning is given somewhere in the passage.

ILLUSTRATION III

Conventional Japanese artists use methods of painting on paper with stone pigments which they learned from visits to China. These are the traditional paintings Westerners often think of or refer to as drawings—though they are not drawings. Conversely, a Japanese painter who works in Western style—painting abstractions, for instance—is seldom a *draftsman:*

Drafters are

    (A) conventional artists.
    (B) non-Japanese.
    (C) abstract.
    (D) artists who draw.
    (E) schooled.

The word *conversely* tells us that a contrast is being presented. One thing is unlike another, and we may find that they are opposites. The contrast is between Japanese artists who work in Western style and Japanese artists who work in a traditional style (in *their* tradition). Those who work in Western style are not often draftsmen, but, it is implied, those who work in traditional style are draftsmen. What, then, is characteristic of the traditional style and is not evident in the Western style? It could be the use of stone pigments, or the fact that the method was learned from the Chinese, or the fact that these works appear to be drawings. If artists can use paint to appear like drawings, they must also be able to draw with drawing materials. None of the other possibilities is among the choices given. Only Choice D relates to the passage.

Note: **Sometimes the meaning of a word can be tracked by following pronoun referents.**

ILLUSTRATION IV

In his strong Scottish burr, he said that he liked a room without *gewgaws* and tin-plate souvenirs from an otherwise unmemorable event. He complained that *these* things tried to appear valuable, but nevertheless were worthless.

A *gewgaw* is

    (A) something from Scotland.
    (B) a World's Fair souvenir.
    (C) a showy trifle.
    (D) a little statue.
    (E) pillows.

Look back in the text for the meaning of *these*. We find *these things* are *gewgaws* and *souvenirs,* so both are described as worthless, but seemingly valuable. A *gewgaw* then, must be a showy trifle. It could be any one of the other things as well, but there is no evidence of what exactly it is.

Note: **Sometimes the meaning of a word is given before it is used.**

ILLUSTRATION V

During the 1974 spring labor offensive, 6,000,000 members of labor unions, either local or national, worked together to organize the most efficient strikes ever reported in the nation. The consequent wage increases, ranging; from 10 percent to 50 percent, added to inflationary pressures. Because of the uncertain economy this year's *shunto* was timid and subdued, and the resulting wage increases much less.

The word *shunto* is closest to

    (A) replacement.
    (B) wage increase.
    (C) labor union.
    (D) yearly push to better wages.
    (E) inflationary pressure

The *shunto* of this year is being compared with that of a previous year. When we look at the only previous year given—1974—we find that what also resulted in wage increases was the *spring labor offensive,* which organized *strikes*. The choices do not offer *strikes*, but Choice D is close to a spring labor offensive.

Note: **Sometimes the entire selection describes a situation which is a definition of a word.**

ILLUSTRATION VI

The problem of *kaso* remains serious. Some villages have disappeared completely; others struggle with continually declining job opportunities. There are, officially, some one thousand such districts. One typical *kaso* town was Ohtaki, which has lost more than half its population in the last 15 years. Its few mines ceased operation several years ago. People continue to work on small farms, with some lumbering on the side. Most young people attend high schools in other towns, and some go on to college, but few come back to work. Ohtaki is beautifully situated in mountains on the edge of a large national park, offering hope of a tourist industry someday. But this kind of development takes time, and, meanwhile, Ohtaki dwindles, like so many others of its kind.

The problem of *kaso* is one of

    (A) decline of population in rural areas.
    (B) poverty.
    (C) poor farming.
    (D) lack of educational opportunity.
    (E) lack of a tourist industry.

Choices B and C are not mentioned, and Choice E could solve the problem—so it is itself not the problem. Ohtaki is an example of *kaso*; therefore, the problem of *kaso* could be Choice D or Choice A. However, educational opportunity is mentioned only once, while a decline of population is mentioned or implied three times. Choice A is best.

Determining Special Techniques Used by the Author

An alert reader expects to find certain techniques in certain kinds of writing. For instance:

In *literature,* writers often:
—create a mood
—present a setting
—describe a character
—narrate an event

In *social studies,* authors frequently:
—use dates to arrange events in sequential order
—point out cause and effect relationships
—make comparisons
—define terms
—propagandize or reason deceptively

In *science,* writers often:
—classify things and events
—try to solve problems
—define technical terms
—discuss experiments and their results

While the purpose of writing determines many of these techniques, no class of writing excludes techniques that may also be found in some other class. Literature offers examples of cause and effect relationships, and a social studies text may try to solve problems. However, the reader who quickly identifies the kind of writing before him expects certain techniques and may recognize them more quickly.

Note: **Some common words indicating *cause and effect*:**

accordingly	final	in short
as a result	hence	lastly
conclusion	in conclusion	therefore
		thus

EXAMPLES

The selection of a design was, *accordingly* ...
As a result, the vote in Congress split ...
The decision is of crucial importance and forces us to the *conclusion* that ...
The *final* outcome of these endeavors ...
Hence, in future conflicts, we believe ...
Therefore, whatever his detractors may imagine, we know ...
Thus, the development of the town followed the route of ...

Note: **Some common words signaling a *comparison* or *contrast*:**

but	nevertheless	still
however	otherwise	yet

EXAMPLES

The philosophy of my youth was progressivism, *but* ...
The study of law fell into disrepute...*however,* after a lapse of a decade ...
Most laboratories use a process ... *Nevertheless,* the method under discussion ...
If this point were strengthened, the defense of the Pacific would ... *otherwise,* the exposure of the West Coast ...
A common means of communication between members of Congress and ...
yet the efficacy ...

Note: **Some common ways to indicate a *change of direction* (a new thought, but not necessarily a comparison nor an effect):**

although	instead of	oddly enough
despite	notwithstanding	regardless
in spite of		

EXAMPLES

Although the passage of the bill was widely acclaimed, its executive ...
Despite a high volume of attendance, the quality of performance ...
Instead of a gentle decline into senescence, the octogenarian ...
The price rise, *notwithstanding,* was indicative of ...
Oddly enough, the product was soon ...

Note also: **Words calling attention to important ideas:**
don't overlook
notice that
of significance is

Words announcing an illustration:

for example	in such cases	namely
for instance	in the same manner	specifically
in other words	just as	

Negative and all-inclusive words:

always	never
at all times	no
entirely	none
every	not
only	under all circumstances

Superlatives:

best	worst

SAMPLE PASSAGES

This section provides 10 sample reading passages. Each passage is followed by one or more questions. The questions include all of the types that are commonly used on the CBEST™.

Read each passage carefully and then try to answer the question or questions that follow. Then check your answers by reading the Analysis that follows each reading passage.

PASSAGE 1

Despite his many hours of hard work at his bench, he realized that his progress was *tenuous.*

We can also describe his progress as

(A) excellent.
(B) laudable.
(C) time-consuming.
(D) steady.
(E) insubstantial.

This sentence indicates that the young man's hard work did not have its expected result. Instead of making excellent, laudable (praiseworthy), or steady progress, he made barely any progress at all; his progress was tenuous, or insubstantial (Choice E). Be aware that words like *despite, although, instead of,* and *unlike* may signal a contrast.

PASSAGE 2

The six-year-old is about the best example that can be found of that type of inquisitiveness that causes irritated adults to exclaim, "Curiosity killed the cat." To him, the world is a fascinating place to be explored and investigated quite thoroughly, but such a world is bounded by the environment in which he or the people he knows live. It is constantly expanding through new experiences, which bring many eager questions from members of any group of first graders, as each one tries to figure out new relationships—to know and accept his place within the family, the school, and the community—to understand all around him. There are adults who find it quite annoying to be presented with such rank inquisitiveness. But this is no purposeless prying, no idle curiosity! It is that quality, characteristic of the successful adult, inherent in the good citizen—intellectual curiosity.

In this passage the author's attitude toward children is one of

(A) despair.
(B) confidence.
(C) indifference.
(D) sharp criticism.
(E) exaggerated optimism.

Although the author discusses the irritation adults sometimes feel at the incessant questions asked by six-year-old children, he feels that these questions are not purposeless. He feels that this intellectual curiosity is a characteristic of the adult citizen, and he is happy and confident when children display this trait (Choice B).

PASSAGE 3

Good American English is simply good English, English that differs a little in pronunciation, vocabulary, and occasionally in idiom from good English as spoken in London or South Africa, but differs no more than our physical surroundings, our political and social institutions, and the other circumstances reflected in language differ from those of other English-speaking areas. It rests upon the same basis as that which the standard speech of England rests upon—the usage of reputable speakers and writers throughout the country. No American student of language is so provincial as to hope, or wish, that the American standard may some day be adopted in England. Nor does he share the views of such in England as think that we would do well to take our standard readymade from them. He will be content with the opinion of Henry Bradley that "the wiser sort among us will not dispute that Americans have acquired the right to frame their own standards of correct English on the usage of their best writers and speakers."

1. The author considers good American English to be

(A) proper for use in America.
(B) superior to the English spoken in South Africa.
(C) inferior to the English spoken in England.
(D) too idiomatic for general acceptance.
(E) suitable as a standard for English-speaking countries.

2. According to the author, correctness in language is determined by

   (A) the majority of those who speak it.
   (B) the dominant social and political institutions.
   (C) geographical conditions.
   (D) good speakers and writers.
   (E) those who wish to standardize the language.

The statement of Henry Bradley in the last sentence justifies the selection of Choice A as the answer to the first question.

The justification for Choice D as the best answer to the second question can be found in two sentences in the passage. Mr. Bradley's quotation mentions the usage of the "best writers and speakers." Likewise, the same thought is found in the second sentence ("the usage of reputable speakers and writers throughout the country").

PASSAGE 4

Today in America vast concourses of youth are flocking to our colleges, eager for something, just what they do not know. It makes much difference what they get. They will be prone to demand something they can immediately use: science, economics, business administration, law in its narrower sense. I submit that the shepherds should not first feed the flock with these. I argue for what used to go as a liberal education—not in the sense that young folks should waste precious years in efforts to master ancient tongues; but I speak for an introduction into the thoughts and deeds of men who have lived before them, in other countries than their own, with other strifes and other needs. This I maintain, not in the interest of that general cultural background which is so often a cloak for the prig, the snob and the pedant. But I submit to you that in some such way alone can we meet and master the high-power salesman of political patent medicines.

The title that best expresses the ideas of this passage is

   (A) *Why Pupils Go to College.*
   (B) *Foreign Languages for Culture.*
   (C) *The Need for Vocational Training.*
   (D) *The Shepherd and His Student Flock.*
   (E) *The Importance of a Liberal Education.*

The author maintains that the young people flocking to our colleges do not know exactly what they are seeking. They often desire materials which they can put to immediate use; they seek subjects which have practical application. The author urges a study of the ideas and actions of men in other countries and other times. This liberal education is valuable not for its snobbishness or pedantry but for the insight it gives the student which will enable him to meet the problems of current society.

By paraphrasing the ideas of the passage in some such manner, the student can see that the writer is stressing "the importance of a liberal education." Thus, Choice E is best. Choice A is inadequate because it is not discussed in the passage. We are told that students are flocking to the colleges but we are not told why. Choice B is mentioned only by indirection. The author talks of mastering ancient tongues. He does not mention the study of contemporary foreign languages in this passage. Similarly, the author does not discuss the need for vocational training. Instead he implies that students, mistakenly, often seek vocational training because of its immediacy of application. Choice D is so broad that it becomes vague. The author is more interested in what the teacher gives his pupils than in the general idea of teacher and pupil.

PASSAGE 5

Many educators argued that a homogeneous grouping of students would improve instruction because the range of student abilities would be limited.

Such a grouping of students would be

    (A) varied.
    (B) irregular.
    (C) cognitive.
    (D) heterodox.
    (E) undiversified.

The roots *homo,* same, and *gen,* kind, indicate that a homogeneous student grouping is made up of students of the same kind or level of ability. It is therefore an *undiversified* group (Choice E).

PASSAGE 6

Most people do not think of fishes and other marine animals as having voices, and of those who are aware of the fact that many of them can "speak," few understand that these "conversations" have significance. Actually, their talk may be as meaningful as much of our own. For example, some sea animals use their "voices" to locate their food in the ocean expanses; others, to let their fellows know of their whereabouts; and still others, as a means of obtaining mates. Sometimes, "speaking" may even mean the difference between life and death to a marine animal. It appears in some cases that when a predator approaches, the prey depends on no more than the sounds it makes to escape.

Fish sounds are important to man, also. By listening to them he can learn a great deal about the habits of the creatures that make them, the size of the schools they form, the patterns of their migrations, and the nature of the environments in which they live. He can also apply this information to the more effective utilization of the listening posts he has set up to detect enemy submarines. A knowledge of fish sounds can avoid confusion and unneeded effort when a "new" sound is picked up and the sound sentry must decide whether or not to call an alert.

1. Which of the following statements is *best* supported by the information given? Noises produced by fish

    (A) are apparently random.
    (B) are used by fishermen to increase their catch.
    (C) can be utilized to tell whether or not a submarine is nearby.
    (D) can confuse users of submarine-detection equipment.

2. Which of the following statements can *best* be inferred from the information given?

    (A) Fish noises cannot be transmitted through air.
    (B) Hearing in fishes is more acute than in people.
    (C) The chief use of "fish voices" is to enable one fish to communicate with another fish.
    (D) The significance of some fish noises has been studied.

1. The passage informs us that the noises produced by fish are "meaningful" and therefore not apparently random. This eliminates Choice A. Statement B may be inferred from the text but is not mentioned in the passage. Fish sounds apparently interfere with listening posts for submarines. These sounds cannot be used to detect submarines. The listener must learn to differentiate between fish sounds and the sounds made by submarines. If he does not differentiate, he will be confused. Thus, D is the best answer.

2. Choice D is best because it is obvious that what we know about fish sounds is based on study. Choices A and B are not mentioned in the text and are therefore assumptions made by the reader. We can object to Choice C because we cannot find any justification for the statement that the "chief" use of these voices is for communication. It is, again, an unwarranted conclusion.

PASSAGE 7

We must discover and develop each student's *intrinsic* talents.

The student's talents are

  (A) inner.
  (B) unwanted.
  (C) objective.
  (D) specious.
  (E) extraneous.

If the student's talents are in need of discovery, they are not obvious talents easily spotted by observers. If they must be developed, we can assume they are not unwanted or specious (deceptive). Choice A is best; the talents are inner and inborn.

PASSAGE 8

A more significant manifestation of the concern of the community with the general welfare is the collection and dissemination of statistics. This statement may cause the reader to smile, for statistics seem to be drab and prosaic things. The great growth of statistics, however, is one of the most remarkable characteristics of the age. Never before has a community kept track from month to month, and in some cases from week to week, of how many people are born, how many die and from what causes, how many are sick, how much is being produced, how much is being sold, how many people are at work, how many people are unemployed, how long they have been out of work, what prices people pay, how much income they receive and from what sources, how much they owe, what they intend to buy. These elaborate attempts of the country to keep informed about what is happening mean that the community is concerned with how its members are faring and with the conditions under which they live. For this reason the present age may take pride in its numerous and regular statistical reports and in the rapid increase in the number of these reports. No other age has evidenced such a keen interest in the conditions of the people.

1. The title below that best expresses the ideas of this passage is:

  (A) *Remarkable Statistics.*
  (B) *The Concerned Community.*

(C) *The Nature of Statistics.*
(D) *Statistics and Human Welfare.*
(E) *How to Keep Informed.*

2. The writer implies that statistics are

(A) too scientific for general use.
(B) too elaborate and too drab.
(C) related to the improvement of living conditions.
(D) frequently misinterpreted.
(E) a product of the machine age.

The author does not describe statistics themselves as remarkable but rather calls their great growth a remarkable characteristic of this age. Similarly, while mentioning several sorts of data gathered, the author does not define the nature of statistics itself. Thus, Choices A and C introduce ideas not presented by the author and are, therefore, unsuitable as appropriate titles. The passage concerns itself with the collection of statistics as a manifestation of a community's concern for the welfare of its members. Thus, any title should include the key word statistics. Choices B and E fail to do so. The best title, therefore, is *Statistics and Human Welfare,* Choice D.

The opening and closing sentences of this passage tell us that statistics are collected out of consideration for the "general welfare" and are the result of a "keen interest in the conditions of the people." Thus, for the second question Choice C is justified. Nowhere in the passage does the author state that statistics are too scientific or misinterpreted. The author, likewise, does not state that statistics are too elaborate. The author does state that they may *seem* drab. The use of the word *seem* implies that the author does not believe that the statement is correct. Choice E is not justified by the text.

PASSAGE 9

As we know the short story today it is largely a product of the nineteenth and twentieth centuries and its development parallels the rapid development of industrialism in America. We have been a busy people, busy principally in evolving a production system supremely efficient. Railroads and factories have blossomed almost overnight; mines and oil fields have been discovered and exploited; mechanical inventions by the thousands have been made and perfected. Speed has been an essential element in our endeavors, and it has affected our lives, our very natures. Leisurely reading has been, for most Americans, impossible. As with our meals, we have grabbed bits of reading standing up, cafeteria style, and gulped down cups of sentiment on the run. We have had to read while hanging on to a strap in a swaying trolley car or in a rushing subway or while tending to a clamoring telephone switchboard. Our popular magazine has been our literary automat and its stories have often been no more substantial than sandwiches.

1. The title below that best expresses the ideas of this paragraph is:

(A) *"Quick-lunch" Literature.*
(B) *Life in the Machine Age.*
(C) *Culture in Modern Life.*
(D) *Reading while Traveling.*
(E) *The Development of Industrialism.*

2. The short story today owes its popularity to its

    (A) settings.
    (B) plots.
    (C) style.
    (D) length.
    (E) characters.

3. The short story has developed because of Americans'

    (A) reactions against the classics.
    (B) need for reassurance.
    (C) lack of culture.
    (D) lack of education.
    (E) taste for speed.

4. From this selection one would assume that the author's attitude toward short stories is one of

    (A) approval.
    (B) indifference.
    (C) contempt.
    (D) impartiality.
    (E) regret.

The opening sentence of this passage defines the topic: the short story as a product of modern, fast-paced society. Any title which does not include both the idea of literature and the idea of speed is incomplete. Only Choice A will do.

If leisurely reading is impossible in modern times, then readers must content themselves with reading matter that is short. Thus, the short story owes its popularity to its length (Choice D).

In answering question 3, we must remember that the author throughout stresses the effects of speed on our lives. Nowhere does the author refer to an American reaction against the classics or a need for reassurance. While the author mentions the sentimentality and lack of substance of our reading matter, he never asserts that these stem from a lack of culture or education on our parts. Instead, it is the author's thesis that the short story grew in response to our fast-paced way of life (Choice E).

If the author believes that Americans have had to read on the run and that their literary tastes have been inevitably affected by the pace of their lives, then his attitude toward the short stories they read is more likely one of regret (Choice E) rather than one of contempt (Choice C). While he would prefer Americans to read more substantial literature than stories in popular magazines, he understands the reasons behind their choice and does not view the short story with scorn. The best answer is Choice E.

PASSAGE 10

Nationalism is not a harmonious natural growth, qualitatively identical with the love for family and home. It is frequently assumed that man loves in widening circles—his family, his village, his tribe or clan, the nation, and finally humanity and the supreme good. But love of home and family is a concrete feeling, accessible to everyone in daily experience, while nationalism, and in an even higher degree cosmopolitanism, is a highly complex and originally an abstract feeling. Nationalism—our identification with the life and aspirations of uncounted millions whom we shall never know, with a territory which we shall never visit in its entirety—is qualitatively different from love of family or of home surroundings. It is qualitatively akin to the love of humanity or of the whole earth.

1. The title below that best expresses the ideas of this paragraph is:

   (A) *A Distinction Without a Difference.*
   (B) *Love of One's Fellow Beings.*
   (C) *The Nature of Nationalism.*
   (D) *An Abstract Affection.*
   (E) *Our Complex Emotions.*

2. Compared with love of family and home, nationalism is more

   (A) natural.
   (B) clannish.
   (C) accessible.
   (D) concrete.
   (E) inclusive.

3. A common assumption regarding nationalism is that it is

   (A) an outgrowth of love of home and family.
   (B) more nearly related to humanity than to the home.
   (C) highly abstract and complex.
   (D) identified with the lives of millions whom we do not know.
   (E) · stimulated by travel within one's own country.

The subject of the opening sentence is nationalism. Only Choice C, *The Nature of Nationalism,* contains this key word. The other choices are too vague to serve as titles for this text.

Love of home and family is described as accessible and concrete. It is contrasted with nationalism, which therefore is neither particularly accessible nor concrete. The opening sentence states that nationalism is not a natural growth. Thus, for question 2 Choices A, C, and D are incorrect. Nationalism is described as our identification with millions of people whom we shall never know; it therefore goes beyond mere clannishness, and can best be described as inclusive (Choice E).

In the third question we are looking for a common assumption about nationalism. Sentence 2 begins "It is frequently assumed that man loves in widening circles—his family, his village,..." The assumption is that love of one's fellows grows out of the love of one's home and family. This is Choice A.

Now take Reading Exam I. Be sure to time yourself. Then, if you need more practice, take Reading Exam II.

Answer Sheet for Reading Exam I

1. Ⓐ Ⓑ Ⓒ Ⓓ Ⓔ
2. Ⓐ Ⓑ Ⓒ Ⓓ Ⓔ
3. Ⓐ Ⓑ Ⓒ Ⓓ Ⓔ
4. Ⓐ Ⓑ Ⓒ Ⓓ Ⓔ
5. Ⓐ Ⓑ Ⓒ Ⓓ Ⓔ
6. Ⓐ Ⓑ Ⓒ Ⓓ Ⓔ
7. Ⓐ Ⓑ Ⓒ Ⓓ Ⓔ
8. Ⓐ Ⓑ Ⓒ Ⓓ Ⓔ
9. Ⓐ Ⓑ Ⓒ Ⓓ Ⓔ
10. Ⓐ Ⓑ Ⓒ Ⓓ Ⓔ
11. Ⓐ Ⓑ Ⓒ Ⓓ Ⓔ
12. Ⓐ Ⓑ Ⓒ Ⓓ Ⓔ
13. Ⓐ Ⓑ Ⓒ Ⓓ Ⓔ
14. Ⓐ Ⓑ Ⓒ Ⓓ Ⓔ
15. Ⓐ Ⓑ Ⓒ Ⓓ Ⓔ
16. Ⓐ Ⓑ Ⓒ Ⓓ Ⓔ
17. Ⓐ Ⓑ Ⓒ Ⓓ Ⓔ

18. Ⓐ Ⓑ Ⓒ Ⓓ Ⓔ
19. Ⓐ Ⓑ Ⓒ Ⓓ Ⓔ
20. Ⓐ Ⓑ Ⓒ Ⓓ Ⓔ
21. Ⓐ Ⓑ Ⓒ Ⓓ Ⓔ
22. Ⓐ Ⓑ Ⓒ Ⓓ Ⓔ
23. Ⓐ Ⓑ Ⓒ Ⓓ Ⓔ
24. Ⓐ Ⓑ Ⓒ Ⓓ Ⓔ
25. Ⓐ Ⓑ Ⓒ Ⓓ Ⓔ
26. Ⓐ Ⓑ Ⓒ Ⓓ Ⓔ
27. Ⓐ Ⓑ Ⓒ Ⓓ Ⓔ
28. Ⓐ Ⓑ Ⓒ Ⓓ Ⓔ
29. Ⓐ Ⓑ Ⓒ Ⓓ Ⓔ
30. Ⓐ Ⓑ Ⓒ Ⓓ Ⓔ
31. Ⓐ Ⓑ Ⓒ Ⓓ Ⓔ
32. Ⓐ Ⓑ Ⓒ Ⓓ Ⓔ
33. Ⓐ Ⓑ Ⓒ Ⓓ Ⓔ
34. Ⓐ Ⓑ Ⓒ Ⓓ Ⓔ

35. Ⓐ Ⓑ Ⓒ Ⓓ Ⓔ
36. Ⓐ Ⓑ Ⓒ Ⓓ Ⓔ
37. Ⓐ Ⓑ Ⓒ Ⓓ Ⓔ
38. Ⓐ Ⓑ Ⓒ Ⓓ Ⓔ
49. Ⓐ Ⓑ Ⓒ Ⓓ Ⓔ
50. Ⓐ Ⓑ Ⓒ Ⓓ Ⓔ
41. Ⓐ Ⓑ Ⓒ Ⓓ Ⓔ
42. Ⓐ Ⓑ Ⓒ Ⓓ Ⓔ
43. Ⓐ Ⓑ Ⓒ Ⓓ Ⓔ
44. Ⓐ Ⓑ Ⓒ Ⓓ Ⓔ
45. Ⓐ Ⓑ Ⓒ Ⓓ Ⓔ
46. Ⓐ Ⓑ Ⓒ Ⓓ Ⓔ
47. Ⓐ Ⓑ Ⓒ Ⓓ Ⓔ
48. Ⓐ Ⓑ Ⓒ Ⓓ Ⓔ
49. Ⓐ Ⓑ Ⓒ Ⓓ Ⓔ
50. Ⓐ Ⓑ Ⓒ Ⓓ Ⓔ

READING EXAM I

Directions: Each passage in this section is followed by a question or questions based on its content. After reading a passage, select the best answer to each question based upon what is stated or implied in the selection. You may spend up to 60 minutes on this section.

Questions 1–5

Many Americans feel that if the clock were turned back to the era just before the turbulent sixties, we would live in a more peaceful and productive nation. In fact, many social pundits bemoan our declining sense of civility and long for a return to the good manners of an earlier generation. Others agree to a point, but fear that this nostalgia might mask a longing for the conditions that existed before civil rights laws were passed, when minorities silently accepted second-class citizenship.

Nevertheless, who can argue that American cities and towns were not safer back in those halcyon days of Eisenhower and Kennedy? Those of us who came of age at that time recall good schools where teachers were respected and students enjoyed reading. We remember communities where the police protected and served without the scrutiny of video cameras, and where doctors still made house calls. But others are quick to remind us that in those good old days our schools were segregated and our police should have been more closely watched. Still, we do have fond memories of a sound dollar that was worth its weight in silver.

Maybe the discomforts of our middle-aged lifestyles are no more than growing pains. Besides, our memories are brighter than what actually occurred. Our children will undoubtedly wonder if they can ever return to the golden age of the nineties.

1. Which of the following best states the theme of the passage?

    (A) Life before the sixties, though not perfect, was better than now.
    (B) Nostalgia for the past is racist.
    (C) People today are not as self-centered and nonproductive as they used to be.
    (D) We are better off living in the past than living in the moment.
    (E) Civil rights laws should be enforced.

2. The best title for the passage would be

    (A) *Past Tense and Future Perfect.*
    (B) *The Past Isn't What It Used to Be.*
    (C) *Decline in Culture Since the Civil Rights Movement.*
    (D) *The Rise in Crime Since the Turbulent Sixties.*
    (E) *Bright Memories: Fact or Fiction.*

3. The word *halcyon* means

    (A) wild.
    (B) exuberant.
    (C) calm.
    (D) restful.
    (E) mythical.

4. The opposite of *pundit* is

    (A) expert.
    (B) genius.
    (C) ignoramus.
    (D) scoundrel.
    (E) cynic.

5. It may be inferred from this passage that

    (A) we only remember what we want.
    (B) we tend to be escapists.
    (C) we will always have a bright past.
    (D) the decline in our lifestyles is related to the increase of our population.
    (E) we should return to the silver standard.

Questions 6–10

Billy Stuart displayed an opprobrious attitude toward his teachers throughout the semester. Cheating, lying, and plagiarizing were only some of the problems. He insulted Ms. Finch and called Mr. Garcia names that cannot be mentioned.

Mrs. Stuart, Billy's mother, claimed that until Mr. Garcia and Ms. Finch were her son's teachers, there had never been a problem. But

Mr. Garcia, scouring student dossiers in the counselor's office, ascertained a propensity for refractory behavior in Billy's history. As far back as kindergarten, Billy had defied authority, and Mrs. Stuart was always present to defend her child against what she saw as endless false charges.

But by defending her son, Mrs. Stuart impeded Billy from maturing. At sixteen, he did not accept correction of class work errors, and he broke class rules. Billy found fault in every teacher and his mother continued to defend her son's behavior.

6. The best meaning of the word *opprobrious* is

    (A) sobering.
    (B) dishonest.
    (C) insolent.
    (D) opportunistic.
    (E) apologetic.

7. According to this passage, this student was

    (A) under the influence of drugs.
    (B) misunderstood.
    (C) victimized by incompetent teachers.
    (D) reproachful.
    (E) popular.

8. Which of these would be a good title for the above passage?

    (A) *A Decline in Civility.*
    (B) *The Problem with Administrators.*
    (C) *Difficult Child, Difficult Parent.*
    (D) *Cheaters Never Prosper.*
    (E) *Improving Teachers.*

9. The best meaning for the opposite of *refractory* is

    (A) manageable.
    (B) deliberate.
    (C) inauspicious.
    (D) joyful.
    (E) determined.

10. The author probably feels that

    (A) Mr. Garcia is prying into other people's business.
    (B) Billy is crying out for help.
    (C) Mrs. Stuart is in a state of denial.
    (D) Ms. Finch and Mr. Garcia are very good teachers.
    (E) Mrs. Stuart is a very concerned mother.

Questions 11–15

Most historians would agree that the first shells spent in the Second World War were, figuratively speaking, discharged in Spain. In fact, much of the political intrigue of the twentieth century can be regarded as having started there. Spain's civil war was the first international conflict fought between extreme ideologies.

The Spanish Civil War divided Spaniards into two main forces. On one side were the Nationalists, made up of the Falange party (Spanish Fascists), militarists, monarchists, landowners, Carlists (traditionalists), and industrialists. All were uniform in their fear and hatred of the radical left. On the other side were the Republicans, consisting of a flaccid association of Republican idealists, socialists, anarchists, and Communists. Often these leftist forces were at odds with each other.

The Nationalists were assisted by Fascist Italy and National Socialist Germany. The Republicans were aided by the Soviet Union and idealist volunteers from all over the world known as the International Brigade.

The war ended in disaster for the Republic. For the right, it marked the end of the threat of Communism in Spain. For the left, it meant the rise of fascism. For the rest of Europe, it meant the beginning of World War II.

Until the recent fall of the Soviet Union, civil wars, like the one fought in Spain, have been repeated over and over again in Central America, Africa, and Asia. Ironically, since the death of Generalissimo Francisco Franco, Spain has found peace and stability through democracy.

11. This passage indicates that

    (A) the Spanish Civil War sometimes saw fighting between Communists and socialists.
    (B) Italy and Germany aided the Spanish Republic.
    (C) the Nationalists were made up of Carlists, anarchists, and free thinkers.
    (D) the Falange party was often at odds with the militarists.
    (E) the Soviet Union was the cause of the Spanish Civil War.

12. The author states that the Spanish Civil War

    (A) was a war of national liberation.
    (B) was fought between the North and the South.
    (C) was the result of a Communist rebellion.
    (D) was an ideological war.
    (E) was not supported by outside interests.

13. The writer mentions all of the items listed below EXCEPT that

    (A) the Soviet Union assisted the Republic against insurgent forces.
    (B) the International Brigade fought Fascists.
    (C) England sided with the Republic.
    (D) monarchists supported the Nationalists.
    (E) Italy was not neutral.

14. The most appropriate title for the passage is

    (A) *The Origins of Fascism.*
    (B) *The Fall of Neocolonialism.*
    (C) *Civil Unrest in Spain.*
    (D) *The International Brigade.*
    (E) *The Many Sides of the Spanish Civil War.*

15. The opposite of *flaccid* as used in the essay is

    (A) firm.
    (B) loose.
    (C) clear.
    (D) terminal.
    (E) determined.

Questions 16–20

Paleontologists theorize that the sauropods of the Mesozoic era, 190 million years ago, evolved from prosauropods just prior to the Jurassic period, during the Triassic period, 225 million years ago. The sauropods were among the largest dinosaurs that ever lived.

   Unlike the carnivores of their era, sauropods did not need to take the lives of other animals to find sustenance. They flourished not because they were ferocious, but because their size alone made them formidable opponents to any would-be predator.

16. The author states that

    (A) sauropods lived during the Triassic period.
    (B) sauropods were carnivores.
    (C) evolution is not a theory but a fact.
    (D) sauropods were vegetarians.
    (E) there is no evidence that sauropods ever existed.

17. The author would disagree that

    (A) sauropods evolved from prosauropods.
    (B) the Jurassic period came after the Triassic.
    (C) all sauropods were herbivorous.
    (D) the sauropods' size protected them from predators.
    (E) prosauropods evolved from sauropods.

18. The word *formidable* means the opposite of

    (A) feeble.
    (B) strong.
    (C) small.
    (D) cowardly.
    (E) shy.

19. Sauropods did which of the following things?

    (A) Evolved into flesh eaters during the Triassic period.
    (B) Evolved into flying prosauropods.
    (C) Became predators.
    (D) Walked upright.
    (E) Flourished during the Triassic period.

20. This passage implies an acceptance of

    (A) creationism as a scientific view.
    (B) the theory of evolution.
    (C) the nonexistence of dinosaurs.
    (D) the survival of carnivores at the expense of sauropods.
    (E) the idea that man evolved from the ape.

Questions 21–25

Undocumented immigrants often live in a timorous state never knowing for certain if they will be discovered. If they are detained by authorities, their dreams can suddenly come to an end. As much as this dilemma evokes a sense of sympathy, the undocumented immigrant is still breaking the law.

But who can blame the immigrant for coming to America? Our pride in political freedom, our industry and financial growth, and our belief in opportunity draw immigrants like a magnet. They come for jobs and education, and for the same reason the Pilgrims came, religious freedom.

Still, they come illegally and create a burden that is hard to carry. Our schools, county hospitals, and welfare rosters swell with people whose names we cannot pronounce and whose faces seem unfamiliar. The level of tolerance of so many sympathetic Americans is strained by taxation to pay for services that citizens from elsewhere incur.

Yet, who is to blame? Homeowners who need cheap labor know where to find help; it's on street corners in poor neighborhoods where eager brown men wait for work. Mothers with careers know where to find easy help; it is found in a Guatemalan woman who will work gratefully for wages an American would not accept. Farmers know where to find help; they've being hiring undocumented workers for a long time. We can buy vegetables and fruit cheaply because illegal aliens will work for less money than Americans.

The great irony in the plight of the illegal alien is that he or she is not alone in breaking the law. We break it too.

21. The word *timorous* means the opposite of

    (A) elegant.
    (B) fearless.
    (C) prosperous.
    (D) frightened.
    (E) unconscious.

22. The author states that

    (A) undocumented immigrants are good for the economy.
    (B) undocumented immigrants are living on welfare.
    (C) undocumented immigrants should not be arrested.
    (D) Americans who employ illegal immigrants are as much to blame for the problem as the illegals.
    (E) everyone has a right to dream.

23. The main idea of this passage might best be stated by which title?

    (A) *Illegal Immigrants: Our Responsibility.*
    (B) *We Share the Blame: Our Immigration Dilemma.*
    (C) *Welfare and the Undocumented Worker.*
    (D) *The Unseen Benefits of Illegal Aliens.*
    (E) *Enough Is Enough: Send Them Home.*

24. You can infer from this essay that

    (A) undocumented workers end up on welfare.
    (B) the children of undocumented workers have overburdened our schools.
    (C) undocumented workers do the real work in this country.
    (D) the undocumented workers' anxiety is everyone's problem.
    (E) we all have a right to dream.

25. The closest meaning to the opposite of *dilemma* is

    (A) quandary.
    (B) solution.
    (C) conclusion.
    (D) sympathy.
    (E) exasperation.

Questions 26–30

The governor of the state of California champions another voucher initiative. He sees it as a panacea for our educational crisis. It will, he believes, make a complacent public school system compete for students and improve its performance.

At the heart of this controversy is an assumption that an expensive public school system has failed to educate a large number of their students, while a streamlined private school system produces competent graduates. This assumption is supported by a belief that an inexpensive means of educating students would be found if public schools were run more like private schools.

However, comparing public and private schools is not fair. Private schools are exclusive and selective by nature, whereas public schools cannot refuse even the most recalcitrant and disturbed students. Is it the fault of teachers or administrators that so many public school students do not do their homework or are often truant? It is difficult for a public school system to maintain high standards when parents complain every time their children feel the stresses of genuine academic anxiety.

Even the assumption that private schools prepare students better than public schools can be disputed. The standard of measurement for each system is very different. Private schools in California are not required to give the same exams given to public school students. How do we know if those private schools truly deliver what they claim? Uniforms and strict rules do not necessarily mean the school produces high test scores.

Still, many parents do not trust their children's education to a public school system that has been criticized for poor test scores, unruly students, and frequent labor disputes between teachers and school districts. While it may be argued that public education is a noble experiment, many parents do not want their children's education to be left to trial and error. The issue remains; however, is it time for such a radical new experiment as the voucher system?

26. According to the author, the governor of California believes

   (A) a voucher system will force public schools to accept all students.
   (B) public schools are accepting the challenge of vouchers.
   (C) private schools are inclusive.
   (D) vouchers will force public schools to improve as they compete for students who might otherwise go to private schools.
   (E) teacher unions are to blame for the poor performance of public schools.

27. The word *complacent* as used in the passage means

   (A) unfair.
   (B) competent.
   (C) unconcerned.
   (D) wasteful.
   (E) tax-supported.

28. Which of the following statements is correct according to the reading passage?

   (A) Private schools are better than public schools.
   (B) Private and public schools are different by nature.
   (C) Vouchers will destroy the public school system.
   (D) Vouchers will help the public schools.
   (E) Teachers need more support.

29. The word *panacea* is the opposite of

   (A) a cure for everything.
   (B) a free society.
   (C) an ineffectual remedy.
   (D) an ill-conceived idea.
   (E) a fair indication.

30. The passage implies that

   (A) public schools are doing a much better job than people think.
   (B) private schools are overrated.
   (C) the voucher is a simple solution to our educational problems.
   (D) public schools are perceived to be failures.
   (E) the governor has a hidden agenda.

Questions 31–35
In spite of the military's success in the past decade with Grenada, Panama, and, more recently, *Desert Storm,* trepidation of a protracted military involvement on foreign shores still lingers in our collective mind because of the Vietnam debacle. Many Americans are too young to recall the nightly news on the war in Vietnam. Those of us who do, recall the horror of it and our fear that our children, siblings, spouses, parents, or neighbors fighting there would return home in body bags or be reported missing in action.

Today we remain understandably circumspect when our leaders threaten to send our soldiers overseas. Yet can we deny the pleas for help from the victims of war crimes? Our history reminds us of more than the Vietnam War; it recalls America's isolationism of the 1930s that turned deaf ears to the pleas of Ethiopians who were fighting fascism and the Chinese who were resisting a Japanese invasion. If we had interceded earlier, perhaps the Holocaust of World War II could have been avoided.

Nevertheless, it is understandable that so many Americans have returned to an isolationist point of view. Even our Founding Fathers warned future generations of "foreign entanglements." But could they have ever foreseen the day when the Atlantic Ocean was not an obstacle to foreign powers? Perhaps every situation calls for a unique response that borrows little from the lessons of history.

31. The author probably feels that

   (A) Americans love a good war.
   (B) many Americans are too young to remember our wars.
   (C) because of the Vietnam War, Americans are prudent about foreign wars.
   (D) the war in Vietnam was a long time ago.
   (E) *Desert Storm* caused a lot of trepidation.

32. The word *protracted* as used in the passage means

   (A) unfriendly.
   (B) brutal.
   (C) circumspect.
   (D) drawn out.
   (E) untimely.

33. The author would agree that

   (A) Americans want to get involved in another land war.
   (B) because of the success in recent wars, Americans have forgotten Vietnam.
   (C) the invasions of Panama, Grenada, and Iraq were protracted wars.
   (D) it is patriotic to support our country's wars.
   (E) the war in Vietnam proved we are not willing to make sacrifices.

34. *Circumspect* as used in the passage means the opposite of

   (A) careless.
   (B) cautious.
   (C) uncommon.
   (D) interested.
   (E) circular.

35. The passage implies that

   (A) Americans are suspicious of their government.
   (B) big business loves war because it improves our economy.
   (C) earlier generations were more patriotic than those who lived through the Vietnam War.
   (D) though Americans might be isolationists at heart, they will fight abroad when necessary.
   (E) war is always wrong.

Questions 36–40

The advantage of purchasing an old house that needs repairs, a *fixer-upper,* as opposed to a new home, is that fixer-uppers are often more affordable. Plus, if you propitiously buy into an economically sound community, you can procure more for your capital and make a reasonable profit when the time comes to sell your home.

However, a fixer-upper can be a fiasco if you do not discern the situation you are about to enter. More often than not, there will be numerous repairs to be made. The roof may need to be replaced; the plumbing and electrical system may also need upgrading. Unless you are willing to hire tradesmen, you will need to be a carpenter, plumber, electrician, painter, and gardener.

When buying a fixer-upper, one way or the other you will have to make a sacrifice; you will either spend a small fortune on hiring tradesmen or spend an enormous amount of time doing the repairs yourself. In the end, though, you could be living in a dream home that you could never have afforded otherwise.

36. The passage illustrates that

   (A) first time home buyers should be very cautious about buying a new home.
   (B) carpenters, electricians, plumbers, painters, and gardeners are usually dishonest.
   (C) fixer-uppers are poor investments with a history of trouble.
   (D) if you are willing to take a risk, buying a fixer-upper can be rewarding.
   (E) when buying a new home, hire a building inspector.

37. The word *propitiously* as used in the passage means

(A) quickly.
(B) fortuitously.
(C) haphazardly.
(D) perceptively.
(E) cautiously.

38. The best title for this essay is

(A) *Pros and Cons of Buying a Fixer-Upper.*
(B) *The Advantages of Buying a Fixer-Upper.*
(C) *The Problems When Buying a Fixer-Upper.*
(D) *Do It Yourself.*
(E) *How to Buy a House.*

39. The word *discern* as used in the passage means the opposite of

(A) discover.
(B) distinguish.
(C) thrive.
(D) disregard.
(E) disrespect.

40. The author probably feels that

(A) there are more advantages in buying a fixer-upper than disadvantages.
(B) there are a few hidden costs with buying a fixer-upper.
(C) home repairs result in rip-offs.
(D) buyers should never buy fixer-uppers.
(E) fixer-uppers are an affordable alternative for the handy home buyer.

Questions 41–45

The sonorous effects and temporal nature of music in conjunction with lyrics make it one of the few art forms that naturally expresses the meaning of time. Paintings, sculpture, and, to some extent, literature, are set in space, and as long as they are not physically altered, remain in time in a concrete form. Music, when recorded, is like cinema in a physical manner. Those recordings, like books, can be reviewed and remembered in the minds of the audience, but music is different from film. Its very nature is expressed in meter. Once expressed, it is out of space and time until it is reclaimed either by the artist or by a recording.

41. The author would agree that music

(A) is a spatial art form that expresses itself in meter.
(B) is nothing of value without meter and lyric.
(C) is a weak art form that does not compare to literature and film.
(D) expresses the meaning of time better than painting and sculpture.
(E) and film have very little in common.

42. The author would disagree that

(A) books and recordings can be remembered.
(B) paintings and sculptures are physical forms and, if unaltered, remain in time.
(C) because of its sonorous quality, music is a unique art form that expressses space better than time.
(D) once recorded, music, like film, can be reviewed and reexperienced.
(E) music is wonderful.

43. The best title for the passage is

(A) *Why Music Is Better Than Art.*
(B) *The Pleasures of Film and Music.*
(C) *The Need for Art in Our Lives.*
(D) *The Problems with Music.*
(E) *Music and Time.*

44. The best meaning of the word *sonorous* is

(A) metrical and melodic.
(B) rhythmic and harmonic.
(C) rich and resonant.
(D) loud and melodic.
(E) harmonic and loud.

45. The author would agree that

(A) music is a timeless art.
(B) sculpting is mathematical.
(C) cinema captures reality.
(D) the temporal arts are ephemeral.
(E) literature is not a concrete art form.

Questions 46–47

Oedipus Rex by Sophocles is a tragedy, not because of its moral statement about patricide and incest, but because the audience experiences a catharsis watching how Oedipus remains noble despite the horrifying consequences of his actions. Oedipus, in his effort to avoid evil, paradoxically fulfills his destiny.

In this paradox, the effort to overcome fate shows how free will is a necessary element to this tragedy. Had Oedipus merely accepted the prophecy that he would kill his father and wed his mother, there would be little to admire. His will to reject his destiny defines him as heroic; he understands the differences between good and evil and rejects evil. By rejecting evil, he desires to be good.

Throughout the play, Oedipus rises to each challenge heroically. He does not shrink away from the truth even when the truth will clearly destroy him. His free will is seen in each choice he makes. Oedipus always rejected the prophecy's fate, although it can be argued that no matter what he did, he was acting out the prophecy. Rejection is an act of defiance, and defiance is an expression of free will. Oedipus' free will allows us to admire him in spite of his sins against nature.

46. *Oedipus Rex* is a tragedy because

    (A) it teaches us what happens when we are immoral.
    (B) it is about a fated soul.
    (C) it leads us to a catharsis.
    (D) it is always tragic when someone commits patricide.
    (E) it is a paradox.

47. The best meaning for the word *catharsis* is

    (A) a climax.
    (B) a relief.
    (C) a denouement.
    (D) a foil.
    (E) a paradox.

Questions 48–50

Most doctors would agree that a daily sustenance of limited sebaceous nourishment, high in vegetable roughage, and combined with regular aerobic exercise can reduce the chances of a blockage in the cardiovascular system.

48. The author would agree that

    (A) doctors recommend sebaceous roughage.
    (B) aerobic exercise alone will reduce the chances of obesity.
    (C) an increase in sebaceous nourishment and inactivity could lead to a blockage in the bloodstream.
    (D) vegetarians live longer.
    (E) an occasional cheeseburger has health benefits.

49. *Sebaceous* foods would be

    (A) nonfat dairy products.
    (B) vitamin B-6.
    (C) sodium chloride.
    (D) legumes.
    (E) pork and beef ribs.

50. A blockage in the cardiovascular system might cause which of the following?

    (A) heartburn.
    (B) anxiety.
    (C) a headache.
    (D) a heart attack.
    (E) obesity.

ANSWERS AND EXPLANATIONS TO READING EXAM I

1. A	14. E	27. C	39. D
2. E	15. A	28. B	40. E
3. C	16. D	29. C	41. D
4. C	17. E	30. D	42. C
5. C	18. A	31. C	43. E
6. C	19. E	32. D	44. C
7. D	20. B	33. E	45. D
8. C	21. B	34. A	46. C
9. A	22. D	35. D	47. B
10. C	23. B	36. D	48. C
11. A	24. D	37. B	49. E
12. D	25. B	38. A	50. D
13. C	26. D		

1. The answer is A because the passage did not claim life was perfect, but saw it as better. It is not B because the passage only suggests that some people see nostalgia as racist. The answer C is wrong because the passage suggests the opposite. Answers D and E were not suggested in the paragraph.

2. The best answer is E because it sums up what the essay is about. Paragraph 3 states, "our memories are brighter than what actually occurred." A is a creative title, but it does not agree with the theme of the passage. B is a tired cliché. C focuses only on one issue from the passage: the Civil Rights issue. D is like C; it focuses only on crime.

3. C is the correct answer. *Halcyon* means *calm*. D is close because a *halcyon* experience might be considered restful, but not all calm experiences lead to rest. A and B mean almost the opposite of *halcyon*. E is an answer totally unrelated to the word.

4. C is the correct answer because a *pundit* is an *expert*; an *ignorant* person is the opposite of a *pundit*. A is incorrect because it is a synonym not an antonym. B is close to the meaning, so it is not its opposite. D is incorrect because *scoundrel* has nothing to do with being or not being a *pundit*. E is incorrect because a *cynic* may or may not be a *pundit* or the opposite of a *pundit*.

5. Choice C is implied in the passage. A is not the best answer because the author remembers the past was not perfect. B is not appropriate as escapism was never mentioned in the passage. D is incorrect because an increase in population was not discussed. E is not the best answer as it represents a minor point only.

6. C is the correct answer because *opprobrious* means *insolent*. The answer can be deduced from the context: It is *insolent* to insult and to call teachers names. Yes, the student was B, *dishonest,* but that was only part of the problem. He was not A, *sobering,* nor E, *apologetic.* He was not D, *opportunistic*; therefore, it has to be C.

7. The best answer is D, *reproachful.* The boy's behavior was in need of correction. A is wrong because there is no mention of the use of drugs. B might be correct if there were more information. C is not correct because nothing in the passage indicates that his teachers were incompetent. E is incorrect as well; there is nothing in the passage that would define the boy's behavior as making him popular.

8. The best title for this passage is C. The passage does discuss A, but only in the narrow confines of a school atmosphere where a difficult parent protects her reproachful child. The passage does not discuss B, administrators, or E, improving teachers. D is wrong, because although the student cheats, cheating is only one of the student's problems.

9. A is the best answer because *refractory* means unmanageable. If asked the opposite of unmanageable, the answer is A, manageable. B, C, D, and E are wrong because these words have nothing to do with *refractory* or its opposite's meaning.

10. The best answer is C, *Mrs. Stuart is in a state of denial,* because she refuses to recognize her son's part in his problems at school. A is incorrect because Mr. Garcia has a responsibility to research Billy's file to understand past behavior. B might be correct if the passage indicated that he wanted help. D might be correct if we had more information. E is wrong because Mrs. Stuart's denial made her a poor parent.

11. The correct answer is A. Many of the elements of the Republic were often "at odds with each other," and since the socialists, anarchists, and Communists made up this

force, it is safe to assume that fighting occurred between Communists and socialists. Besides, B, C, D, and E are wrong. Italy and Germany did not aid the Republic; there were no anarchists and free thinkers on the Nationalists' side; the Falange and militarists were allies; and the Soviet Union did not cause the Spanish Civil War.

12. D is the answer. This war was fought for right- and left-wing ideologies. A and B are wrong: It was not a war of national liberation, nor was it one between North and South. C is incorrect: It was the Nationalists, not the Communists, who rebelled against the government. E is wrong because outside interests played key roles in keeping the war going.

13. C is the correct answer because the author did not make this statement. A, B, D, and E were included in the passage, so they are not the correct choices.

14. E is the best title. A cannot be the best title because the passage implies that fascism had already been established in Italy, and Germany. The passage does not discuss B, the fall of Neocolonialism. In choice C, civil unrest would be an understatement; and in D, the passage dealt with a lot more than just the International Brigade.

15. The opposite of *flaccid* is firm, A. B is wrong because *flaccid* means loose. Choices C, D, and E are irrelevant to the passage.

16. D is correct. The passage indicates that sauropods did not eat meat. A is incorrect because sauropods lived in the Jurassic period, not the Triassic. B is incorrect. Sauropods were not carnivores. The evolution theory in choice C is implied but not stated as fact. E is wrong because the author does not discuss evidence of their existence. The passage is based on the assumption that there is evidence of their existence.

17. The correct answer is E. The author would disagree with E because, as A puts it, sauropods evolved from prosauropods. The author would agree with all of the other statements, B, C, and D; therefore, they are incorrect.

18. The word *formidable* means *strong*; therefore, feeble, choice A is the correct answer.

B is wrong because *strong* means the same as *formidable*. Choice C, small, is wrong because size doesn't equate with strength. Choices D and E, cowardly and shy, might indicate weakness in character or personality but not in physical strength.

19. The correct answer is E. A, B, C, and D were never claimed. According to the passage, all we really know of these choices is that sauropods flourished during the Triassic period.

20. B is the correct answer. The passage states that sauropods *evolved* from prosauropods. "The theory of evolution" is thus implied. A is incorrect because creationism was not discussed. C is incorrect because the essay tells us that dinosaurs did exist. D might be correct, but it is not mentioned. The passage did not touch upon the aspect of evolution given in choice E.

21. The answer is B, *fearless:* the word *timorous* is the opposite of fearless. Associate the word with timid which clearly is the opposite of fearless. Choices A, C, and E are irrelevant to the passage. D is wrong because *timorous* means frightened, not its opposite.

22. The correct answer is D. A, B, and C are wrong because the passage does not make any of those statements. E is wrong because the passage does not discuss the "right to dream."

23. B is the best title. A, C, and D, are clearly not the main ideas of this passage, and E is not discussed in the passage.

24. The correct answer is D. A, B, C, and E are partially correct, but D conveys the essay's underlying message.

25. The opposite of *dilemma* is B, *solution.* A is wrong because a *quandary* is a state of perplexity or doubt. C, *conclusion,* and D, *sympathy,* have nothing to do with the antonym or synonym of *dilemma.* E is incorrect because a person might feel *exasperation* in a *dilemma,* but not in its opposite state.

26. The correct answer is D. The second sentence in the passage clearly makes this statement. A, B, and E are not mentioned in the passage. C is wrong because the passage does not state that the governor believes private schools are inclusive.

27. As used in the passage, *complacent* is best answered correctly in C, *unconcerned*. A and D are wrong because the passage did not suggest that the school system was *unfair* nor *wasteful*. B is wrong because if the school system were *competent,* the governor would see no need to "improve its performance." E has nothing to do with the issue.

28. B is the correct answer. Paragraph 3 of the passage makes this statement clear. A and C are not mentioned by the author. D is claimed by the governor, not the author. E is not mentioned at all.

29. C is correct. *Panacea* means a cure for everything, therefore the opposite is *an ineffectual remedy*. A is the exact meaning, not the opposite. B, D, and E have no relationship to the meaning.

30. D is the best answer because this would not be an issue if public schools were perceived to be successful. A is wrong because public schools, according to the essay, are not doing a better job. B is only partially correct since it is suggested that private schools are not held accountable to the same standards as public schools. C is wrong because the author suggests the opposite. E is wrong because nowhere does the essay hint that the governor has ulterior motives.

31. C is correct. In the first paragraph the author indicates that, in spite of other successes, the memory of the Vietnam War still lingers. A and D are not mentioned. B is only partially correct, as it refers generally to "our wars." The author makes this statement about recalling the Vietnam War in particular. E is wrong. *Desert Storm* did the opposite.

32. The answer is D. *Protracted* means *drawn out*. The other answers can describe a military involvement, but not in this sentence. *Circumspect* means *suspicious*.

33. The correct answer is E. The author suggests that the Vietnam War has instilled fear in our minds. The author would not agree with A, B, and C. D is not mentioned.

34. A is the correct answer. *Circumspect* as used in the passage means *careful*. *Careless* is the opposite. B, *cautious,* is the same as *careful,* not the opposite. C,

uncommon, D, *interested,* and E, *circular,* have no relationship to *circumspect*.

35. D is the correct answer because the essay does not say we always stay out of wars in other parts of the world. Answer A is partially correct: Americans, as suggested in the essay, are suspicious of their government, but it is not a conclusive suggestion. B is wrong because big business was never mentioned. C is wrong because patriotism was not discussed. E is wrong because the morality of war was never discussed.

36. D is the correct answer. You can deduce this answer because choices A, B, C, and E are not suggested. It can be assumed from what the author says that a fixer-upper can be rewarding.

37. B is the correct answer. If you did not already know it, the answer can be deduced because the others do not make sense. *Quickly, haphazardly, perceptively,* and *cautiously* do not make sense when replacing *propitiously* in the sentence.

38. The best title is A because the essay discusses both sides. B is incorrect because the passage does more than discuss the advantages. C is wrong because the passage does more than discuss the problems. D is wrong because the passage does much more than suggest doing it yourself. E is wrong because the passage deals with fixer-uppers.

39. *Discern* means the opposite of D, *disregard*. In the context of the sentence, the word *discern* means to perceive or comprehend; therefore, the opposite would be to miss, pass by, or disregard. Its antonym does not mean *discover, distinguish, thrive,* or *disrespect*.

40. The best answer is E. A is wrong because the passage does not support the position of "more advantages." B is wrong because the passage does not discuss the hidden costs. C is wrong because the passage never mentioned home repair as rip-offs. D is wrong because it offers conclusive advice not supported by the essay.

41. The correct answer is D. The first sentence of the passage supports this statement. B and C are not discussed in the essay. A and E are the exact opposite of what was stated.

42. C is correct. It is similar to what was said, but not the same. The essay never claimed that music expresses space better than other art forms. Its claim was that music expresses time better. The author would agree with the other answers.

43. E is the best answer. A is wrong because the essay never claimed that music is better than art. B is only partially correct. It mentions a pleasure of film and music, but that is not the main idea of the passage. Choices C and D are wrong because the essay does not discuss the need for art nor the problems with music.

44. C is the correct answer. A and B are partially correct, but *sonorous* has more to do with the sound than with the meter or melody of the music. D and E are wrong because the additional concept of *loud* has nothing to do with sonorous.

45. The correct answer is D. The passage supports the idea that the temporal arts are short lived and gone before we know it. A is incorrect because the author never mentioned music as a timeless art. So is B, for the same reason; sculpting and math were never equated. C and E were never mentioned.

46. The best answer is C. A, B, and D are wrong because the author never says that morality or fate make a play a tragedy. E is only partially correct.

47. The best answer is B, *a relief*. The answers A, *a climax,* and C, *a denouement,* are sometimes coincidental, but they do not necessarily equal relief. D is wrong because *a foil* in the dialogue would lead to conflict, not resolution or catharsis. E is wrong because *a paradox* does not offer relief.

48. Choice C is the correct answer because doctors recommend the opposite. A is wrong because there is no mention of *sebaceous* roughage. B is only partly correct; diet is the other factor. D and E are wrong because they are not mentioned in the passage.

49. Since pork and ribs are fatty foods, sebaceous, it can be deduced that answer E is correct. Answers A, B, C, and D are not mentioned; neither is E, but a doctor would probably not recommend limiting nonfat dairy products, vitamin B-6, or legumes. Sodium chloride might be limited but not to the same extent as E, pork and beef ribs, which are high in animal fat.

50. D is the correct answer, which must be deduced. The regimen described in the passage would reduce the chances of D, *a heart attack*, more than it would A, *heartburn*, B, *anxiety*, C, *a headache*, or D, *obesity*.

Answer Sheet for Reading Exam II

1. Ⓐ Ⓑ Ⓒ Ⓓ Ⓔ
2. Ⓐ Ⓑ Ⓒ Ⓓ Ⓔ
3. Ⓐ Ⓑ Ⓒ Ⓓ Ⓔ
4. Ⓐ Ⓑ Ⓒ Ⓓ Ⓔ
5. Ⓐ Ⓑ Ⓒ Ⓓ Ⓔ
6. Ⓐ Ⓑ Ⓒ Ⓓ Ⓔ
7. Ⓐ Ⓑ Ⓒ Ⓓ Ⓔ
8. Ⓐ Ⓑ Ⓒ Ⓓ Ⓔ
9. Ⓐ Ⓑ Ⓒ Ⓓ Ⓔ
10. Ⓐ Ⓑ Ⓒ Ⓓ Ⓔ
11. Ⓐ Ⓑ Ⓒ Ⓓ Ⓔ
12. Ⓐ Ⓑ Ⓒ Ⓓ Ⓔ
13. Ⓐ Ⓑ Ⓒ Ⓓ Ⓔ
14. Ⓐ Ⓑ Ⓒ Ⓓ Ⓔ
15. Ⓐ Ⓑ Ⓒ Ⓓ Ⓔ
16. Ⓐ Ⓑ Ⓒ Ⓓ Ⓔ
17. Ⓐ Ⓑ Ⓒ Ⓓ Ⓔ

18. Ⓐ Ⓑ Ⓒ Ⓓ Ⓔ
19. Ⓐ Ⓑ Ⓒ Ⓓ Ⓔ
20. Ⓐ Ⓑ Ⓒ Ⓓ Ⓔ
21. Ⓐ Ⓑ Ⓒ Ⓓ Ⓔ
22. Ⓐ Ⓑ Ⓒ Ⓓ Ⓔ
23. Ⓐ Ⓑ Ⓒ Ⓓ Ⓔ
24. Ⓐ Ⓑ Ⓒ Ⓓ Ⓔ
25. Ⓐ Ⓑ Ⓒ Ⓓ Ⓔ
26. Ⓐ Ⓑ Ⓒ Ⓓ Ⓔ
27. Ⓐ Ⓑ Ⓒ Ⓓ Ⓔ
28. Ⓐ Ⓑ Ⓒ Ⓓ Ⓔ
29. Ⓐ Ⓑ Ⓒ Ⓓ Ⓔ
30. Ⓐ Ⓑ Ⓒ Ⓓ Ⓔ
31. Ⓐ Ⓑ Ⓒ Ⓓ Ⓔ
32. Ⓐ Ⓑ Ⓒ Ⓓ Ⓔ
33. Ⓐ Ⓑ Ⓒ Ⓓ Ⓔ
34. Ⓐ Ⓑ Ⓒ Ⓓ Ⓔ

35. Ⓐ Ⓑ Ⓒ Ⓓ Ⓔ
36. Ⓐ Ⓑ Ⓒ Ⓓ Ⓔ
37. Ⓐ Ⓑ Ⓒ Ⓓ Ⓔ
38. Ⓐ Ⓑ Ⓒ Ⓓ Ⓔ
49. Ⓐ Ⓑ Ⓒ Ⓓ Ⓔ
50. Ⓐ Ⓑ Ⓒ Ⓓ Ⓔ
41. Ⓐ Ⓑ Ⓒ Ⓓ Ⓔ
42. Ⓐ Ⓑ Ⓒ Ⓓ Ⓔ
43. Ⓐ Ⓑ Ⓒ Ⓓ Ⓔ
44. Ⓐ Ⓑ Ⓒ Ⓓ Ⓔ
45. Ⓐ Ⓑ Ⓒ Ⓓ Ⓔ
46. Ⓐ Ⓑ Ⓒ Ⓓ Ⓔ
47. Ⓐ Ⓑ Ⓒ Ⓓ Ⓔ
48. Ⓐ Ⓑ Ⓒ Ⓓ Ⓔ
49. Ⓐ Ⓑ Ⓒ Ⓓ Ⓔ
50. Ⓐ Ⓑ Ⓒ Ⓓ Ⓔ

READING EXAM II

> **Directions:** Each passage in this section is followed by a question or questions based on its content. After reading a passage, select the best answer to each question based upon what is stated or implied in the selection. You may spend up to 60 minutes on this section.

Questions 1–5

Recently, a number of public schools throughout the state of California have required their students to wear school uniforms. Those who favor uniforms believe that education, not fashion, should be the focus of students while at school, and by wearing uniforms, students' test scores will improve. Others wonder if uniforms can really solve anything other than a wardrobe problem for financially strapped parents who cannot keep up with the demand of teen fashion. Is it really a uniform that makes a student perform well on a standardized test?

Perhaps there is no direct relationship between test scores and uniforms, but the climate on campus can change dramatically with uniforms. For instance, gang members who identify themselves through their attire will not be further distracted by rival colors. But others might argue that uniforms force conformity on students and deny them the chance to express their sense of individuality.

Still, we must weigh our priorities. Is individual expression more important than attempting to solve an academic conundrum? Are we not obligated to try to solve this problem? Though these lyceums of primary and secondary learning where uniforms have been required have yet to improve their test scores, they have reduced violence dramatically. Maybe that is a good enough place to start.

1. The author states that

   (A) school uniforms will help schools improve their test scores.
   (B) all public schools in California recently required students to wear uniforms.
   (C) school uniforms may improve behavior, but limit creativity.
   (D) those who favor school uniforms believe they will avert students' focus from distractions.
   (E) uniforms do not improve test scores.

2. The word that least describes the meaning of *lyceum* is

   (A) school.
   (B) academy.
   (C) office.
   (D) seminary.
   (E) institution.

3. The title that best expresses the main idea of this reading passage is

   (A) *A Uniform Solution to Our Schools.*
   (B) *Eliminating Gangs from Our Schools.*
   (C) *A New Threat to Individuality.*
   (D) *Distractions on Campus.*
   (E) *The Growing Trend of Public School Uniforms.*

4. The best meaning of the word *conundrum* is

   (A) difficulty.
   (B) problem.
   (C) digression.
   (D) alternative.
   (E) differentiation.

5. This essay implies that

   (A) uniforms will make a big difference on test scores.
   (B) uniforms will not make any difference at all on test scores.
   (C) poor test scores are the result of gangsters on campus.
   (D) test scores stand a better chance of improving when the educational climate improves.
   (E) individuality is at risk of being lost.

Questions 6–10

A writing novitiate who dreams of publishing a novel needs to be realistic about her design. Talent alone is not enough. An author must appreciate the publishing market; in other words, she must apprehend what is commercial. But just the word *commercial* is enough for any would-be writer to remonstrate in the name of art.

One might argue that a good book should find a home regardless of the marketplace. However, even an engaging narrative in itself does not translate into success. Editors, for purely arbitrary reasons, often spurn books that eventually become successful at other publishing houses. One can only assume that if so many good books take time to be discovered by publishers, many other worthy manuscripts are never published.

This should not discourage the new writer. If she has talent and is willing to learn what the market dictates, she can eventually succeed. Once she has established a track record, she can rediscover her art. Remember, every litterateur was once a novice who defied the law of averages.

6. According to the above information

   (A) critics are hard on novitiates.
   (B) editors look for talent.
   (C) an agent is essential for establishing a publishing track record.
   (D) talent plus marketing skills will help an author's success.
   (E) engaging narratives should first be translated.

7. The word *novitiate* means

   (A) novice.
   (B) professional.
   (C) editor.
   (D) hobby.
   (E) fiction.

8. In the context of the passage, *litterateur* means

   (A) young literary agent.
   (B) literary editor.
   (C) professional writer.
   (D) artist.
   (E) literary critic.

9. The best title for the above passage would be

   (A) *How to Write a Book: The Ins and Outs to Good Writing.*
   (B) *Pleasing the Literary Critic.*
   (C) *How to Get Published.*
   (D) *Understanding the Literary Market.*
   (E) *An Editor's Dilemma.*

10. The passage is intended to say that

    (A) new writers have a good chance of being published if they have good stories.
    (B) the literary marketplace is overrated.
    (C) editors follow artistic trends.
    (D) new writers should understand the commercial aspect of publishing.
    (E) literary critics dictate the marketplace.

Questions 11–15

Two schools of philosophy have influenced American thinkers in the nineteenth and twentieth centuries: pragmatism and utilitarianism. Pragmatists see experimental or empirical knowledge as preferable to any other form of gathering information. Utilitarians see the greatest good for the greatest number as a means of testing virtue and practicality. Both are noted for their common sense approach to rational thinking.

This rational view, best seen in what is known by philosophers as Occam's razor, is the principle of parsimony. This axiom propounds that if there are two ways of realizing a goal, one direct and the other indirect, the direct approach is preferable. Occam's razor cuts away superfluities. Does this suggest we should always take shortcuts, thereby hastily drawing a conclusion, or that we merely observe what is imperative when attempting any new venture?

11. The author explains that *parsimony* is

    (A) a principle that looks for inexpensive solutions.
    (B) a form of unitarianism.
    (C) an axiom that looks for a indirect and thoughtful solution to a problem.
    (D) a principle that uses a direct line of reasoning, rather than a laborious alternative.
    (E) the easy way out.

12. The author believes that *utilitarians* are

    (A) too pragmatic.
    (B) impractical.
    (C) hasty decision makers.
    (D) practical minded.
    (E) cheap and lazy.

13. The word *propounds* as used in the passage means

   (A) advocates.
   (B) impugns.
   (C) denies.
   (D) decides.
   (E) accuses.

14. The word *empirical* as used in the passage means

   (A) problem solving.
   (B) logical through import.
   (C) learning through experience.
   (D) the ideal form of reasoning.
   (E) textual inquiry.

15. *Occam's razor* is

   (A) very sharp.
   (B) a practical process of problem solving.
   (C) a shortcut leading to failure.
   (D) the difference between utilitarianism and pragmatism.
   (E) a syllogism.

Questions 16–20

The distinction between satire and comedy is as wide as the gap between comedy and tragedy. In fact, satire may have more of a proclivity toward tragedy than toward comedy. Yes, comedy and satire are linked by ironic humor, but where comedy generally chuckles at life, satire howls viciously at society's flaws. Satire, like tragedy, reminds us of our hypocrisy, vanity, greed, and stupidity; but unlike tragedy, satire does not offer us a noble hero. Indeed, a successful satire makes us laugh so we can cope with our shame and embarrassment.

Frequently, readers confuse satire's laughter with the laughter of comedy. But all that comedy and satire have in common is a similar catharsis that arrives at the plot's climax. Otherwise their intentions are very different.

When viewed closely satire and tragedy share a similar role. They tell us to take life seriously. Tragedy teaches us to take life seriously because there is nobility in the aristocratic soul. Satire tells us to take life seriously because there is little dignity in man.

16. Which of the following statements is correct, according to the reading passage?

   (A) comedy and satire laugh at irony.
   (B) satire is not as serious as tragedy.
   (C) tragedy shares a soul with comedy because they utilize irony.
   (D) satire uses humor in order to deal with the darker side of humanity.
   (E) tragedy offers no hope.

17. The writer would agree with the statements listed below EXCEPT that

   (A) satire is not like comedy.
   (B) satire is not like tragedy.
   (C) satire laughs at life.
   (D) tragedy has more in common with satire than comedy.
   (E) satire does not offer us a noble hero.

18. *Proclivity* as used in the passage means the opposite of

   (A) disinclination.
   (B) index.
   (C) spite.
   (D) integrity.
   (E) naturalistic.

19. The author states that

   (A) satire is closer to comedy than to tragedy.
   (B) the climax in tragedy is identical to that found in good satire.
   (C) satire takes a serious look at life.
   (D) comedy ridicules stupid people.
   (E) tragedy is a painful realization that no one is noble.

20. The passage is intended to say that

   (A) comedy is a superior art form.
   (B) satire takes a painful look at life.
   (C) tragedy is overrated.
   (D) the catharsis in comedy is more powerful than that found in satire.
   (E) satire is underrated.

Questions 21–25

To preclude an incursion on that island nation, which would have resulted in at least a million casualties, the commander in chief sanctioned an onerous alternative, making himself the only world leader ever to unleash atomic bombs on a civilian population. President Truman made the difficult decision to bomb Hiroshima and Nagasaki, because in the long run it saved lives.

It is argued by some that it may have been unnecessary to use atomic bombs on Japan. Some revisionists see the act as racist and argue that we never would have used such a weapon on a European nation. They conclude that the bombing of Hiroshima and Nagasaki was not unlike the Holocaust. However, the correlation does not hold up to scrutiny on either a quantitative or moral basis.

First, the scope of A-bomb deaths was not nearly as great as that of the Holocaust. Second, the situation of the Japanese was unlike that of the victims of the Holocaust in Europe. Japan started the war against the United States with a brutal sneak attack on our fleet. Japanese forces also committed horrendous war crimes against American prisoners of war. Finally, Japan had shown itself recalcitrant in coming to the peace table. Though the bombing of two cities was a terrible act, even more Japanese soldiers and civilians would have died in the inevitable invasion.

21. Which of the following statements is correct, according to the reading passage?

(A) Using the atomic bomb on Japan was not much different from the Holocaust in Europe.
(B) The United States was willing to suffer a million casualties.
(C) The death and destruction from A-bombs dropped on Japan were not the same as the atrocities in Europe.
(D) The president saw his decision as auspicious.
(E) Japan started the war and needed to be punished.

22. It may be inferred from this passage that

(A) the immorality of the president's decision was that he dropped bombs on a civilian target.
(B) the decision made the president famous.
(C) the Holocaust in Europe was similar to the use of atomic bombs on Japan.

(D) the moral equation of bombing Japan as equal to the Holocaust does not hold because Japan declared war and committed its own atrocities.
(E) we were more concerned with saving millions of Japanese citizens from dying if we had invaded.

23. The word *onerous* means the opposite of

(A) simple.
(B) biased.
(C) kind.
(D) wretched.
(E) difficult.

24. The best title for expressing the main idea of this essay is

(A) *A Revisionist View of Hiroshima and Nagasaki.*
(B) *The A-Bomb: Hard Choice–Moral Choice.*
(C) *A Simple Solution—An Immoral Solution.*
(D) *The Reluctant President.*
(E) *Revenge and the Bomb.*

25. An *incursion* as used in the passage means

(A) a repellent.
(B) an aversion.
(C) a diversion.
(D) an invasion.
(E) a destruction.

Questions 26–30
Art and music are necessary ingredients to a child's education. Both intensify a child's imagination. Painting, for example, helps a kinesthetic learner express abstract concepts in nonverbal, concrete forms. It can help a pupil understand the real function of geometry. Music teaches discipline, team work, math, and poetry through temporal rhythmic spacing and repetition. Is there anyone who didn't memorize the alphabet through song? Yet, ironically both subjects are the first disciplines to be eliminated from an impecunious school budget.

Too often an uninformed public sees art and music as frivolous expenses that sap the taxpayers. In an effort to streamline school budgets and teach only the basics, we have reduced our curriculum to a lifeless routine of meaningless issues that lack color, size, shapes, sounds, and rhythm.

26. This passage illustrates that

    (A) music and art are essential in educating children.
    (B) kinesthetic learners need more visual aids.
    (C) nonverbal expressions impede the clarity of instruction.
    (D) music and art are inconsequential to the overall interests of a child.
    (E) tight budgets force school districts to eliminate useless subjects.

27. The author would disagree most that

    (A) music teaches cooperation and team work.
    (B) sports, not art and music, should be eliminated from school curriculums.
    (C) music helps students improve their memories.
    (D) art and music are not directly related to math and English.
    (E) art and music are not too expensive.

28. The best title for this passage is

    (A) *Streamlining School Budgets.*
    (B) *Teaching Geometry Through Art.*
    (C) *Improving School Performances.*
    (D) *The Importance of Art and Music.*
    (E) *Kinesthetic Learners and Art.*

29. A *kinesthetic learner* is a

    (A) student who is a troublemaker.
    (B) student who is a visual learner.
    (C) student who is an auditory learner.
    (D) student who learns with his hands.
    (E) student who has severe emotional problems.

30. The word *impecunious* means the opposite of

    (A) wealthy.
    (B) overcrowded.
    (C) innovative.
    (D) poor.
    (E) healthy.

Questions 31–35

Land rich and cash poor, few California ranchers of Mexican heritage found themselves capable of paying the exorbitant property assessments levied by the newly founded California Bear Republic. This arduous tax, combined with an untimely drought, compelled even the most successful ranchers to sell their holdings.

Ironically, after these large ranches were sold to the new American arrivals from the east, property taxes were greatly reduced.

31. Based on the information given, you could assume correctly that

    (A) Mexican ranchers were incapable of paying outrageous import fees.
    (B) Americans unfairly took advantage of Mexico.
    (C) the California Republic unfairly taxed ranchers of Mexican heritage.
    (D) an untimely drought caused the demise of Mexican ranchers in California.
    (E) property taxes have always been unfair.

32. The title that best states the main idea of this reading passage is

    (A) *Manifest Destiny and the Way West.*
    (B) *The End of an Era.*
    (C) *Taxation Without Representation.*
    (D) *The Demise of Mexican Ranchers in California.*
    (E) *Opportunities in California.*

33. The author would agree with everything EXCEPT that

    (A) the land taxes levied in California on the Mexican ranchers were too high.
    (B) the Mexican ranchers in California were wealthy only in land.
    (C) an untimely drought was partly responsible for the demise of these ranchers.
    (D) the tax on the Mexican ranchers was unfair.
    (E) the real reason Mexican ranchers lost their land was due to poor business practices.

34. The opposite meaning of the word *exorbitant* is

    (A) unconscionable.
    (B) modest.
    (C) excessive.
    (D) expensive.
    (E) condemnatory.

35. *Arduous* as used in this passage means

    (A) burdensome.
    (B) facile.
    (C) effete.
    (D) illegal.
    (E) untimely.

Questions 36–40

Igneous rocks, when formed at high temperatures and cooled beneath the surface, are called intrusive. Often, they crystalize coarsely. Granite is probably the best known intrusive rock. Formed aboveground, sedimentary rocks take on different characteristics. These rocks, shaped by ages of exposure to wind, water, and ice are best represented by sandstone. Rocks altered by heat or chemicals are appropriately called metamorphic rocks. These rocks, such as slate, marble, quartzite, and hornfels were pressurized under layers of earth and thus exposed to prolonged heat and permeated by gases; this results in changing their texture and structure.

36. The author says that metamorphic rocks are

    (A) formed at high temperatures.
    (B) formed by wind and rain.
    (C) changed by gases and heat caused by intense pressure.
    (D) cooled below the surface.
    (E) seen in granite.

37. The author says that intrusive rocks are the result of

    (A) compressed sandstone.
    (B) metamorphic marble exposed to wind and water.
    (C) high and low temperatures underground.
    (D) chemicals and permeated gases.
    (E) quartzite and other sedentary rocks.

38. Sedimentary rocks are those that are

    (A) inactive for a long time.
    (B) exposed to the elements.
    (C) exposed to gases and extreme heat.
    (D) filled with minerals.
    (E) exposed to chemicals.

39. Rocks formed at high temperatures beneath the surface are called

    (A) sandstone.
    (B) intrusive.
    (C) exclusive.
    (D) lava.
    (E) precious metal.

40. Slate is formed when

    (A) exposed to water for prolonged periods of time.
    (B) exposed to prolonged heat and gases.
    (C) compressed in foundries.
    (D) exposed to glacier movement.
    (E) chemically formed by man.

Questions 41–45

Unfortunately, corporal punishment at school and at home is still advocated by many people with good intentions. Those in favor of it believe that *if you spare the rod, you spoil the child.* However, many psychologists conclude that corporal punishment is nothing less than child abuse. They argue that when a parent or any adult hits a child, it is usually the result of the adult's inability to control his or her anger.

To assault a child in the name of discipline is to rationalize abuse. Those adults who believe in swatting a child see it as a form of *tough love,* claiming that it hurts the parent more than the child. They might argue that as we have abandoned corporal punishment, our sense of civility has declined. After all, they would ask, how else will we teach our children to respect the law and obey authority. However, those who oppose corporal punishment say that the decline in civility is more apparent in children who are abused than in those who are not.

41. The author probably feels that corporal punishment

    (A) is passé.
    (B) is another word for child abuse.
    (C) is rarely used.
    (D) results in good behavior.
    (E) helps adults cope.

42. The author would agree with everything stated below EXCEPT that

    (A) children should be treated with respect.
    (B) sometimes hitting a child is very desirable.
    (C) the decline in civility is more apparent in abused children than in the non-abused.
    (D) there are better ways to punish a child than corporal punishment.
    (E) corporal punishment is a rationalization for a lack of self-control.

43. The best title for the above passage is

    (A) *Spare the Rod and Spoil the Child.*
    (B) *Corporal Punishment or Child Abuse.*
    (C) *Child Abuse and Civility.*
    (D) *Family Values in America.*
    (E) *The Decline in Civility in Our Schools.*

44. Corporal punishment according to the author is not

    (A) a form of child abuse.
    (B) a result of an adult's inability to control his or her anger.
    (C) an expedient and practical way of raising a child.
    (D) cruel and harmful.
    (E) an adult's rationale for venting his frustrations.

45. The passage is intended to say that

    (A) corporal punishment is a poor form of disciplining a child.
    (B) spare the rod, spoil the child.
    (C) corporal punishment is a carryover from military custom.
    (D) corporal punishment is necessary.
    (E) yelling at kids is better than hitting.

Questions 46–49
Unquestionably, many hardworking people find public assistance an unfair responsibility placed upon taxpayers, even though most recipients are not at fault for their indigent state. Indeed, what makes such programs appear even worse is that the results of massive federal and state spending on poverty have been inauspicious at best.

In fact, some families receive welfare benefits generation after generation, with no hope of escaping poverty. Welfare has not helped but hindered these families' development. The work ethic, the pride of accomplishment, and a sense of independence is lost by those who rely on the government for assistance.

Nevertheless, the majority of welfare recipients are children who cannot fend for themselves. The dilemma remains: Ending public assistance for the needy may relieve the taxpayer's sense of burden, but who will put food on the table of those who are truly needy?

46. The author believes that many hardworking people

    (A) do not question public assistance.
    (B) resent taxes to help the poor.
    (C) are unsuccessful.
    (D) believe in charity.
    (E) understand the need for public assistance.

47. The best meaning of the word *indigent* is

    (A) impoverished.
    (B) unlucky.
    (C) unhappy.
    (D) disenfranchised.
    (E) repugnant.

48. The word *inauspicious* means the opposite of

    (A) insidious.
    (B) successful.
    (C) dubious.
    (D) unlimited.
    (E) fair.

49. The title that best states the main idea of this essay is

    (A) *The Welfare Reform Hoax.*
    (B) *Welfare, Taxes, and the Moral Dilemma.*
    (C) *Welfare Cheats and the Overburdened Taxpayer.*
    (D) *The Greedy and the Needy.*
    (E) *Hungry Children, Lazy Parents.*

Question 50

Although amelioration in agronomics have proliferated, worldwide dissemination of food has lagged behind. Political intrigue and war, even more than economic factors, have isolated pockets of the Third World, thereby rendering many hungry people even more abandoned.

50. The author believes that

(A) farmers cannot keep up with overpopulation.

(B) poverty is the root cause of Third World hunger.

(C) distribution of food to the poor is the real cause of Third World hunger.

(D) drought and pestilence have been eradicated.

(E) more charity can feed the hungry.

ANSWERS AND EXPLANATIONS TO READING EXAM II

1. **D**	14. **C**	27. **D**	39. **B**
2. **C**	15. **B**	28. **D**	40. **B**
3. **E**	16. **D**	29. **D**	41. **B**
4. **B**	17. **C**	30. **A**	42. **B**
5. **D**	18. **A**	31. **C**	43. **B**
6. **D**	19. **C**	32. **D**	44. **C**
7. **A**	20. **B**	33. **E**	45. **A**
8. **C**	21. **C**	34. **B**	46. **B**
9. **D**	22. **D**	35. **A**	47. **A**
10. **D**	23. **A**	36. **C**	48. **B**
11. **D**	24. **B**	37. **C**	49. **B**
12. **D**	25. **D**	38. **B**	50. **C**
13. **A**	26. **A**		

1. The answer is D. The hope is that fashion will not be the focus of attention. Those who advocate uniforms do not claim that they will raise test scores, so A and E are incorrect. The passage says that some schools require uniforms, not all, and does not discuss creativity; therefore, B and C are incorrect.

2. The word *lyceum* is used in reference to school. All of the choices except *office* are a type of school; therefore, C is the correct answer.

3. Answer E is the best choice. Though B and D are partially correct, they do not represent the entire article. C is wrong because the passage only briefly mentions individuality.

4. The best meaning of the word *conundrum* is B, *problem.* Answer A, *difficulty,* is similar to *conundrum,* but *problem* is closer. Answers C, *digression,* D, *alternative,* and E, *differentiation,* have no connection to the synonym or antonym of the word *conundrum.*

5. Answer D is the correct choice. The author states at the end of the passage that reduced violence is a good place to start to improve test scores. The article did not claim A, B, C, or E.

6. D is correct because the article explains that talent and commercial awareness will help. Answer A is incorrect because the article does not discuss the harshness of critics on new writers. B is incorrect because the article says that editors often spurn books that become successful later. C is incorrect because agents are not mentioned in the passage. E is wrong because the article never mentioned translating.

7. Answer A is correct. Both novice and novitiate refer to an inexperienced person. B is wrong because a professional is an experienced person. C, D, and E are not related to the meaning of novitiate.

8. The best choice for *litterateur* is C, *professional writer.* While A, B, and E are also literary people, they are not the author discussed in the passage. D is wrong because it is too broad a definition for *litterateur,* given the context of the passage.

9. The best title for the passage is D. The passage does not discuss A nor B. C is partially correct, but the focus is more on the literary market than on how to get published. While editors are discussed in the passage, their dilemma is not, thus eliminating E.

10. Answer D is implied in this passage. A, B, C, and E are not claimed.

11. The correct answer is D. Choice A is partially correct, but it is not the best choice in the context of the pasage. Choice B was never discussed in the passage. Choice C is wrong because an indirect solution is the opposite of *parsimony.* E is wrong because ease was not discussed and ease cannot be equated with directness.

12. D is the correct answer. The author indicates that "practicality" is one of their goals. The author does not say that they are "too pragmatic," eliminating A. Choice B is the opposite of what the author said. C is wrong because the author is asking a rhetorical question about "hastily drawing a conclusion," not describing utilitarians. E is wrong because cheapness and laziness were never discussed in this passage.

13. The answer is A. *Propound* means to *advocate.* None of the other choices, B–E, makes sense when substituted in the sentence for *propounds.*

14. *Empirical* means C. None of the other choices makes as much sense as C when substituted for *empirical* in the sentence.

15. *Occam's razor* is B. Choice A is wrong because the quality of Occam's razor is not discussed. Choice C is wrong because the principle is not described in the passage as "leading to failure." D is not suggested in the passage. E is wrong because it is not relevant to defining Occam's razor.

16. The correct choice is D. Answer A is partially correct, but D is the more important idea presented in the essay. B is wrong because the author of the essay states that satire is serious. C is incorrect because irony is not discussed in regard to tragedy and comedy. E is incorrect because the essay indicates that tragedy shows nobility, and thereby it offers hope.

17. Answer C is correct because the author claims that comedy laughs at life, but satire laughs at society's flaws. The other answers are wrong because the author would agree with them.

18. The answer is A. *Proclivity* as used in the passage means leaning or inclination; its opposite is disinclination. B, C, D, and E are neither synonyms nor antonyms of *proclivity*.

19. C is the correct answer because the essay supports this statement. Answer A is wrong; it is the opposite of what the author states. B is wrong because the essay said that the climax of satire is like that of comedy, not like that of tragedy. D is wrong; the essay claimed that comedy laughed at life and satire ridiculed people. Based upon the essay, E is a better definition for satire than for tragedy.

20. Choice B is correct. The author implies that while satire keeps us laughing, its message, that there is little dignity in man, is painful. A, C, D, and E are wrong because the superiority or inferiority of the different genres was not discussed.

21. Answer C is correct. The passage supports the differences between the two events, not the similarities. Answer A can be ruled out because the essay supports the opposite idea. B is incorrect because the essay states that the reason for dropping the bombs was to avoid casualties. D is wrong; the passage states that the president looked upon the decision as an "onerous alternative" not as auspicious or favorable.

E is only partially correct as it is just one reason given for dropping the bombs. The larger part of the essay is devoted to demonstrating C, why the atrocities in Europe were not the same as the deaths caused by the A-bombs.

22. D is the correct answer; it is not overtly stated, but it can be inferred from the reasons the president decided to drop the bomb. A is incorrect because nothing in the essay supports the idea that the president's decision was immoral. B is wrong because fame was never mentioned nor hinted at in the passage. C is incorrect because the author emphasizes the differences between the two events, not the similarities. E is wrong because the author states the opposite: "even more Japanese soldiers would have died in the inevitable invasion."

23. A is the answer. *Onerous* means *burdensome* or *troublesome*. In the context of this essay, *simple* could be used as its opposite. B, C, and D are irrelevant. E can be ruled out since it means the same as *onerous*, not the opposite.

24. The best title is B because the essay describes the president's choice to use the A-bomb as a difficult but moral decision. A is wrong because this is not a revisionist view of history; it does not change our vision of the past. C is incorrect because the author does not view the president's decision as either simple or immoral. D is wrong because it limits the scope of the topic. E is wrong because the essay is not about revenge.

25. An *incursion* as used in this passage means an *invasion*, D. It is the opposite of A, *a repellent*, and C, *a diversion*. B is wrong because *an aversion* meaning an antipathy or a repugnance, does not make sense when substituted in the sentence. E, *a destruction*, could happen as the result of an invasion, but not if the invasion was successfully repelled.

26. A is correct because the author sees music and art as very important skills. B and E are correct but are only part of the essay's meaning. C and D are the opposite of what the author claims.

27. D is the answer the author would disagree with most. The author would agree with A, C, and E. The passage does not mention B, the elimination of sports, so it could not be the correct answer.

28. D is the correct answer. The others focus only on part of the issues discussed in the essay, not the entire essay.

29. D is the correct answer because kinesthetic learners do not learn by watching or listening. This rules out B and C. They are not necessarily troublemakers or students with emotional problems. This rules out A and E. This leaves us with D, someone who learns with his hands.

30. *Impecunious* means poor. The opposite of poor is A, *wealthy*. There would be no reason to eliminate disciplines from the school budget if it was wealthy. D is eliminated because it means the same as *impecunious*. The other choices are irrelevant.

31. The gist of this article is that ranchers of Mexican heritage were unfairly taxed; therefore, the answer is C. A is wrong because the article did not mention import fees. B is wrong because the article did not talk about Mexico, but California. D is only partially correct; the essay indicates that taxes were the main culprit. E could not be the correct answer because the author states that there was a drop in property taxes after the Mexican ranchers lost their property.

32. The best title is D because it most accurately describes the main idea of the passage. It does not focus on A, manifest destiny; C, taxation without representation; nor E, opportunities in California. B is a fair answer, but it is not as precise as D.

33. The author would disagree with E. Business practices were not discussed in the passage. A, B, C, and D were reasons given in the paragraph to explain why these ranchers lost their property.

34. The word, *exorbitant,* means excessive. The opposite of excessive is B, *modest.* C can be eliminated because it means the same as *exorbitant,* and D can also be eliminated as it is near to the meaning of exorbitant in this sentence. A and E are irrelevant.

35. A is the correct answer. Answer B, *facile,* means easy, the opposite of *arduous.* Answer C, *effete,* means worn-out and could be the result of an *arduous* task, but it does not mean *arduous.* D, *illegal,* and E, *untimely,* have no relationship to the word *arduous.*

36. The correct answer is C. According to the passage, C best describes metamorphic rocks. Answer A describes metamorphic rocks, but it also describes intrusive rocks. B describes sedimentary rocks. D and E describe intrusive rocks.

37. C is the correct answer. The passage states that intrusive rocks are formed underground by high temperatures and then cooled. A, B, D, and E are wrong because the author never stated nor suggested any of these definitions for intrusive rocks.

38. B is the correct answer. Sedimentary rocks are those that are exposed to the elements, such as wind, water, and ice. A is irrelevant to any of the rocks as described in this passage. C, D, and E describe other types of rocks.

39. The correct answer is B, *intrusive.* Sandstone, answer A is formed differently. Choice C, *exclusive,* was never mentioned in the essay. *Lava* and *precious metal,* D and E, were also not mentioned in the passage.

40. B is the correct answer. Slate is cited as an example of a metamorphic rock that is formed when exposed to prolonged heat and gases. A and D would refer to sedimentary rock. C and E are wrong because foundries and chemical processes developed by man are not mentioned.

41. B is the correct answer. In the last sentence the author equates corporal punishment with abuse. He does not say that it is *passé,* A; *rarely used,* C; *results in good behavior* D; or *helps adults cope,* E.

42. B is the correct answer. It is either stated or implied that the author would agree with all choices except the notion that hitting a child is desirable. A is implied; C is stated in the last sentence; D is implied, although not given; E is stated in the last sentence of the first paragraph.

43. The best title for the passage is B. It explains what the passage is about. The passage does not advocate A, *Spare the Rod and Spoil the Child.* It does partially discuss C, *Child Abuse and Civility,* but this is not the focus of the essay. It does not discuss D, *Family Values in America,* nor E, *The Decline in Civility in Our Schools.*

44. The correct answer is C. It is important to notice the "not" in this question. The author does *not* approve of corporal punishment, so it could *not* be an expedient or practical way to raise a child. The author states or implies all the other choices about corporal punishment.

45. Answer A is the correct choice. B is the belief of people the author does not agree with. C is not discussed in the passage. The author does not believe D. E is not discussed in the passage.

46. B is the correct answer. The essay states that many hardworking people find public assistance an unfair responsibility to taxpayers. Therefore, it can be inferred that they resent taxes to help the poor, B. The essay claims the opposite of A and E. Answers C and D are not claimed in the essay.

47. The word, *indigent* means poor, as does answer A, *impoverished.* It may be *unlucky,* B, to be *indigent,* but that is not a synonym for the word. *Unhappy,* C, is also not a synonym for the word. D, *disenfranchised,* meaning without a vote, does not relate directly to *indigent.* E is not the correct choice. Although being *indigent* may be a repugnant state, repugnant is not a synonym.

48. The word *inauspicious* means the opposite of favorable or *successful,* B. The results of such programs have not been the opposite of A, *insidious,* meaning treacherous or subtle; C, *dubious,* meaning doubtful; D, *unlimited* meaning without limit; or E, *fair,* which means equitable.

49. The best title sums up the entire essay. Answer B, *Welfare, Taxes, and the Moral Dilemma,* sums up the entire essay. A is wrong because neither welfare reform nor hoax is discussed. C is wrong because welfare cheats are not discussed in this essay even though overburdened taxpayers are. D is wrong because no group is identified as being "greedy," although the welfare recipients are identified as being "needy." E is wrong because the essay does not describe the parents of welfare children as "lazy."

50. C is the correct answer because politics and war interfere with food distribution. Answer A is wrong because the essay states farming has improved. B is partially correct, but money is not the main issue in this essay; distribution is. D is not mentioned. E ignores the article's claim that distribution was the problem, not lack of charity.

Chapter 4

Mathematics Review

The mathematics questions on the CBEST™ require you to know mathematical principles and to understand the basics of arithmetic, algebra, and geometry. You should be able to translate verbal problems into mathematical sentences (equations) and to interpret graphs.

The mathematics questions on the CBEST™ can be grouped into three types:

1. Questions that test your *understanding of the processes* that may be used to solve various kinds of mathematical problems.

   What operation would be used to answer the question: How many bus trips must be made to transport 85 students if one bus can carry 24 students? The answer is "division."

   You may be asked to identify an expression or an equation which is a correct interpretation of a verbal problem.

   Which of the following expressions is the interpretation of the phrase, "three less than twice a certain number, n."

   (A) $3 - 2n$
   (B) $3n - 2$
   (C) $2n - 3$
   (D) $2(n - 3)$
   (E) $3 - (n + 2)$

   The answer is C.

2. Questions that test your *ability to solve* various kinds of mathematical *word problems*. These problems may range from arithmetic to algebra and geometry including ratio, proportion, percent, averages, length, width, area, perimeter, etc.

   How many more cookies does Lisa have than Cheryl if Lisa has $2\frac{1}{2}$ dozen cookies and Cheryl has $1\frac{1}{3}$ dozen cookies?

   The answer is 14 cookies.

   If Larry starts jogging at 4 miles per hour at 7:00 A.M. and one half hour later Mitch starts jogging on the same route at 6 miles per hour, at what time will Mitch catch Larry?

   Mitch catches Larry at 8:30 A.M.

An athletic field is in the shape of a rectangle with semicircular ends. If the rectangle is 50 feet wide and 100 feet long, and the semicircular

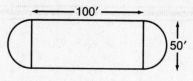

ends are along the 50 foot sides, find the area of the entire field.

The area is $(5000 + 625\pi)$ square feet.

3. Questions which test your *understanding of mathematical concepts and relationships*. There may be questions concerning order and inequality, simple probability, applications of fundamental ideas such as midpoint, similarity, the midpoint formula, distance formula and the Pythagorean theorem, etc.

The vertices of a triangle are $A(0, 0)$, $B(4, 0)$ and $C(4, 4)$. Determine the distance between B and the midpoint of $\overline{AC}$. The distance is $2\sqrt{2}$.

None of the mathematics questions on the CBEST™ are computation questions such as "divide $783 \div 13$." Many problems, however, have some calculation that is necessary to be done to answer the question. This book does not review the elementary operations from arithmetic. If you discover that you need to review those operations, you should do that before you attempt the material in this book.

On the CBEST™, you will have 70 minutes to answer 50 problems. Do the easy problems first. Learn to spot the time-consuming problems quickly so that you can skip them and return to them later if you have the time.

Use this book to review the basics; then try the practice exercises. You should then be well-prepared for the model tests.

REVIEW

This section contains a concise review of the mathematics you need to know for the CBEST™. It is divided into five major sections: Arithmetic, Algebra, Geometry, Formulas, and Math Hints. Many of the sections contain practice questions to help you sharpen your skills.

I. ARITHMETIC

A. Whole Numbers

Definition of Whole Numbers
The set of *whole numbers, W,* differs from the set of counting or *natural numbers, N,* by the number 0.

$$W = \{0, 1, 2, 3, \ldots\}$$
$$N = \{1, 2, 3, \ldots\}$$

There are no fractions or decimals in the set of whole numbers. The number 27 is a whole number, whereas 4.2, 54.302, and $8\frac{2}{3}$ are not.

Factors and Multiples of Whole Numbers

If three whole numbers, a, b, and c are related by the equation $a \times c = b$, then the following four statements have the same meaning:

a divides b
a is a factor of b
b is a multiple of a
b is divisible by a

For example, if $3 \times 4 = 12$, then we can say that 3 divides 12, (also 4 divides 12), 3 is a factor of 12, 12 is a multiple of 3, and 12 is divisible by 3.

Every whole number is a multiple of each of its factors; every whole number is divisible by each of its factors. The set of factors of 20 is {1, 2, 4, 5, 10, 20}. Each number in the set divides 20. The bold terms above are interchangeable, and you should be comfortable with each of them.

Prime and Composite Numbers

A *prime number* is a whole number greater than 1 which has exactly two factors. The two factors of any prime number are always 1 and the number itself. The set of prime numbers is

{2, 3, 5, 7, 11, 13, 17, 19, . . .}.

Memorize the prime numbers up to at least 19. To determine whether or not a number is prime, check for divisibility by the primes up to the point where the quotient becomes smaller than the divisor. For example, let's see whether or not 61 is prime.

$$61 \div 2 = 30 \text{ rem } 1$$
$$61 \div 3 = 20 \text{ rem } 1$$
$$61 \div 5 = 12 \text{ rem } 1$$
$$61 \div 7 = 8 \text{ rem } 5$$
$$61 \div 11 = 5 \text{ rem } 6$$

Notice that, as the divisor increases, the quotient decreases.

Divide 61 by each number in the set of prime numbers until the quotient is smaller than the divisor. Since we have found no other factors (other than 1 and 61), we know that 61 is prime. If any of the prime divisors is a factor of the given number, then the number is not prime.

A whole number greater than 1 that is not prime is called *composite*. The smallest composite number is 4.

The *even* whole numbers are those that have 2 as a factor; all the others that are not divisible by 2 are *odd*.

Two whole numbers are *consecutive* if the larger one is exactly 1 more than the smaller. Seven and 8 are consecutive whole numbers. Thirty, 31, 32, and 33 are four consecutive whole numbers. Generally, consecutive numbers are those that follow in sequence. Thus, 6 and 8 are consecutive even whole numbers; 5, 7, and 9 are consecutive odd whole numbers; 17 and 19 are consecutive prime numbers.

PRACTICE EXERCISE 1

True or false. (1–5)

1. 7 is a multiple of 91.

2. 9 is a factor of 72.

3. 13 divides 143.

4. All prime numbers are odd.

5. 42 is divisible by 14.

Identify the following whole numbers as prime or composite. (6–8)

6. 51

7. 79

8. 1

SOLUTIONS TO PRACTICE EXERCISE 1

1. False. 91 is a multiple of 7: $7 \times 13 = 91$.

2. True. $9 \times 8 = 72$.

3. True. $13 \times 11 = 143$.

4. False. 2 is the only even prime number. All other even numbers are divisible by 2, so therefore they are not prime.

5. True. $14 \times 3 = 42$.

6. 51 is composite. Its factors are 1, 3, 17, and 51.

7. 79 is prime.

8. 1 is neither prime nor composite. There is only one factor of 1, namely 1. Prime numbers must have exactly 2. Composite numbers must be greater than 1.

Prime Factorization

Every composite whole number can be written as a product of its prime factors. Such a product is called the *prime factorization* of the composite whole number. For example, $12 = 2 \times 2 \times 3$. A factor tree can be used to find the prime factorization of any composite whole number.

EXAMPLE 1

To find the prime factorization of 24, first express 24 as a product of any whole numbers. Then express those whole numbers as a product of other whole numbers until a prime number is at the end of each branch of the tree.

So the prime factorization of 24 is $2 \times 2 \times 2 \times 3$.

EXAMPLE 2

Find the prime factorization of 252.

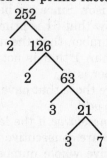

So the prime factorization of 252 is $2 \times 2 \times 3 \times 3 \times 7$

PRACTICE EXERCISE 2

Find the prime factorization of each number. (1–4)

1. 30

2. 63

3. 91

4. 101

SOLUTIONS TO PRACTICE EXERCISE 2

1. $30 = 2 \times 3 \times 5$

2. $63 = 3 \times 3 \times 7$

3. $91 = 7 \times 13$

4. 101 is prime. There is no prime factorization for 101. The answer is *not* 101×1 because 1 is not a prime number.

Lowest Common Multiple

The *lowest common multiple* of two or more numbers can be found by using the prime factorization of the numbers. To find the lowest common multiple of 27 and 63, first write the prime factorization of each number:

$$27 = 3 \times 3 \times 3$$

$$63 = 3 \times 3 \times 7$$

Then use each prime factor the greater number of times that each occurs in either factorization. Since 3 appears three times as a factor in the first factorization and twice as a factor in the second, use three factors of 3. The factor 7 appears at most once, so use one factor of 7. The lowest common multiple of 27 and 63 is $3 \times 3 \times 3 \times 7 = 189$.

To find the lowest common multiple of 24, 36, and 40, first find the prime factorizations:

$$\left.\begin{array}{l} 24 = 2 \times 2 \times 2 \times 3 \\ 36 = 2 \times 2 \times 3 \times 3 \\ 40 = 2 \times 2 \times 2 \times 5 \end{array}\right\}$$ Three factors of 2, two factors of 3, and one factor of 5:

$$2 \times 2 \times 2 \times 3 \times 3 \times 5 = 360$$
$$2 \times 2 \times 2 \times 3 \times 3 \times 5 = 360$$

PRACTICE EXERCISE 3

Find the lowest common multiple of:

1. 45 and 63

2. 24 and 84

3. 8, 12, and 20

SOLUTIONS TO PRACTICE EXERCISE 3
---

1. $\left.\begin{array}{l} 45 = 3 \times 3 \times 5 \\ 63 = 3 \times 3 \times 7 \end{array}\right\}$
   Use two factors of 3, one factor of 5 and one factor of 7: $3 \times 3 \times 5 \times 7 = 315$

2. $\left.\begin{array}{l} 24 = 2 \times 2 \times 2 \times 3 \\ 84 = 2 \times 2 \times 3 \times 7 \end{array}\right\}$
   Use three factors of 2, one factor of 3, and one factor of 7: $2 \times 2 \times 2 \times 3 \times 7 = 168$

3. $\left.\begin{array}{l} 8 = 2 \times 2 \times 2 \\ 12 = 2 \times 2 \times 3 \\ 20 = 2 \times 2 \times 5 \end{array}\right\}$
   Use three factors of 2, one factor of 3, and one factor of 5: $2 \times 2 \times 2 \times 3 \times 5 = 120$

Greatest Common Factor

The *greatest common factor* of two or more numbers can also be determined by using their prime factorizations. To find the greatest common factor of 120 and 252, first determine their prime factorizations:

$$120 = \underline{2} \times \underline{2} \times 2 \times \underline{3} \times 5$$

$$252 = \underline{2} \times \underline{2} \times \underline{3} \times 3 \times 7$$

The product of the *common prime factors* is the greatest common factor of the original numbers. The common prime factors (underlined) are two factors of 2 and one factor of 3. Therefore the greatest common factor of 120 and 252 is $2 \times 2 \times 3 = 12$.

Determine the greatest common factor of:

1. 45 and 63

2. 24 and 84

3. 24, 36, and 40

4. 25 and 16

---

1. $45 = 3 \times 3 \times 5$
   $63 = 3 \times 3 \times 7$

   The common prime factors are two factors of 3. The greatest common factor of 45 and 63 is $3 \times 3 = 9$.

2. $24 = 2 \times 2 \times 2 \times 3$
   $84 = 2 \times 2 \times 3 \times 7$

   There are two factors of 2 and one factor of 3 that are common to both factorizations. The greatest common factor of 24 and 84 is $2 \times 2 \times 3 = 12$.

3. $8 = 2 \times 2 \times 2$
   $12 = 2 \times 2 \times 3$
   $20 = 2 \times 2 \times 5$

   Only two factors of 2 are common to all three factorizations. The greatest common factor of 8, 12, and 20 is $2 \times 2 = 4$.

4. $25 = 5 \times 5$
   $16 = 2 \times 2 \times 2 \times 2$

   There are no prime common factors of these two numbers, but 1 is a factor of every whole number. Therefore, the greatest common factor of 25 and 16 is 1.

B. Fractions

A *fraction* is a number represented as the quotient of two whole numbers, $\frac{a}{b}$, in which the number on top is called the *numerator* and the number on the bottom is called the *denominator*. The denominator of a fraction may not be 0. If the numerator is smaller than the denominator, the fraction is called *proper*. Otherwise, it is called *improper*.

Every whole number can be written as a fraction by placing 1 in the denominator. For example, $12 = \frac{12}{1}$ and $0 = \frac{0}{1}$.

If the numerator and denominator of a fraction are the same number other than 0, the fraction represents 1. For example, $\frac{7}{7} = 1$ and $\frac{12}{12} = 1$. ($\frac{0}{0}$ is undefined.)

Equivalent fractions are two or more fractions that represent the same number.

The *Fundamental Property of Fractions* is a method of forming equivalent fractions by multiplying both the numerator and denominator of a fraction by the same nonzero number.

$$\frac{a}{b} = \frac{a \times k}{b \times k}, \ b \neq 0, \ k \neq 0$$

This property is used primarily in two different ways.

1. To reduce a fraction to the lowest terms, cancel all of the common factors of the numerator and denominator. Cancelling common factors will not change the value of the fraction.

$$\frac{100}{150} = \frac{10 \times 10}{10 \times 15} = \frac{10}{15} = \frac{5 \times 2}{5 \times 3} = \frac{2}{3}$$

Since 2 and 3 have no other common factors (other than 1), we say that $\frac{100}{150}$ has been reduced to $\frac{2}{3}$, and $\frac{2}{3}$ is in the lowest terms.

If you write the numerator and denominator as products of primes, it is easy to cancel all of the common factors.

$$\frac{63}{81} = \frac{3 \times 3 \times 7}{3 \times 3 \times 3 \times 3} = \frac{7}{3 \times 3} = \frac{7}{9}$$

2. To rewrite a fraction so that it has a specific denominator, divide the denominator of the original fraction into the desired denominator. Multiply the quotient by the numerator of the original fraction. The product is the new numerator of the desired fraction.

To rewrite $\frac{7}{8}$ as a fraction with 80 in the denominator, divide 8 into 80 ($80 \div 8 = 10$).

Multiply 10 times 7 ($10 \times 7 = 70$). The new fraction is $\frac{70}{80}$.

Rewrite $\frac{2}{5}$ as a fraction with 30 in the denominator. Divide 5 into 30.

Multiply 6 times 2. The new equivalent fraction is $\frac{12}{30}$.

PRACTICE EXERCISE 5

Reduce the following fractions to lowest terms.

1. $\frac{4}{8}$

2. $\frac{18}{30}$

3. $\frac{105}{120}$

Rewrite each fraction so that it has the indicated denominator.

4. $\frac{2}{3} = \frac{?}{12}$

5. $\frac{5}{8} = \frac{?}{56}$

SOLUTIONS TO PRACTICE EXERCISE 5

1. $\frac{4}{8} = \frac{1 \times 4}{2 \times 4} = \frac{1}{2}$

2. $\frac{18}{30} = \frac{3 \times 6}{5 \times 6} = \frac{3}{5}$

3. $\frac{105}{120} = \frac{5 \times 21}{5 \times 24} = \frac{21}{24} = \frac{3 \times 7}{3 \times 8} = \frac{7}{8}$ The reduction may be done in stages if that is more convenient.

4. $\frac{2}{3} = \frac{?}{12}$ Divide 3 into 12. Multiply the quotient 4 times the numerator 2.

$\frac{2}{3} = \frac{8}{12}$.

5. $\frac{5}{8} = \frac{?}{56}$ Multiply by 7. $\frac{5}{8} = \frac{35}{56}$

Mixed Numbers

A mixed number consists of a whole number and a fraction. For example, $7\frac{1}{4}$ is a mixed number; it means $7 + \frac{1}{4}$. We call $\frac{1}{4}$ the fractional part of the mixed number $7\frac{1}{4}$.

Any mixed number can be changed into an improper fraction:

Step 1 Multiply the whole number by the denominator of the fraction.

Step 2 Add the numerator of the fraction to the result of step 1.

Step 3 Use the result of step 2 as the numerator and use the denominator of the fractional part of the mixed number as the denominator. This fraction is equal to the mixed number.

EXAMPLE 1

Write $7\frac{1}{4}$ as a fraction.

  Step 1 $4 \cdot 7 = 28$

  Step 2 $28 + 1 = 29$

  Step 3   so $7\frac{1}{4} = \frac{29}{4}$

An improper fraction can be changed into a mixed number.

  Step 1   Divide the denominator into the numerator; the quotient is the whole number of the mixed number.

  Step 2   Put the remainder from step 1 over the denominator; this is the fractional part of the mixed number.

  Step 3   Place the results from steps 1 and 2 adjacent to each other.

EXAMPLE 2

Change $\frac{35}{8}$ into a mixed number.

  Step 1   Divide 8 into 35; the quotient is 4 with a remainder of 3.

  Step 2 $\frac{3}{8}$ is the fractional part of the mixed number.

  Step 3   So $\frac{35}{8} = 4\frac{3}{8}$.

PRACTICE EXERCISE 6

Change each mixed number to an improper fraction.

1. $3\frac{2}{3}$

2. $2\frac{3}{8}$

3. $5\frac{7}{12}$

Change each improper fraction to a mixed number.

4. $\frac{25}{7}$

5. $\frac{53}{3}$

6. $\frac{30}{8}$

SOLUTIONS TO PRACTICE EXERCISE 6

1. $3\frac{2}{3} = \frac{3 \times 3 + 2}{3} = \frac{9 + 2}{3} = \frac{11}{3}$

2. $2\frac{3}{8} = \frac{2 \times 8 + 3}{8} = \frac{16 + 3}{8} = \frac{19}{3}$

3. $5\frac{7}{12} = \frac{60 + 7}{12} = \frac{67}{12}$

4. Divide 7 into 25. The quotient is 3 and the remainder is 4. So $\frac{25}{7} = 3\frac{4}{7}$.

5. The quotient is 17 with remainder 2. $\frac{53}{3} = 17\frac{2}{3}$.

6. $\frac{30}{8} = 3\frac{6}{8} = 3\frac{3}{4}$. Be sure to reduce fractions to lowest terms.

Multiplication of Fractions

To multiply two or more fractions, multiply the numerators and multiply the denominators.

$$\frac{a}{b} \times \frac{c}{d} = \frac{a \times c}{b \times d}, \ b \neq 0, \ d \neq 0$$

The resulting fraction should be reduced to lowest terms; the reduction is usually done before the actual multiplication by a procedure called *cancellation.* For example, to multiply $\frac{5}{8} \times \frac{6}{7}$ we should notice that 8 and 6 have a common factor 2. Divide both 8 and 6 by that common factor, then multiply.

$$\frac{5}{8} \times \frac{6}{7} = \frac{5}{\cancel{8}_4} \times \frac{\cancel{6}^3}{7} = \frac{5 \times 3}{4 \times 7} = \frac{15}{28}$$

You can cancel common factors from any numerator and any denominator.

In order to multiply mixed numbers, you must first change them to improper fractions.

$$2\frac{2}{5} \times 3\frac{1}{8} = \frac{12}{5} \times \frac{25}{8} = \frac{\cancel{12}^3}{\cancel{5}_1} \times \frac{\cancel{25}^5}{\cancel{8}_2} = \frac{3 \times 5}{1 \times 2} = \frac{15}{2} = 7\frac{1}{2}$$

$$\frac{4}{9} \times 9\frac{3}{8} = \frac{4}{9} \times \frac{75}{8} = \frac{\cancel{4}^1}{\cancel{9}_3} \times \frac{\cancel{75}^{25}}{\cancel{8}_2} = \frac{1 \times 25}{3 \times 2} = \frac{25}{6} = 4\frac{1}{6}$$

Division of Fractions

A number is the *reciprocal* of a nonzero number if their product is 1.

Fraction	Reciprocal
$\frac{2}{3}$	$\frac{3}{2} = 1\frac{1}{2}$
$2\frac{3}{4}\left(= \frac{11}{4}\right)$	$\frac{4}{11}$
$7\left(= \frac{7}{1}\right)$	$\frac{1}{7}$
$\frac{1}{4}$	$\frac{4}{1}(= 4)$
0	0 has no reciprocal

To find the reciprocal of a fraction, interchange the numerator and denominator. This is sometimes called *inverting* the fraction. When a fraction is inverted, the inverted fraction and the original fraction are reciprocals of each other.

To divide one fraction (the dividend) by another (the divisor), invert the divisor and multiply. For example, to divide $\frac{5}{6}$ by $\frac{3}{4}$, replace $\frac{3}{4}$ by its reciprocal $\frac{4}{3}$ and change the operation to multiplication.

$$\frac{5}{6} \div \frac{3}{4} = \frac{5}{\cancel{6}_3} \times \frac{\cancel{4}^2}{3} = \frac{5 \times 2}{3 \times 3} = \frac{10}{9} = 1\frac{1}{9}$$

A *complex fraction* is a fraction that contains a fraction within its numerator or denominator or both. A complex fraction can be simplified by considering the fraction as the quotient of its numerator divided by its denominator. For example,

$$\frac{2\frac{1}{2}}{1\frac{1}{3}} = 2\frac{1}{2} \div 1\frac{1}{3} = \frac{5}{2} \div \frac{4}{3} = \frac{5}{2} \times \frac{3}{4} = \frac{15}{8} = 1\frac{7}{8}$$

Hints on Word Problems with Fractions

1. The word "of" almost always translates as multiplication.

2. Often it helps to change the numbers in a word problem to values that are easier to work with. Then you can decide which operations and in which order the problem needs to be done. Use whatever operation and order is correct for the easier numbers for the more complicated values given in the problem.

EXAMPLE 1

A worker can make a basket every $\frac{2}{3}$ of an hour. How many baskets can the worker make in $7\frac{1}{2}$ hours?

SOLUTION

(Suppose the problem said "...a basket every 2 hours... How many...in 8 hours?" Clearly the answer would be 4 baskets which is obtained by dividing $8 \div 2$. So divide $7\frac{1}{2}$ by $\frac{2}{3}$.)

$$7\frac{1}{2} \div \frac{2}{3} = \frac{15}{2} \div \frac{2}{3} = \frac{15}{2} \times \frac{3}{2} = \frac{45}{4} = 11\frac{1}{4}$$

If $\frac{1}{4}$ of a basket is not a basket, then the answer is that the worker can make 11 baskets in the given amount of time.

EXAMPLE 2

Jon saves $\frac{1}{3}$ of his weekly salary of $240. How much does he save each week?

SOLUTION

In this case we interpret the word "of" as meaning multiplication. Therefore Jon saves $\frac{1}{3} \times 240 =$

$$\frac{1}{3} \times \frac{240}{1} = \frac{1}{\cancel{3}} \times \frac{\overset{80}{\cancel{240}}}{1} = \frac{80}{1} = 80 \text{ dollars.}$$

Perform the indicated operations.

1. $3\frac{5}{6} \times 1\frac{1}{4}$

2. $4\frac{1}{2} \div 2\frac{1}{4}$

3. $5\frac{1}{3} \div 2\frac{7}{8}$

4. $8 \times \frac{7}{12}$

5. $3\frac{3}{4} \div 5$

6. $\dfrac{4\frac{2}{3}}{1\frac{1}{4}}$

7. A printer can print $1\frac{3}{4}$ pages per minute. How many pages will be printed in 10 minutes?

8. A canister contains $5\frac{1}{2}$ cups of sugar. How many batches of cookies can be made if each batch requires $1\frac{1}{3}$ cups of sugar?

---

1. $3\frac{5}{6} \times 1\frac{1}{4} = \frac{23}{6} \times \frac{5}{4} = \frac{115}{24} = 4\frac{19}{24}$

2. $4\frac{1}{2} \div 2\frac{1}{4} = \frac{9}{2} \div \frac{9}{4} = \frac{9}{2} \times \frac{4}{9} = \frac{\overset{1}{\cancel{9}}}{\underset{1}{\cancel{2}}} \times \frac{\overset{2}{\cancel{4}}}{\underset{1}{\cancel{9}}} = \frac{1 \times 2}{1 \times 1} = \frac{2}{1} = 2$

3. $5\frac{1}{3} \div 2\frac{7}{8} = \frac{16}{3} \div \frac{23}{8} = \frac{16}{3} \times \frac{8}{23} = \frac{16 \times 8}{3 \times 23} = \frac{128}{69} = 1\frac{59}{69}$

4. $8 \times \frac{7}{12} = \frac{8}{1} \times \frac{7}{12} = \frac{\overset{2}{\cancel{8}}}{1} \times \frac{7}{\underset{3}{\cancel{12}}} = \frac{2 \times 7}{1 \times 3} = \frac{14}{3} = 4\frac{2}{3}$

5. $3\frac{3}{4} \div 5 = \frac{15}{4} \div \frac{5}{1} = \frac{15}{4} \times \frac{1}{5} = \frac{\overset{3}{\cancel{15}}}{4} \times \frac{1}{\underset{1}{\cancel{5}}} = \frac{3 \times 1}{4 \times 1} = \frac{3}{4}$

6. $\dfrac{4\frac{2}{3}}{1\frac{1}{4}} = 4\frac{2}{3} \div 1\frac{1}{4} = \frac{14}{3} \div \frac{5}{4} = \frac{14}{3} \times \frac{4}{5} = \frac{56}{15} = 3\frac{11}{15}$

7. $1\frac{3}{4} \times 10 = \frac{7}{4} \times \frac{10}{1} = \frac{7}{\underset{2}{\cancel{4}}} \times \frac{\overset{5}{\cancel{10}}}{1} = \frac{7 \times 5}{2 \times 1} = \frac{35}{2} = 17\frac{1}{2}$

There would be $17\frac{1}{2}$ pages printed in 10 minutes.

8. $5\frac{1}{2} \div 1\frac{1}{3} = \frac{11}{2} \div \frac{4}{3} = \frac{11}{2} \times \frac{3}{4} = \frac{11 \times 3}{2 \times 4} = \frac{33}{8} = 4\frac{1}{8}$

You could make 4 batches of cookies (and have some sugar left).

Addition and Subtraction of Fractions

If two or more fractions have a common denominator, add or subtract the numerators and place the sum or difference over the common denominator. Express the answer in simplest form.

$$\frac{a}{b} + \frac{c}{b} = \frac{a + c}{b} \quad \text{or} \quad \frac{a}{b} - \frac{c}{b} = \frac{a - c}{b}$$

EXAMPLE 1

Perform the indicated operations: $\frac{1}{2} + \frac{2}{3} + \frac{7}{4}$

The lowest common multiple of 2, 3, and 4 is 12. Rewrite each fraction so that the denominator is 12.

$$\frac{1}{2} + \frac{2}{3} + \frac{7}{4} = \frac{?}{12} + \frac{?}{12} + \frac{?}{12} = \frac{6}{12} + \frac{8}{12} + \frac{21}{12} = \frac{6 + 8 + 21}{12} = \frac{35}{12}$$

EXAMPLE 2

Perform the indicated operation: $\frac{3}{5} - \frac{2}{7}$

The lowest common denominator is 35, so rewrite each fraction so that the denominator is 35.

$$\frac{3}{5} - \frac{2}{7} = \frac{?}{35} - \frac{?}{35} = \frac{21}{35} - \frac{10}{35} = \frac{21-10}{35} = \frac{11}{35}$$

EXAMPLE 3

Add as indicated: $1\frac{2}{3} + 3\frac{1}{2}$

SOLUTION

There are two reasonable approaches to this problem.

    a. Rewrite each mixed number as an improper fraction first.

$$1\frac{2}{3} + 3\frac{1}{2} = \frac{5}{3} + \frac{7}{2} = \frac{?}{6} + \frac{?}{6} = \frac{10}{6} + \frac{21}{6} = \frac{31}{6} = 5\frac{1}{6}$$

or

    b. Add the whole numbers and the fractions separately, aligning them vertically.

$$
\begin{array}{cc}
1\frac{2}{3} & 1\frac{4}{6} \\[4pt]
+3\frac{1}{2} & +3\frac{3}{6} \\[4pt]
\hline
 & 4\frac{7}{6} = 4 + 1 + \frac{1}{6} = 5 + \frac{1}{6} = 5\frac{1}{6}
\end{array}
$$

EXAMPLE 4

Subtract as indicated: $8\frac{1}{4} - 5\frac{1}{2}$

SOLUTION

There are the same two options as in the preceding example. We will do this one by subtracting the whole numbers and fractions separately.

$$
\begin{array}{cc}
8\frac{1}{4} & 8\frac{1}{4} \\[4pt]
-5\frac{1}{2} & -5\frac{2}{4} \\[4pt]
\hline
 & 7\frac{5}{4} \\[4pt]
 & -5\frac{2}{4} \\[4pt]
\hline
 & 2\frac{3}{4}
\end{array}
$$

We must borrow $1\left(=\frac{4}{4}\right)$ from the 8.

Add the 1 to the fraction.

PRACTICE EXERCISE 8

Perform the indicated operations.

1. $\frac{5}{8} + \frac{3}{4}$

2. $3\frac{4}{5} + 1\frac{3}{4}$

3. $9\frac{2}{5} - 4\frac{2}{3}$

4. $21 - 9\frac{7}{8}$

5. A restaurant finds that at noon there are $4\frac{1}{2}$ apple pies left. During the afternoon 10 people order apple pie with their meals. If each person who orders apple pie is served $\frac{1}{6}$ of a pie, how much apple pie is left for the evening diners?

SOLUTIONS TO PRACTICE EXERCISE 8

---

1. $\frac{5}{8} + \frac{3}{4} = \frac{5}{8} + \frac{6}{8} = \frac{11}{8} = 1\frac{3}{8}$

2. $3\frac{4}{5} + 1\frac{3}{4} = 3\frac{16}{20} + 1\frac{15}{20} = 4\frac{31}{20} = 4 + 1 + \frac{11}{20} = 5\frac{11}{20}$

3. $9\frac{2}{5} - 4\frac{2}{3} = 9\frac{6}{15} - 4\frac{10}{15} = 8\frac{21}{15} - 4\frac{10}{15} = 4\frac{11}{15}$

4. $21 - 9\frac{7}{8} = 20\frac{8}{8} - 9\frac{7}{8} = 11\frac{1}{8}$

5. Ten people ate $\frac{10}{6} = \frac{5}{3}$ pies. Subtract $\frac{5}{3}$ from $4\frac{1}{2}$.

$$4\frac{1}{2} - \frac{5}{3} = \frac{9}{2} - \frac{5}{3} = \frac{27}{6} - \frac{10}{6} = \frac{17}{6} = 2\frac{5}{6}$$

There are $2\frac{5}{6}$ apple pies left.

C. Ratio and Proportion

Ratio

A *ratio* is a comparison of two numbers by division. For example, the ratio of the number of girls to the number of boys in a classroom that has 8 girls and 10 boys could be expressed as $\frac{8}{10}$ or 8:10 or 8 to 10. The most common form of a ratio is a fraction, so we will use fractions for ratios exclusively in this book. Some other ratios that might be asked for in this example can be seen in the following examples:

The ratio of boys to girls $\qquad$ $\frac{10}{8}$

The ratio of girls to total of students $\qquad$ $\frac{8}{18}$

The ratio of total of students to boys $\qquad$ $\frac{18}{10}$

Any ratio may be treated as any other fraction in a given problem.

Proportions

A *proportion* is an equation that states that two ratios are equal. The proportion $\frac{5}{7} = \frac{10}{14}$ may be read as five is to seven as ten is to fourteen. A proportion $\frac{a}{b} = \frac{c}{d}$ has the property that the equation obtained by *cross-multiplication*; $a \times d = b \times c$ is also true. Therefore, if any three numbers in a proportion are known, then the fourth number can be found using this property.

EXAMPLE 1

Solve for a: $\frac{a}{5} = \frac{14}{35}$

SOLUTION

Cross multiply: $\qquad 35 \times a = 5 \times 14$

$\qquad\qquad\qquad 35 \times a = 70$

Then divide by the number next to the unknown a: $a = 70 \div 35 = 2$

EXAMPLE 2

Solve for y: $\frac{4}{y} = \frac{3}{7}$

SOLUTION

Cross multiply: $3 \times y = 28$

Divide by 3: $\qquad y = \frac{28}{3} = 9\frac{1}{3}$

PRACTICE EXERCISE 9

Solve each of the following proportions.

1. $\frac{2}{5} = \frac{n}{20}$

2. $\frac{x}{12} = \frac{3}{5}$

3. $\frac{a}{18} = \frac{3}{4}$

SOLUTIONS TO PRACTICE EXERCISE 9

---

1. $\frac{2}{5} = \frac{n}{20}$ Cross multiply: $5 \times n = 40$
   Divide by 5: $n = 8$

2. $5 \times x = 36$

   $x = \frac{36}{5} = 7\frac{1}{5}$

3. $4 \times a = 54$

   $a = \frac{54}{4} = \frac{27}{2} = 13\frac{1}{2}$

Applications of Proportions

Proportions may be used to solve many problems. If two quantities both increase or both decrease, they are said to vary directly. Study the following example.

On a map, 2 inches represents 8 miles on the ground. How many inches represent 20 miles on the ground?

SOLUTION

Establish two ratios, one with inches and the other with miles:

$$\text{Inches } \frac{2}{x} \quad \text{Miles } \frac{8}{20}$$

Notice that the numerators are related and the denominators are related by information given in the problem. Write the proportion using these ratios.

$$\frac{2}{x} = \frac{8}{20}$$

Solve this proportion: $8 \times x = 40$

$$x = 5$$

Five inches represent 20 miles on the ground.

In some problems, one quantity decreases as the other increases. Such variations are said to be *indirect or inverse variations*. Study the following example.

It usually takes Mitch 30 minutes to get to work traveling at 50 miles per hour. If he travels at 40 miles per hour, how long will it take him to get to work?

SOLUTION

Establish the two ratios as in the previous direct variation problem:

$$\text{Minutes } \frac{30}{y} \quad \text{Miles per hour } \frac{50}{40}$$

As the speed decreases, the time increases; therefore, this is an inverse variation problem. In that case establish the proportion by inverting only one of the ratios.

$$\frac{30}{y} = \frac{40}{50}$$

Solve this proportion. $40 \times y = 1,500$

$$y = \frac{1,500}{40} = 37\frac{1}{2}$$

It would take Mitch $37\frac{1}{2}$ minutes to get to work at the slower speed.

PRACTICE EXERCISE 10

1. It takes a crew of 4 people 6 hours to clean up an auditorium after a concert. How long would it take 7 people to clean the auditorium?

2. A pump can fill a 4,000-gallon swimming pool in 5 hours. How long would it take the same pump to fill a 5,400-gallon pool?

SOLUTIONS TO PRACTICE EXERCISE 10

1. First ask whether more people would take more or less time. The answer to this question tells us that it is an inverse variation problem.

   Two ratios: People $\frac{4}{7}$ Time $\frac{6}{x}$

   Invert one of the ratios: $\frac{4}{7} = \frac{x}{6}$

   Solve: $7 \times x = 24$

   $$x = \frac{24}{7} = 3\frac{3}{7}$$

   It would take 7 people $3\frac{3}{7}$ hours to clean the auditorium.

2. An increase in the number of gallons means an increase in the time, so this is a direct variation problem.

   Two ratios   Gallons $\frac{4,000}{5,400}$ Time $\frac{5}{x}$

   Write the proportion: $\frac{4,000}{5,400} = \frac{5}{x}$

   Solve: $4,000 \times x = 27,000$

   $$x = \frac{27,000}{4,000} = 6\frac{3}{4}$$

   It would take 6 hours and 45 minutes to fill the bigger pool.

PRACTICE TEST A

The following problems are of the type that may be encountered on the CBEST™.

1. An Erlenmeyer flask can hold 0.6 liters. How many flasks are necessary to hold 3.6 liters?

   (A) 3   (B) 4.2   (C) 6   (D) 12   (E) 21.6

2. At 13° centigrade a cubic centimeter of uranium weighs 18.7 grams. What is the weight (in grams) of 0.1 cubic centimeters of uranium at 13° centigrade?

   (A) 1   (B) 1.87   (C) .187   (D) 100
   (E) 1870

3. If the cost of 500 articles is d dollars, how many of these articles can be bought for x dollars?

   (A) $\dfrac{500d}{x}$ (B) $\dfrac{500}{dx}$ (C) $\dfrac{dx}{500}$

   (D) $\dfrac{500x}{d}$ (E) $\dfrac{d}{500x}$

4. A man left $5,000.00 to his three sons. For every dollar Abraham received, Benjamin received $1.50 and Charles received $2.50. How much money was left to Benjamin?

   (A) $750   (B) $1,000   (C) $1,100
   (D) $1,500   (E) $3,000

5. The Wey of Scotland is equivalent to 40 bushels. How many Weys are there in 4 bushels?

   (A) $\frac{1}{10}$ (B) 1   (C) 10   (D) 44   (E) 160

6. The Japanese ken is equivalent to 5.97 feet. About how many feet are there in 59.7 ken?

   (A) 0.1   (B) 10   (C) 248   (D) 356
   (E) 360

7. 640 acres = 1 square mile

   1 acre = 4,840 square yards

   1 square mile = ? square yards

   (A) $\frac{16}{121}$ (B) $\frac{121}{16}$ (C) 1,760   (D) 309,760
   (E) 3,097,600

8. A bag of chicken feed will feed 18 chickens for 54 days. How long will it feed 12 chickens?

   (A) 36   (B) 37   (C) 53   (D) 72   (E) 81

9. If it requires 9 men 15 days to complete a task, how long would it take to complete this task if three additional men were employed?

   (A) $4\frac{3}{4}$ (B) 10   (C) $11\frac{1}{4}$ (D) 12   (E) 16

10. A man works 5 days a week and binds 35 sets of books each week. If there are 7 books in a set, what is the number of books he binds each day?

    (A) 1   (B) 7   (C) 25   (D) 35   (E) 49

11. Three men invested $2,000, $3,000, and $5,000 respectively upon the formation of a partnership. The net profits at the end of the year amounted to $960.00. How much should the man who invested the least money receive as his share if the profits are divided in accordance with the amount each partner invested?

    (A) $192   (B) $220   (C) $240   (D) $384
    (E) $480

12. Three boys have marbles in the ratio of 19:5:3. If the boy with the least number has 9 marbles, how many marbles does the boy with the greatest number have?

    (A) 27   (B) 33   (C) 57   (D) 81   (E) 171

13. Snow is accumulating f feet per minute. How much snow will fall in h hours if it continues falling at that rate?

    (A) $60fh$ (B) fh (C) $\dfrac{60f}{h}$ (D) $\dfrac{60h}{f}$

    (E) $\dfrac{f}{h}$

14. A diagram of a plane is drawn to the scale of 0.5 inches equal to 80 feet. If the length of the diagram is 4.5 inches the actual length of the plane is

    (A) 320 ft.   (B) 360 ft.   (C) 640 ft.
    (D) 680 ft.   (E) 720 ft.

15. Joan can wire x radios in $\frac{3}{4}$ minute. At this rate, how many radios can she wire in $\frac{3}{4}$ of an hour?

(A) $\dfrac{x}{60}$ (B) $\dfrac{60}{x}$ (C) $60x$ (D) 60

(E) $x + 60$

16. If a light flashes every 6 seconds, how many times will it flash in $\frac{3}{4}$ of an hour?

(A) 225 (B) 250 (C) 360 (D) 450 (E) 480

17. Samuel, Martin, and Miguel invest $5,000, $7,000, and $12,000 respectively in a business. If the profits are distributed proportionately, what share of a $1,111 profit should Miguel receive?

(A) $231.40 (B) $264.00 (C) $333.33
(D) $370.33 (E) $555.50

18. If there are 5 to 8 eggs in a pound, what is the maximum number of eggs in 40 pounds?

(A) 5 (B) 8 (C) 160 (D) 200 (E) 320

19. 24-carat gold is pure gold

18-carat gold is $\frac{3}{4}$ gold

20-carat gold is $\frac{5}{6}$ gold

The ratio of pure gold in 18-carat gold to 20-carat gold is

(A) 5:8 (B) 9:10 (C) 15:24 (D) 8:5
(E) 10:9

20. A cup of oatmeal weighs 3 ounces. A cup of pancake mix weighs 5 ounces. How many cups of oatmeal will have the same weight as 3 cups of pancake mix?

(A) $\frac{3}{5}$ (B) $1\frac{2}{3}$ (C) 3 (D) 5 (E) 15

ANSWER KEY

1. C	6. D	11. A	16. D
2. B	7. E	12. C	17. E
3. D	8. E	13. A	18. E
4. D	9. C	14. E	19. B
5. A	10. E	15. C	20. D

SOLUTIONS TO PRACTICE TEST A

1. **C** This is a direct proportion problem. Set up two ratios:

$$\begin{array}{cc} \#\ of\ flasks & liters \\ \dfrac{1}{x} = & \dfrac{0.6}{3.6} \end{array}$$

$0.6x = 1(3.6)$ Cross multiply.
$6x = 36$ Multiply both sides by 10.
$x = 6$ Divide both sides by 6.

Six Erlenmeyer flasks will hold 3.6 liters.

2. **B** A direct proportion problem:

$$\begin{array}{cc} cubic\ cm & mass \\ \dfrac{1}{0.1} = & \dfrac{18.7}{x} \end{array}$$

$$1x = 0.1(18.7)$$
$$x = 1.87$$

3. **D** $\begin{array}{cc} articles & dollars \\ \dfrac{500}{y} = & \dfrac{d}{x} \end{array}$ Solve for y.

$$dy = 500x$$
$$y = \dfrac{500x}{d}$$

4. **D** Let the amount of money that Abraham receives be x.

Then Benjamin receives $1.5x$ and Charles receives $2.5x$.

The following equation results:

$$x + 1.5x + 2.5x = 5,000$$
$$5x = 5,000$$
$$x = 1,000$$

Be sure to answer the correct question. Benjamin is to receive $1.5(1,000) = 1,500$ dollars.

5. **A** $\begin{array}{cc} Weys & bushels \\ \dfrac{1}{x} = & \dfrac{40}{4} \end{array}$

$$40x = 4$$
$$x = \dfrac{4}{40} = \dfrac{1}{10}$$

6. **D** $\begin{array}{cc} ken & feet \\ \dfrac{1}{59.7} = & \dfrac{5.97}{x} \end{array}$

$$x = (59.7)(5.97) = 356.409$$

7. **E** The easiest way to solve this problem is to recognize that if both sides of the given equation are multiplied by 640, the desired result is obtained.

$$640 \ (1 \ acre) = 640 \ (4{,}840 \ square \ yards)$$
$$1 \ square \ mile = 640 \ (4{,}840) \ square \ yards$$
$$= 3{,}097{,}600 \ square \ yards.$$

8. **E** *chickens   days*

$$\frac{18}{12} \qquad \frac{54}{x}$$

Indirect, so:

$$\frac{18}{12} = \frac{x}{54}$$
$$12x = 18(54)$$
$$x = \frac{18(54)}{12}$$
$$x = 81$$

9. **C** Since, when the number of men *increases* the time *decreases,* this is an indirect proportion problem. After establishing the ratios, invert one of them to form the proportion.

men   days

$$\frac{9}{12} \qquad \frac{15}{x}$$

$$\frac{9}{12} = \frac{x}{15}$$
$$12x = 9(15) = 135$$
$$x = \frac{135}{12} = 11\frac{1}{4}$$

10. **E** There are $35(7) = 245$ books bound in 5 days. Divide 245 by 5. $245 \div 5 = 49$.

11. **A** Since the person who invested \$2,000 has $\frac{2{,}000}{10{,}000} = \frac{1}{5}$ of the investment, then that person should receive $\frac{1}{5}$ of the profit.

$$\frac{1}{5}(960) = 192$$

12. **C** *share   number*

$$\frac{3}{19} = \frac{9}{x}$$

$$3x = 9(19) = 171$$
$$x = 57$$

13. **A** In h hours there are $60h$ minutes. Therefore there will be $60hf$ feet of snow.

14. **E** *inches   feet*

$$\frac{0.5}{4.5} = \frac{80}{x}$$

$$0.5x = 4.5(80) = 360$$
$$x = 720$$

15. **C** *radios   minutes*

$$\frac{x}{y} = \frac{\frac{3}{4}}{45} \qquad \text{Solve for } y.$$

$$\frac{3}{4}y = 45x$$
$$3y = 180x$$
$$y = 60x$$

16. **D** *flashes   seconds*

$$\frac{1}{x} = \frac{6}{2{,}700}$$

$$6x = 2{,}700$$
$$x = 450$$

17. **E** Miguel has $\frac{12{,}000}{24{,}000} = \frac{1}{2}$ of the investment, so he should get $\frac{1}{2}$ of the profit.

$$\frac{1}{2}(1{,}111) = 555.50.$$

18. **E** *eggs   lbs*

$$\frac{8}{x} = \frac{1}{40}$$

$$x = 8(40) = 320$$
$$x = 8(40) = 320$$

19. **B** $\dfrac{gold \ in \ 18\text{-}carat}{gold \ in \ 20\text{-}carat} = \dfrac{\frac{3}{4}}{\frac{5}{6}} = \dfrac{3}{4} \cdot \dfrac{6}{5}$

$$= \frac{18}{20} = \frac{9}{10}$$

20. **D** 3 cups of pancake mix weigh $3(5) = 15$ ounces.

cups of oatmeal   ounces

$$\frac{1}{x} = \frac{3}{15}$$

$$3x = 15$$
$$x = 5$$

D. Decimals

A number that has at least one nonzero digit to the right of the decimal point is called a *decimal fraction* or just a decimal. Every position to the right of the decimal point has a place value according to the scheme:

- *tenths, hundredths, thousandths, ten-thousandths, hundred-thousandths, . . .*

or • $\frac{1}{10}, \frac{1}{100}, \frac{1}{1,000}, \frac{1}{10,000}, \frac{1}{100,000}, \cdots$

To determine the corresponding fraction for any terminating decimal fraction, first determine the place value of the right-most digit, then place the decimal digits over the denominator of that place value. For example,

$0.235 = \frac{235}{1,000}$ and $2.0576 = 2\frac{576}{10,000} = \frac{20,576}{10,000}$.

If the whole number part of a decimal fraction is 0, it need not be written. It is usually included in books for emphasis.

$$0.2891 = .2891$$

You can place any number of zeros to the right of the rightmost digit of a terminating decimal fraction without changing its value.

$$2.35 = 2.350000 = 2.35000000000000$$

Addition and Subtraction of Decimals

To add or subtract decimals, align the decimal points and add as if they were whole numbers.

EXAMPLE 1

25.025 + 1.9834 would be done as follows:

```
2 5 . 0 2 5 0
  1 . 9 8 3 4
2 7 . 0 0 8 4
```

Notice the appended 0 to the first number. The alignment of decimal points assures that we are adding fractions with the same denominator.

EXAMPLE 2

Subtract 8.2 − 2.351

```
8 . 2 0 0
2 . 3 5 1
5 . 8 4 9
```

The appended zeros are necessary in order to borrow properly in the subtraction process.

EXAMPLE 3

Add: 5 + 3.43 + 16.021 + 3.1
Remember that a whole number is understood to have a decimal point immediately after the last digit.

```
   5.000
   3.430
  16.021
+  3.100
  27.551
```

Multiplying Decimals

Decimals are multiplied like whole numbers. The decimal point of the product is placed so that the number of decimal places in the product is equal to the total of the number of decimal places in all of the numbers multiplied.

EXAMPLE 1

What is $5.02 \times .6$?

$(502)(6) = 3012$. There were 2 decimal places in 5.02 and 1 decimal place in .6, so the product must have $2 + 1 = 3$ decimal places. Therefore, $(5.02)(.6) = 3.012$.

EXAMPLE 2

If eggs cost $.06 each, how much should a dozen eggs cost?

Since $12 \times .06 = .72$, a dozen eggs should cost $.72.

Computing Tip. **To multiply a decimal by 10, just move the decimal point to the right one place; to multiply by 100, move the decimal point two places to the right and so on.**

EXAMPLE:

$9,983.456 \times 100 = 998,345.6$

Dividing Decimals

To divide one decimal (the dividend) by another decimal (the divisor) do the following:
  (A) Move the decimal point in the divisor to the right until there is no decimal fraction in the divisor.
  (B) Move the decimal point in the dividend the same number of places to the right as you moved the decimal point in step (A).
  (C) Divide the result of (B) by the result of (A) as if they were whole numbers.
  (D) The decimal point in the quotient should be located immediately above the decimal point in the dividend.

EXAMPLE 1

Divide .05 into 25.155.

  (A) Move the decimal point two places to the right in .05; the result is 5.
  (B) Move the decimal point two places to the right in 25.155; the result is 2515.5.
  (C) Divide 5 into 25155; the result is 5031.
  (D) Since there was one decimal place in the result of (B); the answer is 503.1.

The work for this example might look like this:

$$.05\overline{)25.15\,5} = 503.1$$

You can always check division by multiplying.

$$503.1 \times .05 = 25.155$$

If you write division as a fraction, example 1 would be expressed as $\frac{25.155}{.05}$.

You can multiply both the numerator and denominator by 100 without changing the value of the fraction, so

$$\frac{25.155}{.05} = \frac{25.155 \times 100}{.05 \times 100} = \frac{2515.5}{5}.$$

So steps (A) and (B) always change the division of a decimal by a decimal into the division by a whole number.

To divide a decimal by a whole number, divide them as if they were whole numbers. Then place the decimal point in the quotient so that the quotient has as many decimal places as the decimal (the dividend).

Order of Operations

When an expression with mixed operations is given, the order in which the operations are performed is very important. In arithmetic, the conventional order is as follows:

1. Do any operations inside grouping symbols first. (Grouping symbols may include parentheses (...), brackets [...], braces {...}, and a bar as in $\frac{12 - 4}{6 + 2}$.)

2. Do any roots and exponents in order from left to right.

3. Do multiplications and divisions in order from left to right. (This rule does not say to do all the multiplications before the divisions— do them in order.)

4. Do additions and subtractions in order from left to right.

PRACTICE EXERCISE 11

Perform the indicated operations.

1. $2.3 + 5.42 - 1.57$

2. $2.3 + (5.42 - 1.57)$

3. $0.3 \times 1.2 + 1.1$

4. $0.8 \div 0.4 \times 2$

5. $2.8 + 1.2 \div 2$

SOLUTIONS TO PRACTICE EXERCISE 11

---

1. In order from left to right:
   $2.3 + 5.42 - 1.57 =$
   $7.72 - 1.57 = 6.15$

2. $2.3 + (5.42 - 1.57) =$
   $2.3 + 3.85 =$
   6.15

3. $0.3 \times 1.2 + 1.1 =$ Multiplication before addition.
   $0.36 + 1.1 = 1.46$

4. $0.8 \div 0.4 \times 2$ Multiplication and division in order
   $2 \times 2 = 4$ from left to right.

5. $2.8 + 1.2 \div 2 =$ Division before addition.
   $2.8 + 0.6 = 3.4$

EXAMPLE 2

$$\frac{55.033}{1.1} = \frac{550.33}{11.} = 50.03.$$

EXAMPLE 3

If oranges cost 6¢ each, how many oranges can you buy for $2.52?

$$6¢ = \$.06,$$

so the number of oranges is

$$\frac{2.52}{.06} = \frac{252}{6} = 42.$$

Computing Tip. **To divide a decimal by 10, move the decimal point *to the left* one place; to divide by 100, move the decimal point two places to the left, and so on.**

EXAMPLE

Divide 5,637.6471 by 1,000.

The answer is 5.6376471, since to divide by 1,000 you move the decimal point 3 places to the left.

Converting a Fraction into a Decimal

To convert a fraction into a decimal, divide the denominator into the numerator. For example, $\frac{3}{4}$ = .75. Some fractions give an infinite decimal when you divide the denominator into the numerator for example, $\frac{1}{3}$ = .333 ... where the three dots mean you keep on getting 3 with each step of division. .333 ... is an *infinite decimal*. Another way to write this is $.\overline{3}$. The bar signifies an endlessly repeating decimal.

If a fraction has an infinite decimal, use the fraction in any computation.

EXAMPLE 1

What is $\frac{2}{9}$ of $3,690.90?

Since the decimal for $\frac{2}{9}$ is .2222 ... use the fraction $\frac{2}{9}$.

$\frac{2}{9} \times \$3,690.90 = 2 \times \$410.10 = \$820.20.$

You should know the following decimal equivalents of fractions:

$\frac{1}{100}$ = .01	$\frac{1}{10}$ = .1	$\frac{1}{4}$ = .25	$\frac{5}{8}$ = .625
$\frac{1}{50}$ = .02	$\frac{1}{9}$ = .111...	$\frac{1}{3}$ = .333...	$\frac{2}{3}$ = .666...
$\frac{1}{40}$ = .025	$\frac{1}{8}$ = .125	$\frac{3}{8}$ = .375	$\frac{3}{4}$ = .75
$\frac{1}{25}$ = .04	$\frac{1}{6}$ = .1666...	$\frac{2}{5}$ = .4	$\frac{7}{8}$ = .875
$\frac{1}{20}$ = .05	$\frac{1}{5}$ = .2	$\frac{1}{2}$ = .5	$\frac{3}{2}$ = 1.5
$\frac{1}{12}$ = .0833...			

E. Percent

The word *percent* means "hundredths." Therefore 25% means twenty-five hundredths or 0.25 or $\frac{25}{100} = \frac{1}{4}$.

$$7\% = 0.07 = \frac{7}{100}$$

$$12\frac{1}{2}\% = \frac{25}{2}\% = \frac{\frac{25}{2}}{100} = \frac{25}{2} \times \frac{1}{100} = \frac{\overset{1}{\cancel{25}}}{2} \times \frac{1}{\underset{4}{\cancel{100}}} = \frac{1}{8}$$

also $12\frac{1}{2}\% = 12.5\% = 0.125$

$$16\frac{2}{3}\% = \frac{50}{3}\% = \frac{50}{3} \times \frac{1}{100} = \frac{\overset{1}{\cancel{50}}}{3} \times \frac{1}{\underset{2}{\cancel{100}}} = \frac{1}{6}$$

The decimal value of this percent is not convenient to use in any computation. $16\frac{2}{3}\% = 0.1666666... = 0.1\overline{6}$

You show know the following fractional equivalents of percents:

$1\% = \frac{1}{100}$	$25\% = \frac{1}{4}$	$80\% = \frac{4}{5}$
$2\% = \frac{1}{50}$	$33\frac{1}{3}\% = \frac{1}{3}$	$83\frac{1}{3}\% = \frac{5}{6}$
$4\% = \frac{1}{25}$	$37\frac{1}{2}\% = \frac{3}{8}$	$87\frac{1}{2}\% = \frac{7}{8}$
$5\% = \frac{1}{20}$	$40\% = \frac{2}{5}$	$100\% = 1$
$8\frac{1}{3}\% = \frac{1}{12}$	$50\% = \frac{1}{2}$	$120\% = \frac{6}{5}$
$10\% = \frac{1}{10}$	$60\% = \frac{3}{5}$	$125\% = \frac{5}{4}$
$12\frac{1}{2}\% = \frac{1}{8}$	$62\frac{1}{2}\% = \frac{5}{8}$	$133\frac{1}{3}\% = \frac{4}{3}$
$16\frac{2}{3}\% = \frac{1}{6}$	$66\frac{2}{3}\% = \frac{2}{3}$	$150\% = \frac{3}{2}$
$20\% = \frac{1}{5}$	$75\% = \frac{3}{4}$	

Note, for example, that $133\frac{1}{3}\% = 1.33\frac{1}{3} = 1\frac{1}{3} = \frac{4}{3}$.

Converting Percents to Fractions and Decimals

It is necessary to be able to convert any fraction, decimal, and percent to the other forms. The examples above show percents written as both fractions and decimals. The rules are the following:

1. To change a *percent to a fraction,* drop the percent sign and divide the percent number by 100.

2. To change a *percent to a decimal,* drop the percent sign and move the decimal point two places to the left.

3. To change a *fraction to a percent,* solve the proportion $\dfrac{a}{b} = \dfrac{P}{100}$ for P and attach a percent sign (or change the fraction to a decimal and follow Rule 4).

4. To change a *decimal to a percent,* move the decimal point two places to the right and attach a percent sign.

Every percent problem, perhaps with a little ingenuity, can be phrased "*A* is *P%* of *B*." This sentence immediately gives the percent proportion:

$$\frac{P}{100} = \frac{A}{B}$$

This proportion can then be solved by cross multiplication as done before.

EXAMPLE 1

A company has 6,435 bars of soap. If the company sells 20% of its bars of soap, how many bars of soap did it sell?

The problem can be phrased as follows: The company sold 20% of 6,435 bars of soap. Thus $P = 20$, $B = 6,435$, and A is unknown. The percent proportion is

$$\frac{20}{100} = \frac{A}{6,435}$$
$$100 \times A = 20 \times 6,435$$
$$100 \times A = 128,700$$
$$A = 1,287$$

EXAMPLE 2

In a class of 60 students, 18 students received a grade of B. What percentage of the class received a grade of B?

Phrase the problem as follows: 18 is what percent of 60? $A = 18$, $B = 60$, and P is unknown.

$$\frac{P}{100} = \frac{18}{60}$$
$$60 \times P = 18 \times 100$$
$$60 \times P = 1,800$$
$$P = 30$$

Therefore 30% of the class received B's.

EXAMPLE 3

If the population of Dryden was 10,000 in 1960 and the population of Dryden increased by 15% between 1960 and 1970, what was the population of Dryden in 1970.

"The increase was 15% of 10,000."

$$\frac{15}{100} = \frac{A}{10,000}$$
$$100 \times A = 15 \times 10,000$$
$$100 \times A = 150,000$$
$$A = 1,500$$

So the population was 10,000 + 1,500 = 11,500 in 1970.

A quicker method: the population increased 15%, so the population in 1970 is 115% of the population in 1960. Therefore, the population in 1970 is 115% of 10,000 which is (1.15)(10,000) = 11,500.

"The new population is 115% of 10,000."

$$\frac{115}{100} = \frac{A}{10,000}$$
$$100 \times A = 115 \times 10,000$$
$$100 \times A = 1,150,000$$
$$A = 11,500$$

So the population was 11,500 in 1970.

Interest and Discount

Two of the most common uses of percent are in interest and discount problems.

The rate of interest is usually given as a percent. The basic formula for interest problems is:

INTEREST = AMOUNT × TIME × RATE

You can assume the rate of interest is annual unless the problem states otherwise. Therefore, express the time in years.

EXAMPLE 1

How much interest will $10,000 earn in 9 months at an annual rate of 6%? 9 months is $\frac{3}{4}$ of a year and 6% = $\frac{3}{50}$, so using the formula, the interest is

$10,000 \times \frac{3}{4} \times \frac{3}{50} = \$50 \times 9 = \$450$.

EXAMPLE 2

What annual rate of interest was paid if $5,000 earned $300 in interest in 2 years?

Since the interest was earned in 2 years, $150 is the interest earned in one year.

$$\frac{150}{5,000} = .03 = 3\%, \text{ so the annual rate of interest was 3\%.}$$

This type of interest is called *simple interest.*

There is another method of computing interest called *compound interest.* In computing compound interest, the interest is periodically added to the amount (or principal) which is earning interest.

EXAMPLE 3

What will $1,000 be worth after three years if it earns interest at the rate of 5% compounded annually?

Compounded annually means that the interest earned during one year is added to the amount (or principal) at the end of each year. The interest on $1,000 at 5% for one year is $(1,000)(.05) = $50. So you must compute the interest on $1,050 (not $1,000) for the second year. The interest is $(1,050)(.05) = $52.50. Therefore, during the third year interest will be computed for $1,102.50. During the third year the interest is $(1,102.50)(.05) = $55.125 = $55.13. Therefore, after 3 years the original $1,000 will be worth $1,157.63.

If you calculated simple interest on $1,000 at 5% for three years, the answer would be $(1,000)(.05)(3) = $150. Therefore, using simple interest, $1,000 is worth $1,150 after 3 years. Notice that this is not the same as the money was worth using compound interest.

You can assume that interest means simple interest unless a problem states otherwise.

The basic formula for discount problems is:

DISCOUNT = COST × RATE OF DISCOUNT

EXAMPLE 1

What is the discount if a car which cost $3,000 is discounted 7%?

The discount is $3,000 × .07 = $210.00 since 7% = .07.

If we know the cost of an item and its discounted price, we can find the rate of discount by using the formula

$$\text{rate of discount} = \frac{\text{cost} - \text{price}}{\text{cost}}$$

EXAMPLE 2

What was the rate of discount if a boat which cost $5,000 was sold for $4,800?

Using this formula, we find that the rate of discount equals

$$\frac{5,000 - 4,800}{5,000} = \frac{200}{5,000} = \frac{1}{25} = .04 = 4\%.$$

After an item has been discounted once, it may be discounted again. This procedure is called *successive* discounting.

EXAMPLE 3

A bicycle originally cost $100 and was discounted 10%. After three months it was sold after being discounted another 15%. How much was the bicycle sold for?

After the 10% discount the bicycle was selling for $100(.90) = $90. An item which costs $90 and is discounted 15% will sell for $90(.85) = $76.50, so the bicycle was sold for $76.50.

Notice that if you added the two discounts of 10% and 15% and treated the succesive discounts as a single discount of 25%, your answer would be that the bicycle sold for $75, which is incorrect. Successive discounts are *not* identical to a single discount of the sum of the discounts. The previous example shows that successive discounts of 10% and 15% are not identical to a single discount of 25%.

PRACTICE EXERCISE 12

Express each percent as a fraction and as a decimal. (1–3)

1. 65%

2. 225%

3. 37.5%

Express each fraction as a decimal and as a percent. (4–6)

4. $\dfrac{5}{8}$

5. $\dfrac{13}{20}$

6. $\dfrac{19}{4}$

Express each decimal as a fraction and as a percent. (7–9)

7. 0.37   8. 1.04   9. 0.3925

10. 52 is 40% of what number?

11. 9 is what percent of 30?

12. What is 125% of 84?

13. On a diet, Pete lost 8% of his weight and as a result weighed 138 pounds. What did he weigh at the start of his diet?

14. Ellen received a score of 85% on a test that had 60 questions. How many questions did she get wrong?

15. Robert's salary rose from $540.00 per month to $583.20 per month. What percent raise did Robert receive?

SOLUTIONS TO PRACTICE EXERCISE 12

1. $65\% = \dfrac{65}{100} = \dfrac{13}{20} = 0.65$

2. $225\% = \dfrac{225}{100} = \dfrac{9}{4} = 2\dfrac{1}{4} = 2.25$

3. $37.5\% = \dfrac{37.5}{100} = \dfrac{375}{1,000} = \dfrac{3}{8} = 0.375$

4. $\dfrac{5}{8} = \dfrac{P}{100}$

   $8 \times P = 500$

   $P = \dfrac{500}{8} = 62.5$

   So $\dfrac{5}{8} = 62.5\%$ and $\dfrac{5}{8} = 0.625$

5. $\dfrac{13}{20} = 0.65 = 65\%$

6. $\dfrac{19}{4} = 4.75 = 475\%$

7. $0.37 = \dfrac{37}{100} = 37\%$

8. $1.04 = 1\dfrac{1}{25} = 104\%$

9. $0.3925 = \dfrac{3,925}{10,000} = \dfrac{157}{400} = 39.25\%$

10. Use the percent proportion.

    $\dfrac{52}{B} = \dfrac{40}{100}$

    $40 \times B = 5,200$

    $B = \dfrac{5,200}{40} = 130$

11. $\dfrac{9}{30} = \dfrac{P}{100}$

    $30 \times P = 900$

    $P = 30$ 9 is 30% of 30.

12. $\dfrac{A}{84} = \dfrac{125}{100}$

    $100 \times A = 84 \times 125 = 10,500$

    $A = 105$

13. Since Pete lost 8% of his weight, then he now weighs 92% of his original weight. 138 is 92% of what number?

    $\dfrac{138}{B} = \dfrac{92}{100}$

$92 \times B = 13,800$
$B = 150$
Pete weighed 150 pounds before the diet.

14. If Ellen got 85% correct, then she got 15% wrong. What is 15% of 60?

$$\frac{A}{60} = \frac{15}{100}$$

$100 \times A = 60 \times 15 = 900$
$A = 9$
Ellen got 9 questions wrong.

15. Robert received a raise of $583.20 − $540.00 = $43.20.
43.2 is what percent of 540?

$$\frac{43.2}{540} = \frac{P}{100}$$

$540 \times P = 4,320$
$P = 8$
Robert received an 8% raise.

Rounding Off Numbers

Many times an approximate answer can be found more quickly and may be more useful than the exact answer. For example, if a company had sales of $998,875.63 during a year, it is easier to remember that the sales were about $1 million.

To round off a number to a given place value do the following:

(A) Locate the digit in the position to which you wish to round off.
(B) If the digit in the position immediately to the right is 0, 1, 2, 3, or 4, replace that digit and all others to its right with zeros.
(C) If the digit in the position immediately to the right is 5, 6, 7, 8, or 9, add one to the digit to its left and replace all others to its right with zeros.

EXAMPLE 1

Round off 9,403,420.71 to the nearest hundred.

You must find the multiple of one hundred which is closest to 9,403,420.71.

The answer is 9,403,400.

Most problems dealing with money are rounded off if the answer contains a fractional part of a cent.

EXAMPLE 2

If 16 donuts cost $1.00, how much should three donuts cost?

Three donuts should cost $\frac{3}{16}$ of $1.00. Since $\frac{3}{16} \times 1. = .1875$, the cost would be $.1875. In practice, you would round it up to $.19 or 19¢.

Rounding off numbers can help you get quick, approximate answers. Since many questions require only rough answers, you can sometimes save time on the test by rounding off numbers.

EXAMPLE 3

Round off 43.79 to the nearest tenth.

The place to the right of tenths is hundredths, so look in the hundredths place. Since 9 is bigger than 5, add 1 to the tenths place. Therefore, 43.79 is 43.8 rounded off to the nearest tenth.

F. Signed Numbers

From this point on, multiplication will be indicated not by a × but rather by either a raised dot: $4 \cdot 5 = 20$, parentheses in various ways: $(4)(5) = 20$ or $4(5) = 20$, or by placing symbols side by side with no multiplication sign at all between them: ab, $7x$, $3x^2yz$.

A number preceded by either a positive or a negative sign is called a *signed number*. For example, $+5$, -6, -4.2, and $+\frac{3}{4}$ are all signed numbers. If no sign is given with a number, a positive sign is assumed; thus, 5 is interpreted as $+5$.

Signed numbers can often be used to distinguish different concepts. For example, a profit of $10 can be denoted by $+$10$ and a loss of $10 by $-$10$. A temperature of 20 degrees below zero can be denoted $-20°$.

Much difficulty in mathematics comes from missing or misinterpreting this symbol "$-$". Part of this difficulty is that the symbol really has three different meanings.

1. When it appears to the left of any constant it means "negative."

-7 means "negative seven."

2. When the symbol appears between two numbers it means "minus" or "subtract."

$-7 - 5$ means "negative seven minus five."

3. That symbol in any other location means "opposite" or "additive inverse" or "the negative of." Specifically this means that if it appears to the left of a variable

$-a$ means "the opposite of a."

If it appears to the left of parentheses

$-(x + 2)$ means "the opposite of the quantity x plus 2."

Or if it appears to the left of another operation

-2^2 means "the opposite of two squared."

$-\sqrt{5}$ means "the opposite of the square root of five."

All the numbers which correspond to points to the right of 0 are called *positive numbers*. The sign of a positive number is +.

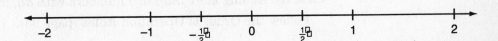

All the numbers which correspond to points to the left of 0 are called *negative numbers*. Negative numbers are signed numbers whose sign is $-$. For example, -3, -5.15, $-.003$ are all negative numbers.

0 is neither positive nor negative; any nonzero number is positive or negative but not both, but $-0 = 0$.

Absolute Value

The absolute value of a signed number is the distance of the number from 0. The absolute value of any nonzero number is *positive*. For example the absolute value of 2 is 2; the absolute value of –2 is 2. The absolute value of a number a is denoted by $|a|$ so $|-2| = 2$. The absolute value of any number can be found by dropping its sign, $|-12| = 12$, $|4| = 4$. *Thus $|-a|$ = $|a|$ for any number a.* The only number whose absolute value is zero is zero.

Adding Signed Numbers

Case I. Adding numbers with the *same sign:*

(A) The sign of the sum is the same as the sign of the numbers being added.
(B) Add the absolute values.
(C) Put the sign from step (A) in front of the number you obtained in step (B).

EXAMPLE 1

What is $-2 + (-3.1) + (-.02)$?

(A) The sign of the sum will be –.
(B) $|-2| = 2$, $|-3.1| = 3.1$, $|-.02| = .02$, and $2 + 3.1 + .02 = 5.12$.
(C) The answer is –5.12.

Case II. Adding two numbers with *different signs:*

(A) The sign of the sum is the sign of the number which is larger in absolute value.
(B) Subtract the absolute value of the number with the smaller absolute value from the absolute value of the number with the larger absolute value.
(C) The answer is the number you obtained in step (B) preceded by the sign from part (A).

EXAMPLE 2

How much is $-5.1 + 3$?

(A) The absolute value of –5.1 is 5.1 and the absolute value of 3 is 3, so the sign of the sum will be –.
(B) 5.1 is larger than 3, and $5.1 - 3 = 2.1$.
(C) The sum is –2.1.

Case III. Adding *more than two* numbers with *different signs:*

Follow the Order of Operation Rules (page 93).

EXAMPLE 3

Find the value of $5 + 52 + (-3) + 7 + (-5.1)$.

SOLUTION

$$5 + 52 + (-3) + 7 + (-5.1) =$$
$$57 + (-3) + 7 + (-5.1) =$$
$$54 + 7 + (-5.1) =$$
$$61 + (-5.1) = 55.9$$

EXAMPLE 4

If a store made a profit of $23.50 on Monday, lost $2.05 on Tuesday, lost $5.03 on Wednesday, made a profit of $30.10 on Thursday, and made a profit of $41.25 on Friday, what was its total profit (or loss) for the week? Use + for profit and − for loss.

SOLUTION

The total is $23.50 + (−2.05) + (−5.03) + 30.10 + 41.25$ which is $94.85 + (−7.08) = 87.77$. So the store made a profit of $87.77.

Subtracting Signed Numbers

(A) Change the sign of the number you are subtracting (the subtrahend).
(B) Add the result of step (A) to the number being subtracted from (the minuend) using the rules of the preceding section.

$$a - b = a + (-b)$$

EXAMPLE 1

Subtract 4.1 from 6.5.

SOLUTION

(A) 4.1 becomes −4.1.
(B) $6.5 + (−4.1) = 2.4$.

EXAMPLE 2

What is $7.8 − (−10.1)$?

SOLUTION

(A) −10.1 becomes 10.1.
(B) $7.8 + 10.1 = 17.9$.

EXAMPLE 3

Perform the indicated operation: $−7.3 − 5.4$

SOLUTION

$−7.3 − 5.4 = −7.3 + (−5.4)$ Follow the rule for addition.
$\qquad = −12.7$

EXAMPLE 4

Perform the indicated operations:

SOLUTION

$11 − 9 + 32 − (−12) + 5$
There are two subtractions to account for:
$\qquad 11 − 9 + 32 − (−12) + 5 =$
$\qquad 11 + (−9) + 32 + 12 + 5 =$
$\qquad 60 + (−9) = 51$

Multiplying Signed Numbers

Case I. Multiplying two numbers:

(A) Multiply the absolute values of the numbers.
(B) If both numbers have the same sign, the result of step (A) is the answer, i.e. the product is positive. If the numbers have different signs, then the answer is opposite the result of step (A).

EXAMPLE 1

$(-5)(-12) = ?$

SOLUTION

(A) $(5)(12) = 60$
(B) Both signs are the same, so the answer is 60.

EXAMPLE 2

$(4)(-3) = ?$

SOLUTION

(A) $(4)(3) = 12$
(B) The signs are different, so the answer is -12. You can remember the sign of the product in the following way:

$$(-)(-) = +$$
$$(+)(+) = +$$
$$(-)(+) = -$$
$$(+)(-) = -$$

Case II. Multiplying more than two numbers:

(A) Multiply the first two factors using Case I.
(B) Multiply the result of (A) by the third factor.
(C) Multiply the result of (B) by the fourth factor.
(D) Continue until you have used each factor.

EXAMPLE 3

$(-5)(4)(2)(-1/2)(3/4) = ?$

SOLUTION

(A) $(-5)(4) = -20$
(B) $(-20)(2) = -40$
(C) $(-40)(-1/2) = 20$
(D) $(20)(3/4) = 15$, so the answer is 15.

The sign of the product is + if there are no negative factors or an even number of negative factors. The sign of the product is – if there are an odd number of negative factors.

Dividing Signed Numbers

Divide the absolute values of the numbers; the sign of the quotient is determined by the same rules as you used to determine the sign of a product. Thus,

$$+ \div + = +$$
$$- \div - = +$$
$$+ \div - = -$$
$$- \div + = -$$

EXAMPLE 1

Divide 53.2 by −4.

53.2 divided by 4 is 13.3. Since one of the numbers is positive and the other negative, the answer is −13.3.

EXAMPLE 2

$$\frac{-5}{-2} = \frac{5}{2}$$

EXAMPLE 3

Perform the indicated operations:

$$-4 + (-8)(-3) - (-1)(5)$$

SOLUTION

Follow the Order of Operation Rules: multiplication before addition or subtraction.

$$-4 + (-8)(-3) - (-1)(5) =$$
$$-4 + 24 - (-5) =$$
$$-4 + 24 + 5 =$$
$$20 + 5 = 25$$

EXAMPLE 4

Perform the indicated operations:

$$\left(\frac{-2}{3}\right) \div (-2)(-4) + \left(\frac{-1}{2}\right)(6)$$

SOLUTION

$$\left(\frac{-2}{3}\right) \div (-2)(-4) + \left(\frac{-1}{2}\right)(6) =$$

$$\left(\frac{-2}{3}\right) \times \left(\frac{-1}{2}\right)(-4) + \left(\frac{-1}{2}\right)\left(\frac{6}{1}\right) =$$

$$\left(\frac{1}{3}\right)(-4) + (-3) =$$

$$\left(\frac{-4}{3}\right) + \left(\frac{-3}{1}\right) =$$

$$\left(\frac{-4}{3}\right) + \left(\frac{-9}{3}\right) = \frac{-13}{3}$$

PRACTICE EXERCISE 13

Perform the indicated operations.

1. $20 - 12 + 8$

2. $15 - 5 \cdot 3$

3. $20 - 2 \cdot 10 + 1$

4. $50 \div [5 \cdot (-2)]$

5. $4 - 4 \cdot 4 - 4$

6. $(18 \div (2 - 5 + 9)) \cdot 2$

---

1. $20 - 12 + 8 = 20 + (-12) + 8 = 8 + 8 = 16$
2. $15 - 5 \cdot 3 = 15 - 15 = 15 + (-15) = 0$
3. $20 - 2 \cdot 10 + 1 = 20 - 20 + 1 = 20 + (-20) + 1 = 0 + 1 = 1$
4. $50 \div [5 \cdot (-2)] = 50 \div [-10] = -5$
5. $4 - 4 \cdot 4 - 4 = 4 - 16 - 4 = 4 + (-16) + (-4) = -12 + (-4) = -16$
6. $(18 \div (2 - 5 + 9)) \cdot 2 = (18 \div (2 + (-5) + 9) \cdot 2 =$

$$(18 \div (-3 + 9) \cdot 2 =$$
$$(18 \div 6) \cdot 2 =$$
$$3 \cdot 2 = 6$$

G. Averages, Medians, Ranges, and Modes

Mean

The *arithmetic mean*, commonly called the average, of a collection of N numbers is the result of dividing the sum of all the numbers in the collection by N.

EXAMPLE 1

The scores of 9 students on a test were 72, 78, 81, 64, 85, 92, 95, 60, and 55. What was the mean score of the students?

Since there are 9 students, the mean is the total of all scores divided by 9.

So the mean is $\frac{1}{9}$ of $(72 + 78 + 81 + 64 + 85 + 92 + 95 + 60 + 55)$, which is $\frac{1}{9}$ of (682) or $75\frac{7}{9}$.

EXAMPLE 2

The temperature at noon in Coldtown, U.S.A. was 5° on Monday, 10° on Tuesday, 2° below zero on Wednesday, 5° below zero on Thursday, 0° on Friday, 4° on Saturday, and 1° below zero on Sunday. What was the average temperature at noon for the week?

Use negative numbers for the temperatures below zero. The average temperature is the average of 5, 10, –2, –5, 0, 4, and –1, which is

$$\frac{5 + 10 + (-2) + (-5) + 0 + 4 + (-1)}{7} = \frac{11}{7} = 1\frac{4}{7}.$$

Therefore, the average temperature at noon for the week is $1\frac{4}{7}°$.

EXAMPLE 3

If the average annual income of 10 workers is $15,665 and two of the workers each made $20,000 for the year, what is the average annual income of the remaining 8 workers?

The total income of all 10 workers is 10 times the average income which is $156,650. The two workers made a total of $40,000, so the total income of the remaining 8 workers was $156,650 – $40,000 = $116,650. Therefore, the average annual income of the 8 remaining workers is

$$\frac{\$116,650}{8} = \$14,581.25.$$

Median

The number in the middle of a collection of numbers if the numbers are arranged in order is called the *median*. In example 1 above, the median score was 78, and in example 2, the median temperature for the week was 0. Notice that the medians were different from the means. In example 3, we don't have enough data to find the median although we know the mean.

In general, the median and the mean of a collection of numbers are different.

If the number of objects in the collection is even, the median is the average of the two numbers in the middle of the ordered array. For example, the median of 64, 66, 72, 75, 76, and 77 is the average of 72 and 75 which is 73.5.

Range

If you subtract the smallest from the largest of a collection of numbers, the result is the range of that collection of numbers. In example 1, the lowest score was 55, and the highest score was 95. The range of scores was $95 - 55 = 40$.

Mode

In a collection of numbers, the most frequently appearing number is the *mode*. If the scores of the 9 students in example 1 were 72, 78, 81, 64, 78, 92, 95, 78, and 55, the mode of these scores would be 78.

H. Powers, Exponents, and Roots

If b is any number and n is a whole number greater than 0, b^n means the product of n factors each of which is equal to b. Thus,

$$b^n = b \cdot b \cdot b \cdot \ldots \cdot b \text{ where there are } n \text{ factors of } b.$$

If $n = 1$, there is only one factor of b so $b^1 = b$. Here are some examples.

$$2^5 = 2 \cdot 2 \cdot 2 \cdot 2 \cdot 2 = 32$$
$$(-4)^3 = (-4) \cdot (-4) \cdot (-4) = -64$$
$$\frac{3^2}{4} = \frac{3 \cdot 3}{4} = \frac{9}{4},$$

$1^n = 1$ for any n, $0^n = 0$ for any n, except 0.

b^n is read "b to the *nth power*."

b^2 is commonly read "b *squared*."

b^3 is commonly read "b *cubed*."

You should know the following squares and cubes:

$1^2 = 1$	$9^2 = 81$	$1^3 = 1$
$2^2 = 4$	$10^2 = 100$	$2^3 = 8$
$3^2 = 9$	$11^2 = 121$	$3^3 = 27$
$4^2 = 16$	$12^2 = 144$	$4^3 = 64$
$5^2 = 25$	$13^2 = 169$	$5^3 = 125$
$6^2 = 36$	$14^2 = 196$	
$7^2 = 49$	$15^2 = 225$	
$8^2 = 64$		

If you raise a fraction, $\dfrac{p}{q}$, to an *nth* power, then $\left(\dfrac{p}{q}\right)^n = \dfrac{p^n}{q^n}$. For example,

$$\left(\frac{5}{4}\right)^3 = \frac{5^3}{4^3} = \frac{125}{64}.$$

Exponents

In the expression b^n, b is called the *base* and n is called the *exponent*. In the expression 2^5, 2 is the base and 5 is the exponent.

The two basic formulas for problems involving exponents are:

(A) $b^n \times b^m = b^{n+m}$

(B) $a^n \times b^n = (a \cdot b)^n$

(C) $\dfrac{b^n}{b^m} = b^{n-m}$

(A), (B) and (C) are called *laws of exponents*.

EXAMPLE 1

What is 6^3?

$$\text{Since } 6 = 3 \times 2, \ 6^3 = 3^3 \times 2^3 = 27 \times 8 = 216.$$
$$\text{or}$$
$$6^3 = 6 \times 6 \times 6 = 216.$$

EXAMPLE 2

Find the value of $2^3 \times 2^2$.

Using (A), $2^3 \times 2^2 = 2^{2+3} = 2^5$ which is 32. You can check this, since $2^3 = 8$ and $2^2 = 4$; $2^3 \times 2^2 = 8 \times 4 = 32$.

Negative Exponents

The following establishes a pattern: decrease the exponent by 1 while dividing the number on the right by 2. (Two is being used only for convenience.)

$$2^4 = 16$$
$$2^3 = 8$$
$$2^2 = 4$$

Continuing, we see that

$$2^1 = 2 \ \text{ and } \ 2^0 = 1.$$

This last equation is frequently misunderstood. Any number (except zero) raised to the zero power is equal to 1, not 0. That is, $7^0 = 1$, $(-15)^0 = 1$ and $\left(\dfrac{-5}{8}\right)^0 = 1$ and so forth. However 0^0 is undefined.

Continuing the pattern above, we see that:

$$2^{-1} = \frac{1}{2} \ \text{ and }$$

$$2^{-2} = \frac{1}{4}\left(\frac{1}{2} \ \text{of} \ \frac{1}{2} \ \text{is} \ \frac{1}{4}\right)$$

$$2^{-3} = \frac{1}{8} = \frac{1}{2^3} \ \text{ and so on.}$$

This suggests the rule for negative exponents:

$$b^{-n} = \frac{1}{b^n}$$

Two results of this rule may be used to simplify some expressions.

1. If a negative exponent appears in a denominator, move the factor to the numerator and change the sign of the exponent.

$$\frac{a}{b^{-n}} = ab^n$$

2. If a negative exponent applies to a fraction, invert the fraction and change the sign of the exponent.

$$\left(\frac{a}{b}\right)^{-n} = \left(\frac{b}{a}\right)^n$$

EXAMPLE 1

$9^0 = 1$

EXAMPLE 2

$$3^{-2} = \frac{1}{3^2} = \frac{1}{9}$$

EXAMPLE 3

$$\left(\frac{3}{4}\right)^{-2} = \left(\frac{4}{3}\right)^2 = \left(\frac{4}{3}\right)\left(\frac{4}{3}\right) = \frac{16}{9}$$

EXAMPLE 4

Find the value of $(2 \cdot 3)^4$

SOLUTION

$(2 \cdot 3)^4 = 6^4 = 6 \cdot 6 \cdot 6 \cdot 6 = 1,296$
or
$(2 \cdot 3)^4 = 2^4 \cdot 3^4 = 16 \cdot 81 = 1,296$

PRACTICE EXERCISE 14

Perform the indicated operations. Recall that exponents are done in rule 2 in the Order of Operation Rules.

1. $7 + 3^2$
2. $(7 + 3)^2$
3. $10 \cdot 2^3$
4. $(10 \cdot 2)^3$
5. $10^3 \cdot 2$
6. $3^3 - 3^0$
7. -2^2
8. $(-2)^2$
9. $\frac{5^6}{5^4}$
10. $(9 - 3) \cdot 2^3 + 50$
11. $80 \div 4^2 + 10$

SOLUTIONS TO PRACTICE EXERCISE 14

1. $7 + 3^2 = 7 + 9 = 16$

2. $(7 + 3)^2 = 10^2 = 100$

3. $10 \cdot 2^3 = 10 \cdot 8 = 80$

4. $(10 \cdot 2)^3 = 20^3 = 8{,}000$

5. $10^3 \cdot 2 = 1{,}000 \cdot 2 = 2{,}000$

6. $3^3 - 3^0 = 27 - 1 = 26$

7. $-2^2 = -(2^2) = -4$

8. $(-2)^2 = (-2)(-2) = 4$

9. $\dfrac{5^6}{5^4} = 5^{6-4} = 5^2 = 25$

10. $(9 - 3) \cdot 2^3 + 5 = 6 \cdot 2^3 + 5 = 6 \cdot 8 + 5 = 48 + 5 = 53$

11. $80 \div 4^2 + 10 = 80 \div 16 + 10 = 5 + 10 = 15$

Roots

If $b = d^n$, then d is called an *nth* root of b. The *nth* root of b is usually written $\sqrt[n]{b}$. The symbol $\sqrt{}$ is called the radical sign; the number n is the index of the radical sign; the number b is called the radicand; and the entire symbol $\sqrt[n]{b}$ is called a radical. Since $2^5 = 32$, then $\sqrt[5]{32} = 2$. The second root is called the square root; the third root is called the cube root.

Since $3^2 = 9$ and $(-3)^2 = 9$, there are two possibilities for the square root of a positive number; the positive one is called the principal square root and it is denoted by the radical sign: $\sqrt{}$. Thus we say $\sqrt{9} = 3$ and $\sqrt{9} \neq -3$.

Since the square of any nonzero real number is positive, *the square root of a negative number is not defined* as a real number. Thus $\sqrt{-2}$ is not a real number. There are cube roots of negative numbers, however $\sqrt[3]{-8} = -2$, because $(-2)^3 = -8$.

You can also write roots as exponents; for example,

$$\sqrt[n]{b} = b^{1/n}; \text{ so } \sqrt{b} = b^{1/2}, \sqrt[3]{b} = b^{1/3}.$$

$\sqrt[n]{a \cdot b} = \sqrt[n]{a} \cdot \sqrt[n]{b}.$ **This formula is the basic formula for simplifying square roots, cube roots, and so on.**

EXAMPLE 1

$\sqrt{54} = ?$

SOLUTION

Since $54 = 9 \cdot 6$, $\sqrt{54} = \sqrt{9 \cdot 6} = \sqrt{9} \cdot \sqrt{6}$. Since $\sqrt{9} = 3$, $\sqrt{54} = 3\sqrt{6}$.

You cannot simplify by adding square roots unless their radicands are the same number. For example,

$$\sqrt{3} + 2\sqrt{3} - 4\sqrt{3} = -\sqrt{3}, \text{ but } \sqrt{3} + \sqrt{2} \text{ is not equal to } \sqrt{5}.$$

EXAMPLE 2

Simplify $6\sqrt{12} + 2\sqrt{75} - 3\sqrt{98}$.

SOLUTION

Since $\sqrt{12} = \sqrt{4 \cdot 3} = \sqrt{4} \cdot \sqrt{3} = 2\sqrt{3}$;

so $\sqrt{75} = \sqrt{25} \cdot \sqrt{3} = 5\sqrt{3}$;

and so $\sqrt{98} = \sqrt{49} \cdot \sqrt{2} = 7\sqrt{2}$.

Therefore, $6\sqrt{12} + 2\sqrt{75} - 3\sqrt{98} = 6 \cdot 2\sqrt{3} + 2 \cdot 5\sqrt{3} - 3 \cdot 7\sqrt{2} = 12\sqrt{3} + 10\sqrt{3} - 21\sqrt{2} = 22\sqrt{3} - 21\sqrt{2}$.

EXAMPLE 3

Simplify $27^{1/3} \times 8^{1/3}$.

SOLUTION

$27^{1/3} = \sqrt[3]{27} = 3$ and $= 8^{1/3} = \sqrt[3]{8} = 2$, so $27^{1/3} \cdot 8^{1/3} = 3 \cdot 2 = 6$.

PRACTICE EXERCISE 15

Simplify.

1. $\sqrt{20}$
2. $\sqrt{72}$
3. $\sqrt[3]{16}$
4. $\sqrt{300}$
5. $\sqrt[4]{64}$

6. $3\sqrt{12}$
7. $\dfrac{-1}{2}\sqrt{18}$
8. $2\sqrt{3} + 4\sqrt{3}$
9. $3\sqrt{8} - 2\sqrt{50}$
10. $5\sqrt{40} - 2\sqrt{100} + \sqrt{90}$

SOLUTIONS TO PRACTICE EXERCISE 15

1. $\sqrt{20} = \sqrt{4 \cdot 5} = \sqrt{4} \cdot \sqrt{5} = 2\sqrt{5}$
2. $\sqrt{72} = \sqrt{36 \cdot 2} = \sqrt{36} \cdot \sqrt{2} = 6\sqrt{2}$

Always find the largest square factor of the radicand.

3. $\sqrt[3]{16} = \sqrt[3]{8 \cdot 2} = \sqrt[3]{8} \cdot \sqrt[3]{2} = 2 \cdot \sqrt[3]{2}$

Find the largest cube factor of the radicand.

4. $\sqrt{300} = \sqrt{100 \cdot 3} = \sqrt{100} \cdot \sqrt{3} = 10\sqrt{3}$
5. $\sqrt[4]{64} = \sqrt[4]{16 \cdot 4} = \sqrt[4]{16} \cdot \sqrt[4]{4} = 2\sqrt[4]{4}$
6. $3\sqrt{12} = 3\sqrt{4 \cdot 3} = 3 \cdot \sqrt{4} \cdot \sqrt{3} = 3 \cdot 2 \cdot \sqrt{3} = 6\sqrt{3}$
7. $\dfrac{-1}{2}\sqrt{18} = \dfrac{-1}{2}\sqrt{9 \cdot 2} = \dfrac{-1}{2}\sqrt{9} \cdot \sqrt{2} = \dfrac{-1}{2} \cdot 3 \cdot \sqrt{2} = \dfrac{-3}{2}\sqrt{2}$
8. $2\sqrt{3} + 4\sqrt{3} = 6\sqrt{3}$
9. $3\sqrt{8} - 2\sqrt{50} = 3\sqrt{4 \cdot 2} - 2\sqrt{25 \cdot 2} = 3 \cdot \sqrt{4} \cdot \sqrt{2} - 2 \cdot \sqrt{25}\sqrt{2} = 3 \cdot 2 \cdot \sqrt{2} - 2 \cdot 5\sqrt{2} = 6\sqrt{2} - 10\sqrt{2} = -4\sqrt{2}$
10. $5\sqrt{40} - 2\sqrt{100} + \sqrt{90} = 5 \cdot 2 \cdot \sqrt{10} - 2 \cdot 10 + 3\sqrt{10} = 10\sqrt{10} - 20 + 3\sqrt{10} = 13\sqrt{10} - 20$

II. ALGEBRA

A. Algebraic Expressions

Often it is necessary to deal with quantities which have a numerical value which is unknown. For example, we may know that Tom's salary is twice as much as Joe's salary. If we let the value of Tom's salary be called T and the value of Joe's salary be J, then T and J are numbers which are unknown. However, we do know that the value of T must be twice the value of J, or $T = 2J$.

T and $2J$ are examples of algebraic expressions. An algebraic expression may involve letters in addition to numbers and symbols; however, *in an algebraic expression a letter always stands for a number.* Therefore, you can multiply, divide, add, subtract, and perform other mathematical operations on a letter. Thus, x^2 would mean x times x. Some examples of algebraic expressions are $2x + y$, $y^3 + 9y$, $z^3 - 5ab$, $c + d + 4$, $5x + 2y(6x - 4y + z)$. When letters or numbers are written together without any sign or symbol between them, multiplication is assumed. Thus $6xy$ means 6 times x times y. $6xy$ is called a term; terms are separated by + or − signs. The expression $5z + 2 + 4x^2$ has three terms, $5z$, 2, and $4x^2$. The letters in an algebraic expression are called *variables* or *unknowns*. When a variable is multiplied by a number, the number is called the *coefficient* of the variable. So in the expression $5x^2 + 2yz$, the coefficient of x^2 is 5, and the coefficient of yz is 2.

Simplifying Algebraic Expressions

You must be able to recognize algebraic expressions which are equal. It will save time when you are solving problems if you can change a complicated expression into a simpler one.

(A) Eliminate any grouping symbols.

Perform the operations inside parentheses first. So $(6x + y) \div x$ means divide the sum of $6x$ and y by x. Notice that $(6x + y) \div x$ is different from $6x + y \div x$.

The main rule for getting rid of parentheses is the distributive law, which is expressed as $a(b + c) = ab + ac$. In other words, if any single term expression is followed by an expression contained in parentheses, then *each* term of the expression inside of the parentheses is multiplied by the one outside of the parentheses. Once we have worked out what is in the parentheses we can proceed.

If an expression has more than one set of parentheses, eliminate the *inner parentheses first* and then *work out* through the rest of the parentheses.

(B) Perform any roots or exponents in order from left to right.

(C) Perform any multiplications or divisions before performing additions or subtractions. Thus, the expression $6x + y \div x$ means add $6x$ to the quotient of y divided by x. Another way of writing the expression would be $6x + \dfrac{y}{x}$. This is not the same as $\dfrac{6x + y}{x}$.

(D) The order in which you multiply numbers and letters in a term does not matter. So $6xy$ is the same as $6yx$.

(E) The order in which you add terms does not matter; for instance, $6x + 2y - x = 6x - x + 2y$.

(F) If there are roots or powers in any terms, you may be able to simplify the term by using the laws of exponents. For example, $5xy \cdot 3x^2y = 15x^3y^2$.

(G) Combine like terms. *Like terms* (or similar terms) are terms which have exactly the same letters raised to the same powers. So x, $-2x$, and $\frac{1}{3}x$ are like terms. For example, $6x - 2x + x + y$ is equal to $5x + y$. In combining like terms, you simply add or subtract the coefficients of the like terms, and the result is the coefficient of that term in the simplified expression. In our example above, the coefficients of x were $+6$, -2, and $+1$; since $6 - 2 + 1 = 5$ the coefficient of x in the simplified expression is 5.

EXAMPLE 1

Simplify $3x^2 - 4\sqrt{x} + \sqrt{4x} + xy + 7x^2 = ?$

$\sqrt{4x} = \sqrt{4}\sqrt{x} = 2\sqrt{x}$.

$3x^2 + 7x^2 = 10x^2, -4\sqrt{x} + 2\sqrt{x} = -2\sqrt{x}$.

The original expression equals $3x^2 + 7x^2 - 4\sqrt{x} + 2\sqrt{x} + xy$. Therefore, the simplified expression is $10x^2 - 2\sqrt{x} + xy$.

EXAMPLE 2

Simplify $\dfrac{21x^4y^2}{3x^6y}$.

$$\dfrac{\overset{7}{\cancel{21}}\,\overset{1}{x^4}\,\overset{y}{y^2}}{\underset{1}{\cancel{3}}\,\underset{x^2}{x^6}\,\underset{1}{y}} = \dfrac{7y}{x^2}$$

EXAMPLE 3

Write $\dfrac{2x}{y} - \dfrac{4}{x}$ as a single fraction.

A common denominator is xy so $\dfrac{2x}{y} = \dfrac{2x \cdot x}{y \cdot x} = \dfrac{2x^2}{xy}$, and $\dfrac{4}{x} = \dfrac{4y}{xy}$.

Therefore, $\dfrac{2x}{y} - \dfrac{4}{x} = \dfrac{2x^2}{xy} - \dfrac{4y}{xy} = \dfrac{2x^2 - 4y}{xy}$

EXAMPLE 4

$2x(6x - 4y + 2) = (2x)(6x) + (2x)(-4y) + (2x)(2) = 12x^2 - 8xy + 4x$.

EXAMPLE 5

$2x - (x + 6(x - 3y) + 4y) = ?$

SOLUTION

To remove the inner parentheses we multiply $6(x - 3y)$ getting $6x - 18y$. Now we have $2x - (x + 6x - 18y + 4y)$ which equals $2x - (7x - 14y)$. Distribute -1 through the parentheses getting $2x - 7x - (-14y) = -5x + 14y$.

Sometimes brackets are used instead of parentheses.

EXAMPLE 6

Simplify $-3x\left[\frac{1}{2}(3x-2y)-2(x(3+y)+4y)\right]$

SOLUTION

$$-3x\left[\frac{1}{2}(3x-2y)-2(x(3+y)+4y)\right]$$

$$-3x\left[\frac{1}{2}(3x-2y)-2(3x+xy+4y)\right]$$

$$=-3x\left[\frac{3}{2}x-y-6x-2xy-8y)\right]$$

$$=-3x\left[-\frac{9}{2}x-2xy-9y\right]$$

$$=\frac{27}{2}x^2+6x^2y+27xy.$$

Adding and Subtracting Algebraic Expressions

Since algebraic expressions represent numbers, they can be added and sub-tracted.

The only algebraic terms which can be combined are like terms.

EXAMPLE 1

$(3x+4y-xy^2)+(3x+2x(x-y)) = ?$

SOLUTION

$(3x+4y-xy^2)+(3x+2x^2-2xy)$ removing inner parentheses
$=3x+4y-xy^2+3x+2x^2-2xy$ removing outer parentheses
$=6x+4y+2x^2-xy^2-2xy$ combining like terms

EXAMPLE 2

$(2a+3a^2-4)-2(4a^2-2(a+4)) = ?$

SOLUTION

$(2a+3a^2-4)-2(4a^2-2a-8)$ removing inner parentheses
$=2a+3a^2-4-8a^2+4a+16$ removing outer parentheses
$=-5a^2+6a+12$ combining like terms

PRACTICE EXERCISE 16

Simplify each algebraic expression.

1. $3(x-2)+4(2x+1)$

2. $(a-b)-(a+b)$

3. $x-[2x-3(x+4)]$

4. $(2x-3y+2)-2(x+2y-4)$

5. $(4x^2y)(-3xy^3)$

6. $\dfrac{1}{2b}-\dfrac{2}{3a}$

---

1. $3(x - 2) + 4(2x + 1) = 3x - 6 + 8x + 4 = 11x - 2$

2. $(a - b) - (a + b) = a - b - a - b = -2b$

3. $x - [2x - 3(x + 4)] = x - [2x - 3x - 12] = x - 2x + 3x + 12 = 2x + 12$

4. $(2x - 3y + 2) - 2(x + 2y - 4) = 2x - 3y + 2 - 2x - 4y + 8 = -7y + 10$

5. $(4x^2y)(-3xy^3) = -12x^3y^4$

6. $\dfrac{1}{2b} - \dfrac{2}{3a} = \dfrac{?}{6ab} = \dfrac{?}{6ab} = \dfrac{3a}{6ab} = \dfrac{4b}{6ab} = \dfrac{3a - 4b}{6ab}$

Multiplying Algebraic Expressions

When you multiply two expressions, you multiply *each term of the first by each term of the second.*

EXAMPLE 1

$(b - 4)(b + a) = b(b + a) - 4(b + a) = ?$
$$= b^2 + ab - 4b - 4a.$$

EXAMPLE 2

$(2h - 4)(h + 2h^2 + h^3) = ?$
$$= 2h(h + 2h^2 + h^3) - 4(h + 2h^2 + h^3)$$
$$= 2h^2 + 4h^3 + 2h^4 - 4h + 8h^2 - 4h^3$$
$$= -4h - 6h^2 + 2h^4$$

Multiplication of two binomials is also an application of the distributive property. It is easily remembered by the acronym FOIL.

EXAMPLE 3

Multiply $(2x + 5)(3x + 4)$.   Multiply:

$2x \cdot 3 = 6x^2$	First terms.
$2x \cdot 4 = 8x$	Outer terms.
$5 \cdot 3x = 15x$	Inner terms.
$5 \cdot 4 = 20$	Last terms.
$8x + 15x = 23x$	Combine Outer and Inner products.

The answer is $6x^2 + 23x + 20$.

EXAMPLE 4

Multiply $(x - 4)(3x + 7)$.   Multiply:

$3x^2$	First terms.
$7x$	Outer terms.
$-12x$	Inner terms.
-28	Last terms.

Combine the outer and inner products: $7x + (-12x) = -5x$.
The answer is $3x^2 - 5x - 28$.

If you need to multiply more than two expressions, multiply the first two expressions, then multiply the result by the third expression, and so on until you have used each factor. Since algebraic expressions can be multiplied, they can be squared, cubed, or raised to other powers.

EXAMPLE 5

$$(x - 2y)^3 = (x - 2y)(x - 2y)(x - 2y).$$

Since $(x - 2y)(x - 2y) = x^2 - 2yx - 2yx + 4y^2$

$$= x^2 - 4yx + 4y^2,$$

$$(x - 2y)^3 = (x^2 - 4xy + 4y^2)(x - 2y)$$

$$= x(x^2 - 4xy + 4y^2) - 2y(x^2 - 4xy + 4y^2)$$

$$= x^3 - 4x^2y + 4xy^2 - 2x^2y + 8xy^2 + 8y^3$$

$$= x^3 - 6x^2y + 12xy^2 - 8y^3.$$

The order in which you multiply algebraic expressions does not matter. Thus $(2a + b)(x^2 + 2x) = (x^2 + 2x)(2a + b)$.

Certain products occur frequently and deserve special attention. The product of two binomials of the type $(A + B)(A - B)$ will always result in the inner and outer products adding to zero. One does not normally think through the FOIL procedure when multiplying such binomials. Merely square the first and last terms and then subtract the second square from the first square.

$$(A + B)(A - B) = A^2 - AB + AB - B^2 = A^2 - B^2$$

Squaring a binomial can be done by following FOIL, but with practice, it can be done directly by following a pattern.

$$(A + B)^2 = A^2 + AB + AB + B^2 = A^2 + 2AB + B^2$$

or

$$(A - B)^2 = A^2 - AB - AB + B^2 = A^2 - 2AB + B^2$$

Cubing a binomial can also be done more easily by following a pattern. Notice that the exponents for the first variable descend from 3 to 0 while the exponents for the second variable ascend from 0 to 3.

$$(A + B)^3 = A^3 + 3A^2B + 3AB^2 + B^3$$

or

$$(A - B)^3 = A^3 - 3A^2B + 3AB^2 - B^3$$

PRACTICE EXERCISE 17

Simplify the following expressions.

1. $(x - 5)(x + 8)$

2. $(3x - 4)(5x + 2)$

3. $(2x - 5)(2x + 5)$

4. $(4x - 3y)(x - 2y)$

5. $(3x - 7)^2$

6. $(x - 2)(x^2 - 3x - 1)$

7. $(x - 2)^3$

SOLUTIONS TO PRACTICE EXERCISE 17

1. $(x - 5)(x + 8) = x^2 + 3x - 40$

2. $(3x - 4)(5x + 2) = 15x^2 - 14^2 - 8$

3. $(2x - 5)(2x + 5) = 4x^2 - 25$

4. $(4x - 3y)(x - 2y) = 4x^2 - 11xy + 6y^2$

5. $(3x - 7)^2 = 9x^2 - 42x + 49$

6. $(x - 2)(x^2 - 3x - 1) = x^3 - 3x^2 - x - 2x^2 + 6x + 2 = x^3 - 5x^2 + 5x + 2$

7. $(x - 2)^3 = x^3 - 6x^2 + 12x - 8$

Factoring Algebraic Expressions

If an algebraic expression is the product of other algebraic expressions, then the expressions are called factors. For instance, we claim that $(2x - 1)$ and $(x + 3)$ are factors of $2x^2 + 5x - 3$. We can always check to see if we have the correct factors by multiplying. We need to be able to factor algebraic expressions in order to solve quadratic equations. It also can be helpful in dividing algebraic expressions.

The following are factoring techniques.

1. *Greatest common factor.* If the terms of an expression all contain a common factor other than 1, use the distributive property to remove the greatest common factor.

$$15x^2 + 12x = 3x(5x + 4)$$

$$24x^3y - 18xy = 6xy(4x^2 - 3)$$

2. *Difference of squares.* If a binomial is the difference of terms, both of which are squares, use the following pattern to factor it.

$$A^2 - B^2 = (A - B)(A + B)$$

$$36x^2 - 49 = (6x - 7)(6x + 7)$$

$$100x^2 - 25 = 25(4x^2 - 1) = 25(2x + 1)(2x - 1)$$

$$x^4 - 81 = (x^2 - 9)(x^2 + 9) = (x - 3)(x + 3)(x^2 + 9)$$

3. *Perfect square trinomial.* If the terms of a trinomial satisfy the pattern for squaring a binomial, then use that pattern to factor it.

$$A^2 \pm 2AB + B^2 = (A \pm B)^2$$

$$16x^2 - 40x + 25 = (4x - 5)^2$$

$$16x^2 - 16x + 4 = 4(4x^2 - 4x + 1) = 4(2x - 1)^2$$

4. *Easy kind of trinomial.* The leading coefficient of this type of trinomial is 1. Look for two numbers whose product is the third term and whose sum (or difference) is the coefficient of the second term.

$$x^2 + 8x + 12 = (x + 2)(x + 6)$$

$$x^2 - 8x + 15 = (x - 5)(x - 3)$$

$$x^2 - 5x - 24 = (x - 8)(x + 3)$$

$$x^2 + 2x - 35 = (x + 7)(x - 5)$$

$$3x^2 - 18x + 24 = 3(x^2 - 6x + 8) = 3(x - 4)(x - 2)$$

5. *Hard kind of trinomial.* The leading coefficient of this type of trinomial is a number other than 1. The procedure is to multiply the first and third terms' coefficients and look for a pair of factors of that number whose sum or difference is the second coefficient. Then rewrite the second term using those numbers, group, and factor.

$2x^2 + 5x - 12$	Multiple 2 times 12.
$24 = 3 \cdot 8$	Look for two factors of 24 whose difference (because the 12 is negative) is 5.
$2x^2 + 8x - 3x - 12$	Rewrite $5x$ as $8x - 3x$.

$(2x^2 + 8x) - (3x + 12)$ Group.

$2x(x + 4) - 3(x + 4)$ Now $(x + 4)$ is a common factor.

$(x + 4)(2x - 3)$

$24x^2 - 14x - 3$ $24 \cdot 3 = 72$ and $72 = 18 \cdot 4$

$24x^2 - 18x + 4x - 3$

$(24x^2 - 18x) + (4x - 3)$

$6x(4x - 3) + 1(4x - 3)$

$(4x - 3)(6x + 1)$

EXAMPLE 1

Factor $(9m^2 - 16)$.

$9m^2 = (3m)^2$ and $16 = 4^2$, so the factors are $(3m - 4)(3m + 4)$.

Since $(3m - 4)(3m + 4) = 9m^2 - 16$, these factors are correct.

EXAMPLE 2

Factor $x^4y^4 - 4z^2$.

$x^4y^4 = (x^2y^2)^2$ and $4z^2 = (2z)^2$, so the factors are $x^2y^2 + 2z$ and $x^2y^2 - 2z$.

You also may need to factor expressions such as $x^2 + 4x + 3$. The factors will be of the form $(x + a)$ and $(x + b)$. Since $(x + a)(x + b) = x^2 + (a + b)x + ab$, you must look for a pair of numbers, a and b, such that $a \cdot b$ is the last term in the expression, and $a + b$ is the coefficient of the middle term (the terms with exponent 1).

EXAMPLE 3

Factor $x^2 + 4x + 3$.

You want numbers whose product is 3 and whose sum is 4. Look at the possible factors of three and check whether they add up to 4. Since $3 = 3 \times 1$ and $3 + 1$ is 4, the factors are $(x + 3)$ and $(x + 1)$. Remember to check by multiplying.

EXAMPLE 4

Factor $y^2 + y - 6$.

Since –6 is negative, the two numbers a and b must be of opposite sign. Possible pairs of factors for –6 are –6 and +1, 6 and –1, 3 and –2, and –3 and 2. Since $-2 + 3 = 1$, the factors are $(y + 3)$ and $(y - 2)$. So $(y + 3)(y - 2) = y^2 + y - 6$.

EXAMPLE 5

Factor $a^3 + 4a^2 + 4a$.

Factor out the common factor a, so $a^3 + 4a^2 + 4a = a(a^2 + 4a + 4)$. Consider $a^2 + 4a + 4$; since $2 + 2 = 4$ and $2 \times 2 = 4$, the factors are $(a + 2)$ and $(a + 2)$. Therefore, $a^3 + 4a^2 + 4a = a(a + 2)^2$.

There are some expressions which cannot be factored; for example, $x_2 + 4x + 6$. In general, if you can't factor something by using the methods given above, don't waste a lot of time on the question. Sometimes you may be able to check the answers given to find out what the correct factors are.

PRACTICE EXERCISE 18

Factor.

1. $x^2 + 10x + 21$

2. $x^2 - 4$

3. $2y^2 + 4y$

4. $z^2 - 7z - 18$

5. $15x^2y - 3xy$

6. $9x^2 - 144$

7. $4x^2y - 8xy^2 + 4x$

8. $4x^2 - 25x + 6$

9. $8 - 2a^2$

10. $15a^2 + 15ab - 30b^2$

11. $a^2 - 24ab + 144b^2$

SOLUTIONS TO PRACTICE EXERCISE 18

---

1. $x^2 + 10x + 21 = (x + 3)(x + 7)$

2. $x^2 - 4 = (x - 2)(x + 2)$

3. $2y^2 + 4y = 2y(y + 2)$

4. $z^2 - 7z - 18 = (z - 9)(z + 2)$

5. $15x^2y - 3xy = 3xy(5x - 1)$

6. $9x^2 - 144 = 9(x^2 - 16) = 9(x - 4)(x + 4)$

7. $4x^2y - 8xy^2 + 4x = 4x(xy - 2y^2 + 1)$

8. $4x^2 - 25x + 6 = (4x - 1)(x - 6)$

9. $8 - 2a^2 = 2(4 - a^2) = 2(2 - a)(2 + a)$

10. $15a^2 + 15ab - 30b^2 = 15(a^2 + ab - 2b^2) = 15(a + 2b)(a - b)$

11. $a^2 - 24ab + 144b^2 = (a - 12b)^2$

Division of Algebraic Expressions

The main things to remember in division are the following:

(1) When you divide a sum, you can get the same result by dividing each term and adding quotients. For example,

$$\frac{9x + 4xy + y^2}{x} = \frac{9x}{x} + \frac{4xy}{x} + \frac{y^2}{x} = 9 + 4y + \frac{y^2}{x}.$$

(2) You can cancel common factors, so the results on factoring will be helpful. For example,

$$\frac{x^2 - 2x}{x - 2} = \frac{x(x - 2)}{x - 2} = x.$$

You can also divide one algebraic expression by another using long division.

EXAMPLE 1

$(15x^2 + 2x - 4) \div (3x - 1)$.

$$
\begin{array}{r}
5x + 2 \\
3x - 1 \overline{\smash{\big)}\ 15x^2 + 2x - 4} \\
\underline{15x^2 - 5x } \\
7x - 4 \\
\underline{6x - 2} \\
x - 2
\end{array}
$$

So the answer is $5x + 2$ with a remainder of $x - 2$.

You can check by multiplying,

$$(5x + 2)(3x - 1) = 15x^2 + 6x - 5x - 2$$

$$= 15x^2 + x - 2; \text{ now add the remainder } x - 2$$

and the result is $15x^2 + x - 2 + x - 2 = 15x^2 + 2x - 4$.

PRACTICE EXERCISE 19

Divide as indicated.

1. $\dfrac{-48x^2y^3z}{-16xy^2z}$

2. $\dfrac{25x^3 - 10x^2 + 5x}{5x}$

3. $\dfrac{2x^2 + 13x + 20}{2x + 7}$

4. $\dfrac{8x^3 + 1}{2x + 1}$

SOLUTIONS TO PRACTICE EXERCISE 19

1. $\dfrac{-48x^2y^3z}{-16xy^2z} = 3xy$

2. $\dfrac{25x^3 - 10x^2 + 5x}{5x} = \dfrac{25x^3}{5x} - \dfrac{10x^2}{5x} + \dfrac{5x}{5x} = 5x^2 - 2x + 1$

3. $\dfrac{2x^2 + 13x + 20}{2x + 7}$ Set up in long division format:

$$
\begin{array}{r}
x + 3 + \dfrac{-1}{2x + 7} \\
2x + 7 \overline{\smash{\big)}\ 2x^2 + 13x + 20} \\
\underline{2x^2 + 13x + 20} \\
2x^2 + 7x \\
\underline{6x + 20} \\
6x + 21 \\
\underline{-1}
\end{array}
$$

4. $\dfrac{8x^3 + 1}{2x + 1}$ You must supply zero terms for the missing second and third terms in the dividend:

$$
\begin{array}{r}
4x^2 - 2x + 1 \\
2x + 1\overline{\smash{\big)}\,8x^3 + 0x^2 + 0x + 1} \\
\underline{8x^3 + 4x^2} \\
-4x^2 + 0x \\
\underline{-4x^2 - 2x} \\
2x + 1 \\
\underline{2x + 1} \\
0
\end{array}
$$

B. Equations

An *equation* is a statement that says two algebraic expressions are equal.

$x + 2 = 3$, $4 + 2 = 6$, $3x^2 + 2x - 6 = 0$, $x^2 + y^2 = z^2$, $\frac{y}{x} = 2 + z$, and $A = LW$

are all examples of equations. We will refer to the algebraic expressions on each side of the equal sign as the left side and the right side of the equation. Thus, in the equation $2x + 4 = 6y + x$, $2x + 4$ is the left side and $6y + x$ is the right side.

Solutions of Equations

If we assign specific numbers to each variable or unknown in an algebraic expression, then the algebraic expression will be equal to a number. This is called *evaluating* the expression. For example, if you evaluate $2x + 4y^2 + 3$ for $x = -1$ and $y = 2$, the expression is equal to $2(-1) + 4 \cdot 2^2 + 3 = -2 + 4 \cdot 4 + 3 = 17$.

If we evaluate each side of an equation and the number obtained is the same for each side of the equation, then the specific values assigned to the unknowns are called *solutions of the equation*. Another way of saying this is that the choices for the unknowns satisfy the equation. The set that contains all of the numbers that make an equation true is called the *solution set*.

EXAMPLE 1

Consider the equation $2x + 3 = 9$.

If $x = 3$, then the left side of the equation becomes $2 \cdot 3 + 3 = 6 + 3 = 9$, so both sides equal 9, and $x = 3$ is a solution of $2x + 3 = 9$. If $x = 4$, then the left side is $2 \cdot 4 + 3 = 11$. Since 11 is not equal to 9, $x = 4$ is *not* a solution of $2x + 3 = 9$.

EXAMPLE 2

Consider the equation $x^2 + y^2 = 5x$.

If $x = 1$ and $y = 2$, then the left side is $1^2 + 2^2$ which equals $1 + 4 = 5$. The right side is $5 \cdot 1 = 5$, since both sides are equal to 5, $x = 1$ and $y = 2$ is a solution.

If $x = 5$ and $y = 0$, then the left side is $5^2 + 0^2 = 25$ and the right side is $5 \cdot 5 = 25$, so $x = 5$ and $y = 0$ is a solution.

If $x = 1$ and $y = 1$, then the left side is $1^2 + 1^2 = 2$ and the right side is $5 \cdot 1 = 5$. Therefore, since $2 \neq 5$, $x = 1$ and $y = 1$ is not a solution.

There are some equations which *do not have any solutions which are real numbers*. Since the square of any real number is positive or zero, the equation $x^2 = -4$ does not have any solutions which are real numbers.

Solving Equations

One equation is *equivalent* to another equation, if they have exactly the same solutions. The basic idea in solving equations is to transform a given equation into an equivalent equation whose solutions are obvious.

The two main tools for solving equations are to form equivalent equations by:

Addition Property of Equality
  (A) Adding or subtracting the same algebraic expression to or from *each* side of an equation.

Multiplication Property of Equality
  (B) Multiplying or dividing both sides of an equation by the same *non-zero* algebraic expression.

The most common type of equation is the linear equation with only one unknown. $6z = 4z - 3$, $3 + a = 2a - 4$, $3b + 2b = b - 4b$, are all examples of linear equations with only one unknown.

The task of solving an equation is to produce a sequence of equivalent equations, the last one of which is of the type

$$x = \text{constant}$$

from which the solution set can easily be found. The rules for generating the equivalent equations are the rules for simplifying algebraic expressions and the Addition Property of Equality and the Multiplication Property of Equality above.

EXAMPLE 1

Solve $6x + 2 = 3$ for x.

SOLUTION

Subtract 2 from each side of the equation. Then $6x + 2 - 2 = 3 - 2$ or $6x = 1$.

Divide each side by 6. Therefore, $x = \dfrac{1}{6}$.

You should always check your answer in the original equation.

Since $6\left(\dfrac{1}{6}\right) + 2 = 1 + 2 = 3$, $x = \dfrac{1}{6}$ is a solution.

EXAMPLE 2

Solve $3x + 15 = 3 - 4x$ for x.
  Add $4x$ to each side:

$$7x + 15 = 3$$

Subtract 15 from both sides:

$$7x = -12$$

Divide both sides by 7:

$$x = \frac{-12}{7}$$

The solutions set is $\left\{\dfrac{-12}{7}\right\}$

Check: $3\left(\dfrac{-12}{7}\right) + 15 = \dfrac{-36}{7} + 15 = \dfrac{69}{7}$ and $3 - 4\left(\dfrac{-12}{7}\right) = 3 + \dfrac{48}{7} = \dfrac{69}{7}$.

If you do the same thing to each side of an equation, the result is still an equation, but it may not be equivalent to the original equation. Be especially careful when you square each side of an equation. For example, $x = -4$ is an equation; square both sides and you get $x^2 = 16$ which has both $x = 4$ and $x = -4$ as solutions. *Always check your answer in the original equation.*

If the equation you want to solve involves square roots, get rid of the square roots by squaring each side of the equation. Remember to check your answer since squaring each side does not always give an equivalent equation.

EXAMPLE 3

Solve $\sqrt{4x + 3} = 5$.

SOLUTION

Square both sides: $\left(\sqrt{4x + 3}\right)^2 = 4x + 3$ and $5^2 = 25$, so the new equation is $4x + 3 = 25$. Subtract 3 from each side to get $4x = 22$ and now divide each side by 4. The solution is $x = \dfrac{22}{4} = 5.5$. Since $4(5.5) + 3 = 25$ and $\sqrt{25} = 5$, $x = 5.5$ is a solution to the equation $\sqrt{4x + 3} = 5$.

If an equation involves fractions, multiply through by a common denominator and then solve. Check your answer to make sure you did not multiply or divide by zero.

EXAMPLE 4

Solve $\dfrac{3}{a} = 9$ for a.

SOLUTION

Multiply each side by a: the result is $3 = 9a$. Divide each side by 9, and you obtain $\dfrac{3}{9} = a$ or $a = \dfrac{1}{3}$. Since $\dfrac{3}{\frac{1}{3}} = 3 \cdot 3 = 9$, $a = \dfrac{1}{3}$ is a solution.

PRACTICE EXERCISE 20

Solve.

1. $3x - 8 = -5$

2. $-11 - 5x = -21$

3. $5x - 18 = 30 - 11x$

4. $4 - 3(x - 1) = 3(x + 1)$

5. $\dfrac{x + 1}{3} - \dfrac{x - 4}{4} = \dfrac{5}{4}$

6. $\sqrt{2x - 3} = 7$

SOLUTIONS TO PRACTICE EXERCISE 20

1. $3x - 8 = -5$. Add 8 to both sides of the equation.

$$3x = 3$$

Divide both sides by 3. $x = 1$

The solution set is {1}.

2. $-11 - 5x = -21$.

Add 11. $-5x = -10$

Divide by -5. $x = 2$

The solution set is {2}.

3. $5x - 18 = 30 - 11x$.

Add 11x. $16x - 18 = 30$

Add 18. $16x = 48$

Divide by 16. $x = 3$

The solution set is {3}.

4. $4 - 3(x - 1) = 3(x + 1)$

Simplify each side of the equation:

$$4 - 3x + 3 = 3x + 3$$

$$-3x + 7 = 3x + 3$$

Add 3x: $7 = 6x + 3$

Subtract 3: $4 = 6x$

Divide by 6: $\dfrac{2}{3} = x$

The solution set is $\left\{\dfrac{2}{3}\right\}$.

5. Multiply by the common denominator 12:

$$12\left(\frac{x+1}{3} - \frac{x-4}{4}\right) = \left(\frac{5}{4}\right)12$$

$$4(x + 1) - 3(x - 4) = 15$$

$$4x + 4 - 3x + 12 = 15$$

$$x + 16 = 15$$

$$x = -1$$

The solution set is {−1}

6. Square both sides:

$$\left(\sqrt{2x-3}\right)^2 = 7^2$$

$$2x - 3 = 49$$

$$2x = 52$$

$$x = 26$$

When you square both sides of an equation, you must check the potential solutions.

$$\sqrt{2(26) - 3} \stackrel{?}{=} 7$$

$$\sqrt{52 - 3} \stackrel{?}{=} 7$$

$$\sqrt{49} \stackrel{?}{=} 7$$

$$7 = 7$$

Since 26 satisfies the original equation, the solution set is {26}.

Systems of Equations

The solution set of a system of linear equations consists of the set of ordered pairs, (x, y), that satisfy both equations. We will review two methods for solving systems of equations:

1. The addition method (also called the elimination method.)

2. The substitution method.

EXAMPLE 1

Use both methods to solve the system:

$$2x + y = 5$$
$$x + y = 4$$

<u>SOLUTION</u>

1. Addition method

Multiply both sides of the second equation by –1:

$$2x + y = 5$$
$$-1(x + y) = (4)(-1)$$

$$2x + y = 5$$
$$-x - y = -4$$

Add the left sides and the right sides of the equations:

$$x = 1$$

Replace x by 1 in either of the original equations, say the first equation:

$$2(1) + y = 5$$
$$2 + y = 5$$
$$y = 3 \qquad \text{The solution set is } \{(1, 3)\}.$$

2. Substitution method

Solve one of the equations for one of its variables. We will solve the first equation for y:

$$y = 5 - 2x$$

Substitute $5 - 2x$ for y in the second equation:

$$x + (5 - 2x) = 4$$

Solve this equation for x:

$$x + 5 - 2x = 4$$
$$-x + 5 = 4$$
$$-x = -1$$
$$x = 1$$

Substitute this value for x in either equation, say the second one, and solve for y: $1 + y = 4$

$$y = 3$$

The solution set is $\{(1, 3)\}$.

Either method can be applied to any system of equations. The substitution method should be used only when one of the equations can easily be solved for one of its variables without introducing fractions. The coefficient of one variable is 1.

PRACTICE EXERCISE 21

Solve the following systems of equations.

1. $2x + 3y = 10$
    $-3x + 2y = 11$

2. $2x = y + 6$
    $y = 5x$

SOLUTIONS TO PRACTICE EXERCISE 21

1. Use the addition method:

Multiply both sides of the first equation by 3 and both sides of the second equation by 2:

$$3(2x + 3y) = (10)(3)$$
$$2(-3x + 2y) = (11)(2)$$
$$6x + 9y = 30$$
$$-6x + 4y = 22$$

Add the left and right sides of the equations:

$$13y = 52$$
$$y = 4$$

Replace y by 4 in the first equation:

$$2x + 3(4) = 10$$
$$2x + 12 = 10$$

$$2x = -2$$
$$x = -1$$

The solution set is $\{(-1, 4)\}$.

2. Use the substitution method:

Substitute $5x$ for y in the first equation:

$$2x = 5x + 6$$
$$-3x = 6$$
$$x = -2$$

then substitute -2 for x in the second equation:

$$y = 2(-2) = -4$$

The solution set is $\{(-2, -4)\}$.

Solving Quadratic Equations

An equation equivalent to $ax^2 + bx + c = 0$, $a \neq 0$ is called *quadratic*. Some examples of quadratic equations are $x^2 + 4x = 3$, $2z^2 - 1 = 3z^2 - 2z$, and $a + 6 = a^2 + 6$.

To solve a quadratic equation:

(A) Write the equation in standard form: $ax^2 + bx + c = 0$
(B) Factor the left side, if possible.
(C) Set each factor equal to 0 separately.
(D) Solve each of the resulting linear equations.
(E) The solution set contains all of the solutions from (D) above.

The method depends on the fact that if a product of expressions is zero then at least one of the expressions must be zero.

EXAMPLE 1

Solve $x^2 + 4x = -3$.

$$x^2 + 4x = 3 = 0$$
$$x^2 + 4x + 3 = (x + 3)(x + 1) = 0$$

So $x + 3 = 0$ or $x + 1 = 0$. Therefore, the solutions are $x = -3$ and $x = -1$.

Check: $(-3)^2 + 4(-3) = 9 - 12 = -3$

$(-1)^2 + 4(-1) = 1 - 4 = -3$, so $x = -3$ and $x = -1$ are solutions.

A quadratic equation will usually have 2 different solutions, but it is possible for a quadratic to have only one solution or even no real solution.

EXAMPLE 2

If $2z^2 - 1 = 3z^2 - 2z$, what is z?

    (A) $0 = 3z^2 - 2z^2 - 2z + 1$
    (B) $z^2 - 2z + 1 = 0$
    (C) $z^2 - 2z + 1 = (z - 1)^2 = 0$
    (D) $z - 1 = 0$ or $z = 1$

Check: $2 \cdot 1^2 - 1 = 2 - 1 = 1$ and $3 \cdot 1^2 - 2 \cdot 1 = 3 - 2 = 1$,

      so $z = 1$ is a solution.

Some equations which may not look like quadratics may be changed into quadratics.

EXAMPLE 3

Find a if $a - 3 = \dfrac{10}{a}$.

Multiply each side of the equation by a to obtain $a^2 - 3a = 10$, which is quadratic.

$$a^2 - 3a - 10 = 0$$

$$a^2 - 3a - 10 = (a - 5)(a + 2)$$

$$\text{So } a - 5 = 0 \text{ or } a + 2 = 0.$$

Therefore, $a = 5$ and $a = -2$ are the solutions.

Check: $5 - 3 = 2 = \dfrac{10}{5}$ so $a = 5$ is a solution.

      $-2 - 3 = -5 = \dfrac{10}{-2}$ so $a = -2$ is a solution.

You can also solve quadratic equations by using the *quadratic formula*. The quadratic formula states that the solutions of the quadratic equation

$ax^2 + bx + c = 0$ are

and
$$x = \frac{1}{2a}\left[-b + \sqrt{b^2 - 4ac}\right]$$

$$x = \frac{1}{2a}\left[-b - \sqrt{b^2 - 4ac}\right].$$

This is usually written $x = \dfrac{-b \pm \sqrt{b^2 - 4ac}}{2a}$

EXAMPLE 4

Find x if $x^2 + 5x = 12 - x^2$.

$$x^2 + 5x + x^2 - 12 = 0$$

$$2x^2 + 5x - 12 = 0$$

So $a = 2$, $b = 5$, and $c = -12$. Substitute these values into the quadratic formula and simplify:

$$x = \frac{-b \pm \sqrt{b^2 - 4ac}}{2a} = \frac{-5 \pm \sqrt{(5)^2 - 4(2)(-12)}}{2(2)} = \frac{-5 + \sqrt{25 - (-96)}}{4}$$

$$= \frac{-5 \pm \sqrt{121}}{4} = \frac{-5 \pm 11}{4}$$

$$= \begin{cases} \dfrac{-5 + 11}{4} = \dfrac{6}{4} = \dfrac{3}{2} \\[2ex] \dfrac{-5 - 11}{4} = \dfrac{-16}{4} = -4 \end{cases}$$
The solution set is $\left\{\dfrac{3}{2}, -4\right\}$.

Note: **If $b^2 - 4ac$ is negative, then the quadratic equation $ax^2 + bx + c = 0$ has no real solutions because negative numbers do not have real square roots.**

The quadratic formula will always give you the solutions to a quadratic equation. If you can factor the equation, factoring will usually give you the solution in less time. Remember, you want to answer as many questions as you can in the time given. So factor if you can. If you don't see the factor immediately, then use the quadratic formula.

PRACTICE EXERCISE 22

Solve the following equations:

1. $x^2 - 3x - 4 = 0$

2. $2x^2 + 5x = 0$

3. $3x^2 - 75 = 0$

4. $x^2 - 2x - 5 = 0$

SOLUTIONS TO PRACTICE EXERCISE 22

1. $x^2 - 3x - 4 = 0$ The left side of this equation is factorable:

   $(x + 1)(x - 4) = 0$ Set each factor equal to 0 separately.

   $x + 1 = 0$ or $x - 4 = 0$

   $x = -1$ $x = 4$ The solution set is $\{-1, 4\}$.

2. $2x^2 + 5x = 0$ The left side is factorable:

   $x(2x + 5 = 0$

   $x = 0$ or $2x + 5 = 0$

   $2x = -5$

   $x = \dfrac{-5}{2}$ The solution set is $\left\{0, \dfrac{-5}{2}\right\}$.

3. $3x^2 - 75 = 0$ The left side is factorable:

   $3(x^2 - 25) = 0$

   $3(x - 5)(x + 5) = 0$

   Set the variable factors equal to 0 separately:

   $x - 5 = 0$ or $x + 5 = 0$

   $x = 5$ $x = -5$ The solution set is $\{5, -5\}$.

4. $x^2 - 2x - 5 = 0$ The left side of this equation is not factorable; therefore, we will use the quadratic formula.

$$a = 1, b = -2, c = -5$$

$$x = \frac{-b \pm \sqrt{b^2 - 4ac}}{2a} = \frac{2 \pm \sqrt{(-2)^2 - 4(1)(-5)}}{2(1)} = \frac{2 + \sqrt{4 - (-20)}}{2}$$

$$= \frac{2 \pm \sqrt{24}}{2} = \frac{2 \pm 2\sqrt{6}}{2} = 1 \pm \sqrt{6}$$

The solution set is $\left\{1 + \sqrt{6},\ 1 - \sqrt{6}\right\}$.

PRACTICE TEST B

The following problems are of the type that may be encountered on the CBEST™.

1. If $r = \dfrac{s}{3}$ and $4r = 5t$, what is s in terms of t?

   (A) $\dfrac{4t}{15}$ (B) $\dfrac{15t}{4}$ (C) $4t$ (D) $5t$ (E) $60t$

2. If $\dfrac{1}{r} = 3$ and $s = 3$, what is r in terms of s?

   (A) s (B) $3 - s$ (C) $\dfrac{1}{s}$ (D) $-s$ (E) $9s$

3. $\dfrac{a}{b} = c$; $b = c$; $b = ?$

   (A) $\dfrac{a}{2}$ (B) $\sqrt{a}$ (C) $\dfrac{a}{6}$ (D) $2a$ (E) a^2

4. $z + \dfrac{1}{z} = 2$; $z = ?$

   (A) $\tfrac{1}{2}$ (B) 1 (C) $1\tfrac{1}{2}$ (D) 2 (E) $2\tfrac{1}{2}$

5. $\dfrac{n}{7} + \dfrac{n}{5} = \dfrac{12}{35}$, what is the numerical value of n?

   (A) 1 (B) $\sqrt{12}$ (C) 6 (D) 17.5 (E) 35

6. $\dfrac{ca^2 - cb^2}{-a - b}$ is equivalent to $cb + ?$

   (A) ac (B) $-ca$ (C) 1 (D) -1 (E) c

7. $x\sqrt{.09} = 3$; $x = ?$

   (A) $\dfrac{1}{10}$ (B) $\dfrac{3}{10}$ (C) $\dfrac{1}{3}$ (D) 1 (E) 10

8. $7x - 5y = 13$

   $2x - 7y = 26$

   $9x - 12y = ?$

   (A) 13 (B) 26 (C) 39 (D) 40 (E) 52

9. $ab - 2cd = p$

   $ab - 2cd = q$

   $6cd - 3ab = r$

   $p = (?)r$

   (A) -3 (B) $-\dfrac{1}{3}$ (C) $\dfrac{1}{3}$ (D) 1 (E) 3

10. $\sqrt{\tfrac{16}{36} + \tfrac{1}{4}} = ?$

    (A) $\dfrac{2}{5}$ (B) $\dfrac{1}{3}$ (C) $\dfrac{5}{6}$ (D) $\dfrac{11}{12}$ (E) $\dfrac{7}{6}$

11. $z + \dfrac{2}{z} = 2z$; $z^2 = ?$

    (A) 1 (B) $\tfrac{1}{2}$ (C) 1 (D) $1\tfrac{1}{2}$ (E) 2

12. $\dfrac{\dfrac{1}{1}}{\dfrac{1}{N}} \div \dfrac{1}{N} = ?$

    (A) 1 (B) $\dfrac{1}{N^2}$ (C) $\dfrac{1}{N}$ (D) N (E) N^2

13. If $\dfrac{1}{x} = \dfrac{a}{b}$ then x equals the

    (A) sum of a and b
    (B) product of a and b
    (C) difference of a and b
    (D) quotient of b and a
    (E) quotient of a and b

14. $x^2 + y = 9$
    $x^2 - y = -1$
    $y = ?$

    (A) 1 (B) ± 3 (C) 5 (D) 8 (E) 10

15. $2x - 4y = -10$
    $5x - 3y = 3$
    $3x - 6y = (?)$

    (A) $\dfrac{3}{5}$ (B) $\dfrac{2}{3}$ (C) -7 (D) 15 (E) -15

16. $5x - 3y = 3$
    $2x - 4y = -10$
    $3x + y = (?)$

    (A) -30 (B) -13 (C) -7 (D) 7 (E) 13

17. $4y - x = 10$
    $3x = 2y$
    $xy = (?)$

    (A) 2 (B) 3 (C) 6 (D) 12 (E) 24

18. $3x + 10 = 9x - 20$
    $(x + 5)^2 = (?)$

    (A) 5 (B) 10 (C) 15 (D) 25 (E) 100

19. $\dfrac{a}{b} = c$; $b = c$. Find b in terms of a.

(A) a (B) b (C) $\pm\sqrt{b}$ (D) $\pm\sqrt{a}$

(E) $\pm\sqrt{ac}$

20. $17xy = 22xy - 5$

$x^2y^2 = (?)$

(A) 0 (B) 1 (C) –5 (D) 5 (E) $7\frac{4}{5}$

SOLUTIONS TO PRACTICE TEST B

1. **B** Substitute:

$r = \left(\dfrac{s}{3}\right)$ and $4r = 5t$

$4\left(\dfrac{s}{3}\right) = 5t$

$4s = 15t$

$s = \dfrac{15t}{4}$

2. **C** $\dfrac{1}{r} = 3$ and $s = 3$ Substitute s for 3

in the first equation.

$\dfrac{1}{r} = s$

$1 = rs$

$\dfrac{1}{s} = r$

3. **B** $\dfrac{a}{b} = c$ and $b = c$ Substitute b for c in the first equation.

$\dfrac{a}{b} = b$

$a = b^2$

$\pm\sqrt{a} = b$

Only the positive value satisfies both equations.

4. **B** $z + \dfrac{1}{z} = 2$

$z^2 + 1 = 2z$

$z^2 - 2z + 1 = 0$

$(z - 1)^2 = 0$

$z - 1 = 0$

$z = 1$

5. **A** $\dfrac{n}{7} + \dfrac{n}{5} = \dfrac{12}{35}$ Multiply both sides by 35.

$35\left(\dfrac{n}{7} + \dfrac{n}{5}\right) = \left(\dfrac{12}{35}\right)35$

$5n + 7n = 12$

$12n = 12$

$n = 1$

6. **B** $\dfrac{ca^2 - cb^2}{-a - b}$

$= \dfrac{c(a^2 - b^2)}{-a - b}$

$= \dfrac{c(a - b)(a + b)}{-1(a + b)}$

$= \dfrac{c(a - b)}{-1}$

$= -c(a - b) = -ac + bc$

Therefore $\dfrac{ca^2 - cb^2}{-a - b} = cb + (-ac)$

7. **E** $x\sqrt{0.09} = 3$ The square root of 0.09 is 0.3.

$0.3x = 3$

$3x = 30$ Multiply both sides by 10.

$x = 10$

8. **C** Add the left and right sides of the equations.

$7x - 5y = 13$
$\underline{2x - 7y = 26}$
$9x - 12y = 39$

9. **B** Multiply both sides of the first equation by –2 and both sides of the second equation by –1.

$-2(ab - 2cd) = (p)(-2)$ $\quad 4cd - 2ab = -1p$
$-1(ab - 2cd) = (q)(-1) \rightarrow 2cd - ab = -q$

Add the left and right sides of the resulting equations, and use the given information that $p = q$ to obtain the following equation.

$6cd - 3ab = -2p - q$
$6cd - 3ab = -2p - q = -3p$

Therefore $-3p = r$ or $p = \dfrac{-1}{3}r$.

10. **C** $\quad \sqrt{\dfrac{16}{36} + \dfrac{1}{4}} = \sqrt{\dfrac{16}{36} + \dfrac{9}{36}} = \sqrt{\dfrac{25}{36}} = \dfrac{5}{6}$

11. **E** $\quad z + \dfrac{2}{z} = 2z^2$ Multiply both sides by z.

$z^2 + 2 = 2z^2$
$2 = z^2$

12. **E** $\quad \dfrac{1}{\dfrac{1}{N}} \div \dfrac{1}{N} = \left(1 \div \dfrac{1}{N}\right) \div \dfrac{1}{N}$

$$= (1 \cdot N) \cdot N = N^2$$

13. **D** Take the reciprocal of both sides of the equation.

$\dfrac{1}{x} = \dfrac{a}{b}$
$\dfrac{x}{1} = \dfrac{b}{a} = x$

14. **C** Add the left and right sides of the equations.

$x^2 + y = 9$
$x^2 - y = -1$
$2x^2 = 8$
$x^2 = 4$

Substitute 4 for x^2 in either equation, say the first one.

$4 + y = 9$
$y = 5$

15. **E** First solve the system by multiplying both sides of the first equation by 5 and both sides of the second equation by -2.

$5(2x - 4y) = (-10)5$
$-2(5x - 3y) = (3)(-2)$
$10x - 20y = -50$
$-10x + 6y = -6$

Add the left and right sides of the equations.

$-14y = -56$
$y = 4$

Substitute 4 into the first equation.

$2x - 16 = -10$
$2x = 6$
$x = 3$

Now substitute $x = 3$ and $y = 4$ into the given expression.

$$3x - 6y = 3(3) - 6(4) = 9 - 24 = -15$$

16. **E** Multiply both sides of the second equation by -1 and add the left and right sides of the equations.

$5x - 3y = 3$
$-2x + 4y = 10$
$3x + y = 13$

17. **C** Solve the first equation for x and substitute into the second equation.

$x = 4y - 10$
$3x = 2y$
$3(4y - 10) = 2y$
$12y - 30 = 2y$
$-30 = -10y$
$3 = y$

Substitute $y = 3$ into the second equation.

$3x = 2(3) = 6$
$x = 2$

So $xy = (2)(3) = 6$.

18. **E** Solve the equation.

$3x + 10 = 9x - 20$
$10 = 6x - 20$
$30 = 6x$
$5 = x$

Then substitute into the expression:

$$(x + 5)^2 = (5 + 5)^2 = 10^2 = 100$$

19. **D** Substitute b for c in the first equation.

$\dfrac{a}{b} = b$

$a = b^2$

$\pm\sqrt{a} = b$

20. **B** $\quad 17xy = 22xy - 5$

$-5xy = -5$
$xy = 1$

Therefore $x^2y^2 = 1$.

C. Verbal Problems

In this section we will solve typical word problems that are found in algebra classes. Here is a general strategy for their solution:

1. Read the problem several times so that the meaning is clear.

2. Make a sketch or a diagram if it makes the problem easier to understand.

3. Choose a variable to represent an unknown quantity in the problem.

    a. Many times the best strategy is to let the variable represent the value of the answer to the question.

    b. If there are several numbers discussed in the problem, it is usually best to let the variable represent the quantity that you know least about.

4. Represent all other unknown quantities in terms of the chosen variable.

5. Write an equation.

    a. Many times a well-known formula e.g., $i = prt$, $d = rt$, $p = 2w + 2\ell$, $A = \pi r^2$, etc. will suggest the correct equation.

    b. Knowledge of measurement and conversion units may help to write an equation. For example, the number of inches in x yards, y feet and z inches is $36x + 12y + z$ and there are $\dfrac{x}{25}$ quarters in x cents.

    c. Sometimes the equation is a literal translation of the words of the problem. Two less than three times a certain number is the same as four more than twice the same number translates as $3x - 2 = 2x + 4$.

6. Solve the equation.

7. Answer the question.

EXAMPLE 1

The sum of two numbers is 20. Find the numbers if the larger number is one less than twice the smaller number.

SOLUTION

Let x be the smaller number.
Then $2x - 1$ is the larger number.
The sum of two numbers equaling 20 is represented by the equation:

$$x + (2x - 1) = 20$$

Solve this equation:

$$x + 2x - 1 = 20$$
$$3x - 1 = 20$$
$$3x = 21$$
$$x = 7$$

The smaller number is 7 and the larger number is $2(7) - 1 = 13$.

Example 2

Mary's salary is 125% of Joe's salary. Tom's salary is 80% of Joe's salary. The total of all three salaries is $61,000. What is Mary's salary?

Let x be Joe's salary (because we know least about his salary).

Then Mary's salary is $1.25x$ and Tom's salary is $0.8x$.

If the total of the three salaries is $61,000 then:

$$x + 1.25x + 0.8x = 61,000$$

Multiply both sides of this equation by 100:

$$100x + 125x + 80x = 6,100,000$$
$$305x = 6,100,000$$
$$x = 20,000$$

So Joe's salary is $20,000, Mary's salary is $1.25(20,000) = $25,000$, and Tom's salary is $0.8(20,000) = $16,000$.

Example 3

Steve weighs 25 pounds more than Jim. Their combined weight is 325 pounds. How much does Jim weigh?

Let Jim's weight be x pounds, then Steve's weight is $x + 25$.

Their combined weight of 325 pounds is represented by the equation:

$$x + (x + 25) = 325$$
$$2x + 25 = 325$$
$$2x = 300$$
$$x = 150$$

So Jim's weight is 150 pounds and Steve's weight is $150 + 25 = 175$ pounds.

Example 4

A carpenter is designing a closet. The floor will be in the shape of a rectangle whose length is 2 feet more than its width. How long should the closet be if the carpenter wants the area of the floor to be 15 square feet?

In most geometric problems, drawing a diagram will be helpful.

If x is the width, then $x + 2$ will represent the length:

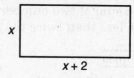

The formula for the area of a rectangle is $A = LW$, and this generates the equation:

$$x(x + 2) = 15$$
$$x^2 + 2x = 15$$
$$x^2 + 2x - 15 = 0$$
$$(x + 5)(x - 3) = 0$$
$$x + 5 = 0 \quad \text{or} \quad x - 3 = 0$$
$$x = -5 \qquad x = 3$$

Since we are seeking the width and length of the rectangle, we reject -5 as an extraneous solution. The width of the rectangle is 3 feet and the length is $3 + 2 = 5$ feet.

PRACTICE TEST C

The following problems are of the type that may be encountered on the CBEST™.

1. How many cents are there in $2x - 1$ dimes?

(A) $10x$ (B) $20x - 10$ (C) $19x$ (D) $\dfrac{2x - 1}{10}$

(E) $\dfrac{x}{5} - 1$

2. How many nickels have the same value as c cents and q quarters?

(A) $\dfrac{c + 25q}{5}$ (B) $5(c + q)$ (C) $5c + \dfrac{q}{5}$

(D) $\dfrac{c + q}{5}$ (E) $c + 25q$

3. How many days are there in w weeks and w days?

(A) $7w^2$ (B) 7 (C) $8w$ (D) $14w$ (E) $7w$

4. How many pupils can be seated in a room with s single seats and d double seats?

(A) sd (B) $2sd$ (C) $2(s + d)$ (D) $2d + s$
(E) $2s + d$

5. A classroom has r rows of desks with d desks in each row. On a particular day when all pupils are present 3 seats are left vacant. The number of pupils in this class is

(A) $dr - 3$ (B) $d + r + 3$ (C) $dr + 3$

(D) $\dfrac{r}{d} + 3$ (E) $\dfrac{d}{r} + 3$

6. A storekeeper had n loaves of bread. By noon he had s loaves left. How many loaves did he sell?

(A) $s - n$ (B) $n - s$ (C) $n + s$ (D) $sn - s$

(E) $\dfrac{n}{s}$

7. A man has d dollars and spends s cents. How many dollars has he left?

(A) $d - s$ (B) $s - d$ (C) $100d - s$

(D) $\dfrac{100d - s}{100}$ (E) $\dfrac{d - s}{100}$

8. How much change (in cents) would a woman receive if she purchases p pounds of sugar at c cents per pound after she gives the clerk a one-dollar bill?

(A) $100 - p - c$ (B) $pc - 100$ (C) $100 - pc$
(D) $100 - p + c$ (E) $pc + 100$

9. Sylvia is two years younger than Mary. If Mary is m years old, how old was Sylvia two years ago?

(A) $m + 2$ (B) $m - 2$ (C) $m - 4$
(D) $m + 4$ (E) $2m - 2$

10. A storekeeper sold n articles at $\$D$ each and thereby made a profit of r dollars. The cost to the storekeeper for each article was

(A) $Dn - r$ (B) $D(n - r)$ (C) $\dfrac{Dn - r}{n}$
(D) $\dfrac{D(n - r)}{n}$ (E) $\dfrac{Dn + r}{n}$

ANSWER KEY

1. B	4. D	7. D	9. C
2. A	5. A	8. C	10. C
3. C	6. B		

SOLUTIONS TO PRACTICE TEST C

1. **B** Each dime is worth 10 cents; therefore there are $10(2x - 1) = 20x - 10$ cents in $2x - 1$ dimes.

2. **A** There are $c + 25q$ cents in c cents and q quarters. To determine the number of nickels that have the same value, divide by 5.

   The number of nickels is $\dfrac{c + 25q}{5}$.

3. **C** In w weeks there are $7w$ days; therefore there are $7w + w = 8w$ days in that amount of time.

4. **D** The number of students that can be seated in s single seats and d double seats is $s + 2d$.

5. **A** There are dr desks in the room. If 3 desks are empty, there must be $dr - 3$ pupils in the room.

6. **B** The number sold is the difference of the number at the beginning of the day minus the number at noon: $n - s$.

7. **D** s cents equals $\dfrac{s}{100}$ dollars. The man has

$$d - \frac{s}{100} = \frac{100d}{100} - \frac{s}{100} = \frac{100d - s}{100} \text{ left.}$$

8. **C** p pounds of sugar at c cents per pound costs pc cents. The amount of change would be the difference between one dollar (100 cents) and pc. Her change is $100 - pc$.

9. **C** Create a chart.

	Now	2 yrs ago
Sylvia	$m - 2$	$(m - 2) - 2 = m - 4$
Mary	m	$m - 2$

Therefore Sylvia was $m - 4$ years old two years.

10. **C** Selling price is equal to cost plus profit.

$nD = nC + r$ (C is the cost of each article.)

Solve for C: $nD - r = nC$

$$\frac{nD - r}{n} = C$$

Uniform Motion Problems

A common type of word problem is a distance or velocity problem. The basic formula is

DISTANCE TRAVELED = RATE · TIME.

The formula is abbreviated $d = rt$.

The distance an object travels is the product of its *average* speed (rate) and the time it is traveling. This formula can be readily converted to express time in terms of distance and rate by dividing each side by r.

$$t = \frac{d}{r}$$

It can also be changed to a formula for rate by dividing it by t,

$$r = \frac{d}{t}.$$

You should memorize the original formula, $d = rt$, and know how to convert it quickly to the others.

EXAMPLE 1

One plane leaves St. Louis going east at 500 miles per hour. A second plane leaves from the same airport at the same time traveling west. If after 3 hours they are 3,375 miles apart, at what speed is the second plane traveling?

SOLUTION

For all uniform motion problems, you should construct a chart based on the formula $d = rt$.

	$d =$	r .	t
Eastbound		500	3
Westbound		x	3

When any two boxes in a row are filled in, use the formula to fill in the third box. In this case, since "rate times time equals distance" we have:

	$d =$	r .	t
Eastbound	1,500	500	3
Westbound	$3x$	x	3

Since the total distance between them after 3 hours is 3,375, the equation is:

$$1,500 + 3x = 3,375$$
$$3x = 1,875$$
$$x = 625$$

The westbound plane traveled 625 miles per hour.

PRACTICE TEST D

The following problems are of the type that may be encountered on the CBEST™.

1. An automobile travels at the rate of 55 miles per hour on the Pennsylvania Turnpike. How many minutes will it take to travel $\frac{2}{3}$ of a mile at this rate?

   (A) 0.2 (B) 0.72 (C) 2.2 (D) 13.5 (E) 22

2. Miguel leaves at 9:00 A.M. and stops for repairs at 9:20 A.M. If the distance covered was 18 miles, what was the average velocity for this part of the trip?

   (A) 5.4 (B) 6 (C) 54 (D) 36 (E) 60

3. A man runs y yards in m minutes. What is his rate in yards per hour?

   (A) $\dfrac{y}{60m}$ (B) $\dfrac{m}{60y}$ (C) $60my$

   (D) $\dfrac{60y}{m}$ (E) $\dfrac{60m}{y}$

4. Ten minutes after a plane leaves the airport, it is reported that the plane is 40 miles away. What is the average speed of the plane, in miles per hour?

   (A) 66 (B) 240 (C) 400 (D) 600 (E) 660

5. An automobile passes City X at 9:55 A.M. and City Y at 10:15 A.M. City X is 30 miles from City Y. What is the average rate of the automobile in miles per hour?

   (A) 10 (B) 30 (C) 90 (D) 120 (E) 360

6. The distance between two cities is 1,800 miles. How many gallons of gasoline will a motorist need, driving an automobile that uses (on the average) 1 gallon of gasoline for each 12 miles?

   (A) 150 (B) 160 (C) 216 (D) 1,500 (E) 2,160

7. How many miles will a car travel if it averages a rate of 35 miles per hour for 3 hours and 24 minutes?

   (A) 109 (B) 112 (C) 113 (D) 119 (E) 129

8. Two cars start towards each other from points 200 miles apart. One car travels at 40 miles an hour and the other travels at 35 miles an hour. How far apart will the two cars be after 4 hours of continuous traveling?

   (A) 20 (B) 40 (C) 75 (D) 100 (E) 160

9. A motorist travels for 3 hours at 40 miles per hour and then covers a distance of 80 miles in 2 hours and 40 minutes. His average rate for the entire trip was

(A) 35 m.p.h. (B) 35.3 m.p.h. (C) 35.5 m.p.h. (D) 36 m.p.h. (E) 37 m.p.h.

10. A man driving a distance of 90 miles, averages 30 miles per hour. On the return trip he averages 45 miles per hour. His average for the round trip in miles per hour is

(A) 34 (B) 36 (C) $37\frac{1}{2}$ (D) 40 (E) 75

11. The El Capitan of the Santa Fe travels a distance of 152.5 miles from La Junta to Garden City in 2 hours. What is the approximate average speed in m.p.h.?

(A) 15.25 (B) 31.5 (C) 30.5 (D) 71 (E) 76.3

12. The distance between Portland, Oregon and Santa Fe, New Mexico is 1,800 miles. How long would it take a train with an average speed of 60 miles per hour to make the trip? (Give answer in hours)

(A) 30 (B) 39 (C) 48 (D) 300 (E) 480

13. A man drives for 5 hours at an average rate of 40 m.p.h. He develops some motor trouble and returns to his original starting point in 10 hours. What was his average rate on the return trip?

(A) 10 (B) 15 (C) 20 (D) 26.6 (E) 40

14. If a man walks W miles in H hours, and then rides R miles in the same length of time, what is his average rate for the entire trip?

(A) $\dfrac{R+W}{H}$ (B) $\dfrac{2(R+W)}{H}$ (C) $\dfrac{R+W}{2H}$

(D) $\dfrac{H}{R-W}$ (E) $\dfrac{RW-H}{2}$

15. How long would it take a car traveling at 30 miles per hour to cover a distance of 44 feet? (1 mile = 5,280 feet)

(A) 1 second (B) 2.64 seconds (C) 5.2 seconds (D) 1 minute (E) 7.7 minutes

ANSWER KEY

1. **B**	6. **A**	11. **E**
2. **C**	7. **D**	12. **A**
3. **D**	8. **D**	13. **C**
4. **B**	9. **B**	14. **C**
5. **C**	10. **B**	15. **A**

SOLUTIONS TO PRACTICE TEST D

1. **B** 55 miles per hour is equivalent to $\dfrac{55}{60}$ miles per minute. From the formula for uniform motion, $d = rt$, we see that time is equal to distance divided by rate, $t = \dfrac{d}{r}$.

So the time to travel $\dfrac{2}{3}$ of a mile is

$$\dfrac{\frac{2}{3}}{\frac{55}{60}} = \dfrac{2}{3} \cdot \dfrac{60}{55} = \dfrac{8}{11} = 0.\overline{72} \text{ minutes.}$$

2. **C** Average velocity is equal to distance divided by time: $r = \dfrac{d}{t}$. Miguel covered 18 miles in 20 minutes or $\dfrac{1}{3}$ of an hour.

Therefore his average velocity is

$$\dfrac{18}{\frac{1}{3}} = 18 \cdot 3 = 54 \text{ miles per hour.}$$

3. **D** $r = \dfrac{d}{t}$. m minutes is equivalent to $\dfrac{m}{60}$ hours. Therefore the man's rate is

$$\dfrac{y}{\frac{m}{60}} = y \cdot \dfrac{60}{m} = \dfrac{60y}{m} \text{ yards per hour.}$$

4. **B** The plane has traveled 40 miles in 10 minutes ($\dfrac{1}{6}$ of an hour).

$$r = \dfrac{d}{t} = \dfrac{40}{\frac{1}{6}} = 40 \cdot 6 = 240 \text{ miles per hour}$$

5. **C** The car traveled 30 miles in 20 minutes ($\frac{1}{3}$ of an hour). Therefore the rate of the car is $r = \dfrac{d}{t} = \dfrac{30}{\frac{1}{3}} = 30 \cdot 3 = 90$ miles per hour.

6. **A** This is a direct proportion problem. Establish two ratios:

gallons   *miles*

$$\frac{1}{x} \qquad \frac{12}{1,800} \qquad\qquad \frac{1}{x} = \frac{12}{1,800}$$
$$12x = 1,800$$
$$x = 150$$

The trip would require about 150 gallons of gasoline.

7. **D** $d = rt = (35)\left(3\dfrac{24}{60}\right) = (35)\left(3\dfrac{2}{5}\right)$

$$= \left(\frac{\overset{7}{\cancel{35}}}{1}\right)\left(\frac{17}{\cancel{5}}\right) = 119 \text{ miles.}$$

8. **D** A diagram will help:

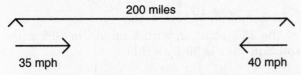

In 4 hours, the car traveling 35 miles per hour will have traveled 140 miles, and the other car will have traveled 160 miles. They will have passed each other and be at the approximate locations as indicated on the diagram:

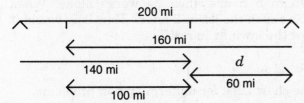

This distance, d, is $200 - 140 = 60$ miles. Therefore the distance between the cars is $160 - 60 = 100$ miles.

9. **B** Average rate is equal to the total distance divided by the total time, $r = \dfrac{d}{t}$. The motorist traveled 3 hours at 40 miles per hour for a distance of 120 miles. Then in $2\frac{2}{3}$ hours another 80 miles was traveled. The total distance traveled was 200 miles in a total time of $5\frac{2}{3}$ hours. Therefore the average rate of travel was

$$\frac{200}{5\frac{2}{3}} = \frac{200}{\frac{17}{3}} = \frac{200}{1} \cdot \frac{3}{17} = \frac{600}{17}$$
$$= 35.294118\ldots \text{ miles per hour.}$$

10. **B** 90 miles at 30 miles per hour takes 3 hours.
90 miles at 45 miles per hour takes 2 hours.
His average rate for the entire trip is

$$\frac{\text{total distance}}{\text{total time}} = \frac{180 \text{ miles}}{5 \text{ hours}}$$
$$= 36 \text{ miles per hour.}$$

The most likely mistake is to average the rates. Generally, rates may not be averaged.

11. **E** $r = \dfrac{d}{t} = \dfrac{152.5}{2} = 76.25$ miles per hour

12. **A** $t = \dfrac{d}{r} = \dfrac{1,800 \text{ miles}}{60 \text{ miles per hour}} = 30$ hours.

13. **C** Traveling for 5 hours at 40 miles per hour, the man travels 200 miles. The return trip in 10 hours would be done at the rate of $\dfrac{200}{10}$ miles per hour.

14. **C** The total distance traveled was $W + R$ miles in a total time of $H + H = 2H$ hours. The average rate is

$$\frac{\text{total distance}}{\text{total time}} = \frac{(W + R) \text{ miles}}{2H \text{ hours}}$$
$$= \frac{W + R}{2H} \text{ miles per hour.}$$

15. **A** 44 feet is equivalent to $\dfrac{44}{5,280}$ miles.

$$t = \frac{d}{r} = \frac{\dfrac{44}{5,280} \text{ miles}}{30 \text{ miles per hour}}$$
$$= 0.0002778 \text{ hours}$$

0.0002778 hours corresponds to $(60)(0.0002778) = 0.01666667$ minutes which corresponds to $(60)(0.016666667) = 1$ second.

Mixture Problems

EXAMPLE

A nurse needs 20 ml of a 30% alcohol solution. The only solutions available are 25% and 50%. How many milliliters of each should be mixed in order to obtain the required solution?

SOLUTION

A diagram of the physical situation will be helpful. Draw three containers, two whose contents will be mixed together to obtain the third. Under each container describe the contents, and inside the containers write the quantity that it holds.

$$\boxed{x \text{ ml}} \quad + \quad \boxed{(20-x) \text{ ml}} \quad = \quad \boxed{20 \text{ ml}}$$
$$ 25\% \qquad\qquad 50\% \qquad\qquad 30\%$$

The amount of alcohol does not change in the process of mixing. This is the basis of the equation. Twenty-five percent of the first container is alcohol; 50% of the second one is alcohol. Together they contain $0.25x + 0.5(20 - x)$ ml of alcohol. Thirty percent of the final mixture, $0.3(20)$, is supposed to be alcohol, so the equation is:

$$0.25x + 0.5(20 - x) = 0.3(20)$$
$$25x + 50(20 - x) = 30(20)$$
$$25x + 1{,}000 - 50x = 600$$
$$-25x + 1{,}000 = 600$$
$$-25x = -400$$
$$x = 16$$

The nurse must mix 16 ml of the 25% solution with 4 ml of the 50% solution to obtain 20 ml of the solution that is 30% alcohol.

Work Problems

The basic formula for work problems states that the amount of work done is equal to the rate at which work is done multiplied by the time spent working, $w = rt$.

EXAMPLE

Marcus can mow the lawn in 5 hours when he works alone. When Carlynne helps him, they can finish the job in 3 hours. How long would it have taken Carlynne to mow the lawn by herself?

SOLUTION

Create a chart similar to the chart used for uniform motion problems.

	$w =$	r	t
Marcus		$\dfrac{1}{5}$	3
Carlynne		$\dfrac{1}{x}$	3

Since Marcus can mow the lawn in 5 hours, then he works at the rate of $\frac{1}{5}$ of the job per hour. If we let x be the number of hours that it takes for Carlynne to mow the lawn alone, then she works at the rate of $\frac{1}{x}$ part of the job per hour. After two boxes in each row are filled in, let the formula fill in the third box.

	$w =$	r	t
Marcus	$\frac{3}{5}$	$\frac{1}{5}$	3
Carlynne	$\frac{3}{x}$	$\frac{1}{x}$	3

Typically the total of the entries of the work column is 1 (one completed job). So the equation is:

$$\frac{3}{5} + \frac{3}{x} = 1$$

Multiply both sides by $5x$:

$$5x\left(\frac{3}{5} + \frac{3}{x}\right) = (1)(5x)$$

$$3x + 15 = 5x$$

$$15 = 2x$$

$$\frac{15}{2} = x$$

It would have taken Carlynne 7 hours and 30 minutes to mow the lawn alone.

Age Problems

EXAMPLE

Lisa is now 6 years older than Cheryl. In two years, Lisa will be twice as old as Cheryl. How old is each girl now?

SOLUTION

A chart will help to organize age problems.

	Now	2 yrs hence
Lisa	$x + 6$	
Cheryl	x	

Let only the heading of the second column fill in that column.

	Now	2 yrs hence
Lisa	$x + 6$	$x + 8$
Cheryl	x	$x + 2$

Since Lisa will be twice as old as Cheryl in two years, the equation is

$$x + 8 = 2(x + 2)$$
$$x + 8 = 2x + 4$$
$$8 = x + 4$$
$$4 = x$$

Cheryl is 4 years old and Lisa is 10.

PRACTICE EXERCISE 23

1. An airplane has just enough fuel for a five-hour flight. How far can it fly on a round-trip on which, during the first leg of the trip, it flies with the wind at 225 miles per hour, and, during the return trip, it flies against the wind at 180 miles per hour?

2. A race car needs a fuel mixture that is 20% alcohol. How many liters of a 10% alcohol fuel mixture must be combined with 100 liters of a 40% alcohol mixture in order to obtain the required percent of alcohol?

3. Find four consecutive even integers whose sum is 100.

4. Find the dimensions of a rectangle whose perimeter is 38 meters and whose area is 84 square meters.

5. Diane was 24 years old when her daughter Heidi was born. In how many years will Diane be four years less than five times Heidi's age?

6. One pipe can fill a tank in four hours. A second pipe can fill the same tank in three hours. If both pipes flow at the same time, how long will it take to fill the tank?

SOLUTIONS TO PRACTICE EXERCISE 23

1. Create a chart. Let x be the number of miles in the one-way distance traveled.

	$d =$	r	t
With wind	x	225	
Against	x	180	

Let the formula fill in the third box:

	$d =$	r	t
With wind	x	225	$\dfrac{x}{225}$
Against	x	180	$\dfrac{x}{180}$

Since the total time must be 5 hours the equation is

$$\frac{x}{225} + \frac{x}{180} = 5$$

Multiply both sides by the lowest common denominator, 900:

$$4x + 5x = 4{,}500$$
$$9x = 4{,}500$$
$$x = 500$$

The total round-trip distance is 2(500) = 1,000 miles.

2. Set up a diagram with the containers:

x liters	+	100	=	$x + 100$
10%		40%		20%

The equation is

$$0.1x + 0.4(100) = 0.2(x + 100)$$
$$x + 4(100) = 2(x + 100)$$
$$x + 400 = 2x + 200$$
$$400 = x + 200$$
$$200 = x$$

One must mix 200 liters of the 10% fuel mixture in order to obtain the required 20% alcohol fuel mixture.

3. The four consecutive even integers can be represented by the following:

$$x$$
$$x + 2$$
$$x + 4$$
$$\text{and} \quad x + 6.$$

Therefore the equation is

$$x + (x + 2) + (x + 4) + (x + 6) = 100$$
$$4x + 12 = 100$$
$$4x = 88$$
$$x = 22$$

The consecutive even integers are 22, 24, 26, and 28.

4. Draw a diagram

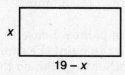

Since the perimeter is 38, then half the perimeter is 19—that is, the length plus the width is 19. So if we let the width be x, then the length is $19 - x$.

The equation is therefore:

$$x(19 - x) = 84$$
$$19x - x^2 = 84$$
$$0 = (x - 7)(x - 12)$$

$$x - 7 = 0 \qquad\qquad x - 12 = 0$$
$$x \quad = 7 \qquad\qquad x = 12$$

Therefore the width is 7 meters and the length is $19 - 7 = 12$ meters.

5. Create a chart.

	Age at birth	x yrs hence
Diane	24	$24 + x$
Heidi	0	x

According to the words of the problem, Diane's age at some point in the future will be 4 years less than 5 times Heidi's age. So the equation is

$$24 + x = 5x - 4$$
$$24 = 4x - 4$$
$$28 = 4x$$
$$7 = x$$

This will happen in 7 years, that is, when Heidi will be 7 years old.

6. Create a chart.

	$w =$	r	t
Pipe 1	$\dfrac{x}{4}$	$\dfrac{1}{4}$	x
Pipe 2	$\dfrac{x}{3}$	$\dfrac{1}{3}$	x

The amount of work done totals 1, so the equation is

$$\frac{x}{4} + \frac{x}{3} = 1 \qquad \text{Multiply by 12.}$$
$$3x + 4x = 12$$
$$7x = 12$$
$$x = \frac{12}{7} = 1\frac{5}{7}$$

The tank will be filled in $1\frac{5}{7}$ hours.

PRACTICE TEST E

The following problems are of the type that may be encountered on the CBEST™.

1. One boy can deliver newspapers on his route in $1\frac{1}{4}$ hours. A boy who takes his place one day finds it takes him 15 minutes longer to deliver these papers. How long would it take to deliver the papers if they worked together?

(A) $22\frac{1}{4}$ min.   (B) $37\frac{1}{2}$ min.   (C) 40 min.
(D) 50 min.   (E) 65 min.

2. A contractor estimates that he can paint a house in 5 days by using 6 men. If he actually uses only 5 men for the job how many days will it take to do this job?

(A) 5   (B) $5\frac{1}{4}$ (C) $5\frac{1}{2}$ (D) 6   (E) $6\frac{1}{2}$

3. A club decided to build a cabin. The job can be done by 3 skilled workmen in 20 days or by 5 of the boys in 30 days. How many days will it take if all work together?

(A) 10 days   (B) 12 days   (C) $12\frac{2}{3}$ days
(D) 14 days   (E) 5 days

4. Andrew can do a piece of work in r days and Bill, who works faster, can do the same work in s days. Which of the following expressions, if any, represents the number of days it would take the two of them to do the work if they worked together?

(A) $\dfrac{r+s}{2}$ (B) $\dfrac{1}{r} + \dfrac{1}{s}$ (C) $r - s$

(D) $\dfrac{rs}{r+s}$ (E) none of these

5. Four tractors working together can plow a field in 12 hours. How long will it take 6 tractors to plow a field of the same size, if all tractors work at the same rate?

(A) 6 hrs.   (B) 9 hrs.   (C) 10 hrs.
(D) 18 hrs.   (E) 8 hrs.

6. A small factory with 3 machines has the job of stamping out a number of pan covers. The newest machine can do the job in 3 days, another machine can do it in 4 days, and the third machine can do it in 6 days. How many days will it take the factory to do the job, using all three machines?

(A) $1\frac{1}{3}$ days   (B) $4\frac{1}{3}$ days   (C) 6 days
(D) 13 days   (E) $1\frac{4}{9}$ days

7. Steven can mow a lawn in 20 minutes and Bernard can mow the same lawn in 30 minutes. How long will it take them, working together, to mow the lawn?

(A) 10 min.   (B) $12\frac{1}{2}$ min.   (C) 15 min.
(D) 25 min.   (E) 12 min.

8. It takes Bert an hour to do a job that Harry can do in 40 minutes. One morning they worked together for 12 minutes; then Bert went away and Harry finished the job. How long did it take him to finish?

(A) 8 min.   (B) 16 min.   (C) 20 min.
(D) 28 min.   (E) 33 min.

9. One man can paint a house in r days, and another man can paint the same house in s days. If together they can do the work in d days, the expression that represents the amount of work done by both men in one day is

(A) $\dfrac{1}{r+s}$ (B) $\dfrac{d}{r+s}$ (C) $\dfrac{r+s}{rs}$

(D) $\dfrac{r+s}{d}$ (E) $\dfrac{d}{rs}$

10. Linda has m minutes of homework in each of her s subjects. What part of her homework does she complete in an hour?

(A) $\dfrac{1}{ms}$ (B) $\dfrac{ms}{60}$ (C) $\dfrac{60}{ms}$ (D) $\dfrac{s}{60m}$

(E) $\dfrac{60m}{s}$

11. Sam can mow a lawn in 20 minutes, while Mark takes 10 minutes longer to mow this lawn. How long will it take them to mow the lawn if they work together?

(A) 10 minutes   (B) 12 minutes
(C) $12\frac{1}{2}$ minutes   (D) 15 minutes
(E) more than 15 minutes

12. It takes h hours to mow a lawn. What part of the lawn is mowed in one hour?

(A) h (B) $\dfrac{h}{x}$ (C) hx (D) $\dfrac{1}{h}$ (E) $\dfrac{x}{h}$

13. If M men can complete a job in H hours, how long will it take 5 men to do this job?

(A) $\dfrac{5M}{H}$ (B) $\dfrac{M}{5H}$ (C) $\dfrac{MH}{5}$

(D) $\dfrac{5}{MH}$ (E) $\dfrac{5H}{M}$

14. Ann can type a manuscript in 10 hours. Florence can type this manuscript in 5 hours. If they type this manuscript together it can be completed in

(A) 2 hours 30 minutes
(B) 3 hours
(C) 3 hours 20 minutes
(D) 5 hours
(E) 7 hours 30 minutes

15. It was calculated that 75 men could complete a section of a new highway in 20 days. When work was scheduled to commence, it was found necessary to send 25 men on another road project. How much additional time will it take to complete the section?

(A) 10 days   (B) 20 days   (C) 30 days
(D) 40 days   (E) 60 days

ANSWER KEY

1. **C**	6. **A**	11. **B**
2. **D**	7. **E**	12. **D**
3. **B**	8. **C**	13. **C**
4. **D**	9. **C**	14. **C**
5. **E**	10. **C**	15. **A**

SOLUTIONS TO PRACTICE TEST E

1. **C** Set up a table. If the first boy can deliver the papers in $1\frac{1}{4} = \frac{5}{4}$ hours, then his rate of work is $\frac{4}{5}$ of the job per hour. The second boy takes $1\frac{1}{2} = \frac{3}{2}$ hours; therefore his rate of work is $\frac{2}{3}$ of the job per hour. The formula fills in the third box in the table.

	$w =$	r	t
1st boy	$\dfrac{4x}{5}$	$\dfrac{4}{5}$	x
2nd boy	$\dfrac{2x}{3}$	$\dfrac{2}{3}$	x

The total of the work column must be 1 (one job completed).

$\dfrac{4x}{5} + \dfrac{2x}{3} = 1$ Multiply both sides by 15.

$$15\left(\dfrac{4x}{5} + \dfrac{2x}{3}\right) = (1)15$$
$$12x + 10x = 15$$
$$22x = 15$$
$$x = \dfrac{15}{22}$$

It would take them $\frac{15}{22}$ hours or $\left(\frac{15}{22}\right)60 = 40.90909\ldots$ minutes to do the job together.

2. **D** As the number of men decreases, the number of days to do the work increases. This is an indirect proportion problem. Establish two ratios, one with men and one with days.

# of men	# of days
$\dfrac{6}{5}$	$\dfrac{5}{x}$

Write the proportion by inverting one of the ratios.

$$\dfrac{6}{5} = \dfrac{x}{5}$$
$$5x = 30$$
$$x = 6$$

3. **B** Each workman works at the rate of $\frac{1}{60}$ of the cabin per day, and each boy works at the rate of $\frac{1}{150}$ of the cabin per day.

	$w =$	r	t
3 workmen	$\dfrac{x}{20}$	$\dfrac{3}{60}$	x
5 boys	$\dfrac{x}{30}$	$\dfrac{5}{150}$	x

The total of the work column must be 1.

$$\frac{x}{20} + \frac{x}{30} = 1 \quad \text{Multiply both sides by 60.}$$

$$60\left(\frac{x}{20} + \frac{x}{30}\right) = (1)60$$

$$3x + 2x = 60$$

$$5x = 60$$

$$x = 12$$

4. **D** Andrew's rate is $\frac{1}{r}$ and Bill's is $\frac{1}{s}$. Create a table.

	$w =$	r	t
Andrew	$\frac{x}{r}$	$\frac{1}{r}$	x
Bill	$\frac{x}{s}$	$\frac{1}{s}$	x

$$\frac{x}{r} + \frac{x}{s} = 1$$

Solve this equation for x. First multiply both sides by rs.

$$rs\left(\frac{x}{r} + \frac{x}{s}\right) = (1)rs$$

$$sx + rx = rs$$

$$x(s + r) = rs$$

$$x = \frac{rs}{r + s}$$

5. **E** $W = rt$. One tractor can plow a field in 48 hours, therefore the rate at which each tractor works is $\frac{1}{48}$ of a field per hour. Six tractors can plow at the combined rate of $\frac{6}{48} = \frac{1}{8}$ of a field per hour. Therefore it would take 8 hours to complete one field.

6. **A** Create a table.

	$w =$	r	t
1st machine	$\frac{x}{3}$	$\frac{1}{3}$	x
2nd machine	$\frac{x}{4}$	$\frac{1}{4}$	x
3rd machine	$\frac{x}{6}$	$\frac{1}{6}$	x

$$\frac{x}{3} + \frac{x}{4} + \frac{x}{6} = 1 \quad \text{Multiply both sides by 12.}$$

$$12\left(\frac{x}{3} + \frac{x}{4} + \frac{x}{6}\right) = (1)12$$

$$4x + 3x + 2x = 12$$

$$9x = 12$$

$$x = \frac{4}{3}$$

The three machines could complete the job in $\frac{4}{3} = 1\frac{1}{3}$ days.

7. **E** Steven and Bernard work at the rates of $\frac{1}{20}$ and $\frac{1}{30}$ of the job per hour, respectively. Create a table.

	$w =$	r	t
Steven	$\frac{x}{20}$	$\frac{1}{20}$	x
Bernard	$\frac{x}{30}$	$\frac{1}{30}$	x

$$\frac{x}{20} + \frac{x}{30} = 1$$

$$\frac{3x}{60} + \frac{2x}{60} = \frac{60}{60}$$

$$5x = 60$$

$$x = 12$$

8. **C** Bert and Harry work at the rates of $\frac{1}{60}$ and $\frac{1}{40}$ of the job per hour, respectively. Create a table.

	$w =$	r	t
Bert	$\frac{12}{60}\left(=\frac{1}{5}\right)$	$\frac{1}{60}$	12
Harry	$\frac{12 + x}{40}$	$\frac{1}{40}$	$12 + x$

$$\frac{1}{5} + \frac{12 + x}{40} = 1$$

$$40\left(\frac{1}{5} + \frac{12 + x}{40}\right) = (1)40$$

$$8 + (12 + x) = 40$$

$$20 + x = 40$$

$$x = 20$$

9. **C** The amount of work that the two men can do in one day is the reciprocal of the amount of time that it takes them to do the work together. Create a table and solve for $\frac{1}{d}$.

	$w =$	r	t
1st man	$\frac{d}{r}$	$\frac{1}{r}$	d
2nd man	$\frac{d}{s}$	$\frac{1}{s}$	d

$\frac{d}{s} + \frac{d}{s} = 1$ Multiply both sides by rs.

$$rs\left(\frac{d}{s} + \frac{d}{s}\right) = (1)rs$$

$$ds + dr = rs$$

$$d(s + r) = rs$$

$$d = \frac{rs}{r + s}$$

$$\frac{1}{d} = \frac{r + s}{rs}$$

10. **C** Try using real numbers to answer this question, and perform the same operations with the variables. Suppose Linda has 5 classes with 15 minutes of homework for each class. She has $(5)(15) = 75$ minutes of homework to do. In one hour she will have done $\frac{60}{75}$ of her homework. It seems that the answer is 60 divided by the product of the the number of classes and the number of minutes of homework for each class: $\frac{60}{ms}$

11. **B** (This is the same type as problem number 7.)
Create a table.

	$w =$	r	t
Sam	$\frac{x}{20}$	$\frac{1}{20}$	x
Mark	$\frac{x}{30}$	$\frac{1}{30}$	x

$$\frac{x}{20} + \frac{x}{30} = 1$$

$$60\left(\frac{x}{20} + \frac{x}{30}\right) = (1)60$$

$$3x + 2x = 60$$

$$5x = 60$$

$$x = 12$$

12. **D** The part of the lawn that is mowed in one hour is the reciprocal of the total time it takes to mow the lawn in hours: $\frac{1}{h}$.

13. **C** Pick some convenient numbers in order to see a solution. Suppose 3 men can complete a job in 8 hours. Assuming that they all work at the same rate, each man works at the rate of $\frac{1}{24}\left(=\frac{1}{3 \cdot 8}\right)$ part of the job per hour. Five men will complete $5\left(\frac{1}{24}\right) = \frac{5}{24}$ part of the job per hour. The total time for them to complete the job is the reciprocal of their rate: $\frac{24}{5} = 4\frac{4}{5}$ hours.

14. **C** (The same type as numbers 7 and 11.) Create a table.

	$w =$	r	t
Ann	$\frac{x}{10}$	$\frac{1}{10}$	x
Florence	$\frac{x}{5}$	$\frac{1}{5}$	x

$$\frac{x}{10} + \frac{x}{5} = 1$$

$$10\left(\frac{x}{10} + \frac{x}{5}\right) = (1)10$$

$$x + 2x = 10$$

$$3x = 10$$

$$x = \frac{10}{3} = 3\frac{1}{3}$$

Three and one-third hours is equivalent to 3 hours and 20 minutes.

15. **A** Each man works at the rate of $\frac{1}{20 \cdot 75} = \frac{1}{1,500}$ part of the job per day. The combined rate for the 50 men is $\frac{50}{1,500} = \frac{1}{30}$ part of the job per day which means that they will finish the job in 30 days, 10 days longer than originally projected.

D. Counting Problems

Here is an example of the first type of counting problem: 50 students signed up for both English and Math; 90 students signed up for either English or Math. If 25 students are taking English but not taking Math, how many students are taking Math but not taking English?

In these problems, "either . . . or . . ." means you can take both, so the people taking both are counted among the people taking either Math or English.

You must avoid counting the same people twice in these problems. The formula is:

the number taking English or Math = the number taking English + the number taking Math − the number taking both.

You have to subtract the number taking both subjects since they are counted once with those taking English and counted again with those taking Math.

A person taking English is either taking Math or not taking Math. So there are 50 + 25 = 75 people taking English, 50 taking English and Math, and 25 taking English but not taking Math. Since 75 are taking English, 90 = 75 + the number taking Math − 50; so there are 90 − 25 = 65 people taking Math. Fifty of the people taking Math are taking English, so 65 − 50 or 15 are taking Math but not English.

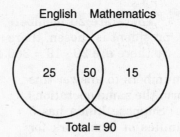

English   Mathematics

25   50   15

Total = 90

The figure shows what is given. Since 90 students signed up for English or Mathematics, 15 must be taking Mathematics but not English.

EXAMPLE 1

In a survey, 60% of those surveyed owned a car and 80% of those surveyed owned a T.V. If 55% owned both a car and a T.V., what percent of those surveyed owned a car or a T.V. but not both?

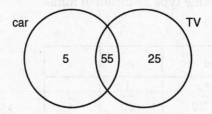

car   TV

5   55   25

The basic formula is:

people who own a car or a T.V. = people who own a car
+ people who own a T.V. − people who own both a car and a T.V.

So the people who own a car or a T.V. = 60% + 80% − 55% = 85%. Therefore, 85% of the people surveyed own either a car or a T.V.

If we just add 60% and 80%, the result is 140% which is impossible. This is because the 55% who own both are counted twice.

If an event can happen in _m_ different ways, and each of the _m_ ways is followed by a second event which can occur in _k_ different ways, then the first event can be followed by the second event in _m · k_ different ways. This is called the _fundamental principle of counting_.

EXAMPLE 1

If there are 3 different roads from Syracuse to Binghamton and 4 different roads from Binghamton to Scranton, how many different routes are there from Syracuse to Scranton which go through Binghamton?

There are 3 different ways to go from Syracuse to Binghamton. Once you are in Binghamton, there are 4 different ways to get to Scranton. So using the fundamental principle of counting, there are $3 \times 4 = 12$ different ways to get from Syracuse to Scranton going through Binghamton.

EXAMPLE 2

A club has 20 members. They are electing a president and a vice president. How many different outcomes of the election are possible? (Assume the president and vice president must be different members of the club.)

There are 20 members, so there are 20 choices for president. Once a president is chosen, there are 19 members left who can be vice president. So there are $20 \cdot 19 = 380$ different possible outcomes of the election.

E. Sequence and Progressions

A _sequence_ is an ordered collection of numbers. For example, 2, 4, 6, 8, 10,… is a sequence. 2, 4, 6, 8, 10 are called the _terms_ of the sequence. We identify the terms by their position in the sequence; so 2 is the first term, 8 is the 4th term, and so on. The dots mean the sequence continues; you should be able to figure out the succeeding terms. In the example, the sequence is the sequence of even integers, and the next term after 10 would be 12.

EXAMPLE 1

What is the eighth term of the sequence 1, 4, 9, 16, 25, …?

Since $1^2 = 1$, $2^2 = 4$, $3^2 = 9$, the sequence is the sequence of squares of integers, so the eighth term is $8^2 = 64$.

An _arithmetic progression_ is a sequence of numbers with the property that the _difference_ of any two consecutive numbers is always the same. The numbers 2, 6, 10, 14, 18, 22, … constitute an arithmetic progression, since each term is 4 more than the term before it—4 is called the _common difference_ of the progression.

If d is the common difference and a is the first term of the progression, then the nth term will be a + (n − 1)d. So a progression with common difference 4 and initial term 5 will have $5 + 6(4) = 29$ as its 7th term. You can check your answer. The sequence would be 5, 9, 13, 17, 21, 25, 29, … so 29 is the seventh term.

A sequence of numbers is called a *geometric progression* if the *ratio* of consecutive terms is always the same. So 3, 6, 12, 24, 48, ... is a geometric progression since

$$\frac{6}{3} = 2 = \frac{12}{6} = \frac{24}{12} = \frac{48}{24}, \dots$$

The *nth term of a geometric series* is

$$ar^{n-1}$$

where a is the first term and r is the common ratio. If a geometric progression started with 2 and the common ratio was 3, then the fifth term should be $2 \cdot 3^4 = 2 \cdot 81 = 162$. The sequence would be 2, 6, 18, 54, 162, ... so 162 is indeed the fifth term of the progression.

We can quickly add the first n terms of a geometric progression which starts with a and has common ratio r. The *formula for the sum of the first n terms* is

$$\frac{ar^n - a}{r - 1}$$

when $r \neq 1$. (If $r = 1$ all the terms are the same so the sum is na.)

EXAMPLE 1

Find the sum of the first 7 terms of the sequence 5, 10, 20, 40, ...

Since $\dfrac{10}{5} = \dfrac{20}{10} = \dfrac{40}{20} = 2$, the sequence is a geometric sequence with

common ratio 2. The first term is 5, so $a = 5$ and the common ratio is 2. The sum of the first seven terms means $n = 7$. Thus, the sum is

$$\frac{5 \cdot 2^7 - 5}{2 - 1} = 5(2^7 - 1) = 5(128 - 1) = 5 \cdot 127 = 635.$$

Check: The first seven terms are 5, 10, 20, 40, 80, 160, 320, and $5 + 10 + 20 + 40 + 80 + 160 + 320 = 635$.

PRACTICE EXERCISE 24

1. Write the first five terms of these sequences whose *nth* term is given:

   a. $a_n = 2n + 1$

   b. $a_n = n^2 - n$

   c. $a_n = 2^n$

2. Which of the sequences in problem 1 above are arithmetic?

3. Which of the sequences in problem 1 above are geometric?

4. Find the 25th term of the sequence whose *nth* term is $a_n = 3n + 1$.

5. Find the eighth term of the geometric sequence whose first three terms are 1, 2, 4.

SOLUTIONS TO PRACTICE EXERCISE 24

---

1. a. Substitute 1, 2, 3, 4, and 5 for n in
   $a_n = 2n + 1$:

   $$3, 5, 7, 9, 11$$

   b. 0, 2, 6, 12, 20

   c. 2, 4, 8, 16, 32

2. The first sequence whose nth term is
   $a_n = 2n + 1$ is arithmetic because there is
   a common difference between successive
   terms.

3. The third sequence whose nth term is
   $a_n = 2^n$ is geometric because there is a
   common ratio between successive terms.

4. Substitute 25 for n in the formula for the
   nth term:

   $$a_n = 3n + 1 = 3(25) + 1 = 75 + 1 = 76$$

5. The geometric sequence whose first three
   terms are 1, 2, 4 has a common ratio of 2.
   Therefore the eighth term is

   $$a_8 = 1(2^{8-1}) = 1(2^7) = 128$$

F. Inequalities

The rules for solving linear inequalities with one variable are similar to those used to solve linear equations. (These are stated as properties with *less than*, however, corresponding statements could be made using *greater than*.

   1. The Addition Property of Inequality
      If $a < b$ then $a + c < b + c$. Any number may be added to both sides of an inequality without changing the sense of the inequality.

   2. The Multiplication Property of Inequality
      If $a < b$, then:

      a. $ac < bc$ if $c > 0$.

      b. $ac > bc$ if $c < 0$.

   If both sides of an inequality are multiplied by a positive number, the sense of the inequality is not changed. However, if both sides are multiplied by a negative number, the sense of the inequality must be reversed.
   The notation $a < x < b$ or $a > x > b$ are always interpreted as *between*. That is, $-1 < x < 3$ means "those numbers between -1 and 3."

EXAMPLE 1

The inequality $2 < 5$ is true.
Add 7 to both sides: $9 < 12$ is also true.
Subtract 5 from both sides: $-3 < 0$ is also true.
Multiply both sides by 3 (a positive number): $6 < 15$ is also true.
Multiply both sides by -2: $-6 < -10$ is false, but $-6 > -10$ is true.

EXAMPLE 2

Solve $5x - 4 < 7x + 2$
Subtract $7x$ from both sides: $-2x - 4 < 2$
Add 4 to both sides: $-2x < 6$
Divide both sides by -2: $x > -3$ (Notice the change in the sense of the inequality—it changed from < to >.)

The solution set $\{x \mid x > -3\}$ can conveniently be shown on a number line.

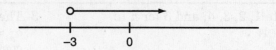

The open circle at -3 is to indicate that the number -3 is not in the solution set. A corresponding closed circle would indicate that the endpoint is included in the solution set, as it would be if the inequality had been $x \geq -3$.

PRACTICE EXERCISE 25

Solve the following inequalities. Graph the solution sets.

1. $3x + 1 > 16$

2. $2(3x - 5) + 7 > x + 12$

3. $\dfrac{3x - 2}{-5} \geq 4$

4. $-6 \leq 2x + 4 \leq 12$

SOLUTIONS TO PRACTICE EXERCISE 25

1. $3x + 1 > 16$

   $3x > 15$

   $x > 5$

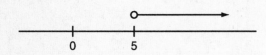

2. $2(3x - 5) + 7 > x + 12$

   $6x - 10 + 7 > x + 12$

   $6x - 3 > x + 12$

   $5x - 3 > 12$

   $5x > 15$

   $x > 3$

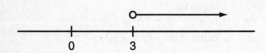

3. $\dfrac{3x - 2}{-5} \geq 4$

   Multiply both sides by -5. Reverse the sense of the inequality:

   $3x - 2 \leq -20$

   $3 \leq -18$

   $x \leq -6$

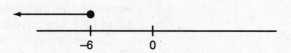

4. $-6 < 2x + 4 \leq 12$

   $-10 \leq 2x \leq 8$

   $-5 \leq x \leq 4$

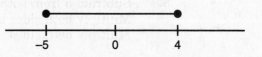

PRACTICE TEST F

The following problems are of the type that may be encountered on the CBEST™.

1. Point P is on line segment AB. Which of the following is always true?

   (A) $AP = PB$ (B) $AP > PB$ (C) $PB > AP$
   (D) $AB > AP$ (E) $AB > AP + PB$

2. If $x < y$ and $a = b$ then

   (A) $x + a = y + b$ (B) $x + a < y + b$
   (C) $x + a > y + b$ (D) $x + a = y$
   (E) $x + a = b$

3. If $x < y$ and $z = \frac{1}{2}x$ and $a = \frac{1}{2}y$ then

   (A) $z > a$ (B) $a > z$ (C) $\frac{1}{2}a = \frac{1}{2}z$
   (D) $2x > 2z$ (E) $2a > y$

4. If $b < d$ and $a = 2b$ and $c = 2d$ then

   (A) $b = d$ (B) $a = c$ (C) $a < c$ (D) $b > d$
   (E) $a > c$

5. If $p < q$ and $r < s$ then

   (A) $p = r > q + s$ (B) $p + r < q + s$
   (C) $pr < qs$ (D) $pr > qs$ (E) $p + r = q + s$

6. If $-1 < x \leq 1$ and x is an integer then the value of x is

   (A) zero only (B) one only
   (C) one and zero
   (D) one value more than one
   (E) one value less than one

7. In the inequality $5x + 2 < 2x + 5$ all of the following may be a value of x except

   (A) 0 (B) 1 (C) –1 (D) –2 (E) –3

8. If $a > b$ and $b > c$ then

   (A) $a < c$ (B) $a > c$ (C) $a = c$ (D) $c > a$
   (E) $b < a$

9. If $a > b > 1$ then which of the following is true?

   (A) $b + a > 2a$ (B) $a^2 < ab$ (C) $a - b < 0$
   (D) $a < b + 1$ (E) $a^2 > b^2$

10. If $2y > 5$ then

    (A) $y > 2.5$ (B) $y < 2.5$ (C) $y = 2.5$
    (D) $y = 10$ (E) $y = 5.2$

11. If $3x - 4 > 8$ then

    (A) $x = 4$ (B) $x = 0$ (C) $x = 4, 0$
    (D) $x > 4$ (E) $x < 4$

12. In triangle ABC, $AB = AC$. All of the following statements are true except

    (A) $AB < AC + BC$ (B) $AC < AB + BC$
    (C) $BC < AB + AC$
    (D) $AC + BC = AB + BC$
    (E) $BC + AC > AB + BC$

13. In triangle KLM, the measure of angle M is greater than the measure of angle L. Which of the following is true?

    (A) $KM > KL$ (B) $KL > KM$ (C) $KL < KM$
    (D) $KM + LM < KL$
    (E) $KL + LM < KM$

14. In triangles ABC and DEF, $AC = DF$, $BC = EF$ and $AB > DE$, then

    (A) m $\angle C$ = m $\angle F$ (B) m $\angle F$ > m $\angle C$
    (C) m $\angle F$ < m $\angle C$ (D) m $\angle A$ = m $\angle D$
    (E) m $\angle B$ = m $\angle E$

15. If $x < y$ and $a < b$, then

    (A) $a + x < b + y$ (B) $a + x > b + y$
    (C) $a = y$ (D) $x = b$ (E) $ax = by$

ANSWER KEY

1. **D**	6. **C**	11. **D**
2. **B**	7. **B**	12. **E**
3. **B**	8. **B**	13. **B**
4. **C**	9. **E**	14. **C**
5. **B**	10. **A**	15. **A**

---

1. **D**

Clearly, $AB > AP$.

2. **B**   The Addition Property of Inequality gives the result

$$x + a < y + b.$$

3. **B**   Multiply both sides of the equations by 2:

$$z - \frac{1}{2}x \rightarrow 2z = x$$

$$a - \frac{1}{2}y \rightarrow 2a = y$$

Substitute for x and y in the inequality, $x < y$:

$2z < 2a$ Divide both sides by 2.

$z < a$ This is equivalent to $a > z$.

4. **C**   Divide both sides of the equations by 2:

$$a = 2b \rightarrow \frac{1}{2}a = b$$

$$c = 2d \rightarrow \frac{1}{2}c = d$$

Substitute for b and d in the inequality, $b < d$:

$\frac{1}{2}a < \frac{1}{2}c$ Multiply both sides by 2.

$a < c$

5. **B**   Add the left sides and the right sides of the inequalities:

$$p + r < q + s$$

6. **C**   Integers in the interval $-1 < x \le 1$ include 0 and 1 only.

7. **B**   Solve the inequality:

$$5x + 2 < 2x + 5$$
$$3x + 2 < 5$$
$$3x < 3$$
$$x < 1$$

The only number among the choices that is not less than 1 is the number 1 itself.

8. **B**   This is a consequence of the transitive property of inequality.

9. **E**   Each of the choices A through D can be eliminated by considering the values $a = 3$ and $b = 2$. There is a theorem which states that for a and b, $a > b > 1$, $a^2 > b^2$.

10. **A**   Divide both sides of the inequality by 2:

$$2y > 5$$
$$y > 2.5$$

11. **D**   Solve the inequality:

$$3x - 4 > 8$$
$$3x > 12$$
$$x > 4$$

12. **E**   Choices A, B, and C are each statements of the theorem that states the length of any side of a triangle must be less than the sum of the lengths of the other two sides. Choice D is the result of the Addition Property of Equality. Choice E is false.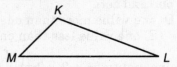

13. **B**   The relevant theorem states that if two angles of a triangle are unequal, then the sides opposite those angles are also unequal with the longer side being opposite the larger angle.

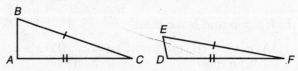

14. **C**   From this diagram it is clear that $m\angle F < m\angle C$.

15. **A**   Add the left and right sides of the inequalities:

$$a + x < b + y$$

III. GEOMETRY

A. Rays and Angles

When a line segment is extended indefinitely in one direction, it is called a *ray*. A ray has one endpoint.

$\overrightarrow{AB}$ is a ray which has A as its endpoint.

Two rays with a common endpoint form an *angle*. The point is called the *vertex* of the angle and the rays are called the *sides* of the angle. The symbol for angle is $\angle$ and an angle can be denoted in the following ways:

(A) $\angle ABC$ where B is the vertex, A is a point on one side, and C a point on the other side.

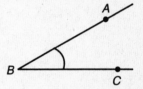

(B) $\angle B$ where B is the vertex.

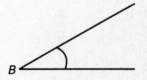

(C) $\angle 1$ or $\angle x$ where x or 1 is written inside the angle.

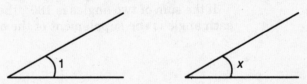

Angles are usually measured in degrees. We say that an angle equals x degrees, when its measure is x degrees. Degrees are denoted by $°$. An angle of 50 degrees is $50°$. Also $60' = 1°$ and $60'' = 1'$ where $'$ is read minutes and $''$ is read seconds.

Angles are congruent ($\cong$) if their measures are equal. That is $\angle ABC \cong \angle DEF$ means $m\angle ABC = m\angle DEF$.

Two angles are *adjacent* if they have the same vertex and a common side and one angle is not inside the other.

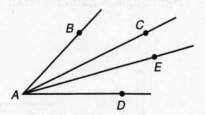

$\angle BAC$ and $\angle CAD$ are adjacent, but $\angle CAD$ and $\angle EAD$ are not adjacent.

If two lines intersect at a point, they form several angles. The angles opposite each other are called *vertical* angles. ∠1 and ∠3 are vertical angles. ∠2 and ∠4 are vertical angles.

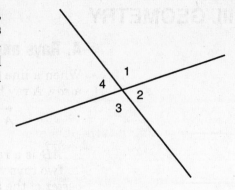

Vertical angles are congruent,

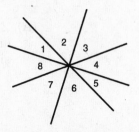

so m∠1 = m∠5, m∠2 = m∠6, m∠3 = m∠7, m∠4 = m∠8.

A straight angle is an angle whose sides lie on a straight line. *A straight angle equals 180°.*

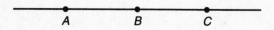

∠ABC is a straight angle.

If the sum of two angles is 180°, then the angles are *supplementary,* and each angle is the supplement of the other.

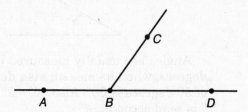

∠ABC and ∠CBD are supplementary.

If an angle of $x°$ and an angle of $y°$ are supplements, then $x + y = 180$.

If two supplementary angles are equal, they are both *right angles.* A right angle is half of a straight angle. The measure of a right angle is 90°.

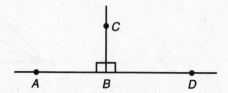

m∠ABC = m∠CBD and they are both right angles. A right angle is denoted by ⌐. When two lines intersect and all four of the angles are equal, then each of the angles is a right angle.

If the sum of two angles is 90°, then the angles are *complementary* and each angle is the complement of the other.

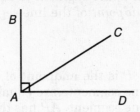

∠*BAC* and ∠*CAD* are complementary.

If an angle of $x°$ and an angle of $y°$ are complementary, then $x + y = 90$.

EXAMPLE 1

If the supplement of an angle is three times as much as the complement of the angle, how many degrees are in the angle?

Let d be the number of degrees in the angle; then the supplement is $(180 - d)°$, and the complement is $(90 - d)°$. Since the supplement is 3 times the complement, $180 - d = 3(90 - d) = 270 - 3d$ which gives $2d = 90$, so $d = 45$.

Therefore, the angle is 45°.

An angle is bisected when it is separated into two congruent angles by a ray, a line, or a segment through the vertex. The ray, line, or segment is called the *angle bisector*.

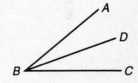

If $\overline{BD}$ bisects ∠*ABC*, then m∠*ABD* = m∠*DBC*.

An *acute angle* is an angle with a measure greater than zero but less than 90 degrees. An *obtuse angle* is an angle with a measure greater than 90 but less than 180 degrees.

∠1 is an acute angle, and ∠2 is an obtuse angle.

B. Lines

A line is understood to be a straight line. A line is assumed to extend indefinitely in both directions. Two points determine a line. There are two ways to denote a line:

(A) by a single letter: l is a line;

(B) by two points on the line:

$\overleftrightarrow{AB}$ is a line.

A *line segment* is the part of a line between two points called *endpoints*. A line segment is denoted by its endpoints.

$\overline{AB}$ is a line segment. The length of $\overline{AB}$ is denoted by AB. If a point P on a line segment is equidistant from the endpoints, then P is called the *midpoint* of the line segment.

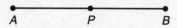

P is the midpoint of $\overline{AB}$ if the length of $\overline{AP}$ = the length of $\overline{PB}$. Two line segments are equal if their lengths are equal; so $AP = PB$ means the line segment $\overline{AP}$ has the same length as the line segment $\overline{PB}$. If two segments have the same length, they are congruent.

P is a *point of intersection* of two lines if P is a point which is on both of the lines. *Two different lines cannot have more than one point of intersection.*

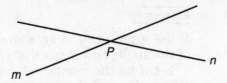

P is the point of intersection of m and n. We also say *m and n intersect at P.*

Two lines in the same plane are parallel if they do not intersect no matter how far they are extended.

Lines m and n are parallel, but k and l are not parallel since if k and l are extended they will intersect. Parallel lines are denoted by the symbol $\parallel$; so $m \parallel n$ means m is parallel to n.

If two lines are parallel to a third line, they are parallel to each other.

If a third line intersects two given lines at different points it is called a *transversal*. A transversal and the two given lines form eight angles. The four inside angles are called *interior* angles. The four outside angles are called *exterior* angles. If two angles are on opposite sides of the transversal they are called *alternate* angles.

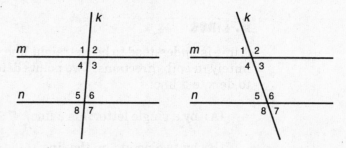

Line k is a transversal with respect to lines m and n. Angles 1, 2, 7, and 8 are the exterior angles, and angles 3, 4, 5, and 6 are the interior angles. $\angle 4$ and $\angle 6$ are an example of a pair of alternate angles. $\angle 1$ and $\angle 5$, $\angle 2$ and $\angle 6$, $\angle 3$ and $\angle 7$, and $\angle 4$ and $\angle 8$ are pairs of *corresponding* angles.

If two parallel lines are intersected by a transversal then:

1. Alternate interior angles are congruent.

2. Corresponding angles are congruent.

3. Interior angles on the same side of the transversal are supplementary.

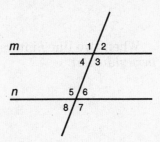

If we use the fact that vertical angles are equal, we can replace "interior" by "exterior" in (1) and (3).

If m is parallel to line n then the following statements are true.

1. $m\angle 4 = m\angle 6$ and $m\angle 3 = m\angle 5$

2. $m\angle 1 = m\angle 5$, $m\angle 2 = m\angle 6$, $m\angle 3 = m\angle 7$ and $m\angle 4 = m\angle 8$

3. $m\angle 3 + m\angle 6 = 180$ and $m\angle 4 + m\angle 5 = 180$

The converses are also true. Let m and n be two lines which have k as a transversal.

1. If a pair of alternate interior angles are congruent, then m and n are parallel.

2. If a pair of corresponding angles are congruent, then m and n are parallel.

3. If a pair of interior angles on the same side of the transversal are supplementary, then m is parallel to n.

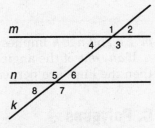

If $m\angle 3 = m\angle 5$, then $m \parallel n$. If $m\angle 4 = m\angle 6$, then $m \parallel n$. If $m\angle 2 = m\angle 6$ then $m \parallel n$. If $m\angle 3 + m\angle 6 = 180°$, then $m \parallel n$.

EXAMPLE 1

If m and n are two parallel lines and angle 1 measures 60°, what is the measure of angle 2?

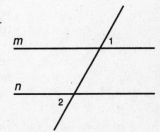

Let $\angle 3$ be the vertical angle equal to angle 2, $m\angle 3 = m\angle 2$. Since m and n are parallel, corresponding angles are equal. Since $\angle 1$ and $\angle 3$ are corresponding angles $m\angle 1 = m\angle 3$. Therefore $m\angle 1 = m\angle 2$, and $m\angle 2$ equals $60°$ since $m\angle 1 = 60°$.

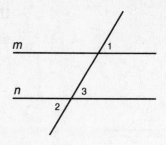

When two lines intersect to form right angles, the lines are said to be *perpendicular*.

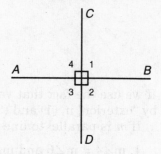

Perpendicular lines form four right angles. $\overline{AB}$ is perpendicular to $\overline{CD}$, and angles 1, 2, 3, and 4 are all right angles. $\perp$ is the symbol for perpendicular; so $\overline{AB} \perp \overline{CD}$.

If two lines in a plane are perpendicular to the same line, then the two lines are parallel.

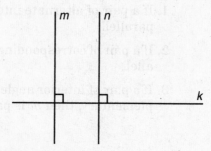

$m \perp k$ and $n \perp k$ implies that $m \parallel n$.

If *any one* of the angles formed when two lines intersect is a right angle, then the lines are perpendicular.

C. Polygons

A *polygon* is a closed figure in a plane composed of line segments which meet only at their endpoints. The line segments are called *sides* of the polygon, and a point where two sides meet is called a *vertex* (plural *vertices*) of the polygon.

ABCDEF is not a polygon since the line segments intersect at points which are not endpoints.

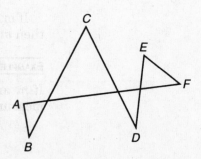

Below are some examples of polygons.

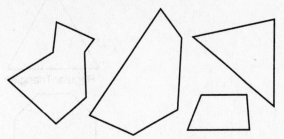

A polygon is usually denoted by the vertices given in order.

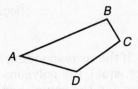

ABCD is a polygon.

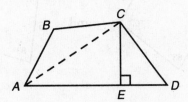

A *diagonal* of a polygon is a line segment whose endpoints are non-adjacent vertices. The *altitude* from a vertex *P* to a side is the line segment with endpoint *P* which is perpendicular to the side.

$\overline{AC}$ is a diagonal, and $\overline{CE}$ is the altitude from *C* to $\overline{AD}$.

Polygons are classified by the number of angles or sides they have. A polygon with three angles is called a *triangle*; a four-sided polygon is a *quadrilateral*; a polygon with five angles is a *pentagon*; a polygon with six angles is a *hexagon*; an eight-sided polygon is an *octagon*. The number of angles is always equal to the number of sides in a polygon, so a six-sided polygon is a hexagon. The term *n*-gon refers to a polygon with *n* sides.

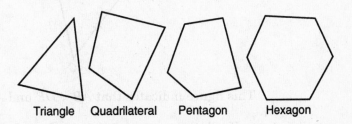

Triangle   Quadrilateral   Pentagon   Hexagon

If the sides of a polygon are all equal in length and if all the angles of a polygon are equal, the polygon is called a *regular* polygon.

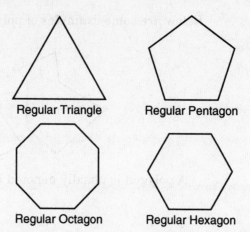

If the corresponding sides and the corresponding angles of two polygons are equal, the polygons are *congruent*. Congruent polygons have the same size and the same shape.

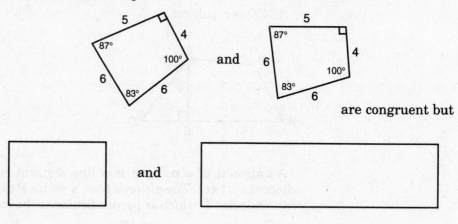

and   are congruent but

and   are not congruent.

In figures for problems on congruence, sides with the same number of strokes through them are equal.

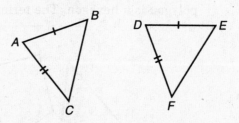

This figure indicates that $AB = DE$ and $AC = DF$.

If all the corresponding angles of two polygons are equal and the lengths of the corresponding sides are proportional, the polygons are said to be *similar*. Similar polygons have the same shape but need not be the same size.

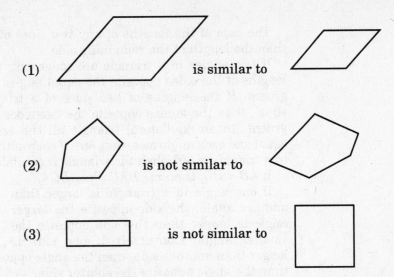

(1)   is similar to

(2)   is not similar to

(3)   is not similar to

In (3) the corresponding angles are equal, but the corresponding sides are not proportional.

 Draw all possible diagonals from one vertex. There will be two fewer triangles formed than the number of sides in the polygon.

The sum of the measures of all the angles of an n-gon is $(n-2)180°$. So the sum of the angles in a hexagon is $(6-2)180° = 720°$.

D. Triangles

A *triangle* is a 3-sided polygon. If at least two sides of a triangle are equal, it is called *isosceles*. If all three sides are equal, it is an *equilateral* triangle. If all of the sides have different lengths, the triangle is *scalene*. When one of the angles in a triangle is a right angle, the triangle is a *right triangle*. If one of the angles is obtuse it is an *obtuse triangle*. If all the angles are acute, it is an *acute triangle*.

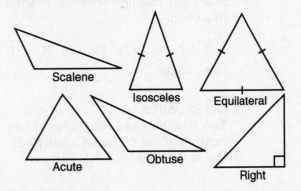

The symbol for a triangle is △; so △ABC means a triangle whose vertices are A, B, and C.

The sum of the angles in a triangle is 180°.

The sum of the lengths of any two sides of a triangle must be greater than the length of the remaining side.

If two angles in a triangle are congruent, then the lengths of the sides opposite the equal angles are congruent. If the lengths of two sides of a triangle are equal, then the angles opposite the two sides are congruent. In an equilateral triangle all the angles are equal and each angle measures 60°. If each of the angles in a triangle is 60°, then the triangle is equilateral.

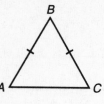

If $AB = BC$, then m$\angle BAC$ = m$\angle BCA$.

If one angle in a triangle is larger than another angle, the side opposite the larger angle is longer than the side opposite the smaller angle. Conversely if one side is longer than another side, then the angle opposite the longer side is larger than the angle opposite the shorter side.

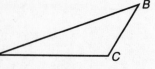

$AB > AC$ implies m$\angle BCA$ > m$\angle ABC$.

In a right triangle, the side opposite the right angle is called the *hypotenuse,* and the remaining two sides are called *legs.*

The Pythagorean theorem If the legs of a right triangle are a and b and the hypotenuse is c, then $a^2 + b^2 = c^2$.

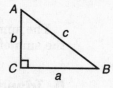

$(BC)^2 = (AB)^2 + (AC)^2$ or $a^2 + b^2 = c^2$

If $AB = 4$ and $AC = 3$ then $(BC)^2 = 4^2 + 3^2 = 25$ so $BC = 5$. If $BC = 13$ and $AC = 5$, then $13^2 = 169 = (AB)^2 + 5^2$. So $(AB)^2 = 169 - 25 = 144$ and $AB = 12$.

If the lengths of the three sides of a triangle are a, b, and c and $a^2 = b^2 + c^2$, then the triangle is a right triangle where a is the length of the hypotenuse.

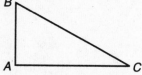

If $AB = 8$, $AC = 15$, and $BC = 17$, then since $17^2 = 8^2 + 15^2$, $\angle BAC$ is a right angle.

Congruence

Two triangles are congruent if two pairs of corresponding sides and the corresponding *included* angles are equal. This is called *Side-Angle-Side* and is denoted by S.A.S.

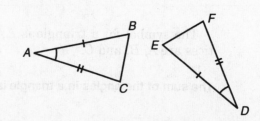

$AB = DE$, $AC = DF$ and m$\angle BAC$ = m$\angle EDF$ imply that $\triangle ABC \cong \triangle DEF$.
$\cong$ means congruent.

Two triangles are congruent if two pairs of corresponding angles and the corresponding *included* side are equal. This is called *Angle-Side-Angle* or A.S.A.

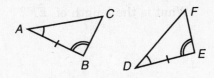

If $AB = DE$, m$\angle BAC$ = m$\angle EDF$, and m$\angle CBA$ = m$\angle FED$ then $\triangle ABC \cong \triangle DEF$.

If all three pairs of corresponding sides of two triangles are equal, then the triangles are congruent. This is called *Side-Side-Side* or S.S.S.

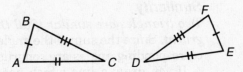

$AB = EF$, $AC = ED$, and $BC = FD$ imply that $\triangle ABC \cong \triangle EFD$.

Because of the Pythagorean theorem, if any two corresponding sides of two right triangles are equal, the third sides are equal and the triangles are congruent.

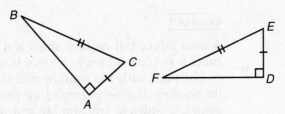

$AC = DE$ and $BC = EF$ imply $\triangle ABC \cong \triangle DFE$.

In general, if two corresponding sides of two triangles are equal, we cannot infer that the triangles are congruent.

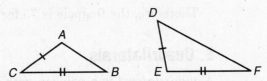

$AC = DE$ and $CB = EF$, but the triangles are not congruent.

If the lengths of two sides of a triangle are equal, then the altitude to the third side divides the triangle into two congruent triangles.

$AB = BC$ and $BD \perp AC$ implies $\triangle ADB \cong \triangle CDB$.

Therefore, m∠ABD = m∠CBD, so BD bisects ∠ABC. Since AD = DC, D is the midpoint of AC so BD is the median from B to AC. A *median* is the segment from a vertex to the midpoint of the side opposite the vertex.

EXAMPLE 1

What is the length of $\overline{EF}$?

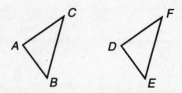

AB = 4, AC = 4.5 and BC = 6, m∠BAC = m∠EDF, DE = 4 and DF = 4.5
Since two pairs of corresponding sides (AB and DE, AC and DF) and the corresponding included angles (∠BAC, ∠EDF) are congruent, the triangles ABC and DEF are congruent by S.A.S. Therefore, EF = BC = 6.

Similarity

Two triangles are similar if all three pairs of corresponding angles are congruent. Since the sum of the angles in a triangle is 180°, it follows that if two corresponding angles are congruent, the third angle must be congruent.

If you draw a line which passes through a triangle and is parallel to one of the sides of the triangle, the triangle formed is similar to the original triangle.

If DE ‖ BC then △ADE ~ △ABC. The symbol ~ means similar.

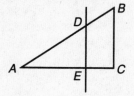

EXAMPLE 1

A man 6 feet tall casts a shadow 4 feet long; at the same time a flagpole casts a shadow which is 50 feet long. How tall is the flagpole?

The man with his shadow and the flagpole with its shadow can be regarded as the pairs of corresponding sides of two similar triangles.

Let h be the height of the flagpole. Since corresponding sides of similar triangles are proportional,

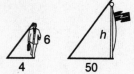

$\frac{4}{50} = \frac{6}{h}$. Cross-multiply getting $4h = 6 \cdot 50 = 300$; so $h = 75$.

Therefore, the flagpole is 75 feet high.

E. Quadrilaterals

A *quadrilateral* is a polygon with four sides. The sum of the measures of the angles in a quadrilateral is 360°. If the opposite sides of a quadrilateral are parallel, the figure is a *parallelogram*.

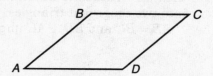

ABCD is a parallelogram.

In a parallelogram:

1. The opposite sides are congruent.

2. The opposite angles are congruent.

3. A diagonal divides the parallelogram into two congruent triangles.

4. The diagonals bisect each other.

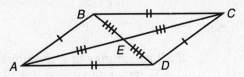

If *ABCD* is a parallelogram, then

1. *AB* = *DC*, *BC* = *AD*.

2. m∠*BCD* = m∠*BAD*, m∠*ABC* = m∠*ADC*.

3. △*ABC* ≅ △*ADC*, △*ABD* ≅ △*CDB*.

4. *AE* = *EC* and *BE* = *ED*.

If *any* of the statements (1), (2), (3), and (4) are true for a quadrilateral, then the quadrilateral is a parallelogram.

If all of the sides of a parallelogram are equal, the figure is called a *rhombus*.

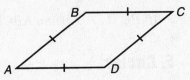

ABCD is a rhombus.
The diagonals of a rhombus are perpendicular.

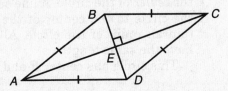

BD ⊥ *AC* so m∠*BEC* = m∠*CED* = m∠*AED* = m∠*AEB* = 90.

If all the angles of a parallelogram are right angles, the figure is a rectangle.

ABCD is a rectangle.

Since the sum of the angles in a quadrilateral is 360°, if *all* the angles of a quadrilateral are equal then the figure is a rectangle. The diagonals

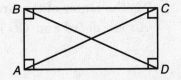

of a rectangle are equal. The length of a diagonal can be found by using the Pythagorean theorem.

If $ABCD$ is a rectangle, $AC = BD$ and $(AC)^2 = (AD)^2 + (DC)^2$.

If all the sides of a rectangle are equal, the figure is a *square*.

$ABCD$ is a square.

If all the angles of a rhombus are equal, the figure is a square. The length of the diagonal of a square is $\sqrt{2}\,s$ where s is the length of a side.

In square $ABCD$, $AC = (\sqrt{2})\,AD$.

A quadrilateral with two parallel sides and two sides which are not parallel is called a *trapezoid*. The parallel sides are called *bases*, and the non-parallel sides are called *legs*.

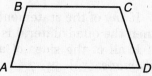

If $\overline{BC} \parallel \overline{AD}$ then $ABCD$ is a trapezoid; $\overline{BC}$ and $\overline{AD}$ are the bases.

F. Circles

A *circle* is a figure in a plane consisting of all the points which are the same distance from a fixed point called the *center* of the circle. A line segment from any point on the circle to the center of the circle is called a *radius* (plural: radii) of the circle. All radii of the same circle have the same length.

This circle has center P and radius $\overline{AP}$.

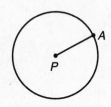

A circle is denoted by a single letter, usually its center. Two circles in a plane with the same center are *concentric*.

C and D are concentric circles.

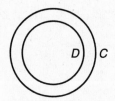

A line segment whose endpoints are on a circle is called a *chord*. A chord which passes through the center of the circle is a *diameter*. The length of a diameter is twice the length of a radius. A diameter divides a circle into two congruent halves which are called *semi-circles*.

P is the center of the circle.

$\overline{AB}$ is a chord and $\overline{CD}$ is a diameter.

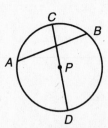

A diameter which is perpendicular to a chord bisects the chord.

O is the center of this circle and $\overline{AB} \perp \overline{CD}$; then $AE = EB$.

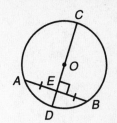

If a line intersects a circle at one and only one point, the line is said to be a *tangent* to the circle. The point common to a circle and a tangent to the circle is called the *point of tangency*. The radius from the center to the point of tangency is perpendicular to the tangent.

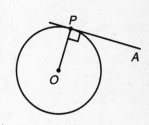

$\overline{AP}$ is tangent to the circle with center O. P is the point of tangency and $\overline{OP} \perp \overline{PA}$.

A polygon is *inscribed* in a circle if all of its vertices are points on the circle.

$ABCDE$ is an inscribed pentagon.

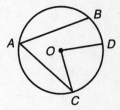

An angle whose vertex is a point on a circle and whose sides are chords of the circle is called an *inscribed angle*. An angle whose vertex is the center of a circle and whose sides are radii of the circle is called a *central angle*.

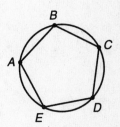

$\angle BAC$ is an inscribed angle.

$\angle DOC$ is a central angle.

An arc is a part of a circle.

Arc ACB is written $\overset{\frown}{ACB}$.

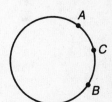

If two letters are used to denote an arc, they represent the smaller of the two possible arcs. So $\overset{\frown}{AB} = \overset{\frown}{ACB}$.

An arc can be measured in degrees. The entire circle is 360°; thus an arc of 120° would be $\frac{1}{3}$ of a circle. The measure of an arc is denoted by $\mathrm{m}\overset{\frown}{AB}$.

A central angle is equal in measure to the arc it intercepts.

$$\mathrm{m}\angle AOB = \mathrm{m}\overset{\frown}{AB}$$

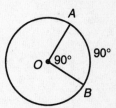

An inscribed angle is equal in measure to $\frac{1}{2}$ the

measure of the arc it intercepts.

$$m\angle ABC = \tfrac{1}{2}\, m\widehat{AC}.$$

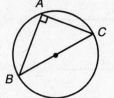

An angle inscribed in a semicircle is a *right angle*.

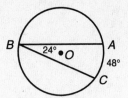

If BC is a diameter, then $m\angle BAC$ is inscribed in a semicircle; so $m\angle BAC = 90°$.

G. Area, Perimeter, and Volume

The area A of a square equals s^2, where s is the length of a side of the square. Thus, $A = s^2$.

If $AD = 5$ inches, the area of square $ABCD$ is 25 square inches.

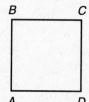

The area of a rectangle equals length times width; if L is the length of one side and W is the length of a perpendicular side, then the area $A = LW$.

If $AB = 5$ feet and $AD = 8$ feet, then the area of rectangle $ABCD$ is 40 square feet.

The area of a parallelogram is base × height; $A = bh$, where b is the length of a side and h is the length of an altitude to the base.

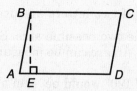

If $AD = 6$ yards and $BE = 4$ yards, then the area of the parallelogram $ABCD$ is 6 · 4 or 24 square yards.

The area of a trapezoid is the (average of the bases)(height).

$$A = \left(\frac{b_1 + b_2}{2}\right)h$$

where b_1 and b_2 are the lengths of the parallel sides and h is the length of an altitude to one of the bases.

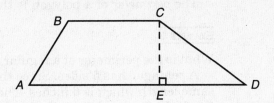

If BC = 3 miles, AD = 7 miles, and CE = 2 miles, then the area of trapezoid $ABCD$ is [(3 + 7)/2] · 2 = 10 square miles.

The area of a triangle is $\frac{1}{2}$ (base)(height); $A = \frac{1}{2}bh$, where b is the length of a side and h is the length of the altitude to that side.

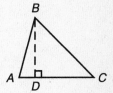

If AC = 5 miles and BD = 4 miles, then the area of the triangle is $\frac{1}{2}(5)(4)$ = 10 square miles.

Since the legs of a right triangle are perpendicular to each other, the area of a right triangle is one half the product of the lengths of the legs.

EXAMPLE 1

If the lengths of the sides of a triangle are 5 feet, 12 feet, and 13 feet, what is the area of the triangle?

Since $5^2 + 12^2 = 25 + 144 = 169 = 13^2$, the triangle is a right triangle (Pythagorean theorem) and the legs are the sides with lengths of 5 feet and 12 feet. Therefore, the area is $\frac{1}{2}(5)(12)$ = 30 square feet.

If we want to find the area of a polygon which is not of a type already mentioned, we break the polygon up into smaller figures such as triangles or rectangles, find the area of each piece, and add these to get the area of the given polygon.

The area of a circle is πr^2 where r is the length of a radius. Since $d = 2r$ where d is the length of a diameter,

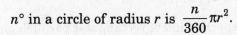

$A = \pi\left(\dfrac{d}{2}\right)^2 = \pi\dfrac{d^2}{4}.$ The number π is an irrational

number often approximated by $\frac{22}{7}$ or 3.14.

If OP = 2 inches, then the area of the circle with center O is $\pi 2^2$ or 4π square inches. The portion of the plane bounded by a circle and a central angle is called a *sector* of the circle.

The shaded region is a sector of the circle with center O. The area of a sector with central angle

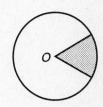

$n°$ in a circle of radius r is $\dfrac{n}{360}\pi r^2.$

If OB = 4 inches and $\angle BOA$ = 100°, then the

area of the sector is $\dfrac{100}{360}\pi \cdot 4^2 = \dfrac{5}{18} \cdot 16\pi = \dfrac{40}{9}\pi$

square inches.

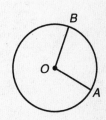

The *perimeter* of a polygon is the sum of the lengths of the sides.

EXAMPLE 1

What is the perimeter of a regular pentagon whose sides are 6 inches long?

A pentagon has 5 sides. Since the pentagon is regular, all sides have the same length which is 6 inches. Therefore, the perimeter of the pentagon is 5×6 which equals 30 inches or 2.5 feet.

The *perimeter of a rectangle is $2(L + W)$* where L is the length and W is the width.

The *perimeter of a square is $4s$* where s is the length of a side of the square.

The *perimeter of a circle* is called the *circumference* of the circle. The *circumference of a circle is πd or $2\pi r$,* where d is the length of a diameter and r is the length of a radius.

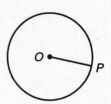

If O is the center of a circle and $OP = 5$ feet, then the circumference of the circle is $2(5)(\pi)$ or 10π feet.

The length of an arc of a circle is $(n/360)\,\pi d$ where the central angle of the arc is $n°$.

If O is the center of a circle where $OA = 5$ yards and $m\angle AOB = 60°$, then the length of arc AB is

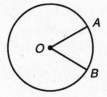

$$\left(\frac{60}{360}\,\pi\right)(10) = \frac{10}{6}\pi = \frac{5}{3}\pi \text{ yards.}$$

EXAMPLE 2

How far will a wheel with a radius of 2 feet travel in 500 revolutions? (Assume the wheel does not slip.)

The diameter of the wheel is 4 feet; so the circumference is 4π feet. Therefore, the wheel will travel $(500)(4\pi)$ or $2,000\pi$ feet in 500 revolutions.

A *rectangular parallelepiped* is a solid figure all of whose faces are rectangles. It has six such faces. Its volume is the product of the length times the width times the height, or $V = LWH$.

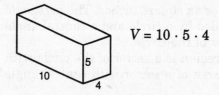

$$V = 10 \cdot 5 \cdot 4$$

A *cube* is a special kind of rectangular parallelepiped with length, width, and height all equal. If x is the length, width, or height, then $V = x^3$.

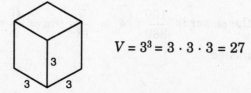

$$V = 3^3 = 3 \cdot 3 \cdot 3 = 27$$

The volume of a *cylinder* is the area of the base multiplied by the height. If the cylinder has a circular base, then $V = h(\pi r^2)$. If two cylinders have the same height and the same base, they will have the same volume regardless of the angle between the base and the line of centers.

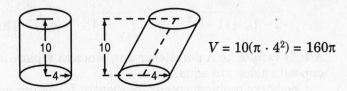

$$V = 10(\pi \cdot 4^2) = 160\pi$$

H. Coordinate Geometry

In coordinate geometry, every point in the plane is associated with an ordered pair of numbers called *coordinates*. Two perpendicular lines are drawn; the horizontal line is called the *x*-axis and the vertical line is called the *y*-axis. The point where the two axes intersect is called the *origin*. Both of the axes are number lines with the origin corresponding to zero. Positive numbers on the *x*-axis are to the right of the origin, negative numbers to the left. Positive numbers on the *y*-axis are above the origin, negative numbers below the origin. The coordinates of a point P are (x, y) if P is located by moving x units along the *x*-axis from the origin and then moving y units up or down. *The distance along the x-axis is always given first.*

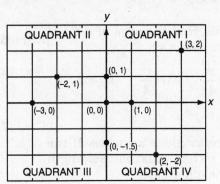

The numbers in parentheses are the coordinates of the point. Thus "$P(3,2)$" means that the coordinates of P are $(3,2)$. *The distance between the point with coordinates (x,y) and the point with coordinates (a,b) is* $\sqrt{(x-a)^2 + (y-b)^2}$. You should be able to answer many questions by using the distance formula.

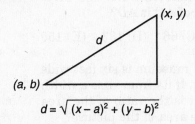

$$d = \sqrt{(x-a)^2 + (y-b)^2}$$

Is $ABCD$ a parallelogram? $A = (3,2)$, $B = (1,-2)$, $C = (-2,1)$, $D = (1,5)$. The length of AB is $\sqrt{(3-1)^2 + (2-(-2))^2} = \sqrt{2^2 + 4^2} = \sqrt{20}$. The length of CD is $\sqrt{(-2-1)^2 + (1-5)^2} = \sqrt{(-3)^2 + (-4)^2} = \sqrt{25}$. Therefore, $AB \neq CD$, so

$ABCD$ cannot be a parallelogram, since in a parallelogram the lengths of opposite sides are equal.

Geometry problems occur frequently. *If you are not provided with a diagram, draw one for yourself.* Think of any conditions which will help you answer the question; perhaps you can see how to answer a different question which will lead to an answer to the original question. It may help to draw in some diagonals, altitudes, or other auxiliary lines in your diagram.

PRACTICE TEST G

The following problems are of the type that may be encountered on the CBEST™.

1. Using formulas
   Circumference = $2\pi r$
   Area = πr^2
   where r = radius, find the area of a circle whose circumference is x.

   (A) $\dfrac{x^2}{4\pi^2}$ (B) $\dfrac{x^2}{4\pi}$ (C) $\dfrac{x^2}{4}$ (D) πx^2

   (E) πx

2. One side of a rectangle is x inches. If the perimeter is p inches, what is the length (in inches) of the other side?

   (A) $p - x$ (B) $p - 2x$ (C) $\dfrac{p-x}{2}$

   (D) $\dfrac{p-2x}{2}$ (E) $2p - 2x$

3. C is the midpoint of segment AE. B and D are on line AE so that $AB = BC$ and $CD = DE$. What percent of AC is AD?

   (A) 33   (B) 50   (C) 66   (D) 133   (E) 150

4. A picture in an art museum is six feet wide and eight feet long. If its frame has a width of six inches, what is the ratio of the area of the frame to the area of the picture?

   (A) $\dfrac{5}{16}$ (B) $\dfrac{5}{4}$ (C) $\dfrac{4}{5}$ (D) $\dfrac{5}{12}$ (E) $\dfrac{3\frac{1}{5}}{1}$

5. To represent a family budget on a circle graph, how many degrees of the circle should be used to represent an item that is 20% of the total budget?

   (A) 20   (B) 36   (C) 60   (D) 72   (E) 90

6. What is the maximum number of glass tumblers (each with a circumference of 4π inches) that can be placed on a table $48'' \times 32''$?

   (A) 36   (B) 48   (C) 92   (D) 96   (E) 192

7. To avoid paying a toll on a direct road, I go west 10 miles, south 5 miles, west 30 miles, and north 35 miles. The length of the toll road is (?) miles.

   (A) 30   (B) 45   (C) 50   (D) 70   (E) 85

8. The length of a rectangle is increased by 50%. By what percent would the width have to be decreased to maintain the same area?

   (A) $33\frac{1}{3}$ (B) 50   (C) $66\frac{2}{3}$ (D) 150
   (E) 200

9. Area of circle $O = 9\pi$. What is the area of $ABCD$?

   (A) 24   (B) 30   (C) 35
   (D) 36   (E) 48

10. A man travels four miles north, twelve miles east, and then twelve miles north. How far (to the nearest mile) is he from the starting point?

(A) 17   (B) 20   (C) 21   (D) 24   (E) 28

11. If angle *DBA* measures 39° and angle *FBE* measures 79°, then angle *GBC* has a measure of

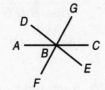

(A) 39°   (B) 51°   (C) 62°
   (D) 118°   (E) 152°

12. The length of a rectangle is *l* and the width is *w*. If the width is increased by 2 units, by how many units will the perimeter be increased?

(A) 2   (B) 4   (C) 2*w*   (D) 2*w* + 2
   (E) 2*w* + 4

13. If the radius of a wheel is *f* feet, how many revolutions does the wheel make per mile? (1 mile equals 5,280 feet)

(A) 5280*f*   (B) $\dfrac{2640}{\pi f}$ (C) 5280πf^2

(D) $\dfrac{\pi f}{2640}$ (E) $\dfrac{\pi f^2}{5280}$

14. The length of a wire fence around a circular flower bed is 100π feet. What is the area (in square feet) of a two-foot concrete walk surrounding this fence?

(A) 98π   (B) 100π   (C) 102π   (D) 202π
   (E) 204π

15. How many tiles (each one foot square) are necessary to form a one-foot border around the inside of a room 24 feet by 14 feet?

(A) 36   (B) 37   (C) 72   (D) 74   (E) 76

16. When the radius of a circle is doubled the area is multiplied by

(A) 2   (B) 2π   (C) 2π*r*   (D) 3.14   (E) 4

17. *AD* = 14
   EF = 6
   BC = ?

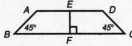

(A) 8   (B) 12
   (C) 20   (D) 26   (E) 36

18. If the diagonal of a table with a square top is 6 feet, what is the area of the table top (in square feet)?

(A) $\sqrt{18}$ (B) 9π   (C) 18   (D) 18$\sqrt{2}$
   (E) 36

19. How many spokes are there in the wheel of a sports car if any two spokes form an angle of 15°?

(A) 12   (B) 15   (C) 22   (D) 24   (E) 36

20. How many degrees are there in an angle formed by the hands of a clock at 2:30?

(A) 100°   (B) 105°   (C) 110°   (D) 115°
   (E) 120°

21. One side of a rectangle is *x* inches. If the perimeter is *p* inches, what is the length (in inches) of the other side? Answer in terms of *p* and *x*.

(A) *p* − *x*   (B) *p* − 2*x*   (C) $\dfrac{p-x}{2}$

(D) $\dfrac{p-2x}{2}$ (E) 2*p* − 2*x*

22. Base $\overline{RT}$ of triangle *RST* is $\frac{4}{5}$ of altitude $\overline{SV}$. If *SV* equals *c*, which of the following is an expression for the area of the triangle *RST*?

(A) $\dfrac{2c}{5}$ (B) $\dfrac{2c^2}{5}$ (C) $\dfrac{c^2}{2}$ (D) $\dfrac{4c^2}{5}$

(E) $\dfrac{8c^2}{5}$

23. A triangle has a base *b* and an altitude *a*. A second triangle has a base twice the altitude of the first triangle, and an altitude twice the base of the first triangle. What is the area of the second triangle?

(A) $\frac{1}{2}ab$ (B) *ab*   (C) 2*ab*   (D) 4*ab*

(E) $\frac{1}{2}a^2b^2$

24. A pond 100 feet in diameter is surrounded by a circular grass walk which is 2 feet wide. How many square feet of grass are there on the walk? (Answer in terms of π.)

(A) 98π   (B) 100π   (C) 102π   (D) 202π
   (E) 204π

25. What is the area of *ABCD*?

(A) 5   (B) 8   (C) 10
(D) 16   (E) 20

26. The distance from *A* to *C* in the square field *ABCD* is 50 feet. What is the area of field *ABCD* in square feet?

(A) $25\sqrt{2}$ (B) 625

(C) 1250   (D) 2500   (E) 5000

27. In the figure at the right, *ABCD* is a square and semicircles are constructed on each side of the square. If *AB* is 2, what is the area of the entire figure?

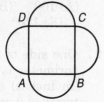

(A) $2 + 4\pi$ (B) $2 - 4\pi$
(C) $4 + 8\pi$
(D) $4 - 2\pi r$ (E) $4 + 2\pi$

28. *O* is the center of the circle at the right. $\overline{XO}$ is perpendicular to $\overline{YO}$ and the area of triangle *XOY* is 32. What is the area of circle *O*?

(A) 16π (B) 32π (C) 64π (D) 128π
(E) 256π

29. Square *QRST* is inscribed in circle *O*.
$OV \perp TS$
$OV = 1$
The area of the shaded portion is

(A) $\pi - 4$ (B) $4\pi - 4$ (C) $2\pi - 4$
(D) $4\pi - 2$ (E) $2\pi - 2$

30. $\overline{QVR} \perp \overline{SVT}$
$m\angle VSR = x°$
$m\angle VRW = (?)°$

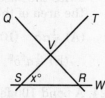

(A) $90 - x$ (B) $90 + x$
(C) $x - 90$ (D) $180 - x$
(E) 135

31. *ABJH*, *JDEF*, *ACEG* are squares

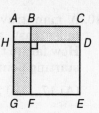

$$\frac{BC}{AB} = 3$$

$$\frac{\text{Area } BCDJ}{\text{Area } HJFG} = ?$$

(A) $\dfrac{1}{9}$ (B) $\dfrac{1}{3}$ (C) 1   (D) 3   (E) 9

32. Rectangle *ABCD* is made up of five equal squares. *AD* = 30. Find *EF*.

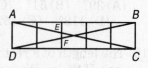

(A) 6   (B) 8   (C) 10   (D) 12   (E) 20

33. Radius *OA* = 6.5
Chord *AC* = 5
Area of triangle *ABC* equals

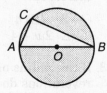

(A) 16   (B) 18   (C) 24
(D) 30   (E) 36

34. Angles *a*, *b*, and *c* are in ratio of 1:3:2.
How many degrees in angle *b*?

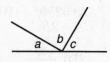

(A) 30   (B) 50   (C) 60   (D) 90   (E) 100

35. *BC* equals one half of *AB*. The area of right triangle *ABC* equals 64 square feet. Find hypotenuse *AC* to the nearest foot.

(A) 12   (B) 14   (C) 18
(D) 24   (E) 32

36. *ABCD* is a square
AE = 2
GC = 8
Shaded area = 44
Area of *FBEJ* = ?

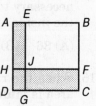

(A) 36   (B) 56
(C) 64   (D) 68   (E) 80

37. The area of a rectangle *KLMN* equals 100. Base *NM* equals 20. What is the area of triangle *ANM* if *A* is any point on *KL*?

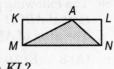

(A) 25   (B) 50   (C) 75   (D) 100
(E) cannot be determined

38. *ABCD* is a rectangle. *AD* = 12, *AB* = 16. *DE* = ?

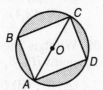

(A) 8   (B) 10   (C) 14
(D) 15   (E) 20

39. *O* is the center of the circle. $\overline{BC}$ is parallel to $\overline{AD}$.
OA = 5
CB = 8

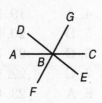

$\dfrac{AB}{AD}$ = ?

(A) $\dfrac{3}{4}$ (B) $\dfrac{4}{5}$ (C) 1   (D) $\dfrac{5}{4}$ (E) $\dfrac{4}{3}$

40. *BA* = 2*BC*
EA = 2*DE*
BE = 14
DC = ?

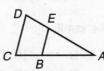

(A) 7   (B) 18   (C) 21   (D) 24   (E) 28

41. If angle *DBG* measures 79° and angle *CBE* measures 39° then angle *GBE* equals

(A) 51°   (B) 62°
(C) 101°   (D) 108°
(E) 202°

42. m∠*A* = (?)°

(A) 15   (B) 45   (C) 60
(D) 80   (E) 120

43. Four circles with diameters of one foot touch at four points as shown in the figure. What is the area of the shaded portion (in square feet)?

(A) $1 - \dfrac{\pi}{4}$ (B) $1 - \pi$ (C) $1 - 4\pi$ (D) π

(E) $\dfrac{\pi}{4}$

44. Perimeter of *ABCD* = 24. The area of the shaded portion is

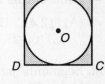

(A) 27π (B) $9\pi - 36$
(C) $9\pi - 24$ (D) $36 - 9\pi$
(E) $24 - 9\pi$

45. *ABIJ*, *BCHI*, *CDGH*, and *DEFG* are congruent rectangles.
AJ = 21
KI = ?

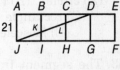

(A) 3   (B) 5.25   (C) 7   (D) 10.5   (E) 14

46. The area of the shaded portion is

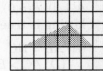

(A) $2r^2(4 - \pi)$
(B) $2r^2(2 - 2\pi)$
(C) $2r^2(\pi - 4)$ (D) $2r^2(\pi - 2)$
(E) $r^2(2 - \pi)$

47. How many square units are there in the shaded triangle?

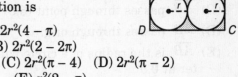

(A) 4   (B) 6   (C) 8
(D) 9   (E) 12

48. $\overline{AE} \perp \overline{ED}$ *ED* = 13
$\overline{CD} \perp \overline{ED}$ *CD* = 3
$\overline{DC} \perp \overline{CB}$ *CB* = 2

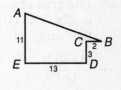

AB = ?   *AE* = 11

(A) 8   (B) 13   (C) 14   (D) 15   (E) 17

49. If an airplane starts at point *R* and travels 14 miles directly north to *S*, then 48 miles directly east to *T*, what is the straight line distance from *T* to *R* in miles?

(A) 25   (B) 34   (C) 50   (D) 62   (E) 2,500

50. The area of a circle with radius r is equal to the area of a rectangle with base b. Find the altitude of the rectangle in terms of π, r, and b.

   (A) $\sqrt{\pi r}$ (B) $\dfrac{2\pi r}{b}$ (C) $\pi r^2 b$

   (D) $\dfrac{\pi r^2}{b}$ (E) $\dfrac{\pi r^2}{b^2}$

51. A line segment is drawn from point $(8,-2)$ to point $(4,6)$. The coordinates of the midpoint of this line segment are

   (A) $(12,4)$ (B) $(12,8)$ (C) $(6,4)$ (D) $(6,2)$
   (E) $(6,-2)$

52. Segments joining points $(-4,0)$, $(0,5)$, and $(4,0)$ will form a (an)

   (A) circle   (B) right triangle
      (C) rectangle   (D) square
        (E) isosceles triangle

53. The segment from A $(-3,-4)$ to B $(3,4)$ is drawn. Which of the following is true?

   (A) the length of $\overline{AB}$ = 5 units

   (B) $\overline{AB}$ is parallel to the X axis

   (C) $\overline{AB}$ passes through point $(6,8)$

   (D) $\overline{AB}$ passes through origin

   (E) $\overline{AB}$ is the radius of a circle with center at 0,0

54. Triangle ABC has the following vertices: $A(1,0)$, $B(5,0)$, and $C(3,4)$. Which of the following is true?

   (A) $AB = BC$ (B) $AB = AC$ (C) $CA = CB$
      (D) $AC > BC$ (E) $AC < BC$

55. The area of a circle whose center is at $(0,0)$ is 25π. The circle passes through all of the following points EXCEPT

   (A) $-5,0$ (B) $5,5$ (C) $5,0$ (D) $0,5$
      (E) $0,-5$

56. The following points are vertices of quadrilateral $ABCD$ $(0,4)$, $(4,0)$, $(0,-4)$ and $(-4,0)$. The area of $ABCD$ is

   (A) 8   (B) 16   (C) 32   (D) 48   (E) 64

57. The vertices of triangle ABC are $(4,3)$, $(4,7)$, and $(8,3)$. The area of triangle ABC equals

   (A) 4   (B) $4\sqrt{3}$ (C) 8   (D) 12.5   (E) 16

58. A line segment $\overline{AB}$ is drawn between $(2,3)$ and $(4,7)$. What are the coordinates of the midpoint?

   (A) $(5,3)$ (B) $(3,5)$ (C) $(6,10)$
      (D) $(2,4)$ (E) $(4,2)$

59. What is the distance from point A $(3,4)$ to point B $(-3,-4)$?

   (A) 0   (B) 5   (C) 10   (D) 13   (E) 14

60. Point P $(4,2)$ is the midpoint of segment $\overline{OPC}$, where O is at origin (O,O). The coordinates of C are

   (A) $(2,1)$ (B) $(4,8)$ (C) $(4,4)$ (D) $(8,2)$
      (E) $(8,4)$

ANSWER KEY

1. B	16. E	31. C	46. A
2. D	17. D	32. A	47. B
3. E	18. C	33. D	48. E
4. A	19. D	34. D	49. C
5. D	20. B	35. C	50. D
6. D	21. D	36. B	51. D
7. C	22. B	37. B	52. E
8. A	23. C	38. B	53. D
9. D	24. E	39. A	54. C
10. B	25. C	40. C	55. B
11. C	26. C	41. C	56. C
12. B	27. E	42. C	57. C
13. B	28. C	43. A	58. B
14. E	29. C	44. D	59. C
15. C	30. B	45. C	60. E

Solutions to Practice Test G

1. B Circumference = $x = 2\pi r$.

Solve for r: $r = \dfrac{x}{2\pi}$

Substitute into the formula for area:

$$A = \pi r^2 = \pi\left(\frac{x}{2\pi}\right)^2 = \pi\left(\frac{x^2}{4\pi^2}\right) = \frac{x^2}{4\pi}$$

2. D The perimeter of a rectangle is given by the formula: $p = 2x + 2L$ Solve this formula for L:

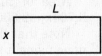

$$p = 2x + 2L$$
$$p - 2x = 2L$$
$$\frac{p - 2x}{2} = L$$

3. E The diagram shows four segments of equal length. Suppose each segment is x units long, then $AC = 2x$ and $AD = 3x$. The question is this: AD is what percent of AC; that is, $3x$ is what percent of $2x$. Write a proportion:

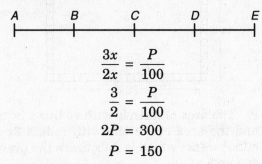

$$\frac{3x}{2x} = \frac{P}{100}$$
$$\frac{3}{2} = \frac{P}{100}$$
$$2P = 300$$
$$P = 150$$

AD is 150% of AC.

4. A The area of the picture is $(6)(8) = 48$ square feet. The area of the picture and frame together is $(7)(9) = 63$ square feet. The area of the frame alone is the difference of these numbers, $63 - 48 = 15$ square feet. The ratio of the area of the frame to the area of the picture is $\dfrac{15}{48} = \dfrac{5}{16}$.

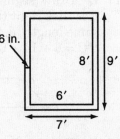

5. D 20% of the budget should be represented by 20% of the total number of degrees in a circle, 360°. What is 20% of 360?

$$\frac{x}{360} = \frac{20}{100}$$
$$100x = 7{,}200$$
$$x = 72$$

6. D Assume that the glasses are arranged as in the diagram. The circumference of each glass is $4\pi = \pi d$; therefore the diameter of each glass is 4 inches. $32 \div 4 = 8$ glasses can be lined up along the width and $48 \div 4 = 12$ glasses can be lined up along the length. Therefore $(12)(8) = 96$ glasses can be placed on the table.

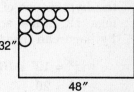

7. C The road from A to B along the toll road would create a right triangle with sides 30 miles and 40 miles. The Pythagorean theorem can be used to find d:

$$d^2 = 30^2 + 40^2$$
$$d^2 = 900 + 1{,}600 = 2{,}500$$
$$d = 50$$

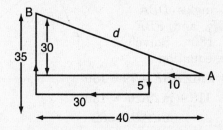

8. A The area of the original rectangle is xy. The area of the altered rectangle is $(y + 0.5y)(x - Px) = 1.5xy(1 - P)$.
Solve the following equation for P.

$xy = 1.5xy(1 - P)$ Divide both sides by xy.
$1 = 1.5(1 - P) = 1.5 - 1.5P$
$-0.5 = -1.5P$
$5 = 15P$
$\dfrac{1}{3} = P$

$\dfrac{1}{3} = 33\dfrac{1}{3}\%$

9. **D** The area of the circle is 9π, so

$$9\pi = \pi r^2$$
$$9 = r^2$$
$$3 = r$$

Since the radius of the circle is 3, the diameter is 6, and the length of the side of the square is equal to the diameter. The area of the square is $6^2 = 36$.

10. **B** The distance from the starting point is the hypotenuse of the right triangle with legs 12 miles and 16 miles. Use the Pythagorean theorem:

$$d^2 = 12^2 + 16^2 = 144 + 256 = 400$$
$$d = 20$$

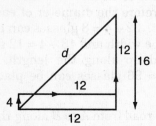

11. **C** $\angle ABF$ and $\angle GBC$ are vertical angles and therefore have the same measure. The sum of angles DBA, ABF, and FBE is $180°$. Solve the equation

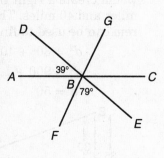

$$39 + m\angle ABF + 79 = 180$$
$$118 + m\angle ABF = 180$$
$$m\angle ABF = 62$$

Therefore $m\angle GBC = 62$.

12. **B** The original perimeter is $2l + 2w$. The new perimeter is $2(l + 2) + 2w = 2l + 4 + 2w$.

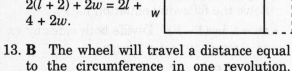

13. **B** The wheel will travel a distance equal to the circumference in one revolution. Divide the circumference into one mile:

$$\frac{5,280}{2\pi f} = \frac{2,640}{\pi f}$$

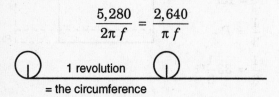

1 revolution
= the circumference

14. **E** If r is the radius of the flower bed, then $100\pi = 2\pi r$ and $r = 50$.

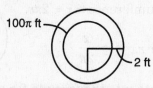

The area of the walk is the difference between the areas of the two circles, one with a radius of 50 feet and the other of 52 feet.

Area of the walk = $\pi(52)^2 - \pi(50)^2 = 2,704\pi - 2,500\pi = 204\pi$

Note that this operation could have been done using a factoring technique:

$$\pi(52)^2 - \pi(50)^2$$
$$= \pi[(52)^2 - \pi(50)^2]$$
$$= \pi(52 - 50)(52 + 50)$$
$$= \pi(2)(102)$$
$$= \pi(204)$$

15. **C** There are two rows of tiles with 14 tiles in each row and two rows of tiles with 22 tiles in each row. The total number of tiles is $2(14) + 2(22) = 28 + 44 = 72$.

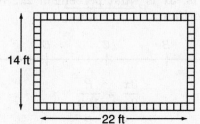

16. **E** The area of a circle with radius x is πx^2 and the area of a circle with radius $2x$ is $\pi(2x)^2 = 4\pi x^2$ which is four times the previous area.

17. **D** Draw segments AG and DH, forming isosceles right triangles whose legs are the same length, 6. Therefore $BC = BG + GH + HC = 6 + 14 + 6 = 26$.

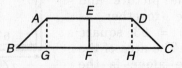

18. **C** Use the Pythagorean theorem to find the value of x^2, the area of the square.

$$x^2 + x^2 = 6^2$$
$$2x^2 = 36$$
$$x^2 = 18$$

19. **D** The number of spokes can be determined by dividing 15 into 360:

$$360 \div 15 = 24.$$

20. **B** The angle between successive numerals on the face of a clock is $360 \div 12 = 30$. At 2:30, the angle includes three and one-half of these intervals which measures $3(30) + 15 = 105$ degrees.

21. **D** Let y be the length of the other side.

$$p = 2x + 2y$$
$$p - 2x = 2y$$
$$\frac{p - 2x}{2} = y$$

22. **B** The area of $\triangle RST = \frac{1}{2}(RT)(SV)$

$$= \frac{1}{2}\left(\frac{4}{5}c\right)(c) = \frac{2c^2}{5}$$

23. **C** The area of any triangle is $\frac{1}{2}$ $(base)(height)$.

The base of the second triangle is $2a$ and the altitude is $2b$, so the area is $\frac{1}{2}(2a)(2b)$ $= 2ab$.

24. **E** (This is the same mathematical problem as number 14.)

25. **C** Separate the region into two triangles, $\triangle ABC$ with base 4 and altitude 2: area $\frac{1}{2}(2)(4) = 4$

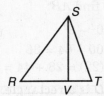

$\triangle ADC$ with base 4 and altitude 3: area $\frac{1}{2}(4)(3) = 6$

26. **C** Let x be the length of the sides of the square. Use the Pythagorean theorem to find the value of x^2 (the area of the square).

$$x^2 + x^2 = 50^2$$
$$2x^2 = 2{,}500$$
$$x^2 = 1{,}250$$

The area is 1,250 square feet.

27. **E** The sides of the square are each 2, so the radius of each semicircle is 1. The four semicircles have the same area as two circles.

Area of the square: $2^2 = 4$ plus
Area of two circles of radius 1: $2(\pi 1^2) = 2\pi$
The total area is: $4 + 2\pi$

28. **C** Let the radius of the circle be r. The area of the triangle is $\frac{1}{2}r^2 = 32$.

$$r^2 = 64$$
$$r = 8$$

The area of the circle is $\pi(8^2) = 64\pi$.

29. **C** Let the radius of the circle be r. Then using the Pythagorean theorem,

$$1^2 + 1^2 = r^2$$
$$2 = r^2$$
$$\sqrt{2} = r$$

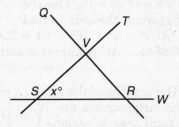

So the area of the shaded portion is the difference between the areas of the circle and the square.

Area of the shaded portion $= \pi r^2 - 2^2 =$
$\pi \left[\sqrt{2}\right]^2 - 4 = 2\pi - 4$

30. **B** Because $\overline{QVR} \perp \overline{SVT}$, $m\angle SVR = 90$.

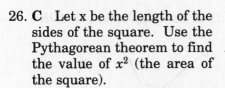

$\angle VRW$ is an exterior angle of $\triangle SVR$. The measure of an exterior angle of a triangle is equal to the sum of measures of the remote interior angles.

$$m\angle VRW = (90 + x)^\circ$$

31. **C** Let $AB = x$, then $BC = 3x$ because $\frac{BC}{AB} = 3$.

Then $HJ = x$ and $BJ = x$ and $FE = 3x$ and $JF = 3x$. So the rectangles are congruent.

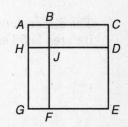

$$\frac{\text{area of } BCDJ}{\text{area of } HJFG} = 1$$

32. A Both diagonals intersect at 6 unit intervals. The segment between the 12 unit segments is $30 - (12 + 12) = 6$.

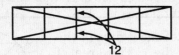

33. D Use the Pythagorean theorem to find BC:

$$(BC)^2 + (AC)^2 = (AB)^2$$
$$(BC)^2 + (5)^2 = 13^2$$
$$(BC)^2 + 25 = 169$$
$$[BC]^2 = 144$$
$$BC = 12$$

The area of $\triangle ABC = \frac{1}{2}(12)(5) = 30$.

34. D For some x, $x + 3x + 2x = 180$.

$$6x = 180$$
$$x = 30$$
$$m\angle b = 3(30) = 90$$

35. C Let $BC = x$, then $AB = 2x$. The area of $\triangle ABC = 64 = \frac{1}{2}(x)(2x) = x^2$.

So $x = 8$ and $2x = 16$. Use the Pythagorean theorem to find AC: $(AC)^2 = 8^2 + 16^2 = 64 + 256 = 320 = 17.888544...$ AC is approximately equal to 18.

36. B The lengths of the sides of the large square are 10. The total area of regions I, II, and III is 44. Use this information to find x. Regions I and II have area 20 and region III has area $8x$.

$$20 + 8x = 44$$
$$8x = 24$$
$$x = 3$$

The dimensions of region IV are 8 by 7, and its area is 56 square units.

37. B By drawing the dashed line in the diagram, we see that the area of regions I and II is always half of the area of the rectangle.

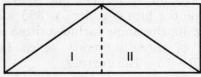

38. B The length of the diagonal of the rectangle can be found by using the Pythagorean theorem:

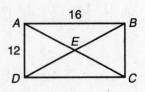

$$(BD)^2 = 12^2 + 16^2 = 144 + 256 = 400$$
$$BD = 20$$

The diagonals of a rectangle bisect each other, so $DE = 10$.

39. A Use the Pythagorean theorem to find AB:

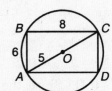

$$(AB)^2 = 10^2 - 8^2$$
$$= 100 - 64 = 36$$
$$AB = 6$$

Since $ABCD$ is a rectangle, $AD = 8$.

40. C Triangles ABE and ACD are similar so the proportion follows:

$$\frac{BE}{CD} = \frac{AB}{AC}$$
$$\frac{14}{CD} = \frac{2x}{3x} = \frac{2}{3}$$
$$2CD = 42$$
$$CD = 21$$

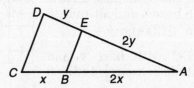

41. C $\angle GBE$ is the supplement of $\angle DBG$.

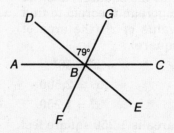

$$m\angle GBE + m\angle DBG = 180$$
$$m\angle GBE + 79 = 180$$
$$m\angle GBE = 101$$

42. **C** The sum of the measures of the angles of any triangle is 180°.

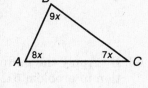

$$7x + 8x + 9x = 180$$
$$24x = 180$$
$$x = 7.5$$

So $m\angle A = 8(7.5) = 60$.

43. **A** The area between the circles is equal to the area of the square with sides one foot minus the area of the four quarter circles with radius $\frac{1}{2}$ foot. The area of

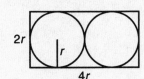

the four quarter circles is equal to the area of one complete circle. The required area is:

$$1^2 - \pi\left(\frac{1}{2}\right)^2 = 1 - \frac{\pi}{4}$$

44. **D** Since the perimeter of the square is 24, then the length of a side is 6 and the radius of the circle is 3. The area inside the square and outside the circle is:

$$6^2 - \pi(3^2) = 36 - 9\pi$$

45. **C** The diagonal separates the parallel segments into thirds. The required length is 7.

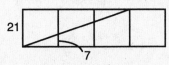

46. **A** The length of the rectangle is $4r$ and its width is $2r$. The area inside the rectangle and outside the circles is:

$$(2r)(4r) - 2[\pi(r)^2] = 8r^2 - 2\pi r^2 = 2r^2(4 - \pi)$$

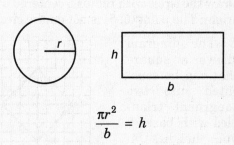

47. **B** The base of the triangle is 6 and its height is 2. The area is:

$$\frac{1}{2}(6)(2) = 6$$

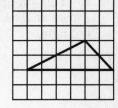

48. **E** Draw the dotted line creating the right triangle with legs 8 and 15. Use the Pythagorean theorem to find x.

$$x^2 = 15^2 + 8^2 = 225 + 64 = 289$$

 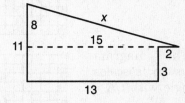

$$x = 17$$

49. **C** Use the Pythagorean theorem:
$$(RT)^2 = 14^2 + 48^2 = 196 + 2{,}304 = 2{,}500$$

$$RT = 50$$

50. **D** Since the areas are equal, $\pi r^2 = bh$. Solve for h.

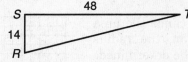

$$\frac{\pi r^2}{b} = h$$

51. **D** The midpoint formula is

$$\left(\frac{x_1 + x_2}{2}, \frac{y_1 + y_2}{2}\right)$$

Apply the formula to the ordered pairs $(8, -2)$ and $(4, 6)$.

$$\left(\frac{8 + 4}{2}, \frac{-2 + 6}{2}\right) = (6, 2)$$

52. **E** The diagram shows an isosceles triangle.

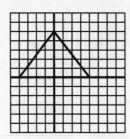

53. **D** The diagram shows the segment passing through the origin.

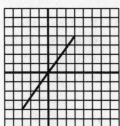

54. **C** The diagram shows an isosceles triangle with $CA = CB$.

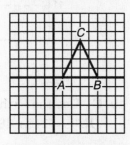

55. **B** Since the area is 25π, the radius can be determined.

$$25\pi = \pi r^2$$

$$25 = r^2$$

$$5 = r$$

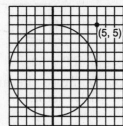

Draw the circle with radius 5 centered at the origin. The point (5, 5) is not on the circle.

56. **C** The diagram shows a square that can be separated into two congruent triangles with bases 8 and heights 4. The area is

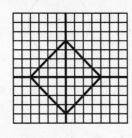

$$2\left[\frac{1}{2}(8)(4)\right] = 32.$$

57. **C** If the triangle has a base of 4 and a height of 4, the area is $\frac{1}{2}(4)(4) = 8$.

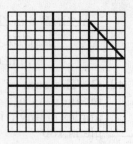

58. **B** Apply the midpoint formula. See solution to problem 51.

$$\left(\frac{2+4}{2}, \frac{3+7}{2}\right) = (3,5)$$

59. **C** Apply the distance formula

$$d = \sqrt{(x_2 - x_1)^2 + (y_2 - y_1)^2}.$$

The distance between points (3,4) and (−3,−4) is:

$$d = \sqrt{(-3-3)^2 + (-4-4)^2} = \sqrt{(-6)^2 + (-8)^2}$$

$$= \sqrt{36+64} = \sqrt{100} = 10$$

60. **E** Let the coordinates of C be (x,y), then using the midpoint formula,

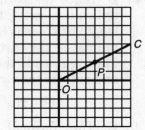

$$(4,2) = \left(\frac{0+x}{2}, \frac{0+y}{2}\right)$$

$$\frac{x}{2} = 4$$

$$\frac{y}{2} = 2$$

so $x = 8$ and $y = 4$. The coordinates of C are (8,4).

FORMULAS

Interest = Amount × Time × Rate

Discount = Cost × Rate of Discount

$$x = \frac{-b \pm \sqrt{b^2 - 4ac}}{2a} \quad \text{(quadratic formula)}$$

Distance = Rate × Time

$a^2 + b^2 = c^2$ when a and b are the legs and c is the hypotenuse of a right triangle (Pythagorean theorem)

Diameter of a circle = 2(Radius)

Area of a square = s^2

Area of a rectangle = LW

Area of a triangle = $\frac{1}{2}bh$

Area of a circle = πr^2

Area of a parallelogram = bh

Area of a trapezoid = $\frac{1}{2}(b_1 + b_2)h$

Circumference of a circle = πd

Perimeter of a square = $4s$

Perimeter of a rectangle = $2(L + W)$

Distance between points (x,y) and (a,b) is $\sqrt{(x-a)^2 + (y-b)^2}$

Volume of a cube = S^3

Volume of a rectangular parallelepiped = LWH

Volume of a cylinder = $\pi r^2 h$

Distance between points (x,y) and (a,b) is $\sqrt{(x-a)^2 + (y-b)^2}$

Hints for Answering Mathematical Questions

1. Reread the question to make sure you have answered the question asked, and not what you anticipated.

2. You may save time by looking at the answers before you begin your computation. Some of the answers may be contrary to fact. Sometimes it is quicker to work back from the answers.

3. Don't waste time on superfluous computations.

4. To save time, estimate the answer whenever you can.

5. Budget your time so you can try all the questions. (Bring a watch.)

6. You may not be able to answer all the questions; don't waste time worrying about it.

7. Do all the problems you know how to work *before* you start to think about those that will take a minute or two to answer.

8. If you skip a question, make sure to skip that number on the answer sheet.

9. Make sure you express your answer in the proper units.

SAMPLE EXERCISES

This section provides two sets of mathematical exercises of mixed type, each with 25 questions. Take these sample exercises, check your answers, and study the answer explanations provided.

The exercises that follow will give you an indication of your ability to handle these mathematical questions. The time for Exercises A and B is 30 minutes each. Scoring for each of the exercises may be interpreted as follows:

20–25	Superior
16–19	Above Average
11–15	Average
7–10	Below Average
0–6	Unsatisfactory

SAMPLE EXERCISE A

1. In 1955, it cost $12 to purchase one hundred pounds of potatoes. In 1975, it cost $34 to purchase one hundred pounds of potatoes. The price of one hundred pounds of potatoes increased X dollars between 1955 and 1975 with X equal to:

   (A) 1.20   (B) 2.20   (C) 3.40   (D) 22

   (E) 34

2. A house cost Ms. Jones C dollars in 1965. Three years later she sold the house for 25% more than she paid for it. She has to pay a tax of 50% of the gain. (The gain is the selling price minus the cost.) How much tax must Ms. Jones pay?

   (A) $\frac{1}{24}C$ (B) $\frac{C}{8}$ (C) $\frac{1}{4}C$ (D) $\frac{C}{2}$

   (E) $.6C$

3. If the length of a rectangle is increased by 20%, and the width of the same rectangle is decreased by 20%, then the area of the rectangle

   (A) decreases by 20%   (B) decreases by 4%
     (C) is unchanged   (D) increases by 20%
       (E) increases by 40%

Use the following graph for questions 4–7.

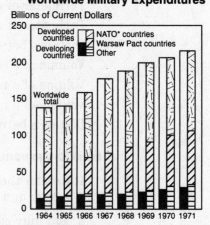

Worldwide Military Expenditures

Billions of Current Dollars

*North Atlantic Treaty Organization

Source: Pocket Data Book, U.S.A. 1973. Bureau of the Census.

4. Between 1964 and 1969, worldwide military expenditures

   (A) increased by about 50%
   (B) roughly doubled
   (C) increased by about 150%
   (D) almost tripled
   (E) increased by 10%

5. The average yearly military expenditure by the developing countries between 1964 and 1971 was approximately how many billions of current dollars?
   (A) 20   (B) 50   (C) 100   (D) 140
     (E) 175

6. Which of the following statements can be inferred from the graph?
   I. The NATO countries have higher incomes than the Warsaw Pact countries.
   II. Worldwide military expenditures have increased each year between 1964 and 1971.
   III. In 1972 worldwide military expenditures were more than 230 billion current dollars.

   (A) I only   (B) II only   (C) I and II only
   (D) II and III only   (E) I, II, and III

7. A speaker claims that the NATO countries customarily spend one-third of their combined incomes on military expenditures. According to the speaker, the combined incomes of the NATO countries (in billions of current dollars) in 1971 was about

   (A) 100   (B) 200   (C) 250   (D) 350
   (E) 500

8. Eight percent of the people eligible to vote are between 18 and 21. In an election, 85% of those eligible to vote who were between 18 and 21 actually voted. In that election, people between 18 and 21 who actually voted were what percent of those people eligible to vote?

   (A) 4.2   (B) 6.4   (C) 6.8   (D) 8   (E) 8.5

9. If n and p are both odd numbers, which of the following numbers *must* be an even number?

   (A) $n + p$ (B) np (C) $np + 2$
   (D) $n + p + 1$ (E) $2n + p$

10. It costs g cents a mile for gasoline and m cents a mile for all other costs to run a car. How many *dollars* will it cost to run the car for 100 miles?

    (A) $\dfrac{g + m}{100}$ (B) $100g + 100m$ (C) $g + m$

    (D) $g + .1m$ (E) g

11. What is the length of the line segment which connects A to B?

    (A) $\sqrt{3}$ (B) 2

    (C) $2\sqrt{2}$ (D) 4

    (E) 8

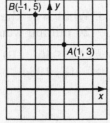

12. A cab driver's income consists of his salary and tips. His salary is $50 a week. During one week his tips were $\frac{5}{4}$ of his salary. What fraction of his income for the week came from tips?

    (A) $\dfrac{4}{9}$ (B) $\dfrac{1}{2}$ (C) $\dfrac{5}{9}$ (D) $\dfrac{5}{8}$ (E) $\dfrac{5}{4}$

Use the table below for questions 13–17.

INCOME (IN DOLLARS)	TAX (IN DOLLARS)
0– 4,000	1% of income
4,000– 6,000	40 + 2% of income over 4,000
6,000– 8,000	80 + 3% of income over 6,000
8,000–10,000	140 + 4% of income over 8,000
10,000–15,000	220 + 5% of income over 10,000
15,000–25,000	470 + 6% of income over 15,000
25,000–50,000	1,070 + 7% of income over 25,000

13. How much tax is due on an income of $7,500?

    (A) $75   (B) $80   (C) $125   (D) $150
    (E) $225

14. Your income for a year is $26,000. You receive a raise so that next year your income will be $29,000. How much *more* will you pay in taxes next year if the tax rate remains the same?

    (A) $70   (B) $180   (C) $200   (D) $210
    (E) $700

15. Joan paid $100 tax. If X was her income, which of the following statements is true?

    (A) $0 < X < 4,000$ (B) $4,000 < X < 6,000$
    (C) $6,000 < X < 8,000$
    (D) $8,000 < X < 10,000$
    (E) $10,000 < X < 15,000$

16. The town of Zenith has a population of 50,000. The average income of a person who lives in Zenith is $3,700 per year. What is the total amount paid in taxes by the people of Zenith? Assume each person pays tax on $3,700.

    (A) $37   (B) $3,700   (C) $50,000
    (D) $185,000   (E) $1,850,000

17. A person who has an income of $10,000 pays what percent (rounding to the nearest percent) of his or her income in taxes?

    (A) 1   (B) 2   (C) 3   (D) 4   (E) 5

18. Given that x and y are real numbers, let $S(x,y) = x^2 - y^2$. Then $S(3, S(3,4)) =$

(A) -40 (B) -7 (C) 40   (D) 49   (E) 56

19. Eggs cost 90¢ a dozen. Peppers cost 20¢ each. An omelet consists of 3 eggs and one-quarter of a pepper. How much will the ingredients for 8 omelets cost?

(A) $.90   (B) $1.30   (C) $1.80   (D) $2.20
(E) $2.70

20. It is 185 miles from Binghamton to New York City. If a bus takes 2 hours to travel the first 85 miles, how long must the bus take to travel the final 100 miles in order to average 50 miles an hour for the entire trip?

(A) 60 min.   (B) 75 min.   (C) 94 min.
(D) 102 min.   (E) 112 min.

21. What is the area of the figure below? $ABDC$ is a rectangle and BDE is an isosceles right triangle.

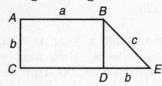

(A) ab (B) ab^2 (C) $b\left(a + \dfrac{b}{2}\right)$ (D) cab

(E) $\dfrac{1}{2}bc$

22. If $2x + y = 5$ then $4x + 2y$ is equal to

(A) 5   (B) 8   (C) 9   (D) 10
(E) none of these

23. In 1967, a new sedan cost $2,500; in 1975, the same type of sedan cost $4,800. The cost of that type of sedan has increased by what percent between 1967 and 1975?

(A) 48   (B) 52   (C) 92   (D) 152   (E) 192

24. What is the area of the square $ABCD$?

(A) 10   (B) 18   (C) 24   (D) 36   (E) 48

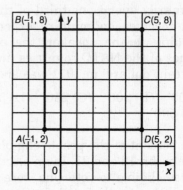

25. If $x + y = 6$ and $3x - y = 4$, then $x - y$ is equal to

(A) -1 (B) 0   (C) 2   (D) 4   (E) 6

SAMPLE EXERCISE B

Use the graphs below for questions 1–5.

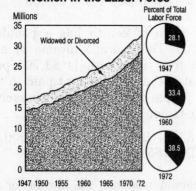

Women in the Labor Force

1947 1950 1955 1960 1965 1970 '72

Source: Pocket Data Book, U.S.A. 1973. Bureau of the Census.

1. The total labor force in 1960 was about y million with y equal to about

(A) 22   (B) 65   (C) 75   (D) 80   (E) 85

2. In 1947, the percentage of women in the labor force who were married was about

(A) 28   (B) 33   (C) 38   (D) 50   (E) 65

3. What was the first year when more than 20 million women were in the labor force?

(A) 1950   (B) 1953   (C) 1956   (D) 1958
(E) 1964

4. Between 1947 and 1972, the number of women in the labor force

   (A) increased by about 50%
   (B) increased by about 100%
   (C) increased by about 150%
   (D) increased by about 200%
   (E) increased by about 250%

5. Which of the following statements about the labor force can be inferred from the graphs?

   I. Between 1947 and 1957, there were no years when more than 5 million widowed or divorced women were in the labor force.
   II. In every year between 1947 and 1972, the number of single women in the labor force has increased.
   III. In 1965, women made up more than one-third of the total labor force.

   (A) I only   (B) II only   (C) I and II only
   (D) I and III only   (E) I, II, and III

6. If $\dfrac{x}{y} = \dfrac{2}{3}$ then $\dfrac{y^2}{x^2}$ is equal to

   (A) $\dfrac{4}{9}$ (B) $\dfrac{2}{3}$ (C) $\dfrac{3}{2}$ (D) $\dfrac{9}{4}$ (E) $\dfrac{5}{2}$

7. In the figure, $\overline{BD}$ is perpendicular to $\overline{AC}$. $\overline{BA}$ and $\overline{BC}$ have a length of a. What is the area of the triangle ABC?

   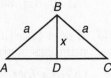

   (A) $2x\sqrt{a^2 - x^2}$ (B) $x\sqrt{a^2 - x^2}$

   (C) $a\sqrt{a^2 - x^2}$ (D) $2a\sqrt{x^2 - a^2}$

   (E) $x\sqrt{x^2 - a^2}$

8. If two places are one inch apart on a map, then they are actually 160 miles apart. (The scale on the map is one inch equals 160 miles.) If Seton is $2\frac{7}{8}$ inches from Monroe on the map, how many miles is it from Seton to Monroe?

   (A) 3   (B) 27   (C) 300   (D) 360   (E) 460

9. In the accompanying diagram $ABCD$ is a rectangle. The area of the isosceles right triangle $ABE = 7$, and $EC = 3(BE)$. The area of $ABCD$ is

   (A) 21   (B) 28   (C) 42   (D) 56   (E) 84

10. An automobile tire has two punctures. The first puncture by itself would make the tire flat in 9 minutes. The second puncture by itself would make the tire flat in 6 minutes. How long will it take for both punctures together to make the tire flat? (Assume the air leaks out at a constant rate.)

    (A) $3\frac{3}{5}$ minutes   (B) 4 minutes

    (C) $5\frac{1}{4}$ minutes   (D) $7\frac{1}{2}$ minutes

    (E) 15 minutes

11. If n^3 is odd, which of the following statements are true?
    I. n is odd.
    II. n^2 is odd.
    III. n^2 is even.

    (A) I only   (B) II only   (C) III only
    (D) I and II only   (E) I and III only

Use the table below for questions 12–15.

Persons in millions. Civilian noninstitutional population as of Nov. 1. Based on post-election surveys of persons reporting whether or not they voted; differs from table 103 data which are based on actual vote counts.

Characteristic	1964 Persons of voting age	1964 Percent voted	1968 Persons of voting age	1968 Percent voted	1972 Persons of voting age	1972 Percent voted
Total	111	69	117	68	136	63
Male	52	72	54	70	64	64
Female	58	67	62	66	72	62
White	99	71	105	69	121	64
Negro and other	11	57	12	56	15	51
Negro	10	58	11	58	13	52
Region:						
North and West........	78	75	82	71	94	66
South	32	57	35	60	43	55
Age:						
18–24 years	10	51	12	50	25	50
25–44 years	45	69	46	67	49	63
45–64 years	38	76	40	75	42	71
65 years and over......	17	66	18	66	20	63

Source: U.S. Bureau of the Census.

12. Which of the following groups had the highest percentage of voters in 1968?

(A) 18–24 years   (B) Female   (C) South
(D) 25–44 years   (E) Male

13. In 1972, what percent (to the nearest percent) of voting age people were female?

(A) 52   (B) 53   (C) 62   (D) 64   (E) 72

14. In 1968, how many males of voting age voted?

(A) 37,440,000   (B) 37,800,000
(C) 42,160,000   (D) 62,000,000
(E) 374,400,000

15. Let X be the number (in millions) of voting age people in the range 25–44 years who lived in the North and West in 1964. Which of the following includes all possible values and only possible values of X?

(A) $0 \leq X \leq 45$ (B) $13 \leq X \leq 45$
(C) $13 \leq X \leq 78$ (D) $45 \leq X \leq 78$
(E) $75 \leq X \leq 78$

16. There are 50 students enrolled in Business 100. Of the enrolled students, 90% took the final exam. Two-thirds of the students who took the final exam passed it. How many students passed the final exam?

(A) 30   (B) 33   (C) 34   (D) 35   (E) 45

17. If a is less than b, which of the following numbers is greater than a and less than b?

(A) $(a + b)/2$ (B) $(ab)/2$ (C) $b^2 - a^2$
(D) ab (E) $b - a$

18. In the figure, $\overline{OR}$ and $\overline{PR}$ are radii of circles. The length of $\overline{OP}$ is 4. If $OR = 2$, what is PR? $\overline{PR}$ is tangent to the circle with center O.

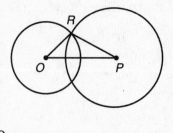

(A) 2   (B) $\dfrac{5}{2}$ (C) 3   (D) $2\sqrt{3}$ (E) $3\sqrt{2}$

19. A bus uses one gallon of gasoline to travel 15 miles. After a tune-up, the bus travels 15% farther on one gallon. How many gallons of gasoline (to the nearest tenth) will it take for the bus to travel 150 miles after a tune-up?

(A) 8.5   (B) 8.7   (C) 8.9   (D) 9.0   (E) 10.0

20. If $x + 2y = 4$ and $x/y = 2$, then x is equal to

(A) 0   (B) $\dfrac{1}{2}$ (C) 1   (D) $\dfrac{3}{2}$ (E) 2

Use the following table for questions 21–23.

SPEED OF A TRAIN OVER A 3-HOUR PERIOD								
TIMED PERIOD (*in minutes*)	0	30	45	60	90	120	150	180
SPEED AT TIME (*in m.p.h.*)	40	45	47.5	50	55	60	65	70

21. How fast was the train traveling $2\frac{1}{2}$ hours after the beginning of the timed period?

(A) 50 m.p.h.   (B) 55 m.p.h.   (C) 60 m.p.h.
(D) 65 m.p.h.   (E) 70 m.p.h.

22. During the three hours shown on the table the speed of the train

(A) increased by 25%
(B) increased by 50%
(C) increased by 75%
(D) increased by 100%
(E) increased by 125%

23. At time t measured in minutes after the beginning of the time period, which of the following gives the speed of the train in accordance with the table?

(A) $\frac{1}{6}t$ (B) $10t$ (C) $40 + t$ (D) $40 + \frac{1}{6}t$
(E) $40 + 10t$

24. It costs $1,000 to make the first thousand copies of a book and x dollars to make each subsequent copy. If it costs a total of $7,230 to make the first 8,000 copies of a book, what is x?

(A) .89   (B) .90375   (C) 1.00   (D) 89
(E) 90.375

25. If 16 workers can finish a job in three hours, how long should it take 5 workers to finish the same job?

(A) $3\frac{1}{2}$ hours   (B) 4 hours   (C) 5 hours
(D) $7\frac{1}{16}$ hours   (E) $9\frac{3}{5}$ hours

ANSWER KEYS

The letter following each question number is the correct answer. A more detailed explanation of all answers follows:

Sample Exercise A

1. D	8. C	14. D	20. D
2. B	9. A	15. C	21. C
3. B	10. C	16. E	22. D
4. A	11. C	17. B	23. C
5. A	12. C	18. A	24. D
6. B	13. C	19. D	25. A
7. D			

Sample Exercise B

1. B	8. E	14. B	20. E
2. D	9. D	15. B	21. D
3. C	10. A	16. A	22. C
4. B	11. D	17. A	23. D
5. A	12. E	18. D	24. A
6. D	13. B	19. B	25. E
7. B			

EXPLANATION OF SOLUTIONS

Sample Exercise A

1. **D** The price increased by $34 - 12 = 22$ dollars.

2. **B** She sold the house for 125% of C or $\frac{5}{4}C$. Thus, the gain is $\frac{5}{4}C - C = \frac{C}{4}$. She must pay a tax of 50% of $\frac{C}{4}$ or $\frac{1}{2}$ of $\frac{C}{4}$. Therefore, the tax is $\frac{C}{8}$. Notice that the three years has nothing to do with the problem. Sometimes a question contains unnecessary information.

3. **B** The area of a rectangle is length times width. Let L and W denote the original length and width. Then the new length is $1.2L$ and the new width is $.8W$. Therefore, the new area is $(1.2L)(.8W) = .96LW$ or 96% of the original area. So the area has decreased by 4%.

4. **A** In 1964 military expenditures were about 140 billion, and by 1969 they had increased to about 200 billion. $\frac{60}{140} = \frac{3}{7}$ which is almost 50%. By using a straight edge, you may see that the bar for 1969 is about half again as long as the bar for 1964.

5. **A** Since the developing countries' military expenditures for every year were less than 30 billion, choice A is the only possible answer. Notice that by reading the possible answers first, you save time. You don't need the exact answer.

6. **B** Statement I cannot be inferred since the graph indicates *only* the dollars spent on military expenditures, not the percent of income and not total income. II is true since each bar is higher than the previous bar to the left. III cannot be inferred since the graph gives no information about 1972. So only statement II can be inferred from the graph.

7. **D** In 1971 the NATO countries spent over 100 billion and less than 150 billion on military expenditures. Since this was one-third of their combined incomes, the combined income is between 300 billion and 450 billion. Thus choice D must be the correct answer.

8. **C** Voters between 18 and 21 who voted are 85% of the 8% of eligible voters. Thus, $(.08)(.85) = .068$, so 6.8% of the eligible voters were voters between 18 and 21 who voted.

9. **A** Odd numbers are of the form $2x + 1$ where x is an integer. Thus if $n = 2x - 1$ and $p = 2k + 1$, then $n + p = 2x + 1 + 2k + 1 = 2x + 2k + 2$ which is even. Using $n = 3$ and $p = 5$, all the other choices give an odd number. In general, if a problem involves odd or even numbers, try using the fact that odd numbers are of the form $2x + 1$ and even numbers of the form $2y$ where x and y are integers.

10. **C** To run a car 100 miles will cost $100(g + m)$ cents. Divide by 100 to convert to dollars. The result is $g + m$.

11. **C** Using the distance formula, the distance from A to B is

$$\sqrt{(1-(-1))^2 + (3-5)^2}$$
$$= \sqrt{4+4} = \sqrt{8} = \sqrt{4 \times 2}$$
$$= \sqrt{4}\sqrt{2} = 2\sqrt{2}.$$

You have to be able to simplify $\sqrt{8}$ in order to obtain the correct answer.

12. **C** Tips for the week were $\frac{5}{4} \cdot 50$, so his total income was $50 + \frac{5}{4}(50) = \frac{9}{4}(50)$. Therefore, tips made up $\frac{\frac{5}{4}(50)}{\frac{9}{4}(50)} = \frac{\frac{5}{4}}{\frac{9}{4}} = \frac{5}{9}$ of his income. *Don't* waste time figuring out the total income and the tip income. You can use the time to answer other questions.

13. **C** An income of 7,500 is in the 6,000–8,000 bracket so the tax will be 80 + 3% of the income over 6,000. Since $7,500 - 6,000 = 1,500$, the income over 6,000 is 1,500. 3% of 1,500 = $(.03)(1,500) = 45$, so the tax is $80 + 45 = 125$.

14. **D** The tax on 26,000 is 1,070 + 7% of $(26,000 - 25,000)$. Thus, the tax is 1,070 +

70 = 1,140. The tax on 29,000 is 1.070 + 7% of (29,000—25,000). Thus, the tax on 29,000 is 1,070 + 280 = 1,350. Therefore, you will pay 1,350 – 1,140 = $210 more in taxes next year. A faster method is to use the fact that the $3,000 raise is income over 25,000, so it will be taxed at 7%. Therefore, the tax on the extra $3,000 will be (.07)(3,000) = 210.

15. **C** If income is less than 6,000, then the tax is less than 80. If income is greater than 8,000, then the tax is greater than 140. Therefore, if the tax is 100, the income must be between 6,000 and 8,000. You *do not* have to calculate her exact income.

16. **E** Each person pays the tax on $3,700 which is 1% of 3,700 or $37. Since there are 50,000 people in Zenith, the total taxes are (37)(50,000) = $1,850,000.

17. **B** The tax on 10,000 is 220, so taxes are

$$\frac{220}{10,000} = .022 = 2.2\% \quad \text{of income. 2.2\% is}$$

2% after rounding to the nearest percent.

18. **A** $S(3,4) = 3^2 - 4^2 = 9 - 16 = -7$. Therefore, $S(3,S(3,4)) = S(3,-7) = 3^2 - (-7)^2 = 9 - 49 = -40$.

19. **D** Eight omelets will use $8 \cdot 3 = 24$ eggs and $8 \cdot \frac{1}{4} = 2$ peppers. Since 24 is two dozen, the cost will be $(2)(90\text{¢}) + (2)(20\text{¢}) = 220\text{¢}$ or $2.20.

20. **D** In order to average 50 m.p.h. for the trip, the bus must make the trip in

$$\frac{185}{50} = 3\frac{7}{10} \quad \text{hours which is 222 minutes.}$$

Since 2 hours or 120 minutes were needed for the first 85 miles, the final 100 miles must be completed in 222 – 120 which is 102 minutes.

21. **C** The area of a rectangle is length times width so the area of *ABDC* is ab. The area of a triangle is one half of the height times the base. Since *BDE* is an isosceles right triangle, the base and height are both equal to b. Thus, the area of *BDE* is $\frac{1}{2}b^2$.

Therefore, the area of the figure is $ab +$

$\frac{1}{2}b^2$ which is equal to $b(a + \frac{b}{2})$. You have to express your answer as one of the possible answers, so you need to be able to simplify.

22. **D** Since $4x + 2y$ is equal to $2(2x + y)$ and $2x + y = 5$, $4x + 2y$ is equal to $2(5)$ or 10.

23. **C** The cost has increased by $4,800 minus $2,500 or $2,300 between 1967 and 1975.

So the cost has increased by $\dfrac{2,300}{2,500}$

which is .92 or 92%. Answer (E) is incorrect. The price in 1975 is 192% of the price in 1967, but the *increase* is 92%.

24. **D** The distance from $(-1,2)$ to $(5,2)$ is 6. (You can use the distance formula or just count the blocks in this case.) The area of a square is the length of a side squared, so the area is 6^2 or 36.

25. **A** Since $x + y = 6$ and $3x - y = 4$, we may add the two equations to obtain $4x = 10$, or $x = 2.5$. Then, because $x + y = 6$, y must be 3.5. Therefore, $x - y = -1$.

Sample Exercise B

1. **B** In 1960 women made up 33.4% or about one-third of the labor force. Using the line graph, there were about 22 million women in the labor force in 1960. So the labor force was about 3(22) or 66 million. The closest answer among the choices is 65 million.

2. **D** In 1947, there were about 16 million women in the labor force, and about $14 - 6$ or 8 million of them were married. Therefore, the percentage of women in the labor force who were married is $\frac{8}{16}$ or 50%.

3. **C** Look at the possible answers first. You can use your pencil and admission card as straight edges.

4. **B** In 1947, there were about 16 million women in the labor force. By 1972 there were about 32 million. Therefore, the number of women doubled which is an increase of 100%. (Not of 200%.)

5. **A** Statement I is true since the width of the band for widowed or divorced women was never more than 5 million between 1947 and 1957. II is false since the number of single women in the labor force decreased from 1947 to 1948. III cannot be inferred since there is no information about the total labor force or women as a percent of it in 1965. Thus, only I can be inferred.

6. **D** If $\dfrac{x}{y}$ is $\dfrac{2}{3}$, then $\dfrac{y}{x}$ is $\dfrac{3}{2}$. Since $\left(\dfrac{y}{x}\right)^2$ is

equal to $\dfrac{y^2}{x^2}$, $\dfrac{y^2}{x^2}\left(\dfrac{3}{2}\right)^2$ or $\dfrac{9}{4}$.

7. **B** The area of a triangle is $\dfrac{1}{2}$ altitude times base. Since $\overline{BD}$ is perpendicular to $\overline{AC}$, x is the altitude. Using the Pythagorean theorem, $x^2 + (AD)^2 = a^2$ and $x^2 + (DC)^2 = a^2$. Thus, $AD = DC$, and $AD = \sqrt{a^2 - x^2}$. So the base is $2 \cdot \sqrt{a^2 - x^2}$. Therefore, the area is $\dfrac{1}{2}(x)(2\sqrt{a^2 - x^2})$ which is choice B.

8. **E** $1:160: 2\dfrac{7}{8}:x.$ $x = 2\dfrac{7}{8}(160).$ $2\dfrac{7}{8}$ is $\dfrac{23}{8}$ so the distance from Seton to Monroe is $\dfrac{23}{8}(160) = 460$ miles.

9. **D** Let $EF = FG = GC$. Therefore, $BE = EF = FG = GC$. Draw perpendiculars $\overline{EH}, \overline{FI}, \overline{GJ}$. Draw diagonals $\overline{HF}, \overline{IG}, \overline{JC}$. The 8 triangles are equal in area since they each have the same altitude ($\overline{AB}$ or $\overline{DC}$) and equal bases ($\overline{BE}, \overline{EF}, \overline{FG}, \overline{GC}, \overline{AH}, \overline{HI}, \overline{IJ}, \overline{JD}$). Since the area of $ABE = 7$, the area of $ABCD = (8)(7)$ or 56.

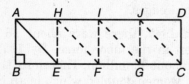

10. **A** In each minute the first puncture will leak $\dfrac{1}{9}$ of the air and the second puncture will leak $\dfrac{1}{6}$ of the air. Together $\dfrac{1}{9} + \dfrac{1}{6} = \dfrac{5}{18}$. So $\dfrac{5}{18}$ of the air will leak out in each minute. In $\dfrac{18}{5}$ or $3\dfrac{3}{5}$ minutes the tire will be flat.

11. **D** Since an even number times any number is even, and n times n^2 is odd, neither n or n^2 can be even. Therefore, n and n^2 must both be odd for n^3 to be odd. I and II are true, and III is false.

12. **E** Look in the fourth column.

13. **B** In 1972 there were 72 million females out of 136 million persons of voting age. $\dfrac{72}{136} = .529$ which is 53% to the nearest percent.

14. **B** In 1968, 70% of the 54 million males of voting age voted, and $(.7)(54,000,000) = 37,800,000$.

15. **B** Since 78 million persons of voting age lived in the North and West in 1964, and there were 65 million persons of voting age not in the 25–44 year range, there must be at least $78 - 65 = 13$ million people in the North and West in the 25–44 year range. X must be greater than or equal to 13. Since there were 45 million people of voting age in the 25–44 year range, X must be less than or equal to 45.

16. **A** 90% of 50 is 45, so 45 students took the final. Two-thirds of 45 is 30. Therefore, 30 students passed the final.

17. **A** The average of two different numbers is always between the two. If $a = 2$ and $b = 3$, then $b^2 - a^2 = 5$, $ab = 6$, and $b - a = 1$; so C, D, and E must be false. If $a = \dfrac{1}{2}$ and $b = 1$, then $(ab)/2 = \dfrac{1}{4}$, so B is also false.

18. **D** Since the radius to the point of tangency is perpendicular to the tangent OR must be perpendicular to PR. Therefore, ORP is a right triangle, and $(PO)^2 = (OR)^2 + (PR)^2$. Then, $(PR)^2 = (PO)^2 - (OR)^2$. Thus, $(PR)^2 = 4^2 - 2^2$, and $PR = \sqrt{16 - 4} = \sqrt{12} = \sqrt{4}\sqrt{3} = 2\sqrt{3}$.

19. **B** After the tune-up, the bus will travel $(1.15)(15) = 17.25$ miles on a gallon of gas. Therefore, it will take $(150) \div (17.25) = 8.7$ (to the nearest tenth) gallons of gasoline to travel 150 miles.

20. **E** If $x/y = 2$, then $x = 2y$, so $x + 2y = 2y + 2y = 4y$. But $x + 2y = 4$, so $4y = 4$, or $y = 1$. Since $x = 2y$, x must be 2.

21. **D** Since $2\frac{1}{2}$ hours is 150 minutes we can see the corresponding speed on the table.

22. **C** The train's speed increased by 70 – 40 which is 30 miles per hour. 30/40 is 75%.

23. **D** When $t = 0$, the speed is 40, so A and B are incorrect. When $t = 180$, the speed is 70, so C and E are incorrect. Choice D gives all the values which appear in the table.

24. **A** The cost of producing the first 8,000 copies is $1,000 + 7,000x$. $1,000 + 7,000x = \$7,230$. Therefore, $7,000x = 6,230$ and $x = .89$.

25. **E** Assume all workers work at the same rate unless given different information. Since 16 workers take 3 hours, each worker does $\frac{1}{48}$ of the job an hour. Thus, the 5 workers will finish $\frac{5}{48}$ of the job each hour. $\frac{5}{48}x = \frac{48}{48}$. It will take $\frac{48}{5} = 9\frac{3}{5}$ hours for them to finish the job.

Self-Assessment: As you went through these practice exercises were you able to finish them in the time allotted? Did you have trouble handling the computations involved? Evaluate your performance. Did you spend so much time on one question that you never got to answer two or three others? Did you forget to leave yourself a minute or two to fill in your guesses? If you fell into these common errors during this practice, be sure to avoid them as you take the model tests.

Chapter 5

Writing Skills Review

PURPOSE OF THE WRITING TEST

1. Writing is thinking on paper. Your ability to reason can be measured by your ability to write. You can, by writing, show your ability to isolate a topic and to support it with examples to make a point.

2. Writing is the best way to determine your understanding and application of the rules of our language.

3. Teachers, like writers, must have the ability to organize interesting lessons, or thoughts, clearly. As a teacher, you will have to think and respond to a variety of unexpected situations where you will be forced to demonstrate your mastery of correct English.

DESIGN OF THE TEST

It is important to remember that your essays will be read not by machines but by people—real people with feelings, moods, likes and dislikes, who have the capacity to laugh, grow angry, and be moved. In most ways, they are probably not much different from you, except that they have had more experience as teachers. Consequently, they will enjoy reading an essay that is informative, entertaining, interesting, and clear. On the other hand, they will be put off by writing that is garbled, phony, or downright dull. As you write, therefore, keep your readers in mind. Write as one human being to another. Let your essays be an exercise in person-to-person communication.

You will respond to two essay topics. One will ask you for your opinion about a statement or a situation. The other will ask you to share a personal experience. You can give yourself as much time as you feel you need within the four-hour time frame, but remember to allow yourself enough time for the math and reading portion of the exam. Most candidates evenly split the hour into 30-minute time frames; however, each writer knows what his or her strengths are and can balance the time accordingly.

You do not need to follow a prescribed pattern, such as the traditional five-paragraph essay. Most successful candidates answer within three to six paragraphs. Your essay should be well organized and interesting. Establish a compelling topic in the first paragraph and develop supporting paragraphs that lead the reader to a logical conclusion. Straying off topic can result in failing the essay exam, no matter how well written the essay.

Evaluating Your Essays

Evaluators are trained to read your essays quickly, without making editing or revision notes. In other words, they read for a quick and general impression. They spend no more than two or three minutes per essay. The strengths and weakness of your work will produce a cumulative effect on the reader. Frequent grammar and spelling errors that impede the clarity of the writing can hurt your score. Evaluating essays is not an exact science. However, most of the readers' judgments will vary little. Your papers will be scored from 1–4. The highest score will earn a 4. A score of 3 is a marginal pass. A score of 2 is a marginal fail, and a score of 1 is unacceptable.

If your English teachers have generally liked your writing, then it's probably safe to assume that you will pass the exam. However, if no one has ever praised your work, this is no time for you to prove that you are the next James Joyce. The evaluators are not going to publish your work, no matter how good your essay is. It will at best earn a 4—nothing more. In short, do not experiment. The readers are simply judging whether the essays are successful or not.

What does it take to write well? Some writers have the uncanny ability to note every detail of an experience and hold our attention through a complex weaving of artistic phrases. Others know what to leave out of a story and still illustrate their point. There is no single answer to what determines good writing, but the readers of the CBEST™ essays will more than likely agree to what is passing and what is not. Usually, an excellent essay demonstrates all of the following skills:

- It has an engaging idea established with an original thesis. This thesis is supported with details, reasons, and examples.

- The paragraphs do not lack unity; there are clear transitions between paragraphs; and the idea comes to a logical conclusion.

- The writer also chooses accurate nouns and adjectives and lively verbs, demonstrating a command of vocabulary.

- His or her sentences vary; the structure is not repetitious and predictable.

- The writing, though not necessarily flawless, is not impeded by frequent grammar, mechanical, or spelling errors.

The type of essay mentioned above would earn a score of 4. A good essay, one earning a score of 3, may demonstrate most of the same elements, but may not be as compelling. Or it may have one too many usage errors.

An adequate essay, which would earn a score of 3, will usually demonstrate the following concerns:

- It is organized around a thesis, but is too general, lacking the details the superior essays demonstrate.

- It is clearly written but does not demonstrate a satisfactory command of vocabulary, variety of sentence structure, and control of grammar.

- It is effective but lacks imagination.

An inadequate essay, earning a score of 2, will usually have the following problems:

- It may not have a thesis; it might ramble without organization.

- There are frequent sentence errors that reveal a lack of writing skill.

- There are serious punctuation errors, usage problems, and misspelled words.

A paper with the problems mentioned above might show potential but does not meet minimal standards. Some review and practice could help the writer improve his chances of passing next time.

A paper scoring a 1 might be off topic, but more than likely it is poorly written. The candidate should take a basic writing course.

THE TESTING MIND-SET

Some candidates claim to be lucky. One told me that she believed the only reason she passed the writing portion was that on that particular day, one of the essay questions excited her imagination. I'm willing to bet that she underestimates her ability to write under pressure. If luck were the trick, then there would be no need to prepare for exams.

Some students love tests because they love a challenge, especially one that will prove their skills, and this is a good way to look at this test. It is good to be confident, but overconfidence can make one careless, and carelessness can lead to failure. Most people experience anxiety before and during an exam, and it can overwhelm them. But anxiety, channeled the right way, can elevate your state of awareness. Somewhere between overconfidence and anxiety is "presence of mind" where one sees clearly and responds accurately. Athletes, Zen Buddhists, and jazz musicians are familiar with this state. Some call it *the zone*. The question is, how do you achieve it?

How do you find *the zone*? Practice and take nothing for granted. Even if you are a published writer, you cannot assume that the writing portion of the test will be a breeze. In fact, a professional writer, who is used to numerous rewrites, might perform poorly at such a task. This test is not looking for a professional essay: it is looking for a clearly written response.

You cannot study for this exam by using rote memorization. You do not know the questions that will be asked of you. But you have a general idea of the type of questions that will be asked, and that should be the help you need.

First, set some time aside for yourself. Second, create a quiet environment. Third, use a kitchen timer, and write an essay in half an hour. In time, write two in an hour.

If you know your weaknesses, work with a tutor. Use the study lessons in this text, but seek a second opinion from a trusted friend or a teacher who can give you an honest assessment of your work.

Before Taking the Writing Skills Exam

Practice writing every day. Write letters to the editor of your local newspaper, to friends, and to politicians. Take a writing course if need be, but practice. If you are a student, take the exam as soon as possible. Your writing skills will probably never be better than they are after immediately completing a writing course. If you're still a student, take another writing course for college credit. If you have practiced writing timed-response essays and feel you are ready to take the exam, apply for the next testing date as soon as possible.

You should assume a positive attitude. Making this test bigger than life will only instill fear and limit your ability to think clearly. Unless you purposely avoided every hard course your college had to offer, you more than likely have mastered the skills necessary to pass this exam. Keep in mind that you could not have come this far in your education unless you had the measurable abilities this exam looks for.

Strategies for the Writing Portion of the Exam

1. When writing, keep to the point. Allow the expansion of your essay to come from the examples and reasons that support your theme. Avoid drifting.

2. Avoid editorializing in your writing response. Do not express your resentments about taking the exam. Stay on topic.

3. Write in the first person, *I,* in your personal response. Use the appropriate person at all times.

4. Assume a serious attitude.

5. Write what you know. It may not be from a personal experience, but you may be aware of a situation that you've read about thoroughly, or you may have a friend who has shared an experience with you.

Getting the Most Out of Thirty Minutes

There are writers who can whip out an essay off the top of their heads with little effort. Some even thrive under pressure. But many good students fritter away their time because they can't organize their thoughts quickly enough.

A good introduction should allow the body and conclusion to follow easily. Practice clarifying your opening statements. But before you write— think.

Revise and edit. Check off the following steps:

Step 1   Often writers force an essay around an idea that does not work. Eliminate any ideas that impede the clarity of your organization.

Step 2   Add ideas. Often your phrasing is missing a point that could clarify your essay and make the difference between confusion or clarity.

Step 3   Sometimes rearranging the order of the ideas can help, but adding ideas and rearranging them can be tricky because of the length of time it may take.

Step 4   After you've made your revision, proofread for errors. If you can fold a piece of paper or use the edge of your test booklet, make a straightedge and, going down line by line, double-check for obvious errors. You may not catch all of them, but the fewer warts remaining, the better your chances of receiving a passing score.

THINK AHEAD

The Length of Your Essay

An essay of 250 to 400 words, though brief, will do. Two hundred and fifty words is approximately one typed page. This is a relatively short essay, so the focus should be tight. Less than 250 might pass, if the writing is exceptional. The quality of your writing is more important than the length. As a rule, essays shorter than 250 words seem anemic and oversimplified.

Structured and Unstructured Exam Questions

There is usually a structure to most of the essay questions. In a sense, they give you the answer. There is a *good* and *bad side* to this. The *good side* is that by answering a structured question, you know the direction of your essay. The *bad side* is that it can be inflexible; that is, by not answering all of the concerns asked in the prompt, you might not complete the writing task. Follow these steps: read the questions carefully, know what is expected from you, check off each issue asked in the prompt, and make sure you've covered each issue as completely as you can.

Example of a Structured Question

You more than likely know someone who has become very successful. This success has in some ways changed him or her. Organize a well written essay in which you do the following:

- Identify and describe this person who became successful and then changed.

- Explain what you believe is different about this person.

- Explain why this person has achieved success, and how he or she is now different.

The above question is structured for you. As you answer it, check off the examples and explanations you've listed. If you are stuck and cannot answer the question, use the six *W*'s: *who, what, how, when, where,* and *why.* For example, it should be easy enough to *identify* the person you are supposed to write about; so answering *who* is not relevant at this point. However, in answering what "is different about this person," use *how, when,* and *where* to illustrate further. When explaining *why* he was successful, use *what, who, when,* and *where* to give more details to the answer.

Unstructured Questions

When there is no plan or specific questions like the one above, the question is unstructured. The direction of the essay is up to you. You will have to create your own guideline. This might be to your advantage because this type of question will free your imagination. However, some people will feel more comfortable with a structured question. If this is the case, the solution is simple: reframe the question in a structured manner.

Example of an Unstructured Question

Contrast the motivation of gun control advocates to those who oppose gun control.

The question is wide open, and for some writers this can lead to panic. To solve this problem, break down the question into a list of questions:

- *What* is gun control and *what* reasons might exist behind both sides of the issue?

- *Who* supports or opposes gun control?

- *Why* do they advocate or oppose gun control?

- *Where* has gun control been successful or unsuccessful?

- *How* is gun control implemented?

- *When* is it necessary to control the ownership of guns?

Remember, just as I suggested using the six W's for the structured questions, you can do the same here. In fact, the six W's might be easier to apply to an unstructured question.

The unstructured question is now structured. You can use this technique any time the essay question seems a bit vague. By asking questions, you can narrow your focus and organize your ideas quickly.

Key Words Used in Essay Questions

ANALYZE: Literally it means to "loosen up" or break down. In practice you will break a single thing or idea into its component parts and then show how those parts are related and essential. Explore connections within the subject of the essay.

COMPARE AND CONTRAST: These methods are usually linked, but may be used separately. A careful user of language will discriminate clearly between them. To compare is to discuss similarities; to contrast is to discuss differences. Comparison-contrast discussions should be balanced.

DEFINE: Set forth the meaning of a thing, idea, or quality by answering the question, "What is it? What does it mean?" After narrowing the thing or idea into a word, put the word into a general classification (*Anger is an emotion*), and then limit its meaning by using description (*How does it look, sound, smell, feel?*); examples (*What other things are like this?*); comparison/contrast (*How is it like/unlike related things?*); value (*What is its function? How important is it?*); and process (*How is it made?*)

DESCRIBE: Create a verbal picture of the subject by relying on the senses of sight, sound, touch, taste, and smell. A careful selection of details is important to satisfy your readers and accomplish your purpose.

DISCUSS: Raise some important issues about a topic and treat them fully over several paragraphs.

EVALUATE: Determine the merit, value, stature, relevance, or truthfulness of a statement or idea. To evaluate a statement, find the thesis, determine what points have been made to support the thesis, and then write a statement declaring whether the points are valid. (*Do they really support the thesis? Are they accurate, current, sound? Are they really relevant to the thesis?*)

EXPLAIN: Clarify an opinion or idea by laying it all out on the table, revealing causes, justifications, and relevant points.

IDENTIFY: Name clearly and specifically the thing that is asked.

PROVE: Determine the truth of an assertion or idea by presenting evidence, logical arguments, or corroborative testimony.

RELATE: Show how things are associated with each other by comparing, matching, equating, or pairing them (as in a cause-and-effect relationship).

STATE: Present the main point clearly and definitively with minimal supporting material.

SUMMARIZE: Condense an argument or discussion by highlighting its main points, omitting supporting material like examples, details, or illustrations which comprise the body of an essay.

Prewriting Strategy

There are numerous prewriting tactics that will help you narrow your topic and expand upon it in an essay. The most important thing to do is to think before you write. Having an idea of what you want to write about and how you want to illustrate it is half the battle. The following are a number of ways you can organize your thoughts quickly.

I. Listing

By listing the ideas that can help develop your focal point, you can see if you have enough material for a well-developed essay. If the topic from the exam asks you to write an argument on drug testing in the workplace, you might quickly jot down the following items:

A. The pros of drug testing in the workplace.
   1. Drug abusers are a danger to others and themselves.
   2. Drug abusers make careless mistakes that cost their employers money.
   3. Many drug abusers have a higher rate of tardiness and absenteeism.
   4. Many workers are demoralized by having to cover for drugged workers who are incapable of performing their jobs properly.

B. The cons of drug testing.
   1. Drug testing is a violation of privacy.
   2. What an individual does at home on his or her own time is no one else's concern.
   3. Alcohol and tobacco use are far more debilitating than drugs like marijuana, but using marijuana could jeopardize your employment; whereas, the use of cigarettes and alcohol is socially tolerated.
   4. There are false positive test readings that can ruin innocent people.
   5. We are giving too much control of our lives to corporations.

It does not matter what order you have the items in at this point. You can prioritize them later. If a list like the one above does not come quickly, or if it is too short, rethink your topic. Remember time is important. You don't want a prizewinning list at the expense of failing the essay.

II. Clustering

If you've attended a high school, a college, or a university in the past decade, you most likely have seen your teachers use a cluster on a chalkboard. In fact, you have probably used it yourself. If you haven't, clustering

EXAMPLE

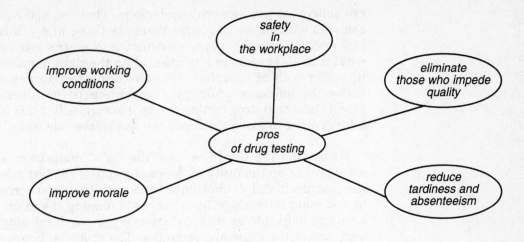

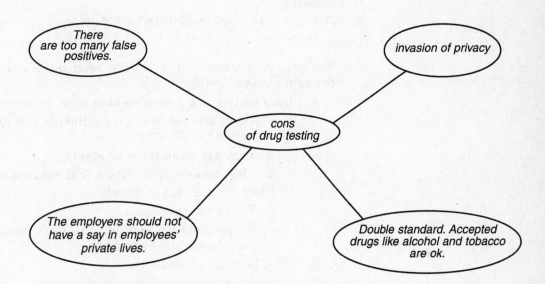

is a way of brainstorming. It's a simple process of starting with a word that comes from your topic; it could include an entire sentence. Circle it and make free associations with the word or concept.

You can prioritize the order any way that suits your writing strategy.

III. Freewriting

Experienced writers often use the freewriting technique because it allows them to jump right into the essay headfirst with eyes closed. If you're comfortable with it, try it. But freewriting often requires lots of revision. It is a process of chipping away mental granite in order to shape a concept. Of course, this requires more time than most test takers have to write a successful essay. Remember, this is not the time to experiment. But if you are a confident freewriter, go for it.

EXAMPLE

Testing workers for drug abuse in the workplace might be an invasion of privacy, but it is becoming necessary. The amount of lost productivity due to the use of drugs hurts everybody. Workers, under the influence of drugs, are dangerous to themselves and others. They can make costly errors that can ruin a business. Of course there are those who will call drug testing just another way for corporate America to control our private lives, but what is at stake is more important than the right to privacy. If productivity suffers, all of us suffer. We can't compete internationally if we are under the influence of drugs. Competition is the American way. Some might claim that drug testing can be inaccurate. But this is a risk we must take in order to make the American workplace safe, sane, and productive.

Notice that the third line from the end—"competition is the American way" breaks up the unity of the paragraph. If the test taker wrote this in the first draft and did not have time to go back and correct the work, he or she could hurt his or her chances of passing the exam. But this could easily be built into an essay; there is a process developing here. The pros and cons of the issue are emerging. The problem, however, is that some topics do not easily allow for the free association of ideas to come into an immediate focus. The writer may meander without developing a point.

IV. Mapping
Mapping is a form of quick and simple outlining.

Thesis:

I. The pros and cons of drug testing need to be examined carefully before making a decision.
  A. Drug testing is a good idea because it improves productivity.
    1. Workers who are under the influence cost employers lots of money.
      a. They are often tardy or absent.
      b. They make serious errors that are costly.
    2. They are a threat to morale.
      a. They cause accidents.
      b. Responsible workers have to work harder to cover the mistakes of the drug users.
  B. Drug testing is a bad idea.
    1. Drug testing is an invasion of privacy.
    2. Drug testing can be wrong.
      a. There are false positive.
      b. Innocent people can be ruined.
    3. There is a double standard to socially accepted substances.
      a. Alcohol and tobacco are socially accepted, but just as bad as other drugs.
      b. Marijuana use could jeopardize employment.

The Impromptu Essay

The impromptu essay can throw a writer off because he or she can never really anticipate the topic. In most writing assignments, the writers can take their time. With few exceptions, most of us write far better at home where we can revise, proofread, edit, and rewrite. At home we can use a grammar text, a dictionary, or a word processor that can check for spelling and grammar as well. Take-home essays can be reviewed by family members or friends. Unlike take-home essays, an impromptu essay takes you by surprise, but some topics are easy to respond to.

Though there are different types of formats for essays, the most standard are the safest. At home you can make certain that your writing includes the basic standards of an essay:

I. Establish a clear beginning with an introductory paragraph.
   A. Begin the introduction with a topic sentence that defines or isolates the issue of your essay.
      1. This topic sentence might be somewhat general in its statement.
         a. Do not confuse it with the thesis sentence.
      2. The introductory paragraph can take several sentences.
      3. It provides details that will be developed throughout the essay.
   B. End your first paragraph with your thesis.
      1. You have narrowed the topic to a particular point of view that will be the focus of your essay.
      2. Your thesis sentence should lay out the main points that will follow in subsequent paragraphs.
II. The body of the essay is detailed, answers the questions, solves the problems, or continues to define the issues proposed in your introduction.
   A. Your second paragraph begins the body of your essay.
      1. It logically connects to the first paragraph,
         a. It will be connected with clear transitions into the following paragraph.
      2. The third and subsequent paragraphs do the same.
   B. The body of the essay leads the reader to a logical conclusion.
III. The conclusion arrives at a final point to sum up all the ideas that the paper has established. It answers the big question or solves a problem posed in the thesis.

Since you won't have the luxury to outline the guideline suggested above, you need to become familiar with the process by practicing at home. A quick way to recall the guideline is to think of it as:

Simple Strategies
1. Define the issue (explain the topic).
2. Develop it (give examples).
3. Draw a conclusion (suggest a solution or answer a question).

Defines	Mike is one of the best students I've ever had and should do well in a university. Like all good
Develops	students, he studies very hard and takes his work seriously. He will be an excellent candi-
Draws Conclusion	date for a top-notch university.

When you are assigned a topic, think about it first. If you can, use the simple steps listed above.

Think of your opening paragraph as a seed from which the ideas grow. In this seed, the genetic code of your essay is formed. By keeping this in mind, unity (beginning, middle, and conclusion) will be easily achieved.

ESSAY TYPES ON THE CBEST™

1. Personal experience

2. Explanatory/Analytic

You will have 60 minutes to write two essays, a personal experience essay and an analytical essay. Either one of the types can be structured or unstructured, but the majority tend to be structured. You will notice in our more detailed look at each of these essay types below, that there is considerable crossover between them.

The Personal Experience Essay

Personal experience essays are by far the most prevalent, requiring personal narratives and descriptions on the part of the writer. Commonly, the student is asked to draw on personal experiences to write these essays. Topics include reminiscences about people or past events, situations at home, school, or in the community, current events and issues, observations about the media, hobbies, personal successes and accomplishments, changes the writer would like to see made, career choices, and the like. Most of these questions are structured so that the student has no doubt about the task at hand.

EXAMPLE

Identify one person who has had a measurable effect on your life. Describe the person and the effect he or she has generated, the means by which the effect was brought about, and the difference the effect has made in your life.

Sample Essay Beginning

There are many people who have had a positive impact on my life, but the one with the most measurable contribution is my high school math teacher, Mr. Newcomb, in whose math classes I spent one semester of my freshman year, and my entire junior and senior years.

(In three developmental sections of the essay, each of which could be written in one or more paragraphs, the writer would then describe Mr. Newcomb and the change he brought about; provide specific and concrete details about the way Mr. Newcomb produced the change, possibly including the ways in which he bolstered the self-confidence of the writer; and then detail the differences Mr. Newcomb's contribution has made in the student's life.)

EXAMPLE

There are very few truly solitary individuals today, so insistently are group activities woven into the patterns of American society. Describe some groups you have been a part of, explaining which you wish you had never joined and which have had a positive influence on your life. Do not merely list the groups. Be sure to describe them specifically, explaining what you did in each group and why you consider each group a good or bad influence.

Sample Essay Beginning

When I was a little girl, my mother eagerly forced me into groups which are to blame for my present feelings of disdain toward softball, gymnastics, karate, and church music. However, I feel I am a stronger, more capable person today because of other groups I was also eagerly forced to join, such as Girl Scouts, 4H, and International Pen Pals.

(In two or three paragraphs for each, the writer can go on to describe the unfavorable groups first, being careful to supply the specific information the question calls for, and then do the same for the beneficial groups, ending the essay with a one- or two-sentence conclusion.)

Here is a full Personal Experience question and essay response:

Describe an incident in which you or someone close to you was cut from a team or rejected in some manner from a group or activity. Be sure to explain the logic behind the reasons for the initial rejection, the reasons you feel the refusal was just or unjust, and the longer-term effect of the incident upon you and your behavior. (30 minutes)

During my first year in college I was cut from the baseball team. To most people that would be a minor bummer in their lives, but to me and my family, it was more of a calamity, in fact, more like a death in the family. To explain why, I need to digress here and explain something about my past few years.

All through my life I have played and excelled at ball, from the time I played T-ball at the Sylmar Independent Baseball League to my first year in college. My mother and father were always a part of my experience; in fact, I have never played a game without one or the other watching. As long ago as my last year in elementary school I was singled out as a real prospect. Two coaches from different high schools used to keep track of me that year when I was pitching for the Broncos, an independent sports organization in the West Valley. Curt Daniels, my coach at that time, said that, in his thirty years of coaching, he had never seen a more promising ballplayer. At Garrison High School in Canoga Park you can still see plaques and cups awarded to me in the trophy room.

During my last season at Garrison High, my coach, Ansel Williams, invited major league scouts to our games. I was offered a job with the Cincinnati and Houston farm systems, but my mother in particular wanted me to go to college. I could have gone practically anywhere, but I settled on USC because of their great baseball tradition.

All this time, I was really playing great. My ERA never dropped below 2.40. The last two seasons of high school ball my elbow had hurt and become swollen after every game, but the pain never kept me from pitching; and the excitement of those years, when I was a hero of the school and even appeared in national sports magazines as a top recruiting prospect, seemed so much more important than a little pain. I never even mentioned the pain to anyone. I just got in the habit of putting ice on my elbow when I got home.

In the first practice game I pitched at USC, disaster struck. Suddenly my arm hurt so badly that I couldn't even lob the ball. Nothing helped—rest, massage, heat, ice—nothing. I was sent by the team doctor to an orthopedic surgeon who did a spread of tests and then told me the bad news. I had literally worn down the cartilage at several key spots in my elbow. There was no quick fix. The elbow could be replaced but at a cost of two to $300,000, and even then there was no guarantee that I could pitch well. The doc said that I had done all the damage when I was much younger, while the cartilage was being formed on the growing bone. The coach had no option but to cut me from the team. I understood. He had other prospects waiting in line who wanted to play. His job was to put the best team together not to wipe the noses of those who cannot play.

Meanwhile, I have had a rebirth of sorts. I never had been much of a student, but suddenly I became interested. I learned a lot about anatomy when all those probes and CAT scans were made of my elbow. I was fascinated by orthopedic medicine. I determined to become a premed major and see what else the world holds for me. So far, it's giving me much more of a kick than baseball.

Evaluation of Essay

This is a well-organized, well-written, natural sounding response to the question. The writer spells out the incident straightforwardly and then effectively shifts to the events leading up to the rejection, in the process supplying enough background information to fulfill each of the points requested in the prompt: the reasons for the rejection, the writer's feelings about the equity of the cut, and the long-term effects. Paragraph 1 clearly proclaims the thesis of the entire essay, which is unwaveringly addressed in every paragraph.

Faults in the essay are its colloquial style, its use of contractions, for example, and slang terms like "doc" and "bummer." The final paragraph is so sparse of detail that it seems abrupt. Likely score: 3 of 4 points.

Here is an example of another personal experience topic developed into an essay:

"Dreams are but the touchstones of our characters."
Henry David Thoreau

A touchstone is a hard, flint-like stone that for centuries was used to test the authenticity of gold or silver. Now, the word touchstone has come to mean any criterion or test used to measure the quality of a thing.

In a well-structured essay, describe a dream you or someone you know well attempted to fulfill, only to discover that the dream did not match the reality. Compare and contrast the dream with its own fulfillment. Show in what ways your life was changed because of your discovery. (30 minutes)

Partial Dream

Ten years ago, when I finally received permission from the Department of Immigration and Naturalization to move to Los Angeles from my native homeland of Seoul, Korea, I thought I was in heaven. Not only was I going to the promised land, America, but I was going to the movie capital of the world, Hollywood. My family and I arrived at Los Angeles International Airport on May 3, 1981, and it was a very few weeks before our lavish dreams were confronted by a very cold reality.

The America I had fabricated in my imagination was the product of American movies, magazines, and advertisements, all a major source of entertainment and information to Koreans. Every day was sunny, and every house was on a beautiful tree-shaded street, each with a large, aquamarine pool in the back yard. The schools (I was a high-school sophomore at the time) were modern facilities with the finest of teachers; standards were high, and the student body was fun-loving, friendly, and eager to learn. How could it be any other way? After all, this was America, the mightiest, the wealthiest, the most scientifically and technologically advanced nation in the history of all mankind. How could such an advanced and learned country possibly maintain itself in such a position of leadership without its young people being students of this quality?

Our first shock came when we drove by taxi to our pre-arranged apartment in North Hollywood. The ride itself was not very pretty. Where were the flowers and wide expanses of green grass? Where was the sunshine? The streets leading to our new home were not clean. There was graffiti all over the walls and houses. Young, aimless men stood around doing nothing, some of them drinking from a can or bottle covered by a small paper bag. We were to learn from our new Korean neighbors that the neighborhood was not safe, and that one had to be careful at all times.

Yet even this was minor compared to what I discovered about the Los Angeles schools. Unlike the high school in Seoul I had just left, where all students were, to be plain, devoting their entire lives to the business of learning, spending nine-hour days in class six days a week, with virtually no time for play, this school was a place of leisure. Students wandered late into each class, and the instructor often sat at the front of the room doing something at his desk while the students chatted for maybe a third of the period. Once the instruction started, if the teacher began asking questions about the assignment or the topic at hand, almost nobody had done the work. If the teacher called on individual students, one after another would say he had not done the homework. The tests on the subject were so easy that a reasonably smart student who had done most of the very easy homework assigned could earn an "A." Once I began to be familiar with the students in the class, I realized how high the absence rate is, and how tolerated it is by the authorities. Eventually I transferred to a magnet school with honors classes, but, while the situation was better, it was still a school with surprisingly low standards and sadly unmotivated students compared to the high school I had left back home.

My general feeling about America is not one of disappointment, as one might expect, but a realization that America needs some help now that maybe I can give. I have chosen education as a career, and I hope that some day I am able to make some changes, even if they are small changes. I hope to be a naturalized citizen soon, and, when I am, I hope to be an active, helpful part of this great nation, and perhaps, just perhaps, move it closer to the ideal I once carried.

Evaluation of Essay

The first paragraph introduces the topic by identifying a dream and hinting at the contrasting reality. The thesis is set forth in the sentence "... it was a very few weeks before our lavish dreams were confronted by a very cold reality," and it is developed in well-detailed paragraphs. The last paragraph holds a surprise ending, a positive statement that runs against the negative grain of the essay, yet manages to help unify and finish it. Likely score: 3½ of 4 points.

The Explanatory/Analytic Essay

An explanatory essay question calls for the writer to explain current issues and ideas, controversies, difficulties, or opinions. A typical question of this type is the following:

The drive for racial equality has been a major factor of the last two decades. Virtually no public institution and few private ones have been unaffected by affirmative action laws and regulations. Explain ways in which your workplace or community has been changed by such human rights regulations.

A more complex dimension is added to such a question when the student is asked to analyze such material; that is, to break it into its component parts and perform a task with those parts such as comparing them or evaluating them or characterizing them in some way.

- Technical analysis answers the question, "How is it put together?" and almost always occurs with functional analysis.
- Functional analysis answers the question, "How does it work?"
- Process analysis answers the question, "How is it done?"
- Causal analysis answers the question, "What caused it?"
- Qualitative analysis answers the questions, "How good or important or true is it?"

Whatever the type of analysis, you can be sure that the question will call for an explosion or segmentation of a single item or idea into its elements. Take the following explanatory/analytic question:

Some people feel the world is advancing too fast and that "modern is not always better." Choose some recent (within 50 years) technological invention or discovery and show that it has some negative spinoffs. Explain how the negative impact of the invention or discovery has affected you and your life. What are the long-term effects of the innovation on the world?

Sample Essay Beginning

The invention of the computer took place about fifty years ago, and, since that time, it has brought the human population of the world untold advantages. Computers keep our bank accounts and issue our pay checks. Computers run our airlines and practically manufacture products like toasters, washing machines, and automobiles. Without computers, this country could not have sent missions to the moon, and without them, we could not perform open-heart surgery, unravel the mysteries of DNA, or watch an event live from the other side of the globe. However, the computerization of man's life on earth has so quickened every transaction and so ruthlessly made every person accountable so frequently, that it has taken a toll of another sort, a toll on the minds and spirits of individuals like you and me.

The writer can now go on to explain how the quickening of transactions and imposition of frequent accountability is taking a toll on our minds and spirits. One way of developing these ideas is to write a paragraph about the "quickening" and another about the "frequent accountability." The writer should always maintain the supremacy of the thesis sentence written in paragraph one: "...the computerization of man's life...has taken a toll." It should also be remembered that the question calls for an analysis of the word computerization, that is, a separation of the word into all of its aspects. In this paper, the writer is locked into negative aspects by the topic. A concluding paragraph might issue some hope for the negative state of affairs.

Here is another explanatory/analytic question.

Please read and give some thought to the following two quotations:

A. "There's one born every minute." P.T. Barnum

B. "It is true that you may fool all the people some of the time; you can even fool some of the people all the time; but you can't fool all of the people all the time." A. Lincoln

Write an essay on the two statements in three parts, as follows:

1. **Compare the statements. Explain what the two statements have in common and how they overlap.**
2. **Contrast the statements. Explain how the two statements differ.**
3. **Explain what your position is regarding the two statements by choosing one or describing the favorable and unfavorable aspects of each. Support your view with examples from your personal experience.**

Sample Essay Beginning

The two quotations above deal with the naiveté and innocence of the public, especially where public pronouncements of famous personalities like politicians and showmen are concerned. However, one quotation differs from the other very clearly because it seems more respectful of the public than the other, and seeks, in fact, to salute it. I believe Lincoln's statement is, upon some analysis, a very astute and credible description of the different stages the public goes through in making political decisions.

The writer can proceed to develop the three parts called for in the question, a paragraph or two about the similarity of the statements and ways in which they overlap, another paragraph or two about their differences, and finally a section dealing with the relative values of the quotations, supported by specific observations the writer has made about the public and politics.

Here is a question and complete essay in the Explanatory/Analytic mode.

We all attempt to make a change for the better at some time in our lives. In fact, all progress made on this planet has been the result of humanity's quest for a better life. Think of a major "change for the better" that you experienced or witnessed in your lifetime, a significant change involving several stages or steps over a period of time. Identify the change, discuss each of its steps, and the effects each step had on you or the principals involved. Be sure to explain how the final outcome was a change for the better.

Student Response

Kadan is a small town in northern Czechoslovakia. It was established in the thirteenth century when King, and also Emperor, Charles IV was traveling through Czech country looking for a piece of beautiful land. I had the good fortune to live in Kadan for twelve years. During those twelve years, I witnessed major changes that were made in the town, most of which affected me profoundly.

I was six years old when my family moved to Kadan. My first impression of the place was one of crushing disappointment. All I could see were several old historical buildings, dingy houses, various churches, and castles in very deteriorated condition. It was like a bad dream. I could not picture myself living and growing up in the middle of this town. There were about ten apartment houses that made up a very large complex. All of them looked exactly the same. It reminded me of boxes that were put together to make a discouraging impression for immigrants coming to town.

The second day after our arrival, we went to see the town. It took us no time to find the central area with an old town hall and a monument to a WWI soldier in the middle of the square. There were not many shops. I remember seeing a police station, an elementary school, a fire station, a few pubs, a very old and unkempt movie theater, and a nondescript hospital.

Without a smile on our faces, my brother and I accepted the reality and started attending elementary school the following Monday. We settled down to routine work in a few days. During the third week or so, we returned home to find a massive construction project beginning right next to our apartment house. Within a couple of months, a beautiful sports complex was completed. We were able to play tennis whenever we wanted, or go swimming all year long. I developed skill at both sports, and won several championships in swimming. My self-confidence began to rise, and I saw life as positive and good.

It did not even take one more year for Kadan to build a truly beautiful hospital with a clean brick and stainless steel design, two more complexes of apartments in more attractive buildings, and a huge shopping center. Life in the town became more enjoyable. The new additions brought jobs, opportunities, and variety to our lives.

A year or so later, a committee made up of well-known architects and other experts evaluated the old historical center of the town. Consequently, most of the buildings were reconstructed from top to bottom, and afterwards, the town center was an incredibly beautiful sight to behold. The committee converted one part of the main castle to a gallery and museum. We people in the town became very interested in the history of our town, and began to take great pride in this captivating place we inhabited.

During the next ten years, Kadan became the most beautiful town in Czechoslovakia, and the most historically exciting. Three new secondary schools were built, and became so popular that students attended from all over the world. A magnificent Greek theater was carved out of a hillside near the town center; within a year, the town was treated to a stunning series of concerts and plays by the world's greatest playwrights and composers. Again, I personally benefited from this innovation. Directly because of the inspiration I received from those wonderful evenings, I became a humanities major and even took up acting.

In the summer months, Kadan was full of tourists and visitors. Parks, tennis courts, and playgrounds were crowded, and it was difficult to eat in any of the wonderful restaurants without a reservation. I could not believe that this was the same bleak town I had moved to just a few years earlier. Suddenly there were so many nice and fascinating places to go, and so many rich and historical treasures to study. The inhabitants of Kadan are proud of their town, and they take good care of it. It is now full of flowers, little parks, and trees. It seems we have all been transformed by the physical changes made in the town.

Evaluation of Essay

This well-organized, well-written essay fulfills in detail the assignment's instructions to write about some progressive changes that took place, in this case, in the Czechoslovakian town of Kadan. The writer is careful to explain the beneficial effect of each change, not only on the people of the town, but on the writer herself, as well as long-term effects of the change. In doing so, the writer writes analytically.

Representative Essays to Sample

The following four essays are student papers that are likely to pass any writing proficiency test, though they vary considerably in quality. Then practice your writing with the sample topics that follow.

Personal Experience

ESSAY 1

Many great stories are based on the events surrounding a natural disaster such as an earthquake, flood, volcanic eruption, tornado, hurricane, or tidal wave. To be sure, many human beings live these dramas daily. What disaster is likely to hit your home? How, or how should you be prepared for such a disaster? What kinds of problems are you liable to encounter in the event of such an occurrence? (30 minutes)

Being aware how many faults lie below us in California makes one realize that earthquakes are a possibility in our lives every living moment we stay in California. California is part of two enormous geologic plates, the Pacific Rim Plate and the Continental Plate. In reality, that means we have two very active forces hitting against each other just beneath us. The last big earthquake we had in this area was the Sylmar earthquake of 1971 which was the result of movement in a fault that had not been active since before the Ice Age and that scientists had labeled extinct.

Being prepared for an earthquake ahead of time can mean the difference between survival with minimum consequences and personal injury, damage, and loss. Preparation means stocking up on essential survival items, taking some important precautions in your home and place of business, and preparing to cope with the psychological trauma a really bad temblor can cause.

To be prepared for an earthquake, a person needs to store a minimum of two weeks of supplies. In a big quake, all services and supply lines are inactive and nonfunctioning. Even gas pumps in gas stations will be out, because there will be no electricity for weeks. Water is the first essential. It may be needed to put fires out, for fires are an ever-present consequence of earthquakes. It may be needed to clean up dangerous spills. If people are hurt, water will be needed to wash their wounds. And, of course, water is personally needed to drink and clean up. Wise people have a water flow tank to store their emergency water supply, that is, a tank of a thousand gallons or so that is part of the normal circulating flow of water to your home and so does not need changing at regular intervals. Otherwise, the swimming pool or hot water tank can be considered a source. At the very least, all families in California should store 25 gallons of water for every person in their family. Canned, freeze dried, MRE paks, and so on is an essential as well, at least enough food to last two weeks. Flashlights and radios with storage-tolerant batteries are an absolute necessity.

Blankets, medical supplies, extra shoes, clothing, pet food if necessary, and money are also essentials to store away, money because cash is king in a natural disaster which will probably be the only tender accepted. Your car should also have a few esssential supplies, particularly water, a flashlight, and a radio in case you are caught far from home.

To physically prepare your home for an earthquake, you need to walk around it and visualize what will move if the house shakes violently. Tie down water heaters with steel straps, anchor large pieces of furniture like clocks or curio cabinets with straps at their tops (most of the time you can do so invisibly). Buy safety latches for cabinets, so they will not open when the shaking starts. At all times be ready to turn off gas and water supplies to the house.

To be psychologically prepared for an earthquake, you need to realize that a large quake has many aftershocks, themselves as strong as regular earthquakes. An earthquake is a profoundly frightening experience. Many people feel an immense malevolence is part of their life after such an experience. Psychiatrists tell us that sharing worries and fears with people around you is one of the best available ways of handling such feelings of anxiety, and, later on, to attend group therapy.

A natural disaster can be a major life shock. A wise and prudent person will try to stave off as much of the pain as possible by taking reasonable precautions.

Essay 2

Some students begin college work successfully. They do well in their classes, they consider themselves "on track," and they are confident. Others do not do well. They are frequently alone, they do poorly in their classes, and they lack self-esteem. What advice would you give entering college students to help them through their first semesters? (30 minutes)

Every change we make in our lives requires us to modify the ways of living we are accustomed to. Sometimes it is very necessary to make minor changes, but other times we have to make drastic changes. One major change undertaken by a student occurs when he decides to go to college.

Like the other circumstances, adjusting to college life is no easy task. It involves going to an unfamiliar place and taking hard, unfamiliar courses with instructors whom you do not know anything about. It also involves going to a place where everybody is a stranger.

Here are some pointers that I have learned during my first two years in college. First, be sure to attend all the orientation activities given by the college. Those meetings will help you to know where to go in case you need help or information. They will aid you in the registration process, which can be frustrating and difficult. You will be told what you need to bring, things you must do beforehand, and information about tests you might need prior to registration. Orientation also gives information about the facilities that are available to students, like the library, tutoring centers, child care center, the bookstore, financial aid office, and the counseling office. All of these are made available to make life a little easier for students.

Second, if you do not know what subjects you need, or if you want to change your major, or a similar problem involving your record, you need to see a counselor. I know many people who wasted much precious time, money, and energy taking unnecessary courses that did not count. Third, you should always attend the first day of classes, because it is a very important day, a day when the professor presents the course and its objectives, as well as the requirements of the class. Fourth, you should try to know someone in your classes; this will allow you to ask questions informally and get another perspective on the class. Fifth, join organizations on the campus. They will also help you feel you belong, and they will help you make friends, and develop collateral interests, all of which will strengthen your investment in and commitment to college life. Through new friends, you will get to know which professors are better than others, which counselors give the correct advice, and which courses are really lively and meaningful.

Finally, organize your time. You need to be sure that you have time both for relaxation and for study. Although college courses require you to study a lot, you should still have time to do what you like, watching your favorite television program, going with your friend to see a movie, and going to parties, for if you do not do so, you will find college life boring. So pay attention to your priorities, and make and follow a study-time schedule. That way, you will be less stressed and you will earn the grades you want.

These are the things I have learned so far. When I first started college work, I would come to campus just before class, and return home just after class. I was always puzzled and lonely. Now, I have seen my counselor, and know exactly what classes to take to transfer to pharmacy school, I have joined the International Students' Club, and everything has changed. I have friends, and I know what professors to take, and I can talk to people about my classes. I do not feel like a stranger anymore. I feel I can say, "This is my college."

Explanatory/Analytic

Essay 3

Consider the following quotations regarding capital punishment:
"The only way to break the chain of violent reaction is to practice non-violence as individuals and collectively through our laws and institutions. Can we expect a decent society if the state is allowed to kill its own people?"
Coretta Scott King

"To be effective, punishment must fit the crime, and the punishment must be certain and swift."
Cesare Beccaria

Write a well-constructed paper in which you argue for or against capital punishment, making sure to acknowledge and counter some of the stronger opposing views. (30 minutes)

I am only 22 years old, but I feel the controversy about capital punishment has been with me all my life. Even in the sixth grade, I remember arguing the issue in class and even taking part in a class vote on the controversy. So, like most of my peers, I have an opinion about the issue. My opinion is very one-sided because, like everyone else in the United States, I have watched every day the increasing murder rate on our streets, in our neighborhoods, and in our homes. My opinion is very simple: death to the killers.

Since the Vietnam War, crime has been increasing in the United States. Mass murders are almost common now, and the daily death of skid-row drunks, young women who are also rape victims, gang members or anyone within fifty feet of them, robbery victims, all-night store clerks, competing lover, you name it, has made life in the U.S.A. much less safe and pleasant. Before we make social or economic progress in this country, we must suppress crime. We need to give a rest to the notion that crime, especially violent crime, is the result of need on the part of starving people. Study after study has shown that poverty is not the cause of crime, but is more often the reason for spectacular feats of recovery, retraining, regeneration within the family. The fact is that most criminals commit their crimes because they choose to do so; in their settings and lifestyles, there are always alternatives for them, but they choose crime.

The broadening of suspect's rights under the Warren Court have resulted in a series of convictions and sentences that are so compromised and light that they do not discourage even the convict himself from resuming a criminal career.

So we have arrived at a need for clear punishment, and, since violent crime has become such a prominent concern to us, we must include capital punishment. Kidnapping was at epidemic levels until it was made punishable by death. Then it almost disappeared. The same is likely to happen with killing if we ever enact a system where justice is certain and swift.

There are those who say that the death penalty is not an effective deterrent, but they have no convincing proof. In fact, they have pretty much had their way over the past twenty-five years, with the number of executions across the country reduced to three or four. What has been the result? An overwhelming explosion in the homicide rate. Opponents of the death penalty, by their very effective campaign, have doomed thousands of innocent people to death. These people talk about a "bloodbath" if executions resume in large number, but they say nothing (and possibly feel nothing) about the "bloodbath" happening now, daily, hourly, in our streets and in our homes. The *Los Angeles Times* this morning published a chilling statistic: in 1991, in Los Angeles City alone, 2340 people were slaughtered, most of them innocent victims.

For years, innocent people have lived with the fear of death, reinforced each day in the news. It is time for potential killers to live with the same fear.

ESSAY 4

Identify some aspect of your work or college or neighborhood that you feel should be changed. Argue for that change, making sure to present some convincing facts and ideas. Present at least one opposing argument along with your counterpoint to that argument. (30 minutes)

Working as a teaching assistant has some advantages. Since I started, working as a TA has helped me develop many skills that will help me to become a better teacher. But because the Los Angeles Unified School District does not offer the assistants benefits, guaranteed hours, or job security, I feel we must form a union. The job we perform is an important one. Most teaching assistants are bilingual, and they help to form a bridge between the students who do not speak English and the teachers, most of whom speak only English. Important threads of rapport form in every classroom between the students and the aide, and between the teacher and the aide. There is a working relationship that results and that will remain only with a stable staff— that is, employees who persevere over several years. However, with low pay and no benefits it is difficult or impossible for all but a few aides to stay on the job for very long. It is a "pin money" job, though its responsibilities are career caliber.

The District employs thousands of people. The largest group of workers are the teachers. These employees have benefits. On the other hand, the second largest group of workers in the Los Angeles District, namely 10,000 teaching assistants, 70% of whom are bilingual, receive no benefits, no vacation, no sick or holiday pay, and no medical or dental coverage. The District knows that, without teaching assistants, the schools would not be able to operate, though the District will not acknowledge the assistants as a unionized group and is avoiding the cost of paying benefits.

The TAs are hired to work an average of three hours a day. Part of their job is to teach reading, math, and science to groups of students. In fact, where a bilingual TA is assisting a monolingual teacher in a totally Spanish-speaking class, the TA does pretty much all of the teaching, if the truth were known. For this reason alone, we deserve better treatment from the District.

The number of teachers is steadily decreasing, and class size is steadily inching upward. Not all students get help from their teachers. There are approximately 38 students per class now, and one teacher alone cannot devote enough time to individual pupils who need attention or nurturing. A TA goes a long way to help this unacceptable situation.

TAs need to help themselves. They need to form a solid union, and then threaten to strike. Then, and only then, will we receive the pay raise and benefits that will stabilize our working relationship with the students and teachers. There are those who look back to the past and say, "Why do we need TAs anyway? We didn't have them years ago, and the schools were great." My answer to them is very simple. That was years ago when everyone was white and English-speaking. Now you have a District that is 65% Hispanic and speaks only Spanish, and another 7% that is Chinese and speaks only Mandarin or Cantonese. The aides are very essential. What will all those English-speaking teachers do with whole classrooms full of students who don't speak their language?

More Personal Experience Topics for Practice

1. The father of a good friend has died. Your friend is too emotionally distraught to write a eulogy. You've been asked to write one, sharing your feelings and thoughts about the passing of a good man. Explain how he affected your life. Give examples of things he did for you.

2. If you owned a restaurant, what type would it be and why? What kind of service would you provide? Describe the food, the decor, and the type of patrons you imagine eating at your place. Above all, why would your restaurant be different or better than someone else's?

3. Your doctor has informed you that though you appear to be healthy, you actually only have two weeks to live. Where would you go; what would you do; who would you do it with; and why would you do it?

4. You've passed the CBEST™, finished your student teaching, and have just been hired by the school of your choice. You love the campus, the teachers—even the students are a pleasant surprise. However, the district has not offered a cost-of-living increase in four years. Many of

the teachers you admire the most are going out on strike. The principal who hired you is counting on you to remain in the classroom. If you stay, you're a traitor. If you strike, you let down the boss and all those kids who think you're wonderful. What do you do?

5. One event in your life stands out in your memory greater than any other. That one event—your marriage to the love of your life, the birth of your first child, the publication of your first novel, the acceptance of a screenplay by George Lucas, or that grand-slam home run you hit in your last season of little league—has changed your life forever. What led up to the event? How did it change your life? What is your life like now as a result of that event? Who was involved? Why was it so significant? Do not forget to include where and when the event occurred.

6. When you were in school, one of your teachers made a big impression on you, not because he was a good teacher, but because he was terrible. The irony of it all is that you've just been hired to teach at your old school, and he is now one of your colleagues. He is still cruel and boring. You are compelled to write him a letter explaining why it's still not too late for him to change.

7. You fear that your son or daughter has been seen socializing with known drug abusers in the neighborhood. How would you discourage your child from becoming a drug user?

8. When you were fifteen, you had a vision as to what you would be at your current age. How did things turn out? Would you have disappointed that fifteen year old who had great expectations, or would you have surprised your former self?

More Explanatory/Analytic Topics for Practice

1. The draft became very unpopular during the Vietnam War. However, generations prior to that event often cited the military as a *rite of passage* that helped young men develop their character. In the army, boys became men because they developed self-confidence, a sense of teamwork, and respect for authority. Considering the current gang culture in our cities, our declining sense of civility, and the pervasive aimlessness of Generation X, isn't it time to reconsider the draft? Whether you are for or against it, explain why. Define your position, give examples, and prove your point with a logical conclusion.

2. Bilingual education has become a political issue in this country. Some argue that it impedes foreign students from learning English. Others believe that it allows students who speak another language to learn important subjects in their native tongue. Should we end bilingual education, or does it play a meaningful role in our schools?

3. Some of our political leaders have proposed that the military discharge members of the armed forces who test positive for HIV. Others argue that those who have this condition have proven them-selves to be loyal and patriotic servicemen. They have also suggested that HIV servicemen and women work stateside in a noncombatant capacity. What is the best solution for this difficult problem?

4. There are various opinions on welfare, ranging from completely eliminating it to expanding existing programs. Some would like to modify it in a way that does not push fathers out of the picture.

Others would like to replace it with a workfare concept, and still others would like to place a time limit on its duration. Offer a solution to this problem.

5. Please read the following line:

   "The weak are strong in cunning."

   William Blake

   What does this line from *The Marriage of Heaven and Hell,* tell you? Analyze it and expound upon it.

6. In August of 1945, President Harry Truman ordered the armed forces in the Pacific to drop the atomic bomb on Japan. Some have argued that this saved the lives of millions of Japanese and Americans who would have fought to their deaths if the United States had invaded Japan. Others believe that the bombing was immoral and that using the A-bomb could have been avoided. What do you think? Was Truman's decision right or wrong? Give reasons why you think it was right or wrong.

7. Some people argue that the intelligence of a child is the result of heredity. They tell us that "the apple does not fall far from the tree." Others hold the environment responsible for forming intelligence, arguing that loving parents can nurture a child's self-esteem which will allow the child to develop emotionally and intellectually. Is it nature or nurture? Are we the end result of predetermined genes, or does our environment play a role in developing our mental capabilities?

8. How many times have you heard the statement, "There ought to be a law!" Describe a contemporary problem in society, politics, or the workplace that could be solved by a new law. Explain what the law should accomplish and how it would be beneficial. Persuade your reader that your point of view is correct.

PRACTICE WRITING SAMPLES

This section provides two sample topics for practice essays. Allow yourself 30 minutes for each essay. Have an honest critic read and respond to each practice essay you complete.

Writing Sample Topic 1

The high school you attended has invited you to its annual College Conference as a speaker. The school would like you to talk about the pros and cons of your college experience because several seniors are thinking of applying to your college and majoring in education. Since you can't make it to the conference, you've decided to send a statement to be read there. Write the remarks that you'd like those high school seniors to hear.

<u>WRITING SAMPLE TOPIC 2</u>

Reading books is one of the vital occupations of an educated person. Choose a book you've read in the last 12 months—not one assigned in a course but one you chose on your own. Ask yourself why the book deserves to be read. In what ways did the book touch your intellect or emotions? Did it alter the way you think or feel? Was it valuable as a commentary on important issues or as an insight into life? Write an essay in which you discuss the effect of the book on your life. Think of your reader as someone who hasn't read the book. Your intent is to persuade that reader to rush home and read the book tonight!

Chapter 6

English Review and Practice

It is important to remember that English usage and mechanics are governed by a set of consistent, logical rules. It is not popular today, at any learning level, to require students to memorize those rules, but they do exist, and they do govern the language that is unquestionably expected of college students, that is, Standard American English. This chapter is dedicated to a comprehensive review of those rules, along with their exceptions, and includes some review exercises to help you determine whether it's all "sinking in." If you find your study of grammar is heavy and vexing, take it slowly. Break this chapter up into smaller bites, and take them one at a time. It really *is* important; everything you study in this chapter has an important bearing on your writing.

If you feel unsure of your prose "ear" (the language sense you've developed over the years), your best strategy is to review this chapter several times. As you examine each section, think of the materials presented to you as a general review of problem areas, rather than as specific data to memorize. The English language has too many options to commit to memory. In each lesson, try to see the general rule and its purpose.

USAGE/MECHANICS

Punctuation

The Comma
Among its many functions, the comma is used to set off independent clauses, items in a series, coordinate adjectives, parenthetical expressions, and nonrestrictive phrases or clauses.

Use a comma to separate independent clauses joined by a coordinating conjunction (*and, but, for, or, nor,* or *yet*).

EXAMPLES

He wanted to be a salesman, but no jobs were available.

The people refused to send their children to school, and the school building stood empty the entire year.

Be sure you understand that this rule applies to the joining of *independent clauses,* that is, complete sentences. The use of the coordinating conjunction to join compound subjects (*Clinton* and *Dole* debated on Columbus Day), pairs of phrases (The service at the shop was performed with *care* and *pride*), compound verbs (Joan *organized* the kitchen and *prepared* the banquet), or the like, does not require the comma.

Use commas to separate items in a series.

EXAMPLES

Friendly, small, and innovative are adjectives that accurately characterize this college.

He went to the basement, set the trap, and returned to the kitchen to wait.

Use a comma to separate coordinate adjectives modifying the same noun.

EXAMPLES

He washed his new, black, shiny pickup.

Himalayan cats have long, silky, heavy fur.

To test whether adjectives are coordinate, reverse their order or insert *and* between them. If the phrase still makes sense. they are coordinate adjectives and require a comma. The first example makes sense using either method: *shiny, black, new pickup,* or *new and shiny and black pickup.*

Non-coordinate adjectives have a special relationship with the nouns they modify. To some degree, they create a word group that itself is modified. They should not be preceded by commas.

EXAMPLE

They all admired the tall, powerful *football player.*

In this sentence, *football* is a non-coordinate adjective, different from the coordinate adjectives *tall* and *powerful.* You cannot put *and* between *powerful* and *football* nor can you move the word *football.* Other examples of non-coordinate adjectives are *doll* house, *art* museum, *computer* science, and *wheat* bread.

Use a comma to set off an introductory phrase or clause from the main clause.

PARTICIPIAL CLAUSE:	Having spent his last penny, Luster tried to borrow a quarter from his boss.
PREPOSITIONAL PHRASE:	At the beginning of each game, a noted singer gives his rendition of "The Star-Spangled Banner."
ADVERBIAL CLAUSE:	When the composer was finished with the prelude, she began work on the first movement.

Use a pair of commas to set off nonrestrictive (amplifying or explanatory) phrases and clauses inserted into a sentence.

EXAMPLES

Mary Jennings, who was my best friend, dropped the class.

The first offer on the Blake house, which had been on the market for almost a month, was very disappointing.

Be sure to distinguish between these *nonrestrictive* interrupters and the *restrictive modifiers,* which are *not* set off by commas. Nonrestrictive modifiers add information but do not limit or change the meaning of the sentence. Note how the meaning changes when the clause is restrictive.

RESTRICTIVE: The young woman who was my best student dropped the class.

The young woman is now identified as the best student. Here is another example of a nonrestrictive clause:

EXAMPLE

Cardiac patients who have artificial valve implants are required to take anticoagulants for the rest of their lives.

Use a comma to set off nonrestrictive phrases and clauses that follow the main clause.

EXAMPLES

Jessica wanted to see the ice show, not the circus.

Few fans thought the reigning heavyweight champion could win, although he was superior to the challenger in every category.

Use the commas to set off an appositive. An appositive is a noun or noun phrase that renames or explains the noun it follows.

EXAMPLE

The novel, a mystery about a secret island off the Washington coast, was an instant bestseller.

Use commas to set off words in direct address. Words in direct address identify the one being spoken to.

EXAMPLE

Excuse me, Beth, but aren't you late for your tennis lesson?

A comma can take the place of an omitted word or phrase.

EXAMPLE

The Capitol Bank is located in a shopping mall; the Investors Bank, in the heart of town.

A comma is sometimes needed for clarity.

EXAMPLES

Ever since, we have taken the plane rather than the train.

In May, Marcia went to Washington, D.C.

PRACTICE EXERCISE 1

Decide whether the punctuation is correct or incorrect at each numbered point in the following paragraph. Then place a check in the proper column.

Correct Incorrect

_____ _____ 1. When a writer begins a
story he must start
1

_____ _____ 2. the pages smoking right
away not bore the
2

_____ _____ 3. reader with verbiage
about setting
3

_____ _____ 4. characterization, and
4
theme. The

_____ _____ 5. author must present a
protagonist, and
5

_____ _____ 6. an antagonist and he
6
must also give

_____ _____ 7. them a cause worth
7
arguing over. The

_____ _____ 8. complication, a series of
8
battles the

_____ _____ 9. protagonist always
loses, comes next
9

_____ _____ 10. just before the crisis, to
10
end all crises. The cli-
max is

Correct Incorrect

_____ _____ 11. the long-awaited, conclusive, high point of
11
the tale.

_____ _____ 12. There cannot be art
without form, and there
12
cannot be form without
careful studied, busi-
nesslike

_____ _____ 13. craft. Any writer, who
13
believes art flows

_____ _____ 14. from emotion alone, is
14
not likely to write

_____ _____ 15. the kind of disciplined,
organized short
15

_____ _____ 16. story, that reflects the
16
real world.

ANSWERS

1. **Incorrect.** An introductory clause is set off by a comma.

2. **Incorrect.** Set off a nonrestrictive phrase that follows the main clause.

3. **Incorrect.** Use commas to separate items in a series.

4. **Correct.** See explanation, item 3.

5. **Incorrect.** Pairs of words (here, the compound objects *protagonist* and *antagonist*).

6. **Incorrect.** Independent clauses linked by a coordinating conjunction are separated from each other by a comma.

7. **Correct.** The phrase *worth arguing over* is restrictive (defines *cause*) and should not be separated from the main clause by a comma.

8. **Correct.** Interrupters, in this case a nonrestrictive appositive, are set off by commas.

9. **Incorrect.** Nonrestrictive concluding phrases are set off by commas.

10. **Incorrect.** The infinitive phrase *to end all crises* is restrictive (defines *crisis*) and should not be set off by a comma.

11. **Incorrect.** The adjective *high* in the phrase *high point* is not a coordinate adjective and should not be preceded by a comma.

12. **Correct.** Use a comma to separate independent clauses joined by a coordinating conjunction.

13. **Incorrect.** The adjective clause *who believes art flows from emotion alone* restricts the meaning of the word *writer* to those writers who hold the same belief. It should not be set off by commas.

14. **Incorrect.** See explanation, item 13. This is the second comma of the pair used mistakenly to set off the adjective clause.

15. **Correct.** The adjective *short* in the phrase *short story* is not a coordinate adjective. It should not be preceded by a comma.

16. **Incorrect.** The adjective clause *that reflects the real world* is restrictive (defines *short story*) and should not be set off by a comma.

The Semicolon

The semicolon is generally used to separate coordinate elements in a sentence, that is, items of the same grammatical nature. Most often, it is used between related ideas that require punctuation weaker than a period, but stronger than a comma. In addition, the semicolon divides three or more items in a series when the items themselves contain commas.

Use a semicolon between related independent clauses not joined by a coordinating conjunction.

EXAMPLES

A mature male gorilla may be six feet tall and weigh 400 pounds or more; his enormous arms can span eight feet.

New York has twelve major stadiums; Los Angeles has fifteen.

Use a semicolon between independent clauses joined by a conjunctive adverb.

Frequently, two independent clauses are joined, not by a coordinating conjunction, but by a transitional word (conjunctive adverb) introducing the second clause. A semicolon must be used between the clauses, because these transitional words (*accordingly, also, consequently, finally, furthermore, however, indeed, meanwhile, nevertheless, similarly, still, therefore, thus,* and the like) are *not* connecting words.

EXAMPLE

A female coyote will not bear pups if her diet consists of fewer than fifty rodents a week; thus, Mother Nature achieves a population balance.

Use a semicolon to separate coordinate clauses if the clauses themselves have commas.

EXAMPLE

The warranty on the car covered extensive repairs to the electrical system, front end, transmission, fuel injection system, and valves; but the amount of time and inconvenience involved in returning each time to the dealer cannot be ignored.

Use a semicolon to separate items in a series when the items themselves contain internal punctuation.

Normally, three or more items in a series are set off by commas; however, when they are made more complex by commas and other punctuation, they are separated by semicolons.

EXAMPLE

The trio was composed of a cellist named Grosz, who had been a European virtuoso for many years; a pianist who had won a major music festival in 1954, 1955, and 1958; and a violinist who had studied in Budapest, Vienna, and Munich.

PRACTICE EXERCISE 2

Each of the following sentences contains a numbered punctuation mark. Decide whether the mark is correct or should be changed to a semicolon. Then check the appropriate space to the left.

Correct Incorrect

_____ _____ 1. He hit the ball well,
^{1}
however, he was not
much of a fielder.

_____ _____ 2. He had played his
entire repertoire: a
short piece by Mozart
that, in spite of its difficulty, was his favorite
sonata; a prelude by
Liszt that once had
caused an audience to
erupt in cheers, in spite
of the fact that he was

Correct Incorrect

_____ _____ not finished, and,
^{2}
finally a mazurka by
Brahms that was popu-
lar with musicians,
composers, and the gen-
eral audience alike.

_____ _____ 3. The movie had seg-
ments unsuitable for
children, including vio-
lent scenes, nudity, and
inappropriate language,
^{3}
but the general theme
was inspirational.

_____ _____ 4. Life is hard work; life
^{4}
can be a pleasure.

ANSWERS

1. **Incorrect.** When a transitional word (conjunctive adverb) is used between clauses, the clauses must be separated by a semicolon.

2. **Incorrect.** This sentence contains a series of items, each a noun modified by an adjective clause, and each containing commas. They should be separated from each other by semicolons.

3. **Incorrect.** The general rule is to use a comma to separate independent clauses joined bya coordinating conjunction. However, when the clauses themselves contain a number of commas, a semicolon is used for clarity.

4. **Correct.** A semicolon is used to separate related independent clauses not linked by a coordinating conjunction.

The Colon, Hyphen, and Apostrophe

The Colon

The colon is a signal that something is to follow: a rephrased statement, a list or series, or a formal quotation. Use a colon in a sentence if you can logically insert *namely* after it.

Use a colon at the end of a complete statement to show anticipation—that is, to show that amplifying details follow, such as a list, a series of items, a formal quotation, or an explanation.

EXAMPLES

Of all the gauges in an airplane cockpit, three are crucial: the altimeter, the gas gauge, and the crash-warning indicator.

After five minutes of silence, the actor uttered those famous words: "To be or not to be; that is the question."

A popover has four common ingredients: flour, milk, salt, and butter.

Problems that occur in the use of the colon usually result from the following lapses:

1. A complete statement (independent clause) does not precede the colon.

Incorrect: Tasks that I must complete today: mow the lawn, read two chapters of history, and tidy my room.

Correct: I must complete several tasks today: mow the lawn, read two chapters of history, and tidy my room.

2. A colon incorrectly separates essential parts of a sentence.

Incorrect: In updating my computer, I added: a hard disk, a laser printer, and a fine-resolution monitor. (The colon separates the verb from its direct objects.)

Correct: In updating my computer, I added some new components: a hard disk, a laser printer, and a fine-resolution monitor.

Also Correct: In updating my computer, I added a hard disk, a laser printer, and a fine-resolution monitor.

3. There is more than one colon in a sentence.

Incorrect: The success of the action depended upon three variables: that the weather would hold out, that the supplies would arrive on time, and that the enemy would be short on three things: planes, ammunition, and food.

Correct: The success of the action depended upon three variables: that the weather would hold out, that the supplies would arrive on time, and that the enemy would be short on planes, ammunition, and food.

Hyphen

The hyphen has two main uses: to divide syllables at the end of a line and to link words in certain combinations. It is also used in compound numbers from twenty-one to ninety-nine.

Hyphenate a compound adjective (an adjective made up of two or more words) when it precedes the noun it modifies. The hyphen is ordinarily not used when the words follow the noun.

EXAMPLES

She wore a well-used raincoat.

BUT

Her raincoat was well used.

The past-due bill lay unnoticed behind the couch.

The bill, past due, lay unnoticed behind the couch.

Note: A compound adjective with an adverbial *-ly* modifier is never hyphenated: the *poorly designed* interchange. When the *-ly* modifier is an adjective, a hyphen is properly used: a *friendly-looking* dog.

Apostrophe

In addition to indicating possession, the apostrophe is used to take the place of omitted numbers (class of '87) and omitted letters or words in contractions (wasn't [was not], o'clock [of the clock]), and sometimes to indicate plurals (A's, I.D.'s).

Use an apostrophe to show the possessive case of nouns and indefinite pronouns.

1. The possessive case of singular nouns (either common or proper) is indicated by adding an apostrophe and an *s*.

EXAMPLES

George's speech, the senator's campaign, anyone's opinion, the boss's office, Charles's book.

2. The possessive case of plural nouns ending in *s* is formed by adding only the apostrophe.

EXAMPLES

the girls' softball team, the waitresses' union, the Harrisons' antique cars.

Note: **Irregular plurals, such as *men* or *children,* form the possessive by adding an apostrophe and an *s*: men's, children's.**

A common error is to confuse possessive pronouns and contractions, particularly *its* and *it's* (meaning *it is*), *their* and *they're* (*they are*), and *whose* and *who's* (*who is*). Possessive pronouns have no apostrophe.

PRACTICE EXERCISE 3

Decide whether the punctuation at each numbered point is correct or incorrect. Then place a check in the proper column.

Correct Incorrect

_____ _____ 1. Into the circus arena paraded all the performers and animals; first the
1

_____ _____ 2. high stepping horses
2
and bareback riders, then the lumbering elephants with their trainers, followed by the cartwheeling clowns and the

_____ _____ 3. brightly costumed
3
trapeze artists.

_____ _____ 4. Louis's expertise at
4
skateboarding amazed his friends.

_____ _____ 5. The long awaited
5
furniture finally

_____ _____ 6. arrived at the Jameses
6
house. In saving a threatened species, a basic

Correct Incorrect

_____ _____ 7. step is the study of it's
7   8
diet, mating and

_____ _____ 8. reproductive processes, range patterns, and social behavior.

ANSWERS

1. **Incorrect.** Use a colon, not a semicolon, to introduce a list after a complete statement.

2. **Incorrect.** Hyphenate a compound adjective that occurs *before* the noun.

3. **Correct.** Do not hyphenate a compound adjective if its first member is an adverb ending in *-ly.*

4. **Correct.** To form the possessive, add an apostrophe and an *s* to a singular noun.

5. **Incorrect.** See explanation, item 2.

6. **Incorrect.** To form the plural possessive of a proper name, add an apostrophe to the plural (Jameses').

7. **Incorrect.** A colon should not be used if it separates essential parts of a sentence (the verb *is* should not be separated from its object, *the study of. . .*).

8. **Incorrect.** The possessive personal pronoun *its* does not take an apostrophe.

The Dash, Question Mark, and Exclamation Point

Dash

The main function of the dash, like parenthesis, is to enclose information within a sentence. Dashes are generally more forceful and therefore should be used sparingly, since they highlight the ideas and items they enclose.

Use dashes to indicate hesitation, or a sudden break in thought or sentence structure, or to set off appositives and other explanatory or parenthetical elements. The dash adds emphasis to any part of a sentence that can be separated from the rest of the sentence.

EXAMPLE

The skydiver—in spite of his broken leg—set a new record for endurance.

Some specific uses of the dash follow:

1. To interrupt continuity of prose

EXAMPLE

"I really can't tolerate—Well, never mind."

2. To emphasize appositives

EXAMPLE

The items she had asked for in the new car—tape deck, mileage computer, stick shift—were all included.

3. To set off phrases or clauses containing commas

When a modifier itself contains commas, dashes can make its boundaries clear.

EXAMPLE

General Motors—which has manufactured tanks, cannons, and mobile cranes—has always been far more than an automobile assembler.

4. To set off parenthetical elements

EXAMPLE

The child was sitting—actually sprawling—at his desk.

Question Mark

A question mark indicates the end of a direct question. A question mark in parentheses signals doubt or uncertainty about a fact such as a date or a number.

Use a question mark after a direct question.

EXAMPLES

When are we going to eat?

Ask yourself, what are the odds of winning?

(It is also correct to capitalize the word *what*.)

A question mark in parentheses may be used to express doubt.

EXAMPLE

The Dean's notes, published in 1774 (?), are considered the novel's origin.

The question mark is unlikely to cause you trouble on the English test. Problems mainly occur (a) because of failure to distinguish between *direct* and *indirect* questions (an *indirect* question is always followed by a period: *My friend asked why I didn't have my car.*) or (b) because of mistaken combination of question marks with other punctuation marks. A question mark should never be combined with a comma, period, exclamation point, or other question mark.

Exclamation Point

An exclamation point is an indicator of strong *emotional* feelings, such as anger, joy, shock, surprise, or fear. It may also be used to express irony or emphasis. Like the dash, it should be used sparingly.

Use an exclamation point after a command, an interjection, an exclamation, or some other expression of strong emotion.

COMMAND: Stop!

INTERJECTION: Wow! Fire! Help!

EMOTIONAL EXPRESSION: Don't tell me you did it again! How wonderful!

An exclamation point should not be used with commas, periods, other exclamation points, or question marks.

PRACTICE EXERCISE 4

Decide whether the punctuation at each numbered point is correct or incorrect. Then place a check in the proper column.

Correct Incorrect

_____ _____ 1. The tornado headed—
                 1
              no, *hurtled*—our way.

_____ _____ 2. The doctor—an
                 2
              imposter, actually—
                 2
              cleared his throat.

_____ _____ 3. The book—which was
                 3
              expensive—had been
                 3
              his favorite for many
              years.

_____ _____ 4. Don't tell me you're
              leaving already.
                 4

_____ _____ 5. Is this the building you
              want to study!
                 5

_____ _____ 6. Mr. Williams asked
              when I could rake his
              lawn?
                 6

_____ _____ 7. Last Tuesday, I'll never
                 7
              forget it, was the first
                 7
              time we saw Michael
              Jordan play.

Correct Incorrect

_____ _____ 8. The famous diva—who
                 8
              had performed in such
              eminent opera houses
              as the Met, LaScala,
              and Covent Garden—
                 8
              was not willing to sing
              at our school.

ANSWERS

1. **Correct.** Dashes can be used to signal a dramatic or emphatic shift in tone.

2. **Correct.** Dashes can be used to emphasize an appositive.

3. **Incorrect.** Commas, not dashes, should be used to set off simple adjective clauses such as this one. Remember, though, that dashes *can* be used to set off adjective and other clauses that contain commas or other marks of punctuation.

4. **Incorrect.** An exclamation point is called for here, to show dismay.

5. **Incorrect.** This sentence is a direct question and requires a question mark.

6. **Incorrect.** An indirect question takes a period, not a question mark.

7. **Incorrect.** Use dashes to signal an abrupt change of thought.

8. **Correct.** Nonrestrictive clauses that are long and contain internal commas can properly be set off by dashes.

Quotation Marks and Parentheses

Quotation Marks

One of the main uses of quotation marks is to signal the exact words of a writer or speaker. Quotation marks are also used to enclose the titles of short literary or musical works (articles, short stories or poems, songs), as well as words used in a special way.

Enclose direct quotations in quotation marks.

EXAMPLE

"We will wage war wherever it takes us," Winston Churchill pledged.

Quotation marks should enclose only the exact words of the person quoted.

EXAMPLE

Winston Churchill pledged that "we will wage war wherever it takes us." (NOT . . .pledged "that we will. . .")

Note: When a quoted sentence is interrupted by a phrase such as *he said* or *she replied,* two pairs of quotation marks must be used, one for each part of the quotation. The first word of the second part of the quoted material should not be capitalized unless it is a proper noun or the pronoun *I.*

EXAMPLE

"There are two sorts of contests between men," John Locke argued, "one managed by law, the other by force."

Commas and periods *always* belong *inside* quotation marks; semicolons and colons, outside. Question marks and exclamation points are placed inside the quotation marks when they are part of the quotation; otherwise, they are placed outside.

EXAMPLES

What did he mean when he said, "I know the answer already"?

"The case is closed!" the attorney exclaimed.

Parentheses

Parentheses, like dashes, are used to set off words of explanation and other secondary supporting details—figures, data, examples—that are not really part of the main sentence or paragraph. Parentheses are less emphatic than dashes and should be reserved for ideas that have no essential connection with the rest of the sentence.

Use parentheses to enclose an explanatory or parenthetical element that is not closely connected with the rest of the sentence.

EXAMPLE

The speech that she gave on Sunday (under extremely difficult circumstances, it should be noted) was her best.

If the parenthetical item is an independent sentence that stands alone, capitalize the first word and place a period inside the end parenthesis. If it is a complete sentence within another complete sentence, do not begin it with a capital letter or end it with a period. A question mark or exclamation point that is part of the parenthetical element should be placed inside the parenthesis.

EXAMPLES

On Easter, I always think of the hot cross buns I used to buy for two cents apiece. (At the time, the year was 1939, and I was three years old.)

A speech decrying the lack of basic skills on campuses today was given by Congressman Jones (he was the man who once proposed having no entrance standards for community college students).

The absurd placement of the child-care center (fifteen feet from a class-room building!) was amateur architecture at its worst.

Capitalization

Take the trouble to capitalize words only according to standard principles. Do not capitalize words unnecessarily.

The rules of capitalization are generally clear and less subject to exceptions than most rules of language. Nevertheless, if you encounter problems, an up-to-date dictionary should help you, especially where the capitalization of a word depends upon its use: "the bible of show business" but "the Holy Bible," "my big brother" but "your Big Brother in Washington."

Proper Names

Note that common nouns like boulevard, heights, university, park, and store are capitalized when they accompany proper nouns.

1. Names of persons, specific entities, and trademarks

EXAMPLES

Sarah Kaltgrad, J. P. Morgan, Mohammed, Nissan Maxima, William the Conqueror, the Constitution, English 101, Peabody Award, the Statue of Liberty, Cherrios

2. Geographical names

EXAMPLES

Little Neck, New York, the Southwest, Colorado, Niagara Falls, Quebec, Rocky Mountains, Yellowstone Park, MacArthur Park, Zuma Beach, Coney Island, Germany, Europe, Asia, Missouri River, Bermuda Triangle, Rodeo Drive, Cape Fear

3. Specific nations, cultures, ethnic groups, and languages use a proper adjective.

EXAMPLES

Mexican, Thai, Cherokee, English, Afro-American, Pacific Islanders, Tahitians, Chinese, Koreans, Bosnians, Iranians, Farsi, English, Russian, Armenian, Spanish, Chinese, Swedish

4. Schools, institutions, government divisions and agencies, and companies

EXAMPLES

United Way, Library of Congress, UCLA, Securities and Exchange Commission, Houston Oilers, General Mills, Kent School, Red Cross, Rotary Club, Medicare, Coast Guard

5. Days, months, commemorative days, and holidays

EXAMPLES

Monday, March, Veterans' Day, Father's Day, Thanksgiving

6. Significant events or periods, historical documents

EXAMPLES

the Fourteenth Amendment, Middle Ages, Operation Desert Storm, the Bill of Rights, the Great Depression, Prohibition, the Constitution

7. Religious references to documents, holidays, personages, and deities

EXAMPLES

the Bible, Koran, Upanishads, Genesis, Revelations, Easter, Allah, Messiah, Christian, Hindu, Moslem, Judaic, Mormon, Christmas, Yom Kippur

8. Words used in a special sense

EXAMPLES

We all know that *Time* waits for no man.

Only the all-consuming, obsessive drive for *Money* remains as a motivation.

Abbreviations and Acronyms
- Capitalize abbreviations or shortened forms of capitalized words.

EXAMPLES

USC, NBC, IBM, AT&T, CA, NYC, NFL, MADD, UNESCO

- Capitalize Titles Indicating Rank or Relationship

- Capitalize titles and words denoting family relationships that precede the name but not those that follow it.

EXAMPLES

Mama McCaslin, Cousin Jenny, President William Clinton; the president of the United States, Governor Pete Wilson, General Taylor, George West, the captain, Phillip Stein, our governor, Aunt Adrienne, Adrienne, my aunt.

When words indicating family relationships are substituted for proper names, they are usually capitalized:

EXAMPLE

Well, *Father*, you certainly did well on the course today!

- Capitalize the First Word and All Other Important Words in Titles

Articles (*the, a, an*), coordinating conjunctions (*and, but, for, or, yet*), prepositions (*in, to, for, around, up, under*), and the *to* in infinitives are not normally capitalized.

- Always Capitalize the First Word in a Sentence and the First Word in Directly Quoted Speech

EXAMPLES

Never have so many viewers tuned in to one program.

Are you sure? *Well*, then, let's cancel the wedding. *I'm* serious.

Father Mike often says, "*Blessed* are those who are funny."

Without hesitation, *Elizabeth* shouted, "*Down* with the *Bruins!*"

- Avoid Unnecessary Capitals

Keep in mind this handy rule:

Note: Common (uncapitalized) nouns are often preceded by articles (*a, an, the*) or by limiting words like *each, many, several, every,* or *some.*

Capitalization Review Chart

Capitals	No Capitals
Lieutenant Cameron Winston	the lieutenant in charge, every lieutenant
the Korean War	the gas wars of the 70's
German, Swedish, Tagalong	foreign languages
East-West University	your local university
the U.S. Army	a rough and ready army
March, St. Patrick's Day	spring, holiday
the Midwest, Midwesterners	to fly west, midwestern states
the Retail Merchants Association	an association for merchants

Capitals	No Capitals
Tay-Sachs disease	cancer, colds, pneumonia
a Himalayan, Toyota trucks	cats, small trucks
several Republican hopefuls	democratic movements
our Declaration of Independence	the women's declaration of independence

PRACTICE EXERCISE 5

Decide whether the punctuation or capitalization at each numbered point is correct or incorrect. Then place a check in the proper column.

Correct Incorrect

_____ _____ 1. He had said that "he
                    1
            was nobody to fool
            with."

_____ _____ 2. Fred wrote a poem for
            Barbara, which he enti-
            tled "Barbaric
                2
            Barbara."
                2

_____ _____ 3. Joseph Pummell (he
            was the senator who
            authored the antifraud
            bill.) offered to speak at
                3
            our first meeting.

_____ _____ 4. "I knew for sure," she
            said, "when he didn't
            ask me to the prom".
                4

_____ _____ 5. The measure designed
            to lower inflationary
            pressures on the econo-
            my resulted in a
            cost-of-living increase of
            12 percent (some mea-
            sure, some reduction!).
                5

Correct Incorrect

_____ _____ 6. "There is no doubt," he
            asserted, "That the
                6
            enormous national debt
            will be a major problem
            in the next century."

ANSWERS

1. **Incorrect.** Only the actual words spoken can be in quotation marks. *He was* would not be part of the speaker's words.

2. **Correct.** Quotation marks are used in titles of shorter literary works.

3. **Incorrect.** A complete sentence enclosed in parentheses within another sentence does not take a period.

4. **Incorrect.** A period always belongs inside the quotation mark.

5. **Correct.** An exclamation point that is part of the parenthetical phrase is placed within the parentheses.

6. **Incorrect.** The second part of a direct quotation that is interrupted by a phrase like *he asserted* does not begin with a capital unless the first word is a proper noun or *I*.

CUMULATIVE REVIEW I

What lies behind the creative genius of our

greatest <u>authors</u> has been the subject of

1

speculation over the past two centuries. There

is little doubt that many of the <u>worlds</u> creative

       2

geniuses experienced miserable <u>lives</u> most

       3

often, they suffered a personal and extreme

brand of deprivation that profoundly affected

the quality of their daily lives. Almost <u>always,</u>

       4

the depth of their misery is related to the

greatness of their genius. One who reads both

Emily Bronte's *Wuthering Heights* and the

       5

<u>best known</u> critical discussions about her

6

work cannot escape the <u>conclusion,</u> that Emily

       7

was the product of a punitive and abusive

<u>environment,</u> it is difficult to avoid the further

8

conclusion that the strength and authenticity

of her <u>novel</u> the vulnerabilities and palpable

    9

yearnings of its main characters—are <u>related</u>

          10

<u>however, faintly</u> to her personal affliction.

10

1. (A) NO CHANGE
   (B) authors'
   (C) authors,
   (D) author's

2. (A) NO CHANGE
   (B) world's
   (C) worlds'
   (D) world's,

3. (A) NO CHANGE
   (B) lives:
   (C) lives;
   (D) lives,

4. (A) NO CHANGE
   (B) always;
   (C) always—
   (D) always:

5. (A) NO CHANGE
   (B) "Wuthering Heights"
   (C) Wuthering Heights
   (D) Wuthering-Heights

6. (A) NO CHANGE
   (B) best, known
   (C) best-known
   (D) "best known"

7. (A) NO CHANGE
   (B) conclusion:
   (C) conclusion—
   (D) conclusion

8. (A) NO CHANGE
   (B) environment;
   (C) environment—
   (D) environment?

9. (A) NO CHANGE
   (B) novel;
   (C) novel—
   (D) novel:

10. (A) NO CHANGE
    (B) related; however faintly,
    (C) related, however faintly,
    (D) related (however faintly)

Answers for Cumulative Review I

1. **A** The noun *authors* is a simple object in this sentence and requires no punctuation.

2. **B** The plural *geniuses* are a possession of the world and require that it signal that possession with an apostrophe.

3. **B** The words occurring after *lives* form an independent clause and so must be set off with a stronger mark of punctuation. The colon is the best choice in this context because the following statement gives specific focus to the general statement made in the sentence's introductory clause.

4. **A** Set off introductory phrases with a comma.

5. **A** Underline (set in italics) novels and other larger works of literature.

6. **C** Hyphenate compound adjectives preceding the noun they modify.

7. **D** The adjective clause following the noun *conclusion* is a restrictive modifier and so does not take separating punctuation.

8. **B** The clause that follows necessitates a strong mark of punctuation. Since it is closely related in meaning to the previous independent clause, the most appropriate choice is the semicolon.

9. **C** The dash at the end of this phrase requires a matching dash at the beginning. Dashes are appropriately used to give special emphasis to parenthetical phrases such as this one.

10. **C** The phrase *however faintly* is parenthetical and must be set off by commas.

BASIC GRAMMAR

Subject-Verb Agreement

Nouns, verbs, and pronouns often have special forms or endings that indicate *number*—that is, whether the word is singular or plural. A verb must agree in number with the noun or pronoun that is its subject.

- A verb agrees in number with its subject. A singular subject requires a singular verb; a plural subject, a plural verb.

SINGULAR	**PLURAL**
The *house has* three bathrooms.	Many *houses have* more than one bathroom.
UCLA is my choice.	*UCLA, Berkeley, and Stanford are* my favorites.
My *cat,* a Persian named Gus, *is* awake all night.	*Cats,* according to this article, *are* almost always nocturnal.
Mandy, together with the other girls, *wants* a pizza for lunch.	*Mandy and the other girls want* a pizza for lunch.

- Do not let intervening words obscure the relationship between subject and verb. Find the subject and make the verb agree with it.

EXAMPLES

A column of wounded prisoners, townspeople, and exhausted soldiers *was spotted* struggling over the horizon. (*Was spotted* agrees with its subject, *column,* not with the intervening plural nouns.)

She, her brother, and her friends from upstate *have* always *bought* tickets to the rock concert. (The verb agrees with the plural subject.)

- Singular subjects followed by such words and phrases as *along with, as well as, in addition to, together with,* or *with* require singular verbs.

EXAMPLE

The *carrier,* together with three destroyers and two frigates, *was dispatched* to the Mediterranean Sea.

- Indefinite pronouns like *anybody, each, either, everyone, neither,* and *one* are always singular, and take a singular verb, regardless of intervening words. Other indefinite pronouns, like *all, any, none* or *some* may be either singular or plural. *Both, few, many,* and *several* are always plural.

EXAMPLES

Neither of my children *has* an interest in music.

All is not lost BUT *all* of us *are* going.

Few of the golfers *were* professionals.

- Compound subjects joined by *and* usually take a plural verb. (An exception is a compound subject that names one person, thing, or idea: *Ham and eggs is* a favorite breakfast.)

EXAMPLES

The *Toyota* and the *Ford are* low on gas.

The *Pendletons,* the *Riveras,* and the *Kleins are coming* to dinner.

- In sentences that begin with *there is* or *there are,* the subject follows the verb, and the verb must agree with it.

EXAMPLES

There *are* (verb) many *reasons* (subject) for the war in the Middle East.

- Singular subjects joined by *or* or *nor* take a singular verb. If one subject is singular and the other plural, the verb should agree with the nearer subject.

EXAMPLES

Either the *vegetable* or the *pan is creating* this awful taste. (Singular subjects)

Either the *pan* or the *vegetables are creating* this awful taste. (The verb agrees with the nearer subject.)

- Collective nouns (bunch, committee, family, group, herd, jury, number, team) may be either singular or plural, depending upon whether the group is regarded as a unit or as individuals.

SINGULAR: The number of homeless families *increases* every year. The *committee has* the serious responsibility of selecting a new dean.

<u>Notice that the same nouns are considered rural when the reference is to individual members or the group.</u>

PLURAL: A *number* of homeless people *were* ill enough to require hospitalization. The *committee have* not *agreed* on a date for the picnic.

Note: **A good rule to follow with *number, total,* and similar nouns is that, preceded by *the, number* is singular; preceded by *a,* it is plural. Another test: *A number of* should be treated as plural if it signifies several or many.**

Words like *aeronautics, cybernetics, mathematics,* and *physics* or like *news* and *dollars,* are plural in form but usually singular in usage.

EXAMPLES

Mathematics is a subject essential to the sciences.

Eighty-five *dollars* for that coat *is* a bargain.

PRACTICE EXERCISE 6

Decide whether the verb in the following sentences should be singular or plural. Then indicate your answer by placing a check in the appropriate space.

1. Some of us is( ) are( ) studying for the test.

2. The Board of Trustees is( ) are( ) making a decision about tuition increases this Wednesday.

3. The committee is( ) are( ) arriving in Chicago at different times.

4. There is( ) are( ) several options available to the opera buff in Chicago.

5. A large shipment of automotive parts has( ) have( ) been delayed.

6. Peanuts is( ) are( ) high in cholesterol.

7. Neither the mechanics nor the shop manager was( ) were( ) able to solve the problem.

8. Hospital expense, as well as doctor's, is( ) are( ) skyrocketing.

9. The cat and the dog is( ) are( ) getting a flea bath today.

10. Few of us realize( ) realizes( ) how much work went into the senior prom.

ANSWERS

1. ARE studying. The indefinite pronoun *some* here signifies more than one and consequently requires a plural verb.

2. IS making. The Board of Trustees is a single body acting officially as a legal entity.

3. ARE arriving. The reference is clearly to individual members of the committee; therefore, the verb is plural.

4. ARE. The subject of the sentence is *options,* and the plural verb *are* agrees in number.

5. HAS been delayed. The subject of the sentence, *shipment* requires a singular verb.

6. ARE. The plural subject *peanuts* requires a plural verb.

7. WAS. If a singular subject and a plural subject are joined by *nor*, the verb agrees with the nearer subject ("manager *was*").

8. IS skyrocketing. The singular subject *expense* requires a singular verb.

9. ARE getting. Use a plural verb with two singular subjects joined by *and*.

10. REALIZE. The subject of this sentence is the indefinite pronoun *few*, which requires the plural verb *realize*.

Principal Parts of Verbs

All verbs have four principal parts: the *present* (NOW), the *past* (YESTERDAY), the *present participle* (the -ING form of the verb), and the *past participle* (the form of the verb with HAVE). To find the principal parts of the verb, just remember the clues NOW, YESTERDAY, -ING, and HAVE.

PRESENT:	(you) *work* (NOW)
PAST:	(you) *worked* (YESTERDAY)
PRESENT PARTICIPLE:	(you are) *workING*
PAST PARTICIPLE:	(you HAVE) *worked*

PRESENT:	(he) *buys* (NOW)
PAST:	(he) *bought* (YESTERDAY)
PRESENT PARTICIPLE:	(he is) *buyING*
PAST PARTICIPLE:	(he HAS) *bought*

Participles are used:

1. as part of the main verb of the sentence

EXAMPLES

Sylvia *was buying* a dress.

Ed *had swum* a mile last Sunday.

2. as an adjective

EXAMPLE

Protesting loudly at the podium, Mr. McCracken insisted that an environmental study be held. (The present participle *protesting* modifies the noun *Mr. McCracken*.)

3. as a noun

A gerund is the present participle, or *-ing* form of the verb, used as a noun.

EXAMPLE

Smoking is indisputably a danger to one's health. (The gerund *smoking* is the subject of this sentence.)

When the main verb is separated from its helping verbs (like *has, have, be, does*) by intervening parts of a sentence, sometimes, through omission, an error in verb formation results. The verb formation *did not swum,* for example, is obviously wrong when seen out of context, but notice how difficult it is to spot in a sentence.

INCORRECT: Florence Chadwick *had swum* the English Channel twice before in treacherously cold weather, but last winter she *did not.*

CORRECT: Florence Chadwick *had swum* the English Channel twice before in treacherously cold weather, but last winter she *did not swim.*

INCORRECT: The rebel groups never *have* and never *will surrender* to any government forces.

CORRECT: The rebel groups never *have surrendered* and never *will surrender* to any government forces.

Another error involving principal parts of verbs results from a confusion of the simple past and the past participle. As in the preceding examples, such errors are more likely to occur in sentences where subject and verb are separated by modifiers. Note the following examples:

EXAMPLES

	PRESENT	PAST	PAST PARTICIPLE
We *saw* (not *seen*) the dog just last week.	see	saw	seen
The Dodgers finally *did* (not *done*) it.	do	did	done
My family had *gone* (not *went*) there for several summers.	go	went	gone
The music *began* (not *begun*) as the ship slid into the sea.	begin	began	begun
Jose Canseco had *broken* (not *broke*) his favorite bat.	break	broke	broken
The guests had *eaten* (not *ate*) before the wedding party arrived.	eat	ate	eaten
The Liberty Bell had *rung* (not *rang*) every Fourth of July for a century.	ring	rang	rung

Verbs like *sit, set, rise, raise, lie,* and *lay* cause trouble because of similarity of form.

EXAMPLES

	PRESENT	PAST	PAST PARTICIPLE
My cats usually *lie* (not *lay*) in the sun.	lie	lay	lain
The president *lay* (not *laid*) down for his afternoon rest.	(to recline)		
The wounded soldier had *lain* (not *laid*) on the battlefield for three days.			
If you *lay* (not *lie*) your jacket on the counter, it may become soiled.	lay	laid	laid
Phillip *laid* (not *lay*) the new sod on the prepared soil.	(to place)		

EXAMPLES

	PRESENT	PAST	PAST PARTICIPLE

The contractors have recently *laid* (not *lain*) the fresh cement for our new driveway.

At the sound of "Hail to the Chief," everyone usually *rises* (not *raises*).

	PRESENT	PAST	PAST PARTICIPLE
	rise (to get up or move up)	rose	risen

The flag *rose* (not *raised*) to the strains of "The Marine Hymn."

We feel that the faculty and staff have *risen* (not *raised*) to the challenge.

The college trustees intend to *raise* (not *rise*) student fees.

	raise (to cause to rise)	raised	raised

The students *raised* (not *rose*) the dress code issue again.

The neighbors had *raised* (not *risen*) the third side of the barn by noon.

Some errors arise from the confusion of the present tense with another principal part. Look at the following examples:

EXAMPLES

The students protested that the test was *supposed* (not *suppose*) to be on Chapter Three.

They *used* (not *use*) to have dinner together every Friday.

Shirley *came* (not *come*) to see how you are.

The following list of principal parts features verbs that sometimes cause trouble in speaking and writing.

PRESENT	PAST	PAST PARTICIPLE
become	became	become
begin	began	begun
bid (offer)	bid	bid
bid (command)	bade	bidden
bite	bit	bit, bitten
blow	blew	blown
break	broke	broken
bring	brought	brought
burst	burst	burst
catch	caught	caught
choose	chose	chosen
come	came	come
dive	dived, dove	dived
do	did	done

PRESENT	PAST	PAST PARTICIPLE
drag	dragged	dragged
draw	drew	drawn
drink	drank	drunk
drive	drove	driven
eat	ate	eaten
fall	fell	fallen
fly	flew	flown
forget	forgot	forgot, forgotten
freeze	froze	frozen
get	got	got, gotten
give	gave	given
go	went	gone
grow	grew	grown
hang (suspend)	hung	hung
hang (execute)	hanged	hanged
know	knew	known
lay	laid	laid
lead	led	led
lend	lent	lent
lie (recline)	lay	lain
lie (speak falsely)	lied	lied
lose	lost	lost
pay	paid	paid
prove	proved	proved, proven
raise	raised	raised
ride	rode	ridden
ring	rang, rung	rung
rise	rose	risen
run	ran	run
see	saw	seen
shake	shook	shaken
shrink	shrank	shrunk
sing	sang, sung	sung
sink	sank, sunk	sunk
speak	spoke	spoken
spring	sprang	sprung
steal	stole	stolen
swim	swam	swum
swing	swung	swung
take	took	taken
tear	tore	torn
throw	threw	thrown
wear	wore	worn
weave	wove	woven
wring	wrung	wrung
write	wrote	written

Find the verb errors in the following sentences. Not every sentence has an error. Place a check in the appropriate column.

Correct Incorrect

_____ _____ 1. Within five minutes, the fireman had climbed the ladder, plowed his way through mountains of debris, and did the impossible by putting out the fire.

_____ _____ 2. The play was completely staged by July and began in early August.

_____ _____ 3. She was very weary and simply wanted to lay down until dinner.

_____ _____ 4. The price of football tickets had rose dramatically since 1974.

_____ _____ 5. The New Zealand crew had lost a man overboard and tore the spinnaker.

_____ _____ 6. He had driven his bike to the trail head, run to the lake, and swum to the base camp.

Correct Incorrect

_____ _____ 7. When we were down at the lake on weekends, we use to sit on the sand and watch the girls.

_____ _____ 8. After my mother removed the sheets from the washer, my sister hanged them on the line.

ANSWERS

1. **Incorrect.** *Had climbed,* [had] *plowed,* and [had] *done.*

2. **Incorrect.** *Was staged* and [was] *begun.*

3. **Incorrect.** The infinitive form of the verb *lie* (meaning *to recline*) is *to lie.*

4. **Incorrect.** *Rose* is the past tense of the verb *rise;* the past participle required here is *risen.*

5. **Incorrect.** *Had lost* and [had] *torn.*

6. **Correct.**

7. **Incorrect.** The past tense *used* is needed here.

8. **Incorrect.** The past tense of *hang* (to suspend) is *hung.*

Verb Forms and Verbals

A high percentage of verb-related errors occurs because the reader confuses *verb forms*—that is, the different forms that an action word can assume—with entirely different structures known as *verbals*—words formed from verbs but not used as verbs in a sentence. Known as *participles, gerunds,* and *infinitives,* verbals form important phrases within the sentence.

Infinitives

An infinitive is ordinarily preceded by *to* and is used as a noun, an adjective, or an adverb.

NOUN: *To err* is human. (Subject)

ADJECTIVE: The survivors had little *to celebrate*. (*To celebrate* modifies the noun *little*.)

ADVERB: *To please* his children, Jerry bought a new pool. (*To please* modifies the verb *bought*.)

Sometimes, infinitives omit the word *to*.

EXAMPLES

Who dares [to] *challenge* a champion?

Please [to] *go*.

Make him [to] turn on the radio.

We saw him [to] leave.

Because both gerunds and participles have an *-ing* ending, they can be harder to distinguish between. However, a sentence that equates the two presents an error in parallel structure. If you understand the function of each in the sentence, you will be sure to spot this error if it occurs on the English test.

Gerunds

A gerund always ends in ring and functions as a noun.

SUBJECT: *Writing* is very rewarding.
SUBJECTIVE COMPLEMENT: My favorite occupation is *binding* books.
DIRECT OBJECT: He now regrets *resigning*.
OBJECT OF PREPOSITION: After *sealing* the letter, he went for a walk.

Participle

A participle acts as an adjective in the sentence.

EXAMPLES

Growling threateningly, the gorilla intimidated the crowd. (*Growling* modifies *gorilla*.)

The floor *invaded* by termites was made of oak. (*Invaded* modifies *floor*.)

There are two forms of participles, present and past. Present participles end in *-ing;* past participles assume many different forms (e.g., *bought, granted, shown, heard, hung, hidden, shot, torn*).

Other verb forms that may give trouble are the progressive and the passive. Progressive verb forms are regular action words that emphasize continuing action: "I *am running*" rather than "I *run*." Passive verbs transform the sentence in such a way that the subject is receiving action instead of performing it: "I *was given*" instead of "I *gave*."

Note the similarities of form in the following groups:

VERBS:
Simple—I *hit* the clay target fifty times.
Progressive—I *am hitting* the ball better than ever.
Passive—I *was hit* by a snowball.

VERBALS:
Infinitive—*To hit* a child is considered criminal.
Gerund—*Hitting* golf balls at a driving range is essential preparation for a match.
Participle—The man *hitting the ball* is also the coach.

PRACTICE EXERCISE 8

The following items may have errors in the use of verbals and verb forms. Indicate with a check in the proper column, whether the sentence is correct or incorrect.

Correct Incorrect

_____ _____ 1. By providing day care will help the working mother, as well as the economy.

_____ _____ 2. He made me to see this was a mistake.

_____ _____ 3. Sue is playing golf this morning, having lunch at the clubhouse, and expected home at three.

_____ _____ 4. Sylvia has traveled often, taking her little sister with her.

_____ _____ 5. To give underprivileged children gifts at Christmas and serving poor people a meal at this holiday made him happy.

_____ _____ 6. He wanted to start a cooperative family grocery outlet and selling a variety of household products.

ANSWERS

1. **Incorrect.** Although the gerund *providing* seems to be the subject of the verb *will help,* it is not. It is the object of the preposition *by.* To correct the sentence, omit *by.*

2. **Incorrect.** Drop the *to* of the infinitive after the verb *make* ("He made me see. . .")

3. **Incorrect.** The progressive forms *is playing* and [*is*] *having* are incorrectly made parallel with the passive form [*is*] *expected.* The correction is to use the progressive form: "[*is*] *expecting* to arrive home at three."

4. **Correct.** The participle *taking* modifies *Sylvia.*

5. **Incorrect.** The infinitive *to give* is not parallel with the gerund *helping* in the compound subject of this sentence. The verbals must both be infinitives or must both be gerunds.

6. **Incorrect.** The compound direct object of this sentence combines an infinitive (*to start*) and a gerund (*selling*). The elements must be parallel (*to start* and *to sell*).

Pronouns

Pronouns are most often employed as substitutes for nouns, but some can also be used as adjectives or conjunctions. To master pronouns and be able to spot errors in their use, you need to understand pronoun *case* (nominative, possessive, objective), pronoun *number* (singular or plural), and pronoun *class* (personal, demonstrative, interrogative, relative, indefinite).

Personal Pronouns

A personal pronoun indicates by its form the person or thing it takes the place of: the person speaking (first person), the person spoken to (second person), or the person or thing spoken about (third person).

First-Person Pronouns

	SINGULAR	PLURAL
Nominative case	I	we
Possessive case	my, mine	our, ours
Objective case	me	us

Second-Person Pronouns

	SINGULAR	PLURAL
Nominative case	you	you
Possessive case	your, yours	your, yours
Objective case	you	you

Third-Person Pronouns

	SINGULAR	PLURAL
Nominative case	he, she, it	they
Possessive case	his, hers, its	their, theirs
Objective case	him, her, it	them

Some common errors in pronoun case occur frequently in everyday speech and may well appear on the writing test. Study the following applications to see if you have been using the correct forms.

Use the nominative case of a pronoun in a compound subject.

EXAMPLE

Betty and *I* watched the Olympics on television.

Use the nominative case of a pronoun following any form of the verb *to be*. This use may not sound right to you, but it is standard written English, the language of the writing test.

EXAMPLES

It is *she*.

The winner was *I*.

Use the objective case when the pronoun is the object of a preposition.

This is just between you and *me*.

Doug looks like *me*. (Like, as well as *but,* can be used as a preposition.)

Nadine made coffee for Allan, Ken, and *me*.

When there are intervening words, eliminate them to find the correct pronoun to use. "Nadine made coffee for *I*" sounds ridiculous, yet some people might say, "Nadine made coffee for *Allan, Ken, and I.*" Similarly, in the sentence *"We (Us) homeowners want better roads,"* eliminate the word *homeowners* to find the correct word: *"We want better roads."*

Use the objective case when the pronoun is the object of a verb.

The noise frightened Karen and *me*.

Use the nominative case for pronouns that are subjects of elliptical clauses (clauses that are incomplete or unexpressed).

My children are as excited as *I* [am].

She raked more than *he* [raked].

As and *than* are subordinating conjunctions that introduce elliptical clauses. Complete the clause to determine the pronoun case.

Use a possessive pronoun before a gerund. Just as you would say *My car,* you would also say *My smoking* bothers her.

We have always regretted *her* leaving for California.

Demonstrative Pronouns

Demonstrative pronouns (*this, that, these, those*) take the place of things being pointed out.

These are Mary's.

I don't like *this.*

They are called demonstrative adjectives when used before nouns:

These seats are comfortable.

INCORRECT: *Them* are the new watches I ordered.

CORRECT: *Those* are the new watches I ordered.
            (Demonstrative pronoun)

Do not substitute a personal pronoun for a demonstrative pronoun or a demonstrative adjective.

INCORRECT: Look at *them* diamonds!

CORRECT: Look at *those* diamonds!
            (Demonstrative adjective)

Interrogative Pronouns

Interrogative pronouns (*who, whom, whose, which*, and *what*) are used in questions. *Who, which,* and *what* are used as subjects and are in the nominative case. *Whose* is in the possessive case. *Whom* is in the objective case, and, like all objects, it is the receiver of action in the sentence.

The most common error involving interrogative pronouns is the tendency to use *who* instead of *whom*.

When the pronoun is receiving the action, the objective form *whom* must be used.

INCORRECT: *Who* did you contact?

CORRECT: *Whom* did you contact? (You did contact whom?)

When the pronoun is performing the action, the nominative *who* must be used.

INCORRECT: *Whom* did you say is running the dance?

CORRECT: *Who* did you say is running the dance?
            (*Who* is the subject of *is running*.)

Relative Pronouns

Relative pronouns (*who, whom, whose, which, what,* and *that*) refer to people and things. When a relative pronoun is the subject of a subordinate clause, the clause becomes an adjective modifying a noun in the sentence.

EXAMPLE

The rumor *that plagued him all his life* was a lie. (*That* [subject] *plagued him all his life* modifies *rumor*.)

Which and *that* can also act as conjunctions to introduce subordinate clauses.

EXAMPLE

Bob knew *that* Boston would win.

Indefinite Pronouns

Indefinite pronouns (*all, another, any, both, each, either, everyone, many, neither, one, several, some,* and similar words) represent an indefinite number of persons or things. Many of these words also function as adjectives ("*several* men").

Indefinite pronouns present few problems. One thing to remember:

Use a singular pronoun with an indefinite antecedent like *one,* ***everyone,* and *anybody.***

INCORRECT: Everyone needs to prepare *themselves* for retirement.

CORRECT: Everyone needs to prepare *himself* (or *herself*) for retirement.

And a final caution:

The antecedent of a pronoun should be clear, specific, and close to the pronoun. Reword the sentence if necessary.

CONFUSING: The coach told Eric that *he* could practice after school.
CLEAR: The coach said that Eric could practice after school.

Possessive Pronoun–Gerund Combination Drill

If you have the habit of using objective-case pronouns with gerunds and gerund phrases, a very common error, try to remember this: *Gerunds are always nouns; therefore any pronoun placed before them must always be a possessive pronoun.* Here is an easy way to develop an ear for the use of the correct pronoun case. The following sentences are all correct. Just read the list several times, preferably aloud.

1. She resented *my* going out and having business lunches.

2. *Your* wanting to get up and leave was obvious to everyone.

3. *Her* having to cook dinner as well as take care of the children was the last straw.

4. The girls were irritated at *our* referring to the old fraternity all evening.

5. *Your* wanting to rebuild the city is very moving to me.

6. George resented *their* imposing a filing fee for new candidates.

7. The commission ruled against *my* giving away free balloons at the fair.

8. *Your* car-pooling can help rid the city of gridlock.

9. Edna began to feel embarrassed at *his* jumping into every conversation and immediately monopolizing it.

10. *Our* letting Brock eat table scraps from the table produced a spoiled animal.

11. *Your* sponsoring our son will not be forgotten.

12. *Their* having turned their backs on Kuwait and Saudi Arabia could possibly signify the end of the PLO.

13. *My* getting married should have no impact on you.

14. He felt strongly that he did not have to explain *his* enlisting in the Navy to anyone.

15. The world in general deeply resents *Saddam Hussein's* setting those oil fires and causing the world's largest oil spill.

16. The *industrial world's* treating oil as the only economical source of energy has brought us to a critical state of dependence.

17. *Janet's* brushing her hair every night has certainly made a difference in her appearance.

18. The house mistress felt that *Yvonne's* obvious flaunting of her intelligence would lead to some animosity among the women.

19. *Her* knowing that he did not have much money, yet ordering prime rib and lobster tails, was an example of raw greed.

20. *Bertha's* consuming four entire chickens in front of the Jungle Chicken stand was not the kind of endorsement the management hoped for.

21. Mary thinks *Phil's* chewing gum is the reason they did not get the part.

22. *Jill's* losing her wallet started off a very bad day.

23. The whole city was shocked by *his* refusing to take the oath.

24. *Their* running and jumping on our grass is going to ruin our front lawn.

25. *My* taking lunch to work every day has saved hundreds of dollars so far.

PRACTICE EXERCISE 9

Find the pronoun errors in the following sentences. Not every sentence has an error. Place a check in the appropriate column to indicate whether the sentence is correct or incorrect.

Correct   Incorrect

_____   _____   1. Who do you think is coming?

_____   _____   2. I can tell the culprit. It was he.

_____   _____   3. I play more tennis than her, but she has a natural talent.

Correct   Incorrect

_____   _____   4. They nominated everybody but Rosa and he.

_____   _____   5. Frank and him have been using the word processor.

_____   _____   6. Everyone must pat themselves on the back once in a while.

_____   _____   7. The broker was surprised at him wanting to buy 5,000 shares of that penny stock.

Correct Incorrect

_____ _____ 8. Who did you see in the play.

_____ _____ 9. The IRS required Lee, Carlotta, and I to produce more detailed records.

_____ _____ 10. Us Chicagoans don't appreciate our city nearly enough.

ANSWERS

1. **Correct.** *Who,* the subject of *is coming,* is performing the action.

2. **Correct.** The nominative case is used with all forms of the verb *to be. He* is correct.

3. **Incorrect.** To correct this sentence, supply the missing verb: "I play more tennis than *she* [does]. . ."

4. **Incorrect.** *But* in this sentence is used as a preposition; its object must be in the objective case (*him*), not the nominative.

5. **Incorrect.** Use the nominative case for a pronoun in a compound subject (Frank and *he*).

6. **Incorrect.** The pronoun should be *himself* (or *herself*) to agree with the singular form *everyone.*

7. **Incorrect.** *Wanting to buy stock* is a gerund phrase; it takes the possessive pronoun *his.*

8. **Incorrect.** *Whom* is needed, because it is the object of *did see.*

9. **Incorrect.** The pronoun *I* should be in the objective case (*me*) because it is a direct object of *required.*

10. **Incorrect.** The pronoun us should be in the nominative case (*we*) because it modifies *Chicagoans,* the subject of the sentence.

CUMULATIVE REVIEW II

Operators and manufacturers of nuclear

reactor power facilities are making increased

use of robots to improve operations and

maintenance, lower operating costs,

<u>increasing</u> plant availability and equipment
  1
reliability, <u>enhanced</u> worker safety, and
  2
reduce worker exposure to radiation. There is

no doubt in the field that advanced telerobotic

systems <u>can have made</u> more effective use of
  3
human operators, expert systems, and

intelligent machines; in fact, <u>few</u> of the world's
  4

1. (A) NO CHANGE
   (B) increases
   (C) increase
   (D) increased

2. (A) NO CHANGE
   (B) enhancing
   (C) enhances
   (D) enhance

3. (A) NO CHANGE
   (B) can make
   (C) can be made
   (D) can be making

4. (A) NO CHANGE
   (B) some
   (C) one
   (D) none

leading nuclear plant designers believe that a facility without modern robotic and telerobotic systems <u>will have become</u> obsolete in a very
5
few years. The design of future nuclear plants and supporting facilities—particularly <u>these</u>
6
involving fuel recycling—should incorporate considerations for use of robotic systems.

A committee of scientists critical of the move toward robotics <u>believe</u> that existing
7
methods for controlling and preprogramming the typical robot <u>is</u> appropriate for only a
8
limited number of jobs in nuclear facilities, mainly because <u>it simply require</u> too much
9
supervision. In addition, existing robots are limited in their ability to sense their surroundings and <u>interpreting</u> sensor data, a
10
prerequisite for handling unexpected problems during the routine executions of tasks.

5. (A) NO CHANGE
   (B) would have become
   (C) becomes
   (D) will become

6. (A) NO CHANGE
   (B) they
   (C) those
   (D) that

7. (A) NO CHANGE
   (B) believes
   (C) believed
   (D) have believed

8. (A) NO CHANGE
   (B) were
   (C) are
   (D) will be

9. (A) NO CHANGE
   (B) it simply required
   (C) they simply require
   (D) it simply requires

10. (A) NO CHANGE
    (B) interpret
    (C) interpreted
    (D) has interpreted

1. **C**   The verb *increase* needs to be an infinitive to be parallel with the series of infinitive phrases that comprise the end of the sentence.

2. **D**   The verb *enhance* needs to be an infinitive to be parallel with the series of infinitive phrases that comprise the end of the sentence.

3. **B**   The passage is written in the present tense, and employs the present tense in generally true statements.

4. **B**   *Some* is the more logical choice of indefinite pronoun here: the use of *few* in the text renders the sentence meaningless.

5. **D**   The future tense is made necessary by the trailing phrase "in a very few years."

6. **C**   Demonstrative pronouns take the place of things *being pointed out*. In this case, the word *those* is more appropriate for the antecedent *facilities* because those facilities will be built in the future.

7. **B**   The subject of the verb is the singular noun *committee*.

8. **C**   The subject of the verb is the plural noun *methods*.

9. **D**   The subject of the verb is the singular personal pronoun *it,* the antecedent of which is the noun *robot*.

10. **B**   *Interpret* is one of a pair of parallel infinitives (*to sense* and *to interpret*) modifying the noun *ability*.

SENTENCE STRUCTURE

In addition to a NO CHANGE response, the questions on the writing test that deal with sentence structure will offer three alternatives, each one a restructuring of the underlined part. Errors in sentence structure include such items as sentence fragments, run-on sentences, misplaced modifiers, and lack of parallelism. These topics are reviewed in this section.

Sentence Fragments

A sentence fragment is a part of a sentence that has been punctuated as if it were a complete sentence. It does not express a complete thought but depends upon a nearby independent clause for its full meaning. It should be made a part of that complete sentence.

INCORRECT: I was not able to pick up my child at her school. *Having been caught in heavy traffic.* (Participial phrase)

REVISED: Having been caught in heavy traffic, I was not able to pick up my child at her school.

OR

I was not able to pick up my child at her school. I had been caught in heavy traffic.

INCORRECT: The cat sat on the water heater. *Unable to get warm.* (Adjective phrase)

REVISED: Unable to get warm, the cat sat on the water heater.

INCORRECT:	The salesman tightened the wire around the burlap feed bag with a spinner. *Which twists wire loops until they are secure.* (Adjective clause)
REVISED:	The salesman tightened the wire around the burlap feed bag with a spinner, which twists wire loops until they are secure.
INCORRECT:	We will probably try to find another insurance company. *When our policy expires.* (Adverb clause)
REVISED:	When our policy expires, we will probably try to find another insurance company.

Run-on Sentences

Probably the most common error in writing occurs when two sentences are run together as one. There are two types of run-on sentences: the *fused* sentence, which has no punctuation mark between its two independent clauses, and the *comma splice,* which substitutes a comma where either a period or a semicolon is needed.

FUSED:	Jean had no luck at the store they were out of raincoats.
COMMA SPLICE:	She surprised us all with her visit, she was on her way to New York.

To correct a run-on sentence, use a period, a semicolon, or a coordinating conjunction (*and, but, or, nor, for*) to separate independent clauses.

Note the following examples of run-on sentences and the suggested revisions.

FUSED:	Eric is a bodybuilder he eats only large amounts of meat.
REVISED:	Eric is a bodybuilder; he eats only large amounts of meat.
COMMA SPLICE:	He had never seen Alex so prepared, he even had backup copies of his study sheets!
REVISED:	He had never seen Alex so prepared. He even had back-up copies of his study sheets!
COMMA SPLICE:	His father was an artist, his mother was an accountant.
REVISED:	His father was an artist, and his mother was an accountant.

PRACTICE EXERCISE 10

Most of the following items contain sentence fragments or run-on sentences. Place a check in the proper column to indicate whether the item is correct or incorrect.

Correct   Incorrect

_____   _____   1. Bert used his manuscript for scratch paper. Having received rejection notices from twelve publishers.

_____   _____   2. The bank changed its hours and hired more security officers. After a wave of bank robberies hit the neighborhood.

_____   _____   3. We have to leave now it will be dark soon.

_____   _____   4. Having been declared fit by his doctor, Cleveland planned a weekend hike to the top of Mount Washington.

_____   _____   5. It was an embarrassment to hear Colonel Wilkinson talk about the medals he won with his marching corps. In front of all those wounded veterans!

_____   _____   6. Erica played softball for Taft High School, she hit a home run every week.

_____   _____   7. Our Himalayan cat Mathilda gave birth to seven beautiful kittens. All little white bundles of purring fluff.

_____   _____   8. Boris accidentally stepped on the little girl's foot he felt terrible.

Correct   Incorrect

_____   _____   9. It is necessary to vacuum around and under your refrigerator at least once a month. To prevent it from overheating.

_____   _____   10. Several of us want to give Dr. Kellogg a birthday party. Because he is so kind and generous.

_____   _____   11. Human cloning will soon become a reality; people will be able to produce improved versions of themselves.

_____   _____   12. Jared was warned, he was offending too many of his superiors.

ANSWERS

1. **Incorrect.** *Having received rejection notices from twelve publishers* is a participial phrase modifying the proper noun *Bert* and must be attached to the main clause.

2. **Incorrect.** The adverb clause *After a wave of bank robberies hit the neighborhood* modifies the verbs *changed* and *hired,* and should be joined to the rest of the sentence.

3. **Incorrect.** This is a fused sentence, which needs a period, semicolon, or coordinating conjunction between the words *now* and *it.* If a period is used, the word *it* should begin with a capital letter.

4. **Correct.** The dependent phrases, *Having been declared fit by his doctor* and *to the top of Mount Washington,* have been included in one complete sentence.

5. **Incorrect.** *In front of all those wounded veterans* is a prepositional phrase that should be made part of the sentence containing the word it modifies, *talk.*

6. **Incorrect.** This sentence is a comma splice; that is, a comma is used where a stronger mark of separation belongs, such as a period, semicolon, or coordinating conjunction.

7. **Incorrect.** *All little white bundles of purring fluff* is an appositive phrase modifying *kittens*. It cannot stand alone.

8. **Incorrect.** See explanation, item 3.

9. **Incorrect.** The infinitive phrase *To prevent it from overheating* should be part of the previous sentence.

10. **Incorrect.** *Because he is so kind and generous* is a dependent adverb clause that should be attached to the independent clause containing the verb it modifies.

11. **Correct.** The independent clauses are properly separated by a semicolon.

12. **Incorrect.** See explanation, item 6.

Connectives

Connectives that join elements of equal rank are called coordinating conjunctions (*and, but, or, nor, for, yet*). Connectives that introduce a less important element are called subordinating conjunctions (*after, although, since, when*).

Coordinating conjunctions link words, phrases, and clauses that are of equal importance.

EXAMPLES

The pilot *and* the crew boarded the plane.

The road ran through the valley *and* along the river.

Compound sentences are formed when coordinating conjunctions link two independent clauses.

EXAMPLE

You can sign the loan papers on Friday, *or* you can sign them on Monday.

Subordinating conjunctions are used in sentences to connect clauses that are not equal in rank—that is, in sentences in which one idea is made subordinate to another. There are many subordinating conjunctions. Some of the important ones are *after, as, because, before, if, in order that, once, since, unless, until, whenever,* and *wherever.*

EXAMPLES

We covered up the newly planted citrus trees *when* the temperature began to drop.

Until I saw her in person, I thought Cher was a tall woman.

Another form of connective is the *conjunctive adverb*. It is actually an adverb that functions as a coordinating conjunction. The principal conjunctive adverbs are *accordingly, also, besides, certainly, consequently, finally, furthermore, however, incidentally, instead, likewise, nevertheless, otherwise, similarly,* and *undoubtedly.* When they join clauses, conjunctive adverbs are usually preceded by a semicolon and followed by a comma.

EXAMPLE

I understand you wish to see a Broadway musical; *undoubtedly,* you'll have to get tickets far in advance for one of the hit shows.

Coordination can be overdone. If every significant idea in every sentence is given equal weight, there is no *main* idea.

FAULTY
COORDINATION: The real power in the company lies with Mr. Stark, and he currently owns 55 percent of the stock; in addition to that, his mother is semiretired as president of the firm.

REVISED: The real power in the company lies with Mr. Stark, who currently owns 55 percent of the stock and whose mother is semiretired as president of the firm.

Notice that subordinating two of the independent clauses tightens the sentence and adds focus.

Subordination of too many parts of a sentence, however, can be just as confusing. Look at the following examples:

EXCESSIVE
SUBORDINATION: Standing on the corner were many aliens who had entered the country illegally, and most of whom had applied for amnesty, and even more important to them though, who had families back in Mexico or El Salvador who needed food and shelter.

REVISED: Standing on the corner were many illegal aliens, most of whom had applied for amnesty. Even more important to them, though, was the fact that they had families needing food and shelter back in Mexico or El Salvador.

Notice how proper coordination and subordination helps clarify a confusing stream of excessively entwined modifiers.

You must also keep in mind the *logic* of subordination. What you choose to subordinate in a sentence has to make sense to the reader. For example, the sentence "Sue happened to glance at the sky, amazed to see an enormous flying saucer hovering over the barn" gives greater importance to the fact that Sue glanced at the sky. A more logical version of that sentence is, "Happening to glance at the sky, Sue was amazed to see an enormous flying saucer hovering over the barn."

BACKWARD
SUBORDINATION: She studied medicine with great intensity for fifteen years, becoming a doctor.

LOGICAL REVISION: She became a doctor, having studied medicine with great intensity for fifteen years.

BACKWARD
SUBORDINATION: The pitcher momentarily let the runner on first base take a wide lead, when he stole second.

LOGICAL REVISION: The runner stole second when the pitcher momentarily let him take a wide lead.

BACKWARD
SUBORDINATION: He ran over with a fire extinguisher, saving the driver's life.

LOGICAL REVISION: Running over with a fire extinguisher, he saved the driver's life.

PRACTICE EXERCISE 11

Most of the following sentences contain either faulty coordination or subordination, or backward subordination. Place a check in the appropriate column to indicate whether the sentence is correct or faulty.

Correct Faulty

_____ _____ 1. I had prepared myself by practicing, and I was able to beat Phil at racquetball.

_____ _____ 2. Realizing that the mob does not forgive breaches of security, Lefty went into hiding.

_____ _____ 3. As a terrible storm began, we were eating.

_____ _____ 4. George found out about the burglary, and he was so shocked at first, and he could not remember his telephone number.

_____ _____ 5. Between Big Sur and Carmel, the roads were in very bad condition, because the State Highway Agency is repairing them.

Correct Faulty

_____ _____ 6. He bought a second-hand car, which had a sun roof, and it began to leak, so he took the car back to the dealer, who replaced the roof.

_____ _____ 7. The V-2 Project was manned by prisoners who had no contact with the outside world, because it was completed in total secrecy.

_____ _____ 8. Janine is a ballet dancer, and her sister is a gymnast.

ANSWERS

1. **Faulty.** This sentence is an example of faulty coordination. The sentence would be improved by subordinating the less important idea: Having prepared myself by practicing, I was able to beat Phil at racquetball.

2. **Correct.** In this sentence, the less important idea is properly subordinated.

3. **Faulty.** This sentence is an example of illogical or backward subordination. The important idea is the storm, not the eating: A terrible storm began as we were eating.

4. **Faulty.** This sentence is an example of faulty coordination. Improve it by subordinating two of the independent clauses: When George found out about the burglary, he was so shocked at first that he could not remember his telephone number.

5. **Faulty.** This is an example of illogical or backward subordination. The fact that the roads were being repaired is the main idea of the sentence. We know that, because the other clause gives the reason that the roads are being repaired. *Revised:* Because the roads between Big Sur and Carmel were in very bad condition, the State Highway Agency is repairing them.

6. **Faulty.** This is an example of both faulty coordination and excessive subordination. *Revised:* He bought a secondhand car with a sun roof. When the sun roof began to leak, he took the car back to the dealer, who replaced the roof.

7. **Faulty.** This sentence is an example of illogical subordination. Of the two ideas, *The V-2 Project was manned by prisoners* and *it was completed in total secrecy,* the second is the more important one. *Revised:* Because the V-2 Project ... world, it ...

8. **Correct.** This is an acceptable compound sentence, pairing two equal ideas logically.

Modifiers

Adjectives and Adverbs

The purpose of adjectives and adverbs is to describe, limit, color—in other words, to *modify* other words. Adjectives modify nouns or pronouns, and generally precede the words they modify. Adverbs describe verbs, adjectives or other adverbs. Some words can be used as either adjectives (He has an *early appointment*) or adverbs (He arrived *early*).

ADJECTIVES: *fuzzy* peach
impressive view
sour milk

ADVERBS: He grumbled *loudly.*
She smiled *broadly.*
It poured *unmercifully.*

Although most adverbs end in *-ly,* some do not (*fast, hard, long, straight*). A few adjectives also have an *-ly* ending (*lovely* day, *lively* discussion).

Adjectives

Problems that students face with adjectives frequently relate to the use of degrees of comparison. There are three degrees: the *positive*—the original form of the word (*straight*); the *comparative*—used to compare two persons or things (*straighter*); and the *superlative*—used to compare more than two persons or things (*straightest*). If not understood, the spelling and form changes involved can sometimes confuse the unwary student.

1. Most adjectives form the comparative and superlative degrees by adding *-er* and *-est:*

POSITIVE: nice
COMPARATIVE: nicer
SUPERLATIVE: nicest

2. Other adjectives form the comparative and superlative by using more and most:

POSITIVE: challenging
COMPARATIVE: more challenging
SUPERLATIVE: most challenging

3. Some adjectives change completely as they form the comparative and superlative degrees:

POSITIVE: little
COMPARATIVE: less
SUPERLATIVE: least

Be alert for double comparisons, which incorrectly use *more* or *most* with adjectives that already express a degree: *more softer* or *most strongest*.

Also, watch for the illogical use of the comparative or the superlative with adjectives that cannot be compared, such as *square, round, perfect, unique*. It is meaningless to write *rounder* or *most perfect*.

When comparing only two nouns, use the comparative degree: Mars is the *larger* of the two planets. When comparing more than two, use the superlative: Gibson is the *most dangerous* hitter on their team.

Adverbs

Adverbs (either as words, phrases, or clauses) describe the words they modify by indicating *when, how, where, why, in what order,* or *how often*. Adverbs also tell to what degree.

WHEN: He studied *until 10:00 every night*.
TO WHAT DEGREE: She is *too pretty* for words.
HOW: She testified *with quiet dignity*.
WHERE: Bring the paper *here*.
WHY: They rejected the offer *because it was too little*.
IN WHAT ORDER: *One after another*, the townspeople told the judge their story.

Note: *Anywheres, nowheres,* **and** *somewheres* **are incorrect adverb forms. Use** *anywhere, nowhere, somewhere.*

The adjectives *good* and *bad* should not be used as adverbs.

NOT
She doesn't sing so *good*.
He wants that job *bad*.

BUT
She doesn't sing so *well*.
He wants that job *badly*.

Standard English requires the use of a formal adverb form rather than a colloquial version.

NOT
This was a *real* good clambake.
He *sure* doesn't look happy.

BUT
This was a *really* good clambake.
He *surely* doesn't look happy.

PRACTICE EXERCISE 12

Some of the following sentences combine errors in the use of adjectives or adverbs. Determine whether a or b is the correct word to use. Then place a check in the appropriate column.

    a   *b*

_____ _____ 1. The new Turbo-B ran *real/really* well during
         a   b
     the first race.

_____ _____ 2. Mike is the *more/most*
               a   b
     active of the twins.

_____ _____ 3. I *sure/surely* would like
         a   b
     that leather jacket.

_____ _____ 4. Portia was even more *fussier/fussy* than
         a   b
     Elena.

_____ _____ 5. These earrings are *unique/most unique!*
         a   b

    a   *b*

_____ _____ 6. He had many friends in Chicago, where he lived *previous/previously.*
         a   b

ANSWERS

1. **b** The adverb *really* is needed to modify the adverb *well*. (Only adverbs can modify other adverbs.)

2. **a** The comparative degree is used when two are compared.

3. **b** In colloquial speech, the word *sure* is accepted. In the writing test, as in all secondary school and college writing, the norm is standard English, which requires the adverb *surely* in a construction like this.

4. **b** With the comparative degree *more*, only the positive degree *fussy* is correct. *More fussier* is a double comparison.

5. **a** It is illogical to add degrees to absolutes like *unique*. Something is either unique or not unique.

6. **b** The adverb *previously* is the correct choice to modify the verb *lived*. *Previous*, an adjective, cannot modify a verb.

Probably the most persistent and frustrating errors in the English language involve either *incorrect modification* or else *inexact modification* that is difficult to pin down.

In most cases, if you can keep your eye on the *word or phrase being modified*, it is easier to avoid the following pitfalls.

Misplaced Modifiers
To avoid confusion or ambiguity, place the modifying words, phrases, or clauses near the words they modify.

Misplaced Adverb Modifiers
Adverbs like *scarcely, nearly, merely, just, even,* and *almost* must be placed near the words they modify.

CONFUSED:	Last week during the cold spell, I *nearly* lost all of my flowers.
CLEAR:	Last week during the cold spell, I lost *nearly* all of my flowers. (The adverb *nearly* modifies the pronoun *all*.)
CONFUSED:	Acme *just* cleaned my rugs last month.
CLEAR:	cleaned my rugs *just* last month. (The adverb *just* modifies the adverbial phrase *last month*.)

Misplaced Phrase Modifiers

CONFUSED:	*To plant tomatoes,* it was a good growing year.
CLEAR:	It was a good growing year *to plant tomatoes.*
CONFUSED:	*Like a sleek projectile,* the passengers saw the new train approach the station.
CLEAR:	The passengers saw the new train approach the station *like a sleek projectile.*

Misplaced Clause Modifiers

CONFUSED:	He packed all of his books and documents into his van, *which he was donating to the library.*
CLEAR:	He packed all of his books and documents, *which he was donating to the library,* into his van.
CONFUSED:	The new series of seminars will focus on how to prevent inflation, *which will benefit us all.*
CLEAR:	The new series of seminars, *which will benefit us all,* will focus on how to prevent inflation.

Dangling Constructions

A dangling modifier literally hangs in the air; there is no logical word in the sentence for it to modify. Frequently it is placed close to the wrong noun or verb, causing the sentence to sound ridiculous: *Driving through the park, several chipmunks could be seen.*

Dangling Participles

A participle is a form of the verb that is used as an adjective. Unless there is a logical word for it to modify, the participial phrase will dangle, modifying either the wrong noun or none at all.

INCORRECT:	Having run out of gas, John was late for dinner.
REVISED:	Because the car ran out of gas, John was late for dinner.
INCORRECT:	Driving along the parkway, several deer were spotted.
REVISED:	Driving along the parkway, we spotted several deer.

Dangling Gerunds

A gerund is the *-ing* form of a verb serving as a noun (*Smoking is bad for your health*). When a gerund is used as the object of a preposition ("by *hiding*," "after *escaping*," "upon *realizing*"), the phrase can dangle if the actor that it modifies is missing.

INCORRECT:	After putting a bloodworm on my hook, the flounders began to bite.
REVISED:	After putting a bloodworm on my hook, I found that the flounders began to bite.
INCORRECT:	In designing our house addition, a bathroom was forgotten.
REVISED:	In designing our house addition, we forgot to add a bathroom.

Dangling Infinitives

Unlike the participle and the gerund, the infinitive performs more than one job in a sentence. While the participle acts like an adjective, and the gerund like a noun, the infinitive phrase can take the part of a noun, adjective, or adverb. Note the following examples of dangling infinitive phrases:

INCORRECT:	To skate like a champion, practice is essential.
REVISED:	To skate like a champion, one must practice.
INCORRECT:	To make a good impression, a shirt and tie should be worn to the interview.
REVISED:	To make a good impression, Jeff should wear a shirt and tie to the interview.

Illogical Comparisons

Occasionally, a writer will mistakenly compare items that are not comparable.

INCORRECT:	Her *salary* was lower than a clerk. (The *salary* is incorrectly compared with a *clerk*.)
CORRECT:	Her *salary* was lower than a *clerk's*.
INCORRECT:	The cultural *events* in Orlando are as diversified as *any other large city*. *Events* are being compared with a large city.
CORRECT:	The cultural events in Orlando are as diversified as *those in any other large city*.

Another form of illogical comparison results when a writer fails to exclude from the rest of the group the item being compared.

INCORRECT:	She is taller than *any girl* in her class.
CORRECT:	She is taller than *any other girl* in her class.

PRACTICE EXERCISE 13

In the following sentences, find the errors that involve modifiers. Not every sentence has an error. Place a check in the appropriate column to indicate whether the sentence is correct or incorrect.

Correct Incorrect

_____ _____ 1. The corn was roasted by the boys skewered on the ends of long, pointed sticks.

_____ _____ 2. t was still pouring, so Uncle Maurice went out to the sty to feed the hogs with an umbrella.

_____ _____ 3. Coming nearer to it, the building certainly seemed dilapidated.

_____ _____ 4. Henry's sales record will be as good as any of the top salespeople.

_____ _____ 5. Coiled in a corner of the garage and ready to spring, Mrs. Lampert was surprised by a rattlesnake.

_____ _____ 6. Having been asked to speak at the senior dinner, Fred spent many evenings preparing his speech.

_____ _____ 7. To be well baked, you have to leave the pork roast in the oven for three hours.

_____ _____ 8. We saw the impressive Concorde on the porch this morning.

ANSWERS

1. **Incorrect.** The participial phrase *skewered on the ends of long, pointed sticks* should be placed closer to corn, the noun it is intended to modify: *Skewered... sticks, the corn...*

2. **Incorrect.** The prepositional phrase *with an umbrella* is misplaced. It seems to modify the *hogs* or *to feed* but should modify the verb *went*.

3. **Incorrect.** This sentence is missing the noun that the participial phrase *Coming nearer to it* is meant to modify. A corrected version might be *Coming nearer to the building, we noticed that it certainly seemed dilapidated.*

4. **Incorrect.** This sentence contains an illogical comparison. The correct sentence should include the pronoun *that: Henry's sales record will be as good as that of any of the top salespeople.*

5. **Incorrect.** The participial phrase beginning this sentence seems to modify *Mrs. Lampert.* It should modify *rattlesnake.* The correction, of course, is to place the word *rattlesnake* close to the participial phrase.

6. **Correct.** The participial phrase is placed close to *Fred,* the noun it logically modifies.

7. **Incorrect.** The infinitive phrase *To be well baked* here incorrectly modifies *you* instead of *roast,* the noun it is intended for.

8. **Incorrect.** The Concorde was not on the porch, as this sentence seems to imply. *Revised: As we sat on the porch this morning, we saw the impressive Concorde.*

CUMULATIVE REVIEW III

The life of famed watchmaker Abraham-Louis Breguet was, from beginning to end (1747–1823). A steady progression toward [1] fame and fortune. Breguet soon revealed a lively interest that developed into a veritable passion for things mechanical in his step- [2] father's shop. He studied with the famed jeweler Abbot Marie for twelve years, his [3] vocation was henceforth decided. Living in [4] the Swiss cantons on the French border, watch-making had already been developed on a large scale by refugee French families, because it was limited almost exclusively to [5] inexpensive products. Young Breguet, on the [6] contrary, demonstrating very early a decided [6] disgust for shoddy workmanship, as well as a [6] genius for precision work, had an attitude he [6] never lost. [6]

1. **(A)** NO CHANGE
   (B) (1747–1823), a
   (C) (1747–1823) a
   (D) (1747–1823); a

2. **(A)** NO CHANGE
   (B) (Place at the beginning of the sentence).
   (C) (Place after the verb revealed).
   (D) (Delete altogether; the phrase is not related).

3. **(A)** NO CHANGE
   (B) years his vocation
   (C) years, then his vocation
   (D) years, and his vocation

4. **(A)** NO CHANGE
   (B) (Place this phrase after border).
   (C) (Place this phrase after families).
   (D) Delete altogether; the phrase is not related).

5. **(A)** NO CHANGE
   (B) but
   (C) even though
   (D) however

6. **(A)** NO CHANGE
   (B) Young Breguet, on the contrary, demonstrating very early a decided disgust for shoddy workmanship, as well as a genius for precision work, an attitude he never lost.
   (C) Young Breguet, on the contrary, demonstrated very early a decided disgust for shoddy workmanship, as well as a genius for precision work, an attitude he never lost.
   (D) Young Breguet, on the contrary, demonstrated very early a decided disgust for shoddy workmanship, as well as a genius for precision work, and had an attitude he never lost.

In 1802, Breguet, receiving the gold medal
<u>   </u>
                    7
at an exhibition of industrial products, sat at
<u>   </u>
                    7
the table of the first consul. Throughout his
<u>   </u>
        7
reign, Napoleon's interest in the works of the

watch master, principally those of high

precision, never slackened. The face studded
                              <u>   </u>
                                    8
with brilliant diamonds and rubies, Napoleon
<u>   </u>
                    8
acquired Breguet's most ambitious creation
<u>   </u>
                    8
the day after it was completed.
<u>   </u>
            8

The fall of the empire did not affect either
<u>   </u>
                  9
his fortunes adversely or his renown, which
<u>   </u>
                9
had spread throughout Europe. The
<u>   </u>
            9
exhibition of 1819 in which Breguet presented

a collection of his most important works was

a triumphant compendium of his life, by then
                                     <u>   </u>
                                        10
more than seventy years old.
<u>   </u>
        10

7. **(A)** NO CHANGE
   (B) In 1802, Breguet, receiving the gold medal at an exhibition of industrial products, sitting at the table of the first consul.
   (C) In 1802, Breguet received the gold medal at an exhibition of industrial products, and sat at the table of the first consul.
   (D) In 1802, Breguet sat at the table of the first consul, receiving the gold medal at an exhibition of industrial products.

8. **(A)** NO CHANGE
   (B) The face studded with brilliant diamonds and rubies, Breguet's most ambitious creation, the day after it was completed, was acquired by Napoleon.
   (C) The face studded with brilliant diamonds and rubies the day after it was completed, Napoleon acquired Breguet's most ambitious creation.
   (D) Napoleon acquired Breguet's most ambitious creation, the face studded with brilliant diamonds and rubies, the day after it was completed.

9. **(A)** NO CHANGE
   (B) The fall of the empire did not adversely affect either his fortunes or his renown, which had spread throughout Europe.
   (C) Adversely, the fall of the empire did not affect either his fortunes or his renown, which had spread throughout Europe.
   (D) The fall of the empire did not affect either his fortunes or his renown adversely, which had spread throughout Europe.

10. **(A)** NO CHANGE
    (B) (Place this phrase at the beginning of the sentence).
    (C) (Place this phrase, bracketed with commas, after the word *Breguet*).
    (D) (Delete this phrase; it is not relevant).

ANSWERS FOR CUMULATIVE REVIEW III

1. **B** This sentence contains the parenthetical interruption *from beginning to end (1747–1823),* which must be set off by commas. Any stronger mark of punctuation after the parentheses results in two fragmented sentences.

2. **B** The only logical position in this sentence for the prepositional phrase *in his stepfather's shop* is at the beginning of the sentence where it will correctly modify the noun *Breguet.*

3. **D** A compound sentence is the most appropriate vehicle for these two ideas of equal importance. A comma is used before the coordinating conjunction that joins coordinate clauses.

4. **C** The only logical position in this sentence for the participial phrase *Living in the Swiss cantons* is next to the noun it logically modifies, *families.*

5. **B** Only a connective signaling contrast like *but* makes sense in this context, especially in the light of the next sentence.

6. **C** This choice allows the main clause to emphasize the major characteristic of the subject, and correctly subordinates the parenthetical phrase, *an attitude he never lost.*

7. **C** The act of receiving the gold medal is logically as important as sitting with the first consul, and should not be subordinated in a participial phrase.

8. **D** The phrase *The face studded with brilliant diamonds and rubies* modifies the noun *creation* and so must be placed next to it.

9. **B** The adverb *adversely* logically modifies only the verb *affect* and should be placed near it.

10. **C** The phrase *By then more than seventy years old* appropriately modifies the noun *Breguet* and should be placed next to it, set off by commas since it is a parenthetical addition.

CONSISTENCY AND TENSE

Verbs in Subordinate Clauses

Because *tense* indicates the time of the action and *voice* indicates whether the subject is the agent of the action (*active:* Tom *saw*) or the recipient of the action (*passive:* Tom *was seen*), both of these verb forms are central to the consistency of a sentence or passage.

Tense

A verb in a subordinate clause should relate logically in tense to the verb in the principal clause. Avoid any unnecessary shift.

INCORRECT:	As the wedding *began* [past], the bride's mother *starts* [present] to cry.
CORRECT:	As the wedding *began* [past], the bride's mother *started* [past] to cry.
INCORRECT:	He *had intended* [past perfect] to finish his third novel by the end of the year, but he *has been very sick* [present perfect] until Thanksgiving.
CORRECT:	He *had intended* [past perfect] to finish his third novel by the end of the year, but he *had been very sick* [past perfect] until Thanksgiving.

INCORRECT: By the time the fire *had been extinguished* [past perfect], the priceless paintings *had been destroyed* [past perfect].

CORRECT: By the time the fire *was extinguished* [past], the priceless paintings *had been destroyed* [past perfect]. (The past perfect expresses action that took place before the simple past.)

Voice

A verb in a subordinate clause should relate logically in voice to the verb in the main clause. It is generally better to avoid voice shifts within a sentence.

INCORRECT: Sighs of appreciation *could be heard* [passive] as the waiters *brought* [active] huge trays of roast beef and Yorkshire pudding.

CORRECT: The guests *sighed* [active] with appreciation as the waiters *brought* [active] huge trays of roast beef and Yorkshire pudding.

INCORRECT: If the fishing boat *had been reached* [passive] in time, the Coast Guard *might have saved* [active] it with floats. (Note that the subject shifts as well as the voice.)

CORRECT: If it *had reached* [active] the fishing boat in time, the Coast Guard *might have saved* [active] it with floats.

The Present Infinitive

Always use the present infinitive (*to run, to see*), after a perfect tense (a tense that uses some form of the helping verb *have* or *had*).

EXAMPLES

He *has decided to order* the Jaguar Model S-1. (Present Perfect + Present Infinitive)

They *had hoped to hold* a spring picnic. (Past Perfect + Present Infinitive)

Keep in mind that the test offers three substitute choices for each underlined part. Frequently, even though you may not remember the grammatical terms involved, your prose sense will lead you to the right answer.

Look at the following set of responses. Which is correct?

(A) Fran would of wanted to see the show.
(B) Fran would have wanted to had seen the show.
(C) Fran would have wanted to have seen the show.
(D) Fran would have wanted to see the show.

Choice D is correct. If you selected this answer, did you apply the grammatical principle involved (use the present infinitive after a perfect tense), or were you guided by your prose "ear"? Chances are that it may have been your own language sense that suggested this answer. The point is that you already possess language sense that should help you on the test. With more preparation, you should do even better.

The Subjunctive Mood
Verbs may be expressed in one of three moods: the *indicative,* used to declare a fact or ask a question; the *imperative,* used to express a command; and the *subjunctive,* generally used to indicate doubt or to express a wish or request or a condition contrary to fact. The first two moods are fairly clear-cut.

INDICATIVE: This cake is tasty. Who baked it?

IMPERATIVE: Please leave now. Go home.

Note: **The imperative mood has only one subject (*you*) and one tense (*the present*).**

The subjunctive mood presents more of a problem. It suggests *possibilities, maybes, could have beens,* or *wishes that it had been,* and its uses are sometimes more difficult to understand. The subjunctive mood appears more frequently in formal English than in standard written English.
Notice the following uses, including some traditional ones:

EXAMPLES

I insist that the new road *be started* this spring.

The company requires that the check *be certified.*

Had she *been* certain of her facts, she would have challenged the teacher.

If need *be,* we can use our pension money.

Should the swarm *reappear,* I will call a beekeeper.

If he *were* honest, he would return all the money.

I move that the budget *be accepted.*

Far *be* it from me to suggest that he is lying.

Would that I *were* sixteen again!

I wish I *were* on a plane to Tahiti.

Note: **Today, the subjunctive is most often used to express doubt, wishes, or conditions contrary to fact. However, the indicative can also be used for some of these same feelings.**

SUBJUNCTIVE MOOD: If it *be* true, I will be delighted.

INDICATIVE MOOD: If it *is* true, I will be delighted.

Special Use of the Present Tense
Use the present tense to express universally true statements or timeless facts.

EXAMPLES

Ice *forms* at 32°F.

The rainy season seldom *arrives* in California.

She told the campers that mosquitos *are* part of nature.

The Historical Present
In writing about a poem or describing events in fiction or plays, use the present tense. This convention is called the historical present.

EXAMPLE

In *A Tale of Two Cities,* Dr. Manette *is restored* to his daughter after twenty years in jail.

PRACTICE EXERCISE 14

In the following sentences, find any errors in mood or tense. Not every sentence has an error. Place a check in the appropriate column to indicate whether the sentence is correct or incorrect.

Correct Incorrect

_____ _____ 1. If I knew about winning the lottery, I would not have sold my boat.

_____ _____ 2. In his poem *In Memoriam,* Tennyson wrote a eulogy for his friend Arthur Henry Hallam.

_____ _____ 3. The children have gone fishing for trout.

_____ _____ 4. By the time the tide had covered the sand castles, we had already put the children to bed.

_____ _____ 5. Groans and catcalls could be heard as the opposing team took the field.

_____ _____ 6. When the earthquake struck, we all run out of our houses.

_____ _____ 7. If I was you, I would take the job.

_____ _____ 8. If we reach an accord by Monday, we will offer it to the membership by Monday night.

ANSWERS

1. **Incorrect.** The past tense *knew* does not go back in time far enough to permit the use of the present perfect tense later in the sentence. The correction is to change *knew* to *had known* (the past perfect).

2. **Incorrect.** Use the historical present for statements about literary works (*poet. . . writes*).

3. **Incorrect.** Use the present infinitive after a perfect tense: The children have gone *to fish* for trout.

4. **Incorrect.** Watch the sequence of tenses: The children had been put to bed *before* the tide covered the sand castles. *Covered* is the correct tense.

5. **Incorrect.** Both the subject and the voice shift in this sentence. *Revised:* The opposing team heard groans and catcalls as they took the field.

6. **Incorrect.** Maintain a consistent verb tense: When the earthquake struck [past], we all *ran* [past] out of our houses.

7. **Incorrect.** Use the subjunctive mood for a condition contrary to fact: If I *were* you. . .

8. **Correct.** There are no awkward shifts of subject or voice in this sentence. The sequence of tenses is also correct.

Predication

Predication refers to the process of joining the *naming* part of the sentence (the *subject*) to the *doing* or *describing* part of the sentence (the *predicate*).

SUBJECT	PREDICATE
People	are buying more fish.
Cecelia	is a counselor.

It is not likely that a writer or reader will have trouble linking the subjects and predicates of sentences as short as these. It is in the use of longer, more detailed sentences that predication errors come about. Illogical predication equates unlike constructions and ideas. Look at the following incorrect examples.

INCORRECT: By working at such technical plants as Lockheed and Bendix gives the engineering students insight into what will be expected of them. (*By working* does not give them insight; *working* does.)

According to one authority, the ages of thirty to forty are subject to the most pressures concerning self-identity. (The *ages* are not subject to the pressures, but rather the *people* of those ages.)

The sheer simplicity of frozen food may soon replace home-cooked meals. (*Simplicity* will not replace the meals; *frozen food* will, *because* of its simplicity of preparation.)

Paying bills on time causes many worries for young families. (*Paying* bills does not cause worries, but *not paying* them does.)

Is When, Is Where, Is Because

The use of *is when, is where, is because* is always incorrect. The reason is simple: *when, where,* and *because* introduce adverbial clauses; and a noun subject followed by a form of the verb *to be* must be equated with a noun structure, not with an adverb clause.

INCORRECT: Lepidopterology *is where you study butterflies and moths.*

CORRECT: Lepidopterology *is the study of butterflies* and moths (Here, the adverb clause *where you study* . . . has been changed to a subject complement: *lepidopterology = study.*)

INCORRECT: The reason they won *is because they had better coaching.*

CORRECT: The reason they won *is that they had better coaching.* (The noun clause that *they had better coaching* equates with the noun *reason.*)

OR

They *won because* they had better coaching. (The adverb clause modifies the verb *won.*)

PRACTICE EXERCISE 15

In the following sentences, find any errors in predication. Not every sentence has an error. Place a check in the appropriate column to indicate whether the sentence is correct or incorrect.

Correct Incorrect

_____ _____ 1. By building a more efficient engine will save fuel.

_____ _____ 2. Maintaining a healthy weight causes problems for many millions of Americans.

_____ _____ 3. Vertigo is when a person becomes dizzy and is unable to maintain his balance.

_____ _____ 4. Heart failure results from the inability of the heart to pump enough blood to maintain normal bodily functions.

_____ _____ 5. My first sight of Niagara Falls was inspiring, joyful, emotional.

Correct Incorrect

_____ _____ 6. The reason that our team did not win was because our key players had injuries.

ANSWERS

1. **Incorrect.** *Building* a more efficient engine may save fuel, but not *by building*.

2. **Incorrect.** The problem does not lie in *maintaining* a healthy weight. It lies in *not maintaining* a healthy weight.

3. **Incorrect.** *Is when* is always incorrect. *Revised:* Vertigo is a condition which...

4. **Correct.** This sentence has no errors in predications.

5. **Incorrect.** The *sight* was not inspiring, joyful, or emotional; the speaker's *feelings* were.

6. **Incorrect.** Equate a noun (*reason*) with a noun structure (the clause *that our key players had injuries*).

Parallelism

Parallel ideas in a sentence should be expressed in the same grammatical form. If they are not, the sentence will be unbalanced.

A series of coordinated elements should be parallel in form.

INCORRECT: He enjoys *plays, exhibitions,* and *to walk* every morning. (An infinitive is paired with two nouns.)

CORRECT: He enjoys *going* to plays, *visiting* exhibitions, and *walking* every morning.

OR

He enjoys *plays, exhibitions,* and morning *walks.*

INCORRECT: The union wanted *pay increases for every employee* and *that there would be shorter working hours.* (A noun is paired with a noun clause.)

CORRECT: The union wanted *pay increases* for every employee and shorter *working hours.*

The constructions that follow correlative conjunctions (*both-and, either-or, neither-nor, not only-but also, whether-or*) should be parallel in form.

INCORRECT: He was *neither qualified* to lead this country *nor was he willing*.

CORRECT: He was *neither qualified nor willing* to lead this country.

Do not use *and* before *which* or *who* unless the sentence has a previously expressed *which* or *who* clause with which to be parallel.

INCORRECT: She is a well-known surgeon from New York, and who has written many books on brain surgery.

CORRECT: She is a well-known surgeon from New York, who has lectured at many medical schools and who has written many books on brain surgery.

Note: A sentence may lack parallelism even though its parts are *grammatically* parallel. If the ideas are not logically equal, then the flow of ideas is not parallel.

INCORRECT: The dean introduced new faculty members, explained some curriculum strategies, began an exploratory discussion of the accreditation process, *spilled coffee on his tie,* reviewed the budget for the fiscal year, and *went to lunch with Don Love.* (Although the italicized phrases are grammatically parallel, they are not parallel with the other ideas expressed.)

PRACTICE EXERCISE 16

In the following sentences, find any errors in parallelism. Not every sentence has an error. Place a check in the appropriate column to indicate whether the sentence is correct or incorrect.

Correct Incorrect

_____ _____ 1. William Faulkner wrote *As I Lay Dying, The Sound and the Fury, Sartoris,* and he was also the author of *The Reivers.*

_____ _____ 2. Cluster secretaries answer calls about special programs, file important papers, sort mail, and they do typing and stuffing envelopes.

Correct Incorrect

_____ _____ 3. He bought a new scooter with an electric starter, and which has dual pipes and a digital clock.

_____ _____ 4. My sister's tamale pie is made with ground meat, chili seasoning, olives, and it has onions and beans as well.

_____ _____ 5. Playing racquetball is more taxing than to jog or play basketball.

_____ _____ 6. The union stood firm on its demands for a realistic wage, a better health plan, and a more generous pension package.

Correct Incorrect

_____ _____ 7. The pool is eighteen feet in length and twelve feet wide.

_____ _____ 8. Most citizens felt gas rationing to be a necessity and fair.

ANSWERS

1. **Incorrect.** *Made parallel:* William Faulkner wrote *As I Lay Dying, The Sound and the Fury, Sartoris,* and *The Reivers.* (*He was also the author of* is unnecessary.)

2. **Incorrect.** *Made parallel:* Cluster secretaries answer calls about special programs, file important papers, sort mail, type, and stuff envelopes.

3. **Incorrect.** *Made parallel:* He bought a new scooter with an electric starter, dual pipes, and a digital clock. (A sentence that contains *and which* is not parallel unless it has a previously expressed *which* clause.)

4. **Incorrect.** *Made parallel:* My sister's tamale pie is made with ground meat, chili seasoning, olives, onions, and beans.

5. **Incorrect.** *Made parallel:* Playing racquetball is more taxing than jogging or playing basketball. (In the original, the infinitives *to jog* and [*to*] *play* are not parallel with the gerund phrase *playing racquetball.*

6. **Correct.** The structures in this sentence—*wage, plan,* and *package*—are parallel.

7. **Incorrect.** *Made parallel:* The pool is eighteen feet long and twelve feet wide. (Or match the phrase *in length* with the phrase *in width.*)

8. **Incorrect.** *Made parallel:* Most citizens felt gas rationing to be necessary and fair. (In the original sentence, an adjective, *fair,* is paired with a noun, *necessity.*

Transitional Words and Phrases

Words of transition are clues that help the reader to follow the writer's flow of ideas. Confusion can result, however, when an illogical or incorrect connective is used. The following list includes more commonly used transitional words and phrases, and the concepts they suggest.

Concept

Addition	also, furthermore, moreover, similarly, too
Cause and Effect	accordingly, as a result, consequently, hence, so, therefore, thus
Concession	granted that, it is true that, no doubt, to be sure
Conclusion	in short, that is, to conclude, to sum up
Contrast	although, but, however, nevertheless, on the contrary, on the other hand
Example	for example, for instance

Watch for errors in logical use of transitional words. For example:

INCORRECT: At many gas stations, drivers have to pump their own gasoline; *therefore,* at Ken's Union Station, full service is still the rule.

CORRECT: At many gas stations, drivers have to pump their own gasoline; *however,* at Ken's Union Station, full service is still the rule.

PRACTICE EXERCISE 17

In the following sentences, find any transition errors. Not every sentence has an error. Place a check in the appropriate column to indicate whether the sentence is correct or incorrect.

Correct Incorrect

_____ _____ 1. Her apple pie won a blue ribbon at the county fair; nevertheless, we all wanted the recipe.

_____ _____ 2. Bud and Jake climbed to the top of the falls, and Jake had a fear of heights.

_____ _____ 3. I have been meaning to learn more about electronics, so I just bought a book on the subject.

_____ _____ 4. I have just finished preparing my tax return after four weeks of figuring and frustration; furthermore, I refuse to fill out any other forms for at least a month!

Correct Incorrect

_____ _____ 5. Maria has spent almost twelve years of her academic life studying medicine; however, she feels well qualified to treat sick people.

Answers

1. **Incorrect.** The connective *nevertheless* is obviously illogical here, with its implication of contrast. A better transitional word might be *consequently*.

2. **Incorrect.** A contrast like *although* is needed in this sentence.

3. **Correct.** This is a typical cause-and-effect sentence, correctly using the word *so*.

4. **Incorrect.** The speaker refuses to fill out another form *because of* his work on the tax return. Needed here is a causal transition like *as a result*.

5. **Incorrect.** The connective *however* does not make sense here because it implies contrast. A causal word like *accordingly* is required.

CUMULATIVE REVIEW IV

Crime and Punishment by Fyodor Dostoevsky

is a topical novel dealing with philosophical

doctrines, <u>political</u>, and social issues widely
      1

discussed in Russia just after the 1861 reforms.

<u>By most critical essays</u>, treating Dostoevsky's
      2

work <u>has employed</u> psychological or biological
      3

points of view. Because *Crime and Punishment*

is a passionate, masterly portrayal of internal

1. **(A)** NO CHANGE
   (B) politically
   (C) politics
   (D) that are political

2. **(A)** NO CHANGE
   (B) Because of most critical essays
   (C) Most critical essays,
   (D) Most critical essays

3. **(A)** NO CHANGE
   (B) have employed
   (C) should employ
   (D) employ

psychological conflict, a general assumption

has evolved in the general critical world that

the author wrote, at least in part, from

personal experience. Nevertheless,
              4
Dostoevsky's biography has been endlessly

probed, explored, and it was thoroughly
                   5
analyze.
   5
   In 1849, Dostoevsky was convicted of

consorting with known radical factions;
                                6
however, he was sentenced to a four-year
   6
prison term. Many critical commentaries on

Crime and Punishment consider this

experience formative and essential, certainly a

major source of the creative impulses

that eventually resulted in the execution of the

novel. The epilogue of the novel had been set
                                        7
in Siberia, where he was imprisoned. If,

indeed, he were talking to his fellow prisoners,
        8
then he must have focused on crime and guilt,

and thought about the psychology of the

criminal mind granted that he lived among
              9
hardened convicts. One must ask, though, why

he waited until 1865 to write *Crime and*

Punishment. One possible answer is because
                                       10
he wrote the novel in part to speak against

foreign ideas adopted by the Russian radicals

of the 1860s.

4. **(A)** NO CHANGE
   (B) Hence,
   (C) On the contrary,
   (D) Furthermore

5. **(A)** NO CHANGE
   (B) and being analyzed.
   (C) and analyzed.
   (D) subject to analysis.

6. **(A)** NO CHANGE
   (B) factions, yet, he was sentenced
   (C) factions and was sentenced
   (D) factions; moreover, he was sentenced

7. **(A)** NO CHANGE
   (B) is set
   (C) was set
   (D) has been set

8. **(A)** NO CHANGE
   (B) he was talking
   (C) he had talked
   (D) he had been talking

9. **(A)** NO CHANGE
   (B) as he
   (C) knowing that
   (D) considering that

10. **(A)** NO CHANGE
    (B) is when
    (C) is where
    (D) is that

1. **C** A noun is necessary in this postion to be parallel with the other noun objects in this series, *doctrines* and *issues*.

2. **D** As it stands, this sentence contains an error in predication, beginning with one construction. *By most critical essays,* and continuing with a different one, *treating Dostoevsky's work has employed . . . points of view.* It is incorrect to separate a subject from its verb, as in choice C.

3. **D** The verb must agree with its plural subject *essays* and maintain the established present tense.

4. **B** The logic of the sentence requires a cause/effect transitional marker like *Hence,* not the contrast or addition markers suggested by the alternative choices.

5. **C** The parallel series of past participles in this sentence requires this option: *has been probed, explored, and analyzed.*

6. **C** The logic of this sentence requires a transitional word suggesting either *cause* or *addition.* Since the acts of *conviction* and *sentencing* seems to be of equal weight, the conjunction *and* is a sound choice.

7. **B** Use the historical present tense when relating events that occur in fiction.

8. **A** The subjunctive is the logical choice of mood in this *if* clause because it expresses a suppostion.

9. **B** The use of the subordinating conjunction *as* is a sound choice in this position because it creates an adverb clause that modifies the verbs *focused* and *thought.* The other choices create modifiers of the subject to little effect.

10. **D** Only the use of the words *is that* in this spot forms a noun structure that equate with the noun *answer.* The other choices form adverb clauses that cannot equate with the noun.

WORD CHOICE

Diction

Some of the questions on the writing test will require you to decide the appropriateness of a word in its context. In a technical passage about the development of the transistor, for example, the use of a flowery or ornate word or phrase would stand out as inappropriate. Similarly, words that are illiterate or colloquial, or used in spoken English, for the most part, are not appropriate in a formal literary passage.

A word is *appropriate* if it fits the reader, occasion, and purpose for which the writing is intended. In general, most language can be categorized as either formal, informal (colloquial), or popular.

Formal Diction

Formal diction is seldom used in everyday conversation and writing. It is found in writing that serves a serious purpose (for example, a research paper) and concerns weighty or substantial topics, such as death, crime, philosophy, scholarship, science, and literature.

Formal language employs a more scholarly vocabulary than popular English (*eccentric* for *strange, extenuation* for *excuse, immaculate* for *clean, tantamount* for *equivalent,* and so on). Another characteristic is grammatical exactness.

Informal Diction

Informal diction is *colloquial* language, that is, the language of everyday conversation. It includes contractions (always improper in formal writing), slang, colloquialisms, dialect and turns of phrase peculiar to local areas (*provincialisms,* and shortened word forms (*TV* for *television*), *phone* for *telephone, stereo* for *stereophonic set,* and so on).

Popular Diction

Popular diction lies somewhere between formal and informal (colloquial) diction. It is not as free as colloquial, nor does it include slang or provincialisms, but it relaxes many of the rules and restrictions of formal written English. Generally, popular diction is the language of mass-media publications. Its aim is to appeal to and communicate clearly with the average reader.

The following expressions have no place in formal prose.

Cool it.	year
guys	guts
spaced-out	I've had it!
for sure	stuck-up
creep	an awful lot

This list contains some common misspellings, provincialisms, illiterate expressions, and incorrect forms to be avoided.

NOT	BUT
aggravate	annoy; exasperate
a half an hour	a half hour or half an hour
alot	a lot
alright	all right
and etc.	etc. or et cetera
anywheres	anywhere
being that, being as how	as, because, since
can't seem to	seem unable to
considerable sick	quite sick
dark-complected	dark-complexioned
different than	different from
hadn't ought	ought not
heighth	height
irregardless	regardless, irrespective
no-account: no-good	worthless
off of	off, from
out loud	aloud
outside of	except; beside
should of, would of	should have, would have
the reason is because	the reason is that
tote	carry
try and give	try to give
use to	used to
visit with	visit
won him	beat him

Some colloquialisms and short forms are appropriate in everyday conversation and informal writing, but should not be used in formal written English.

NOT	BUT
ad	advertisement
at about: at around	about: around
can't help but	cannot help but
center around	center on
get going	go
guess so, reckon so	think, suppose
has got to go	has to go
he is liable to be there	he is likely to be there
hold on	wait
kids	children
kind of a, sort of a	kind of, sort of
mighty hard	very hard
okay	all right
out loud	aloud
packs quite a punch	delivers a strong blow
phone	telephone
show up	appear to be superior
TV	television
wait a bit	wait

Here is a list of frequently misused or confused words. Be sure you can distinguish their meanings.

accept: to receive; to agree to
except: to exclude
except: a preposition meaning *but, other than*

affect: to influence
effect: to bring about
effect: a noun meaning *result*

allusion: indirect reference
illusion: false perception or image

all ready: everything is ready
already: by this time

alumna: a female graduate
alumnae: two or more female graduates
alumnus: a male graduate
alumni: two or more male graduates; also, a universal term for college graduate

amount: used for noncountable bulk or weight (an amount of milk)
number: used for things that can be counted as individual units (a number of gallons of milk)

compare: to deal with similarities
contrast: to deal with differences

complement: to complete or strengthen
compliment: to praise

continual: frequently repeated
continuous: without interruption; never ending

emigrate: to move out of a country or region
immigrate: to move into a country or region

fiancé: engaged man (plural: fiancés)
fiancée: engaged woman (plural: financées)

former: first
latter: last

healthful: giving health
healthy: having good health

imply: to suggest or hint by word or manner (He *implied*, by the way he ignored me, that he did not want to talk to me.)
infer: to gain an opinion or understanding from what one reads or hears (I *inferred* from the mayor's announcement that he was going to run.)

incredible: unbelievable (A story is *incredible*.)
incredulous: unwilling or unable to believe (A person is *incredulous*.)

less: used with noncountable items (We had *less* information about the earthquake than they did.)
fewer: used with countable items (There were *fewer* students every year.)

principal: main, most important; a sum of money; a school official
principle: a rule of conduct; a general truth

than: a conjunction used to express a comparison
then: at that time; therefore

List of Commonly Misspelled Words

absence	amateur	attendance	carrying
accidentally	among	audience	certain
accommodate	amount	bachelor	changeable
accompanying	analyze	balance	changing
accomplish	annual	before	characteristic
accustom	answer	beginning	clothes
achievement	apartment	believe	coming
acknowledge	apology	benefited	committee
across	apparent	breathe	comparison
address	appearance	brilliant	competition
a lot	approaching	bureau	conceive
all right	arctic	buried	conferred
always	argument	business	conscience
almost	ascend	calendar	conscientious
although	association	candidate	consciousness
altogether	athlete	career	convenient

course	familiar	meant	recommend
courteous	fascinating	minute	referred
criticism	February	mischievous	relieve
criticize	foreign	necessary	religious
curiosity	formerly	ninth	restaurant
dealt	forty	noticeable	rhythm
definite	fourth	nowadays	schedule
desirable	friend	occasionally	separate
despair	generally	occurred	sergeant
desperate	genius	occurrence	severely
dictionary	government	original	sophomore
different	grammar	paid	speech
dining	guidance	parallel	stopped
disagree	handle	particularly	strength
disappear	height	pastime	stretch
disappoint	humorous	perform	studying
disastrous	imagination	perhaps	succeed
discipline	immediately	piece	surpise
dissatisfied	indefinitely	pleasant	temperature
dormitory	independent	possible	thorough
eighth	inevitable	preferred	till
eligible	infinite	prejudice	together
embarrass	intelligent	principal	tragedy
enthusiastic	interesting	principle	truly
environment	itself	privilege	Tuesday
equipped	knowledge	probably	unnecessarily
especially	laboratory	proceed	until
exaggerated	led	professor	usually
excellent	lightning	psychology	weather
existence	literature	quantity	whether
experience	loneliness	quiet	wholly
explanation	loose	quite	woman
extraordinary	lose	really	writing
extremely	mathematics	receive	written

Imagery and Figurative Language

Writers in search of clear, vivid, and forceful prose often use devices called figures of speech to gain a desired effect. Note the image conveyed by Phillip Wylie's description of a very thin woman as "a trellis for varicose veins." Among the important figures of speech are *simile, metaphor, synecdoche, metonymy,* and *personification.* Inappropriate expressions that you may need to *rule out* on the writing test could involve misuse of these figures of speech.

Simile

A simile is a figure of speech that uses *like* or *as* to compare two dissimilar things.

EXAMPLES

". . .mountains like thirsty giants"—*National Geographic*

"a complexion like the belly of a fish"—*Charles Dickens*

Some similes have been used so much that they are no longer effective and are considered clichés.

INEFFECTIVE SIMILES: old as the hills
dull as dishwater
American as apple pie
teeth like pearls

Metaphor

A metaphor is a figure of speech that suggests a likeness between two ideas or objects. *As* or *like* is not used.

EXAMPLES

This monstrous human error, the megalopolis. . .
"She is the rose, the glory of the day."—*Edmund Spenser*

As with similes, some metaphors have become trite through overuse.

INEFFECTIVE METAPHORS: the black sheep of the family
a wolf in sheep's clothing
a sea of troubles

A mixed metaphor results when metaphors occurring in the same sentence or paragraph create ludicrous images. If a woman is said to be a rose, and her arms petals, then she cannot be a jewel in the next sentence.

EXAMPLES

The floodgates of atheism and permissiveness are stalking arm in arm throughout the land. (Floodgates cannot stalk.)

The harvest sown by the crooked politicians came home to roost. (Two mixed metaphors here: *seeds,* not a *harvest,* are sown, and *chickens,* not a *harvest,* come home to roost.)

Synecdoche

Synecdoche uses the part to represent the whole: *ranch hands,* for example, for a group of men performing labor with their hands, or *daily bread* for food. Here are a few more synecdoches:

EXAMPLES

The pen [writing] is mightier than the sword [fighting].

Five hundred souls [people] were lost.

Metonymy

Metonymy substitutes something closely related for the thing actually meant. The *White House* stands for the president, for example; *the Blue and the Gray,* for the Union and Confederate forces.

EXAMPLES

"Scepter and crown [the king] must tumble down."

The Dodgers need to add more bats [good hitters] to their team.

I'm going to complain directly to City Hall.

Personification

Personification is a form of metaphor in which an inanimate object or abstract idea—for example, a car, or a quality like love—is treated as if it has human characteristics, feelings, or actions.

EXAMPLES

"I have seen the ambitious ocean swell and rage and foam."

William Shakespeare

Justice hung her head.

We use personification often in daily conversation when we speak of the "bitter wind," "nasty weather," "gentle breeze," "cruel sea," "unforgiving clock," or "bountiful Mother Nature."

Errors involving these figures of speech on one of the writing tests will most probably consist of mixed or confused examples, so be alert for any absurd, illogical, or meaningless expressions or comparisons.

PRACTICE EXERCISE 18

Most of the following sentences contain errors in diction, imagery, or logical expression. Place a check in the appropriate space to indicate whether the sentence contains appropriate diction and sound expressions, or uses faulty language or flawed expressions. Note that all sentences should be in standard written English.

Correct | Faulty or Flawed

_____ _____ 1. It was a near perfect day to have a picnic.

_____ _____ 2. Quick as a flash, the horse and rider jumped the gun and sailed around the track at full steam.

_____ _____ 3. Paul excepted the invitation to compete in the biathlon.

_____ _____ 4. The college has finally untangled itself from the briar bush of debt and is now in smooth water.

_____ _____ 5. I was tickled pink to discover that the Senate had passed the revised income tax legislation.

_____ _____ 6. He use to be a catcher for the Mets.

Correct | Faulty or Flawed

_____ _____ 7. You hadn't ought to aggravate the Doberman!

_____ _____ 8. Though the other political party keeps dragging the national debt red herring across our path, it misfires every time.

_____ _____ 9. The issue of increased subway fares has become a political football.

_____ _____ 10. They discovered a large amount of gold coins.

ANSWERS

1. **Faulty.** This is a colloquial use of *near* (an adjective), instead of *nearly* (an adverb), to modify *perfect*.

2. **Flawed.** This sentence contains two overused expressions (the simile *Quick as a flash* and the metaphor *jumped the gun* and a mixed metaphor (*sailed . . . at full steam*).

3. **Faulty.** The correct word to use here is *accepted* (agreed), not *excepted* (excluded from).

4. **Flawed.** The college is likened first to an animal or person becoming tangled in a bush, then to a ship at sea.

5. **Faulty.** *Tickled pink* is a colloquial expression.

6. **Faulty.** *Use to* should be changed to *used to.*

7. **Faulty.** Use *ought not,* not *hadn't ought.* *Annoy* is a better word choice than *aggravate.*

8. **Flawed.** A red herring cannot fire (or misfire) like a gun.

9. **Correct.** The metaphor presents a clear, vivid picture of an unpopular issue that is being tossed back and forth by politicians.

10. **Faulty.** *Number* is used for a countable noun like *coins.* (But it would be correct to use *a large amount of gold.*)

Wordiness

To avoid wordiness, eliminate language that either duplicates what has already been expressed or adds nothing to the sense of the statement.

WORDY: At the present time, you can call up the library on the telephone if you want to receive that particular information.

REVISED: Now you can call the library for that information.

WORDY: A factor in the cause of the decline in stock prices was unwarranted growth.

REVISED: One cause of the decline in stock prices was unwarranted growth.

OR

A factor in the decline in stock prices. . .

WORDY: As a pet, the llama is easygoing in its habits and has a friendly personality.

REVISED: As a pet, the llama is easygoing and friendly.

Expressions like *there are* and *it is* can add unnecessary words to your sentences.

EXAMPLES

[There are] several people at school [who] have promised to help with the gardening at the new campus.

[It is] the way you swing the club [that] amazes me.

A *redundant* expression is characterized by unnecessary repetition. To say *adequate enough* is to be redundant, because *adequate* and *enough* have nearly the same meaning.

EXAMPLES

The two clubs joined [together] to feed the poor at Christmas.

They circled [around] the field.

For a list of ski areas in the state, refer [back] to page 25.

Avoid redundancies and roundabout phrases (*circumlocutions*) like the following:

WORDY	CONCISE
advance planning	planning
contributing factor	factor
due to the fact that	because
during the course of	during
exact same symptoms	same symptoms; exact symptoms
for the purpose of	for
in the event that	if
in the near future	soon
large in size	large
past experience	experience
past history	history
revert back	revert
sufficient enough	sufficient; enough

Omissions

A common error in written English is the careless omission, especially the omission acceptable in speech but not in writing. Some of the errors on the writing test are likely to be such omissions.

The Careless Omission
Do not omit a needed verb, preposition, or conjunction.

FAULTY: The Coast Guard always has and always will assist boaters in distress.

CORRECT: The Coast Guard always has *assisted* and always will assist boaters in distress.

FAULTY: Carol will graduate high school in June.

CORRECT: Carol will graduate *from* high school in June.

FAULTY: Liza was both allergic and fond of cats.

CORRECT: Liza was both allergic *to* and fond of cats.

FAULTY: He eats as much or more than anyone else in the family.

CORRECT: He eats as much *as* or more than anyone else in the family.

The Incomplete Comparison
Include every word needed to make a complete comparison.

It may seem obvious to state that a comparison expresses a relationship between *two* things: for example, *Johnny is older than Sue.* A surprisingly common error, however, is the incomplete comparison.

INCOMPLETE:	Our new lawn requires less water.
REVISED:	Our new lawn requires less water *than our old one did.*
INCOMPLETE:	A subcompact's mileage is better than a large sedan.
REVISED:	A subcompact's mileage is better *than that of* a large sedan.
INCOMPLETE:	He wanted that medal more than his competitors. (Did he want the medal or the competitors?)
REVISED:	He wanted that medal more than his competitors *did* [want].

The Missing Transition

Without logical transitions, the flow of ideas can lack natural progression and unity. Note the following.

WITHOUT TRANSITION:	He wanted so much to do well on the test; he had not studied enough.
REVISED:	He wanted so much to do well on the test, *but* he had not studied enough.
WITHOUT TRANSITION:	The multimillionaire Getty lived in London; most of his holdings were in the United States.
REVISED:	The multimillionaire Getty lived in London, *although* most of his holdings were in the United States.

Sexist Language

Throughout most of the history of the English language, masculine pronouns have been used to represent either sex. In addition, women have been routinely excluded from many nouns intended to represent humanity. Still worse, traditional use of sexist language tends to place men and women in stereotyped roles.

It is not necessary to begin using awkward terms to avoid sexist language. Terms like *mail carrier, firefighter,* or *police officer* are reasonable alternatives to *mailman, fireman,* and *policeman.*

The use of the sexist pronoun is more difficult to avoid. One alternative is to use the plural: instead of *A voter must do his duty,* say, *Voters must do their duty.* An occasional use of *he* or *she* is acceptable, though the phrase tends to be cumbersome.

EXAMPLE

When a person is called by the IRS for an audit, *he or she* should go over last year's return.

You can avoid the construction by rewording the sentence.

EXAMPLE

A person called by the IRS for an audit should go over the past year's return.

PRACTICE EXERCISE 19

Most of these sentences are either wordy or incomplete in some way. Place a check in the appropriate column to indicate whether the sentence is correct or faulty.

Correct Faulty

_____ _____ 1. His appeal was his good looks as well as his natural charm.

_____ _____ 2. Mexican food is as well liked by Europeans as Americans.

_____ _____ 3. Because of the unlikely possibility that rain will occur this weekend, we will not venture to have the canoe race.

_____ _____ 4. The teacher impatiently repeated the answer again.

_____ _____ 5. Is it true that snow tires are safer?

_____ _____ 6. She always let her cat out at 5 A.M. in the morning.

_____ _____ 7. The comma, semicolon, and colon are punctuation marks used to separate components of a sentence.

_____ _____ 8. New materials to construct long-lasting batteries have and continue to be developed by Bell scientists.

_____ _____ 9. In my opinion, I think the autobiography of her life would make a good movie.

_____ _____ 10. I admire Dylan more than Cherie does.

Correct Faulty

_____ _____ 11. The baby was crying as if she were hungry; she had been fed only an hour ago.

_____ _____ 12. The motion picture *Gone With the Wind* is a movie that still has great audience appeal.

ANSWERS

1. **Faulty.** Revised: His appeal was *due* to his good looks as well as his natural charm.

2. **Faulty.** Revised: Mexican food is as well liked by Europeans as *it is by* Americans.

3. **Faulty.** Revised: Because of the possibility of rain this weekend, we will not have the canoe race. (Excessive words omitted.)

4. **Faulty.** *Repeated . . . again* is redundant.

5. **Faulty.** Revised: Is it true that snow tires are safer *than other types of tires?*

6. **Faulty.** *In the morning* is unnecessary with *A.M.*

7. **Correct.** This sentence is neither wordy nor incomplete.

8. **Faulty.** Revised: New materials to construct long-lasting batteries have *been* and continue to be developed by Bell scientists.

9. **Faulty.** *In my opinion* and *I think* express the same idea. Also, *autobiography of her life* is a redundant phrase.

10. **Correct.** The thought in this sentence is complete.

11. **Faulty.** A transitional word like *yet* is needed in this sentence.

12. **Faulty.** Revised: The motion picture *Gone With the Wind* still has great audience appeal.

Chapter 7

ESL Tips

If English is your second language, writing an essay in English may sometimes seem like a losing battle. However, with a little guidance, a lot of your errors can be eliminated. The purpose of this section is to give you insights into some of the aspects of English grammar that are probably giving you problems. Therefore, in part I, we will begin with an examination of the meaning and use of linking words. In part II, we will study relative clauses. Part III will deal with the use of articles in English. Part IV will give you a quick review of verb tenses. Last of all, in part V there will be a series of exercises that will teach you to correct (or edit) your paper while reviewing those aspects of English that tend to give students problems. Well, let's begin!

I. LINKING WORDS

If ESL writers understand the meanings and usage of linking words, the tone of their papers will greatly improve. You probably have a fairly good command of such common linking words as *and, but,* and *or,* but in this section you will improve your knowledge of a wide range of linking words and learn to use them correctly. Thus, you will have a greater selection to choose from when you are writing. Also, your writing will be more cohesive. That is to say that your essay will be more unified and fluent.

Before discussing linking words, it is necessary to have a clear understanding of phrases and clauses, which are the basic building blocks of sentences. Then, we will be ready to examine the meaning and usage of coordinating conjunctions, subordinating conjunctions, and conjunctive adverbs. Last of all, we will discuss five simple ways to punctuate sentences.

A. Phrases

First of all, you may have words in your language that sound like *phrase* and *clause,* but try to clear your mind of what these words mean in your language because you may get confused. In fact, in some languages *phrase* may mean *sentence,* and such is not the case in English.

If a phrase is <u>not</u> a sentence, what is it? Simply stated, it is a group of words that does not have <u>both</u> a subject and a predicate (verb). If it had <u>both</u> a subject and a predicate (verb), it would be a clause (we will talk about clauses later). Phrases can be as small as two words or as long as you please if there is a lot of modification. Phrases are important because they are the basic building blocks (elements) from which sentences are made.

There are many types of phrases. Let's take a close look at each type.

Noun phrases

The most important element in a noun phrase is a noun. Remember, a noun refers to a person (Peter, girl), place (school, New York), thing (pen, computer), action (typing), event (graduation) or concept/feeling (liberty, love). This noun may be surrounded by many words that modify (or give information about) the noun. In the following examples, the main nouns are underlined.

a **boy**

the **boy** with glasses

the nice **boy** with glasses

the nice **boy** with glasses that I spoke to

Did you notice how the noun can be preceded (precede = to go before) by words or followed by words that tell us about the boy? Did you ask yourself how the last example can be considered as a noun phrase when it has a subject and a verb, *I spoke,* in it? Don't get confused. The main element is still the noun **boy,** and *that I spoke to* is a relative clause (which will be discussed in section B) that tells about the noun **boy.** Let's take a look at the other elements in the phrases.

the nice **boy** (with glasses) (that I spoke to)

article adjective **noun** prepositional phrase relative clause

Verb phrases

Verb phrases consist of a main verb (remember a verb states mental or physical actions and conditions) and all of the helping verbs (auxiliaries) that precede it. The main verb in the following examples is the verb **to do.**

have **done**

should have **done**

may have **done**

Adjective phrases

Yes, you have guessed that the main element in these phrases is an adjective. Remember an adjective gives extra information about a noun or pronoun. For example, in *a red dress,* the word *red* is an adjective because it tells which color the dress is. The adjective may also be surrounded by elements that add information to the adjective (or modify the adjective). For example:

very **hot** indeed (the word *indeed* means really)

Adverb phrases

These are similar to adjective phrases in structure, but they have an adverb as the main word. Remember an adverb usually modifies a verb. For example, notice the role that the adverb *frequently* plays in the following sentence:

He **frequently** telephoned.

In this example, the adverb *frequently* tells us about the verb *tele-phoned*. Specifically, it tells us how often he telephoned. Here are some other examples of adverb phrases:

very **softly**

quite **clearly**

Prepositional phrases

These begin with prepositions, which are words that show relationships (often of time and space) between words. Such words as *on, under, before, toward, into,* and *at,* are all prepositions. Examples of prepositional phrases would be:

in the papers

with his friends

after the dinner

Gerund phrases

This type of phrase begins with a gerund, which you know as the "ing" form of the verb.

going to school

running home

playing the game

Infinitive phrases

Yes, you are catching on! Infinitive phrases begin with an infinitive, which is the base, or pure form of the verb.

to play ball

to say the answer

to find the way

Participle phrases

These phrases begin with a participle. When you first started to study English, you may have memorized verb forms. For example, the verb *to see* has three forms: to see (infinitive), saw (past), seen (participle). The third form *seen* is the participle. Here are some examples of participle phrases:

seen from above

played with great spirit

Now that you have learned about the various types of phrases, read the following paragraph and see if you can identify each underlined phrase. Write your answers directly below each phrase.

(1) On March 5, 1770, which was (2) five years (3) before the American Revolution, there was (4) a bloody encounter (meeting) (5) between British soldiers and the colonists of Boston. (6) This event is commonly

referred to as (7) <u>the Boston Massacre.</u> It all began when citizens, who (8) <u>were protesting</u> (9) <u>new taxes</u> (10) <u>imposed (put on them) by Britain,</u> began (11) <u>to harass (bother) the British soldiers</u> who (12) <u>had been sent</u> (13) <u>to stop the demonstrations.</u> After the colonists struck (14) <u>a squad (group) of British soldiers</u> (15) <u>with missiles,</u> the soldiers fired (shot) (16) <u>into the crowd</u> and killed five colonists. Eight soldiers and their commander (17) <u>were tried</u> (put on trial) for murder, and two (18) <u>were found</u> guilty. This event is (19) <u>especially significant</u> because it served (20) <u>to get support</u> (21) <u>for the movement</u> (22) <u>to break away</u> from Britain.

You may have noticed that not all of the phrases were underlined. Here are the answers:

1. Prepositional phrase (tells when)
2. Noun phrase (noun = years)
3. Prepositional phrase (tells about years)
4. Noun phrase (noun = encounter)
5. Prepositional phrase (notice how the preposition *between* is followed by two noun phrases *British soldiers* and *the colonists* and a prepositional phrase *of Boston*)
6. Noun phrase (noun = event)
7. Noun phrase (noun = massacre)
8. Verb phrase (verb = protest)
9. Noun phrase (noun = taxes)
10. Participle phrase (participle = imposed)
11. Infinitive phrase (infinitive = to harass)
12. Verb phrase (verb = sent)
13. Infinitive phrase (infinitive = to stop)
14. Noun phrase (noun = squad) the prepositional phrase of British soldiers tells us about the squad
15. Prepositional phrase
16. Prepositional phrase
17. Verb phrase (verb = tried)
18. Verb phrase (verb = found)
19. Adjective phrase (adjective = significant)
20. Infinitive phrase
21. Prepositional phrase
22. Infinitive phrase

You probably noticed that many times a phrase includes another phrase. For example, in the phrase *five years before the American Revolution,* the main noun is *years* and it is followed by the prepositional phrase *before the American Revolution,* which tells us about the noun *years.* Phrases give a lot of extra information and make your writing colorful and rich. Use them abundantly when you write!

B. Clauses

The next basic building block of the sentence is a clause. As was previously stated, a clause has <u>both</u> a subject and a verb. Clauses may be either independent or dependent. An independent clause is a complete thought and can stand on its own. A dependent clause must always be linked with an independent clause. To understand the difference, try comparing the following:

Column 1	Column 2
There was a bloody battle (fight).	<u>Because</u> there was a bloody battle
Soldiers fired at the citizens.	<u>Even though</u> soldiers fired at the citizens
The soldiers were tried for murder.	<u>After</u> the soldiers were tried for murder

All of the clauses in the first column are independent because they are complete thoughts. The clauses in the second column are dependent because they are incomplete thoughts. In fact, if you read *Because there was a bloody battle,* you will probably ask yourself, "What happened because there was a bloody battle?"

Also, notice that the clauses in column 2 are identical to the ones in column 1, but all the clauses in column 2 have a word which has been added on. This word makes the clause dependent and is called a subordinating conjunction. In these examples, the subordinators are *because, even though,* and *after.*

PRACTICE EXERCISE 1

Identify the following as being either a phrase or a clause. If it is a clause, be sure to identify it as being either dependent or independent.

	Phrase	Clause Independent/Dependent	
1.	_____	_____ _____	After the first day of the fifth month of the year
2.	_____	_____ _____	Since he was called the best player on the team
3.	_____	_____ _____	They never thought that they would win the game
4.	_____	_____ _____	A game between the White Sox and the Orioles
5.	_____	_____ _____	As soon as they came home
6.	_____	_____ _____	The team that won the game
7.	_____	_____ _____	All is fair in love and war
8.	_____	_____ _____	Although he did not know the answer
9.	_____	_____ _____	It did not seem logical that they could do so well
10.	_____	_____ _____	The odd situation in which he found himself the other day

1. **Phrase** - This is a very long prepositional phrase. Notice how *after the first
day* is followed by two more prepositional
phrases (*of the fifth month* and *of the
year*). This is a very long string of prepositional phrases. Many times students will
write phrases like this and punctuate
them as sentences. Be careful!

2. **Dependent clause** - The subject is *he,*
and the complete verb is *was called,* so
this is a clause. However, the word *since*
makes the clause dependent.

3. **Independent clause** - The subject is
they, and the verb is *thought,* so this is a
clause. *That they would win the game* is a
relative clause which is acting as the
object of the verb *thought.* We will speak
about relative clause soon.

4. **Noun phrase** - The main noun is *game,*
and it is followed by the prepositonal
phrase *between the White Sox and the
Orioles.*

5. **Dependent clause** - The subject is *they,*
and the verb is *came.* It is dependent
because of the subordinating conjunction
as soon as.

6. **Noun phrase** - The main noun is *team,*
and it is followed by the relative clause
that won the game.

7. **Independent clause** - The subject is *all,*
and the verb is *is.*

8. **Dependent clause** - The subject is *he,*
and the complete verb is *did not know.*
The word *although* makes the clause
dependent.

9. **Independent clause** - The subject is *it,*
and the complete verb is *did not seem.*

10. **Noun phrase** - The main noun is *situation,* and it is followed by a relative clause.

Now go back and place periods at the end of
all of the independent clauses (3 - 7 - 9). It is
very important to be able to distinguish
between a phrase, dependent clause, and
independent clause in order to correctly punctuate your writing. Also, phrases and dependent clauses are fragments, so do not treat
them as full sentences!

C. Coordinating Conjunctions: *and, but, yet, or, nor, (neither ... nor) for, so*

EXAMPLE 1

She graduated, and her parents are happy.
   (Clause A)   (Clause B)

Can Clause A, *She graduated,* stand alone as a complete sentence?
Can Clause B, *her parents are happy.* stand alone?

The answer to both questions is of course, yes. In fact, both clauses are
independent and the word *and,* which unites these two clauses, is a *coordinating conjunction.*

Our task is to examine the meanings of the seven coordinating conjunctions by defining the relationships that may exist between clauses. Thus,
you will be able to use these linking words properly.

And

This is by far the most commonly used coordinating conjunction probably
because it has the possibility of representing a number of relationships.

Consider the uses that follow.

EXAMPLE 2

He bought the cake, and they paid for it.
  (Clause A)   (Clause B)

In the preceding sentence *and* is adding the information of Clause A to the information of Clause B. This linkage is known as an *additive* relationship.

EXAMPLE 3

He bought the cake, and she ate it.

In example 3 *and* represents that the two actions happened at the same time. This is a relationship of time which is called a *temporal* relationship (temp = time).

EXAMPLE 4

He ate the cake, and there is no more left.

Last of all, the word *and* in example 4 represents the cause and effect relationship that exists between the two clauses. This kind of pairing is known as a *causal* relationship. Notice the word *cause* in *causal*.

Keep in mind the three basic relationships: *additive* (add), *temporal* (time), and *causal* (cause). These definitions will serve us later on to define the sometimes obscure meanings of other linking words.

But

This conjunction also has the possibility of representing several meanings. Consider the following sentences.

EXAMPLE 5

His book was interesting, *but* hers was extremely boring.

In example 5, a simple contrast is being made between two books. One is interesting, and the other is boring.

EXAMPLE 6

She played the piano beautifully, *but* she could not read sheet music.

Normally, we expect that if someone is able to play the piano well, he or she will be able to read sheet music. Given the information in the first clause, the information in the second clause is not expected.

EXAMPLE 7

Her husband collapsed at the dinner table, *but* she continued to eat her dinner.

EXAMPLE 8

He suffers from heart problems, *but* he jogs as if he were twenty years old.

Examples 5, 6, 7, and 8 show us how *but* can represent either a contrast or a contradiction (an *adversative* relationship).

Yet

You are probably familiar with this word as an adverb as found in the following sentences:

He has not arrived yet. (until now)
Do not turn off the radio yet. (at the present time)

However, this word can also function as a conjunction, and it has the same meaning as *but* has in example 6. In fact, these two conjunctions are interchangeable when used to introduce information that is not expected.

EXAMPLE 9

She studied all week, {but she did not pass the exam.
                    , {yet

EXAMPLE 10

He did well in law school, {yet he has failed his state bar exams.
                         , {but

EXAMPLE 11

She worked overtime every day, {yet she still did not have enough money.
                            , {but

Or

This conjunction establishes a choice between two possibilities.

EXAMPLE 12

She can pursue her degree, or she can attempt to get some experience in her field.

Nor

This conjunction is not a negative form of *or*. In fact its meaning is the same as *and* + *not*. Whenever you have *not* in two clauses that are joined by *and,* you should join the two sentences with *nor.* Your writing will sound more sophisticated. For example:

EXAMPLE 13

He is **not** a doctor, **and** he is **not** a lawyer.
He is **not** a doctor, **nor** is he a lawyer.

Notice how the word order changed in the second clause:

He is not a doctor, and he is not a lawyer.

He is not a doctor, nor is he a lawyer.

To get the correct word order for the second clause, ask yourself how you would make a question out of that clause. For example:

He is a lawyer. ————— Is he a lawyer?

It is this question form that is used after *nor.*

He is not a doctor, nor **is he a lawyer.**
question form

Let's try combining some other clauses with *nor.*

EXAMPLE 14

She does **not** understand democracy, **and** she does **not** value freedom.

Follow these simple steps:

1. Substitute *and* for *nor.*
2. Eliminate the word *not* in the second clause.
3. Change the second clause to the question word order:

does she value freedom

Your sentence should look like this:

She does not understand democracy, **nor does she value** freedom.

EXAMPLE 15

She did **not** eat her meat, **and** she did **not** touch her vegetables.

Combine these two clauses by following the above steps. Your answer should be:

She did not eat her meat, **nor did she touch** her vegetables.

Now try to combine these two clauses with nor:

EXAMPLE 16

He did **not** settle the trade problem, **and** he did **not** impress the American people.

Your answer should be:

He did not settle the trade problem, **nor did he impress** the American people.

Let's take this transformation one step further by using the structure *neither...nor.* Note how our previous sentences would change.

#13. He is not a doctor, nor is he a lawyer.
He is **neither** a doctor **nor** (is he) a lawyer.

Is he need not be repeated the second time. If you drop the verb and subject, you may drop the comma.

#14. She does not understand democracy, nor does she value freedom.
    She **neither** understands democracy, **nor** values freedom.

If the verb is still in the second clause, keep the comma. Also, you may have noted that **neither** was placed before the verb *understands*. In contrast, **neither** was placed after the verb *is* in example #13. **Neither** is very mobile. For simplicity:

A. Place **neither** after the verbs, *to be, to have* and modals.
    • Peter is **neither** smart **nor** clever.
    • I have **neither** patience **nor** fortitude.
    • He can **neither** swim **nor** run.
B. Place **neither** after the verb whenever two simple items are being listed:
    • He speaks **neither** French **nor** German.
    • The president wants **neither** pity **nor** blame.
C. In all other cases, place **neither** before all other verbs (see #15 & #16).

#15. She did not eat her meat, nor did she touch her vegetables.
    She **neither** *ate* (use simple past because we are not using *did*) her meat, **nor** *touched* (use simple past) her vegetables.

#16. He did not settle the trade problem, nor did he impress the American people.
    He **neither** *settled* (use simple past) the trade problem, **nor** *impressed* the American people.

Now, try to join the following clauses first with **nor** then with **neither ... nor**

PRACTICE EXERCISE 2

---

1. In Africa, European languages are **not** spoken in family circles, **and** they are **not** spoken at tribal meetings.

Join the two clauses with **nor**. _____

_____

Answer: In Africa, European languages are not spoken in family circles, **nor** are they spoken at tribal meetings.

Join the clauses with **neither ... nor**. _____

_____

Answer: In Africa, European languages are **neither** spoken in family circles **nor** at tribal meetings. (It is not necessary to repeat *are they spoken*.)

2. Ali Baba, the main protagonist of *Arabian Nights,* is **not** evil, **and** he is not greedy.

Join the two clauses with **nor**. _____

_____

Answer: Ali Baba, the main protagonist of *Arabian Nights,* is not evil, **nor** is he greedy.

Join the two clauses with **neither** ... **nor**. _____

_____

Answer: Ali Baba, the main protagonist of *Arabian Nights,* is **neither** evil **nor** greedy.

3. The media does **not** consider the effects of violent programs on children, **and** it does **not** consider how it influences public opinion.

Join the two clauses with **nor**. _____

_____

Answer: The media does not consider the effects of violent programs on children, **nor** does it consider how it influences public opinion.
Join the clauses with **neither** ... **nor**. _____

_____

Answer: The media considers **neither** the effects of violent programs on children **nor** how it influences public opinion. (In this case, place **neither** after the verb because we are creating a list.)

4. He did **not** want to sell his home, **and** he did **not** want to refinance it.

Join the two clauses with **nor**. _____

_____

Answer: He did not want to sell his home, **nor** did he want to refinance it.

Join the two clauses with **neither** ... **nor**. _____

_____

Answer: He wanted **neither** to sell his home **nor** to refinance it.

For

You are familiar with *for* used as a preposition. However, since this conjunction is not commonly used in spoken English, you may not be aware that this word may be used as a coordinating conjunction. In fact, it follows a statement and gives a reason much in the same way that the word *because* does. ***Because* subordinates a clause whereas *for* coordinates it.**

EXAMPLE 17

The production of grain was low in 1988, *for* there was a drought.

EXAMPLE 18

The production of grain was low in 1988 *because* there was a drought.

Note: **There is no comma before *because*.**

So

When this word is used as a conjunction, it introduces the *result* of the first clause.

EXAMPLE 19

The anesthesia wore off, *so the doctor had to administer a second dose.* (The clause in italics is the result.)

EXAMPLE 20

They argued all day long, *so they decided to look for new roommates.*

PRACTICE EXERCISE 3

Combine the following sentences by means of one of the seven coordinating conjunctions: *and, but, yet, or, nor, for,* or *so.* Do not forget that these conjunctions are preceded by a comma and followed by a word that begins with a lowercase letter. At times, two different conjunctions may be acceptable.

1. The concept of the "discovery of the New World" is absurd to Native Americans. Their ancestors had inhabited the New World many centuries before the Europeans landed on the Eastern seaboard.

   _____

   _____

2. Many refer to the discovery of the New World as an Age of Discovery. This period should be more appropriately called an Age of Destruction, given the impact that the Europeans had on Native Americans.

   _____

   _____

   _____

3. The Europeans did not value the cultures that they found in the New World. They did not respect the ancient rites of the natives.

   _____

   _____

   _____

4. The Europeans felt that the natives were heathens (godless). It was their obligation to convert the Indians to Christianity.

   _____

   _____

5. The Indians could be submissive to the newcomers. They could attempt to fight for the preservation of their rights.

_____

_____

_____

ANSWERS

1. Clause 1 is a statement. Clause 2 is the explanation that supports what is stated in clause 1. Use _for_ to connect the two clauses.
   * The concept of the "discovery of the New World" is absurd to Native Americans, for their ancestors had inhabited the New World for many centuries before the Europeans landed on the Eastern seaboard.
2. The information in the second clause is in contradiction to the information in the first clause. This is an adversative relationship. Either _but_ or _yet_ could have been used to join these two clauses.
   * Many refer to the discovery of the New World as an Age of Discovery,
      {but this period...
      {yet this period...
3. Either _and_ (if we wish to make this an additive relationship), or _nor_ (if we wish to stress that both clauses are negative) may be used.
   * The Europeans did not value the cultures that they found in the New World, and they did not respect the ancient rites of the natives.
   * The Europeans did not value the cultures that they found in the New World, nor did they respect the ancient rites of the natives.

Note: **The negative drops from the second clause, and question word order is used for the second clause.**

   * The Europeans neither valued the cultures that they found in the New World, nor respected the rites of the natives.

4. _And_ may be used if you want to establish a simple additive relationship.
   * The Europeans felt that the natives were heathens, and it was their responsibility to convert them to Christianity.

   _So_ may be used to state that the second clause is the result of the first.
   * The Europeans felt that the natives were heathens, so it was their responsibility to convert them to Christianity.

5. _Or_ should be used to emphasize the fact that the Indians had two choices.
   * The Indians could be submissive to the newcomers, or they could fight for the preservation of their rights.

PRACTICE EXERCISE 4

Use a coordinating conjunction _(and, but, yet, or, nor, for, so)_ to unite the following pairs of sentences.

1. It is interesting to try exotic cuisine.
   On a cold wintry night, a dish of hot soup is always satisfying.

_____

_____

2. That restaurant is famous for its split pea soup.
People drive hundreds of miles to try it.

_____

_____

3. I did not appreciate the red decor.
I did not find the food particularly tasty.

_____

_____

4. I could not try their famous soup recipe.
They had stopped making it the month before.

_____

_____

5. We could not get what we had come for. (Here, *for* is a preposition not a conjunction)
We decided to go home.

_____

_____

ANSWERS

1. [..., but ...] or [..., yet ...]

2. [..., and ...] or [..., so ...]

3. I did not appreciate the red decor, *nor did I* find the food to be particularly tasty.
   (Do not forget to put auxiliary + subject.)

   or:

   I neither appreciated the red decor, *nor* found the food to be particularly tasty.

4. [..., for ...]

5. [..., so ...]

D. Subordinating Conjunctions

EXAMPLE 1

He could not bring the painting out of the country
(Clause A)
because the government would not allow him.
(Clause B)

Clause A is an independent clause and can stand alone. Clause B cannot stand by itself because the word *because* makes this clause dependent. The linking word *because* is a subordinating conjunction. For a full discussion of subordinating conjunctions see section B of part I.

Note: **ESL writers often make two mistakes when using this type of linking word. First of all, they place a comma before *because*. Remember, commas are only placed before coordinating conjunctions. Also, since in other languages a subject need not be stated (especially in a secondary clause),** many ESL writers are tempted to leave out the subject after the linking word. This is not acceptable because in English every clause must have a subject that is stated.

EXAMPLE 2

INCORRECT: She left, because was tired.
CORRECT: She left because she was tired.

Be sure to check your writing for these two common errors.
    In addition, the order of the two clauses can be reversed:

EXAMPLE 3

Because she was tired, she went home.

Most people would prefer to use "since" instead of because at the beginning of a sentence.

Note: The dependent clause is followed by a comma. The rule is:
   • **Dependent clause, Independent clause**
   • **Independent clause Dependent clause (no comma)**

In short, these conjunctions represent specific relationships of time *(temporal)*, cause and effect *(causal)* or contrast/contradiction *(adversative)*. Let's begin our discussion with an examination of subordinating conjunctions that represent time relationships.

Time (Temporal) Subordinating Conjunctions

The most common temporal conjunctions are the following: *after, since, before, by the time, when, whenever, while, as, as long as, so long as, now that, until, once,* and *as soon as.*

All of these linking words establish *when* the action of the two clauses took place in relationship to one another. The meaning of many of these linking words should be very clear to advanced ESL writers. Let's concentrate on those linking words that might not be known to you. Also, we will look at some of the verb tenses normally used with these words. (For a review of tenses and their usage, see part IV.)

Since:

EXAMPLE 4

Since he left, he *has telephoned* three times.

Note: Do not forget to use the present perfect (or the present perfect progressive) for the verb in the independent clause. Refer to part IV for a review of the tenses. Remember *since* may also be used to give a cause.

PRACTICE EXERCISE 5

The following sentences consist of two clauses joined by *since*. Fill in the blanks with the present perfect form of the verbs given in parentheses.

1. Since the last great war finished, there _____ (*to be*) several small wars.

2. The temperature _____ (*to increase*) since the winds stopped blowing.

3. Since she _____ (*to move*) to Los Angeles, she cannot find decent employment.

ANSWERS

1. *have been*

2. *has increased*

3. *has moved*

By the time:

EXAMPLE 5

By the time they *got* home, the fire *had already destroyed* the building.

This expression implies that the action in the first clause took a long time. Also, when referring to the past, the simple past is used with the first clause (*got*), and the past perfect is used in the second clause (*had destroyed*). Both actions took place in the past, but emphasis is given to the fact that one action was completed before the other action took place.

PRACTICE EXERCISE 6

The following sentences consist of two clauses joined by *by the time*. Fill in the blanks with either the simple past or past perfect forms of the verbs given in parentheses.

1. By the time he _____ (*to come*), the war _____ (*to finish*).

2. By the time Columbus _____ (*to leave*), he _____ (*to collect*) a vast number of plant species.

3. She _____ (*to develop*) stomach problems by the time she _____ (*to reach*) high school.

ANSWERS

1. *came, had finished*

2. *left, had collected*

3. *had developed, reached*

This expression may also be used to speak about the future and the present habitual.

EXAMPLE 6

By the time he <u>gets</u> here, we <u>will have finished</u> the project.
      (simple present   (future perfect)
           for
      the near future)

When/Whenever:

These two linking verbs differ slightly in meaning.

EXAMPLE 7

When he finished his work, he left. (At that precise moment)

EXAMPLE 8

Whenever you finish your work, you may leave. (At any time)

Whenever I see that painting, I think of my grandmother. (It stresses *every* time.)

PRACTICE EXERCISE 7

Choose either *when* or *whenever* whenever to fill the blanks in the following sentences.

1. _____ he comes home from work, he reads the newspaper.

2. _____ they go to New York, they visit Central Park.

3. She gets a horrid skin rash _____ she eats berries.

ANSWERS

---

1. *when* (at that moment. If you use *whenever,* it sounds as if he does not come home from work very often.)

2. *when* or *whenever* (*Whenever* stresses *every* time.)

3. *when* or *whenever* (*Whenever,* stresses the fact that it happens *every* time.)

While/As/As long as/So long as:

All of these conjunctions denote that the action of the two clauses happened at the same time.

EXAMPLE 9

While he went to law school, he worked at the docks.
While implies an action that lasted a long period of time (durative).

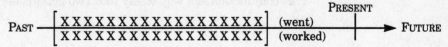

EXAMPLE 10

As the graduates stood up, the crowd cheered.
As implies at the same time.

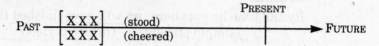

EXAMPLE 11

As/so long as he was attending college, he worked an extra twenty hours a week.
This conjunction is a lot like *while*. It emphasizes that he worked an extra twenty hours only while he attended college.

EXAMPLE 12

So long as we were coworkers, she never invited me to her home.
(This statement implies that we are no longer coworkers.)

For all four of these conjunctions, the two actions may also take place in the present or future.
Present: While I *clean* the house, she *shops*.
Future: While I *am* in France, she *will be* in Italy. (The simple present *am* may refer to the future.)

Until:

As a conjunction, this word means the period of time before something happened.

EXAMPLE 13

Until laws were established, countries did not hesitate to throw chemical waste into the Mediterranean Sea.
Until laws are established, countries will not hesitate to throw chemical waste into the Mediterranean Sea.

Once:

This linking word refers to the period of time after which something happens.

EXAMPLE 14

Once laws were established, countries could no longer legally throw chemical waste into the Mediterranean Sea.
Once laws are established, countries will no longer legally throw chemical waste into the Mediterranean Sea.

As soon as:

This conjunction is a way to say that two actions began at the very same time.

EXAMPLE 15

As soon as the new pollution laws came into effect, five countries were fined for polluting the Mediterranean Sea.
As soon as the new pollution laws come into effect, five countries will be fined for polluting the Mediterranean Sea.

PRACTICE EXERCISE 8

Choose among *since, by the time, when, whenever, while, as, as/so long as, until, once, as soon as* to fill the blanks in the following sentences.

1. _____ I heard the news, I ran to her house.

2. _____ she finished her degree, she applied for medical school.

3. _____ they got to Los Angeles, the sun had already risen.

4. _____ he hears her name, he begins to cry.

5. Her accomplice waited at the door _____ she robbed the bank.

6. _____ they learn to save money, they will never be able to afford a house.

7. _____ her parents are willing to support her financially, she will never make a serious effort to find employment.

ANSWERS

---

1. *when* or *as soon as*

2. *when, once, as soon as*

3. *by the time*

4. *when* or (even better) *whenever* (stresses every time)

5. *while, as*

6. *until*

7. *as/so long as*

Cause/Effect (Causal) Subordinating Conjunctions

Some of the most frequently used conjunctions in this category are *because, since, as, inasmuch, so (that), in order that.*

Because: This linking word introduces a direct reason.

EXAMPLE 16

She left school *because* she no longer had money for tuition.

Since/As/Inasmuch as:

Circumstances that led to an event or action are expressed with these conjunctions.

EXAMPLE 17

They sold their house *since* they had run out of money.

EXAMPLE 18

They sold their house *as* they had run out of money.

EXAMPLE 19

They sold their house *inasmuch* as they had run out of money.

Note: *Since* **and** *as* **may also represent time relationships as well.**

So (that)/In order that/In order to

These words introduce the desired result. In the independent clause, what was done to obtain the desired result is stated.

EXAMPLE 20

He took out a loan so that he could pay his tuition.
what was done   desired result

Note: *So that* **is a subordinating conjunction. Unlike** *so* **(the coordinating conjunction)** *so that* **is not preceded by a comma.**

EXAMPLE 21

He took out a loan *in order that* he could pay his tuition.

PRACTICE EXERCISE 9

Choose among *because, since, as, inasmuch as, so...that,* or *in order that,* to fill the blanks in the following sentences.

1. _____ she is such a fantastic instructor, all of her courses are full.

2. The grapes had to be harvested immediately _____ a storm was coming in.

3. He had to take four units of American history _____ he might graduate.

ANSWERS

---

1. *since, as, inasmuch as* (*Because* is not commonly found at the beginning of a sentence.)

2. *because, since, as, inasmuch as*

3. *so that, in order that*

Contrast/Contradiction (Adversative) Subordinating Conjunctions
The most common contrast/contradiction conjunctions are *although, even though, though,* and *whereas.*

Although/Even though/Though:

These three conjunctions have the same meaning and are interchangeable. They introduce a truth which is then denied or contradicted in the independent clause.

EXAMPLE 22

<u>Although he studied diligently,</u> <u>he did not pass the exam.</u>
     (Truth)   (In contradiction with
                               the first clause)

Note: **Notice that the same relationship is represented by the coordinating conjunction *but*; however, *but* introduces the clause in which the contradiction is given.**

EXAMPLE 23

<u>He studied diligently,</u> *but* <u>he did not pass the exam.</u>
    (Truth)   (Contradiction)

EXAMPLE 24

Even though she carefully took the medicine for ten days, she still had the ear infection.

EXAMPLE 25

She carefully took the medicine for ten days, *but* she still had the ear infection.

Whereas:

This word means *while on the contrary*.

EXAMPLE 26

One parent arrived on time *whereas* the others were tardy.

EXAMPLE 27

Public universities are affordable *whereas* private universities are not.

PRACTICE EXERCISE 10

Choose either *although, even though, though* or *whereas* to fill the blanks in the following sentences.

1. My sister wore a red dress _____ I wore a blue one.

2. _____ they had lived next door to each other for twenty years, they had never spoken to one another.

3. _____ a university degree takes about four years to complete, a community college degree takes about two years.

ANSWERS

1. *whereas*

2. *even though, though, although*

3. *whereas*

PRACTICE EXERCISE 11

Choose the appropriate subordinating conjunction given in parentheses for each of the following sentences. Answers and explanations are below.

1. Tarquin was an Etruscan king who ruled Rome with a strong hand. _____ Roman nobles rebelled against King Tarquin, Romans had little freedom. (*until, since, by the time*)

2. _____ Tarquin was driven out of Rome. the Romans had already suffered for many years. (*When, While, Until, By the time*)

3. _____ Etruscan royalty left Rome, Rome became a republic. (*By the time, When, Before, After, Whenever*)

4. Roman generals brought back great wealth to Rome _____ Rome fought other powerful states. (*since, whenever, when*)

Note: The conjunction is in the middle of the sentence and there is no comma before it.

5. First Julius Caesar defeated his rivals. Then he ruled Rome. _____ Julius Caesar defeated his rivals, Caesar ruled Rome as a dictator. (*So long as, Once, As soon as*)

6. Other states feared Rome _____ Rome was ruled by Caesar. (*so long as, until, whenever*)

7. Roman soldiers are called legionnaires _____ the Roman army was divided into legions. (*so, although, because*)

8. The emperors treated the soldiers with extreme care _____ there was always great danger of mutiny. (*because, so, since*)

9. The legionnaires had specially designed sandals _____ they would be able to march for miles. (*because, even though, so, in order that*)

10. _____ legionnaires were not allowed to be married, many soldiers had unofficial wives and offspring (children). (*Since, Even though, Although*)

11. _____ Roman women slaves had few rights, wealthy Roman women enjoyed many privileges. (*Whereas, Even though*)

ANSWERS

1. **Until.** This is a temporal relationship with the meaning of "for the entire time before the Romans rebelled."

2. **By the time.** This is a temporal relationship with the meaning that "the Romans had suffered over the period of time before Tarquin was driven out." (Note how the past perfect is used in the second clause.)

3. **When** or **After.** This is a temporal relationship, and either conjunction makes sense although the meaning changes in accordance with the conjunction that is chosen.
    when—at the same time
    after—first the Etruscans left, then Rome became a republic.

4. **Whenever** or **When.** This is a temporal relationship. The best answer is *whenever,* because it emphasizes that great wealth was brought back to Rome *every time* Rome fought other states.

5. **Once** or **As soon as.** This is a temporal relationship. Both give the idea that the moment Caesar defeated his rivals, he began his rule as a dictator, which lasted thereafter.

6. **So long as.** This is a temporal relationship. This conjunction signifies that the actions of the two clauses took place over the same period of time.

7. **Because.** This is a causal relationship. The conjunction introduces a direct reason.

8. **Because** or **Since.** This is a causal relationship. Both conjunctions will do just fine.

9. **So** or **In order that.** This is a causal relationship. These conjunctions introduce the why behind the action in the first clause, that is, why legionnaires had specially designed sandals.

10. **Even though** or **Although.** This is a causal relationship. These two conjunctions are interchangeable.

11. **Whereas.** This is an adversative relationship. *Whereas* is the best choice because it emphasizes the contrast which existed between the two groups of women.

E. Conjunctive Adverbs

ESL writers must be especially careful with the group of linking words called conjunctive adverbs, which link together paragraphs, clauses, or even parts of phrases. Again, as in our previous discussion, we will deal with these linking words from the viewpoint of meaning (semantics) since the meanings of these connectors may not be evident to a nonnative speaker. The following chart shows the function of these connecting words.

Function	Conjunctive Adverbs
To list or rank The asterisk marks items that are used as a group. For example, if you start a paragraph with *on one hand*, the next paragraph must begin with *on the other hand.*	*first, second, third… *first of all, second of all… *on one hand, on the other hand… to begin with next, then to conclude, finally, lastly last of all
To introduce similar thoughts or thoughts that follow the same logic	equally, likewise, correspondingly, similarly, by the same token

EXAMPLE 1

The dumping of toxic waste must be curbed. Likewise, the emission of deadly fumes must be strictly regulated.

To reinforce or develop an idea	also, furthermore, moreover, in addition

EXAMPLE 2

The committee did not approve the amendments; furthermore, it mandated that all future amendments be sent to a subcommittee.

To summarize or develop a conclusion	therefore, thus, (these two are interchangeable) to sum up, to summarize, to conclude, in conclusion (this group is usually used at the end of an essay)
To illustrate a point the example of rewording	for instance, for example, that is, that is to say, in other words

EXAMPLE 3

He has one semester to raise his grade point average. In other words, if he does not get better grades, he will not get into graduate school.

To introduce a result   consequently, therefore, thus, hence (formal), as a consequence, in consequence, as a result

EXAMPLE 4

He did not raise his grades; therefore, he did not get into graduate school.

To show a contrast   on the contrary, in contrast, by contrast, in comparison, by comparison

EXAMPLE 5

She owned her own house. In comparison, her sister did not own anything.

To introduce a statement that is   however, nonetheless,
unexpected in light of what was   nevertheless, in any event,
just said   in any case, at any rate

EXAMPLE 6

The country has a substantial national debt; nevertheless, government officials are increasing defense contracts.

Many times writers confuse conjunctive adverbs with subordinating and coordinating conjunctions. Conjunctive adverbs are very different in that they give information about the verb, and they cannot hold independent clauses together. A conjunctive adverb is very mobile, and it may be placed at the beginning, middle, or end of a sentence. For example:

However, the army was not prepared for the attack.
However is followed by a comma.
The army, **however,** was not prepared for the attack.
Commas are placed before and after *however.*
The army was not prepared for the attack, **however.**
The comma is placed before *however.*

As in these examples, commas always set off the conjunctive adverb from the rest of the sentence.

If the conjunctive adverb is at the beginning of a sentence, it may be preceded by either a period or a semicolon. For example:

Peter loved Jane. **However,** Jane did not share the same sentiments.
Peter loved Jane; **however,** Jane did not share the same sentiments.
Notice how the *h* after a semicolon is not a capital letter.

A conjunctive adverb at the beginning of a sentence or an independent clause will never be preceded by a comma. Remember it is not a coordinating conjunction! When a comma instead of a period is placed between two independent clauses, we have what is called a comma splice. A comma cannot hold sentences together. Use either a period or a semicolon between sentences.

INCORRECT: He studied, **however,** he did not know the answer.

The comma before "however" must be replaced by either a period or a semicolon.

CORRECT: He studied; **however,** he did not know the answer.
He studied. **However,** he did not know the answer.

PRACTICE EXERCISE 12

Look at the following sentences and try to decide which ones are incorrectly punctuated.

1. Antibiotics will not help a sore throat that is caused by a virus. Consequently, doctors should not prescribe antibiotics for this type of ailment (medical problem).

2. Antibiotics will not help a sore throat that is caused by a virus, consequently, doctors should not prescribe antibiotics for this type of ailment.

3. Antibiotics will not help a sore throat that is caused by a virus; consequently, doctors should not prescribe antibiotics for this type of ailment.

4. Antibiotics will not help a sore throat that is caused by a virus. Doctors, consequently, should not prescribe antibiotics for this type of ailment.

5. Antibiotics will not help a sore throat that is caused by a virus; Consequently, doctors should not prescribe antibiotics for this type of ailment.

ANSWERS

1. Correct - *Consequently* begins the second clause and is preceded by the period of the preceding clause.

2. Incorrect - Again *consequently* begins the second clause and must be preceded by either a period or a semicolon.

3. Correct

4. Correct - The conjunctive adverb has been placed closer to the verb and is marked off by commas. Do not get confused. If it were at the beginning of the clause, it would not be possible to place a comma before it.

5. Incorrect - When the conjunctive adverb follows a semicolon, do not capitalize the first letter.

PRACTICE EXERCISE 13

Use a conjunctive adverb to fill in the blank spaces.

1. In most western countries the deceased (dead) were either buried or cremated. _____ (A), in New Guinea the deceased were smoked, mummified, covered with clay, and placed on a scaffold (a high shelflike construction) out in the open. _____ (B), the remains of villagers were placed on exhibit for all to see.

2. The sting of Africanized or "killer" bees is no more dangerous than that of a European bee. _____ (A), Africanized bees are deadly because they tend to attack in mass. _____ (B) if you are attacked by this type of bee, your best defense is to seek shelter in a car or building. You will still get stung, but the number of stings will be reduced.

3. The giant figures which are etched in the deserts of the U.S. Southwest were created

about A.D. 890. _____ (A), scientists believe that the figures are a representation of prehistoric Indian myths.

4. White-throated swifts (a type of bird) are threatened by the toxic chemical DDT; _____ (A), the peregrine falcon, which is found on the coasts of California, is also endangered by DDT.

5. _____ (A), consumers are attracted to the price and quality of foreign automobiles. _____ (B), these same consumers are intent upon buying American products to boost the American economy.

6. Student loans greatly benefit university students. _____ (A), the money obtained from these loans allows students to pursue their education. _____ (B), since students do not have to work full time to support themselves, they are able to finish their studies earlier and enter the work force. _____ (C), students with loans do not have to depend on parental financial support.

ANSWERS

---

1. A. On the contrary, In/By contrast, In/By comparison

   B. In other words, That is, That is to say

2. A. However, Nonetheless, Nevertheless

   B. Accordingly, Consequently, Hence, Therefore, Thus, As a consequence, As a result

3. A. Also, Furthermore, Moreover, In addition

4. A. equally, likewise, correspondingly, similarly, by the same token

   or:

   also, furthermore, moreover, in addition

5. A. On one hand

   B. On the other hand

6. A and B. First ... Second, or First of all ... Second of all

   C. Finally, Lastly, Last of all

F. A Summary of Linking Words

It is now clear that coordinating conjunctions, subordinating conjunctions, and conjunctive adverbs all link parts of sentences, full sentences, or even paragraphs together. The writer chooses each one of these connectors in accordance with the relationships that he or she is establishing.

Remember: A clause has both a subject and a predicate (verb).

Note: **All three types of connectors are followed by clauses that must have a subject that is explicitly stated.**

The following chart summarizes the three types of connectives according to type (coordinating conjunction, subordinating conjunction, or conjunctive adverb) and function. As a writer, the choice is up to you!

Function	Coordinating Conjunctions __, conj __.	Subordinating Conjunctions Ind. Clause Dep. Clause. Dep. Clause, Ind. Clause.	Conjunctive adverbs __. Conj. adverb, __. __; conj. adverb, __.
Additive To add together two pieces of information	and		Listing: first, second, third… first of all, second of all… on one hand, on the other hand… to begin with, next, then, to conclude, finally, lastly, last of all
Adversative Two pieces of infomation are in contrast	but, yet or, nor	although, even though, though [introduce the truth] whereas [contrast]	Equative: equally, likewise, correspondingly, similarly, by the same token Reinforcing: also, furthermore, moreover, in addition, however, nonetheless, nevertheless, in any event, in any case, at any rate. on the contrary, in/by contrast, in/by comparison
Causal To give a cause or reason	for [gives a reason] so [gives a result]	because [gives a reason] since, as, inasmuch as [gives the circumstances]	consequently, therefore, hence, thus, as a consequence, in consequence, as a result
Temporal To give *when* something happened		after, since, before, by the time, when, whenever, while, as, as long as, so long as, now that, until, once, as soon as	
Summative To make a summary			therefore, thus, to sum up, to summarize, to conclude, in conclusion, in a nutshell
Exemplificative— To give an example			for instance, for example
Rewording— To Reword			that is, that is to say, in other words

G. A Summary of Sentence Punctuation

Once you understand how sentences are made, punctuation is fairly easy. Basically, there are four ways that sentences may be punctuated.

1. Between two independent clauses (or sentences), you may place a period. This is by far the most common situation.

> Peter studied all night. The next day he passed the exam.

Think of a traffic light. A period is a full stop similar to a red light on the road. In fact, in Britain a period is called *full stop*. Use it when you want the reader to stop and take a pause between two complete and separate thoughts.

2. Between two full clauses, it is also possible to place a semicolon (;). Be careful. This type of punctuation is not very common. It is used only when the two sentences are very close in meaning or strongly related in some way. Since in the preceding example the second sentence is a consequence of the first, it would be possible to separate the two with a semicolon.

> Peter studied all night; the next day he passed the exam.

Notice how the word after the semicolon is not capitalized. Think of the semicolon as being a yellow traffic light. The reader takes a short pause between the two sentences but does not come to a complete stop. Do not overuse semicolons!

3. Let's now talk about how to punctuate those sentences that are made up of a dependent and independent clause. If the dependent clause is first, place a comma before the independent clause. For example:

> If she comes to New York, she will stay with me.
>
> DEPENDENT   INDEPENDENT

If the independent clause comes first, there is no comma:

> She will stay with me if she comes to New York.

4. Last of all, if there is a conjunctive adverb. These are the possible types of punctuation:

   a. Peter studied all night. Consequently, he passed the exam.

   b. Peter studied all night; consequently, he passed the exam.

   c. Peter studied all night. He, consequently, passed the exam.

   d. Peter studied all night. He passed the exam, consequently.

II. RELATIVE CLAUSES

Before we finish our discussion of clauses, we must examine relative clauses which serve to make our writing more concise and colorful. We will concentrate on those relative clauses which function as adjectives in that they modify nouns or pronouns.

A. What is a Relative Clause?

A relative clause is a complete sentence which has been placed within another sentence.
For example:
   The boy is my brother.
   The boy is sitting on the rock.
It is awkward to repeat the subject *boy* two times, and it is possible to take the information of the second sentence and insert it into the first. Whenever you find that you are repeating the same subject over and over again, you should ask yourself if you can avoid repetition by using a relative clause. In the above example, let's take the second sentence, *the boy is sitting on the rock,* and insert it into the first. When you do so, you must always place the new relative clause immediately after the noun that it refers to. Thus, we now have:
   The boy (the boy is sitting on the rock) is my brother.
Now it is necessary to replace *the boy* in the relative clause with a relative pronoun:
   The boy <u>who</u> is sitting on the rock is my brother.

B. Relative Pronouns (*Who, That,* and *Which*) and Restrictive Clauses

You have probably been taught that **who** is used to take the place of a person, **which** is used to take the place of things and **that** may be used for people and things. In other words:

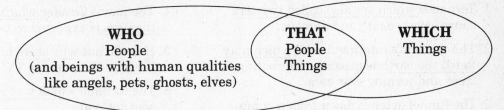

WHO
People
(and beings with human qualities like angels, pets, ghosts, elves)

THAT
People
Things

WHICH
Things

This rule is true, but *that* cannot <u>always</u> be used in place of *who* and *which.* In fact, *that* can only be used in **restrictive** clauses. So our diagram should read:

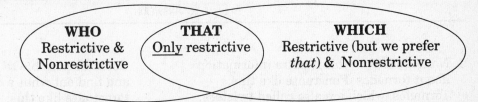

WHO
Restrictive &
Nonrestrictive

THAT
<u>Only</u> restrictive

WHICH
Restrictive (but we prefer *that*) & Nonrestrictive

Now, in order to understand what restrictive and nonrestrictive clauses are, let's examine the following sentence.

   The women <u>who is giving the speech</u> is a good friend of mine.

The relative clause <u>who is giving the speech</u> is very important information because it lets the listener know which woman is my friend. In this case this information is *restrictive;* it is necessary in order to identify the woman. If we take this clause out, we will not know which woman is being referred to. Since restrictive clauses are an important part of the sentence, we do not place commas either before or after the clause. Commas are like parentheses, and they indicate that the information within is not necessary. In the case of restrictive clauses, the information is not extra; it is necessary.

Often, <u>but not always,</u> nonrestrictive clauses are found after proper nouns. For example:

Marconi, <u>who died in 1937,</u> invented the telegraph.

Even if we do not know who Marconi is, it is possible, with this last name, to go to an encyclopedia and find out the identity of this person. The information, *who died in 1937,* is extra or unnecessary information for identifying Marconi. Thus, it is a nonrestrictive clause, and it is preceded and followed by commas.

PRACTICE EXERCISE 14

To see if you have clearly understood, study the following sentences and determine if the clauses are restrictive or nonrestrictive. Then add commas before and after the clause as necessary.
Remember:

| RESTRICTIVE CLAUSES | — | NECESSARY INFORMATION | — | NO COMMAS |
| NONRESTRICTIVE CLAUSES | — | EXTRA INFORMATION | — | PUT COMMAS |

1. Tornados <u>which are also called twisters</u> cause severe death and damage.

2. The tornado's rotating funnel <u>which may touch the earth</u> is capable of uprooting trees and turning over cars.

3. The funnel extends down from a cumulonimbus cloud <u>which often forms in the middle or the latter part of the day.</u>

4. The movie *Twister* <u>which is presently in the theaters</u> is expected to be a box office hit.

5. Helen Hunt <u>who stars in the movie</u> is also the star of a popular TV show.

6. The tornado <u>which was seen in the movie</u> was not real.

7. Meteorologists <u>who specialize in tornado prediction</u> have saved thousands of lives.

ANSWERS

1. Nonrestrictive - this is extra information about tornados. Punctuate like this:
Tornados, which are also called twisters, cause severe death and damage.

2. Nonrestrictive - this is extra information. Punctuate like this:
The tornado's rotating funnel, which may touch the earth, is capable of uprooting trees and turning over cars.

3. Nonrestrictive - this is extra information. It would be possible to go to a reference book and find out what a cumulonimbus cloud is. Punctuate like this:
The funnel extends down from a cumulonimbus cloud, which often forms in the middle or the latter part of the day.

4. Nonrestrictive - *Twister* is a proper noun. Punctuate like this:
The movie *Twister,* which is presently in the theaters, is expected to be a box office hit.

5. Nonrestrictive - Helen Hunt is a proper noun. Punctuate like this:
   Helen Hunt, who stars in the movie, is also the star of a popular TV show.

6. Restrictive - it tells us which tornado. Punctuate like this:
   The tornado which was seen in the movie was not real. (no commas)

7. Restrictive - it tells which meteorologists. Punctuate like this:
   Meteorologists who specialize in tornado prediction have saved thousands of lives. (no commas)

In which sentences can the relative pronouns be replaced with *that*?
Answer: *That* may be used only in restrictive clauses, #6 & 7

6. The tornado *that* was seen in the movie was not real.
   This clause is restrictive because without the information *that was seen in the movie,* we would not know which tornado is being referred to.

7. Meteorologists *that* specialize in tornado prediction have saved thousands of lives.

This clause is restrictive because it tells us exactly which meteorologists.

C. When Should I Use the Relative Pronoun *Whom*?

The relative pronoun *whom* often confuses ESL students. We already have the pronoun *who* for people, so when do we use the *whom* form? The answer is simple. *Who* is the only pronoun in English that has an object form, and every time *who* is functioning as an object, you must use the form *whom* in written English (informal spoken English does not always stick to this rule).

The next step is to decide when *who* is functioning as an object. There are two possibilities. *Who* may be the object of a verb or a preposition.

EXAMPLE 1

The person *whom I saw* was wearing a big green hat.

Let's examine the clause *whom I saw.* The subject of this clause is *I.* The predicate (or verb) is *saw,* and *whom* is the object of the verb *saw.* ESL students get confused because they sometimes think that they must examine *whom* in relation with the main clause, which in this case would be: *The person was wearing a big green hat.*

Handy Hint: **If the pronoun *who* is followed by a subject pronoun or a subject noun, we know immediately that *who* is an object, and we must use the form *whom*.**

Also, many verbs, such as *speak to, be with,* and *call on* are followed by prepositions, and *who* can be the object of that preposition.

EXAMPLE 2

This is the man *whom I spoke of.* In this clause, *I* is the subject, and the predicate is *spoke of.*

Whom is the object of the preposition *of*: I spoke of *the man.* I spoke of *whom.*

These verbs are phrasal verbs, and prepositions may be placed either immediately after the verbs or immediately before the pronoun *whom.*

EXAMPLE 3

This is the man whom I spoke *of*. (immediately after the verb)

EXAMPLE 4

This is the man *of* whom I spoke. (immediately before whom)

Handy Hint: Whenever *who* is preceded by a preposition, use the form *whom*.

PRACTICE EXERCISE 15

Decide in the following clauses if *who* or *whom* should be used. Also, add commas if the clause is nonrestrictive.

1. The man from _____ I received the call is very concerned about his child's progress.

2. The man _____ I received the call from is very concerned about his child's progress.

3. The man _____ called me is very concerned about his child's progress.

4. Mr. Canter _____ called me last night is very concerned.

5. The young student ____ sent the telegram did not know of the danger.

6. The young student to ____ I sent the letter is my sister.

7. The young student _____ I sent the letter to is my sister.

8. Cosimo Mizzi _____ sent a letter last week is an excellent student.

9. I finally met the elderly woman of _____ you spoke.

10. I finally met the elderly woman _____ you spoke of.

ANSWERS

1. Whom - restrictive - no commas. Notice there is the preposition <u>from</u> before and the subject <u>I</u> after the pronoun.

2. Whom - restrictive - no commas. Notice the pronoun is followed by the subject I.

3. Who - restrictive - no commas. *Who* is the subject of the clause - - - - called me.

4. Who - nonrestrictive - commas. *Mr. Canter* is a proper noun. Thus, the following clause is nonrestrictive.

5. Who - restrictive - no commas. *Who* is the subject of the clause - - - - sent the telegram.

6. Whom - restrictive - no commas. The relative pronoun is preceded by the preposition *to* and followed by the subject pronoun *I*.

7. Whom - restrictive - no commas. The relative pronoun is followed by the subject *I*.

8. Who - nonrestrictive - commas. Cosimo Mizzi is a proper noun, and the clause that follows will be nonrestrictive.

9. Whom - restrictive - no commas. *Whom* follows the preposition *of* which is part of the verb to speak.

10. Whom - restrictive - no commas. *Whom* is followed by the subject of the clause - - - - you spoke of.

D. When Can We Omit (Delete or Eliminate) the Relative Pronoun?

You may have noticed that sometimes the relative pronoun is omitted, and you may have some questions about when it is proper to omit the pronoun. Here are two times when it is common to omit the pronoun.

1. Whenever the pronoun is immediately followed by the verb *to be* (which means that the pronoun is functioning as the subject of the clause), the pronoun and the verb may be omitted. It does not matter what tense the verb *to be* is.

EXAMPLE 1

The young man, *who was* sensitive to the needs of others, decided to join the Peace Corps.

May become: The young man, sensitive to the needs of others, decided to join the Peace Corps.

However, if the relative clause is reduced to a simple adjective or a list of adjectives, we do not normally omit the relative pronoun.

EXAMPLE 2

You would not say: The young man, <u>sensitive,</u> decided to join the Peace Corps.

In this case, the remaining adjective would simply be placed before the noun:

The <u>sensitive</u> young man decided to join the Peace Corps.

2. In <u>restrictive</u> clauses, if the relative pronoun (who, which or that) is acting as an object, it is possible to omit the relative pronoun.

EXAMPLE 3

He has not read the book <u>that</u> you recommended. (*that* is the object of *you recommended*)

May become: He has not read the book you recommended.

Note: It is perfectly fine to leave out the relative pronoun in these sentences. It is important that you recognize that reduction is possible, and most native speakers would automatically omit the pronoun in these situations.

PRACTICE EXERCISE 16

Try to decide if pronoun omission (leaving out) is possible in the following sentences. Ask yourself the following questions:

- Is the relative pronoun directly followed by the verb *to be?*
- Is the clause restrictive and the pronoun acting as an object within that clause?

If the answer to either question is *yes,* omit the pronoun (and the verb *to be*).

1. Mozart, who was born on January 27, 1756, was an Austrian composer.

2. Mozart's father was Leopold Mozart, who was a celebrated musician.

3. Leopold took his son on concert tours that introduced the young boy to the royalty of Europe.

4. By the time Mozart was six years old, he had already written several piano pieces which became very popular.

5. At the age of fourteen, he was paid to produce *Mithridate,* which was his first serious opera, which he produced in Milan.

6. Mozart, who produced over 600 musical works, had a life which was full of financial difficulties.

ANSWERS

1. Since we have *who + was,* it is possible to write:

   Mozart, born on January 27, 1756, was an Austrian composer.

2. Since we have *who + was,* it is possible to write:

   Mozart's father was Leopold Mozart, a celebrated musician.

3. This is a restrictive clause, but *that* is the subject of the verb *introduced.* We cannot omit the pronoun.

4. This is a restrictive clause, but *which* is the subject of the verb *became.* We cannot omit the pronoun.

5. *Which was his first serious opera:* since we have *which + was,* we may omit *which was.*

Which he produced in Milan, may not be reduced because it is a nonrestrictive clause.

So the sentence may look like this:

At the age of fourteen, he was paid to produce *Mithridate,* his first serious opera, which he produced in Milan.

6. The clause *who produced over 600 musical works* is nonrestrictive. No omission is possible. Since in the restrictive clause we have *which + was,* it is possible to omit the relative pronoun + *was.* Thus, the sentence could read:

Mozart, who produced over 600 musical works, had a life full of financial difficulties.

III. THE USE OF ARTICLES

How many times have you found yourself confused as to whether or not you should use an article before a noun? Well, you are not alone since, for most ESL writers, article usage is a very bewildering affair. To make matters worse, most explanations of the subject are very complicated. In this section, we will examine article usage from the viewpoint of *specification*. That is to say, we will try to understand whether or not a noun is *specific* in the mind of the writer and reader. You will find that if you develop a clear idea of specification, article usage will become much easier for you.

First of all, however, let us take a good look at how the article may be used with singular and plural, countable nouns (objects like pens, chairs, desks, and books) and noncountable nouns (salt, oil, rice, and sugar). You will want to refer to the following charts throughout our discussion.

Singular Countable Nouns

A or An **If emphasis is on "one"**
He bought *a car.* (Meaning *one*)
They are planning *a vacation.*

The **If the noun is specific**
The car he bought is expensive (the one he bought)
The vacation lasted six weeks. (Here it is understood from previous conversation which vacation is being referred to.)

Plural Countable Nouns
Noncountable Nouns (mass, abstract, etc.)

No article **If the reference is general**
Books are very expensive. (Books in general)
Honesty is the best policy. (Honesty in general)
Students should consider all options. (Students in general)

The **If the noun is specific**
The books required for this course have not arrived yet.
The people of this country should all vote.
The generosity that she demonstrated will never be forgotten.

A. The Function of the Article *the*

Note: In this section we will speak about *the.* This article is used when you want to point out a person or thing. If, instead, you want to stress that there is only *one* of these objects, you will use the article *a.* In many of the examples given in this section, it is possible to use *a,* but we will talk only about the article *the* and keep the discussion of *a* for the next section (B).

This article is used when the speaker (or writer) has in mind (and wants to point out) a very specific person (the man), group of people (the teachers), object (the table), group of objects (the tables), a feeling (the pain), and so on. In fact, this article is very closely related to the adjectives *this, that, these,* and *those.* In contrast, if a subject is being spoken about in general, no definite article is used. Consider the sentences that follow:

EXAMPLE 1

Beer is produced in the state of Washington. (No article is used because we are talking about beer in general.)

EXAMPLE 2

The beer produced in the state of Washington is known for its purity. (Here we use the article with *beer* because we are speaking specifically of the beer in Washington as opposed to beer produced in other states.)

In example 2, *the beer in Washington* is being singled out and set apart from all other types of beer. In this case the word *beer* is specified by a prepositional phrase *in Washington.* There are many ways in which a noun may become specific. The next six sections will give you a clear idea of this subject.

Specification that is directly given in a sentence

A noun may be made specific by information contained in a sentence.

EXAMPLE 3

The book *on the table* is mine.   *prepositional phrase*

EXAMPLE 4

The book *that I told you about* is written   *relative clause*
by Bill Stanley.

EXAMPLE 5

The *red and green* book is mine.   *adjective*

Note: **Modification does *not* necessarily make a noun specific. Always keep in mind whether the noun is being spoken of in general, or if a specific object or person is being referred to. Compare the phrases that follow.**

Spanish literature	(The writer is talking about Spanish literature in general.)
The literature of Spain	(The writer with this construction is specifying the literature of Spain as opposed to that of other countries.)
Seventeenth century poetry	(in general)
The poetry of the seventeenth century	(as opposed to the poetry of other centuries)
Women who smoke *The women* who smoke a pack a day	(all women who smoke in general) (a specific group as opposed to women in the same group who do not smoke a pack a day)

Note: As a general rule, when the noun is followed by *of,* you will use either the article *the* or the article *a.*

Specification that comes from an immediate situation
It is possible that a noun is specific even though there is no modification of the noun in the sentence.

EXAMPLE 6

The dishes are dirty.

In this example, the listener would know which dishes the speaker is referring to because they have just spoken about the dishes or possibly the speaker is pointing to the dishes.

Specification that comes from shared knowledge
Sometimes the person or thing being referred to is specific to the listener or speaker because all the members of that culture or group are familiar with that person or object.

EXAMPLE 7

The president was seen at Camp David last week.

If both the speaker and the listener are inhabitants of the United States, both will understand that the president of the United States is being referred to. If the speaker were speaking of the president of another country, either the country or the name of the president would be mentioned.

EXAMPLE 8

The president of Mexico was in Washington D.C. last week.

Specification that is the result of the fact that only one such object or person exists in the world
At times an object, person, or group is specific because it is unique and the only such object or person in the world, for example:

the sun	the earth	the north
the Equator	the universe	the west
the south	the east	the Acropolis
the White House	the Vatican	the Prince of Wales
the Renaissance	the Roman gods	

Note: The word *earth* is often used without an article especially when we use expressions like *falling down, return to* and the preposition *down:*

> The meteorite *fell to earth.*
> The proposal is very *down to earth.* (meaning logical)
> What *on earth* are you doing? (informal expression)
> Keeping this principle in mind, it is logical that the definite article be used with such expressions as the following:
> • the first, the second

- the last, the first
- the same, the only
- the most, the least, the best, the most beautiful (Now it should be perfectly clear why the superlative adjective must be preceded by the article *the*!)

Specification given by a preceding text (what you just wrote)

Very often the first time a noun is mentioned in a text it carries an indefinite article. The second time the noun is mentioned, it is given a definite article because both the writer and the reader know specifically to whom or to what the noun is referring.

EXAMPLE 9

A young *man* and *an* elderly *woman* got on the tram at Fourth Street. *The man* was wearing a green coat, and *the lady* was wearing an old pink sweater, which looked as if it had served her for many years.

EXAMPLE 10

Agostina bought *a* new *car* last summer. When she arrived home from the dealer, she found that *the ignition* was not working properly.

In the latter example, *ignition* is given a definite article because from the previous text we know that this is the ignition of the car that Agostina bought. This is indirect previous (anaphoric) reference.

Note: Once a topic is introduced, everything that refers to that topic becomes specific.

EXAMPLE 11

At *an* American university *graduation, the students* and *the professors* usually wear caps on their heads and long black hooded gowns. *The colors* on *the hoods* represent academic rank and the college attended by *the wearer.*

In example 11, the subject is the description of a graduation. Once the subject is announced, all of the elements relating to that subject require a definite article: the student, the professors, the colors, the hoods, the wearer.

Institutions and mass communication

Cultural institutions and aspects of mass communication and transportation are usually considered to be specific and require the article *the,* for example:

the cinema	the theater	the movies
the novel	the ballad	the drama
the opera	*the radio	the television (Here, *the* may be deleted.)
the paper(s)	the press	the news (Here, *the* may be deleted.)
*the bus	*the train	the mail

Note: The asterisk denotes items with which the article is omitted if the word is preceded by the preposition *by* as you can see in the next two sentences.

EXAMPLE 12

They travel to school by *bus* every day.

EXAMPLE 13

The news of the disaster was first communicated by *radio*.

As regards cultural institutions such as *the cinema,* at times the reference may be to the building in which a movie is being shown. In any case the article *the* is still used.

EXAMPLE 14

She went to *the cinema* on Broadway. (i.e., the building)

EXAMPLE 15

She loves to go to *the cinema*. (In other words, she likes to see films in general.)

The same principle holds true for some of the other nouns listed.

EXAMPLE 16

The mail came in at six o'clock. (The actual letters)

EXAMPLE 17

The mail should be privately owned. (The institution)

Class nouns

These nouns are generally considered to be specific: *the poor, the lonely, the rich, the wealthy, the dead, the middle class, the abused, the sick,* and so forth.

EXAMPLE 18

The homeless of this city need immediate assistance.

EXAMPLE 19

The hungry need to be fed.

EXAMPLE 20

The illiterate should be taught.

PRACTICE EXERCISE 17

Now that we have thoroughly examined what makes a noun specific, it is time to do a practice exercise.

In the following sentences, insert the article *the* where necessary. The answers will directly follow the exercise, so you will be able to correct yourself immediately. *Note:* ø means that no article is needed.

1. _____ potatoes that come from Idaho sell very well.

2. _____ Italian art is fascinating.

3. _____ people of America should vote.

4. _____ students who study at this university should keep careful _____ financial records.

5. _____ plants in this garden are all drought resistant.

6. _____ plants should be chosen according to their resistance to drought.

7. _____ Constitution provides for _____ liberty and _____ justice.

8. _____ constitutions establish the principles through which laws are made.

9. _____ earth revolves around _____ sun.

10. _____ sun rises to _____ east.

11. An American wedding is full of _____ tradition. _____ bride usually wears a white gown, and _____ groom wears a tuxedo. _____ best man brings _____ wedding ring to _____ church, and _____ maid of honor helps _____ bride dress for _____ ceremony.

12. Last night they all went to _____ theater.

They greatly enjoyed _____ play. They also frequent both _____ opera and _____ cinema.

13. Some believe that _____ poor, meek, and _____ humble shall be the first to enter _____ kingdom of God.

14. Without _____ air we cannot live.

15. _____ air over Los Angeles is very polluted.

16. Is _____ art an imitation of _____ life?

17. _____ literature of _____ nineteenth century tends towards _____ realism.

18. _____ agriculture is important to our society.

19. _____ small farms are greatly in danger.

20. Many of _____ small farms of California have disappeared.

21. For engineering _____ math is essential.

22. _____ humanity has always struggled for _____ survival.

23. _____ Japanese cars are very popular in the United States.

24. _____ practice makes perfect.

25. _____ modern art is very difficult to understand.

ANSWERS

1. Two answers are possible:

    The potatoes = as compared to those grown in other states

    ø potatoes = potatoes from Idaho in general

    The choice you make actually changes the meaning.

2. ø Italian art = this type in general

3. The people of America (Remember, if there is *of* after the noun you will most likely need *the*.)

4. The students or ø students (see answer 1) ø financial records (in general)

5. The plants (*in this garden* makes it specific)

6. ø plants (in general). ø drought resistant (in general)

7. The Constitution (It is specific because we are speaking about the U.S. Constitution.) ø liberty, ø justice (concepts in general)

8. ø constitutions (in general)

9. the earth, the sun (only one such object)

10. the sun, the east (only one such object)

11. ø tradition (in general) Every noun after *tradition* has the article the. Once the topic of *an American wedding* has been specified, every noun referring to that wedding is specific.

12. the theater, the play, the opera, the cinema (All are cultural institutions.)

13. the poor, the meek, the humble (class nouns) the kingdom of God (Remember, *of* usually makes a noun specific.)

14. ø air (in general)

15. The air (specifically *over Los Angeles*)

16. ø art, ø life (in general)

17. The literature *of the* nineteenth century, ø, realism (in general)

18. ø agriculture (in general)

19. ø small farms (in general)

20. the small farms (*of* makes it specific)

21. ø math (in general)

22. ø humanity, ø survival (in general)

23. ø Japanese cars (in general)

24. ø practice (in general)

25. ø modern art (in general)

B. The Function of the Article *a/an*

The indefinite article *a/an* is used whenever a countable singular noun is *not* specific. Thus, the usage of this article is exactly the opposite of that of the definite article. Compare the two articles in the following sentences:

EXAMPLE 1

A child should be taught manners.

In example 1 we are speaking about children in general. We are making a generalization.

EXAMPLE 2

The child should be taught manners.

In the preceding sentence the speaker has a specific child in mind. Either he or she has just spoken about the child, or both the speaker and the listener have just seen the child.

The indefinite article is derived from the word *one*. Very often this article is used with the meaning of *one*.

EXAMPLE 3

She walked *a mile* to school. (meaning one mile)

EXAMPLE 4

He found *a dollar* in his pocket. (one dollar)

EXAMPLE 5

The Wilsons have *a house* in Los Angeles and *a villa* in France.

Also, do not forget that when you state the profession of a person and use the verb *to be,* you must use an indefinite article before the profession. In many other languages this is not the case.

EXAMPLE 6

He is *an engineer.*

EXAMPLE 7

She is *a medical doctor.*

PRACTICE EXERCISE 18

Fill in the blank spaces in the following sentences with *a, an,* or *the.*

1. Some people do not even drink _____ single glass of water a day.

2. _____ car that I have never seen before drove away.

3. _____ car that I bought last week is at the mechanic's for repairs.

4. John is _____ artist of great renown.

5. Peter is _____ man that changed my life.

6. She fixed _____ car last week that was worth as much as my house.

7. _____ gentleman approached him and asked him the way to London.

8. _____ gentleman was wearing a funny green plaid jacket.

9. I left _____ newspaper on the table. Have you seen it?

10. I would like _____ glass of water.

ANSWERS

---

1. a single glass *(one)*
2. A car *(generic one)*
3. The car *(specific)*
4. an artist *(profession)*
5. the man *(specific)*

6. a car *(generic, one)*
7. A gentleman *(generic, one)*
8. The gentleman (here, *he is specific*)
9. a newspaper *(one),* the newspaper
10. a glass *(one)*

C. When Do We Use No Article At All? (Zero Article)

Of course we have seen how any noun that is neither specific nor carries the meaning of *one* will not have an article. Here are some other cases that do not require an article:

Certain institutions, if preceded by at, in, on, to. Consider the following:

He went to town.
    to church.
    to college.
    to school.
    to sea.

He went to jail.
    to bed.
    to class.

(ALSO: He went downtown.)

Nouns denoting times of day and night, after at, by, after, *and* before.

He came *at midnight.*
It happened *before dawn.*
Come home *by noon.*
Do not return *after dark.*

Meals, unless you are speaking of one particular meal.

Come to my house for *dinner.* vs. *The dinner* we ate was horrid.
Breakfast is served at 8:00. vs. *The breakfast,* which was served at 8:00, consisted of coffee and toast.

D. How Is the Article Used When Referring to a Group?

Examine the following possibilities:
    A rose is a delicate flower. (One rose represents the group of roses.)
    Roses are delicate flowers. (Roses as an entire group.)
    The rose is a delicate flower. (The rose as compared to other flowers.)

In all three preceding examples the noun represents the whole group. We are speaking about roses in general. Very often in essays, we speak about a subject in general. Is it possible to use any one of these three forms whenever we want? The answer is no. Let us look carefully at each type.

A rose

In order to represent the group, *a rose* must be the subject of the sentence. In the following example and a subsequent one (both marked with an asterisk), *a rose* is NOT in the subject position, and it cannot represent the group.

*People are learning to appreciate *a rose*. (As an object, *a rose* will not represent the group.)
People are learning to appreciate *roses*.

Study the construction in which you can use a noun—in this case, *a rose*—to represent the group:
A rose *is a* symbol of love.
or:
A... is a...

We cannot use "a rose" to represent the group of roses if we do not have the preceding construction as the following sentence shows:
*A rose is popular. (There is no *a* after the verb.)
Roses are popular.

Notice the differences between the following sentences:

the novel.	(As a group.)
John has studied novels.	(As a group.)
a novel.	(*One* novel not the group.)

Noncount Nouns

Using a plural noun or a noncount noun without an article is the most common way to speak of a class of things.

Teachers have many duties. (Teachers as a group.)
Parents must monitor their children. (Parents as a group.)
Students should study hard. (Students as a group.)
Women must fight for their rights. (Women in general.)
Honesty is the best policy. (Honesty in general.)
Hunger is a prime mover. (Hunger in general.)
Research has proven that cigarettes are deadly. (All cigarettes)

Note: **This usage with no article is by far the most common in an essay since usually you will be asked to discuss a topic in general.**

Nouns with the article "the" are used for the following categories:

musical instruments:	Peter plays *the piano* very well.
dances:	Elizabeth loves to dance *the waltz*.
nationalities:	*The British* love to drink tea.
adjective/noun:	*The poor* need shelter.

PRACTICE EXERCISE 19

Fill the blanks in the following sentences with *the* or ø where no article at all is needed.

1. In the past _____ young men went to _____ sea for _____ adventure.

2. _____ sea is _____ food source of _____ future.

3. He came to _____ school late. _____ students laughed as he opened _____ door. _____ teacher had little _____ patience for his antics.

4. Before _____ dawn _____ athletes began to practice _____ for big game.

5. _____ peace will not be a reality until _____ soldiers relinquish their arms.

6. _____ dinner served at _____ White House was very special indeed.

7. _____ breakfast should be eaten by all if _____ energy levels are to be kept high.

8. _____ parents have long recognized _____ importance of treating _____ children with _____ love and _____ respect.

9. _____ bananas have _____ minerals and _____ vitamins which make them a very rich food.

10. _____ banana I ate yesterday was from Panama.

11. _____ cat is a highly intelligent animal.

12. _____ words are _____ symbols that represent _____ actions or _____ things.

13. _____ Chinese have great respect for _____ elderly.

14. _____ samba is a fun dance to learn.

15. _____ microwave ovens should not be used to cook _____ eggs._____ children risk terrible facial burns if they attempt to eat _____ microwaved eggs that have not been properly prepared. In fact, _____ yolks might explode in their faces.

ANSWERS

1. ø, young men, ø sea, ø adventure

2. the sea, the food source, the future

3. ø school

   the students, the door, the teacher (all become specific), ø patience (in general)

4. ø dawn, the athletes, the big game

5. ø peace, ø soldiers (in general) *or* the soldiers (who are fighting)

6. the dinner, the White House

7. ø breakfast, ø energy levels

8. ø parents, the importance, ø children, ø love, ø respect

9. ø bananas, ø minerals. ø vitamins

10. The banana

11. The cat

12. ø words, ø symbols, ø actions, ø things

13. The Chinese, the elderly

14. The samba

15. ø microwave ovens, ø eggs, ø children, ø microwaved eggs, the yolks

E. The Article with Proper Nouns

Proper nouns are the names of specific people, (Peter Smith), places (New York), days (Monday), and so on.

One rule of thumb is that a proper noun is specific in itself, and it does not generally need an article. If for some reason the reference is not clear you need to use an article.

- Are you speaking of the Susan Stowski that I know?

Note: Also, if the proper noun has a common noun as a base, you will normally need the article *the,* for example:

• the *Queen* of England	vs.	Queen Elizabeth
• the Italian *Republic*	vs.	Italy
• the *President*	vs.	President Clinton
• the Metropolitan *Museum* of Art		
• the United *States* of America	vs.	America
• the Suez *Canal*		

- the *University* of California (If the modification precedes the name of the university the article is usually not needed: Stanford University, Yale University, but there are exceptions.)
- the Atlantic (*Ocean*)
- the Mediterranean (*Sea*)
- the Soviet *Union*
- the North *Pole*

• the *City* of Los Angeles	vs.	Los Angeles
• the Nile (*River*)		

There are groups of proper nouns that are usually preceded by the article **the.** They are as follows:

- Plural islands, lakes, and mountains: *the* Bahamas, *the* Great Lakes, *the* Alps
- Buildings, businesses, and holidays, which can either have or not have an article, for example:

NO ARTICLE	ARTICLE
Los Angeles City Hall	the Empire State Building
Independence Hall	the Forum
Memorial Stadium	the Civic Auditorium
Sears Roebuck	The Hilton
Christmas	the Fourth of July

- Newspapers: *The Times, The Observer, The Daily News* (magazines do not carry the article *the.*)
- Family name in the plural:
  the Fultons
  the Murphys

This is a general guideline that will help you to make a reasonable decision. Of course, there are exceptions that must be memorized as you encounter them.

PRACTICE EXERCISE 20

Fill in the blanks in the following sentences with *the* or ø where no article at all is needed.

1. _____ Colemans will be here for _____ Christmas.

2. _____ *Los Angeles Times* has a separate edition for _____ San Fernando Valley.

3. _____ Lake Erie is _____ southernmost lake of _____ Great Lakes.

4. _____ Department of Building and Safety of _____ City of Los Angeles has many offices all over _____ metropolitan area.

5. _____ Memorial Day is not as celebrated as _____ Fourth of July.

6. _____ Pacific Ocean has long been a favorite spot for _____ summer tourists.

7. _____ Rome was founded by _____ Romulus and _____ Remus.

8. _____ Madonna Inn is located on _____ Pacific Coast.

9. _____ Canary Islands are a group of islands off _____ coast of _____ Africa, in _____ Atlantic.

10. _____ Queen Elizabeth is well loved by _____ British.

11. _____ John Thompson who came to _____ interview was not a polite young man!

12. _____ College of Fine Arts at _____ University of New Mexico has a fine reputation.

13. _____ Soviet Union underwent great social reform.

14. _____ Notre Dame is a famous gothic cathedral in _____ Paris.

15. _____ Nutcracker Suite was arranged by _____ Peter Tchaikovsky.

ANSWERS

1. The Colemans, ø Christmas

2. The *Los Angeles Times,* the San Fernando Valley

3. ø Lake Erie, the southernmost lake, the Great Lakes

4. The Department of Building and Safety, the City of Los Angeles, the metropolitan area

5. ø Memorial Day, the Fourth of July

6. The Pacific Ocean, ø summer tourists (in general) *or* the summer tourists (as opposed to the winter ones)

7. ø Rome, ø Romulus, ø Remus

8. The Madonna Inn, the Pacific Ocean

9. The Canary Islands, the coast of ø Africa, the Atlantic

10. ø Queen Elizabeth, the British

11. The John Thompson, the interview

12. The College of Fine Arts, the University of New Mexico

13. The Soviet Union

14. ø Notre Dame, ø Paris

15. The Nutcracker Suite, ø Peter Tchaikovsky

IV. A QUICK REVIEW OF THE MAJOR VERB TENSES

A. The Present—Simple Present

General Truths

You will find that the simple present is often used in essays because it serves to speak about *general truths*.

So if you are writing a description, a classification, a definition, a comparison and contrast, a cause and effect or a persuasion, you will most likely be using the simple present (unless you are referring to the past or future). Look at the following example of comparison and contrast:

Phonics and whole language *are* two methods teachers *use* to teach young children how to read. Phonics *involves* the teaching of the relationships that *exist* between sounds and symbols. By contrast, whole language *is* a philosophy of education that focuses on language as a means of communication.

Perceptions and States of Being

The simple present is also used to write about sensations and states that are occurring at the moment of speaking.

EXAMPLE 1

The wind feels cold against my face. The rain *chills* my very soul.

Habitual Actions

Also, the simple present is used to speak about actions that are repeated all the time, that is, habitual actions.

EXAMPLE 2

The news *is* broadcasted every hour on the hour.

B. The Present—Present Progressive

The present progressive tense is used to emphasize the fact that an action is happening now.

EXAMPLE 1

The condition *is getting* progressively worse.

EXAMPLE 2

The president *is coming* to Los Angeles at this moment.

Note: **Both the simple present and the present progressive may be used to speak about the future.**

EXAMPLE 3

The train *leaves* at three o'clock. (near future)

EXAMPLE 4

Next summer I *am going* to Brazil.

In these cases, there is usually an adverb indicating time (today, tomorrow, next year, and so on) which accompanies the verb.

Fill in the blanks in the following sentences with the appropriate tense—either *simple present* or *present progressive*—of the verbs given in parentheses.

1. A great number of the roads in Europe _____ (*to be*) a tribute to the Roman soldiers that built them.

2. Many countries _____ (*rebuild*) these roads which _____ (*to be*) in desperate need of repair.

3. The family _____ (*wait*) for the doctor to arrive.

4. He _____ (*hope*) that the doctor will have a cure.

5. The swallows _____ (*return*) to Capistrano every year.

6. The bus _____ (*depart*) at two o'clock this afternoon.

ANSWERS

---

1. *are* (fact or truth)

2. *are rebuilding* (in the process); *are* (fact or truth)

3. *is waiting* (in the process)

4. *hopes* (state of mind) or *is hoping* (to emphasize the duration of the act)

5. *return* (habitual action)

6. *departs* or *is departing* (for the future)

C. The Past—Simple Past

This tense is used for actions or states of being that occurred in the past and have finished. The action may have lasted over a period of time, and it may have even been a repeated action. Most important of all, the action must no longer be taking place.

EXAMPLE 1

They *received* an eviction notice.

EXAMPLE 2

They *received* seven eviction notices.

EXAMPLE 3

It *took* three years to evict them.

Note: *used to* + the simple form of the verb may be used to speak about states of conditions and habitual actions that happened in the past.

EXAMPLE 4

I *used to eat* in restaurants every day.

EXAMPLE 5

She *used to be* very short.

D. The Past—Past Progressive

This tense is very often misused by ESL writers. In order to use this tense, there must be *two* actions (or an action and a specific time). The action must be in progress when the other action takes place. This usage may be very different from that in your language.

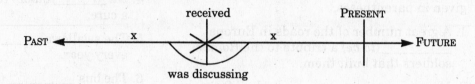

EXAMPLE 1

The council *was discussing* security, when they *received* an anonymous call, which indicated that there was a bomb in the building.

EXAMPLE 2

At five o'clock, the witness *was leaving* for work.

PRACTICE EXERCISE 22

Fill in the blanks in the following sentences with either the *simple past* or the *past progressive* tense of the verbs given in parentheses.

1. The crows _____ (*to come*) as the sun _____ (*to begin*) to set. They _____ (*to swoop*) out of the sky and _____ (*to settle*) in the branches of the old oak trees. Their cries _____ (*deafen*) all who _____ (*be*) within a quarter of a mile.

2. During the course of his last year at the university, he _____ (*to receive*) three job offers.

3. Last summer, they _____ (*to spend*) their vacation looking for a house to buy.

4. Emily _____ (*to live*) in New York City.

5. The merchant _____ (*to count*) the day's earnings when a thief _____ (*to enter*) the shop.

6. At ten o'clock I _____ (*to leave*) the office.

7. Last year she _____ (*to study*) at the university when she _____ (*to decide*) to move to Europe.

ANSWERS

1. *came, began, swooped, settled, deafened, were* (All these actions happened and finished over a period of time in the past.)

2. *received*

3. *spent* (happened and finished over a period of time)

4. *lived* or *used to live* (state of condition)

5. *was counting, entered* (The counting was in progress when it was interrupted by the thief.)

6. *left*

7. *was studying, decided* (The studying was interrupted by her decision.)

E. The Future—Simple Future

There are several ways to indicate the future in English. Consider these examples:

Example 1

I will go. (Definite intention)

Example 2

I am going to go shopping. (Intention to do something)

Example 3

I go at noon. (Simple present with an adverb of time)

F. The Future—Future Progressive

Just like the past progressive, the future progressive may be used to indicate something that will be in progress when another action takes place or at a specific time. Also, we use this tense to stress that an action will be lasting a long time in the future (duration).

Example 1

He *will be traveling* in Spain when I arrive in Europe.

Example 2

Next summer, she *will be studying* for her university exit exams.

Example 3

By this time next week, I *will be leaving* for the Orient.

Practice Exercise 23

Fill in the blanks in the following sentences with either the *simple future* or the *future progressive* tense of the verbs given in parentheses.

1. She _____ (*to earn*) a large income next year.

2. They _____ (*to finish*) their studies in two months.

3. The president _____ (*to visit*) Japan at the end of the month.

Answers

---

1. *will earn* or *is going to earn* or *will be earning*

2. *will finish* or *are going to finish* or *will be finishing*

3. *will visit* or *is going to visit* or *will be visiting*

G. The Perfect Forms—Present Perfect

Note: Some other languages have a tense that may resemble the present perfect in form, but the usage is probably very different. The best way to understand this tense is to not make comparisons with other languages.

There are three main times when we use the present perfect.

We use this tense for actions that began in the past and are still continuing now.

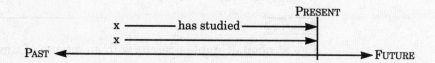

EXAMPLE 1

He *has studied* ballet for three years.

EXAMPLE 2

They *have known* Pat for three years.

EXAMPLE 3

She *has played soccer* since she was a child.

We also use the present perfect for an action that happened in the past, but when this action occurred is either unknown or not indicated.

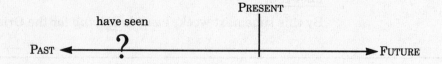

EXAMPLE 4

I *have seen* this movie. (I do not remember when.)

EXAMPLE 5

I *have been* to Europe several times. (The exact times are irrelevant to the discourse.)

Note: This form is also used for actions that never occurred, and for actions that we do not know whether or not they occurred.

EXAMPLE 6

Have you *been* to Tokyo?

EXAMPLE 7

I *have* never *been* to Tokyo.

Last of all, the present perfect is used for actions that have *just* finished or finished a short time ago.

EXAMPLE 8

They *have* just *finished* their dinner.

EXAMPLE 9

Mary *has* just *finished* her law degree.

Note: **Many times several tenses could be grammatically correct in a sentence. The tense you choose gives added meaning to the verb. Look at the differences of meaning that exists between these two sentences:**

I *went* to New York.	The speaker knows in his mind exactly when he went even though he doesn't say exactly when.
I *have been* to New York.	In this case, the speaker does not know when he went to New York, or perhaps when the action occurred is not important to the discourse.

Now, try to identify the difference in meaning between the following two sentences:

Has Pete *gone* to Los Angeles?	vs.	*Did* Pete *go* to Los Angeles?
(present perfect)		(simple past)

Again, both sentences are grammatically correct. In the first, the speaker has no specific time in mind. Perhaps the action never even took place. In the second sentence, the speaker has a specific time in mind and is sure that there is a good chance that Pete actually went to Los Angeles. Maybe the speaker knows that Pete spent his vacation in California, and there is a good chance that he went to Los Angeles. Or it is possible that Pete told the speaker that he intended to go to Los Angeles. As you can see, the choice of verb tense brings different meaning to the sentence. The choice is up to you.

Note: **The SIMPLE PAST is used for a definite time in the past (at least in the mind of the speaker).**

The PRESENT PERFECT is used for an indefinite time in the past (maybe the action never even occurred).

H. The Present Forms—Present Perfect Progressive

The present perfect progressive is used in just about the same ways as the present perfect. The difference between the two is that the progressive form is used to emphasize the continuous nature of the action.

EXAMPLE 1

He *has studied* English for three years. (He began three years ago and is still studying.)

EXAMPLE 2

He *has been studying* English for three years. (He began three years ago and is still studying day, after day, after day.)

Fill in the blanks in the following sentences with either the *present perfect,* the *present perfect progressive,* or the *simple past* of the verbs given in parentheses. In some cases, all three may be grammatically correct.

1. They _____ (*to visit*) Scotland.

2. In 1987, Nancy _____ (*to finish*) her degree.

3. They _____ (*to study*) at NYU for two years.

4. That famous actor from the 1930s _____ (*to die*).

ANSWERS

---

1. *visited.* If the time is definite in your mind.
   have visited. If the time is indefinite in your mind.
   have been visiting. If they started visiting a while ago, and they are still visiting. Here you want to emphasize the duration of the act.

2. *finished.* The time is definite.

3. *studied.* If the action was in the past and finished.
   have studied. Either the time is indefinite, or they are still studying.

have been studying. They started a while ago and are still studying. Emphasis is given to the duration of the action.

4. *died.* If you remember when.
   has died. If you don't remember when.
   has been dying. This form would rarely be used. It means that the person is very ill and has been in the process of dying for a long time. It sounds very sarcastic. Some verbs that involve actions that happen and finish quickly (to finish, to start, to die) do not usually go into the present perfect progressive form.

Note: The tense we choose gives different meanings to the sentences.

I. The Perfect Forms—Past Perfect

This form is used to show how an action happened before another action or time in the past. Therefore, in order to use this form it is necessary to have actions or an action and a specific time in the past.

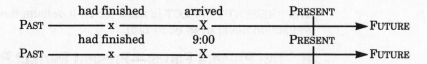

EXAMPLE 1

They *had finished* their homework before we *arrived.*

EXAMPLE 2

They *had finished* their homework before *nine o'clock.*

J. The Perfect Forms—Past Perfect Progressive

When we want to stress the fact that the past perfect action continued for a period of time, then we use the past perfect progressive form.

EXAMPLE 3

He *had been watching* television before you arrived.

EXAMPLE 4

They *had been studying* English before the phone rang.

PRACTICE EXERCISE 25

Fill in the blanks in the following sentences with either the *past perfect* or the *past perfect progressive* form of the verbs given in parentheses.

1. They _____ (*to meet*) before they graduated from the university.

2. By the time you arrived home, she _____ (*to finish*) all of the dessert.

3. Before 1985, they ____ (*to live*) in California for ten years.

4. Before their mother returned, they _____ (*to complete*) all of their chores.

ANSWERS

---

1. *had met.* With a verb like *to meet,* you probably would not use a progressive form unless you want to emphasize the fact that they continually meet each other.

2. *had finished*

3. *had lived* or *had been living*

4. *had completed* (finished) or *had been completing* (in the act of completing)

K. The Perfect Forms—Future Perfect

Much like the form that we have just discussed, this form is used to speak about an action that will occur before another action or time in the future.

EXAMPLE 1

They *will have finished* dinner before you return.

EXAMPLE 2

They *will have finished* dinner before nine o'clock.

L. The Perfect Forms—The Future Perfect Progressive

This form is used just like the preceding one; however, since it is a progressive form, it emphasizes the continuous nature of the action.

EXAMPLE 1

They *will have been studying* for one year in China, before they will return home.

EXAMPLE 2

She *will have been waiting* seven hours by midnight.

PRACTICE EXERCISE 26

Fill in the blanks in the following sentences with either the *future perfect* or the *future perfect progressive* form of the verbs given in parentheses.

1. Barbara _____ (*to arrive*) in Korea by this time tomorrow.

2. Before you get home this evening. I _____ (*to cook*) dinner.

3. By the year 2000, I _____ (*to study*) for twelve years.

4. By his action he _____ (*to prove*) his intentions.

ANSWERS

1. *will have arrived*

2. *will have cooked*

3. *will have studied* or *will have been studying*

4. *will have proven*

Verb Tense Summary

Simple Present
- General truths
  Example: The sky *is* blue.
- Perceptions and states of being.
  Example: It *tastes* delicious.
- Habitual actions
  Example: I always *go* to New York on vacation.

Present Progressive
- The action is happening now.
  Example: I *am sitting*.

Simple Past
- The action occurred in the past. The speaker knows when it took place, and the action is finished.
  Example: I *visited* Spain. (I know that I went there last month)

Past Progressive
- One action was in progress in the past when another action took place.
  Example: I *was studying* for the exam when the telephone rang.

Future
- Use for an action that will take place in the future.
  Example: Enza *will return* to Rome next year.
  Example: Enza *is going to go* to Rome next year.

Future Progressive
- Use for an action that will be in progress in the future when another action takes place.
  Example: Peter *will be working* at Hughes when he graduates.

Present Perfect

- Use for an action that started in the past and is still in progress.
  Example: Susan *has studied* English for three years.
- Use when we do not know when an action took place in the past.
  Example: I *have seen* this movie. (I don't remember when.)

Present Perfect Progressive

- It has the same use as the present perfect, but it is used to emphasize the fact that the action has been continuous.
  Example: Susan *has been studying* English for three years.

Past Perfect

- Use for an action that took place before another action in the past.
  Example: He *had been* to the United States three times before he moved there.

Past Perfect Progressive

- This tense has the same use as the past perfect, but it is used to stress the continuous nature of the action.
  Example: He *had been living* in the United States for ten years before he became a citizen.

V. LEARNING TO CORRECT YOUR COMPOSITION BY YOURSELF

To greatly improve your writing, you must reserve a part of the time given to you for the correction of your paper. All of us have our weak spots. That is to say, we all tend to repeat the same mistakes constantly. You should get out your old essays from your various classes and study the errors that you made. Try to categorize your mistakes. Answer the following questions to try to pinpoint where your weaknesses lie.

1. Do you have trouble with verb tenses? (See part IV.)   ☐ yes ☐ no

2. Do your subjects and verbs normally agree?   ☐ yes ☐ no

3. Do you have trouble with prepositions?   ☐ yes ☐ no

4. Do you often choose an incorrect article? (See part III.) ☐ yes ☐ no

5. Do you have trouble with linking words? (See part I.)   ☐ yes ☐ no

6. Do you use relative clauses correctly? (See part II.)   ☐ yes ☐ no

7. Do you have trouble with reported speech?
   (Putting someone else's words into your words.)   ☐ yes ☐ no

8. Do you make mistakes when the sentence you are
   writing contains the word *if?*   ☐ yes ☐ no

9. Do you have trouble with choosing the correct forms
   of words? (Parts of speech)   ☐ yes ☐ no

10. Do you find that you tend to repeat the same
    words over and over again?   ☐ yes ☐ no

11. Do you use a lot of words that fill space but say
    very little?   ☐ yes ☐ no

12. Is it always clear to whom or what you are referring?   ☐ yes ☐ no

Once you know what type of mistakes you make, you will be able to proofread your essay specifically for these mistakes.

In this section, we will review some of the topics just mentioned. Also, we will practice correcting (or editing) papers that contain some commonly made mistakes.

PRACTICE EXERCISE 27

Read the following introduction to an essay and decide what its main structural defects are. Later we will examine its grammatical errors.

Raising Children in the United States

The family is always been the basic unit of society in any country. It is the most important factor in any community. Any professional can tell that in a family, it is important to observe the relationship of parents to their children. There are so many duties and responsibilities that parents are facing especially here in the United States when raising their children.

Since in the United States, the culture, values and traditions are very different as compared to any other countries, parents have a different way of raising their children too. They got a different way to give their children the material things that they need, a different interpretation of what is freedom and the way to discipline their children.

What are your comments about this introduction from the point of view of structure and content?

_____

_____

_____

The person who wrote this piece knows the language fairly well and has some good thoughts on the subject. However, it seems that the writer is so tied up in words, that he is giving little thought to what he is actually saying. In fact, much of the first paragraph can be eliminated. We really don't know the thesis statement until the second paragraph. This is a common problem with ESL writers. When you write in a foreign language it is easy to over concentrate on grammar, word choice and word order to the point of losing sight of what you are actually trying to say. If you *think* and *plan* carefully before you begin to write, you will avoid this type of common error.

Pointer 1.   **Plan exactly what you are going to say *before* you begin to write. Use your words wisely. Be concise. (See Chapter 3.)**

Now let's take a look at some of the grammatical mistakes in the two sample paragraphs. What are the problems that this writer must pay particular attention to?

Your comments:
_____
_____
_____

If you guessed tenses, repetition, and unclear reference, then you have done a fine job analyzing this sample. Now, make your corrections directly onto the following text.

Raising Children in the United States

The family <u>is always been</u> the basic unit of society in any country. <u>It is
1
the most important factor in any community.</u> <u>Any professional can tell that</u>
2 3
in a family, it is important to observe the relationship of parents <u>to</u> their
4
children. There are so many duties and responsibilities that parents <u>are

facing</u> especially here in the United States when raising <u>their</u> children.
5 6
Since in the United States, the culture, values and traditions are very

different <u>as compared to any other countries,</u> <u>parents</u> have a different
7 8
way of raising their children too. <u>They got a different way to give their
9
children the material things that they need, a different interpretation of
9
what is freedom and the way to discipline their children.</u>
9

ANSWERS

(The corrections are underlined.)

1. *is the.* Usually, when writing about a topic in general, we use the simple present tense. However, if you want to use the word *always*, you must use *has always been.*

2. This sentence repeats the thought of the first sentence. Eliminate it.

3. This phrase is wordy. Get straight to the point.

4. *with.* You have a relationship *with* someone.

5. *face.* Use the simple present for general truths.

6. Misplaced: "... <u>face when raising children in the United States</u>."

7. In this sentence, it seems that the writer is comparing *culture, values,* and *traditions* to *countries.* Probably the writer intended the comparison to be between *culture, values,* and *traditions in the United States* and *culture, values,* and *traditions in other countries.* Thus, the sentence should read "... <u>from those in other countries</u>."

8. Which parents are being spoken of? <u>American parents</u>.

9. Repetition. When you find that you are repeating the same exact words, something is wrong. Get straight to the point! Moreover, in the rest of the essay, which does not appear here, the writer goes on to speak about the value of hard work and not the value of material things. Freedom and discipline are overlapping topics in this essay.

Here is an example of how the writer could have written the introduction in Practice Exercise 27:

Since every culture has different values and traditions, the way parents raise their children greatly varies in each country. Visitors to the United States are quick to notice that American parents have a unique way of raising their children, especially as regards their methods of disciplining their children and teaching their children the value of work.

As you can see, the content of the original introductory paragraphs was very limited.

PRACTICE EXERCISE 28

Study the next composition. See if you can correct all of the underlined sections of the text.

Why People Come to the United States

In many countries <u>in all over the world</u> there are a lot of problems, <u>such</u>
1
<u>as politicals, socials, and economics.</u> These problems make <u>people to leave</u>
2   3   4
their countries. For example, <u>Nicaragua and El Salvador for the civil war.</u>
5
Chile, Argentina, Paraguay. Uruguay and Peru, among others, are countries that <u>lost</u> a lot of people. <u>They had to leave their own countries</u> <u>for</u> the
6   7   8
military dictatorships. In Africa and <u>oriental countries</u> <u>is happening the</u>
9   10
<u>same situation.</u> Although in Europe there are many countries where people <u>could</u> get a good education and <u>they could get good jobs</u>, the people
11   12
still <u>came</u> to the United States for many reasons. <u>For example, the United</u>
13   14
<u>States is a country whose government is chosen democratically by the</u>
14
<u>people, the United States is a country which respects everyone and any-</u>
14
<u>body can manifest his/her ideas. And in the United States there are a lot</u>
14
<u>of possibilities to work and study.</u>
14

ANSWERS

1. <u>All over the world</u> or <u>In many countries there...</u>

2. <u>....there are a lot of political, social, and economic problems.</u> It is much better form to use the three words as adjectives.

Pointer 2. Be careful how you use the expression *such as*. It always follows a general noun, and it gives subtypes of that noun. For example, *companies, machines,* and *professions* are all general nouns in the following sentences. Notice how *such as* introduces specific subtypes. Note the punctuation that is used.

COMPANIES, *such as IBM and NCR,* have large research departments.
A secretary must know how to operate many MACHINES, *such as photocopiers and word processors.*
There are many dangerous PROFESSIONS, *such as that of the soldier and the law enforcement agent.*
Notice how in the essay that we are working on *such as* was incorrectly used to introduce three adjectives, not three noun subtypes.

3 and 4. <u>...and economic problems that make people leave their countries.</u>

Pointer 3. Pay special attention to preposition usage after "two-verb verbs."

Certain verbs, such as *to make, to let,* and *to help,* are usually followed by another verb to complete their meaning. Sometimes, the second verb is preceded by *to,* and sometimes it is not. The rule is very simple. The verbs *to make, to let,* and *to have (someone do something)* are not followed by *to.* With *to help, to* is optional. Observe the following examples.

to is excluded
They *made* him *go* to the university   no *to* is used
They *let* him *finish* his dinner.   no *to* is used
They *had* him *do* the work.   no *to* is used
to is optional
They *helped* him *finish* his degree.
    OR   *to* can be omitted or used
They *helped* him *(to) finish* his degree.
All other verbs require (to)
He *permitted* him *(to) go.*
We *asked* him *(to) stay.*
He *was obliged (to) tell* the truth.
They *were told (to) stop* fighting.
Lucretia *got* the company *(to) donate* money.
Bill *wants* you *(to) fix* the sink.
John *expects* his children *(to) do* well.

5. This is not a full sentence. It should be:
<u>People leave Nicaragua and El Salvador because of the civil war.</u>
Note that "<u>for</u> the civil war" becomes "<u>because of</u> the civil war"

Pointer 4. **Notice that in English, *for* does not introduce a reason as it often does in other languages.**

INCORRECT: He came to the United States *for to get a better job.*
CORRECT: He came to the United States *to get a better job.* (two-verb verb: see Pointer 3)
INCORRECT: He came to the United States *for the war.*
CORRECT: He came to the United States *because of the war.* (because of + noun)

6. <u>have lost</u>. Use the present perfect because the time is very indefinite. Also, this tense emphasizes the fact that the action has occurred over many years until the present.

7. Again, if a concept must be repeated, you must stop and try to make your writing more concise. Sentences 6 and 7 should be combined to read <u>...have lost a lot of people who disagreed with the governing military regimes.</u>

Pointer 5. **Prepositional phrases, relative clauses, and compound verbs all serve to make your writing concise.**

CHOPPY: He left for school. It was five o'clock.
IMPROVED: <u>At five o'clock</u>, he left for school.
　　　　 (Prepositional phrase)
CHOPPY: The children passed the exam. The exam was given yesterday.
IMPROVED: The children passed <u>the exam that was given yesterday.</u>
　　　　　　　　　　　　　　 (Relative clause)
REPETITIOUS: Louis ran. *Louis* tripped. *Louis* fell.
IMPROVED: Louis <u>ran, tripped, and fell.</u>
　　　　　　 (Compound verb)
Learn to use these three structures effectively!

8. *For* cannot be used with the meaning of *because of*.

9. <u>In Africa and Asia.</u> When you make a list, each element must be similar to the other ones. If the first two items are nouns, then the third item must be a noun. If the first item is a continent, then the next one must also be a continent.

10. <u>the same situation is happening</u>. Unless you are using a special construction, such as a yes/no question, in English statements usually the subject will come before the verb. Be careful because in your language a verb/subject sequence may be perfectly normal. If we change the verb, it sounds even better: <u>...the same situation prevails.</u>

11. <u>can</u>. Use the simple present when speaking of generalities.

12. <u>a good education and jobs</u>. Be concise!

13. <u>come</u>. Again, use the simple present.

14. Notice how <u>the United States</u> is repeated three times. Besides the fact that the punctuation of this section of text is extremely poor, something must be done to put all of this information into one concise sentence. Here is one solution:

Democracy, freedom of speech, and the possibility of self-advancement are three reasons why so many people from all over the world choose to make the United States their home.

Notice how the three concepts were neatly summarized by three nouns: democracy, freedom of speech, and self-advancement. This sentence also serves as a thesis sentence in that it tells the reader, in a clear, concise manner, that the following essay will deal with democracy, freedom of speech, and self-advancement in the United States.

Now let's take a look at a revised version of the original paragraph:

All over the world, there are a lot of political, social and economic problems that make people leave their countries. For example, people leave Nicaragua and El Salvador because of the civil war. Chile, Argentina, Paraguay, Uruguay and Peru, among others, are countries that have lost a lot of people who disagreed with the governing military regimes. In Africa and Asia, the same situation prevails. Although in Europe there are many countries where people can get a good education and jobs, many Europeans still come to the United States. In reality, democracy, freedom of speech, and the possibility of self-advancement are three reasons why so many people from all over the world choose to make the United States their home.

The preceding paragraph could be further improved, but this revision is grammatically correct and directly reflects the original version.

In summary, after you have written your first draft, always read your paper carefully. Make sure you avoid the problems that we have just discussed. With a serious effort, you will greatly improve the quality of your writing. Remember that it is important that you make your paper as logical, coherent, and gramatically correct as possible. However, the readers of your paper do not expect grammatical correctness 100 percent of the time and will not be focusing on individual grammatical errors. Your paper will be judged on your overall ability to organize your thoughts and make yourself understood.

Answer Sheet— Model Test One

Reading

1. Ⓐ Ⓑ Ⓒ Ⓓ Ⓔ
2. Ⓐ Ⓑ Ⓒ Ⓓ Ⓔ
3. Ⓐ Ⓑ Ⓒ Ⓓ Ⓔ
4. Ⓐ Ⓑ Ⓒ Ⓓ Ⓔ
5. Ⓐ Ⓑ Ⓒ Ⓓ Ⓔ
6. Ⓐ Ⓑ Ⓒ Ⓓ Ⓔ
7. Ⓐ Ⓑ Ⓒ Ⓓ Ⓔ
8. Ⓐ Ⓑ Ⓒ Ⓓ Ⓔ
9. Ⓐ Ⓑ Ⓒ Ⓓ Ⓔ
10. Ⓐ Ⓑ Ⓒ Ⓓ Ⓔ
11. Ⓐ Ⓑ Ⓒ Ⓓ Ⓔ
12. Ⓐ Ⓑ Ⓒ Ⓓ Ⓔ
13. Ⓐ Ⓑ Ⓒ Ⓓ Ⓔ
14. Ⓐ Ⓑ Ⓒ Ⓓ Ⓔ
15. Ⓐ Ⓑ Ⓒ Ⓓ Ⓔ
16. Ⓐ Ⓑ Ⓒ Ⓓ Ⓔ
17. Ⓐ Ⓑ Ⓒ Ⓓ Ⓔ

18. Ⓐ Ⓑ Ⓒ Ⓓ Ⓔ
19. Ⓐ Ⓑ Ⓒ Ⓓ Ⓔ
20. Ⓐ Ⓑ Ⓒ Ⓓ Ⓔ
21. Ⓐ Ⓑ Ⓒ Ⓓ Ⓔ
22. Ⓐ Ⓑ Ⓒ Ⓓ Ⓔ
23. Ⓐ Ⓑ Ⓒ Ⓓ Ⓔ
24. Ⓐ Ⓑ Ⓒ Ⓓ Ⓔ
25. Ⓐ Ⓑ Ⓒ Ⓓ Ⓔ
26. Ⓐ Ⓑ Ⓒ Ⓓ Ⓔ
27. Ⓐ Ⓑ Ⓒ Ⓓ Ⓔ
28. Ⓐ Ⓑ Ⓒ Ⓓ Ⓔ
29. Ⓐ Ⓑ Ⓒ Ⓓ Ⓔ
30. Ⓐ Ⓑ Ⓒ Ⓓ Ⓔ
31. Ⓐ Ⓑ Ⓒ Ⓓ Ⓔ
32. Ⓐ Ⓑ Ⓒ Ⓓ Ⓔ
33. Ⓐ Ⓑ Ⓒ Ⓓ Ⓔ
34. Ⓐ Ⓑ Ⓒ Ⓓ Ⓔ

35. Ⓐ Ⓑ Ⓒ Ⓓ Ⓔ
36. Ⓐ Ⓑ Ⓒ Ⓓ Ⓔ
37. Ⓐ Ⓑ Ⓒ Ⓓ Ⓔ
38. Ⓐ Ⓑ Ⓒ Ⓓ Ⓔ
49. Ⓐ Ⓑ Ⓒ Ⓓ Ⓔ
50. Ⓐ Ⓑ Ⓒ Ⓓ Ⓔ
41. Ⓐ Ⓑ Ⓒ Ⓓ Ⓔ
42. Ⓐ Ⓑ Ⓒ Ⓓ Ⓔ
43. Ⓐ Ⓑ Ⓒ Ⓓ Ⓔ
44. Ⓐ Ⓑ Ⓒ Ⓓ Ⓔ
45. Ⓐ Ⓑ Ⓒ Ⓓ Ⓔ
46. Ⓐ Ⓑ Ⓒ Ⓓ Ⓔ
47. Ⓐ Ⓑ Ⓒ Ⓓ Ⓔ
48. Ⓐ Ⓑ Ⓒ Ⓓ Ⓔ
49. Ⓐ Ⓑ Ⓒ Ⓓ Ⓔ
50. Ⓐ Ⓑ Ⓒ Ⓓ Ⓔ

Mathematics

1. Ⓐ Ⓑ Ⓒ Ⓓ Ⓔ
2. Ⓐ Ⓑ Ⓒ Ⓓ Ⓔ
3. Ⓐ Ⓑ Ⓒ Ⓓ Ⓔ
4. Ⓐ Ⓑ Ⓒ Ⓓ Ⓔ
5. Ⓐ Ⓑ Ⓒ Ⓓ Ⓔ
6. Ⓐ Ⓑ Ⓒ Ⓓ Ⓔ
7. Ⓐ Ⓑ Ⓒ Ⓓ Ⓔ
8. Ⓐ Ⓑ Ⓒ Ⓓ Ⓔ
9. Ⓐ Ⓑ Ⓒ Ⓓ Ⓔ
10. Ⓐ Ⓑ Ⓒ Ⓓ Ⓔ
11. Ⓐ Ⓑ Ⓒ Ⓓ Ⓔ
12. Ⓐ Ⓑ Ⓒ Ⓓ Ⓔ
13. Ⓐ Ⓑ Ⓒ Ⓓ Ⓔ
14. Ⓐ Ⓑ Ⓒ Ⓓ Ⓔ
15. Ⓐ Ⓑ Ⓒ Ⓓ Ⓔ
16. Ⓐ Ⓑ Ⓒ Ⓓ Ⓔ
17. Ⓐ Ⓑ Ⓒ Ⓓ Ⓔ

18. Ⓐ Ⓑ Ⓒ Ⓓ Ⓔ
19. Ⓐ Ⓑ Ⓒ Ⓓ Ⓔ
20. Ⓐ Ⓑ Ⓒ Ⓓ Ⓔ
21. Ⓐ Ⓑ Ⓒ Ⓓ Ⓔ
22. Ⓐ Ⓑ Ⓒ Ⓓ Ⓔ
23. Ⓐ Ⓑ Ⓒ Ⓓ Ⓔ
24. Ⓐ Ⓑ Ⓒ Ⓓ Ⓔ
25. Ⓐ Ⓑ Ⓒ Ⓓ Ⓔ
26. Ⓐ Ⓑ Ⓒ Ⓓ Ⓔ
27. Ⓐ Ⓑ Ⓒ Ⓓ Ⓔ
28. Ⓐ Ⓑ Ⓒ Ⓓ Ⓔ
29. Ⓐ Ⓑ Ⓒ Ⓓ Ⓔ
30. Ⓐ Ⓑ Ⓒ Ⓓ Ⓔ
31. Ⓐ Ⓑ Ⓒ Ⓓ Ⓔ
32. Ⓐ Ⓑ Ⓒ Ⓓ Ⓔ
33. Ⓐ Ⓑ Ⓒ Ⓓ Ⓔ
34. Ⓐ Ⓑ Ⓒ Ⓓ Ⓔ

35. Ⓐ Ⓑ Ⓒ Ⓓ Ⓔ
36. Ⓐ Ⓑ Ⓒ Ⓓ Ⓔ
37. Ⓐ Ⓑ Ⓒ Ⓓ Ⓔ
38. Ⓐ Ⓑ Ⓒ Ⓓ Ⓔ
49. Ⓐ Ⓑ Ⓒ Ⓓ Ⓔ
50. Ⓐ Ⓑ Ⓒ Ⓓ Ⓔ
41. Ⓐ Ⓑ Ⓒ Ⓓ Ⓔ
42. Ⓐ Ⓑ Ⓒ Ⓓ Ⓔ
43. Ⓐ Ⓑ Ⓒ Ⓓ Ⓔ
44. Ⓐ Ⓑ Ⓒ Ⓓ Ⓔ
45. Ⓐ Ⓑ Ⓒ Ⓓ Ⓔ
46. Ⓐ Ⓑ Ⓒ Ⓓ Ⓔ
47. Ⓐ Ⓑ Ⓒ Ⓓ Ⓔ
48. Ⓐ Ⓑ Ⓒ Ⓓ Ⓔ
49. Ⓐ Ⓑ Ⓒ Ⓓ Ⓔ
50. Ⓐ Ⓑ Ⓒ Ⓓ Ⓔ

Chapter 8

Model Test One

READING

> **Directions:** Each passage in this section is followed by a question or questions about its content. Select the best answer to each question based on what is stated or implied in the selection. You may spend up to 60 minutes on this section.

1. Throughout America, on campuses and in the streets, people express their opinions on everything from foreign policy to meteorological forecasting to drug addiction. Americans have invented many techniques of expression. Although speechmaking remains the most common, newer forms, such as silent sit-ins, passive non-violence, and sign-carrying marches, are also used.

The author would probably agree that

(A) techniques for expressing one's opinion in public have been developed in America only because of the constitutional right to freedom of speech.
(B) the proliferation of techniques for expressing opinions in America has probably clouded many issues.
(C) speechmaking is still commonly used as a persuasive technique, but it has become largely ineffective.
(D) people choose topics on which to voice their opinions without careful consideration or research.
(E) the use of newer techniques of expression for the purpose of swaying public opinion is perhaps more common in the United States than elsewhere.

Questions 2–3

MEDIAN PERCENTAGE OF SUCCESS BY THEMES FOR FOUR AGE GROUPS

THEME	POSITION	NATIONAL MEDIAN
9-YEAR-OLDS		
1. Word Meanings	1	87%
2. Visual Aids	2	85%
3. Written Directions	3	81%
4. Reference Materials	5	64%
5. Facts from Passages	6	60%
6. Main Ideas from Passages	8	45%
7. Drawing Inferences from Passages	4	78%
8. Critical Reading	7	58%
Range of Medians		**45–87**
		(42)
13-YEAR-OLDS		
1. Word Meanings	2	76%
2. Visual Aids	4	72%
3. Written Directions	1	83%
4. Reference Materials	3	74%
5. Facts from Passages	5	71%
6. Main Ideas from Passages	8	51%
7. Drawing Inferences from Passages	7	59%
8. Critical Reading	6	60%
Range of Medians		**51–83**
		(32)

THEME	POSITION	NATIONAL MEDIAN
17-YEAR-OLDS		
1. Word Meanings	6	68%
2. Visual Aids	2	84%
3. Written Directions	3	84%
4. Reference Materials	1	84%
5. Facts from Passages	4	84%
6. Main Ideas from Passages	7	68%
7. Drawing Inferences from Passages	8	68%
8. Critical Reading	5	72%
Range of Medians		**68–84**
		(16)

ADULTS		
1. Word Meanings	6	72%
2. Visual Aids	4	80%
3. Written Directions	3	86%
4. Reference Materials	1	93%
5. Facts from Passages	2	88%
6. Main Ideals from Passages	5	75%
7. Drawing Inferences from Passages	8	50%
8. Critical Reading	7	70%
Range of Medians		**50–93**
		(43)

SOURCE: National Assessment of Educational Progress

2. According to this table, 9-year-olds and 13-year-olds

   (A) did better than 17-year-olds in "Written Directions."
   (B) both did least well in "Main Ideas from Passages."
   (C) did best in "Word Meanings."
   (D) did better than adults in all but one category.
   (E) did better in the skill area (theme) of "Reference Materials" than older groups.

3. The range of median scores is smallest for

   (A) 9-year-olds.
   (B) 9-year-olds and adults.
   (C) 13-year-olds and adults.
   (D) 17-year-olds.
   (E) adults.

Questions 4–5
Almost unnoticed, scientists are reconstructing the world of plants. A new technique using colchicine, a poisonous drug, has allowed scientists to remodel many kinds of flowers, fruits, vegetables, and trees, creating new varieties with unexpected frequency. Even plants native to other countries are used to obtain the desired effects.

4. One can conclude from this passage that

   (A) the reconstruction of so many plants will be detrimental to the environment.
   (B) the new strains of plants that are produced are often better in some way.
   (C) the remodeling of plants is a controversial activity.
   (D) the creation of new varieties of plants rarely happens.
   (E) scientists must satisfy rigid requirements in order to experiment with plant varieties.

5. The title that best fits this passage is

   (A) Concern for Plant Life.
   (B) Dangers in Plant Drugs.
   (C) Reconstructing Plant Life.
   (D) Plant Growth and Heredity.
   (E) Renewing the Earth.

Questions 6–7
Conserving natural resources can be a formidable task in our national community. The preservation of small bits of irreplaceable biotic communities is so entangled with economic and social considerations that in the time spent resolving jurisdictional questions, some specimens may be permanently lost.

6. The author's attitude is one of

   (A) unhappy remorse.
   (B) uninformed naivete.
   (C) overzealous devotion.
   (D) detached disregard.
   (E) concerned interest.

7. As used in this passage, the best definition of "biotic" is

   (A) neighboring.
   (B) animal.
   (C) life.
   (D) growth.
   (E) environment

8. In response to the student's request for clarification of the theory, he wrote a paper couched in such formal circumlocutions that the student was as perplexed as he had been before. The best meaning for "circumlocutions" as used in this passage is

(A) judgments.
(B) indirect language.
(C) uninhibited expressions.
(D) assumptions.
(E) references.

Questions 9–10

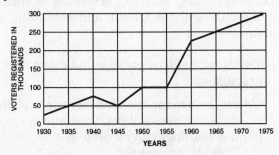

The graph shows the number of voters registered in one state between 1930 and 1975. Refer to the graph to answer the following questions.

9. Between what two periods was the increase in voter registration the greatest?

(A) 1930 and 1940
(B) 1955 and 1960
(C) 1945 and 1950
(D) 1960 and 1975
(E) 1930 and 1950

10. How much of a difference was there between voter registration in 1950 and 1975?

(A) 50,000 voters
(B) 225,000 voters
(C) 15,000 voters
(D) 150,000 voters
(E) 200,000 voters

Questions 11–13
A debate has gone on for centuries that focuses on the question of how much financial or other assistance should be given to the poor. The argument on one side emphasizes the misfortunes and deprivations those of low income must endure and appeals to the moral instincts of those in policy-making positions to use compassion in their judgments. On the other side, people speak about the role that indolence has played in engendering poverty and how public assistance programs vitiate incentives to work and to save.

11. A word that could meaningfully replace "vitiate" as used in this passage is

(A) support.
(B) impair.
(C) outline.
(D) manifest.
(E) implicate.

12. According to this passage, providing assistance for the poor is

(A) a debatable question.
(B) a poor choice.
(C) not up to those in policy-making positions.
(D) merely perpetuating poverty.
(E) an essential ingredient of a democracy.

13. Which of the following would be a good title for the ideas in this passage?

(A) Human Rights
(B) When Is Enough Too Much?
(C) Compassion in Government
(D) How Much Should Be Given to the Poor?
(E) Poverty and the Poor

Questions 14–16
Psychologists often refer to a certain phenomenon, one that has existed in every society and in every period of history, as an expression of the "evil eye syndrome." It is reflected in and referred to as the fear of success, or, in some instances, as the need to fail. It may be thought of as the general fear that calamity waits in the wings in the hour of success and rejoicing. It is interesting to consider how this ancient heritage actively influences us today.

14. The "evil eye syndrome" can be equated with

(A) witchcraft.
(B) a fear of failure.
(C) a fear of success.
(D) paranoia.
(E) the need for success.

15. One example of a class of behaviors that might be manifested over the years as a reaction to the "evil eye syndrome" would be

(A) superstitions.
(B) celebrations.
(C) funeral rites.
(D) reunions.
(E) legal actions.

16. Which one of the following statements best expresses an idea found in this passage?

(A) Success and failure are one and the same.
(B) Misfortune has ever existed.
(C) The future determines the present.
(D) Joy and sadness work hand in hand.
(E) Disaster often follows triumph.

Questions 17–18

The presence in most higher-order land animals of prehensile organs for grasping and exploring the environment creates the impression that intelligence is the sole province of animals with this characteristic. This generalization, then, makes it seem surprising that an animal with as superior a brain as the porpoise is not accompanied by any type of manipulative organ.

17. In a continuation of this paragraph, it would be reasonable for the writer to discuss

(A) the intelligent echo-sounding ability of porpoises.
(B) the uniqueness of the thumb as a prehensile organ.
(C) the differences between higher-order land animals.
(D) the intelligence levels of animals with manipulative characteristics.
(E) the mating habits of porpoises.

18. The author's main point is that

(A) porpoises exhibit the same characteristics as many land animals.
(B) people assume incorrectly that because the more intelligent animals have a prehensile organ that only animals with this characteristic manifest a high degree of intelligence.

(C) superior brains reside only in animals with prehensile organs.
(D) the presence of a prehensile tail or other organ is an essential attribute for animals with higher levels of intelligence.
(E) no one characteristic can be identified as the criterion for rating the level of intelligence in animals.

Questions 19–20

One is so helpless in the face of propaganda. The possibility of manipulating the minds of the public by withholding or distorting the facts is appalling. How can one think or speak intelligently without a clear understanding of the facts?

19. The author of this passage indicates that propaganda

(A) can be used most effectively only if the facts are manipulated in subtle ways.
(B) is a tool that can be used in a frightening manner.
(C) is only effective with those who are uninformed, who have no understanding of the facts.
(D) manipulates the public's mind by presenting issues that detract from the main issue of interest.
(E) makes one helpless by inundating the public with pieces that present contradictory information.

20. Which of the following could be the next sentence in this paragraph?

(A) One needs to elicit from propaganda the facts which are most accurate.
(B) Distorting facts to suit one's purpose is contrary to the fundamental beliefs of all systems of government.
(C) How can one participate in the development of propaganda without knowing the facts?
(D) Withholding information from the public is illegal.
(E) The control of information is ruinous in a democracy, and it becomes a farce.

Questions 21–22

Writers have often been told that the vitality of literary expression rests on authentic experience. It is likely that this demand does nag fitfully at writers' consciences, but creativity, at its most mysterious, is profound and inexplicable. Can anyone seriously believe that it is necessary to become a soldier of fortune or sail on the high seas in order to feel the pain, the bewilderment or the joy of the human predicament?

21. One idea presented in the passage is that

(A) creative instincts do not come easily to a writer.
(B) the creativity required in writing is responsible for great mysteries.
(C) the creative ability of a writer compensates for any supposed lack of actual experience.
(D) all creative writers have a depth that is not the result of a writing experience.
(E) the conscience of a creative writer is not bothered by his critics.

22. The author of this passage does NOT feel that

(A) writers are concerned with the need to base their writing on experience.
(B) the only worthwhile writing is based on real experience.
(C) it is necessary to know something about being a soldier in order to write about being a soldier.
(D) the human predicament can be written about without suffering.
(E) writers should dwell on personal experience in their writing.

Questions 23–25

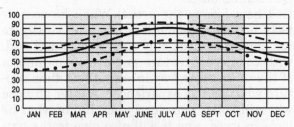

– – – RANGE OF COMFORTABLE TEMPERATURE
– · – AFTERNOON MAXIMUM TEMPERATURE
——— AVERAGE DAILY TEMPERATURE
– • – MORNING MINIMUM TEMPERATURE
▓▓▓ COMFORTABLE PERIODS IN THE YEAR BASED ON TEMPERATURE

The graph represents average temperature conditions in Tampa, Florida. Refer to the graph to answer the following questions.

23. According to the graph, in Tampa,

(A) the highest temperatures occur in the afternoon in September and May.
(B) periods of comfortable temperatures occur in March and September.
(C) average daily temperatures are lowest in February.
(D) May and June are the warmest months.
(E) morning temperatures range from 30° to 60°.

24. The range of year-round temperatures for Tampa is approximately

(A) 50°– 85°.
(B) 70°– 90°.
(C) 40°– 90°.
(D) 38°– 95°.
(E) 40°– 65°.

25. This graph could reasonably be used to

(A) determine the appropriateness of solar applications to a building.
(B) determine the potential for use of a windmill in this area.
(C) identify risk of hurricane damage in this area.
(D) plot barometric ratings for different times of the year.
(E) find out how temperatures vary during storm activity.

26. In the absence of any empirical evidence of how people reacted to seeing the war on television, it is just as plausible to suggest that television promoted support for the war as to say it promoted opposition.

As used in this passage, the most appropriate definition for "empirical" is

(A) clearly incorrect.
(B) foreboding.
(C) taken from unfamiliar material.
(D) based on research.
(E) original.

27. There is much pent-up frustration in this country, and the opposing frustrations which inflict religion and politics are expressed in feelings of nostalgia as well as jeremiads of the one against the other.

From the context of this passage, it is possible to conclude that the best definition of "jeremiad" is

(A) great journey.
(B) embellishment.
(C) tale of woe.
(D) donation.
(E) sigh of relief.

Questions 28–30

Conformity is not considered desirable in many areas of life, so why do we think that it is necessary to eliminate the variations of language that are provided by dialects? Does equality come by eliminating those that are different or by removing the differences? In recent years, black people have rejected hair straighteners and other applications only because they are asking for the basic human right of respecting themselves. It would sometimes seem as if the inability of children to learn grammatical rules is the result of a subconscious refusal to deny their own identity, to deny a part of themselves. If we tell them that the way they use language is wrong, are we not asking them to do just that? Freedom is not real if it is simply the freedom to conform to everyone else.

28. The author's main point is that

(A) the right of a person to speak like himself may be violated by teaching him that there is only one correct way to speak.
(B) children have difficulty learning grammar because the rules are difficult to apply.
(C) equality can be achieved more easily by establishing better lines of communication.
(D) teaching the grammar of one dialect is an essential aspect of providing education for all.
(E) one must express some conformity if effective communication is the goal.

29. The author's attitude in this passage reflects

(A) generosity.
(B) some confusion.
(C) a clear bias.
(D) disgust.
(E) ambivalence.

30. In order to make his point, the writer uses the technique of

(A) contrast.
(B) examples.
(C) logical exclusion.
(D) comparison.
(E) detailed analysis.

Questions 31–32

Nature evidently expected us to take a daily dose of radiation in much the same way that we experience the cuts and bruises of ordinary living. There was never any intention for man to experiment with radioactive elements as concentrated extracts. As a result of this experimentation, man has had to develop various devices to extend his perception and detect untoward situations involving radiation.

31. The "devices" mentioned in this passage refer to

(A) radioactive elements.
(B) optical equipment.
(C) "sixth sense."
(D) tools used to detect radioactivity.
(E) equipment used in nuclear reactors.

32. According to the author, we are exposed to radiation daily

(A) only if we live in industrialized areas.
(B) as a result of man's experimentation.
(C) in concentrated extracts.
(D) more frequently than we get cuts and bruises.
(E) in very small doses.

Questions 33–35

God how I envy the artist! When he sees or feels or senses something that is worthy to remember, he need only turn to his easel and, with colors and texture and even a minimum of talent, in some way interpret and thus capture what he has experienced. A later glimpse will still make him clearly mindful of what he had observed, and it will also give to the outsider an idea of what he is displaying, varying in depth and intensity according to the degree of the artist's talent.

The lonely writer, however, sees, feels, or senses, and then is forced to search deep and longingly for those special words that are the exact ones to convey or interpret what he has experienced. If words are not chosen with extreme care, a later glimpse will not enable him to recall exactly what the feeling or emotion was, and moreover, will not give the outsider the all-important idea or understanding of the experience the writer wished to share with him.

33. The writer of this passage would probably agree that

   (A) the artist has difficulty creating an impression because of his many choices of medium and color.
   (B) capturing the essence of a feeling in words or in colors is equally difficult.
   (C) less competent artists may present an impression that is far from accurate.
   (D) returning to a piece of written or artistic work after it has been completed never arouses the same impression.
   (E) writing is a very special and demanding talent.

34. The tone of this passage could be identified as

   (A) ambivalent.
   (B) flippant.
   (C) despairing.
   (D) indifferent.
   (E) determined.

35. The author makes his point by the use of

   (A) comparison and contrast.
   (B) logical explanation.
   (C) examples and details.
   (D) generalization.
   (E) fact and opinion.

Questions 36–38
It is estimated that for the expert mastery of a specialized field, about 50,000 pieces of information, an amount about equivalent to the recognition vocabulary of college-educated readers, may be required. In order to gain literacy in many demanding endeavors, it is essential that abstract groups of items be "chunked" to make it possible to process them efficiently. This skill is the greatest advantage for the expert and, conversely, the greatest problem for the beginner.

36. According to the author, "chunking" information

   (A) is only required in specialized fields.
   (B) prevents the clear discrimination of details.
   (C) enables one to gain a basic level of literacy.
   (D) makes it possible to learn more.
   (E) is a skill learned in college.

37. One reason that the skill described in this passage might be a problem for the beginner is that

   (A) the beginner has not yet developed a command of the skill of estimating.
   (B) the unfamiliarity of the material makes it difficult to "chunk" information in meaningful ways, and there are, therefore, too many isolated bits to remember.
   (C) beginners in this field are often not college-educated.
   (D) even readers with a large recognition vocabulary have difficulty with this type of material.
   (E) information essential to understanding the demands of a task must be acquired from other sources.

38. By "chunking," the author means

   (A) putting of literary works into specialized groups.
   (B) developing abridged versions of work manuals.
   (C) cutting down the size of written passages.
   (D) transforming abstract information into more concrete terms.
   (E) grouping pieces of information in meaningful patterns.

Questions 39–41
As an alternative to the experimental approach, one that offers the opportunity for a radically different view of things, the ethnographic approach is being used more and more frequently. No "variables" or "controls" are part of such an approach, since all of the elements which make up the context of situation, including the experimenter, are integral parts of the process and of the phenomena one wishes to explain.

39. One can conclude from this passage that

    (A) the experimental approach is more productive than the ethnographic approach.
    (B) variables and controls are associated with the experimental approach.
    (C) an opportunity to use the ethnographic approach is not often found.
    (D) elements which make up the situational context are extraneous in the ethnographic approach.
    (E) the phenomena observed in the experimental approach are of little interest.

40. Which of the following statements could have preceded this passage?

    (A) The ethnographic approach was often used in conjunction with the experimental approach.
    (B) The experimental approach offers the only viable possibility for studying unexplained phenomena.
    (C) When one wishes to change or control variables, the ethnographic approach is more appropriate.
    (D) One assumption underlying the experimental approach is that variables can be broken down and studied in isolation.
    (E) Methodological differences between the two approaches result in very different findings.

41. In the ethnographic approach, the experimenter

    (A) is considered part of the situational context.
    (B) is removed.
    (C) creates the phenomena.
    (D) can be ignored because he is not part of the process.
    (E) controls variables by distorting relationships.

Questions 42–44

The leap of a grasshopper is so prodigious—150 times its one-inch length—that an equivalent feat for a man would be a casual jump, from a standing position, over the Washington Monument. Its skeleton, worn on the outside like all insects, is composed of a chemical com-

pound called chitin. This sheath is extremely tough and resistant to alkali and acid compounds that would eat the clothing, flesh, and bones of man. Muscles are attached to this outside armor and arranged around catapult-like hind legs so as to permit their astonishing jumps.

42. The best meaning for "prodigious" as used in this passage is

    (A) immense.
    (B) innocuous.
    (C) original.
    (D) fluid.
    (E) intense.

43. Chitin is

    (A) a sheath consisting of an acid and an alkali.
    (B) a substance in the outside coating of a grasshopper.
    (C) part of the muscle of a grasshopper.
    (D) a catapult structure.
    (E) a chemical in all insects.

44. According to the author, the grasshopper is

    (A) a lowly insect.
    (B) a troublesome nuisance.
    (C) inclined to damage clothing and other goods.
    (D) made up of chemicals.
    (E) a small creature of amazing strength.

Questions 45–48

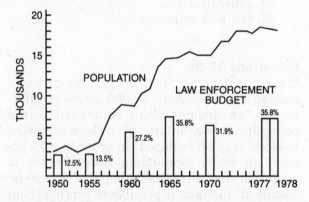

The graph represents the growth in population in one U.S. city and the percent of the budget of that city allocated to law enforcement. Refer to the graph to answer the following questions.

45. For the period between 1950 and 1978 in this city,

    (A) the increase in the population was not matched by a similar increase in money spent on law enforcement.
    (B) the growth in the population outstripped the increase in law enforcement monies by 3 to 1.
    (C) the law enforcement budget showed a consistent increase while the population showed a dramatic increase.
    (D) the population doubled while the law enforcement budget only increased by about 10%.
    (E) the population and the law enforcement budget rose in about equal increments.

46. In the period covered by the graph, the population in the city grew by approximately

    (A) 10,000.
    (B) 15,000
    (C) 25,000.
    (D) 30,000
    (E) 35,000.

47. According to the graph, it may be concluded that the amount of the budget reserved for law enforcement

    (A) rose sharply between 1950 and 1955.
    (B) decreased between 1960 and 1965.
    (C) almost tripled between the first and last years shown.
    (D) doubled since 1965.
    (E) remained stable between 1955 and 1965.

48. The greatest increase in the city's population occurred during the period

    (A) 1950–1955.
    (B) 1956–1960.
    (C) 1960–1963.
    (D) 1966–1970.
    (E) 1974–1978.

Questions 49–50

Two, then, appears to be the magic number. At every level of biological organization, the significance of pairs is evident. There is a pairing of chemical substances in DNA, a pairing of chromosomes in the nucleus of a cell, and the pairing of individuals in sexual reproduction. Part of the theory holds that simple characters, ones which separate in an all-or-none fashion, are regulated by two particles (genes), one from each parent organism. When the particles are different, the offspring will show one or the other character, but not a mixture of both.

49. One can conclude that the topic of this paragraph is

    (A) numerology.
    (B) DNA.
    (C) genetics.
    (D) living organisms.
    (E) biology.

50. From the information presented in this passage, one could determine that an example of a "simple" character would be

    (A) height.
    (B) eye color.
    (C) sex.
    (D) intelligence.
    (E) build.

MATHEMATICS

Directions: Select the best answer to each of the following questions. Any figures provided are there as reference; they are approximations and are not drawn to scale except when stated.

You may refer to the following information during this section of the test.

= is equal to
≠ is unequal to
< is less than
> is greater than
≤ is less than or equal to
≥ is greater than or equal to

√ square root of
° degrees
‖ is parallel to
⊥ is perpendicular to
π pi, approximately 3.14

Circle: Radius = r; Circumference = $2\pi r$; Area = πr^2; a circle contains 360°

Triangle: In triangle ABC, $\angle BDA$ is a right angle,

Area of $\triangle ABC = \dfrac{(AC)(BD)}{2}$;

Perimeter of $\triangle ABC = AB + BC + CA$
Sum of the measures of the three angles is 180°.

Rectangle: Area = $L \times W$; Perimeter = $2(L + W)$

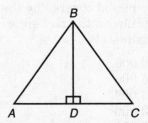

1. Which of the following numbers is closest to 27?

   (A) $26\frac{1}{4}$
   (B) 26.3
   (C) 26.74
   (D) 27.28
   (E) $27\frac{1}{4}$

2. 7□ (4 □ 2) = 14
   What operations go in the boxes?

   (A) ×, +
   (B) +, +
   (C) +, ×
   (D) −, +
   (E) ×, −

3. Which of the following is the numerical form for "fourteen thousand fourteen"?

   (A) 14,000,14
   (B) 14,014
   (C) 1414
   (D) 140,014
   (E) 1,400,014

4. In which of the following numerals does 7 have the greatest value?

   (A) 74.03
   (B) 237.46
   (C) 3347.98
   (D) 9.9997
   (E) 1709.46

5. What is the cube root of $(2^2)(2)$?

   (A) 2
   (B) 4
   (C) 8
   (D) 2 · 2
   (E) 512

6. The sum of 3 numbers, A, B, and C is 100. Also, a 4th number, D, is greater than A. Which of the following statements can you be certain is true?

   (A) $D + B + C < 100$
   (B) $D + B + C > 100$
   (C) $A + D + B > 100$
   (D) $A + D + C > 100$
   (E) $D + B + C = 100$

7. If there are C cats and D dogs in a pet store, what is the ratio of the number of cats to the total number of dogs and cats in the pet store?

(A) $\dfrac{C - D}{C + D}$

(B) $\dfrac{C}{C + D}$

(C) $\dfrac{C}{D}$

(D) $\dfrac{D}{C}$

(E) $\dfrac{C + D}{C}$

8. If the average of six x's is 6, what is the average of twelve x's?

(A) $\frac{1}{6}$
(B) $\frac{1}{2}$
(C) 1
(D) 6
(E) 12

9. $150 is 75% of what amount?

(A) $11.25
(B) $2000.00
(C) $112.50
(D) $200.00
(E) None of the above

10. Which of the following numbers are primes?
   I. 9
   II. 13
   III. 113
   IV. 121

(A) I and II only
(B) II and III only
(C) II, III, and IV only
(D) III and IV only
(E) All are prime.

11. If $x = -5 - (-6)$, what is the additive inverse (opposite) of x?

(A) 0
(B) 1
(C) –1
(D) 11
(E) –11

12. An ice cream parlor has 6 different flavors of ice cream and 3 different toppings. A sundae is defined as: two scoops of ice cream of different flavors and one topping. How many different sundaes can be made?

(A) 18
(B) 36
(C) 108
(D) 90
(E) 200

13. This tank holds 16 gallons and the car averages 22 miles per gallon.

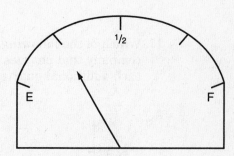

How much farther can the car travel?

(A) 264 miles
(B) 88 miles
(C) 22 miles
(D) 64 miles
(E) None of the above

14. In a game of darts, Marie threw 3 darts. If each one landed in a different ring, which score would have been impossible for her to have gotten?

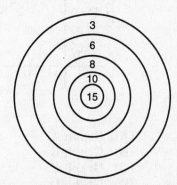

(A) An odd score greater than 30.
(B) An even score greater than 30.
(C) An odd score less than 20.
(D) A score of 19.
(E) A score of 24.

15. A rubber ball is dropped from the top of a tree 16 feet high. Sam is keeping track of how many times the ball hits the ground. He knows that every time it hits the ground it bounces back up half as high as the distance it fell. Also, it is caught when it bounces to a high point of 1 foot. How many times will Sam record the ball hitting the ground?

(A) 6 times
(B) 5 times
(C) 4 times
(D) 2 times
(E) 1 time

16. Scuba divers are concerned about the water temperatures because the water gets colder the deeper they go. This drop in temperature averages 4.5 degrees for every 1000 feet down. If the temperature at 6000 feet under water is 37 degrees, what is the temperature at sea level?

(A) 10 degrees
(B) 27 degrees
(C) 64 degrees
(D) 75 degrees
(E) None of the above

17. Which of the following graphs represents the taxi rates for a company that charges $.50 for the first quarter mile and $.25 for each additional quarter of a mile?

A.

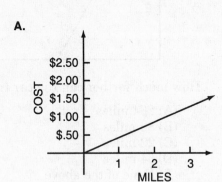

B.

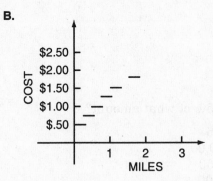

C.

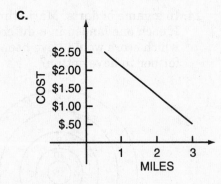

D.

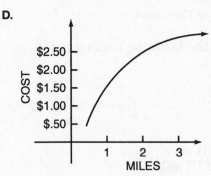

(A) Graph A
(B) Graph B
(C) Graph C
(D) Graph D
(E) None of the above

18. If $\frac{2}{3}$ of the capacity of a tank is 60 gallons, what is the total capacity of the tank?

 (A) 30 gallons
 (B) 40 gallons
 (C) 90 gallons
 (D) 120 gallons
 (E) None of the above

19. We need to divide $2100.00 among 3 people, Shelley, Mario, and Pat, so that Mario receives double what Shelley receives and Pat receives double what Mario receives. How much will Pat receive?

 (A) $300.00
 (B) $600.00
 (C) $900.00
 (D) $1200.00
 (E) None of the above

20. Ms. White spent $5.04 on dinner. This included 5% tax. How much of the bill was for tax?

 (A) $.25
 (B) $.26
 (C) $.20
 (D) $.21
 (E) None of the above

21. Harold decided to keep a record of the money he collects from his newspaper route. Using the information given, how much money does Harold collect in the month of February? (Note: Assume February has 28 days and that February 1 was on a Sunday.)

DELIVERY DAYS	WEEKLY RATE	NUMBER OF CUSTOMERS
Daily except Sunday	$1.75	20
Sunday only	$1.00	30
All week (daily & Sunday)	$2.50	50

 (A) $190
 (B) $525
 (C) $21
 (D) $760
 (E) None of the above

22. Which of the following expressions is a simplified form of
$(3x + 5) - [3x - (-x + 1) - 3]$?

 (A) $x - 7$
 (B) $3x + 7$
 (C) $-x + 9$
 (D) $x + 9$
 (E) $x + 1$

23. Subtract $3x^2 - 2x + 3$ from $2x^2 - 2$. The result is:

 (A) $-x^2 + 2x - 5$
 (B) $-x^2 - 2x - 5$
 (C) $x^2 + 2x + 1$
 (D) $-x^2 + 2x + 1$
 (E) $x^2 - 2x + 5$

24. Lemon drops come in packs of 8 for 72¢. Chocolate mints come in packs of 6 for 45¢. Ruth bought 48 pieces of candy. How many of each kind of candy did she buy, if she spent $3.96? (Choose the *best* answer.)

 (A) 6 packs of lemon drops, no chocolate mints
 (B) 8 packs of chocolate mints, no lemon drops
 (C) 3 packs of lemon drops, 4 packs of chocolate mints
 (D) Choices A, B, and C are possibilities.
 (E) None of the above is a possibility.

25. A factor of $3x^2 + 2x - 5$ is:

 (A) $x + 1$
 (B) $x + 5$
 (C) $3x + 1$
 (D) $3x - 1$
 (E) $3x + 5$

26. What is the value of $x^2y - xy^2$ when $x = 4$ and $y = 2$?

 (A) 24
 (B) 16
 (C) 0
 (D) –8
 (E) –32

27. If $\sqrt{x - 5} - 3 = 0$, then x is:

(A) 4
(B) 11
(C) 8
(D) 14
(E) There is no solution for x.

28. The formula given by $F = \frac{9}{5}C + 32°$ gives the relationship between Celsius (C) and Fahrenheit (F) temperature. If the temperature is 68 degrees Fahrenheit, what is the corresponding Celsius temperature?

(A) 64.8°
(B) 20°
(C) 154.4°
(D) 198°
(E) None of the above

29. If a function is defined by the set of ordered pairs (1, 2), (2, 4), (3, 8), (4, 16), (5, y), then the value of y is:

(A) 20
(B) 24
(C) 28
(D) 32
(E) 36

30. If $.5x - 3 = 7$ then $x = ?$

(A) 20
(B) 8
(C) 2
(D) .8
(E) .2

31. If $m > 0$ and $n < 0$, which of the following is true?

(A) $\dfrac{m}{n} > 0$

(B) $m \cdot n > 0$

(C) $\dfrac{1}{m} > \dfrac{1}{n}$

(D) $\dfrac{1}{n} > \dfrac{1}{m}$

(E) $m \cdot n = 0$

32. Mr. Jones wants to make a rectangular garden in his backyard. He has determined that the garden will measure 21 feet by 27 feet. In order to increase the fertility of the soil he will add 4 inches of topsoil. How many cubic yards of soil will he add?

(A) 252
(B) 2268
(C) 189
(D) 63
(E) None of the above

33. In the figure, angle y is more than 90 degrees and less than 180 degrees. Side x is between which 2 numbers?

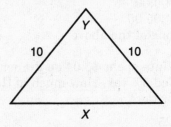

(A) 0, 10

(B) 0, $10\sqrt{2}$

(C) 10, $10\sqrt{2}$

(D) $10\sqrt{2}$, 20

(E) Both B and C

34. In the graph, if a straight line passes through point $P(6, 2)$ and point $Q(9, 0)$ it should also pass through what point on the y axis?

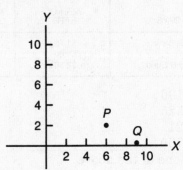

(A) (0, 2)
(B) (0, 4)
(C) (0, 5)
(D) (0, 6)
(E) (0, 9)

35. How many degrees are there in the angle formed by the hands of a clock at 5:00 p.m.?

(A) 100
(B) 114
(C) 120
(D) 150
(E) 175

36. Suppose a flagpole has a 25-foot shadow and a yardstick next to the flagpole has a 5-foot shadow at the same time. How tall is the flagpole?

(A) 10 feet
(B) 15 feet
(C) 20 feet
(D) Not enough information given
(E) None of the above

37. In the figure, triangle *ABC* is a right triangle with right angle at *B*. What is the area of triangle *ABC*?

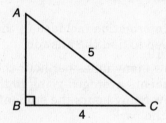

(A) 12 square units
(B) 20 square units
(C) 10 square units
(D) 6 square units
(E) 15 square units

38. Which of the following triples of numbers could *not* be the lengths of the sides of a triangle?
   I. (1, 2, 3)
   II. (3, 4, 5)
   III. (5, 12, 13)
   IV. (2, 4, 10)

(A) I only
(B) I and III only
(C) II and III only
(D) I and IV only
(E) IV only

39. A square and an equilateral triangle have equal perimeters. What is the length of a side of the triangle if the area of the square is 9 square units?

(A) 3 units
(B) 4 units
(C) 6 units
(D) 9 units
(E) 12 units

40. For which of the following lengths of a side of a square would the perimeter be divisible by both 3 and 4?

(A) $\frac{1}{4}$
(B) 2
(C) 4
(D) 7
(E) None of the above

41. Suppose you bought a side of beef weighing 500 pounds at a cost of $1.25 per pound. At no additional cost the butcher removed the waste and packaged the meat. If the waste was 33% of the total weight, how much did you pay for a pound of packaged beef?

Which statement is another way of asking what you are trying to find out in this problem?

(A) What is 33% of 500 pounds?
(B) How many pounds of waste are in a 500-pound side of beef?
(C) How much does one pound of edible meat cost if you know the total cost for all of the meat?
(D) How much does it cost to buy one pound of packaged meat at $1.25 per pound?
(E) None of the above

42. Last week the student bus took two hours to travel to a school 100 miles away for a football game. How long can we expect the bus to take to travel to a school 80 miles away?

What is another way of stating the problem?

(A) If it takes two hours to travel 100 miles, how long will it take to travel 80 miles?
(B) If it takes two hours to travel 80 miles, how long will it take to travel 100 miles?
(C) If it takes two hours to travel 100 miles, how long will the entire trip take?
(D) If one school is 100 miles away and another is 80 miles away, how much longer does it take to travel to the school 100 miles away'?
(E) None of the above

43. During Elmhurst High School's annual candy sale, Bert sold the most boxes of candy. Joan sold one box less than Bert, and Rhonda sold half as many boxes as Bert. Together the three sold 89 boxes.

Let B be the number of boxes sold by Bert. Which expression best represents the number sold by Joan?

(A) $\dfrac{B}{1}$
(B) $B - 1$
(C) $1 - B$
(D) $B \times 1$
(E) None of the above

44. What equation would you use to find the number of boxes sold by Bert?

(A) $\dfrac{B}{1} + (\tfrac{1}{2})B + B = 89$

(B) $(B - 1) + (\tfrac{1}{2})B + B = 89$

(C) $(1 - B) + (\tfrac{1}{2})B + B = 89$

(D) $(B - 1) + 2B + B = 89$
(E) None of the above

45. The 8th grade Outdoors Skills class took a bike trip to the county park. They averaged nine miles an hour on the way to the park and, because of a downhill grade, averaged 10 miles per hour on the return trip. They spent some time at the park hiking and eating lunch before returning to school. How long did it take to bike from the park back to school?

What additional information is needed to determine how long it took to bike from the park back to school?

(A) How many miles per hour the students averaged going to the park.
(B) How many hours the students spent at the park.
(C) How many miles per hour the students averaged on the trip back to school.
(D) How long they spent hiking and eating lunch.
(E) How many miles it is from the school to the park.

46. What information included in the problem is needed to find the answer?

(A) How many miles per hour the students averaged going to the park.
(B) How many hours the students spent at the park.
(C) How many miles per hour the students averaged on the trip back to school.
(D) How many miles it is from the school to the park.
(E) All of the above information is needed.

47. A farmer has 6 more hens than dogs. The total number of dogs and hens is 132. To find the number of each, guess that there are as many hens as dogs—66 of each. Then add 3 to the number of hens and subtract 3 from the number of dogs. So, 66 + 3 = 69 hens and 66 − 3 = 63 dogs.

Which problem below could be solved using exactly the same steps?

(A) Bill earns $6 more per week than Lou. If Bill earns $132 per week, how much does Lou earn?
(B) Bill earns $6 more per week than Lou. If Lou earns $132 per week, how much does Bill earn?
(C) Bill earns $6 more per week than Lou. Together they earn $132. How much does each earn per week?
(D) Bill earns $6 more per week than Lou. Together they earn $132. How much less does Lou earn than Bill?
(E) None of the above

48. Clara and Herb, 2 young parents, took their 3 children to Disneyland. Adult tickets cost $12 each and child tickets cost $8 each. Senior citizens can get tickets for 1/2 the adult ticket price and groups of 4 or more persons get a 20% discount on the total ticket cost. How much did they pay for tickets altogether?

Which information is needed to solve this problem?

(A) All you need are the prices of the tickets for adults and children.
(B) All you need is the total number of people who bought tickets.
(C) All you need are the total prices for the tickets, the number of adults, and the discount for groups of 4 or more.
(D) All you need are the number of adults, the number of children, the price of senior citizen tickets, and the price of adult and child tickets.
(E) All you need are the number of adults, the number of children, the price of adult and children tickets, and the discount for groups of 4 or more.

49. In a recent survey of 250 people, 130 preferred *Softie* paper towels to *Kleenup* paper towels, 100 people had no preference, and the remainder preferred *Kleenup*. What percent of those surveyed preferred *Kleenup* paper towels?
Answer: 40%

Which statement best describes why the answer given is *not* reasonable?

(A) Only 20% of those surveyed preferred *Kleenup*.
(B) 130 is 52% of 250.
(C) 100 people had no preference and 100 is 40% of 250.
(D) Only 20 people preferred *Kleenup* and 20 is 8% of 250.
(E) There is not enough information to determine what percent preferred *Kleenup*.

50. Harvey started a savings account. At the beginning of the year he put $284 in the account and left it for one year. At the end of the year he had earned $10\frac{1}{4}\%$ interest. How much money did he have in his savings account at the end of the year?
Answer: $313.11

Which statement best describes why the answer given for this problem is reasonable?

(A) The answer must be greater than $284.
(B) $313.11 is almost $30 greater than $284.
(C) $313.11 rounds to $310 and $310 − $284 = $26; to the nearest ten $26 rounds to $30.
(D) 10% of $284 is $28.40; $284 + $28.40 = $312.40; the answer will be a little more than $312.40.
(E) Because he should get at least $313 if he leaves his money in a savings account for an entire year.

WRITING

Directions: You will have 60 minutes to write an essay on each of the following two topics. Try to spend approximately 30 minutes on each topic, as they are of equal value in the evaluation. While quantity is not as important as quality, the topics selected will probably require an essay rather than just a paragraph or two. Organization is an integral part of effective writing, so you may want to use some of the allotted time to plan your work. Support your ideas with clear, specific examples or explanations. Write legibly, and do not skip lines.

FIRST TOPIC:

A lack of discipline in the schools, from unruliness in the classroom to vandalism on school property, is a constant topic of discussion among parents and educators. Discuss what you feel are the reasons for discipline problems.

SECOND TOPIC:

Describe one person you have known well who has significantly influenced your life.

ANSWER KEY

Reading

1. E	11. B	21. C	31. D	41. A
2. B	12. A	22. B	32. E	42. A
3. D	13. D	23. B	33. E	43. B
4. B	14. C	24. C	34. C	44. E
5. C	15. A	25. A	35. A	45. A
6. E	16. E	26. D	36. D	46. B
7. C	17. A	27. C	37. B	47. C
8. B	18. B	28. A	38. E	48. B
9. B	19. B	29. C	39. B	49. C
10. E	20. E	30. D	40. D	50. C

Mathematics

1. E	11. C	21. D	31. C	41. C
2. E	12. D	22. C	32. E	42. A
3. B	13. B	23. A	33. D	43. B
4. E	14. B	24. C	34. D	44. B
5. A	15. C	25. E	35. D	45. E
6. B	16. C	26. B	36. B	46. C
7. B	17. B	27. D	37. D	47. C
8. D	18. C	28. B	38. D	48. E
9. D	19. D	29. D	39. B	49. D
10. B	20. E	30. A	40. E	50. D

ANALYSIS OF ERRORS

The following table lists the subject matter covered in each question of the Reading and Mathematics sections of the test. Find the question numbers that you got wrong and review the subject matter covered in those questions again.

SECTION	QUESTION NUMBERS	SUBJECT AREA
READING		
	5, 13, 16, 18, 28, 49	Finding the Main Idea
	12, 14, 19, 21, 31, 32, 36, 37, 41, 43, 50	Finding Specific Details
	1, 4, 6, 15, 17, 20, 22, 29, 33, 34, 39, 40, 44	Finding Implications
	7, 8, 11, 26, 27, 31, 38, 42	Determining the Meaning of Strange Words
	30, 35	Determining Special Techniques
	2, 3, 9, 10, 23, 24, 25, 45, 46, 47, 48	Interpreting Tables and Graphs

SECTION	QUESTION NUMBERS	SUBJECT AREA
MATHEMATICS		
Arithmetic	2, 3, 10, 13, 14, 15, 16	Whole Numbers
	13, 18	Fractions
	4, 16, 21	Decimals
	9, 20	Percentage
	1	Rounding Off Numbers
	11	Signed Numbers
	8	Averages, Medians, Ranges, and Modes
	5	Powers, Exponents, and Roots
Algebra	22, 23, 25, 26, 43, 47, 48, 49, 50	Algebraic Expressions
	27, 30, 44	Equations
	19, 24, 41, 42, 45, 46	Verbal Problems
	12	Counting Problems
	7, 36	Ratio and Proportion
		Sequence and Progression
	6, 14, 31	Inequalities
Geometry	35	Angles
		Lines
		Polygons
	33, 38	Triangles
		Quadrilaterals
		Circles
	32, 37, 39, 40	Area, Perimeter, and Volume
	29, 34	Coordinate Geometry
Formulas	28	Formulas
Other	17	Interpreting Graphs (see Reading Section)

ANSWER EXPLANATIONS

Reading

1. **E** It is implied that the freedom to protest creatively is uniquely American. Answer A limits the reasons for protest and B, C, and D are not mentioned in the passage.

2. **B** The table shows that the median percentage for 9-year-olds in "Main Ideas from Passages" was 45% (8th position) and for 13-year-olds, it was 51% (8th position).

3. **D** The last line of the table must be used, which shows the range of medians for each age group. The range for 17-year-olds is 68–84, a range of only 16 points, the smallest of all the ranges.

4. **B** The passage implies that the scientists' goal in creating new varieties of plants is to improve upon them. Answers A, C, and E are not mentioned in the passage. D is inaccurate.

5. **C** The other titles are too specific or too general. The passage is mainly about the reconstruction process.

6. **E** The author apparently is concerned that debates over jurisdiction may delay the taking of action to prevent the loss of living specimens. Answer A is too strong, and B, C, and D are inaccurate.

7. **C** It is safe to conclude that biotic refers to a more general classification, i.e., pertaining to life.

8. **B** The idea that the student asked for a clarification and was still confused suggests that the language was unclear or indirect.

9. **B** In 1955, voter registration was 100,000. This increased to approximately 225,000 in 1960, the greatest increase for any one period.

10. **E** In 1950, voter registration was 100,000, and in 1975, it was 300,000, an increase of 200,000 voters.

11. **B** In discussing the "other side," the author indicates that providing assistance may get in the way of (impair) the development of a motivation to work and save.

12. **A** The author does not support either side but presents the issue as a debatable question, with two sides.

13. **D** The issue discussed is whether it is helpful to provide assistance to the poor, i.e., how much should they be given and how much should they be encouraged to work for themselves? Answers A, C, and E are too general; answer B is too specific.

14. **C** The writer states in the second sentence that the syndrome is sometimes referred to as a fear of success or as the need to fail. Paranoia (D) is too strong a statement.

15. **A** It is not stated, but one could easily conclude that it is the best answer because people always have believed in superstitious acts to ward off evil spirits or to keep from being jinxed.

16. **E** A paraphrase of the statement, "calamity waits in the wings in the hour of success," would be the idea that disaster often follows triumph.

17. **A** The last sentence in the passage allows one to assume that the author will go on to talk about the behavior of porpoises as an indication of their superior brains. The earlier references to prehensile organs are used to emphasize how surprising it is that porpoises are so intelligent.

18. **B** The author wishes to make the point that the correlation in animals between a high level of intelligence and the presence of a prehensile organ does not necessarily mean that the absence of such an organ is an indication of the absence of intelligence. Answer C states the opposite.

19. **B** The author states that using propaganda to manipulate minds is appalling.

20. **E** The author could most appropriately go on to talk about the adverse effect of propaganda in a democracy. It is unlikely that he would say it was contrary to *all* systems of government.

21. **C** It is implied that, although some people suggest that writers must base their writing on actual experience, their amazing creativity can compensate for any lack of experience.

22. **B** The writer seems to feel that personal experience is important but that writing which is worthwhile can be based on other, probably more important, creative instincts as well. The author does not advocate writing about subjects about which one is totally ignorant, so C is a poor choice.

23. **B** The shaded area of the graph, including the months of March and September, show the comfortable periods of the year. The other answers are not supported by the graph.

24. **C** The lowest temperature shown on the graph is 40° and the highest is about 90°.

25. **A** No wind, storm, or barometric pressure information is provided on the graph. It can be assumed, however, that the warm temperatures are a result of sunshine, so answer A is a viable use for this graph.

26. **D** Since the writer says it is plausible to suggest either of two sides of a question, one can conclude that there is no research evidence to support either side.

27. **C** The writer indicates that feelings of frustration have led to looking back with a fondness for the past and relating tales of woe that tend to blame the other side.

28. **A** The author feels that insisting that people conform to a dialect different from their own may be a violation of their rights.

29. **C** It is clear in the passage that the writer is biased against the attempt to eliminate variations in language.

30. **D** To make his point, the writer compares children's resistance to denying their own dialect to the rejection by black people of processes which deny their identity.

31. **D** The author's lament that man's experimentation has led to the exposure to

greater dangers from radioactivity includes a reference to the need for tools to detect radioactivity.

32. **E** We are exposed to small doses of radiation that are part of our natural environment. Answer A is never mentioned, and answers B and C are clearly not daily occurrences for most people. Answer D is inaccurate.

33. **E** The author reflects his bias that it is much more difficult and demanding to create an image with words.

34. **C** The author feels his work is difficult to the point where it is nearly impossible to achieve the goals a writer sets out to accomplish.

35. **A** The writer compares and contrasts his task with that of the artist.

36. **D** It is emphasized that the only way one can master all of the information in a specialized field is to "chunk," or group it, into meaningful units, thus to process and learn more.

37. **B** Beginners, by definition, are unfamiliar with new material and, therefore, they cannot group bits of information, making it very difficult for them to remember so many pieces.

38. **E** The meaning of "chunking" is quite clearly implied in the passage as the grouping of pieces of information in order to make them more manageable.

39. **B** Since the writer is comparing the two approaches and states that variables and controls are not part of the ethnographic approach, one can assume that they belong to the other.

40. **D** One can assume that the writer discussed the experimental approach preceding this passage, but he introduces the ethnographic approach here, so he would not have written about it before.

41. **A** The writer is clear that the unique aspect of the ethnographic approach is that all elements are seen as part of the process.

42. **A** In explaining how much of a jump this would represent for man, the writer is indicating that the grasshopper's leap is immense.

43. **B** The writer specifies that chitin is a chemical compound found in the outside skeleton of the grasshopper.

44. **E** The writer is clearly respectful of the grasshopper's strong qualities.

45. **A** The population of the city increased by almost five times while the law enforcement budget only increased by about three times for the period shown.

46. **B** In 1950, the population was 3,000, and in 1978, it was about 18,000, an increase of 15,000 citizens.

47. **C** The amount of the budget for law enforcement was 12.5% in 1950, and 35.8% in 1978. This is an increase of almost three times.

48. **B** A careful reading of the graph shows that the population increased from 4,000 to 9,000 during these years.

49. **C** Enough information is presented and specific terms used that, even if it is not stated, one could conclude that the passage is about genetics.

50. **C** The writer states that *simple* characters are ones that are acquired in their entirety or not at all. The would be true of maleness or femaleness. The genes determine that one is either a male or a female. The other answers all could encompass a range of possible characteristics.

Mathematics

1. **E** $27\frac{1}{4} = 27.25$ which is .25 greater than 27. All other choices are further from 27 than .25.

2. **E** $7 \boxed{\times} (4 \boxed{-} 2)$
   $= 7 \times 2$
   $= 14$

3. **B** Answer A is not written as a number (has only 2 digits after the last comma).
   Answer C is one thousand four hundred fourteen.
   Answer D is one hundred forty thousand fourteen.
   Answer E is one million four hundred thousand fourteen.

4. **E** The value of the 7 in each of the numerals is: (A) 70, (B) 7, (C) 7, (D) 0.0007 $\frac{7}{10000}$, (E) 700.

5. **A** The cube root r of a number n is that number such that $r^3 = n$ (i.e., $r \times r \times r = n$). Clearly $2 \times 2 \times 2 = (2^2 \times 2)$ or 8. So the cube root of $(2^2 \times 2)$ is 2.

6. **B** We are given that $A + B + C = 100$. If we replace A with D, which is greater than A, then the sum will be greater than 100 (i.e., $D + B + C > 100$).

7. **B** C = number of cats

   $C + D$ = total number of cats and dogs

   $\dfrac{C}{C + D}$ = ratio of cats to total number of cats and dogs.

8. **D** Whenever a group of identical numbers, x, are averaged, the average will equal x. Thus, in this problem, no matter how many x's are averaged, the average must be 6.

9. **D** Let A be the amount we need to know.
   $$150 = \tfrac{75}{100} \times A$$
   $$\tfrac{100}{75} \times 150 = \tfrac{100}{75} \times \tfrac{75}{100} \times A$$
   $$200 = A$$

10. **B** A prime is a whole number that is divisible only by itself and 1.
    I. $9 = 3 \times 3$ (not prime)
    II. 13 has only 1 and 13 as factors, thus is prime.
    III. 113 has only 1 and 113 as factors, thus is prime.
    IV. $121 = 11 \times 11$ (not prime)

11. **C** $x = -5 - (-6)$
    $x = -5 + 6$
    $x = 1$

    The additive inverse (opposite) of a number n is the number m such that $n + m = 0$. So the opposite of 1 is –1.

12. **D** The number of choices for first ice cream scoop = 6, for second scoop = 5, and for the topping = 3. The number of different sundaes
    = $6 \times 5 \times 3$
    = 90

13. **B** The tank is $\tfrac{1}{4}$ full, so it has 4 gallons ($\tfrac{1}{4} \times 16 = 4$). Since the car averages 22 miles per gallon, it can go $4 \times 22 = 88$ miles.

14. **B** Try to create a score for each choice.
    A. $15 + 10 + 8 > 30$ and is odd.
    B. It is impossible to get a score greater than 30 without using 15, but if you use 15

and want an even score, you must also use 3. However, the largest score possible using 15 and 3 is $15 + 3 + 10 = 28$, which is smaller than 30.
C. $8 + 6 + 3 < 20$ and is odd.
D. $10 + 6 + 3 = 19$
E. $10 + 8 + 6 = 24$

15. **C** Draw a sketch and count the bounces.

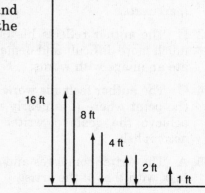

16. **C** If the temperature drops 4.5° for every 1000 feet, for 6000 feet it will have dropped $6 \times 4.5° = 27°$. If the underwater temperature is 37° and is 27° lower than at the surface, then the surface temperature is 37° + 27° = 64°.

17. **B** Only graph B is constantly \$.50 from 0 to $\tfrac{1}{4}$ mile and then rises at a rate of \$.25 for each quarter mile thereafter.

18. **C** If $\tfrac{2}{3}$ of the capacity is 60 gallons, then $\tfrac{1}{3}$ of the capacity is 30 gallons ($60 \div 2$). So the total capacity ($\tfrac{3}{3}$) must be 3×30 or 90 gallons.

19. **D** Think of each person's share in terms of Shelley's share, S. Shelley gets S, Mario gets $2S$, and Pat gets $2 \times (2S)$ or $4S$. Since the total amount of money is \$2100, we have

    $S + 2S + 4S = 2100$

    $7S = 2100$

    $5 = \tfrac{2100}{7}$

    $S = 300$

    So Shelley gets \$300. Since Pat gets $4S$, then Pat gets $4 \times 300 = \$1200$.

20. **E** Suppose x represents the cost of the dinner (not including tax). Then the tax is $.05x$. Ms. White paid \$5.04 which included the cost of the dinner (x) and the tax ($.05x$). So, $x + .05x = 5.04$
    $1.05x = 5.04$
    $x = \tfrac{5.04}{1.05}$
    $x = 4.80$

The dinner cost $4.80. So the tax was $.24.
($5.04 − 4.80 = $.24 or .05 × $4.80 = $.24)

21. **D** If February 1 is a Sunday and there are
28 days in the month, there are four
Sundays and four full weeks in the month.
Daily except Sunday, Harold gets $1.75 ×
20 × 4 = $140.00. Sunday only, Harold gets
$1.00 × 30 × 4 = $120.00. All week, Harold
gets $2.50 × 50 × 4 = $500.00. Adding
these 3 amounts gives a total for the month
of $760.

22. **C** $(3x + 5) − [3x − (−x + 1) − 3]$
$= (3x + 5) − [3x + x − 1 − 3]$
$= (3x + 5) − [4x − 4]$
$= 3x + 5 − 4x + 4$
$= −x + 9$

23. **A** $(2x^2 − 2) − (3x^2 − 2x + 3)$
$= 2x^2 − 2 − 3x^2 + 2x − 3$
$= −x^2 + 2x − 5$

24. **C** Try each of the choices.
A. $6 × 8 = 48$ candies (OK) and $6 × $.72 =
4.32 (not OK)
B. $8 × 6 = 48$ candies (OK) and $8 × $.45 =
3.60 (not OK)
C. $(3 × 8) + (4 × 6) = 48$ candies (OK) and
$(3 × $.72) + (4 × $.45) = 3.96 (OK)

25. **E** Try to match each choice with another
linear factor to give the product $3x^2 + 2x −
5$. In each case, except E, whenever a factor
gives the correct first and last terms, the
middle term is incorrect.
(A) $(x + 1)(3x − 5) = 3x^2 − 2x − 5$
(B) $(x + 5)(3x − 1) = 3x^2 + 14x − 5$
(C) $(3x + 1)(x − 5) = 3x^2 − 14x − 5$
(D) $(3x − 1)(x + 5) = 3x^2 + 14x − 5$
(E) $(3x + 5)(x − 1) = 3x^2 + 2x − 5$

26. **B** Given: $x = 4, y = 2$
Substituting into: $x^2y − xy^2$
We obtain: $(4)^2 2 − 4 (2)^2$
$= 16 · 2 − 4 · 4$
$= 32 − 16 = 16$

27. **D** $\sqrt{x − 5} − 3 = 0$
$\sqrt{x − 5} = 3$
$\left(\sqrt{x − 5}\right)^2 = 3^2$
$x − 5 = 9$
$x = 9 + 5$
$x = 14$

28. **B** Given: $F = \left(\frac{9}{5}\right)C + 32°$
$F = 68°$
Substituting: $68° = \left(\frac{9}{5}\right)C + 32°$
$\left(\frac{9}{5}\right)C = 68° − 32°$
$\left(\frac{9}{5}\right)C = 36°$
$\left(\frac{5}{9}\right)\left(\frac{9}{5}\right)C = \left(\frac{5}{9}\right)\left(\frac{36°}{1}\right)$
$(1)C = \left(\frac{180°}{9}\right)$
$C = 20°$

29. **D** The pattern is such that each pair (x, y)
is determined by $y = 2^x$. So $y = 2^5$, $y = 32$.

30. **A** $.5x − 3 = 7$
$.5x = 7 + 3$
$.5x = 10$
$x = \left(\frac{10}{.5}\right)$
$x = 20$

31. **C** Given: $m > 0$ and $n < 0$
In other words, m is positive and n is negative. $\frac{1}{m}$ is positive, $\frac{1}{n}$ is negative so
$\frac{1}{m} > \frac{1}{n}$. (Any positive number is greater
than any negative number.)

32. **E** In order to determine the number of
cubic yards (i.e. volume) we must transform all the measurements into the same
units. Since 3 feet = 1 yard we have:
21 feet = 7 yards
27 feet = 9 yards
and since 36 inches = 1 yard
4 inches = $\frac{1}{9}$ yard
The volume is the product of all the measurements of the garden: Volume = $\frac{1}{9} × 7 ×
9 = 7$ cubic yards

33. **D** Examine the extreme cases for y. If y
were exactly 90 the Pythagorean theorem
could be used to find x:
$x^2 = 10^2 + 10^2$
$x = 2 · 10^2$
$x = 10\sqrt{2}$
If y were exactly 180, the side would form
a straight line of length 20.
So, in order to form a triangle according to
the restrictions of the problem, side x must
be between $10\sqrt{2}$ and 20.

34. **D** The straight line PQ and the x and y axes form similar triangles, for all points on PQ. So the triangle PQR is similar to triangle SOQ, where S is the point on the y axis. The coordinates of point S can be determined by the following proportion:

$$\frac{3}{9} = \frac{2}{y}$$
$$3y = 18$$
$$y = 6$$

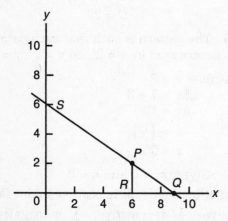

35. **D** The face of the clock (total of 360°) is subdivided into 12 equal parts (30° each). Each hour the hour hand moves exactly 30°. So at 5 o'clock the hands of the clock form an angle of:

$$5 \times 30° = 150°$$

36. **B** The figures below represent the flagpole and yardstick and the shadows they cast, respectively. The situation involves similar triangles for which the following proportions can be written:

$$\frac{x}{25} = \frac{3}{5}$$
$$5x = 3 \times 25$$
$$5x = 75$$
$$x = 15$$

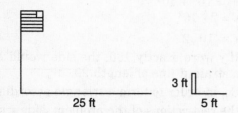

So, the flagpole is 15 feet high.

37. **D** Triangle ABC is a right triangle. In order to find the measure of side AB we can use the Pythagorean theorem:

$$(AB)^2 + 4^2 = 5^2$$
$$(AB)^2 + 16 = 25$$
$$(AB)^2 = 25 - 16$$
$$(AB)^2 = 9$$
$$(AB) = 3$$

The area of a right triangle is:

Area = $\frac{1}{2}$ × base × height

Area = $\frac{1}{2} \times 3 \times 4 = \frac{12}{2}$

Area = 6 square units

38. **D** In order for a triple of numbers to qualify as sides of a triangle the sum of any two of the numbers must be greater than the third. Only choices II and III satisfy this condition. So choices I and IV could not be the lengths of the sides of a triangle.

39. **B** P_s: Perimeter of square = $4 \times s$
A_s: Area of square = $s \times s$
P_t: Perimeter of an equilateral triangle = $3 \times t$
$A_s = s \times s = 9$ units
$s = 3$ units
$P_s = 4 \times s = 12$ units
$P_t = 3 \times t = 12$ units
$t = 4$ units
So, the side of the triangle measures 4 units.

40. **E** If the side of the square is s, the perimeter will be $4s$. Because it has a factor of 4, the perimeter will always be divisible by 4. But, if the perimeter is also to be divisible by 3 it must have a factor of 3 as well. So s must be a multiple of 3 (e.g., 3, 6, 9, 12, etc.) None of choices A–D is a multiple of 3.

41. **C** The problem asks us to find the price per pound of beef which has had the waste removed, given that we know the price per pound of the beef including the waste. Choice C is the only one that asks this same question.

42. **A** We are told that it takes two hours to travel 100 miles, and asked how long it would take to travel 80 miles. Only choice A rephrases this same question.

43. **B** Bert sold B boxes. Joan sold one box less than Bert. So, the number of boxes sold by Joan is $B - 1$.

44. **B** Bert sold B boxes. Joan sold $B - 1$ boxes (one box less than Bert). Rhonda sold $\left(\frac{1}{2}\right)B$ boxes (half as many boxes as Bert). Altogether they sold 89 boxes. Thus, $B + B - 1 + \left(\frac{1}{2}\right)B = 89$.

45. **E** (Recall: Distance = Rate × Time or Time = Distance/Rate) To determine how long it took to bike from the park to school, we would need to divide the distance by the rate (10 m.p.h.). However, the distance between the park and the school is not given. This additional information is necessary to answer the question.

46. **C** Refer to the explanation of problem 45. It is necessary to know both the distance and the rate to find the time. The rate (10 miles per hour) is included in the problem.

47. **C** Choice C can be solved as follows:
Begin by guessing that Bill and Lou make the same amount, $66 each. Then (since Bill actually earns $6 more) add $3 to Bill's salary and subtract $3 from Lou's salary. So 66 + 3 = 69 is Bill's salary and 66 − 3 = 63 is Lou's salary. These steps are exactly the same as those used in the farmer problem.

48. **E** The answer would be found by first multiplying the number of adults (2) times the price per adult (12), next multiplying the number of children (3) times the price per child ($8) and then adding the two results (24 + 24 = 48). Since the family has more than 5 persons, we would then subtract the 20% discount (.20 × 48) from the total ticket price to obtain the final total price. Choice E includes all the information necessary for this solution.

49. **D** If, in a survey of 250 people, 130 people preferred *Softie* and 100 people had no preference then 20 people preferred *Kleenup* (250 − 130 − 100). Twenty people of a total of 250 people is less than 10% (10% of 250 is 25), so 40% is clearly not a reasonable answer. Choice D outlines this line of reasoning.

50. **D** Harvey earned $10\frac{1}{4}$% interest—just slightly more than 10%. It is easy to figure 10% of 284—multiply .10 × 284 = 28.4 (just move the decimal point in 284 one place to the left). So Harvey will have slightly more than $284 + $28.40 ($312.40) at the end of one year. Choice D explains this line of reasoning.

Writing

The following essay outlines have been written to demonstrate the planning of well-written answers to the topics given. Use these only as guidelines to evaluating your own organization. Many different organization patterns and plans could work equally well for the topics given.

FIRST TOPIC

A lack of discipline in the schools, from unruliness in the classroom to vandalism on school property, is a constant topic of discussion among parents and educators. Discuss what you feel are the reasons for discipline problems.

Essay Outline:

A. Introduction
1. General description of background information; presentation of setting for thesis.
2. Presentation of thesis or point of view.

B. Reasons
1. State reason in clear, concise terms. (Ex.: "A lack of discipline in the schools, whether it is manifested as distracting behavior in the classroom or violent aggressiveness on school grounds, can be attributed to specific situations in the home.")
   a. Elaborate idea presented by giving more information, stating the position another way, or explaining more.
   b. Support thesis with examples.
2. Present additional reasons in same manner as above.

C. Summary and conclusions
1. Restate in brief terms the reasons stated in the body of the paper.
2. Give conclusions in the form of implications, prognosis, or recommendations.

Describe one person you have known well who has significantly influenced your life.

Essay Outline:

A. Introduction
   1. Introduce person by giving a personal anecdote or unique characteristic of the person.
   2. Give an indication of how your life was changed by this person.

B. Description in more extensive detail
   1. Special qualities

   2. Context of acquaintance
   3. Nature of relationship

C. Influence—positive or negative
   1. Direction and nature of influence
   2. Personal reaction to person's influence
   3. Specific examples

D. Conclusions
   1. Summarize what has been said about person's influence.
   2. Conclude with general feelings currently about person's influence.

Answer Sheet— Model Test Two

Reading

1. Ⓐ Ⓑ Ⓒ Ⓓ Ⓔ
2. Ⓐ Ⓑ Ⓒ Ⓓ Ⓔ
3. Ⓐ Ⓑ Ⓒ Ⓓ Ⓔ
4. Ⓐ Ⓑ Ⓒ Ⓓ Ⓔ
5. Ⓐ Ⓑ Ⓒ Ⓓ Ⓔ
6. Ⓐ Ⓑ Ⓒ Ⓓ Ⓔ
7. Ⓐ Ⓑ Ⓒ Ⓓ Ⓔ
8. Ⓐ Ⓑ Ⓒ Ⓓ Ⓔ
9. Ⓐ Ⓑ Ⓒ Ⓓ Ⓔ
10. Ⓐ Ⓑ Ⓒ Ⓓ Ⓔ
11. Ⓐ Ⓑ Ⓒ Ⓓ Ⓔ
12. Ⓐ Ⓑ Ⓒ Ⓓ Ⓔ
13. Ⓐ Ⓑ Ⓒ Ⓓ Ⓔ
14. Ⓐ Ⓑ Ⓒ Ⓓ Ⓔ
15. Ⓐ Ⓑ Ⓒ Ⓓ Ⓔ
16. Ⓐ Ⓑ Ⓒ Ⓓ Ⓔ
17. Ⓐ Ⓑ Ⓒ Ⓓ Ⓔ

18. Ⓐ Ⓑ Ⓒ Ⓓ Ⓔ
19. Ⓐ Ⓑ Ⓒ Ⓓ Ⓔ
20. Ⓐ Ⓑ Ⓒ Ⓓ Ⓔ
21. Ⓐ Ⓑ Ⓒ Ⓓ Ⓔ
22. Ⓐ Ⓑ Ⓒ Ⓓ Ⓔ
23. Ⓐ Ⓑ Ⓒ Ⓓ Ⓔ
24. Ⓐ Ⓑ Ⓒ Ⓓ Ⓔ
25. Ⓐ Ⓑ Ⓒ Ⓓ Ⓔ
26. Ⓐ Ⓑ Ⓒ Ⓓ Ⓔ
27. Ⓐ Ⓑ Ⓒ Ⓓ Ⓔ
28. Ⓐ Ⓑ Ⓒ Ⓓ Ⓔ
29. Ⓐ Ⓑ Ⓒ Ⓓ Ⓔ
30. Ⓐ Ⓑ Ⓒ Ⓓ Ⓔ
31. Ⓐ Ⓑ Ⓒ Ⓓ Ⓔ
32. Ⓐ Ⓑ Ⓒ Ⓓ Ⓔ
33. Ⓐ Ⓑ Ⓒ Ⓓ Ⓔ
34. Ⓐ Ⓑ Ⓒ Ⓓ Ⓔ

35. Ⓐ Ⓑ Ⓒ Ⓓ Ⓔ
36. Ⓐ Ⓑ Ⓒ Ⓓ Ⓔ
37. Ⓐ Ⓑ Ⓒ Ⓓ Ⓔ
38. Ⓐ Ⓑ Ⓒ Ⓓ Ⓔ
49. Ⓐ Ⓑ Ⓒ Ⓓ Ⓔ
50. Ⓐ Ⓑ Ⓒ Ⓓ Ⓔ
41. Ⓐ Ⓑ Ⓒ Ⓓ Ⓔ
42. Ⓐ Ⓑ Ⓒ Ⓓ Ⓔ
43. Ⓐ Ⓑ Ⓒ Ⓓ Ⓔ
44. Ⓐ Ⓑ Ⓒ Ⓓ Ⓔ
45. Ⓐ Ⓑ Ⓒ Ⓓ Ⓔ
46. Ⓐ Ⓑ Ⓒ Ⓓ Ⓔ
47. Ⓐ Ⓑ Ⓒ Ⓓ Ⓔ
48. Ⓐ Ⓑ Ⓒ Ⓓ Ⓔ
49. Ⓐ Ⓑ Ⓒ Ⓓ Ⓔ
50. Ⓐ Ⓑ Ⓒ Ⓓ Ⓔ

Mathematics

1. Ⓐ Ⓑ Ⓒ Ⓓ Ⓔ
2. Ⓐ Ⓑ Ⓒ Ⓓ Ⓔ
3. Ⓐ Ⓑ Ⓒ Ⓓ Ⓔ
4. Ⓐ Ⓑ Ⓒ Ⓓ Ⓔ
5. Ⓐ Ⓑ Ⓒ Ⓓ Ⓔ
6. Ⓐ Ⓑ Ⓒ Ⓓ Ⓔ
7. Ⓐ Ⓑ Ⓒ Ⓓ Ⓔ
8. Ⓐ Ⓑ Ⓒ Ⓓ Ⓔ
9. Ⓐ Ⓑ Ⓒ Ⓓ Ⓔ
10. Ⓐ Ⓑ Ⓒ Ⓓ Ⓔ
11. Ⓐ Ⓑ Ⓒ Ⓓ Ⓔ
12. Ⓐ Ⓑ Ⓒ Ⓓ Ⓔ
13. Ⓐ Ⓑ Ⓒ Ⓓ Ⓔ
14. Ⓐ Ⓑ Ⓒ Ⓓ Ⓔ
15. Ⓐ Ⓑ Ⓒ Ⓓ Ⓔ
16. Ⓐ Ⓑ Ⓒ Ⓓ Ⓔ
17. Ⓐ Ⓑ Ⓒ Ⓓ Ⓔ

18. Ⓐ Ⓑ Ⓒ Ⓓ Ⓔ
19. Ⓐ Ⓑ Ⓒ Ⓓ Ⓔ
20. Ⓐ Ⓑ Ⓒ Ⓓ Ⓔ
21. Ⓐ Ⓑ Ⓒ Ⓓ Ⓔ
22. Ⓐ Ⓑ Ⓒ Ⓓ Ⓔ
23. Ⓐ Ⓑ Ⓒ Ⓓ Ⓔ
24. Ⓐ Ⓑ Ⓒ Ⓓ Ⓔ
25. Ⓐ Ⓑ Ⓒ Ⓓ Ⓔ
26. Ⓐ Ⓑ Ⓒ Ⓓ Ⓔ
27. Ⓐ Ⓑ Ⓒ Ⓓ Ⓔ
28. Ⓐ Ⓑ Ⓒ Ⓓ Ⓔ
29. Ⓐ Ⓑ Ⓒ Ⓓ Ⓔ
30. Ⓐ Ⓑ Ⓒ Ⓓ Ⓔ
31. Ⓐ Ⓑ Ⓒ Ⓓ Ⓔ
32. Ⓐ Ⓑ Ⓒ Ⓓ Ⓔ
33. Ⓐ Ⓑ Ⓒ Ⓓ Ⓔ
34. Ⓐ Ⓑ Ⓒ Ⓓ Ⓔ

35. Ⓐ Ⓑ Ⓒ Ⓓ Ⓔ
36. Ⓐ Ⓑ Ⓒ Ⓓ Ⓔ
37. Ⓐ Ⓑ Ⓒ Ⓓ Ⓔ
38. Ⓐ Ⓑ Ⓒ Ⓓ Ⓔ
49. Ⓐ Ⓑ Ⓒ Ⓓ Ⓔ
50. Ⓐ Ⓑ Ⓒ Ⓓ Ⓔ
41. Ⓐ Ⓑ Ⓒ Ⓓ Ⓔ
42. Ⓐ Ⓑ Ⓒ Ⓓ Ⓔ
43. Ⓐ Ⓑ Ⓒ Ⓓ Ⓔ
44. Ⓐ Ⓑ Ⓒ Ⓓ Ⓔ
45. Ⓐ Ⓑ Ⓒ Ⓓ Ⓔ
46. Ⓐ Ⓑ Ⓒ Ⓓ Ⓔ
47. Ⓐ Ⓑ Ⓒ Ⓓ Ⓔ
48. Ⓐ Ⓑ Ⓒ Ⓓ Ⓔ
49. Ⓐ Ⓑ Ⓒ Ⓓ Ⓔ
50. Ⓐ Ⓑ Ⓒ Ⓓ Ⓔ

Chapter 9

Model Test Two

READING

Directions: Each passage in this section is followed by a question or questions about its content. Select the best answer to each question based on what is stated or implied in the selection. You may spend up to 60 minutes on this section.

Questions 1–2
A new form of painting developed by a group of former illustrators in 1909 was called the "Ashcan School." The name was derived from the fact that these artists portrayed distinctly unglamorous subjects. Their works often depicted the harsh reality of life faced by those who live in large urban areas—especially New York City.

1. The nickname borne by the group of artists mentioned in the passage

   (A) was not the one adopted by the artists themselves.
   (B) was given to them by a teacher from the original school.
   (C) identified them as former newspaper men.
   (D) resulted from their unpleasant subjects.
   (E) reflected the opinion of the artistic community.

2. Any of the following might be included in works by artists of the "Ashcan School" EXCEPT

   (A) slum dwellings.
   (B) city beautification projects.
   (C) littered sidewalks.
   (D) subway entrances.
   (E) crowded downtown sidewalks.

Questions 3–4
Recent archeological findings have suggested the fact that humans and the apes have a common ancestor which is less simian than creatures previously considered to be the human ancestor. The discovery of a 17-million-year-old fossil in Africa brings into question the long-held idea that humans evolved from the apes. Since it predates the time when the two species are supposed to have branched apart, it suggests a common ancestor which is more humanlike than apelike.

3. According to the passage, it is possible that

   (A) more fossils which support the theory will soon be found.
   (B) apes evolved from humans.
   (C) the discovered fossil predates all other findings.
   (D) the human species evolved from simians.
   (E) the fossil is not really 17 million years old.

4. Which of the following statements is most appropriate as a continuation of this passage?

   (A) Fossil jawbones and molars provide dental evidence to support this suggestion.

(B) It calls into question the use of anatomical traits to determine ancestry.

(C) Scanning primal remains with electron microscopes reveals its simian characteristics.

(D) Both species, then, can be considered to be the likely progenitor.

(E) The new family tree will show orangutans, rather than chimps, to be the closest relative.

Questions 5–7

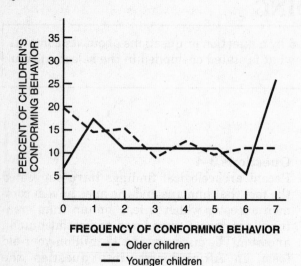

FREQUENCY OF CONFORMING BEHAVIOR

-- Older children
— Younger children

The graph shows the results of an experiment that studied the effects on a child's judgment of being in a group which unanimously gives wrong answers. The experimenter's purpose was to find out how often younger and older children yield to group influences. Refer to the graph to answer the questions.

5. From the graph, one could say that

(A) 4% of the older children exhibit conforming behavior.

(B) about 18% of the younger children conformed to the group in one instance.

(C) 20% of the younger children and about 6% of the older children never followed the group.

(D) there was no evidence that either younger or older children changed their judgments in order to conform to the group.

(E) the younger children were influenced by the older children.

6. The findings show that, in general,

(A) the experiment was too complicated to reveal anything.

(B) the effect of peer pressure is much more evident in the older children.

(C) the influence of the group was more pronounced on the younger than on the older children.

(D) children cannot make accurate judgments when they are in a group of their peers.

(E) children will stick with an answer if they are sure they are right.

7. The experimenter found that when a child had given what was obviously a correct response and the group (as instructed) gave an incorrect response, the child would show signs of discomfort: fidget in his seat, rub his eyes, etc. From this, and the findings as shown on the graph, the experimenter could conclude that

(A) the effect of a group's judgment on a child is not very strong.

(B) a willingness to change judgments to conform to a group is not evident in children.

(C) incorrect responses make a child feel uncomfortable.

(D) there is a strong tendency of children to conform to a group, but it is not easy for them to do so.

(E) pressuring a child to respond when he is uncertain of an answer is an unfair tactic.

Questions 8–11

The possibility of the existence of black holes in space has generated a vast amount of speculation, debate, and research since it was first suggested in the 1930's. Signals from deep in space have been detected by an orbiting satellite that indicate the presence of an object smaller than the earth, but with a degree of energy 1,000 times greater than the sun. Having named it Cygmus X-1, scientists generally agree that forces being exerted to slacken the pace of disintegrating galaxies probably originate in black holes such as this one. When thermonuclear fires that power very large stars are extinguished, the star's atoms compress with such a tremendous force that only the nuclei remain, nuclei with the same amount of matter and the same gravitational force. The force, however, is so intensely focused that no light can escape, and the star literally turns itself inside out, becoming a black hole.

8. Cygmus X-1 is

   (A) an orbiting satellite.
   (B) a black hole.
   (C) a force.
   (D) an object floating in space.
   (E) a disintegrating galaxy.

9. From this passage, one could conclude that

   (A) the presence of such an object in space is a great danger to space travellers.
   (B) information about black holes is based on speculation, and there is little agreement among scientists about their origin.
   (C) the nucleus of an extinguished star eventually breaks apart.
   (D) black holes are referred to in this way because no light from them reaches our eyes.
   (E) all stars eventually burn out.

10. The writer implies that

    (A) galaxies are disintegrating at a decreasing rate.
    (B) signals in space are often unidentified.
    (C) objects entering a black hole move only in one direction.
    (D) as a star shrinks, its gravitational force abates.
    (E) time and space are extended within a black hole.

11. Which of the following statements is most appropriate as a continuation of the passage?

    (A) Thermonuclear fires are extinguished, and the star's gravitational force begins to increase.
    (B) While the gravitational force exerted outside the hole is a "pulling" one, inside it becomes a "pushing" force, and an object pulled in is lost forever in space.
    (C) The force created by this action is so tremendous that the star may be drawn into this vacuum in space.

    (D) This black hole no longer exhibits any gravitational force or any form of energy.
    (E) The gravitational radius is the point where the star's compacting action is at its limit, and the creation of a black hole is no longer possible.

Questions 12–13

Why children everywhere throughout history have invariably exhibited the unconscious inclination, at some specific point in learning to draw, to draw a circle with an X or cross in it, known as a *mandala,* is unknown. Art can be an expression of feeling or ideas, and it is often an index of a time and a culture. People have always drawn mandalas in association with very intense experiences.

12. An idea that is expressed in this passage is that

    (A) art is an unconscious expression of hostility.
    (B) art transcends all time.
    (C) children's art provides keys to the history of a culture.
    (D) children draw mandalas without thinking or learning about them.
    (E) symbols represent intense feelings.

13. According to the author, all of the following are true about mandalas EXCEPT

    (A) they are commonly drawn by children.
    (B) they can be used to study cultures.
    (C) they can be circular or elliptical.
    (D) they have been used throughout history.
    (E) no one knows why children draw them.

Questions 14–15

When two lions made a raid on the village, three English officers and several natives were off in pursuit the very next day. After a very few hours, one of the pair had been killed, but the other escaped into the jungle. When one of the officers caught a glimpse of the lion, he instantly fired, enraging the beast so that it rushed toward him at full speed. The captain saw its movement and knew that if he tried to get into a better position for firing, he would be directly in the way of the charge. He decided to stand transfixed, trusting that when the lion passed by him unaware, he could shoot to advantage. He was, however, deceived.

14. Which of the following sentences would be most appropriate as a continuation of this passage?

   (A) Unlike his adversary, his efforts were thwarted.
   (B) The animal saw him and flew at him in a dreadful rage.
   (C) The villagers suddenly appeared shouting their objections.
   (D) The other officer turned and fired at him.
   (E) The lion cowered and fell to the ground.

15. The best title for this selection is

   (A) The Captain's Misjudgment.
   (B) Hunting.
   (C) Revenge by a Lion.
   (D) Raid on a Village.
   (E) Escape to the Jungle.

Questions 16–18
It is sometimes lost sight of that the importance of educational endeavors, of studying and pushing the mind not only to remember, but to grasp and calculate, is not in the number of facts retained, since most are not, but in the development of a better and more powerful instrument. The mind, like the body, is a thing whereof the powers are developed by effort.

16. The author makes the point that many of the facts acquired through study

   (A) are of dubious value.
   (B) are too changeable to be considered important.
   (C) will be forgotten.
   (D) will be of more use later in life.
   (E) will contribute to a broader understanding of life.

17. The "instrument" referred to by the author is

   (A) the body.
   (B) a calculator.
   (C) something which processes information, such as a computer.
   (D) something used to solve simple problems, such as a ruler.
   (E) the mind.

18. The "powers" in line 8 could be referred to as

   (A) the powers that be.
   (B) the powers at large.
   (C) the powers generated.
   (D) the powers of the mind.
   (E) muscle power.

Questions 19–20
The majority of the population of the Near East lives in the villages. The villager is rooted to the land, land which is not owned by the villagers but by landlords or the government. The vagaries of the seasons, along with high rentals and taxes, have made village farming difficult. When difficulties arise, nomads can move to escape those difficulties, but, tied as they are to the land, villagers find it almost impossible, making them more exploitable.

19. A good title for this selection would be

   (A) Plight of the Villagers in the Near East.
   (B) Land Exploitation in the Near East.
   (C) Village Life in the Third World.
   (D) Farming and the Nomads.
   (E) Agricultural Progress in the Near East.

20. A word that could be used in place of "vagaries" as used in this passage is

   (A) temperatures.
   (B) precipitation.
   (C) significance.
   (D) changeableness.
   (E) conditions.

Questions 21–22
The elements found in plant and animal cells—oxygen, hydrogen, nitrogen, carbon, phosphorus, sulfur, and trace elements—are, in themselves, nonliving or inorganic. Combined in the right proportions, however, they become part of a living system. The nucleus of the cell, which contains the vital chromosomal material, determines, indirectly, the biochemical activity and specific characteristics of all cellular organisms.

21. Substances in the nuclei of cells are

   (A) combined with chromosomal material.
   (B) in different proportions depending on their activity.
   (C) essential to life.
   (D) biochemical.
   (E) all organic when found in isolation.

22. The author stresses

    (A) the unique composition of the nucleus of a plant or animal cell.
    (B) the interaction of substances in living cells.
    (C) the effect of chromosomal activity in cellular organisms.
    (D) the contrast between organic and inorganic substances in cells.
    (E) the characteristics determined by chromosomes.

Questions 23–25

The upsurge of interest in reading comprehension has been so dramatic in recent years that it is difficult to review pertinent information from related disciplines, analyze it for commonalities and interrelationships, and make generalizations or draw any conclusions. Current references by educators to relevant information from the varying disciplines of psycholinguistics, sociolinguistics, and cognitive psychology do not seem to be amenable to any language of coherence. Researchers in the related disciplines are either looking at language processing in very general terms or are analyzing small bits and pieces, or they are only beginning to consider certain aspects of language. Psycholinguists, for example, spent a considerable amount of time investigating the psychological reality of various linguistic units and the processing of these units and, only recently, have begun to consider the role of semantics.

23. According to the writer, information from related disciplines

    (A) has provided the most important facts about reading comprehension.
    (B) has no bearing at all on the study of reading comprehension.
    (C) has been largely unproductive thus far.
    (D) is based on poorly done research.
    (E) allows researchers to form a specific model of comprehension.

24. By "language of coherence," the author means

    (A) colloquial expressions.
    (B) mutually intelligible languages.
    (C) terms for putting divergent ideas together.
    (D) specialized jargons.
    (E) a related language and its derivatives.

25. The writer implies that

    (A) knowing if a linguistic element, such as a phoneme, is psychologically real contributes little to an overall understanding of comprehension.
    (B) it is difficult to understand the research of unrelated disciplines.
    (C) researchers do not apply what they learn from research in any practical way.
    (D) as with other information from related fields, semantics will not be a productive area.
    (E) sociolinguists and psycholinguists cannot speak the same language.

Questions 26–27

One of the most powerful forces in the human psyche, phobias are enigmatic because they also will loosen their grip on a person quite readily. This fact accounts for their common identification as a set of symptoms, rather than as a neurosis with a ponderous label. Therapists, in fact, have taken the position that, in most cases, the symptoms are, themselves, the disease. As such, they can be treated and often with relatively quick results. The woman who has withdrawn into the shell of her house for a period of thirty years because she is terrified of going out may, with a very short period of treatment, be back on the streets.

26. The main point of this passage is that

    (A) phobias afflict a large proportion of people in modern society.
    (B) while a phobia may handicap a person for a long time, it can be alleviated easily.
    (C) the cause for phobias has not been determined.
    (D) like alcoholism, a phobia is a disease that resists treatment.
    (E) a phobia is a neurosis that mainly afflicts women.

27. The author makes his point by use of

    (A) example.
    (B) allusion.
    (C) exaggeration.
    (D) logic.
    (E) analogy.

Questions 28–30

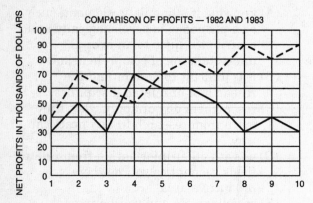

COMPARISON OF PROFITS — 1982 AND 1983

NET PROFITS IN THOUSANDS OF DOLLARS

28. A small company wants to compare profits for two different years of operation. The solid line on the graph represents its profits in 1982. The broken line represents profits for 1983. According to the graph, profits for 1982 were lower than 1983 for every month except the month numbered

(A) 3
(B) 8
(C) 4
(D) 7
(E) 5

29. How much more were the profits for the best month in 1983 over the best month in 1982?

(A) $20,000
(B) $10,000
(C) $40,000
(D) $15,000
(E) $30,000

30. Which pair of figures below represents the comparison of average monthly profits for 1982 and 1983?

(A) $45,000–$70,000
(B) $35,000–$65,000
(C) $10,000–$30,000
(D) $30,000–$90,000
(E) $50,000–$85,000

Questions 31–33

Without constant and active participation, not necessarily in an official capacity, in the details of politics on the part of the most intelligent citizens, there is the danger that the conduct of public affairs will fall under the control of selfish and ignorant or crafty and venal men. The duties and services which, when selfishly and ignorantly performed, stigmatize a man as a mere politician, ensure the success of democracy when performed with honor and vigilance.

31. In this passage, the term "politician" is used with

(A) respect.
(B) the best intentions.
(C) disdain.
(D) amusement.
(E) some degree of compassion.

32. It is clear in this passage that the author is in favor of

(A) control of services by politicians.
(B) vigilant monitoring of committees.
(C) less involvement in public affairs by those who are uninformed.
(D) democratic participation by interested citizens.
(E) more emphasis on the needs of the community at large.

33. A word that could be used in place of "venal" in this passage is

(A) vengeful.
(B) rebellious.
(C) corrupt.
(D) progressive.
(E) naive.

Questions 34–36

Students who are considered gifted need to be concerned with the structure and form of literature, and they are able to deal with the poet's technique in a way that is not possible with less able students. Yet they are not different from other students so far as interests and rewards sought in reading are concerned. It is possible for bright students to present glib technical analyses of literary selections without really developing a mature understanding of literature as a reconstruction of experience. Depth should be the goal.

34. Which of the following sentences is most appropriate as a continuation of the paragraph?

(A) Literature study for gifted students should be planned to avoid this pitfall.

(B) If instead, the goal is merely to cover the most material, many important works will be given a surface reading, without any real understanding or appreciation as the result.

(C) It is better for these students to study a wide range of selections in the interest of forming many bases of comparison than to attempt to develop a thorough understanding of one piece.

(D) In literature, the needs of gifted students can be met by using procedures for differentiating instruction.

(E) At the same time, comparative study of similar genres will provide additional information.

35. The author's purpose is to

(A) convince the reader that technical analyses of literary selections do not enhance one's understanding of them.

(B) direct the teacher to help students to develop their ability to analyze literary form and structure.

(C) explain the difference in literary interests between gifted and less able students.

(D) encourage the teacher to explore literature with gifted students in ways that will ensure their understanding.

(E) provide specific ideas for differentiating instruction.

36. The statements made in this passage seem most to represent

(A) facts based on specific examples.

(B) facts gathered from different sources.

(C) both fact and opinion.

(D) opinions based on experience.

(E) opinions based on stated research.

Questions 37–38

There was, perhaps, some degree of association between the perfecting of symmetry as art form and the discovery of perspective, both of them contributions from the Arab world. The Arabs were captivated by calculations and played with ingenious symmetrical design, as evidenced in their architecture. Perspective was a concept that vitalized both art and mathematics, and it provided a new tool for the artist to capture on canvas a particular view of reality.

37. The writer indicates that

(A) the Arabs had no mathematical ability.

(B) symmetry and perspective were borrowed from other cultures.

(C) perspective was discovered by the Arabs.

(D) Arab architecture was all advanced.

(E) symmetry is evident in nature.

38. Which of the following statements represents an idea that could be part of this paragraph?

(A) Calculus, the mathematics of change, captures the changing character of nature.

(B) There is unity and harmony in nature that can be described through numbers.

(C) The Arab world preserved the mathematical knowledge of ancient civilizations.

(D) The eye of the artist and the mind of the mathematician bridged the gap from a static to a dynamic concept of nature.

(E) The scientist needed a new mathematics to capture instantaneous motion.

Questions 39–40

An interesting distinction existed in the language of the ancient Greeks, having to do with the study of mathematics. They differentiated something called *arithmetic* from something called *logistic*. Arithmetic was more of an investigation of the world of numbers, while logistic was merely a set of rules to memorize and use for doing rote operations. Arithmetic then, was seen as a science, open to endless investigation. Logistic was more of a dull craft, needed for bookkeeping and other such practices.

39. Based on the information in the passage, which of the following points could the writer support?

(A) There is little difference between the way mathematics was taught in ancient Greece and the way it is taught today.

(B) The world of numbers was not accessible to the ancient Greeks.

(C) What is commonly taught in the early years of schools today is mainly logistic and, as such, it does not promote inquiry.

(D) Rote operations can be performed without learning rules considered by the ancient Greeks to be part of logistic.

(E) The science of logistic could not be taught in the public schools with the curriculum as it is today.

40. The writer implies that, in the distinction the Greeks made in the study of mathematics,

(A) information was lost.
(B) arithmetic was more interesting.
(C) mathematical rules were clarified.
(D) logistic was too difficult for small children to deal with.
(E) arithmetic was more elementary than logistic.

Questions 41–43

Theater reviewers, often unjustly stigmatized as baleful and destructive fiends, should really be allowed their occasional verbal eruptions when one considers that they must scrutinize everything offered up for public inspection. The column space that might yesterday have seemed wholly inadequate to contain a reviewer's comments on *Long Day's Journey into Night* is about the same as that which, today, must tax the reader's patience with the verdict on the latest scrap that has chanced to find for itself a backer with a hundred thousand dollars to lose.

41. The author's attitude toward the "fiends" is

(A) argumentative.
(B) antagonistic.
(C) resentful.
(D) sympathetic.
(E) contemptuous.

42. The passage suggests that the drama critic is

(A) affected adversely by the requirements of his job.
(B) aware of the value of public opinion.
(C) suspicious of criticism directed at him.
(D) captivated by most of what he sees.
(E) interested in obliging the backers of plays.

43. The writer implies that the play, *Long Day's Journey into Night,* was

(A) poorly written.
(B) too long.
(C) inconsequential.
(D) momentous.
(E) pleasant.

Questions 44–46

PRIORITIES OF SCHOOL BOARDS AND THE PUBLIC

SCHOOL BOARD MEMBERS CONCERNS	PERCENT
Declining enrollment	39.0
Collective bargaining	29.7
Curriculum reform	23.2
Discipline	22.8
Federal interference	19.3
Declining tax base	18.8
Outmoded facilities	15.3
Drug abuse	9.6
Teacher militancy	7.2
Student legal rights	2.9
Desegregation	2.4

PUBLIC OPINION POLL CONCERNS	
Discipline	24.0
Drug abuse	13.0
Declining tax base	12.0
Curriculum reform	11.0
Poor teachers	10.0
Crime/vandalism	4.0
Overcrowded schools/classes	4.0
Alcoholism	2.0
Mismanagement	2.0
Outmoded facilities	2.0
Federal interference	2.0
Declining enrollment	1.0

44. In general, the table shows that

(A) "discipline" in the schools is a high-priority concern both of school boards and of the public.
(B) the public is more concerned about schools than are school boards.
(C) the priority of school board concerns is completely different from that of the public.
(D) a "declining tax base" and "declining enrollment" are, as would be expected, high-priority concerns, both for school boards and for the public.
(E) the public needs to be more involved with and concerned about school needs.

45. According to the table, "drug abuse"

    (A) is a greater concern to the public than to school boards.
    (B) is a low-priority concern, both for school boards and for the public.
    (C) is, for the public, a less significant concern than the curriculum or the quality of teachers.
    (D) is a concern for 13% of the school board members surveyed in the poll.
    (E) is the greatest problem in schools today.

46. From the table, one can determine that

    (A) "federal interference" is a concern of 19.3% of the people responding to the poll.
    (B) 10% of board members are concerned about "poor teachers."
    (C) because of "declining enrollment," "overcrowded schools" is not a concern of either the public or of school boards.
    (D) "declining enrollment" is a concern for 39% of school board members who responded to the poll.
    (E) the percentage of board members and of the public concerned about "outmoded facilities" is about the same.

Questions 47–50

Many researchers have become increasingly aware of the fact that early experiences of many kinds can have permanent effects on an animal's behavior. The idea of imprinting as an early experience during which a young animal forms a strong social attachment to a mother-object has aroused a great deal of interest and research. Although the effort to formulate laws of learning has demonstrated that behaviors which were once thought to be instinctive are modifiable by learning, behaviors such as imprinting are so persistent in character and resistant to alteration by reinforcement that they cannot be explained by conventional laws of learning. Other explanatory devices must be constructed.

In a broad sense, imprinting refers to an early experience that has a profound influence on the later adult social behavior of an animal. Although imprinting has been studied mainly in birds, it also has been observed in other animals. It seems that processes very much like imprinting exist in every social species, particularly those in which there are parent-young relationships.

47. The title that best expresses the ideas of this selection is

    (A) Effects of Early Experiences on Animals.
    (B) Research Results on Imprinting.
    (C) Instinctive Behaviors in Animals.
    (D) The Process of Imprinting.
    (E) Social Behaviors of Animals.

48. From the style of this selection, one would assume that it was taken from

    (A) a research report on reinforcement techniques.
    (B) a psychology textbook.
    (C) an informal essay.
    (D) a book on the care of animals.
    (E) a treatise on the validity of behavioral techniques.

49. The author indicates that

    (A) all animal behaviors can be easily explained.
    (B) the adult social behavior of animals is mostly conditioned behavior.
    (C) imprinting provides valuable information about learning.
    (D) imprinting never occurs in bird species.
    (E) strong social attachments between different species are never formed.

50. Which of the following could be considered to be an example of imprinting?

    (A) Recognition of parents by their young even when separated at birth.
    (B) Kittens which are not handled by adults just after their eyes are open remain wild and fearful of people for their whole life.
    (C) Ducks making associations between adults similar in appearance.
    (D) A young animal's preference for one food over another, even when it has not ever tasted the ones offered.
    (E) A mother gull's tendency to stop laying eggs if all eggs are removed from her nest.

MATHEMATICS

Directions: Select the best answer to each of the following questions. Any figures provided are there as reference; they are approximations and are not drawn to scale except when stated.

You may refer to the following information during this section of the test.

= is equal to
≠ is unequal to
< is less than
> is greater than
≤ is less than or equal to
≥ is greater than or equal to

√ square root of
° degrees
‖ is parallel to
⊥ is perpendicular to
π pi, approximately 3.14

Circle: Radius = r; Circumference = $2\pi r$; Area = πr^2; a circle contains 360°

Triangle: In triangle ABC, $\angle BDA$ is a right angle,

Area of $\triangle ABC = \dfrac{(AC)(BD)}{2}$;

Perimeter of $\triangle ABC = AB + BC + CA$
Sum of the measures of the three angles is 180°.

Rectangle: Area = $L \times W$; Perimeter = $2(L + W)$

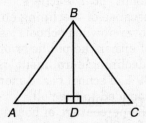

1. Which of these fractions is the largest?

   (A) $\frac{3}{8}$

   (B) $\frac{4}{7}$

   (C) $\frac{4}{9}$

   (D) $\frac{3}{5}$

   (E) $\frac{1}{3}$

2. Last week the lowest temperature was 15°F. This week it was 21 degrees colder. What was the lowest temperature this week?

   (A) 6°F
   (B) –6°F
   (C) 36°F
   (D) –36°F
   (E) None of the above

3. How would this numeral be read: 6,004,005?

   (A) Six hundred thousand four hundred five
   (B) Six thousand four thousand five
   (C) Six million four thousand five
   (D) Six thousand four and five thousandths
   (E) None of the above

4. 42,578.1502
In the numeral above, the value of the 2 to the left of the decimal point is how many times greater than the value of the 2 to the right of the decimal point?

   (A) 10^3 times greater
   (B) 10^6 times greater
   (C) 10^7 times greater
   (D) 10^{-6} times greater
   (E) None of the above

5. What number is the square of 16?

   (A) 256
   (B) 4
   (C) 32
   (D) 4 or –4
   (E) None of the above

6. Put in order (least to greatest):
$$-\tfrac{5}{3}, \; -.3, \; \tfrac{1}{3}, \; \tfrac{1}{5}, \; .5$$

(A) $-\tfrac{5}{3}, \; -.3, \; \tfrac{1}{5}, \; \tfrac{1}{3}, \; .5$

(B) $-\tfrac{5}{3}, \; -.3, \; .5, \; \tfrac{1}{3}, \; \tfrac{1}{5}$

(C) $-.3, \; -\tfrac{5}{3}, \; \tfrac{1}{5}, \; \tfrac{1}{3}, \; .5$

(D) $-\tfrac{5}{3}, \; -.3, \; \tfrac{1}{5}, \; .5, \; \tfrac{1}{3}$

(E) None of the above

7. In a glass we have 180 grams of milk with sugar. If there are 20 grams of sugar in the solution, what is the ratio of pure milk to milk and sugar?

(A) $\dfrac{180}{180 + 20}$

(B) $\dfrac{180}{20}$

(C) $\dfrac{20}{180}$

(D) $\dfrac{20}{180 + 20}$

(E) $\dfrac{180 - 20}{180}$

8. After 3 swimming tests, Mark's times were 78 seconds, 81 seconds, and 73 seconds. What must be his time on the fourth test to have an average of 76 seconds?

(A) 66
(B) 70
(C) 74
(D) 76
(E) None of the above

9. In an election with three candidates, Tom received 240 votes, Donna received 100 votes, and Gregory received 60 votes. What percent of the total number did Tom receive?

(A) 6%
(B) 30%
(C) 50%
(D) 60%
(E) 120%

10. If x, y, and z are all numbers which are divisible by 5, which of the following must be divisible by 5?

I. $x + y$
II. $x \cdot y$
III. $x + y + z$

(A) I only
(B) II only
(C) III only
(D) II and III only
(E) I, II, and III

11. $-2 \cdot \left[\dfrac{-63}{-7} - (6 - 12) \right] =$

(A) 18
(B) −30
(C) 6
(D) −12
(E) None of the above

12. How many different amounts of money can be created from one penny, one nickel, one dime, and one quarter by choosing 2 coins at a time?

(A) 6
(B) 4
(C) 3
(D) 8
(E) None of the above

13. A wading pool holds 100 gallons of water. The pool is three-fourths empty. If a hose can fill the pool at a rate of 20 gallons per hour, how long will it take to fill the pool?

(A) 2 hours 30 minutes
(B) 3 hours
(C) 3 hours 30 minutes
(D) 3 hours 45 minutes
(E) None of the above

14. If the digits of a two digit number are reversed, the new number is greater by 54. Which choice could have been the original number?

(A) 64
(B) 49
(C) 37
(D) 28
(E) 82

15. There are eight basketball teams in a tournament. Each team will play each of the other teams only once. How many games will be played?

   (A) 28
   (B) 56
   (C) 64
   (D) Impossible to determine
   (E) None of the above

16. John owes Jerry $126.50. If John is going to pay it back at a rate of $5.50 a month, how many months will it take?

   (A) 23 months
   (B) 18 months
   (C) 30 months
   (D) Not enough information
   (E) None of the above

17. Which of the following graphs represents a postage rate schedule where letters of $\frac{1}{2}$ ounce or less cost 20¢ and each additional $\frac{1}{2}$ ounce costs 15¢ more?

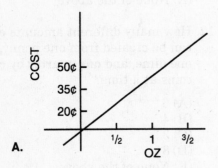

A.

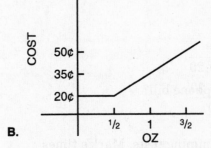

B.

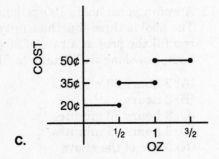

C.

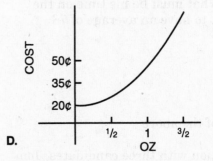

D.

   (A) Graph A
   (B) Graph B
   (C) Graph C
   (D) Graph D
   (E) None of the above

18. A government owed $\frac{3}{4}$ billion dollars and has paid $\frac{1}{6}$ billion.
    How much does it still owe?

    (A) $\frac{7}{12}$ billion dollars

    (B) $\frac{1}{2}$ billion dollars

    (C) $\frac{4}{10}$ billion dollars

    (D) $\frac{11}{12}$ billion dollars

    (E) None of the above

19. Separate 56 into two parts such that three times the smaller is 7 more than one half of the larger number. The two numbers are:

    (A) 45 and 11
    (B) 33 and 23
    (C) 36 and 20
    (D) 46 and 10
    (E) None of the above

20. The telephone company gave a 0.9% discount on all bills which were paid on time. What would be the discount on a $23.75 telephone bill?

    (A) $.25
    (B) $23.54
    (C) $.21
    (D) $26.39
    (E) $2.14

21. "Boy's black Schwinn bike, five speed, basket, light, good condition, call 338-1462." How much would it cost to run this ad for one day?

    Classified Ad Rates
    To figure cost multiply the number of words (including address and/or phone number) times the appropriate rate given below. Cost equals (number of words) × (rate per word). Minimum ad 10 words, $2.80.

    1–3 days ....$.28 per word

    5 days ....$.315 per word

    10 days ....$.40 per word

    30 days ....$.84 per word

    (A) $.56
    (B) $3.36
    (C) $3.78
    (D) $6.72
    (E) None of the above

22. Annie has $0.99 consisting of 15 coins. If her coins are only nickels, dimes, and pennies and she has twice as many dimes as pennies, how many nickels does she have?

    (A) 1
    (B) 2
    (C) 3
    (D) 4
    (E) Cannot tell from the information given

23. $r = mn - 2pq$
    $s = 10pq - 5mn$
    $r = (?) \times s$

    (A) -5

    (B) $-\frac{1}{5}$

    (C) $\frac{1}{5}$

    (D) 5

    (E) None of the above

24. Which of the following equals $\frac{x}{y} - \frac{x}{z}$?

    (A) $\dfrac{1}{y - z}$

    (B) $\dfrac{1}{yz}$

    (C) $\dfrac{xz - xy}{yz}$

    (D) $\dfrac{x}{y - z}$

    (E) $\dfrac{xy - xz}{yz}$

25. $(x - 7)(2x - 3) = ?$

    (A) $2x^2 - 17x + 21$
    (B) $2x^2 + 21$
    (C) $2x^2 - 17x - 21$
    (D) $2x^2 + 21$
    (E) None of the above

26. If $x = \frac{2}{3}$ and $y = 5$, then $\dfrac{x + y}{x} = ?$

    (A) 5

    (B) $\frac{34}{9}$

    (C) $8\frac{1}{2}$

    (D) $17\frac{1}{2}$

    (E) None of the above

27. If $3.5x = 70$, then $x = ?$

   (A) 2
   (B) 20
   (C) 245
   (D) 200
   (E) None of the above

28. We wish to write a formula which will reflect the total cost of operating a motorcycle. If gasoline costs x cents per mile and other expenses total y cents per mile, how many *dollars* will it cost to run the motorcycle 200 miles?

   (A) $2(x + y)$
   (B) $(100)(200)(x + y)$
   (C) $200x + 200y$
   (D) $\dfrac{x + y}{100}$
   (E) None of the above

29. If $y = 2x + 3$ what is $3y$?

   (A) $6x + 6$
   (B) $6x + 9$
   (C) $2x + 9$
   (D) $6x + 3$
   (E) None of the above

30. If $\dfrac{5t}{2} = \dfrac{3}{2}$, then $t = ?$

   (A) $-\frac{3}{5}$
   (B) $\frac{3}{5}$
   (C) 4
   (D) −4
   (E) None of the above

31. If x^3 is odd which of the following is (are) true?

   I. $(x - 1)$ is even.
   II. x is odd.
   III. x is even.

   (A) I only
   (B) II only
   (C) III only
   (D) I and II only
   (E) I and III only

32. If the volume of a cone is given by $V = \frac{1}{3}\pi r^2 \cdot h$ (where r is the radius of the base and h is the height), what is the height of a cone with volume = 24 cubic centimeters and radius of base = 3 centimeters?

   (A) 24 centimeters
   (B) 8π centimeters
   (C) $\dfrac{8}{\pi}$ centimeters
   (D) 8 centimeters
   (E) None of the above

33. If the radius of a circle is tripled, how many times larger will the area of the circle be?

   (A) 3
   (B) 6
   (C) 9
   (D) 12
   (E) None of the above

34. Point P, with coordinates $(6, 8)$ is on a circle with center at the origin $(0, 0)$. If point Q is on the circle and has coordinates $(x, 0)$, what is x?

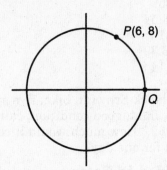

   (A) 6
   (B) 10
   (C) 8
   (D) $\sqrt{10}$
   (E) $\sqrt{14}$

35. A regular hexagon (six-sided figure with all sides the same length) can be divided into 6 triangles as shown. What is the measure, x, of the angle formed by 2 sides of the hexagon?

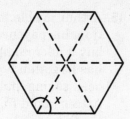

(A) 120°
(B) 60°
(C) 90°
(D) 150°
(E) Cannot be determined from information given

36. On Frank's map 1 inch represents 10 miles. If the distance from Bloomingdale to Watersedge on the map is $3\frac{1}{2}$ inches, what is the real distance between the towns?

(A) $3\frac{1}{2}$ miles
(B) 155 miles
(C) 35 miles
(D) 350 miles
(E) None of the above

37. A rectangle has a perimeter of 56 meters. If one of its sides measures 12 meters, then its area is equal to:

(A) 112 square meters
(B) 114 square meters
(C) 168 square meters
(D) 192 square meters
(E) None of the above

38. Which of the following triples of numbers could be the sides of a right triangle?

I. 10, 24, 26
II. 6, 6, 6
III. 9, 12, 15
IV. 5, 5, $5\sqrt{2}$

(A) I only
(B) II and III only
(C) I and III only
(D) I, II, and III only
(E) I, III, and IV only

39. A dangerous watchdog is tied to a stake by a chain that is 15 meters long. How many square meters of area does the dog have to walk around in?

(A) 225π
(B) 225
(C) 30π
(D) 112.5
(E) None of the above

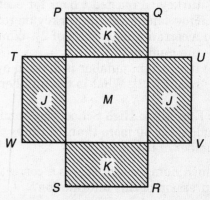

40. Rectangle $PQRS$ has the same area as rectangle $TUVW$. The areas of the small shaded rectangles are J and K, as shown. $K = J \times$?

(A) $\frac{1}{2}$
(B) $\frac{2}{3}$
(C) $\frac{3}{4}$
(D) 1
(E) $\frac{3}{2}$

41. Ms. Rodriquez gave a math test of 25 items. She gave three points for each correct answer and subtracted two points for each wrong answer. Hal answered all the questions and got a score of zero. How many items did Hal answer wrong?

In solving this problem, Rhonda guesses that Hal had 15 right and 10 wrong. Why is Rhonda's guess wrong'?

(A) It gives more than 25 items.
(B) It gives less than 25 items.
(C) The test score would be more than 0.
(D) The test score would be less than 0.
(E) None of the above is a valid reason.

42. Which of the following statements can be represented by the equation $\frac{1}{3} \times n = 2\frac{1}{2}$?

    (A) Only $2\frac{1}{2}$ sticks of gum were left after $\frac{1}{3}$ of a pack was chewed. How many sticks were in the pack originally?
    (B) A cookbook recommends that a turkey be roasted $\frac{1}{3}$ hour for each pound of turkey. How large a turkey could be cooked in $2\frac{1}{2}$ hours?
    (C) A cookbook recommends that a $2\frac{1}{2}$ kg turkey be roasted $\frac{1}{3}$ hour for each kg. How long must the turkey be roasted?
    (D) A certain number is $\frac{1}{3}$ of $2\frac{1}{2}$. What is the number?
    (E) If a certain number is divided by $\frac{1}{3}$, the result is $2\frac{1}{2}$. What is the number?

43. At Elm Ridge High School the number of students is 40 more than 16 times the number of teachers.

    Which number sentence is a correct expression of this information?

    (A) $16s = t + 40$
    (B) $16s + 40 = t$
    (C) $16s - 40 = t$
    (D) $s = 16t + 40$
    (E) $16t = s + 40$

44. If 60 feet of telephone cable weighs 140 pounds, what is the weight of 150 feet of this wire? Which of the following procedures will give a correct solution?

    I. $\dfrac{60}{n} = \dfrac{140}{150}$

    II. $\dfrac{60}{140} = \dfrac{n}{150}$

    III. $\dfrac{60}{140} = \dfrac{150}{n}$

    IV. Since $60 + 60 + 30 = 150$, then the weight is equal to $140 + 140 + 70$.
    V. Since $60 \times 150 = 9000$, then the weight is $9000 + 140$.

    (A) I only
    (B) II only
    (C) I and II only
    (D) III and IV only
    (E) I, II, and V only

45. Arthur is able to save $125 per month from his paycheck. He needs $425 more to buy a microcomputer that costs $1800. He has forgotten how many months he has been saving, but he would like to know. Arthur could find out if he did which of the following?

    (A) Subtract $425 from $1800 and divide $125 into the answer.
    (B) Divide $125 into $1800 and add $425 to the answer.
    (C) Divide $125 into $425 and subtract the answer from $1800.
    (D) Multiply $125 times $425 and divide the answer into $1800.
    (E) Multiply $125 times $425 and subtract the answer from $1800.

46. Ivan saved money from his monthly paycheck for 7 consecutive months to buy a new television. At the end of the 7 months he had saved $315. The total cost of the television he wanted, including tax, was $289.49. How much money did Ivan have after he bought the television? Answer: $604.49.

    Which statement describes best why the answer given for this problem is *not* reasonable?

    (A) The television cost $289.49.
    (B) If he had $315, he spent $289.49.
    (C) If he had $315 and spent $289.49, the amount left must be less than $315.
    (D) If the television cost $289.49, he saved more money than the television actually cost.
    (E) Because there is not enough information to answer the question.

47. Harriet was washing her car when she noticed that George was washing his car also. It happens that Harriet washes her car every 9 days and George washes his every 12 days. How many days will pass before they next wash their cars on the same day?

    Which of the following solution methods is most likely to give a correct solution?

(A)

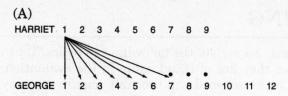

(B) 9 + 12 = 21

(C)

HARRIET	9	18	27	36	45		
GEORGE	12	24	36	48	60		

(D)

(E) 9 × 12 = 108

48. What does the California Electric Co. charge for each kilowatt-hour used?

CALIFORNIA ELECTRIC COMPANY

FOR OCT. 4 THROUGH NOV. 5

PREVIOUS BILL $132.56
CREDITS $132.56
BALANCE ....$ 0.00

PRESENT READING (KW-H)	PREVIOUS READING (KW-H)	KW-H USED	AMOUNT
9682	11526	1844	$175.18

AMOUNT DUE:
IF PAID BY DEC. 1.................$175.18
AFTER DEC. 1 ....$180.18

Which statement indicates a correct operation to perform to answer this question?

(A) $175.18 ÷ 11526 = $0.015
(B) $175.18 ÷ 1844 = $0.095
(C) $175.18 ÷ 9682 = $0.018
(D) $175.18 − $132.56 = $42.62
(E) 1844 ÷ 9682 = 0.19

49. It takes Lisa 28 minutes to get to and from school each day. She wondered how many minutes she spends going to and from school in an entire school year.

Lisa could solve this problem if she also knew . . .

(A) There are 60 minutes in an hour.
(B) There are 180 school days in a year.
(C) The school is half a mile from Lisa's house.
(D) There are 5 school days in a week.
(E) How many days she goes to school in an entire school year.

50. The following problem statement has insufficient information. From a piece of cardboard in the shape of a square the largest possible circle is cut out. What is the area of the circle?

This problem can be solved if you also know;

   I. The thickness of the cardboard.
  II. The length of a side of the cardboard.
 III. The area of the piece of cardboard.

(A) I and II
(B) I and III
(C) II and III
(D) Only I is needed.
(E) Either II or III is needed.

WRITING

Directions: You will have 60 minutes to write an essay on each of the following two topics. Try to spend approximately 30 minutes on each topic, as they are of equal value in the evaluation. While quantity is not as important as quality, the topics selected will probably require an essay rather than just a paragraph or two. Organization is an integral part of effective writing, so you may want to use some of the allotted time to plan your work. Support your ideas with clear, specific examples or explanations. Write legibly, and do not skip lines.

FIRST TOPIC:

Some educators feel that declaring a moratorium on testing, or halting the use of tests in schools for a period of time, would be helpful. It would give people time to consider the uses and misuses of testing and its value. Discuss whether you agree or disagree with this position.

SECOND TOPIC:

Everyone has, at one time or another, suffered from a fear of some sort. Describe one situation in which you experienced this emotion.

ANSWER KEY

Reading

1. D	11. B	21. C	31. C	41. D
2. B	12. D	22. A	32. D	42. A
3. B	13. C	23. C	33. C	43. D
4. A	14. B	24. C	34. B	44. C
5. B	15. A	25. A	35. D	45. A
6. C	16. C	26. B	36. D	46. D
7. D	17. E	27. A	37. C	47. D
8. B	18. D	28. C	38. D	48. B
9. D	19. A	29. A	39. C	49. C
10. A	20. D	30. A	40. B	50. B

Mathematics

1. D	11. B	21. B	31. D	41. C
2. B	12. A	22. C	32. C	42. B
3. C	13. D	23. B	33. C	43. D
4. C	14. D	24. C	34. B	44. D
5. A	15. A	25. A	35. A	45. A
6. A	16. A	26. C	36. C	46. C
7. E	17. C	27. B	37. D	47. C
8. E	18. A	28. A	38. E	48. B
9. D	19. D	29. B	39. A	49. E
10. E	20. C	30. B	40. D	50. E

ANALYSIS OF ERRORS

The following table lists the subject matter covered in each question of the Reading and Mathematics sections of the test. Find the question numbers that you got wrong and review the subject matter covered in those questions again.

SECTION	QUESTION NUMBERS	SUBJECT AREA
READING		
	12, 15, 19, 26, 35, 47	Finding the Main Idea
	1, 8, 13, 16, 21, 37, 49	Finding Specific Details
	2, 3, 4, 9, 10, 11, 14, 23, 25, 31, 32, 34, 38, 39, 40, 41, 42, 43, 48, 50	Finding Implications
	17, 18, 20, 24, 33, 27, 36	Determining the Meaning of Strange Words
	27, 36	Determining Special Techniques
	5, 6, 7, 28, 29, 30, 44, 45, 46	Interpreting Tables and Graphs

SECTION	QUESTION NUMBERS	SUBJECT AREA
MATHEMATICS Arithmetic	3, 5, 10	Whole Numbers
	1, 6, 13, 18	Fractions
	4, 6, 16, 21	Decimals
	9, 20	Percentage
		Rounding Off Numbers
	2, 6, 11	Signed Numbers
	8	Averages, Medians, Ranges, and Modes
	4, 31	Powers, Exponents, and Roots
Algebra	23, 24, 25, 26, 28, 29	Algebraic Expressions
	27	Equations
	14, 19, 22, 41, 42, 43, 45, 46, 47, 48, 49, 50	Verbal Problems
	12, 15	Counting Problems
	7, 30, 36, 44	Ratio and Proportion
		Sequence and Progression
		Inequalities
Geometry		Angles
		Lines
	35	Polygons
	38	Triangles
		Quadrilaterals
	34	Circles
	32, 33, 37, 39, 40	Area, Perimeter, and Volume
	34	Coordinate Geometry
Formulas		Formulas
Other	17, 48	Interpreting Graphs and Tables (see Reading Section)

ANSWER EXPLANATIONS

Reading

1. **D** It is stated in the passage that the name came from the fact that they painted unpleasant subjects.

2. **B** One could conclude that the artists' works portrayed only the unpleasant side of urban living and not anything as optimistic as a beautification project.

3. **B** The most significant point here is that the discovery of the fossil, which is more humanlike than apelike, suggests the possibility that the common ancestor of apes and humans was human.

4. **A** It is likely that the writer will suggest supporting evidence, and also refers back to the "suggestion" of the previous sentence.

5. **B** Reading the graph carefully, one can see that the solid line representing the younger children indicates that 18% of them conformed to the group only once (frequency of one on the bottom line).

6. **C** The line representing the younger children shows that a larger percent of them (25%) conformed to the group's influences the greatest number of times (7).

7. **D** The results of the study, as given on the graph, show that there is, in fact, evidence that children are influenced by a group, but the observations stated indicate that it is not an easy thing for them to do.

8. **B** "Having named *it*" (line 9), the author states, this object detected in space is a black hole, "such as this one." (line 12)

9. **D**   Since no light escapes from this extinguished star, it is safe to conclude that that is why they are so named.

10. **A**   None of the other implications is supported by the passage, and the author does say that the forces of black holes are "slackening the pace of disintegrating galaxies."

11. **B**   The gravitational force remains the same, so A is wrong; a great deal of energy is given off from black holes, 1,000 times more than from the sun, so D is wrong. The black hole already has been created at this point in the description, so E is inappropriate. The author could very well discuss the type of gravitational force that is exerted once the black hole is created.

12. **D**   The author states this (lines 2–3). The other statements are not accurate based on the passage or are merely implied.

13. **C**   While all of the other statements represent references made in the passage, no reference is made to any variation in shape.

14. **B**   This is the only response that represents how he was deceived. that is, how his plan did not work.

15. **A**   B and E are too general; D is inaccurate; revenge by the lion (C) is never mentioned.

16. **C**   The author states (lines 3–4) that most facts are not retained.

17. **E**   The author's main point is that studying helps to develop the powers of the mind, here referred to as an instrument.

18. **D**   The author discusses the need for study to develop the powers of the mind. A, B, and C do not refer to powers. Muscle power (E) is used as comparison.

19. **A**   The passage describes the problems faced by the village farmers in the Near East. Answers B, D, and E are too general; the Third World (C) is not mentioned.

20. **D**   Answers A and B are too specific. Inconsistent weather conditions are a serious problem for farmers.

21. **C**   The writer mentions that the substances in the nuclei of cells are, in some way, responsible for biochemical activity and characteristics; hence, they are essential to life.

22. **A**   The passage focuses on the unique way in which the substances are combined and how they contribute to life.

23. **C**   Although the writer indicates that the information has not been integrated thus far and has, therefore, been largely unproductive, he does imply that it is important to know about.

24. **C**   The need, the author points out, is to find a means to put divergent ideas together and determine what they all say about the process.

25. **A**   The writer states that psycholinguists have been investigating small units and their reality and have not considered the larger picture.

26. **B**   All of the ideas presented by the writer—that a phobia is considered a set of symptoms, that it is enigmatic, and that it can be treated with quick results—focus on this point.

27. **A**   The last sentence in the passage provides an example of the point the author is making.

28. **C**   In only one case, month number 4, is the solid line representing 1982 above the broken line representing 1983.

29. **A**   The best profits for one month in 1983 were $90,000, and in 1982 the best profits for one month were $70,000, so the difference is $20,000.

30. **A**   It is necessary to average the monthly profits for each year, but the sum is easily divided by 10.

31. **C**   In suggesting that concerned citizens must participate in government, the writer implies a general distrust of the stereotyped politician by use of the word "mere." (line 6)

32. **D**   The author's point is that if concerned and intelligent citizens do not participate in government affairs, they leave them in the hands of those who may be less than honest.

33. **C**   The terms used in reference to the individuals who might gain control of public affairs if honest people do nothing include

"selfish, ignorant, and crafty," a category into which "corrupt" fits well.

34. **B** The author wants to make the point that developing a real appreciation and understanding of literature is more important than covering a large number or wide range of selections. Answers A and D are too general; answer E is bringing up a new subject; answer C conflicts with the author's main point.

35. **D** The author wants the teacher to go beyond technical analyses of literature with gifted students.

36. **D** The author's statement are all opinions based apparently on some teaching experience. No facts or research results are presented.

37. **C** The writer states that both the perfecting of symmetry and the "discovery of perspective" came from the Arab world.

38. **D** Since the passage focuses on the discovery and use of both symmetry and perspective, it is reasonable to make a generalization about how these two concepts changed man's perception of the world.

39. **C** The author's purpose in writing this passage could easily be to make the point that the way math is taught in the schools today is limited and limiting. Answers A, B, and D conflict with statements in the passage. E conflicts with what is implied.

40. **B** The writer speaks of *logistic* in dull terms and seems to imply that *arithmetic* was much more interesting.

41. **D** The writer is sympathetic to drama critics because he understands the problems they confront.

42. **A** It is indicated that the drama critic is occasionally vicious only because he must review so much that is of no value.

43. **D** The writer's statement that the column space allocated in the past would have been wholly inadequate indicates that the drama critic was reviewing a very worthwhile play.

44. **C** It seems the most noteworthy finding of the poll is that the concerns of school boards and of the public do not match at all.

45. **A** Since it is a concern of 13% of the people polled from the public sector, and only 9.6% of school board members listed it as a concern, one could conclude that it is a greater concern for the public.

46. **D** The table shows that 39% of school board members are concerned about "declining enrollment"; it is their greatest concern.

47. **D** Although social behavior is discussed and early experiences are mentioned, the passage, in general, is about imprinting.

48. **B** The information is presented in a general way to give background facts. It is not limited to reinforcement or behavioral techniques (A and E), and does not deal with the care of animals (D); nor is the tone casual enough for answer (C).

49. **C** The author indicated that there is much interest in imprinting because it is a unique process and reveals a great deal about learning.

50. **B** Although the author does not mention an example of a negative experience of imprinting, he does specify that imprinting is an early experience that affects the social behavior of an animal, even into adulthood. The other answers do not deal directly with the early learning from parent-offspring attachments.

Mathematics

1. **D** Choices A, C, and E are smaller than $\frac{1}{2}$, and choices B and D are greater than $\frac{1}{2}$. So, we need only decide which is the larger of B and D.

$$\frac{4}{7} \times \frac{5}{5} = \frac{20}{35} \qquad \frac{3}{5} \times \frac{7}{7} = \frac{21}{35}$$
Since, $\frac{21}{35} > \frac{20}{35}$, $\qquad \frac{3}{5} > \frac{4}{7}$

2. **B** $15° - 21° = 15° + -21° = -6°$

3. **C** A is 600,405.
B is not a standard way of expressing any number.
D is 6,004.005.

4. **C** The value of each place in a decimal numeral is 10 times greater than the place to its immediate right. Therefore, we need only count how many places apart the twos are to obtain the answer. 42, 578. 1502 The

answer is $10 \times 10 \times 10 \times 10 \times 10 \times 10 \times 10$ or 10^7.

5. **A**   The square of a number n is the number $n \times n$ or n^2.

$$16^2 = 256$$

6. **A**   First write all of the numerals in decimal form (divide top by bottom).

$$-\frac{5}{3} = -1.66 \quad \frac{1}{3} = .33 \quad \frac{1}{5} = .2$$

Arrange on a number line. Negatives go to the left of zero, and the larger in absolute value (ignoring sign) the further from zero.

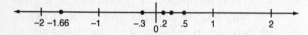

7. **E**   Total weight of milk and sugar is 180 grams. Sugar weighs 20 grams. Thus pure milk weighs $180 - 20$ (or 160 grams). Ratio of pure milk to milk and sugar is

$$\frac{180 - 20}{180}$$

8. **E**   Let t = Mark's time on the fourth test.

$$(78 + 81 + 73 + t)/4 = 76$$
$$78 + 81 + 73 + t = 4(76)$$
$$232 + t = 304$$
$$t = 304 - 232$$
$$t = 72$$

9. **D**   Total votes = $240 + 100 + 60 = 400$

Tom's percentage $= \frac{240}{400} = \frac{240}{400} \div \frac{4}{4}$

$$= \frac{60}{100} = 60\%$$

10. **E**   If a whole number n is divisible by 5, then it can be written $n = 5 \times m$ for some whole number m.

So, x, y, and z can be written as

$$x = 5 \cdot a$$
$$y = 5 \cdot b$$
$$z = 5 \cdot c$$

Then

I. $x + y = 5a + 5b = 5(a + b)$
   So, $x + y$ is divisible by 5.
II. $x \cdot y = 5a \cdot 5b = 5 \cdot 5 \cdot a \cdot b$
   So, $x \cdot y$ is divisible by 5.
III. $x + y + z = 5a + 5b + 5c = 5(a + b + c)$
   So, $x + y + z$ is divisible by 5.

11. **B** $-2\left[\frac{-63}{-7} - (6 - 12)\right]$

$$= -2 [9 - (-6)]$$
$$= -2 [9 + 6]$$
$$= -2 \times 15$$
$$= -30$$

12. **A**   Listing the different amounts of money, we have the following number of cents: 6, 11, 26, 15, 30, 35.

13. **D**   100 gallons to start. $\frac{3}{4} \times 100 = 75$ gallons missing.
The hose pumps 20 gallons per hour.

$$\frac{75}{20} = 3\frac{15}{20} = 3\frac{3}{4} \text{ hours to fill the 75 gallons.}$$

(3 hours 45 minutes)

14. **D**   It is easy and quick to just test each of the choices. The original number is 28, since $82 - 28 = 54$.

15. **A**   Each team will play each of the 7 other teams. Thus each of the 8 teams has 7 games on its schedule. So there are $7 \times 8 = 56$ games listed on the schedules. But, of course a game between teams A and B is the same as a game between teams B and A (i.e. every game is listed on 2 schedules). So there are actually only $\frac{56}{2} = 28$ different games.

16. **A** $\$126.50 \div \$5.50 = 23$
It will take 23 months.

17. **C**   Only graph C is 20¢ for letters up to $\frac{1}{2}$ ounce, 35¢ for letters between $\frac{1}{2}$ ounce and 1 ounce, 50¢ for letters between 1 ounce and $1\frac{1}{2}$ ounce, etc.

18. **A**   We need to figure $\frac{3}{4}$ billion $- \frac{1}{6}$ billion.
The answer will clearly be in billions of dollars. We need only to figure $\frac{3}{4} - \frac{1}{6}$.

$$\frac{3}{4} - \frac{1}{6} = \frac{9}{12} - \frac{2}{12} = \frac{7}{12}$$

19. **D**   Rather than using algebra, it is easiest to examine each of the choices. Notice that each pair presented does total 56 as required. Only choice D satisfies the condition that 3 times the smaller is 7 more than $\frac{1}{2}$ the larger. $(3 \times 10 = \frac{1}{2} \times 4 + 7)$

20. **C**   The discount is only slightly less than 1%, so we expect it to be a little less than

24¢ (.01 × $23.75 = .2375; just move the decimal point two places to the left). Thus choice C seems most likely (more precisely, .9% × 23.75 = .009 × 23.75 = .21375, so the discount is about 21¢).

21. **B** The ad contains 12 words. The cost per word (for 1 day) is 28¢. So the ad cost is $12 \times .28 = \$3.36$.

22. **C** Suppose Annie has x pennies. Then she has $2x$ dimes and $(15 - 3x)$ nickels. An equation is

$$x + 10(2x) + 5(15 - 3x) = 99$$
$$x + 20x + 75 - 15x = 99$$
$$6x + 75 = 99$$
$$6x = 24$$
$$x = 4$$

There are 4 pennies, 8 dimes, and $(15 - 3(4)) = 3$ nickels.

23. **B** The question asks, what can we multiply times s to get r? Notice that both r and s contain terms involving mn and pq. In fact if we multiply r by -5 we get s. In other words, $-5 \times r = s$. So, $r = \left(-\frac{1}{5}\right) \times s$.

24. **C** This problem involves 2 fractions to be subtracted. Their common denominator is yz.

$$\frac{x}{y} - \frac{x}{z} = \left(\frac{x}{y} \cdot \frac{z}{z}\right) - \left(\frac{x}{z} \cdot \frac{y}{y}\right)$$
$$= \frac{xz}{yz} - \frac{xy}{yz}$$
$$= \frac{xz - xy}{yz}$$

25. **A** $(x - 7)(2x - 3) = x(2x) - 3(x) - 7(2x) - 7(-3)$
$$= 2x^2 - 3x - 14x + 21$$
$$= 2x^2 - 17x + 21$$

26. **C** $x = \frac{2}{3}$ and $y = 5$

Substituting into the given formula $\dfrac{x + y}{x}$ we obtain:

$$\frac{\frac{2}{3} + 5}{\frac{2}{3}}$$
$$= \left(\frac{2}{3} + 5\right) \times \frac{3}{2}$$
$$= \frac{17}{3} \times \frac{3}{2}$$
$$= \frac{17}{2}$$
$$= 8\frac{1}{2}$$

27. **B** Given: $3.5x = 70$

Solving for x:

$$x = \frac{70}{3.5}$$
$$x = 20$$

28. **A** gasoline = x cents per mile
total expenses = y cents per mile
dollars to run the motorcycle 200 miles = ?
$x + y$ = total cents per mile

$$\frac{(x + y)}{100} = \text{total dollars per mile}$$

$$200 \times \frac{(x + y)}{100} = \text{total dollars for 200 miles}$$

Simplifying: $2(x + y)$ = total dollars to run 200 miles

29. **B** Given: $y = 2x + 3$
Question: $3y = ?$
Substituting: $3y = 3(2x + 3)$
$$= 6x + 9$$

30. **B** Given $\dfrac{5t}{2} = \dfrac{3}{2}$

$$2 \times 5t = 2 \times 3$$
$$10t = 6$$
$$t = \frac{6}{10} = \frac{3}{5}$$

31. **D** Given: x^3 is odd
This implies that x is odd
If x is odd then:

   I. "$(x - 1)$" is even is a true statement.
  II. "x is odd" is a true statement.
 III. "x is even" is a false statement.

32. **C** Volume of cone: $V = \frac{1}{3}\pi \cdot r^2 \cdot h$
$$h = ?$$
$$V = 24 \text{ cm}^3$$
$$r = 3 \text{ cm}$$
Substituting: $24 = \frac{1}{3}\pi \cdot 32 \cdot h$
$$h = \frac{24 \cdot 3}{9 \cdot \pi} = \frac{8}{\pi} \text{ cm}$$

33. **C** Area of circle = $a = \pi \cdot r^2$
If the radius is tripled, then the new radius R is:
$$R = 3r$$
so the new area will be:
$$A = \pi \cdot R^2$$
substituting: $A = \pi \cdot (3r)^2$
$$A = \pi \cdot 9r^2$$
$$A = 9 \cdot \pi \cdot r^2 = 9a$$
so the new area is 9 times larger than the previous area.

34. **B** From Point P with coordinates $(6, 8)$ we determine the radius of the circle, using the Pythagorean theorem.

$$r^2 = 6^2 + 8^2$$
$$r^2 = 36 + 64$$
$$r^2 = 100$$
$$r = 10$$

So the x coordinate at point Q is 10.

35. **A** The triangles formed are equilateral triangles. (Triangles with equal angles and equal sides.) Since the angles of a triangle always add up to 180°, each angle in these triangles must measure 60°. Angle x is the angle formed by two adjacent, equal angles of 60° each. Hence, angle x measures $2 \times 60° = 120°$.

36. **C** 1 inch represents 10 miles.

So, $3\frac{1}{2}$ inches represents $(3\frac{1}{2}) \times 10$ miles
$= \frac{7}{2} \times 10$ miles $= 35$ miles.

37. **D** The perimeter of this rectangle is:
$2a + 2b = 56$
If $a = 12$ then $b = 16$.
The area of this rectangle is $a \times b$.
So area $= 12 \times 16 = 192$ m^2

38. **E** To be the sides of a right triangle the numbers must satisfy the Pythagorean theorem, or be multiples of the sides of a triangle that satisfies the Pythagorean theorem. We must examine each triple:

I. $(10, 24, 26)$ is a multiple of $(5, 12, 13)$

$$5^2 + 12^2 = 13^2$$
$$25 + 144 = 169$$
$$169 = 169$$

So, $(10, 24, 26)$ can be a right triangle.

II. $(6, 6, 6)$ is an equilateral triangle (triangle with 3 equal sides). Each angle in any equilateral triangle measures 60°. So an equilateral triangle can never be a right triangle.

III. $(9, 12, 15)$ is a multiple of $(3, 4, 5)$ for which
$$3^2 + 4^2 = 5^2$$
$$9 + 16 = 25$$
So, $(9, 12, 15)$ can be a right triangle.

IV. $(5, 5, 5\sqrt{2})$ is a multiple of $(1, 1, \sqrt{2})$ for which
$$1^2 + 1^2 = (\sqrt{2})^2$$
$$1 + 1 = 2$$
So, $(5, 5, 5\sqrt{2})$ can be a right triangle.

39. **A** The watchdog will have access to the region within the circle of radius $r = 15$. The area of this region is:

$A = \pi \cdot r^2$
$A = \pi \cdot (15)^2$
$A = 225 \cdot \pi$

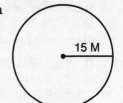

40. **D** The areas of the large rectangles are the same.

Area of $(PQRS) = $ Area of $(TUVW)$
Area of $(PQRS) = M + 2K$
Area of $(TUVW) = M + 2J$

Since the areas are the same:

$$M + 2J = M + 2K$$
$$\text{So, } 2J = 2K$$
$$J = K$$
$$\text{or } K = J \times 1$$

41. **C** There are two conditions that must be checked for in this item.
   I. The total number of items must be exactly 25.
   II. Score for right answers $= 3 \times$ the number of right answers (r) and score for wrong answers $= -2 \times$ the number of wrong answers (w).

Since Hal got a score of zero, the equation $3r + (-2)w = 0$ represents Hal's performances.

Rhonda guessed that Hal had 15 right and 10 wrong answers.

Let's check the above conditions:
   I. $10 + 15 = 25$ (condition satisfied)
   II. $3 \times 15 + (-2) \times 10 = 45 - 20 = 25$

Hal would get a score of 25, not 0.

So answer C is correct, Hal's score would be more than 0.

42. **B** $\frac{1}{3} \times n = 2\frac{1}{2}$

1 pound of turkey takes $\frac{1}{3} \times 1$ hours to cook

2 pounds of turkey takes $\frac{1}{3} \times 2$ hours to cook

n pounds of turkey takes $\frac{1}{3} \times n$ to cook

Since we know that it takes $2\frac{1}{2}$ hours to cook a turkey, we set up the equation:

$\frac{1}{3} \times n = 2\frac{1}{2}$

43. **D** Number of students $= 16 \times$ number of teachers $+ 40$

$$s = 16t + 40$$

44. **D**   60 feet of cable weigh 140 pounds.
150 feet of cable weigh?
This can be set up as a ratio in the following way:

$$\frac{60}{140} = \frac{150}{n}$$

or 150 feet = 60 feet + 60 feet + 30 feet and in weight this is equivalent to:

150 feet weighs 140 pounds + 140 pounds + 70 pounds

(Since 30 feet is $\frac{1}{2}$ of 60 feet, the weight of 30 feet should be $\frac{1}{2}$ of 140 pounds or 70 pounds.) So answers III and IV are correct.

45. **A**   To find how much he has saved Arthur should subtract $425 from $1800. Since he saves $125 a month, to find out how many months he has been saving he should divide the answer above by $125.

46. **C**   Once you spend some of the money that you've saved, the amount left must be less than what you had saved. Since Ivan had saved $315 and spent part of that, the amount left must be less than $315.

47. **C**   Since Harriet washes her car every 9 days, she washes it on days 9, 18, 27, 36, 45, etc. Since George washes his car every 12 days he washes it on days 12, 24, 36, 48, etc. The only suggested solution that shows these two patterns is choice C.

48. **B**   There were 1844 kilowatt-hours used and the company charged a total of $175.18. The amount paid for each kilowatt-hour is $175.18 ÷ 1844 = $0.095.

49. **E**   Lisa can solve the problem by multiplying 28 times the number of days she goes to school in a year. To solve this problem Lisa must know the number of days she goes to school in an entire year. (Note: Choice B does not consider the possibility that she may be absent on some days.)

50. **E**   In order to find the area of the circle, all we need to know is the radius of the circle to be cut. The radius is $\frac{1}{2}$ the side of the square. If we knew the side of the square we would have the solution. It would also be enough to know the area of the cardboard (since we know it is a square, and thus we can figure the length of each side of the square).

Writing

The following essay outlines have been written to demonstrate the planning of well-written answers to the topics given. Use these only as guidelines to evaluating your own organization. Many different organization patterns and plans could work equally well for the topics given.

FIRST TOPIC

Some educators feel that declaring a moratorium on testing, or halting the use of tests in schools for a period of time, would be helpful. It would give people time to consider the uses and misuses of testing and its value. Discuss whether you agree or disagree with this position.

Essay Outline:

A. Introduction

1. General statements on testing in the schools, background, i.e., give a general context for the thesis being presented.

2. Presentation of thesis statement or point of view—a moratorium on testing would/would not be helpful.

B. Reasons: pro or con

1. State each reason in clear, specific terms. (Ex.: "Tests are misused when they are used to place students in reading groups.")

a. Elaborate or explain more about how the reason supports your point of view.

b. Support with specific examples.

2. Present additional reasons in same manner as above.

C. Summary and conclusions

1. Restate your point of view in brief terms.

2. Conclude with statement about likelihood of such a moratorium, future of schools with or without tests, or recommendations for alternative solutions.

Everyone has, at one time or another, suffered from a fear of some sort. Describe one situation in which you experienced this emotion.

Essay Outline

A. Introduction

1. Describe, in general terms, the type of situation in which you have found yourself when you experienced this particular fear.

2. Discuss, in general terms, the nature and quality of the fear.

3. Give the reader a strong impression of the fear you have felt and interest him in reading further.

B. Elaboration

1. Extend explanation of situation and fear which attended it.

2. Give additional information to support description.

3. Use comparison/contrast to give reader a more exact sense of how you felt.

4. Discuss how this experience influenced your behavior or other aspects of your life.

C. Summary and conclusions

1. Restate your experience in very brief terms.

2. Conclude by indicating how you have assimilated this experience.

Answer Sheet— Model Test Three

Reading

1. Ⓐ Ⓑ Ⓒ Ⓓ Ⓔ
2. Ⓐ Ⓑ Ⓒ Ⓓ Ⓔ
3. Ⓐ Ⓑ Ⓒ Ⓓ Ⓔ
4. Ⓐ Ⓑ Ⓒ Ⓓ Ⓔ
5. Ⓐ Ⓑ Ⓒ Ⓓ Ⓔ
6. Ⓐ Ⓑ Ⓒ Ⓓ Ⓔ
7. Ⓐ Ⓑ Ⓒ Ⓓ Ⓔ
8. Ⓐ Ⓑ Ⓒ Ⓓ Ⓔ
9. Ⓐ Ⓑ Ⓒ Ⓓ Ⓔ
10. Ⓐ Ⓑ Ⓒ Ⓓ Ⓔ
11. Ⓐ Ⓑ Ⓒ Ⓓ Ⓔ
12. Ⓐ Ⓑ Ⓒ Ⓓ Ⓔ
13. Ⓐ Ⓑ Ⓒ Ⓓ Ⓔ
14. Ⓐ Ⓑ Ⓒ Ⓓ Ⓔ
15. Ⓐ Ⓑ Ⓒ Ⓓ Ⓔ
16. Ⓐ Ⓑ Ⓒ Ⓓ Ⓔ
17. Ⓐ Ⓑ Ⓒ Ⓓ Ⓔ

18. Ⓐ Ⓑ Ⓒ Ⓓ Ⓔ
19. Ⓐ Ⓑ Ⓒ Ⓓ Ⓔ
20. Ⓐ Ⓑ Ⓒ Ⓓ Ⓔ
21. Ⓐ Ⓑ Ⓒ Ⓓ Ⓔ
22. Ⓐ Ⓑ Ⓒ Ⓓ Ⓔ
23. Ⓐ Ⓑ Ⓒ Ⓓ Ⓔ
24. Ⓐ Ⓑ Ⓒ Ⓓ Ⓔ
25. Ⓐ Ⓑ Ⓒ Ⓓ Ⓔ
26. Ⓐ Ⓑ Ⓒ Ⓓ Ⓔ
27. Ⓐ Ⓑ Ⓒ Ⓓ Ⓔ
28. Ⓐ Ⓑ Ⓒ Ⓓ Ⓔ
29. Ⓐ Ⓑ Ⓒ Ⓓ Ⓔ
30. Ⓐ Ⓑ Ⓒ Ⓓ Ⓔ
31. Ⓐ Ⓑ Ⓒ Ⓓ Ⓔ
32. Ⓐ Ⓑ Ⓒ Ⓓ Ⓔ
33. Ⓐ Ⓑ Ⓒ Ⓓ Ⓔ
34. Ⓐ Ⓑ Ⓒ Ⓓ Ⓔ

35. Ⓐ Ⓑ Ⓒ Ⓓ Ⓔ
36. Ⓐ Ⓑ Ⓒ Ⓓ Ⓔ
37. Ⓐ Ⓑ Ⓒ Ⓓ Ⓔ
38. Ⓐ Ⓑ Ⓒ Ⓓ Ⓔ
49. Ⓐ Ⓑ Ⓒ Ⓓ Ⓔ
50. Ⓐ Ⓑ Ⓒ Ⓓ Ⓔ
41. Ⓐ Ⓑ Ⓒ Ⓓ Ⓔ
42. Ⓐ Ⓑ Ⓒ Ⓓ Ⓔ
43. Ⓐ Ⓑ Ⓒ Ⓓ Ⓔ
44. Ⓐ Ⓑ Ⓒ Ⓓ Ⓔ
45. Ⓐ Ⓑ Ⓒ Ⓓ Ⓔ
46. Ⓐ Ⓑ Ⓒ Ⓓ Ⓔ
47. Ⓐ Ⓑ Ⓒ Ⓓ Ⓔ
48. Ⓐ Ⓑ Ⓒ Ⓓ Ⓔ
49. Ⓐ Ⓑ Ⓒ Ⓓ Ⓔ
50. Ⓐ Ⓑ Ⓒ Ⓓ Ⓔ

Mathematics

1. Ⓐ Ⓑ Ⓒ Ⓓ Ⓔ
2. Ⓐ Ⓑ Ⓒ Ⓓ Ⓔ
3. Ⓐ Ⓑ Ⓒ Ⓓ Ⓔ
4. Ⓐ Ⓑ Ⓒ Ⓓ Ⓔ
5. Ⓐ Ⓑ Ⓒ Ⓓ Ⓔ
6. Ⓐ Ⓑ Ⓒ Ⓓ Ⓔ
7. Ⓐ Ⓑ Ⓒ Ⓓ Ⓔ
8. Ⓐ Ⓑ Ⓒ Ⓓ Ⓔ
9. Ⓐ Ⓑ Ⓒ Ⓓ Ⓔ
10. Ⓐ Ⓑ Ⓒ Ⓓ Ⓔ
11. Ⓐ Ⓑ Ⓒ Ⓓ Ⓔ
12. Ⓐ Ⓑ Ⓒ Ⓓ Ⓔ
13. Ⓐ Ⓑ Ⓒ Ⓓ Ⓔ
14. Ⓐ Ⓑ Ⓒ Ⓓ Ⓔ
15. Ⓐ Ⓑ Ⓒ Ⓓ Ⓔ
16. Ⓐ Ⓑ Ⓒ Ⓓ Ⓔ
17. Ⓐ Ⓑ Ⓒ Ⓓ Ⓔ

18. Ⓐ Ⓑ Ⓒ Ⓓ Ⓔ
19. Ⓐ Ⓑ Ⓒ Ⓓ Ⓔ
20. Ⓐ Ⓑ Ⓒ Ⓓ Ⓔ
21. Ⓐ Ⓑ Ⓒ Ⓓ Ⓔ
22. Ⓐ Ⓑ Ⓒ Ⓓ Ⓔ
23. Ⓐ Ⓑ Ⓒ Ⓓ Ⓔ
24. Ⓐ Ⓑ Ⓒ Ⓓ Ⓔ
25. Ⓐ Ⓑ Ⓒ Ⓓ Ⓔ
26. Ⓐ Ⓑ Ⓒ Ⓓ Ⓔ
27. Ⓐ Ⓑ Ⓒ Ⓓ Ⓔ
28. Ⓐ Ⓑ Ⓒ Ⓓ Ⓔ
29. Ⓐ Ⓑ Ⓒ Ⓓ Ⓔ
30. Ⓐ Ⓑ Ⓒ Ⓓ Ⓔ
31. Ⓐ Ⓑ Ⓒ Ⓓ Ⓔ
32. Ⓐ Ⓑ Ⓒ Ⓓ Ⓔ
33. Ⓐ Ⓑ Ⓒ Ⓓ Ⓔ
34. Ⓐ Ⓑ Ⓒ Ⓓ Ⓔ

35. Ⓐ Ⓑ Ⓒ Ⓓ Ⓔ
36. Ⓐ Ⓑ Ⓒ Ⓓ Ⓔ
37. Ⓐ Ⓑ Ⓒ Ⓓ Ⓔ
38. Ⓐ Ⓑ Ⓒ Ⓓ Ⓔ
49. Ⓐ Ⓑ Ⓒ Ⓓ Ⓔ
50. Ⓐ Ⓑ Ⓒ Ⓓ Ⓔ
41. Ⓐ Ⓑ Ⓒ Ⓓ Ⓔ
42. Ⓐ Ⓑ Ⓒ Ⓓ Ⓔ
43. Ⓐ Ⓑ Ⓒ Ⓓ Ⓔ
44. Ⓐ Ⓑ Ⓒ Ⓓ Ⓔ
45. Ⓐ Ⓑ Ⓒ Ⓓ Ⓔ
46. Ⓐ Ⓑ Ⓒ Ⓓ Ⓔ
47. Ⓐ Ⓑ Ⓒ Ⓓ Ⓔ
48. Ⓐ Ⓑ Ⓒ Ⓓ Ⓔ
49. Ⓐ Ⓑ Ⓒ Ⓓ Ⓔ
50. Ⓐ Ⓑ Ⓒ Ⓓ Ⓔ

Chapter 10

Model Test Three

READING

> **Directions:** Each passage in this section is followed by a question or questions about its content. Select the best answer to each question based on what is stated or implied in the selection. You may spend up to 60 minutes on this section.

Questions 1–2

The development of the scientific attitude in an ever-increasing number of people resulted from achievements of science and invention. Marked by a spirit of open-mindedness and critical-mindedness, the scientific attitude emphasizes the need to review an issue carefully, to understand the relationship between cause and effect, and to refrain from drawing conclusions until all facts have been presented and weighed carefully. Such an attitude is vital in a democratic government since the choice between principles and policies demands a careful and open-minded consideration of issues and the ultimate choice rests with the majority of the people.

1. The author's attitude toward the scientific attitude and democratic government could best be described as

    (A) pessimistic.
    (B) confused.
    (C) ambivalent.
    (D) positive.
    (E) critical.

2. The author would probably agree with all of the following statements EXCEPT which one of the following?

(A) The use of the scientific method has had a favorable influence on the establishment of democratic government.
(B) In a democracy, the opportunity to consider issues carefully is actually precluded by the need for expediency.
(C) The practice of democracy and the development of a new scientific invention require a similar approach.
(D) The open-mindedness and painstaking research demanded by the scientific method can be used by people participating in a democratic government.
(E) Since decisions in a democracy are made by a majority of the people, many points of view need to be considered.

Questions 3–4

Linguists who study the development of language in children note that child speech deviates from adult speech in a systematic fashion. These deviations are constructed by the child on the basis of his or her own partial analysis of language and the cognitive tendencies of the child's mind. The occurrence of overregularizations, instances when irregular verbs are inflected for past tense as if they were regular, demonstrates that this systematic process is going on as children learn language.

3. An example of an "overregularization" in a child's speech would be

   (A) "broke."
   (B) "comed."
   (C) "no I go."
   (D) "walked."
   (E) "coat on."

4. The main point of this passage is that

   (A) children make many errors when learning language.
   (B) children's overcorrections reveal that they are figuring out the rules of language.
   (C) child speech is similar to adult speech and is really an imitation.
   (D) a child's mind is overburdened by the volume of rules he must learn to master language.
   (E) no one can teach a child language as well as he can learn it by himself.

Questions 5–6

Television is often cited as a dominant force in changing our political structure. At its worst, it turns a system of parties into a contest of personalities, exchanging a concern with ideas and policies for a preoccupation with images and styles.

5. This passage primarily discusses

   (A) public policies and television polls.
   (B) general reactions to the force of television.
   (C) the system of political parties in the U.S.
   (D) political dominance as portrayed in television programs.
   (E) the negative effect television can have on politics.

6. An idea presented in this passage is that

   (A) political parties do not benefit from television coverage of campaigns.
   (B) television coverage of politics focuses attention on physical images rather than mental concepts.
   (C) the need for an alteration of political structure is more evident when television reviews politics.

   (D) the interest in political images has made television a natural medium for politics.
   (E) television and politics do not mix.

Questions 7–8

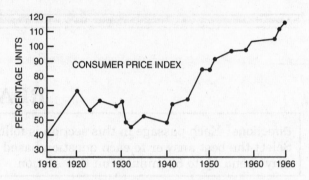

The graph represents the Consumer Price Index for the period 1916 to 1966. Refer to the graph to answer the following questions.

7. If the dots represent specific points when the Consumer Price Index was "read," then the number of times (one dot to another) that the index went down was

   (A) one.
   (B) three.
   (C) four.
   (D) six.
   (E) eight.

8. In 1950, the Consumer Price Index was approximately

   (A) 93%.
   (B) 82%.
   (C) 100%.
   (D) 65%.
   (E) 74%.

Questions 9–10

Impulsive, unconventional, boundlessly energetic, Alice Roosevelt pursued pleasure with the same abandon that Roosevelt demonstrated in his activities. She kept the newspaper-reading public captivated. Alice lived by her own law. She smoked, a habit considered most unladylike at that time. She was often reported to be involved in the sort of adventures not commonly associated with a president's daughter.

9. The author's attitude toward Alice Roosevelt could best be identified as

(A) reserved.
(B) uncanny.
(C) respectful.
(D) naive.
(E) conservative.

10. One conclusion that could be drawn from this passage is that

(A) Alice Roosevelt was not very well thought of because of her outrageous behavior.
(B) President Roosevelt and his daughter were not on good terms for the term of his presidency.
(C) Alice Roosevelt's activities provoked the antagonism of law enforcement officials.
(D) journalists found Alice Roosevelt to be a rich topic for newspaper copy.
(E) a president's family members are not free to participate in activities that are detrimental to the presidential image.

Questions 11–12
Root and stem have no need of a calendar to inform them that the calm days of midsummer have arrived. They themselves are marks on the calendar of time, there in field and meadow for anyone to observe and take note.

11. The author's attitude is one of

(A) confusion.
(B) ecstasy.
(C) pessimism.
(D) regret.
(E) confidence.

12. The author compares the parts of a plant to

(A) midsummer days.
(B) numbers on a calendar.
(C) the parts of a day.
(D) seasons of the year.
(E) flowers in a field.

Questions 13–14
If a group is to get on with its work, whether it is working out a new budget or learning about physics, indirect processes may require special attention. Difficulties often emerge which have no direct relation to the budget or to physics. Problems in communication often develop when a group assembles to do a particular job, even though the language is clear.

13. According to the author, "indirect processes" are

(A) only apparent to people working in a group.
(B) ones which can interfere with group communications.
(C) sometimes attributable to the work of the group.
(D) those that can be carried out best in a group.
(E) the tasks undertaken by a specific group.

14. In writing this passage, the author's purpose seems to be

(A) to argue the point that the work of a group, such as a committee, cannot be effective because of inhibiting factors.
(B) to discuss the pros and cons of studying physics in a group.
(C) to report the results of an experiment in group dynamics.
(D) to provide information about group dynamics or factors that influence communication in a group.
(E) to entertain the reader with a sarcastic comment on group dynamics.

Questions 15–18
The laser is a fairly recent technological discovery, but it is proving to be a revolutionary alternative in a great many fields. To understand why, it is important to understand the nature of the laser beam. It is an extremely narrow beam of light, but it is significantly different in quality from ordinary light, which consists of waves referred to as "incoherent" light. The "coherent" light waves produced by the laser are parallel and of the same size and frequency, each wave fitting closely to the contiguous one. While the waves of ordinary light fly off in every direction, the laser can travel long distances without scattering. The waves of a laser also have extremely short wavelengths, allowing a much greater amount of information to be carried.

The laser serves as a carrier of information, capable of transmitting the messages carried by telephone, radio, and television combined.

In the medical field, the laser is being used to perform bloodless, painless surgery. Hard substances, such as diamonds, can be cut with a laser, and enormous distances can be measured to within a few feet. It is evident that only the surface of this gem has been scratched in finding new and beneficial uses.

15. Laser is different from ordinary light in

(A) shape and sensation.
(B) type and nature.
(C) hue and color.
(D) order and influx.
(E) repetition and regularity.

16. Each of the following terms could be used to describe ordinary light EXCEPT

(A) scattered.
(B) not parallel.
(C) coherent.
(D) restricted substance.
(E) dispersed.

17. From this passage, it can reasonably be concluded that laser beams could be used to do all of the following EXCEPT

(A) calculate the distance from the moon to the earth.
(B) remove a wart.
(C) transmit television programs.
(D) guide a spaceship.
(E) convert sea water into drinking water.

18. The writer most likely used the figurative expression in the last sentence of the passage to

(A) refer to the use of the laser in surgery.
(B) allude to the ability of the laser to cut diamonds.
(C) emphasize the need to find additional uses for the laser.
(D) identify characteristics of the laser beam.
(E) clarify specific uses of the laser not mentioned previously in the passage.

Questions 19–21
Tax shelters with real economic value may eventually begin to show profits. In this case, the investor will gain, not only from the tax deductions, but from the profits as well. As a rule, when the profits start to accrue, it is time to look for another investment to shelter those profits.

19. Which one of the following statements best expresses an idea found in this selection?

(A) Sheltering the profits from another tax shelter is not a recommended action.
(B) Profits and deductions both constitute gains from tax shelters.
(C) Profits will increase when deductions decrease.
(D) Investing in tax shelters is no longer beneficial if the shelters show profits.
(E) The real value of tax shelters is negligible.

20. The author would agree that most tax shelters

(A) produce profits.
(B) are sources for reinvestment.
(C) permit tax deductions.
(D) are illegal.
(E) result in financial gains but not significant ones.

21. The word "accrue" in line 5 could be replaced most accurately by

(A) combine.
(B) operate.
(C) hold.
(D) dissipate.
(E) accumulate.

Questions 22–23
The civilization of the 20th century, highly technical as it is, is like an airplane in flight, supported by its forward motion. It cannot stop without falling.

22. To extend the simile in this passage, one might say which of the following?

(A) As the airplane becomes larger and travels longer distances, flight technology must improve to keep pace with the increased demands.
(B) The need for man to "spread his wings" will be satisfied only by longer and more productive airplane flights.

(C) Falling without a parachute available to rescue him from certain death, man will find ways to improve the state of civilization.

(D) The technology needed to keep an airplane aloft is not adequate to meet the demands of modern technological society.

(E) Referring to basic laws of motion, one can see that the airplane is headed toward disaster.

23. The author would agree that

(A) the world's use of natural resources will decline as techniques are improved.

(B) the curve of scientific progress will ultimately lead to the world's destruction.

(C) to stop science would create more problems than solutions.

(D) twentieth century civilization has not really progressed as much as the degree of technology would indicate.

(E) present techniques used in science are so undependable that they cannot possibly effect improvements in society.

Questions 24–26

Refer to the diagram to answer the next three questions.

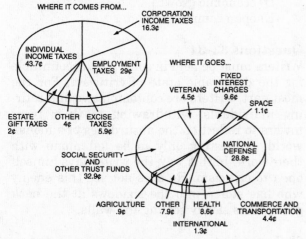

TYPICAL BUDGET DOLLAR

WHERE IT COMES FROM...

CORPORATION INCOME TAXES 16.3¢

INDIVIDUAL INCOME TAXES 43.7¢

EMPLOYMENT TAXES 29¢

WHERE IT GOES...

FIXED INTEREST CHARGES 9.6¢

VETERANS 4.5¢

SPACE 1.1¢

ESTATE GIFT TAXES 2¢

OTHER 4¢

EXCISE TAXES 5.9¢

NATIONAL DEFENSE 28.8¢

SOCIAL SECURITY AND OTHER TRUST FUNDS 32.9¢

AGRICULTURE .9¢

OTHER 7.9¢

HEALTH 8.6¢

COMMERCE AND TRANSPORTATION 4.4¢

INTERNATIONAL 1.3¢

24. Next to individual income taxes, the greatest amount of money to run the government comes from

(A) employment taxes.
(B) social security.

(C) corporation income taxes.
(D) fixed interest charges.
(E) excise taxes.

25. If National Defense spending were reduced by 8.0¢, and this 8.0¢ were added to the health budget, the budget amount for health would then be

(A) 17.6¢.
(B) 37.4¢.
(C) 8.6¢.
(D) 18.4¢.
(E) 16.6¢.

26. In the budget of the U.S. government, income from employment taxes is about equal to

(A) individual income taxes.
(B) national defense spending.
(C) all other taxes combined.
(D) social security costs.
(E) health and agriculture spending.

Questions 27–28

It is important to remember that almost all accidents are psychological in origin, not mechanical. Eighty-four percent of all vehicles involved in fatal accidents are found to be in good condition. The fact that, in the other 16 percent, the defects are usually in brakes, lights, or tires, most of which the driver probably knows about, and that he or she goes on driving anyhow, makes these accidents seem to be appropriately characterized as ones in which there is also a strong psychological factor.

27. All of the following facts are included in the passage EXCEPT which one of the following?

(A) Sixteen percent of vehicles involved in accidents have defects.

(B) Drivers usually know when their vehicles have problems with brakes, lights, or tires.

(C) Mechanical factors contribute to accidents much more often than psychological factors.

(D) Vehicles in good condition are involved in 84 percent of all fatal accidents.

(E) Defects in brakes, lights, or tires are found in most of the cars in which mechanical problems result in an accident.

28. The author implies that

(A) when a driver knows that his or her car has a defect and drives it anyway, the accident that may result could be attributed to psychological, not mechanical, factors.

(B) 84 percent of all accidents could be prevented if mechanical defects were corrected.

(C) failures in brakes, lights, or tires do not result in accidents.

(D) drivers cannot be held responsible for accidents caused by mechanical failure.

(E) accidents are caused by psychological factors 16 percent of the time.

Questions 29–30

After seemingly endless hours of practice, after years of planning and hoping, he stood in a daze, awaiting the judge's decision. The moment of trial had finally come. Suddenly, it was over. The results were read, carefully and deliberately. I've actually won, he repeated incredulously to himself.

29. Which of the following sentences best completes the paragraph?

(A) Like a defendant awaiting a verdict, he slowly rose to his feet and turned to face his judges.

(B) Suddenly, he was overwhelmed with a sense of timidity and turned and fled from the scene.

(C) As if he were a victorious warrior from times past, he raised his arms to embrace the applause from the crowd.

(D) Like a child in need of approval, he jumped to his feet and ran to his teammates, expecting their congratulations.

(E) Filled with a quiet sense of exaltation, unmatched by anything he had ever known, he turned and approached the judges' platform.

30. The passage describes how a person feels who

(A) has to endure a trial.

(B) has to spend hours waiting.

(C) is required to serve as a judge.

(D) has won a competition.

(E) has completed years of work on a project.

Questions 31–32

The dramatic increase in the earth's population—since 1750, it has more than tripled—has not been a biologically-caused evolutionary phenomenon. The evolution has occurred in the world's economic organization. That the human population has tripled in seven generations can be attributed to the amelioration in economic unification. A cooperating world society moves goods across the earth's surface with great ease and, thereby, supports its inhabitants.

31. The main point of this passage is that

(A) the earth's population is three times what it was in 1750.

(B) the world's economic system has unified the world.

(C) the improvement in the economic organization of the world has been the primary cause of the increase in population since 1750.

(D) cooperation among the countries of the world has been erratic, but there is, nonetheless, greater economic unification.

(E) achieving world unification is an evolutionary process.

32. In the writer's opinion, trade is necessary for

(A) democracy.

(B) self-preservation.

(C) political unity.

(D) economic growth.

(E) open communication.

Questions 33–34

Writers must be held in some part accountable for the deplorable state of criticism. For the most part, writers are contemplative and retiring individuals, withdrawing to their ivory towers to reflect on the absurdities of a foolish world, requesting only to be left alone with their work. In this way, the writer lays himself open to criticism. He does not see this enemy who has stolen into the shadows at the back gate and is slowly scaling the walls.

33. In the last sentence of this passage, the image created by the author is used to

(A) explain the effects of a writer's personality on his works.

(B) emphasize the need for monitoring the works of writers more closely.

(C) describe how critics assault writers while they are unaware or unprepared.

(D) highlight the contribution of constructive criticism to the literary world.

(E) create the impression that writers are isolated from the world and have no understanding of it.

34. From the passage, one could conclude that the author would identify critics as

(A) ivory tower dwellers.
(B) retirees.
(C) absurdities of a foolish world.
(D) the "enemy."
(E) a necessary evil.

Questions 35–38

It is not in the interest of that general cultural background, used so often as a cloak for the snob or the pedant, that I argue for the experience of a liberal education. I speak for an introduction to the thoughts and actions of those who have gone before, to the inhabitants of countries other than their own with different struggles and needs, and to concepts divorced from their primary interests.

35. A writer with an opposing point of view to that of the author of this passage might argue for

(A) the inclusion of courses in a broad, rather than narrow or specific, range of curricular areas.
(B) a course of education which leads to something of immediate practical use.
(C) a college curriculum that allows students to structure their program to meet their own needs.
(D) a traditional course of study often reserved only for those who become known as snobs or eggheads.
(E) a program focused on great books, the classics, history, or the humanities.

36. In this passage, the word "pedant" is used to refer to

(A) a respected scholar.
(B) one who is pretentious about his learning.
(C) an educator.
(D) someone who does not work for a living.
(E) an educated patent medicine peddler.

37. Which of the following would be an accurate paraphrase of the first sentence in this passage?

(A) It is not that I am indifferent to the need for a cultural background, but rather that I don't think it can be equated with a liberal education.
(B) I am not in favor of an education that pursues the past in the interest only of creating the impression of being educated.
(C) A liberal education can lead to a derogatory classification of those suffering from a cultured background.
(D) The pedant is one who pursues a liberal education for the purpose of appearing cultured.
(E) I am in favor of a liberal education, but not in the interest of providing a cause for snobbery.

38. In a word, the author's purpose in writing this passage is to

(A) persuade.
(B) entertain.
(C) report.
(D) describe.
(E) quibble.

Questions 39–40

There are at least two quite different kinds of things we learn when we learn our language. We learn the language itself, which includes the sound system, the syntax, and the vocabulary. We also learn something which is, perhaps, not as apparent. We learn how to manipulate our language so that we can communicate effectively and efficiently with others. That is not quite the same thing as having learned the language.

39. The writer of the passage implies that

(A) one does not "know" a language until he knows how to use the language in social situations.
(B) once you have mastered the basic structures of a language, the ability to use it effectively follows naturally.
(C) learning a language is one of the most difficult things an individual can do.
(D) communicating effectively requires a mastery of all the basic elements of a language.

(E) a person who knows more than one language gains a greater ability to use any language effectively.

40. This passage is most likely taken from

(A) a textbook for English grammar instruction.
(B) an article on linguistics and language development.
(C) a paper on topics for speech-making.
(D) a review of a communications textbook.
(E) a manual for ham radio operators.

Questions 41–42

There seems to be a tendency to induce all children to write with their right hands. Both parents and teachers have evidenced an antipathy to a child using his or her left hand. Some psychologists, however, believe that to compel a left-handed child to write with his or her right hand may result in emotional damage.

41. The author of this passage would agree with all of the following statements EXCEPT which one of the following?

(A) Children should be allowed to use their left hand if they have a tendency to do so.
(B) The parents of left-handed children often exhibit a negative reaction to their using their left hand.
(C) Psychologists do not support the contention that encouraging a child to switch from a natural use of his left hand to the use of his right hand presents any problems.
(D) The tendency to encourage children to switch to the use of their right hand has been exhibited by both parents and teachers.
(E) To compel a child to use his right instead of his left hand may not be a good idea.

42. As used in line 4, the best synonym for the word, "antipathy," is

(A) aversion.
(B) indifference.
(C) gentleness.
(D) prejudice.
(E) recurrence.

Questions 43–44

In the interest of making test results for a group more meaningful, information other than the raw scores are often provided. The median or midpoint, which indicates the central tendency of a distribution, may be given, along with so-called measures of dispersion, statistics which indicate whether the scores cluster close to the center or are dispersed at some distance from the center.

43. One group of statistical indicators which tells how test scores are distributed in a group is called

(A) the median.
(B) the test score midpoint.
(C) measures of dispersion.
(D) distribution markers.
(E) measures of central tendency.

44. According to this passage,

(A) tests are useful for measuring academic growth.
(B) test scores have more meaning when the range of scores for the group is known.
(C) test developers need to increase the reliability of tests.
(D) test scores are meaningless without other information about classroom performance.
(E) cluster scores provide more valuable information than individual test scores.

Questions 45–46

When the desire to write overwhelms you, never deny it. What you are able to put into words may not be worthy of a prize, but at least you have succeeded in doing something few people ever attempt—capturing forever something that may only be experienced once—a feeling, a sensation, an emotion, an idea.

45. In this passage, the writer's tone is one of

(A) indifference.
(B) delight.
(C) scorn.
(D) encouragement.
(E) pessimism.

46. Which of the following statements is most appropriate as a continuation of the paragraph?

    (A) The rewards are few, but the need to accomplish something new can be met.
    (B) What one accomplishes as a result of this work will be duplicated.
    (C) These are far more precious than anything tangible as they attribute life to the mind.
    (D) No one of these goals can be worth more effort than the others.
    (E) At such a time, the only appropriate response may be to silence one's longings.

Questions 47–49

It is generally acknowledged that the United States, although it remains powerful, no longer stands at the top of various status rankings that measure a country's position in the world. Whether the nation is judged on political, economic, or military criteria, it is evident that it has lost its number one status. National attention has turned to a search for ways to halt the decline. Reasons for the decline are offered in every sector. Businessmen point to government interference in the free market; religious leaders focus on declining moral standards; parents complain about an inadequate public education system; the party out of power blames the party in power, and the party in power blames everyone else. Some few realists—or defeatists, as the case may be— suggest that the dominance enjoyed by this country was purely an accident of history and not the result of some special quality of the American people or of some unique destiny.

47. The title that best expresses the ideas of this selection is

    (A) National Priorities.
    (B) Historical Accident.
    (C) U.S. Decline in Position.
    (D) World Status for Nations.
    (E) Democratic Flaws.

48. Reasons for the current U.S. status in the world are

    (A) not given.
    (B) easily specified.
    (C) abundant.
    (D) offered by other nations.
    (E) found primarily in the military.

49. In this selection, the author does NOT mention

    (A) statistics supporting the U.S. position.
    (B) education as a factor affecting the U.S. position.
    (C) the opinion of politicians.
    (D) the factors on which a national ranking is based.
    (E) any attempts to explain how the U.S. achieved its current ranking.

50. Education has been, from the beginning, a sort of American obsession. Even the first colonists brought with them a respect for education. Americans were among the first to assert that all children would be educated in elementary schools.

    Which of the following sentences is most appropriate as a continuation of the paragraph?

    (A) Although these schools were public, they were not "free," except to those students who could not pay.
    (B) Book learning for girls was almost totally neglected in the colonial period.
    (C) It took a long time, but today the majority of Americans receives at least an elementary education.
    (D) As registration increased, the high school changed.
    (E) Education is a process by which the individual is influenced by informal and formal means.

MATHEMATICS

Directions: Select the best answer to each of the following questions. Any figures provided are there as reference; they are approximations and are not drawn to scale except when stated.

You may refer to the following information during this section of the test.

= is equal to
≠ is unequal to
< is less than
> is greater than
≤ is less than or equal to
≥ is greater than or equal to

√ square root of
° degrees
‖ is parallel to
⊥ is perpendicular to
π pi, approximately 3.14

Circle: Radius = r; Circumference = $2\pi r$; Area = πr^2; a circle contains 360°

Triangle: In triangle ABC, $\angle BDA$ is a right angle,

Area of $\triangle ABC = \dfrac{(AC)(BD)}{2}$;

Perimeter of $\triangle ABC = AB + BC + CA$
Sum of the measures of the three angles is 180°.

Rectangle: Area = $L \times W$; Perimeter = $2(L + W)$

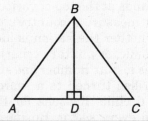

1. Which of the following is less than N, if N is any positive number?

   (A) $1 \times N$
   (B) $1\frac{1}{4} \times N$
   (C) $\frac{3}{2} \times N$
   (D) $\frac{3}{4} \times N$
   (E) $N \div \frac{3}{4}$

2. $3 + 5 \times 6 - 4 \div 2 = ?$

   (A) 22
   (B) 46
   (C) 31
   (D) 14.5
   (E) None of the above

3. Which of the following is the numeral for "five thousand two hundred and eight tenths?"

   (A) 5,280
   (B) 5,000.208
   (C) 5,200.08
   (D) 5,200.8
   (E) None of the above

4. In the numeral below, which digit is in the hundredths place?

   3457.682

   (A) 2
   (B) 4
   (C) 6
   (D) 8
   (E) None of the above

5. What is the square root of 324?

   (A) 324
   (B) 162
   (C) 18
   (D) 648
   (E) None of the above

6. Which of the following is smaller than and closest to $\frac{1}{2}$?

   (A) $\frac{2}{7}$
   (B) $\frac{3}{7}$
   (C) $\frac{4}{7}$
   (D) $\frac{1}{3}$
   (E) $\frac{2}{3}$

7. A factory has 320 daytime workers and the number of night workers is one-fourth the number of daytime workers. What is the ratio of day workers to total workers?

   (A) $\frac{320}{400}$

   (B) $\frac{80}{320}$

   (C) $\frac{320}{80}$

   (D) $\frac{320}{480}$

   (E) None of the above

8. In which of the following sequences does the average of the sequence equal one of the terms of the sequence?

   I. $x, x + 1, x + 2$
   II. $x, x + 2, x + 4$
   III. $x, x + 1, x + 3$
   IV. $x, x + 2, x + 4, x + 6$

   (A) I only
   (B) II only
   (C) I and II only
   (D) I, II, and III only
   (E) II and IV only

9. The school football team lost 25% of the games it played. If it won 18 games, how many games did it lose?

   (A) 4
   (B) 24
   (C) 6
   (D) 7
   (E) None of the above

10. In which of the following is 360 written as a product of prime numbers?

    (A) 10×36
    (B) $2 \times 2 \times 2 \times 5 \times 9$
    (C) $5 \times 8 \times 9$
    (D) $2 \times 2 \times 2 \times 3 \times 3 \times 5$
    (E) None of the above

11. $(\frac{1}{3} - 1) \times \square = 1$
    Which number goes in the box to make a true statement?

    (A) $\frac{2}{3}$

    (B) $-\frac{3}{2}$

    (C) $-\frac{2}{3}$

    (D) 2

    (E) None of the above

12. Sally has 2 skirts, 5 blouses, and 3 dresses. If Sally wears either a dress or a skirt and blouse, how many different outfits does she have?

    (A) 10
    (B) 30
    (C) 13
    (D) 17
    (E) None of the above

13. Our backyard is 225 square meters in area. We have mowed $\frac{2}{3}$ of it. If it takes us 5 minutes to mow 25 square meters, how long will we need to mow to finish the job?

    (A) 10 minutes
    (B) 15 minutes
    (C) 30 minutes
    (D) 45 minutes
    (E) None of the above

14. A number, X, is more than 30, but less than 50. The sum of its digits is 8. X is even. What number is X?

    (A) 53
    (B) 62
    (C) 71
    (D) 44
    (E) None of the above

15. Mary's 5th grade class is planning a chess tournament. If there are 4 people who signed up to play, how many games must be played so that every person plays every other person just once?

    (A) 12
    (B) 5
    (C) 16
    (D) 8
    (E) None of the above

16. A car that has a 16 gallon tank was filled with 12.5 gallons of gas at $1.08 a gallon. How much was spent on gas?

    (A) $17.28
    (B) $3.78
    (C) $13.50
    (D) $22.50
    (E) None of the above

17. Which of the following is the graph of $y = x^2 + 2$?

A.

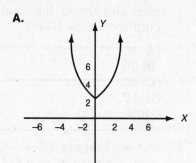

B.

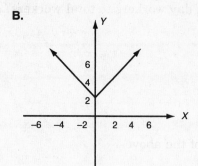

C.

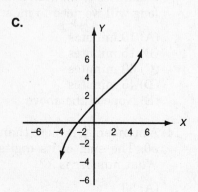

D.

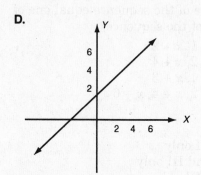

(A) Graph A
(B) Graph B
(C) Graph C
(D) Graph D
(E) None of the above

18. $\frac{1}{5}$ of a keg of beer was used at a party last Saturday. Yesterday, $\frac{1}{2}$ of what was left was drunk. How much of the keg still remains?

(A) $\frac{2}{5}$
(B) $\frac{3}{5}$
(C) $\frac{1}{2}$
(D) $\frac{3}{10}$
(E) $\frac{7}{10}$

19. Three times the lesser of two consecutive whole numbers is less than twice the greater. Which of these is the only possibility for the greater?

(A) 3
(B) 6
(C) 4
(D) 2
(E) 0

20. A suit which is regularly $105.00 is on sale for 20% off. How much do you save on the suit?

(A) $2.10
(B) $5.25
(C) $84.00
(D) $20.00
(E) None of the above

21. Martha worked in a fast food restaurant for ten weeks during her summer vacation. She was paid $4.25 per hour and made from $10 to $15 a day on tips. She lived at home and was able to save most of her money to buy a used car that cost $1800 (taxes included). After all deductions, Martha averaged $3.50 per hour take home pay. She also averaged $54 per week in tips. By the end of the ten weeks, what is the minimum number

of hours Martha must have worked to buy the car?

(A) 360 hours
(B) 297 hours
(C) 515 hours
(D) 400 hours
(E) Not enough information is given.

22. George went to the drugstore and bought gumballs and stickers. The gumballs cost 5¢ each and the stickers cost 8¢ each. He spent 60¢. How many gumballs did he buy?

(A) 3 gumballs
(B) 4 gumballs
(C) 5 gumballs
(D) 7 gumballs
(E) 1 gumball

23. $\frac{x}{y} = y$, so $y = ?$

(A) x
(B) $2x$
(C) $\frac{x}{6}$
(D) $\sqrt{x}$
(E) $\frac{x}{2}$

24. If $\frac{1}{x} = 14$ and $y = 7$, what is x in terms of y?

(A) $2y$
(B) $\frac{1}{2y}$
(C) $-2y$
(D) $\frac{y}{2}$
(E) None of the above

25. $x^2 - 16 = ?$

(A) $(x - 4)^2$
(B) $(x + 4)^2$
(C) $(x - 4)(x + 4)$
(D) $(x + 8)(x - 2)$
(E) None of the above

26. If $x = 3$, then $5x - 2x^2 = ?$

(A) 117
(B) 24
(C) −21
(D) −3
(E) None of the above

27. If $3x - 5 = 2$, then $x - \frac{1}{3} = ?$

(A) 2
(B) $2\frac{1}{3}$
(C) 3
(D) $7\frac{1}{3}$
(E) 7

28. The circumference of a circle of radius, R, is given by $C = 2 \cdot \pi \cdot R$. Which expression gives the value of the radius if you know the circumference?

(A) $R = \dfrac{C}{\pi}$

(B) $R = \dfrac{\pi C}{2R}$

(C) $R = \dfrac{C}{2 \cdot \pi}$

(D) $R = C + 2$

(E) $R = C - 2$

29. Which of the following equations gives the relationship shown in the table below?

(A) $y = 2x + 1$
(B) $y = x^2 - 1$
(C) $y = (x + 1)^2$
(D) $y = x^2 + 1$
(E) None of the above

X	0	1	2	3	4	5
Y	1	2	5	10	17	26

30. If $\dfrac{15}{45} = \dfrac{50}{x}$, then $x = ?$

(A) 30
(B) 70
(C) 200
(D) 110
(E) 150

31. If $m < 0$ and $n > 0$ and n is even, which of the following is (are) definitely a negative even number?

 I. $m \cdot n$
 II. $m - n$
 III. $2m$

(A) I only
(B) II only
(C) III only
(D) I and II only
(E) I and III only

32. If the volume of a cylinder is found by multiplying the area of its base times its height, what is the volume of the cylinder

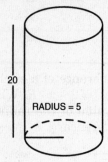

pictured?

(A) 25×20
(B) $25 \times 20 \times \pi$
(C) $10 \times 20 \times \pi$
(D) $5 \times 20 \times \pi$
(E) None of the above

33. A and B are two regular pentagons (five sided figures with all angles and sides equal). If pentagon B is twice as large as pentagon A, and the angles of A measure 108° each, what is the measure of each

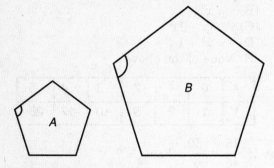

angle in pentagon B?
(A) 216°
(B) 54°
(C) 108°
(D) 72°
(E) None of the above

34. Suppose the line PQ is parallel to the line MN. If the coordinates of N are $(5, y)$,

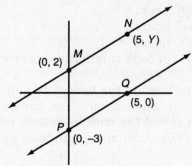

then y must be equal to ?

(A) 5
(B) 4
(C) 3
(D) 2
(E) None of the above

35. In the figure you see triangle ABC and the measures of two of its angles. What is x (the measure of angle BCD)?

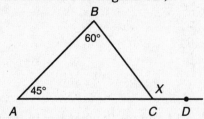

(A) 75
(B) 60
(C) 135
(D) 105
(E) Cannot be determined from information given

36. Sam is going to make a scale drawing of his rectangular garden. The graph paper he will use is $8\frac{1}{2}$ inches by 11 inches and has squares that are $\frac{1}{4}$ inch on each side. He decides that he will let each square represent 1 square foot. If he can use only 1 sheet of graph paper, which of the following sizes of gardens can he draw to scale?

   I. 30 feet × 42 feet
  II. 35 feet × 40 feet
 III. 21 feet × 43 feet

(A) I only
(B) II only
(C) III only
(D) I and II only
(E) I and III only

37. A rectangular painting which measures 12 centimeters by 30 centimeters needs framing. If we want a frame 2 centimeters wide, what will the area of the frame itself be in square centimeters?

(A) 448
(B) 360
(C) 184
(D) 88
(E) None of the above

38. Which of the following could be lengths of the sides of a parallelogram (that is, a 4-sided figure in which the opposite sides are parallel)?

   I. 5, 10, 5, 10
  II. 5, 10, 5, 15
 III. 5, 6, 5, 6

(A) I only
(B) II only
(C) III only
(D) I and III only
(E) I and II only

39. The area of a small square in the figure is 16. The perimeter of the figure is:

(A) 24
(B) 40
(C) 44
(D) 48
(E) 56

40. A square has a side of $3 \cdot \sqrt{\pi}$ centimeters. Find the radius of a circle that would have an area equal to that of the square.

(A) 9 centimeters
(B) 3 centimeters
(C) $3 \cdot \pi$ centimeters
(D) $3 \sqrt{\pi}$ centimeters
(E) None of the above

41. Harry has only quarters and dimes. Some kids made guesses about how much money Harry could have. Which guess does not belong?

(A) Lisa guessed 55¢.
(B) Laura guessed 35¢.
(C) Kim guessed 75¢.
(D) Heather guessed 45¢.
(E) Carrie guessed 30¢.

42. Which problem statement can be solved using the number sentence

$$3n + 2 = 35?$$

(A) Mario's father's age is 2 years more than 3 times Mario's age. Mario's father is 35 years old. How old is Mario?
(B) Mario's father is 35 years old. Two years from now Mario's father will be 3 times as old as Mario. How old is Mario?
(C) There are 35 cats and dogs in a pet store. There are 2 dogs and 3 times as many cats. How many cats are there?
(D) There are n cats in a pet store. If you add 2 to this number and multiply by 3, you get 35. How many cats are there?
(E) Two more than 35 is 3 times a number.

43. There are 152 students who study French, Spanish, or German at Lincoln High School. Of these, 37 take only French, 60 take only Spanish, and 22 take only German. Also, 17 take both French and Spanish but not German, 3 take both Spanish and German but not French, and 9 take French and German but not Spanish. How many students study all 3 languages?

Which diagram(s) correctly represent(s) the information stated in this problem?

I.

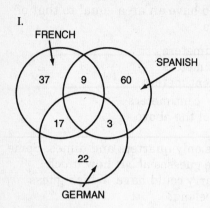

II.

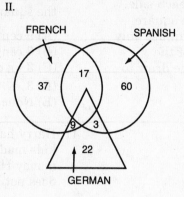

III.

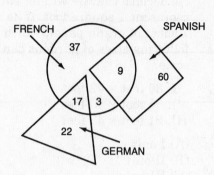

(A) I only
(B) II only
(C) III only
(D) I and II only
(E) II and III only

44. Ooey Gooey Gum is on sale at 8 pieces for $.59. At this rate, how many pieces could Terry buy for $1.00?

Which of the following equations could be used to solve this problem?

(A) $\frac{8}{59} = \frac{100}{n}$

(B) $\frac{n}{8} = \frac{59}{100}$

(C) $\frac{8}{59} = \frac{n}{100}$

(D) $\frac{8}{100} = \frac{n}{59}$

(E) None of the above

45. The farmer could find the length of one side of a farm if he also knew:

(A) Two sides of the farm have the same length.
(B) 1 acre = 4840 square yards.
(C) The farm has an area of 50 acres.
(D) The farm is triangular in shape.
(E) The farm is rectangular in shape.

46. Jim, Ruth, and Peter took turns driving home from the lake. Ruth drove 40 miles more than Jim. Jim drove twice as far as Peter. Peter drove 86 miles. How far was the total drive? Answer: 126

Which statement best describes why the answer given for this problem is *not* reasonable?

(A) Jim drove more than Peter.
(B) Ruth drove 40 miles more than Jim.
(C) Peter drove 86 miles himself.
(D) Because there is not enough information to answer the question.
(E) Because you want to find the total distance.

47. Box seats for the World Series cost $40 each and grandstand seats cost $18 each. Luis ordered 3 box seats and 7 grandstand seats. Orders for more than $150 received 10% discount on the purchase price. What did Luis have to pay for all the seats he ordered?

Which is an appropriate first step in solving the problem?

(A) Find the total number of seats.
(B) Find 10% of $150.
(C) Find 10% of the total cost of the seats.
(D) Find the total cost for 3 box seats.
(E) Subtract $150 from the total cost of the 10 seats.

48. Carla bought all of the available bell trim fabric and $2\frac{1}{3}$ yard of the lace at a remnant sale. She paid for the items with a $5 bill. How much change should she get?

REMNANT SALE

Bell trim $5\frac{1}{2}$ yards............40¢ per yard
Ribbon $4\frac{1}{4}$ yards...........25¢ per yard
Lace $2\frac{3}{4}$ yards............60¢ per yard

Which solution method is correct for this problem?

(A) 40¢ + 60¢ = \$1.00 → \$5 − \$1 = \$4
(B) $5\frac{1}{2} + 2\frac{1}{3} = 7\frac{5}{6}$
(C) $5\frac{1}{2} \times 40¢ = \$2.20$ ⎱ \$2.20 + \$1.40 = \$3.60
     $2\frac{1}{3} \times 60¢ = \$1.40$ ⎰ → \$5 − \$3.60 = \$1.40
(D) $5\frac{1}{2} + 2\frac{1}{3} = 7\frac{5}{6}$ → \$1 + $7\frac{5}{6}$ = \$7.83
     40¢ + 60¢ = \$1
(E) $5\frac{1}{2} \times 40¢ = \$2.20$ ⎱ → \$2.20 + \$1.65 = \$3.85
     $2\frac{3}{4} \times 60¢ = \$1.65$ ⎰ → \$5 − \$3.85 = \$1.15

49. Two of the cash registers in a grocery store contain a total of \$740. If you shift \$45 from the first register to the second, the two registers then contain equal amounts.

Which question(s) could be answered using this information?

  I. How much money is in each register before the money is shifted?
  II. How much money is in each register after the money is shifted?
  III. How many cash registers are there in the grocery store?

(A) I only
(B) I and II only
(C) II only
(D) III only
(E) I, II, and III

50. Julie's Juice Joint is open 7 days per week and sells an average of 1400 glasses of freshly squeezed orange juice per week. Each week, 1050 pounds of oranges and 950 pounds of grapefruits are used. Julie bought 750 pounds of oranges on Wednesday. How many days supply is this? To solve this problem, you need to know:

  I. Julie's Juice Joint is open 7 days a week.
  II. 1400 glasses of orange juice are sold each week.
  III. 1050 pounds of oranges are used each week.
  IV. 950 pounds of grapefruit are used each week.
  V. 750 pounds of oranges were bought one day.

(A) I, II, and III only
(B) I, II, III, and IV only
(C) I, III, and V only
(D) I, II, III, and V only
(E) I, II, III, IV, and V

WRITING

Directions: You will have 60 minutes to write an essay on each of the following two topics. Try to spend approximately 30 minutes on each topic, as they are of equal value in the evaluation. While quantity is not as important as quality, the topics selected will probably require an essay rather than just a paragraph or two. Organization is an integral part of effective writing, so you may want to use some of the allotted time to plan your work. Support your ideas with clear, specific examples or explanations. Write legibly, and do not skip lines.

First Topic:

Research studies on effective teaching usually demonstrate that it is the teacher that "makes the difference," but it has been difficult to identify specific qualities that are evident in a "good" teacher. Discuss qualities which you think an effective teacher should have.

SECOND TOPIC:

At one time or another, everyone has had an experience that did not turn out as expected. Describe one such experience you have had and how it affected you.

ANSWER KEY

Reading

1. D	11. E	21. E	31. C	41. C
2. B	12. B	22. A	32. B	42. A
3. B	13. B	23. C	33. C	43. C
4. B	14. D	24. A	34. D	44. B
5. E	15. B	25. E	35. B	45. D
6. B	16. C	26. B	36. B	46. C
7. D	17. E	27. C	37. E	47. C
8. B	18. B	28. A	38. A	48. C
9. C	19. B	29. E	39. A	49. A
10. D	20. C	30. D	40. B	50. C

Mathematics

1. D	11. B	21. A	31. E	41. E
2. C	12. C	22. B	32. B	42. A
3. D	13. B	23. D	33. C	43. B
4. D	14. D	24. B	34. A	44. C
5. C	15. E	25. C	35. D	45. E
6. B	16. C	26. D	36. E	46. E
7. A	17. A	27. A	37. C	47. D
8. C	18. A	28. C	38. D	48. C
9. C	19. D	29. D	39. E	49. B
10. D	20. E	30. E	40. B	50. C

ANALYSIS OF ERRORS

The following table lists the subject matter covered in each question of the Reading and Mathematics sections of the test. Find the question numbers that you got wrong and review the subject matter covered in those questions again.

SECTION	QUESTION NUMBERS	SUBJECT AREA
READING	4, 5, 14, 31, 37, 39, 44, 47	Finding the Main Idea
	3, 6, 12, 15, 16, 19, 27, 41, 43, 44, 48, 49	Finding Specific Details
	1, 2, 9, 10, 11, 13, 17, 20, 23, 28, 29, 30, 32, 34, 35, 38, 39, 40, 45, 46, 50	Finding Implications
	13, 21, 36, 42	Determining the Meaning of Strange Words
	18, 22, 33	Determining Special Techniques
	7, 8, 24, 25, 26	Interpreting Tables and Graphs

SECTION	QUESTION NUMBERS	SUBJECT AREA
MATHEMATICS Arithmetic	2, 5, 10	Whole Numbers
	1, 6, 13, 18	Fractions
	3, 4, 16	Decimals
	9, 20	Percentage
		Rounding Off Numbers
	11, 31	Signed Numbers
	8	Averages, Medians, Ranges, and Modes
		Powers, Exponents, and Roots
Algebra	23, 24, 25, 26	Algebraic Expressions
	27, 29, 42	Equations
	14, 19, 21, 22, 23, 41, 45, 46, 47, 48, 49, 50	Verbal Problems
	12, 15	Counting Problems
	7, 30	Ratio and Proportion
		Sequence and Progression
	19	Inequalities
Geometry		Angles
		Lines
	33	Polygons
	35	Triangles
	38	Quadrilaterals
	28	Circles
	32, 37, 39, 40	Area, Perimeter, and Volume
	17, 34	Coordinate Geometry
Formulas		Formulas

ANSWER EXPLANATIONS

Reading

1. **D** The author suggests that the development of the scientific attitude works well in a democratic government.

2. **B** In this passage, the author does not acknowledge that the need for expediency may prevent the idealistic use of procedures guided by a scientific attitude.

3. **B** The writer defines an overregularization as the inflection of an irregular verb ("come") with a regular verb ending ("-ed") (instead of saying "came").

4. **B** The author wishes to make the point that children are analyzing the language they hear and figuring out the rules, as evidenced by their over-application of the rules. The author infers no judgment on teaching techniques, so E would be a wrong answer. A is true but is not a main point. C and D are inaccurate.

5. **E** The author suggests that television can focus on personality factors and divert attention away from the real issues. Polls (A) are never mentioned; B and C are too general, and D introduces a new aspect.

6. **B** The nature of the medium, focusing attention on appearance, style, voice, and manner, leads the viewer away from the contemplation of ideas. A is inaccurate.

7. **D** Counting carefully, from dot to dot, the times the line goes down, one should get six.

8. **B** It is necessary to follow very carefully up from 1950 and straight across. It is about 82%.

9. **C** The author writes with admiration of Alice Roosevelt's free-spirited attitude.

10. **D** Since the author speaks of the "newspaper-reading public," and her activities are clearly ones that would draw attention, reporters would enjoy writing about her. B, C, and E are not mentioned in the passage, and A is portrayed as secondary to how interesting she was.

11. **E** The author expresses the confidence that the growth of plants has gone on and will continue on nature's schedule. B is an exaggeration of the feelings the author displays.

12. **B** The growth of plants occurs with such regularity over time that it is compared to marks on a calendar.

13. **B** The writer implies that communication problems are factors outside of the immediate task, an example of "indirect processes."

14. **D** The purpose is merely to discuss group dynamics and how factors interact to affect the workings of a group.

15. **B** The passage explains the differences in terms of quality, using terms like coherence, frequency, size, etc.

16. **C** The writer distinguishes laser from ordinary light on the basis of "coherence," a quality of the former.

17. **E** All of the other possibilities could be predicted from the uses mentioned in the passage.

18. **B** The use of the terms, "scratch" and "gem," bring to mind the laser's use in cutting diamonds.

19. **B** The principal advantage of tax shelters is in tax deductions, but the author points out that profits also can be made. The other answers contradict points made by the author.

20. **C** The author refers to tax shelters in a way that implies that they all permit tax deductions.

21. **E** From the context, as the author suggests that profits accrued should be reinvested, it is clear that "accumulate" is the best definition.

22. **A** The comparison suggests that technology must "fly on"; as the needs of society increase, so must technology's answers to the questions that arise with society's increasing complexity.

23. **C** The author implies that science must go forward to find ever-new technologies so that civilization is not left without resources.

24. **A** As displayed in the symbolic dollar on the left, Employment Taxes, at 29¢ per dollar, is second only to Individual Income Taxes.

25. **E** If 8.0¢ from the defense budget is added to the 8.6¢ allocated to the health budget, the result is 16.6¢.

26. **B** Income from employment taxes is 29¢ and national defense spending is 28.8¢, the closest of all the answers given.

27. **C** The author states in the first sentence that the reverse is the case.

28. **A** The author implies that even those accidents where mechanical failure is involved could be attributed to psychological factors since the driver often knows about the car's defects.

29. **E** This sentence fits the style and situation of the passage best. A is incorrect from the description of his position; B and C do not fit the style nor one's predictions of what might happen; the passage does not convey the impression that he would act (D) like this or, in fact, that there are teammates.

30. **D** Since the passage describes practice, planning, and judges' decision, it seems clear that it is a competition. While a competition may be a "trial" to some extent, D is the clearer answer.

31. **C** The *main* point is that the large population increase is due to economic factors.

32. **B** The writer is suggesting that, without an efficient exchange of goods, preserving the human race is difficult, if not impossible. Political considerations (A and C) and communication (E) are not mentioned. Economic growth is part of trade in this passage, so (D) is not the best answer.

33. **C** The author's main point is that writers largely try to remain aloof from the world and, therefore, allow critics to sneak in while they're not watching.

34. **D** The author describes literary critics as the villains who attack the poor unsuspecting writer. A and B would best fit the author's description of writers; C his view of writers' subject matter; and E is not appropriate.

35. **B** The writer is in favor of a liberal education, while an opponent would favor a more practical course of study in business, science, law, or the like. Answers A, D, and E advocate courses of study more or less consistent with the author's view. Answer C is irrelevant.

36. **B** By definition, a "pedant" is one who is pretentious about his learning. In addition, paired as it is with "snob," answers A and C would be inconsistent with its meaning. D and E are inaccurate.

37. **E** The author supports a liberal education because of the knowledge that it provides, not because of the air of snobbery which some may use it to create.

38. **A** The passage could be part of a written debate, and the author is arguing his case.

39. **A** The writer's main point is that one must and does learn more than just the basic structures of a language; he must know how to use the language. It must be learned, so B is wrong. C and D are too general, and E may be true but is not mentioned in the passage.

40. **B** The topic is primarily language, how and why it is developed in people.

41. **C** The writer does, in fact, report that psychologists suggest the possibility of emotional damage.

42. **A** Antipathy means aversion, and the passage suggests that parents and teachers have a strong negative reaction.

43. **C** Measures of dispersion are mentioned in the passage as ones which indicate where the scores are grouped, near or far away from the center.

44. **B** The passage emphasizes the need to know more than raw scores in order to understand a group's performance.

45. **D** The author is trying to encourage others to respond to their penchants for writing.

46. **C** "These" refers to "feeling, sensation, emotion, idea," and the sentence explains the value of and reward for putting words on paper.

47. **C** Although the passage mentions world status, the primary focus is on the decline of the U.S. position and reasons for it.

48. **C** As the writer indicates in lines 10–16, there is no shortage of explanations offered for the decline in U.S. status.

49. **A** The author describes the U.S. status and reasons for it, but does not include any statistics supporting it.

50. **C** The author is presenting background facts on the general progress and history of American education. Subjects B and D are not directly on the subject; E is too general; A is defeating the author's purpose by showing limits to public education.

Mathematics

1. **D** Multiplying N by a number smaller than 1 will always give a product smaller than N, whereas multiplying by a number larger than 1 will give a product larger than N.
   In choices A, B, and C, N is multiplied by 1 or by a number larger than 1. In choice E, $N \div \frac{3}{4} = N \times \frac{4}{3}$, so the product is larger than N. Only in choice D is N multiplied by a number smaller than 1.

2. **C** The standard order of operations is (from left to right)
   1. Multiplications and divisions
   2. Additions and subtractions
   Therefore,
   $$3 + 5 \times 6 - 4 \div 2 = 3 + (5 \times 6) - (4 \div 2)$$
   $$= 3 + 30 - 2$$
   $$= 33 - 2$$
   $$= 31$$

3. **D** A is five thousand two hundred eighty.
   B is five thousand and two hundred eight thousandths.
   C is five thousand two hundred and eight hundredths.

4. **D** The places are:
   thousands   (3)
   hundreds   (4)

tens	(5)
ones	(7)
tenths	(6)
hundredths	(8)
thousandths	(2)

5. C Clearly, A, B, and D are all too large to give 324 when multiplied by themselves. The only possible correct answer listed is 18. And, in fact $18 \times 18 = 324$.

6. B C ($\frac{4}{7}$) and E ($\frac{2}{3}$) are both larger than $\frac{1}{2}$. B ($\frac{3}{7}$) is larger than A ($\frac{2}{7}$), thus closer to $\frac{1}{2}$. Thus, we need only to compare B ($\frac{3}{7}$) and D ($\frac{1}{3}$) and to choose the larger. A common denominator for these two is 21.

$$\frac{3}{7} \times \frac{3}{3} = \frac{9}{21}$$
$$\frac{1}{3} \times \frac{7}{7} = \frac{7}{21}$$
$$\frac{9}{21} > \frac{7}{21}, \text{ so } \frac{3}{7} > \frac{1}{3}$$

7. A Let N = number of night workers
$$N = (\tfrac{1}{4})(320) = 80$$
Thus, the total number of workers is:
$320 + 80 = 400$
The ratio of day workers to total workers =
$\frac{320}{400}$

8. C
(yes)

I.
$$\frac{x + (x + 1) + (x + 2)}{3}$$
$$= \frac{3x + 3}{3} = \frac{3(x + 1)}{3} = x + 1$$

(yes)

II.
$$\frac{x + (x + 2) + (x + 4)}{3}$$
$$= \frac{3x + 6}{3} = \frac{3(x + 2)}{3} = x + 2$$

(no)

III.
$$\frac{x + (x + 1) + (x + 3)}{3}$$
$$= \frac{3x + 4}{3} = \frac{3(x + \frac{4}{3})}{3} = x + \frac{4}{3}$$

(no)

IV.
$$\frac{x + (x + 2) + (x + 4) + (x + 6)}{4}$$
$$= \frac{4x + 12}{4} = \frac{4(x + 3)}{4} = x + 3$$

9. C The team lost 25% or $\frac{1}{4}$ of its games ($25\% = \frac{25}{100} = \frac{1}{4}$). So they must have won $\frac{3}{4}$ of their games. In other words, they won three times as many games as they lost. They won 18 games. So $\frac{18}{3}$ = the number of games lost. They lost 6 games.

10. D Each of the choices has product 360. We need to find the one which consists entirely of prime numbers (numbers whose only factors are themselves and 1).
In A neither 10 nor 36 is prime.
($10 = 2 \times 5$), ($36 = 6 \times 6$)
In B 9 is not prime ($9 = 3 \times 3$)
In C neither 8 nor 9 is prime.
($8 = 2 \times 4$), ($9 = 3 \times 3$)
In D all the factors are prime.

11. B $\left(\frac{1}{3} - 1\right) \times \square = 1$
$$-\frac{2}{3} \times \square = 1$$
$$-\frac{2}{3} \times -\frac{3}{2} = \frac{6}{6} = 1$$

12. C Sally has $2 \times 5 = 10$ blouse-skirt combinations, and 3 dresses. So she has $10 + 3 = 13$ different outfits.

13. B Since $\frac{2}{3}$ of the yard is mowed, $\frac{1}{3}$ remains to be done. So, $\frac{1}{3} \times 225 = 75$ square meters remains to be done. If 25 square meters can be done in 5 minutes, then 75 square meters can be done in $15(3 \times 5)$ minutes.

14. D It is easiest here to simply examine the choices. None of A, B, or C is less than 50. Choice D (44) satisfies all the given criteria (more than 30, less than 50, sum of digits $(4 + 4)$ is 8).

15. E The answer is $3 + 2 + 1 = 6$. Imagine telling children what order they will play in. The first child must be assigned a time to play each of the other 3 children. The second child needs only 2 assignments (because she already has an assignment for child number 1). The third child already is scheduled to play children #1 and #2, so needs only 1 assignment. The fourth child's schedule is fully determined by the arrangements already made.

16. C $\$1.08 \times 12.5 = \$13.50$

17. A Make a table containing several ordered pairs which satisfy the equation $y = x^2 + 2$.

x	y
−2	6
−1	3
0	2
1	3
2	6

Check which of the graphs contain all the points in your table.

18. **A** $\frac{1}{5}$ was used Saturday. (So, $1 - \frac{1}{5} = \frac{4}{5}$ remained.) Half of the remainder was drunk, so the other half of the remainder still remains. In other words,

$$\frac{1}{2} \times \frac{4}{5} = \frac{4}{10} = \frac{2}{5}$$

still remains.

19. **D**   Rather than using algebra, it is easiest to examine the choices here.
   (A) If 3 is the greater, then 2 is the lesser. Is $3 \times 2 < 2 \times 3$? NO (6 = 6)
   (B) If 6 is the greater, then 5 is the lesser. Is $3 \times 5 < 2 \times 6$? NO (15 > 12)
   (C) If 4 is the greater, then 3 is the lesser. Is $3 \times 3 < 2 \times 4$? NO (9 > 8)
   (D) If 2 is the greater, then 1 is the lesser. Is $3 \times 1 < 2 \times 2$? YES (3 < 4)

20. **E**   You save 20% of $105.
   $105 \times 20\% = \$21$

21. **A**   Martha needed $1800. In ten weeks she made $10 \times 54 = \$540$ in tips. Since $1800 − $540 = 1260, she needed to make $1260 in wages. She was paid $3.50 per hour (take-home pay). So she needed to work $1260 ÷ 3.50 = 360$ hours to have enough money for the car.

22. **B**   Given: gumballs are 5¢ each (g)
   stickers are 8¢ each (s)
   Total George spent was 60¢
   $5 \times g + 8 \times s = 60$
   Analyzing this equation we realize that if we substitute an odd number of gumballs in the equation, $5 \times g$ will be odd, so $8 \times s$ will have to be odd. But this is impossible since 8 is even. This means the number of gumballs will necessarily have to be even. The only choice is, thus, choice B.

23. **D** $y \cdot \dfrac{x}{y} = y + y$

   $x = y^2$

   $\sqrt{x} = y$

24. **B** $\frac{1}{x} = 14$

   $\frac{x}{1} = \frac{1}{14}$

   Since $y = 7$, then $2y = 14$

   $\frac{x}{1} = \frac{1}{2y}$

   $x = \frac{1}{2y}$

25. **C**   If you recognize this expression as the "difference of squares" $x^2 - a^2$, you may recall that $x^2 - a^2 = (x - a)(x + a)$. Thus $x^2 - 16 = (x - 4)(x + 4)$. If you do not recall this relationship multiply out each choice.

26. **D**   Given: $x = 3$
   Substituting: $5(3) - 2(3)$
   $= 15 - 2(9)$
   $= 15 - 18 = -3$

27. **A** $3x - 5 = 2$
   $3x = 7$
   $x = \frac{7}{3}$
   Then $x - \frac{1}{3} = \frac{7}{3} - \frac{1}{3} = \frac{6}{3} = 2$

28. **C** $C = 2 \cdot \pi \cdot R$

   $\dfrac{C}{2 \cdot \pi} = \dfrac{2 \cdot \pi \cdot R}{2 \cdot \pi}$

   $R = \dfrac{C}{2 \cdot \pi}$

29. **D**   Substitute the value of x and y given in the table into each of the equations given. Choice D is the only equation which is true when each pair of values is substituted for x and y.

30. **E** $\dfrac{15}{45} = \dfrac{50}{x}$

   Cross multiply: $15x = 45 \cdot 50$

   and solve $x = \dfrac{45 \cdot 50}{15}$

   $x = 150$

31. **E** m is negative.
   n is positive and even.
   I. $m \cdot n$ is negative and even.
   II. $m - n$ is negative but not necessarily even.
   III. $2 \cdot m$ is negative and even.
   So, I and III are negative even numbers.

32. **B**   The area of the base is the area of the circle of radius 5.

$A = \pi \cdot r^2$
$A = \pi \cdot (5)^2 = 25 \cdot \pi$
height = 20
volume = area of base × height
volume = $25 \cdot \pi \times 20 = 25 \times 20 \times \pi$

33. **C** Each angle of any regular pentagon measures 108°. The reason for this is that the pentagon can be divided into 3 triangles (180° each) totaling 540° (3 × 180°). Since the regular pentagon has 5 equal angles each one is 540 ÷ 5 = 108°.

34. **A** Since the lines MN and PQ are parallel their slopes are equal. So we set up the following proportions:
$$\frac{0 - (-3)}{5 - 0} = \frac{y - 2}{5 - 0}$$
Hence, $\frac{3}{5} = \frac{y - 2}{5}$
$$5y - 10 = 15$$
$$5y = 25$$
so $y = 5$

35. **D** The sum of the interior angles of the triangle is 180° ($A + B + C = 180°$). So angle BCA is 180° − (60° + 45°) = 75°. So x, which is the supplement of angle BCA (together they form a straight angle of 180°) is 180° − 75° = 105°.

36. **E** To determine the measures of the largest possible garden we imagine it taking up the entire page. In this case $8\frac{1}{2}$ inches is equivalent to:
$$\left(8\frac{1}{2}\right) \div \frac{1}{4} = \frac{17}{2} \times \frac{4}{1} = 34 \text{ feet}$$
11″ is equivalent to: $11 \div \frac{1}{4} = 11 \times \frac{4}{1} = 44$ feet. So the largest possible dimensions are 34 feet × 44 feet. I and III represent gardens with dimensions that fit on this paper, using the scale given.

37. **C** The area of the frame will be equal to the difference between the areas of the two rectangles indicated in the figure.
$$(34 \times 16) - (30 \times 12) = 544 - 360 = 184$$

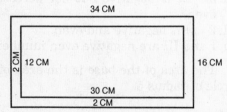

34 CM
2 CM 12 CM   16 CM
30 CM
2 CM

Area of the frame is 184 square centimeters.

38. **D** If both pairs of opposite sides are parallel then the measures of opposite sides must be the same. I and III are the only possibilities.

39. **E** The area of each small square is 16. This implies that the side of each small square is 4. Since the perimeter is the distance all the way around the figure, perimeter = 14 × 4 = 56

40. **B** Area of the square = (side)² = $(3 \cdot \sqrt{\pi})^2$
= $9 \cdot \pi$
Area of the circle = $\pi \cdot r^2 = 9 \cdot \pi$
$$r^2 = 9 \cdot \pi/\pi$$
$$r^2 = 9$$
$$r = 3$$

41. **E** Since Harry has only quarters and dimes the least he could have is one of each, which is equal to 35¢. Carrie's guess is unreasonable because it is less than the minimum Harry could have.

42. **A** Problem statement A is the only one that could be solved using the number sentence given. Suppose n is Mario's age. Three times Mario's age plus 2 years is equal to 35, which is his father's age, as indicated by the number sentence $3n + 2 = 35$.

43. **B** Diagram I is incorrect because it represents 17 students taking French and German but not Spanish.
Diagram II is correct.
Diagram III is incorrect because it represents the intersection of all three languages to be Ø. If this is the case then we don't have enough students represented in the diagram.
Since 37 + 9 + 17 + 60 + 3 + 22 < 152.

44. **C** Determine an equation which represents the proportion: 8 is to $.59 as an unknown amount is to $1.00. The equation would be:
$\frac{8}{59} = \frac{n}{100}$, which is choice C.

45. **E** The farmer needs to know the shape of the farm. However, if it were a triangle he would also need to know how the sides of the triangle were related. If it is a rectangle by knowing one side he can determine the other.

46. **E** Ruth drove 40 miles more than Jim. Jim drove twice as far as Peter. Peter drove

86 miles. The total distance is the sum of everyone's driving. The answer given of 126 miles is only Peter's and part of Ruth's distances driven. So answer E explains this error.

47. **D** The first thing you want to determine is how much would be paid for either the box seats or the grandstand seats.

48. **C** First, find the amount paid for the bell trim fabric:

$$5\tfrac{1}{2} \times 40¢ = \tfrac{11}{12} \times 40¢ = \$2.20$$

Second, find the amount paid for the lace:

$$2\tfrac{1}{3} \times 60¢ = \tfrac{7}{3} \times 60¢ = \$1.40$$

Finally, add the amount spent on both the lace and bell trim fabric and subtract from $5.00.

$$\$2.20 + \$1.40 = \$3.60$$
$$\$5.00 - \$3.60 = \$1.40$$

Answer C has all these steps.

49. **B** There is no way to determine how many cash registers there are in the store, so choice III can be eliminated. Both I and II can be determined. (Let A and B be the amounts in the 2 registers at first. $A + B = \$740$ and $A = B + \$45$. Solving these 2 equations gives $A = \$392.50$, $B = \$347.50$.)

50. **C** She uses 1050 pounds of oranges in 1 week (7 days). This information will allow us to find the number of pounds used per day. Once this information is obtained, divide it into 750 pounds of oranges bought and determine how many days that is equivalent to. Answer C includes these 3 pieces of information.

Writing

The following essay outlines have been written to demonstrate the planning of well-written answers to the topics given. Use these only as guidelines to evaluating your own organization. Many different organization patterns and plans could work equally well for the topics given.

FIRST TOPIC

Research studies on effective teaching usually demonstrate that it is the teacher that "makes the difference," but it has been difficult to identify specific qualities that are evident in a "good" teacher. Discuss qualities which you think an effective teacher should have.

Essay Outline:

A. Introduction
   1. Give background information to lead in to the thesis, perhaps reiterating the point others have made that the teacher "makes the difference."
   2. Present thesis or point of view to be given in paper.
B. Effective qualities
   1. State each quality in clear, concise terms.
   2. Support each quality you suggest with a rationale and supporting details or examples from your own experience or that of others.
C. Summary and conclusions
   1. Restate in brief terms the main point made in the body of the paper.
   2. Suggest conclusions to draw, implications, or recommendations.

SECOND TOPIC

At one time or another, everyone has an experience that did not turn out as expected. Describe one such experience you have had and how it affected you.

Essay Outline:

A. Introduction
   1. Give background information to provide setting for theme of paper.
   2. State theme of paper, i.e., the main idea or gist of the experience to be described.
B. Description of the experience
   1. Lead in to the description by setting the scene, giving the context.
   2. Continue the description with supporting details.
   3. Describe the effects on you produced by the experience.
C. Summary and conclusions
   1. Restate experience and effects in brief terms.
   2. State conclusions in the form of comparisons to other experiences, lessons learned, resolutions made, or recommendations.

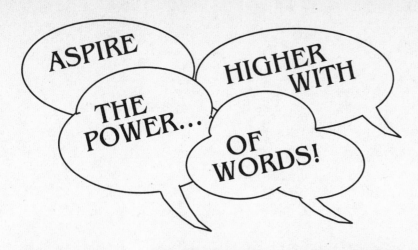

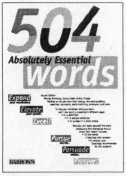

No One Can Build
Your Writing Skills Better
Than We Can....

Essentials of English, 4th Edition
$9.95, Can. $12.95 (0-8120-4378-2)
The comprehensive program for effective writing skills.

Essentials of Writing, 4th Edition
$9.95, Can. $12.95 (0-8120-4630-7)
A companion workbook for the material in *Essentials of English.*

10 Steps in Writing the Research Paper, 5th Edition
$9.95, Can. $12.95 (0-8120-1868-0)
The easy step-by-step guide for writing research papers. It includes a section on how to avoid plagiarism.

How to Write Themes and Term Papers, 3rd Edition
$10.95, Can. $14.50 (0-8120-4268-9)
The perfect, logical approach to handling theme projects.

The Art of Styling Sentences: 20 Patterns to Success, 3rd Edition
$8.95, Can. $11.95 (0-8120-1448-0)
How to write with flair, imagination and clarity, by imitating 20 sentence patterns and variations.

Writing The Easy Way, 2nd Edition
$11.95, Can. $15.95 (0-8120-4615-3)
The quick and convenient way to enhance writing skills.

Basic Word List, 3rd Edition
$5.95, Can. $7.95 (0-8120-9649-5)
More than 2,000 words that are found on the most recent major standardized tests are thoroughly reviewed.

BARRON'S EDUCATIONAL SERIES, INC.
250 Wireless Boulevard • Hauppauge, New York 11788
In Canada: Georgetown Book Warehouse
34 Armstrong Avenue • Georgetown, Ontario L7G 4R9

(#15) R 2/97